Piano

AN EASY GUIDE

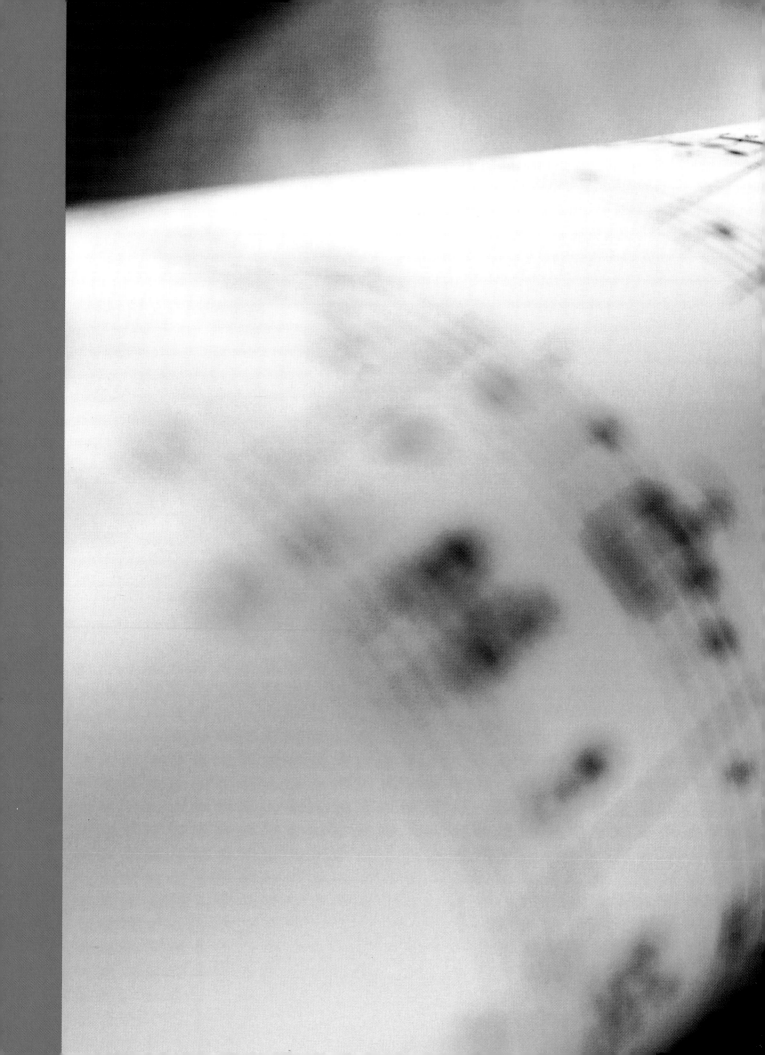

Piano

AN EASY
GUIDE

NEW HOLLAND

chris coetzee

First published in 2003 by
New Holland Publishers
London • Cape Town • Sydney • Auckland
www.newhollandpublishers.com

86 Edgware Rd
London W2 2EA
United Kingdom

80 McKenzie Street
Cape Town 8001
South Africa

14 Aquatic Drive
Frenchs Forest, NSW 2086
Australia

218 Lake Road
Northcote, Auckland
New Zealand

ISBN 1 84330 366 3 (HB); 1 84330 367 1 (PB)

Reproduction by Unifoto Pty Ltd
Printed and bound by Times Malaysia
2 4 6 8 10 9 7 5 3

Publisher: Mariëlle Renssen
Publishing managers: Claudia Dos Santos, Simon Pooley
Commissioning editors: Karyn Richards, Alfred LeMaitre
Managing art editor and designer:
Richard MacArthur
Design concept: Peter Bosman
Editor: Gill Gordon
Picture researcher: Karla Kik
Proofreader: Vanessa Rogers
Production: Myrna Collins
Consultant: Jenny Stern ARCM, LRSM, B.Mus, M.Mus

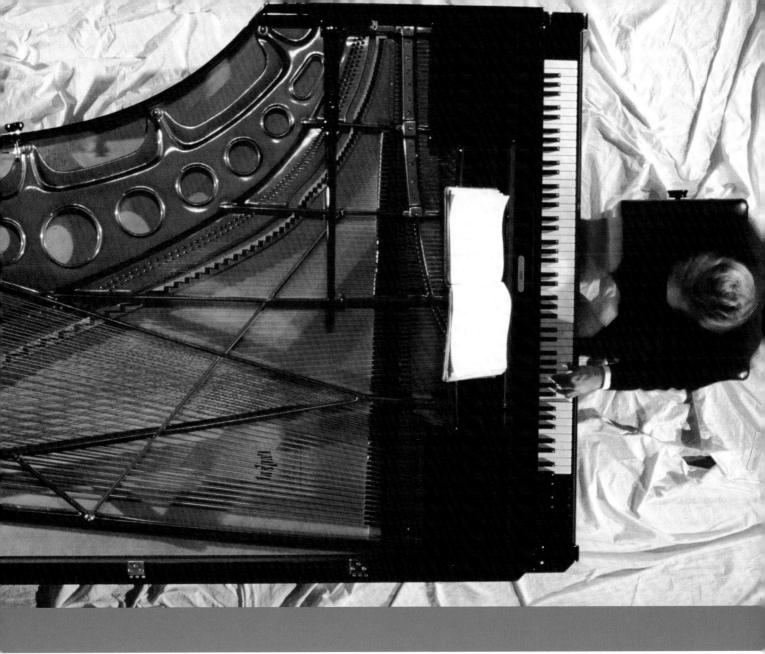

AUTHOR'S DEDICATION

This book is dedicated to my parents: my mother, for giving me the bug, and my father for allowing me to pursue it. Also to my teacher, Roucher du Toit, whose wisdom and boundless knowledge permeate these pages. Thank you to my friends, Sanet Liebenberg and Ernst Gouws, who have taught me more than they realize. Lastly, it is also dedicated to Annatjie Moolman, for her help in interesting times.

contents

mf

𝄐ₑ𝄐.

TAKING UP THE PIANO

LEARNING TO PLAY THE PIANO can be a very rewarding experience, but it does not happen overnight. Learning to play really well requires many years of patient study and diligent practice, something for which you may have neither the time nor the inclination. This book has one purpose: to make it as easy as possible for you to discover the enjoyment that comes with being able to make music.

Adults often take up hobbies that stimulate their creative sides, that allow them to explore activities they may have missed out on in childhood, or that provide an opportunity to escape, even momentarily, from the stresses of daily life. Many give up fairly quickly, as the amount of time required to learn a new skill or activity is often more than they anticipated, or they are unable to progress on their own and must rely on teachers and classes with fixed times and schedules. Music is an ideal hobby to pursue in your own time and at your own pace. Once you have mastered the basic skills and techniques of playing and sight-reading, you will be free to explore and discover the wealth of music out there.

Many books on learning music are either very vague, or too technical for beginners, but this one is written in language that anyone can understand. While it does not attempt to offer a complete course in music theory, it gives a wider perspective on many aspects of playing the piano. It looks at the development of the piano and how the instrument makes its sound. It explains the essentials of how to read music without going into the unnecessary complexities of theory, and shows where your hands and feet should go. A chapter on interpreting classical, jazz and popular music includes pieces from various periods so that by playing them, you can understand some of the influences and techniques that shaped musical history. It also gives useful information on how to buy sheet music, what to look for in recorded music and includes a glossary of music terms as well as some details of music websites and magazines.

The author, an amateur pianist for the past 16 years, has done his utmost to make the text clear, concise and interesting so that any person, no matter what his or her musical background, can discover the thrill and pleasure of playing the piano.

OPPOSITE The beauty of a piano's sound is rivalled only by its intricacy of operation.

ORIGIN OF THE PIANO

It took many talented and inventive men hundreds of years to bring the piano to its current state of near-perfection and experiments are still being made to design the perfect piano. Isolated attempts at piano design were initiated by the mid-15th century, however these early versions were not at all the same as the modern instrument. They remained a bit of a curiosity in many European palaces, as the nobility preferred the harpsichord (a keyboard instrument where the strings are plucked instead of struck) because of its agreeable sound when used for chamber music.

As a boy, Mozart began by playing the harpsichord.

Clavichords produce a soft sound and a subtle tone.

The first instrument that resembled the modern piano was designed in about 1709 by Bartolomeo Cristofori, the keeper of instruments at the Medici court in Florence. He named it the *gravicembalo col pian' e forte* ('harpsichord with soft and loud') from which the words 'pianoforte' and later just 'piano' are derived. The reason for this name was the fact that the instrument could produce soft and loud sounds simply by varying the pressure of the fingers and the velocity with which one struck the keys of the keyboard. It was also capable of producing varying gradations in volume within a single musical phrase. This gave it a great advantage over the harpsichord, on which this was not possible. But these characteristics were not new. Another predecessor of the piano was the clavichord, on which the strings were struck by metal blades called tangents, instead of by a felt-tipped hammer. The volume could be varied by changing the pressure applied by the fingers. The sound of the clavichord was so soft, however, that it was only used as a practising instrument or for the most intimate forms of music-making.

Not many people took note of Cristofori's invention at first. However, as the design of the pianoforte improved it began to gain acceptance. JS Bach did not initially approve of an early piano made by Gottfried Silbermann in the early 1740s, but when he played a later instrument by the same maker, he openly sang its praises. During the 18th century, there were many families of piano builders in Europe, each of whom had their own design or modification of Cristofori's original idea. In this competitive atmosphere, great strides were made in pianoforte construction. By the 1770s, German piano maker Johann Andreas Stein had significantly improved Cristofori's escapement system (which facilitates the rapid repetition of notes, see p13). A decade later, led by John Broadwood, the English school of piano making strengthened the piano's overall design. In 1818, a Frenchman, Sébastien Erard, devised the double-escapement action which is still being used today.

The harpsichord has a more delicate sound than the piano.

These improvements caused a surge in the popularity of the instrument in the late 18th century. Mozart, who lived through this time, played the harpsichord as a boy but, by the time he died in 1791, aged just 35, the piano had completely replaced the harpsichord as the most important keyboard instrument in Europe. One of the reasons for this was the ascendancy of the middle class after the French Revolution (1789–99). Music began to move away from the court and into the public concert hall. In these large spaces the harpsichord, which had an intimate sound better suited to smaller chambers, sounded too soft and its place was soon usurped by the pianoforte. As the piano developed further, the many shades of sound it could produce inspired composers to write music for it. Beethoven's earliest sonatas are written to be played on either harpsichord or pianoforte, but he soon switched to composing for the piano alone. Other Romantic composers and performers who quickly adopted the piano as their preferred instrument, include Chopin, Mendelssohn and Liszt.

The Industrial Revolution that began in England in the latter half of the 18th century created a prosperous middle class. As pianos became more affordable, they soon became the standard instrument for making music in the home. During the Victorian era, learning to play the piano was an indispensable part of a well-born lady's education.

Jelly Roll Morton (on the piano) & the Red Hot Peppers.

Until the advent of radio and television, domestic music-making was an important form of social interaction. But, by the mid-20th century, as lifestyles changed and alternative forms of entertainment evolved, fewer people continued to play the piano as a hobby or have a piano in the home. The piano retained some prominence in the jazz style, but once rock and roll took hold in the 1950s, the piano came to be seen largely as an instrument for 'serious music'.

When electronic keyboards became popular in the 1970s it was not so much for their intrinsic piano sound, but rather as a means by which musicians could produce electronically created sounds. However, singer-songwriters such as Elton John, Billy Joel, Carole King, Enya, Tori Amos, Alicia Keys and others continue to compose and perform on the piano, ensuring that it remains a vital part of modern music.

A Victorian family enjoys an evening's home entertainment.

Elton John is one of the best known modern pop pianists.

11

HOW A PIANO WORKS

All musicians should have a thorough working knowledge of their instrument. This gives them the means to avoid certain musical disadvantages which are linked to the design of the instrument and to exploit beneficial characteristics.

Keyboard instruments produce sound in different ways: on an organ, the keys are depressed by the fingers, thereby permitting air into the pipes; a harpsichord's strings are plucked when the keys are depressed; and on a clavichord the strings are stuck with a metal tangent. Piano strings vibrate when they are struck with a felt-tipped hammer after a key is depressed.

The modern form of the keyboard, with its arrangement of keys in two rows (the lower consisting of white keys and the upper of black keys arranged in groups of two and three), developed over many centuries. It probably had its origins in the Greek *hydraulis* (hydraulic organ) and eventually became standardized after the 15th century. In the Middle Ages, you did not simply depress the keys with your fingers; they were very large and were operated by banging down on them with a fist covered in a protective leather glove; not a very subtle way to produce a sound.

The case, or outer wooden part, of a piano protects it and gives each piano its distinctive appearance. The shape of the

The metal frame, strings, wrest plank, tuning pins and hammers of an upright piano.

case classifies a piano as either a grand or an upright. Within the case is the frame, which houses all the working elements. Frames used to be made of wood, such as mahogany, but as the tension exerted on the frame by the strings increased (it is approximately 30 tonnes on a modern concert grand piano), manufacturers turned to metal.

The strings are fastened into a string plate located at one end of the frame (the rear of a grand piano and the bottom of an upright). At the opposite end is the wrest plank, where the tuning pins are found. These pins are turned to regulate the tension and resultant pitch of the string.

There are three strings to a note for the higher notes (see opposite top). They are tuned in unison, meaning that they sound the same pitch. This is to increase the resonance of the high notes, which would otherwise sound very thin and soft. There are two strings for the notes in the middle and only one string for the resonant low notes.

The soundboard lies beneath the strings. It is usually made of fine-grained spruce and acts as an amplifier for the vibrations of the strings.

The strings and metal frame of a grand piano with the sound board showing behind it.

On a piano, thick single strings (left) sound the lowest, or bass, notes; thinner strings, in pairs (centre), provide the middle notes; the highest notes come from the thinnest strings, which are arranged in groups of three (right).

A piano's action, or how it makes its sound, comprises all the individual parts that cause a string to vibrate freely when a key is depressed. On an upright piano, the action is vertical (see photographs below left), and on a grand piano, the action is horizontal (see photographs below).

A key acts as a lever which balances on a balancing pin. When a key is depressed, its opposite side lifts, causing two main things to happen. Firstly, a felt damper is lifted off the corresponding string, allowing it to vibrate freely. Secondly, the action causes a felt-tipped hammer to strike the string. This is a problem because, once the key is fully depressed, the hammer would be against the string, stopping the vibrations.

The escapement action was devised so that the hammer would only be propelled to a certain point and then velocity would allow it to complete the journey and strike the string. It then rebounds off the string, leaving it free to vibrate. The backcheck stops the hammer from rebounding again.

When a key is released, the damper stops the string from vibrating and the hammer returns to its original position (this occurs as a result of gravity on a grand and with the help of springs and other mechanisms on an upright piano).

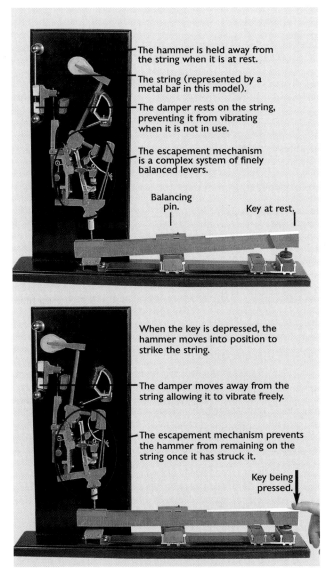

The hammer is held away from the string when it is at rest.

The string (represented by a metal bar in this model).

The damper rests on the string, preventing it from vibrating when it is not in use.

The escapement mechanism is a complex system of finely balanced levers.

Balancing pin.

Key at rest.

When the key is depressed, the hammer moves into position to strike the string.

The damper moves away from the string allowing it to vibrate freely.

The escapement mechanism prevents the hammer from remaining on the string once it has struck it.

Key being pressed.

A model of the action on an upright piano showing how it makes its sound when a key is depressed.

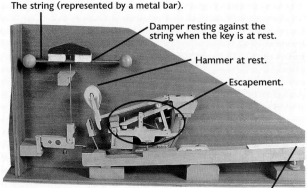

The string (represented by a metal bar).

Damper resting against the string when the key is at rest.

Hammer at rest.

Escapement.

Key at rest.

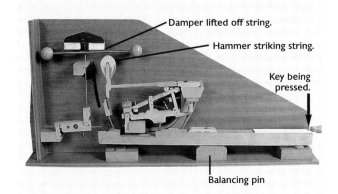

Damper lifted off string.

Hammer striking string.

Key being pressed.

Balancing pin

A grand piano has a similar action to an upright, but the shape of the instrument makes the operation look different.

The pedals are levers that are controlled by the player's feet. The right pedal is the damper (or sustaining) pedal. When it is depressed, it lifts all the dampers off the strings, allowing them to vibrate. The left pedal is the soft pedal. On a grand piano it shifts the hammers slightly to one side. This means the hammers now strike one string less than usual, diminishing the sound and changing its tone. When the left pedal is depressed, the single-stringed low notes are struck slightly off-centre. On most upright pianos, the left pedal moves the hammers closer to the strings.

Some pianos have a middle pedal. On a grand piano it has the same function as the damper pedal, but only lifts the dampers off keys that are being depressed at the same time as the pedal. On some upright pianos, the middle pedal places a strip of felt between all the hammers and the strings, greatly reducing the sound – a useful feature if you want to practise without annoying your neighbours.

The left pedal is the soft pedal; the right sustains the sound.

On a grand piano, the middle pedal sustains certain notes.

The wrest plank and tuning pins of a grand piano.

Vibrating strings

Sound consists of vibrations travelling through the air. Sound is measured in hertz, representing the number of vibrations per second (frequency). The pitch of a sound depends on the number of vibrations, therefore if the frequency is high, the note will be high, and vice versa.

When a piano string vibrates, it produces a sound. If the vibrations are regular and stable, a note is the result. The properties of a note are influenced by the properties of the string. A thick, heavy string vibrates more slowly than a thin one, and produces a lower note. This is why copper wire is wound around the low strings, to make them heavier. A long string also vibrates more slowly than a short string, producing a lower note. Looking inside a piano will confirm this. Depressing a key on the far left of the keyboard produces a low sound because that is where the long thick strings are situated, while the short thin strings on the far right produce the high notes. A grand piano is shaped to accommodate the steady lengthening of strings from one side to the other. The longest strings are situated diagonally above the others to save space. The upright piano is a more compact version of the same principle.

The string plate, strings and frame of a grand piano. Note how the thick strings are set at an angle above the others.

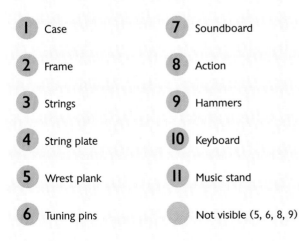

A modern piano is a precision-engineered instrument designed to produce the best possible sound. It comprises various parts, which are indicated in these photographs of an upright piano (above and above right, in detail), and a modern concert grand piano (right).

1 Case

2 Frame

3 Strings

4 String plate

5 Wrest plank

6 Tuning pins

7 Soundboard

8 Action

9 Hammers

10 Keyboard

11 Music stand

Not visible (5, 6, 8, 9)

LEARNING THE LANGUAGE

MUSIC IS LIKE ANY OTHER LANGUAGE. In order to communicate effectively you need a basic grasp of grammar and vocabulary. Luckily, the language of music is simple. If you know the first seven letters of the English alphabet and can multiply and divide by two, then you already know more than half of what you need to read music. Learning music should not be a chore. It can be exciting to learn a new language, and this one can be learned very quickly. Of course, it is not possible to cover everything in a few pages, but what has been included should enable you to figure out more advanced musical structures on your own. Various aspects of reading music are explained and accompanied by diagrams for easy reference.

It is a characteristic of Western music to write down an approximation of what you hear. The development of musical notation (the marks on the page) began in the Middle Ages, when the Church was the centre of musical activity in Europe. Traditionally, the service was chanted or sung by the clergy, assisted by a choir. They sang from memory but, as the liturgy expanded and the number of hymns increased, they soon found themselves unable to remember everything. Many systems were devised to overcome this, such as using hand signals to remind the choir of the melody, but writing down the melodies was the next step.

Hymns were written with marks above the words, ascending and descending as the melody did. This sufficed, but it was an imprecise system since it did not show on which note or pitch to begin. In the 11th century, a horizontal line was used to represent a single note. All the marks on the line were sung on that specified note. The higher the marks were above the line, the higher the notes were sung and vice versa. Soon a second line was added, representing a second note and reducing the number of notes between the two lines. More lines were added and by the 16th century we had the five lines constituting the modern musical stave. The marks became formalized and developed into the notes we know today.

The modern means of notating music has been accepted worldwide and can be read by musicians throughout the world. Music is probably the world's only universal language and it is the means by which a composer who lived 300 years ago can communicate his inspiration to a living performer today.

OPPOSITE This Renaissance hymnal is a good example of early music notation. Although the notes look different from modern notation, the contour of the melody is clear.

Accipit Calicem manu dextera, & eo se signans, dicit:

SAnguis Dómini nostri Jesu Christi custódiat ánimam meam in vitam ætérnam. Amen.

Sumit totum Sanguinem cum partícula. Quo sumpto, si qui sunt communicandi, eos communicet, antequam se purificet. Posteà dicit:

QUod ore súmpsimus, Dómine, pura mente capiámus : & de múnere temporáli fiat nobis remédium sempitérnum.

Interim porrigit Calicem minístro, qui infundit in eo parum vini, quo se purificat : deinde prosequitur:

COrpus tuum, Dómine, quod sumpsi, & Sanguis, quem potávi, adhæreat viscéribus meis : & præsta, ut in me non remáneat scélerum mácula, quem pura & sancta refecérunt sacraménta. Qui vivis & regnas in sæcula sæculórum. Amen.

Abluit digitos, extergit, & sumit ablutionem : extergit os, & Calicem, quem operit, & plicato

Corporáli, collocat in Altári ut priùs : deinde prosequitur Missam.

Dicto, post ultimam Oratiónem, Dóminus vobíscum. ℞. Et cum spíritu tuo, dicit pro Missæ qualitate, vel, Ite missa est, vel, Benedicámus Dómino. ℞. Deo grátias.

In Missis Defunctorum dicit Requiéscant in pace. ℞. Amen.

Tempore Paschali, hoc est, à Missa Sabbati sancti usque ad Sabbatum in Albis inclusive.

Ite missa est, alle lú ia, al le lú ia.

In Festis Solemnibus.

I te e e e e mis sa est.

RHYTHM

The value of the notes

Imagine an orange. It is round and if you leave it alone it will remain one whole orange. Similarly, one uncoloured circle constitutes one whole note (or semibreve; the older English terms are still used occasionally and are given in brackets). If you were to divide the orange into two equal parts, you would have two half oranges. To make a half note (minim), add a stem to a whole note. Dividing the half note equally, you would have two quarter notes (crotchets), which look like half notes, but with the circle coloured in. Dividing one quarter note results in two eighth notes (quavers), each looking like a quarter note with a flag, or tail, attached to the end of the stem. A sixteenth note (semiquaver) has two flags, while a thirty-second note (demisemiquaver) has three, and a sixty-fourth note (hemidemisemiquaver!) has four flags. So, all you need to do is multiply by two. Simple, isn't it?

NOTE VALUES

- = Whole note (semibreve)
- = Half note (minim)
- = Quarter note (crotchet)
- = Eighth note (quaver)
- = Sixteenth note (semiquaver)
- = Thirty-second note (demisemiquaver)
- = Sixty-fourth note (hemidemisemiquaver)

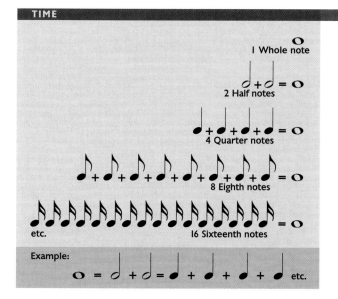

TIME

1 Whole note

2 Half notes

4 Quarter notes

8 Eighth notes

etc.   16 Sixteenth notes

Example: etc.

Time

Music takes place in time, and as an art form, it cannot exist without it. Thus, one quarter note will sound just as long as two eighth notes *in the same piece of music*. In the same way, one quarter note will sound only half the length of one half note. This very basic manifestation of mathematics is the foundation of all time in music. Time is a measurement of the general movement of a piece of music and learning to keep time is essential if you are to develop your playing skills.

In the accompanying graphic (left), the notes shown on each line all add up to the equivalent of one whole note (as shown on the top line).

The bar

This is not a place where you can order a martini, but the space between two bar lines. A bar line is a vertical line that runs from the top to the bottom of a stave (the five horizontal lines on which music is written, see p22) and can often span several staves. Each bar has a number (usually starting with one) and is the musician's means of finding a certain place in a piece of music. Two bar lines of equal thickness next to one another constitute a double bar line, which is used to divide a piece into sections. The final bar line has a thick second line and usually occurs at the end of a piece.

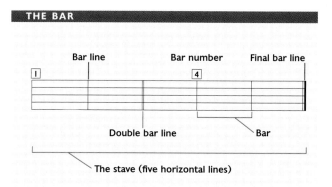

THE BAR

Bar line   Bar number   Final bar line

Double bar line   Bar

The stave (five horizontal lines)

Time signature

Most music pieces have a time signature at the beginning.. It is written as one number above another and divides each bar into equal beats. The top number (usually between 2 and 12) gives the number of beats per bar. The bottom number (any multiple of two) gives the value of a beat. A two signifies a half note per beat; a four, a quarter note per beat; an eight, an eighth note, and so on. There are various ways of counting beats and rhythm, including the French time-name method (ta, ta-te etc.). This book uses numbers to denote beats.

TIME SIGNATURE

$\frac{4}{4}$ time is sometimes notated as common time, derived from an old way of denoting time values (C = $\frac{4}{4}$, ₵ = $\frac{2}{2}$). There are four quarter notes (crotchets) to the bar in both examples above.

BEAT VALUES PER BAR

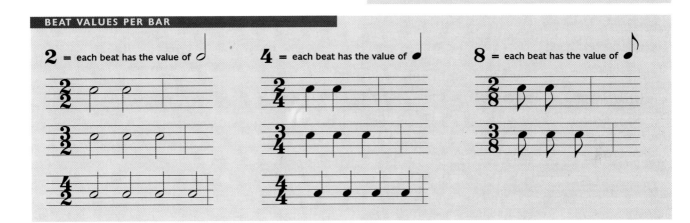

Counting the beats

It is imperative to count out loud the beats of a bar while you play, making sure that all beats are equal in length. In the examples, beats are indicated by a number above the note that takes the main beat, while subdivisions of the beat are marked with an + sign (spoken as 'and', not 'plus').

In the first example below, each bar should be counted as follows: 'One and two and three and'.

Whether you count out loud or tap out the beats with your fingers or toes, it is useful to establish the rhythm of a piece before you begin playing it.

An instrument called a metronome (see pp35 and 93) can help you keep a steady beat when you are learning, but it is essential that you are able to maintain a stable beat without it if your playing is to progress.

COUNTING THE BEATS

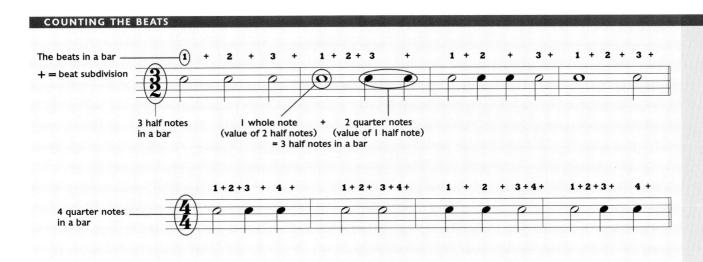

Rests

Music has to breathe, and composers use rests within the bars to achieve this. Just as note values indicate the duration of a note, so there are rest signs to indicate where there is silence. Each note value has a corresponding rest sign.

The whole note rest sign looks like a small black rectangle 'hanging' from a line. A half note rest looks the same, but 'sits' on the line. A quarter note rest looks like a squiggle (or a back-to-front eighth rest), while the rests for the flagged notes (eighths, sixteenths, etc.) look like a '7', with the top indicating the number of flags. However, if an entire bar is to remain silent, a whole note rest is used, no matter what the time signature of the piece is.

RESTS

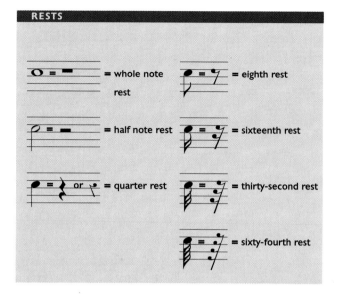

DOTTED NOTES

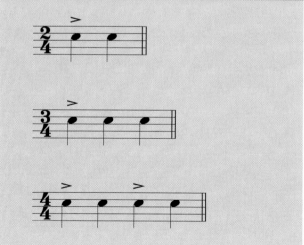

Dotted half note = one half note + one quarter note.

Dotted quarter note = one quarter note + one eighth note.

Dotted eighth note = one eighth note + one sixteenth note.

Double-dotted note = one quarter + one eighth + one sixteenth.

Dots

A dot to the immediate right of a note lengthens the note by half its value. Thus a dotted half note will be equal in length to one half note plus one quarter note (or three quarter notes). This rule applies to rests as well.

If a second dot (called a double dot) appears to the immediate right of the first dot, it will further lengthen the note's value by half of the first dot. Thus, a double-dotted half note will sound the composite length of a half note plus a quarter note plus an eighth note (or seven eighth notes).

In Baroque music (see p40), dotted notes are usually played as double-dotted notes, to increase the vitality of the music.

Accents

In a piece of music with a regular beat, some beats are more important than others. In a piece with two beats to a bar (like a march), the first beat is usually more important than the second. In a piece with three beats to a bar (like a waltz), the first beat is usually more important than the second or third beats. When there are four beats to a bar, the first beat is usually the most important, the third beat is the next most important, and the second and fourth beats the least important.

The sign used to make a note more important is called an accent (>). It looks like an arrowhead or sideways triangle and is written close to the head of the note it is accenting.

ACCENTS

Groups

Notes are grouped in a certain way within the bar. If there are three beats to a bar, the notes will be grouped into three groups. This only applies to notes that are equal to or smaller in value than the value of a beat. Notice how the beam (the line that joins two or more notes) links the notes together. Only notes with flags (tails) get beamed together, with the number of beams corresponding to the number of flags. This looks neater than writing each flagged note separately.

Time signatures with a 2, 3 or 4 as the top value are called simple times, because there are only as many groups of notes as there are beats. Time signatures with a 6, 9 or 12 as the top value are called compound times, because there are three beats to a group.

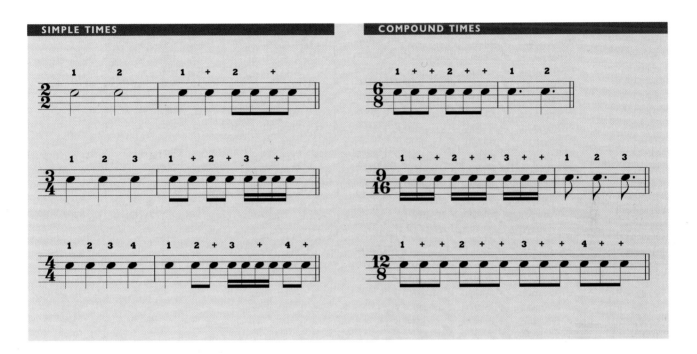

Rhythm exercises

Congratulations! You are now halfway through your journey of learning to read music. The three exercises below should help you to read musical rhythm.

Using the beats provided as a guideline, first count the beats out loudly (one and two and three and etc.), keeping a steady pulse, then simultaneously count and clap the rhythm of the notes. Go slowly, otherwise you'll get very mixed up.

PITCH

The Keyboard

The arrangement of the keyboard into two rows of white and black keys (the black keys in groups of two and three) was standardized by the 15th century. On many older instruments, like harpsichords and organs, the colours are reversed, simply because ebony was more readily available than ivory. The grouping of black keys is consistent across the entire keyboard (except at the extreme edges). This is because the white keys are named after the first seven letters of the alphabet. Every white note to the immediate right of the middle black note in the groups of three is the note A. The next white note, to the right of A, is B. The next white note is C, and so on as far as G, after which the next note is A, once again to the right of the middle black note. Adjacent A's are said to be an octave apart because there are eight white notes from the one to the other (from the Latin *octo* meaning eight).

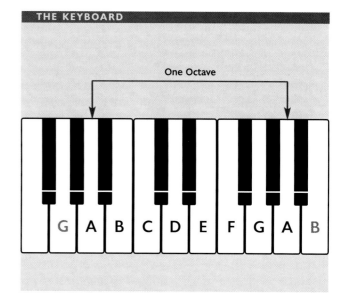

THE KEYBOARD

One Octave

G A B C D E F G A B

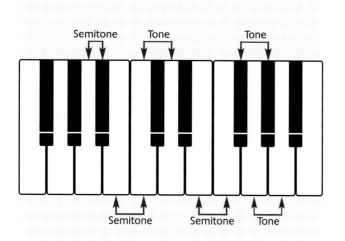

TONES AND SEMITONES

Semitone   Tone   Tone

Semitone   Semitone   Tone

Tones and semitones

If you count all the notes (including the black keys) in an octave, you will get 12. These are the twelve semitones that make up an octave. Adjacent notes are a semitone apart. The distance between two notes that are separated by one note is a whole tone. Thus two semitones form a whole tone.

The stave

The stave, or staff, consists of five horizontal lines. A note is either on a line or in the space between two lines. If notes go higher or lower than the stave allows, a ledger line is used (see opposite page). This has the same function as the other lines, but is only used for the specific note.

Clef signs

Clef signs are used to specify the register of notes. The treble, or soprano, clef (𝄞) is generally used for notes above middle C (the C in the middle of the keyboard), while the bass clef (𝄢) is generally used for notes below middle C. (There are other clefs, but these are the only ones used in modern editions of piano music.)

In the treble clef, middle C is notated on the first ledger line below the stave, making the note on the first line of the stave (the bottom line) the E above it. In the bass clef, middle C is notated on the first ledger line above the stave and the note on the bottom line is the G an octave and a half below middle C. The grand stave consists of both these staves.

Knowing your way around a keyboard is a fundamental skill.

POSITION OF THE NOTES ON THE GRAND STAVE

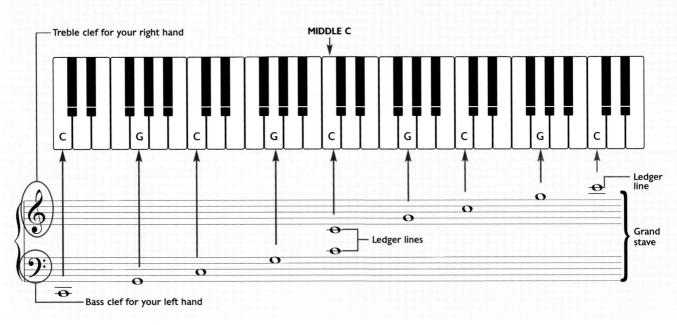

Treble clef for your right hand

MIDDLE C

Ledger line

Ledger lines

Grand stave

Bass clef for your left hand

Accidentals

These are signs that alter the pitch of any note they are written in front of. A sharp sign (♯) raises a note by one semitone, while a flat sign (♭) lowers a note by one semitone. Thus a G♯, (the middle of the three black notes), will be a semitone above a G. If one note in a bar is sharpened, for instance a C, then all subsequent C's in that bar are also sharpened.

A bar line (see p18) cancels all accidentals that occur in the previous bar. If a sharp or flat is cancelled in the same bar, a natural sign (♮) is used. All notes are natural (that is, in their 'natural' state) unless flattened or sharpened, but we do not write out the natural sign for each one.

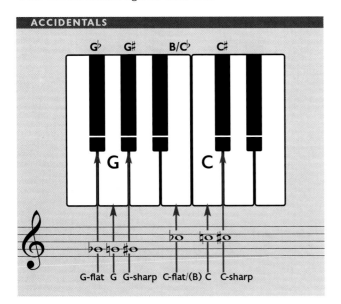

ACCIDENTALS

G♭   G♯   B/C♭   C♯

G   C

G-flat G G-sharp C-flat/(B) C C-sharp

Key signatures

A key signature is a collection of sharps or flats written at the beginning of a piece of music, and indicating that all the subsequent notes on that pitch are altered. Thus, if an F-sharp occurs at the beginning of a piece as a key signature, all Fs in the piece are sharpened unless they are altered by a natural sign. (Remember that a natural sign will only alter subsequent notes in the same bar, after which the bar line once again enforces the key signature.)

Sharps and flats are always introduced into a key signature in a definite order. For sharps, this is F, C, G, D, A, E and B. The first sharp will always be F-sharp and the second one will be C-sharp. Therefore, if a piece has a key signature of only one sharp it will always be F-sharp, if it has two sharps they will be F-sharp and C-sharp, and so on.

The order in which flats are introduced into a key signature is exactly the opposite (B, E, A, D, G, C, F).

KEY SIGNATURE

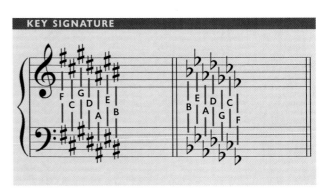

F G D E
   C   A B

E D C
B A G F

23

Pitch exercises

These exercises will help you learn to read pitch. The rhythm of all the notes is equal, so you don't need to concentrate too much on that. Bear in mind that the names of the notes in both clefs are the same, but they are two octaves apart on the keyboard. Remember to look at the key signature.

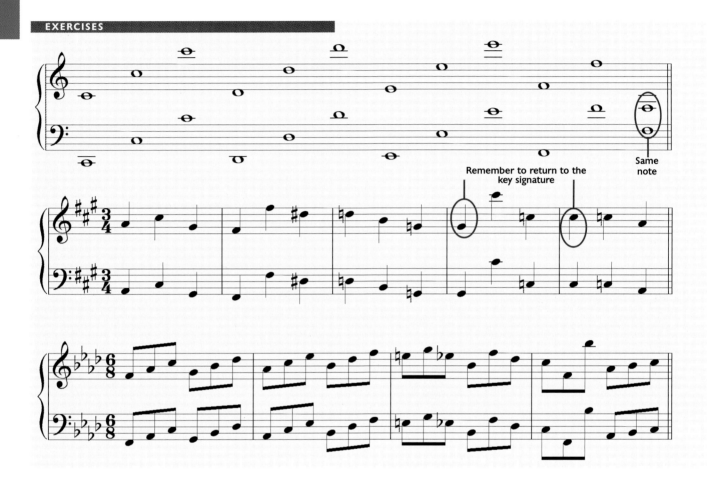

EXERCISES

Remember to return to the key signature

Same note

Tempo

These are words that are written in the top left-hand corner of a piece of music. They describe how fast or slow the piece should be played. A piece with many sections can have multiple tempo indications, but they are always written above the top stave. Some of the most commonly used words are given below. Consult the glossary on p92 for others.

TEMPO

Adagio – Slowly (at a relaxed pace, at leisure)
Andante – Moderately slow (at a steady, walking pace)
Allegro – In a fast and lively manner
Presto – Very fast, rapidly
Accelerando (accel.) – Getting gradually faster
Ritardando (rit.) – Getting gradually slower

Dynamics

These are words or abbreviations that indicate the dynamics (variations in loudness and softness) of a piece or between groups of notes. Dynamics are usually written between the two staves of the grand stave, but if each hand plays different dynamics, they are written below the respective stave. As with tempo and articulation, most of the terms are Italian in origin.

DYNAMICS

Fortissimo (very loud) – $\boldsymbol{f\!f}$
Forte (loud) – $\boldsymbol{f}$
Mezzo forte (moderately loud) – $\boldsymbol{mf}$
Piano (soft), pianissimo (very soft) – $\boldsymbol{p}$, $\boldsymbol{pp}$
Crescendo (cresc.) – Getting gradually louder
Decrescendo (decresc.) – Getting gradually softer

Articulation

There are various signs and words (mostly Italian in origin) that alter the length of notes, both individually and in relationship to one another. As far as the piano is concerned, these articulation signs refer to the manner in which you play the notes on the keyboard.

Legato The 'normal' way of playing consecutive notes with very little silence between them and as smoothly as possible (imagine oil flowing over a smooth surface). The nature of legato playing differs according to the style of music you play. (See also exercise 2 on p31.)

Staccato A dot *above* a note (not to be confused with the dot *next to* a note that lengthens its value, see p20), indicates that the note should be played shorter than written (usually only half its length). It is used to cancel out all the rest signs that one would otherwise have had to use, and gives the note a breathless, almost 'clipped' sound.

Tenuto A short horizontal line above a note, meaning the note should be held for its full value and played with feeling.

The tie A short curved line connecting two notes with the same pitch, either from different groups in the same bar or on either side of a bar line. The tie makes the two notes sound like one note of composite length.

The slur A curved line written above a collection of notes of different pitch. It can span several bars and indicates that the notes written beneath it form a single musical unity or phrase and should therefore be played legato.

PUTTING IT ALL TOGETHER

The most important thing to remember is that rhythm and pitch are equal partners in music and both are indispensable. The most difficult thing to do when reading music is to concentrate on both. Luckily this skill can be practiced. Here are some tips on how to practise sight-reading effectively.

• Read as much music as possible. Just as your reading speed increases if you read a lot of books, the more music you read, the easier it becomes.

• Read from the lowest note to the highest note. For most people, the left hand is less agile than the right. The sooner you find your left-hand notes, the better.

• Try to keep your eyes one bar ahead of your hands.

• Concentrate on rhythm first because you can read it faster than pitch. When reading ahead, assess the rhythm of the entire bar instantaneously (it is easier than you think). This leaves you free to concentrate on pitch.

The ability to read music develops over time, so do not be disheartened if you do not achieve results immediately.

That, in a nutshell, is everything you need to know in order to read music. The glossary (see p92), explains many terms you might come across in your initial exploration of music. If you encounter terms that you do not understand, it is time to invest in a musical dictionary or reference book.

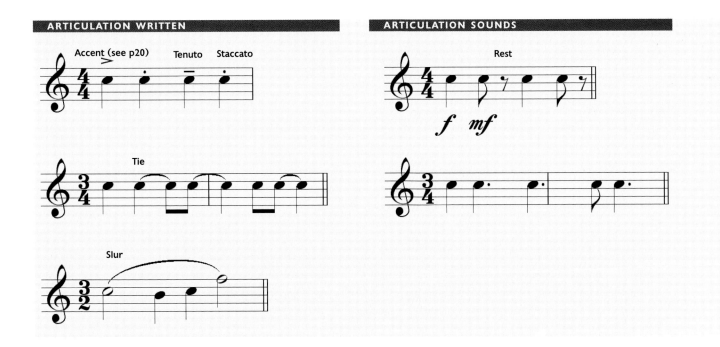

ARTICULATION WRITTEN

ARTICULATION SOUNDS

25

chapter three

PRACTISE BEFORE PLAYING

THERE ARE AS MANY WAYS TO PLAY THE PIANO as there are teachers to teach it. All teachers and experienced players have their own ideas of what constitutes 'proper' piano playing and what does not. Every teacher develops his or her own style. One teacher might demand that your wrists are lowered, while another would have you raise them. As a beginner though, the most important thing is to play the piano in the manner that gives you the greatest joy and pleasure. The legendary jazz maestro Louis Armstrong was quite sensible when he stated, 'There's only two ways to sum up music: either it's good or it's bad, and if it's good you don't mess around with it, you just enjoy it.'

When you are learning, it may be tempting to disregard conventional practices in the belief that you will pick them up as you go along, but it is much harder to correct mistakes later than it is to learn to do things the right way; so start as you mean to continue. Maintaining the correct posture and hand positions might seem tedious, and will probably be tiring until your body adapts, but in time, your fingers will start to move fluidly and you will automatically sit correctly at the keyboard. Without realizing it, your playing will have moved to the next level.

In the past, it was common for two outstanding pianists to belittle each other because of the way the other played. While the public usually enjoyed this mutual antagonism, they often could not figure out the difference between the two players, for individual nuances of style and interpretation can be very subtle indeed and are the result of dedicated and intense practice over many years.

As a beginner, you will probably have neither the time nor the inclination to spend hours practising scales and other exercises but, as with any sport or other activity, the more you practise, the easier it becomes, so do try to set aside an hour or two on a regular basis. You'll soon see the results in your playing.

This chapter is devoted to the actual mechanics of piano playing. It highlights some of the difficulties of playing the piano and suggests how these can be overcome. Some technical exercises are included to help promote a sound technique (way of playing) by strengthening the fingers and developing their agility.

OPPOSITE Many beginners are put off by the thought of repetitive practising, but if you get into a regular routine, practising will become less of a chore.

GENERAL POSTURE

Posture refers to the general way in which we hold or position our bodies. As far as the piano is concerned, posture refers mostly to the way you sit when you play.

• Relax. A bit of tension is good, but the most important thing is to be as comfortable as possible. Your chair should be comfortable, level and in line with the keyboard.

• Imagine a straight line running from the top of your head to the point where your buttocks make contact with the chair. You should endeavour to keep the line straight but not rigid.

• Your navel should be level with the top of the white keys.

• To ensure that you are sitting at an appropriate distance from the piano, make your hands into fists and extend your arms. Your fists should just touch the back of the keyboard.

• Your knees should be comfortably apart. Your right foot should rest flat on the floor with the toes almost touching the right pedal. The toes of the left foot should be in a straight line with the back of the right foot and a foot's width should separate the two. This will help you remain balanced and ensure you do not fall off your chair if you sway from side to side as you play. Leaning slightly forwards also helps your balance, as does sitting three-quarters of the way into your chair.

This is an ideal posture from which to begin playing.

Establish the correct distance from the piano before you play.

Hands, arms and shoulders

The most important parts of a pianist's body are the hands, arms and shoulders. It is here that you find the most variation between what different teachers recommend.

• Put both hands on your knees. Remove them and, keeping the rounded form of your fingers, place them lightly on the keyboard with one finger to each of five adjacent white notes. This is called the 'high' hand position. It is good for beginners as it promotes finger work (when depressing the keys the hand should remain still and only the fingers should move).

• With your hands still in contact with the keys, gently lift your elbows about a fist-and-a-half's width from your sides. This space gives your arms some buoyancy and stops you from exerting too much weight on the hands alone. This is a good starting position for beginners. It may feel uncomfortable at first, but it will become easier as your shoulder and back muscles become stronger. If you feel yourself tensing up while playing, stop and relax, then take up the position again. It will soon become second nature, leaving you free to concentrate on the music.

• Keep your nails short. You can break them while playing, and long nails clicking on the keys can be very irritating.

USING THE PEDALS

When you start playing the piano, you may think that using the pedals is very complicated. As a beginner, it is probably better to concentrate on playing the correct notes and rhythms, but if you want to use the pedals, bear the following in mind:

• The pedals are depressed with the front (ball) of the foot, while the heel remains in contact with the floor.

• The soft pedal (the left-hand one) reduces the sound by causing the hammers to strike fewer strings (see p14). Don't use it in soft passages. Your fingers are capable of playing softly and composers only ask for this pedal because of the change in tone it facilitates.

• The sustaining pedal (on the right) enriches tones, increases the resonance of individual notes and helps to facilitate long legato passages (see p25). Use this pedal with discretion. If it falls into the wrong hands (or feet), it can muddy the sound and you could lose the beautiful harmonies of the music.

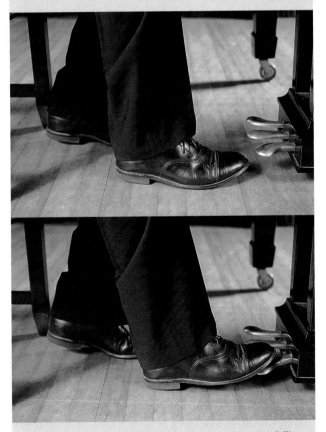

ABOVE Keep your spine as straight as possible when playing.
TOP The high hand position is a good starting point.

ABOVE Your heel should be on the ground when pedalling.
TOP Have your feet in the right position before playing.

29

WHY PRACTISE TECHNICAL EXERCISES?

Technical exercises teach you to control the movement of your fingers and train them to move in certain ways. They also make your fingers stronger and more flexible. If you have ever noticed a concert pianist's fingers moving so fast that you can't see them, you will realize that many hours of technical exercises have made his or her fingers that agile.

All pianists should know the standard way of playing typical passages such as scales, arpeggios and chords. Two-hand exercises teach your hands to be independent of each other. Do not be worried if your left hand wants to move in the same direction as your right or vice versa. This is natural and takes practice to overcome.

The main objective behind technical exercises is to learn to translate thought into action. Each note has a corresponding action to create it. A quick, fluid translation is important if you are to learn to play more advanced pieces.

Play technical exercises frequently in order to reap their benefits. Repetitive practice however, is very boring, so leave the task of practising scales hour after hour to the serious musicians. Spend as much time on these exercises as you are able to, but if your mind starts wandering, stop and do something more interesting. Many people give up playing the piano because teachers over emphasize repetitive practice. It takes all the fun out of it and, if you do not enjoy something, you should not waste a second of your life doing it. Remember though, that these exercises do have many advantages and it would be a shame not to use them to help you play better. Achieving the results you want is directly proportional to the amount of time that you are willing to spend.

In the exercises, fingering marks are written near the notes. The number 1 always refers to the thumb (of either hand) and 5 to the little finger. All the exercises can be transposed. This means that it is possible to start them on any of the 12 notes within an octave, as long as the distance between the different notes remains the same (see below).

TRANSPOSITION

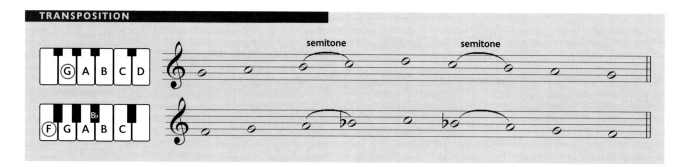

Exercise 1 – Finger position

Take up the correct hand position and place your right hand (RH) with your thumb on the G above middle C and the rest of your fingers on the four adjacent white notes. Press your hand down, making sure that all the notes sound simultaneously and are equally loud. Your hand should stay in the same form and your fingers should not buckle. The notes should be loud and clear. This exercise will strengthen your fingers and teach them what the distance between the white notes feels like. You can also lift your hand high into the air and bring it down again on the same notes. This 'target practice' teaches you to aim for the right notes. Play the exercise on any five adjacent white notes. Repeat it with the left hand and then with both hands simultaneously.

This exercise can also be used to familiarize yourself with the action of a piano which you have not played before.

FINGER POSITION

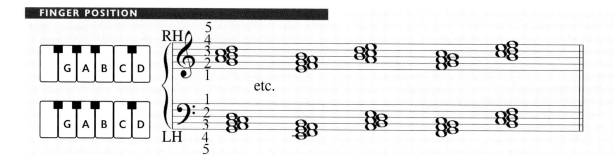

Exercise 2 – Individual notes

Start with your hand in the same position as for the previous exercise. This time, play each note separately, starting with your thumb. Only the finger that has a note to play should be doing the work. Keep the other four fingers relaxed and in light contact with the keys. When releasing a key, simply relax the playing finger and allow the key to push your finger back to its starting position. Try at all times to keep your fingers relaxed and in contact with the keys, even when they are not playing. Then go on to the next finger and repeat the process.

Practise the exercise in two ways. First play semi-staccato, meaning that you make a small break between each note (see p25); and then legato, where you press down the next finger at the exact instant you lift the previous one (think of the action a see-saw makes). This exercise is meant to teach the fingers to move separately, as well as teach you the difference between playing in a detached style and a legato style.

Play the exercise with separate hands first, then both hands simultaneously, so that the left hand plays in the opposite direction to the right hand.

Exercise 3 – Swinging thumb

This series of exercises strengthens your fingers and makes them more flexible. Practise each hand separately until you are comfortable with the action and then play both hands together. Start by pressing any note with your third finger (once again this counts for both hands) and play the notes on either side with your thumb (3a). Remember to keep your hand high so that your thumb can fit beneath the third finger. This swinging action is important in many scale passages.

The other forms of this exercise (3b, 3c, 3d) are based on the same principle, whereby one note is depressed and the adjacent fingers play adjacent notes while the remaining two fingers are relaxed. At first, this is a lot more difficult than it looks, because you suddenly become aware that you have more fingers on one hand than you can concentrate on. In the final exercise (3d), you will find that your fifth finger can't move very far without help from the fourth finger. Don't worry, it does get easier!

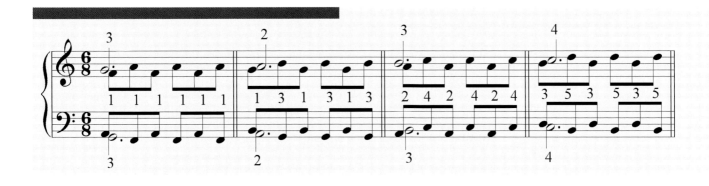

Exercise 4 – Recognizing patterns

This teaches you to translate thought into action. It warms up your fingers and teaches them to recognize patterns that may seem illogical to the brain. You will have to concentrate in the beginning, until your fingers get used to the movements. Work with each hand separately and then play both hands together, either as written below, or an octave apart. Go slowly – if you start too fast you will get very mixed up.

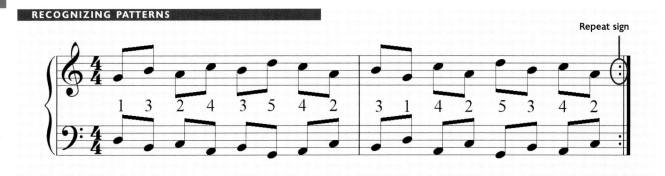

Exercise 5 – Scales

The word scale comes from the Latin *scala*, meaning ladder. The most important thing about a scale is that it begins and ends on the same note. The first form of the scale is called the major (5a). It is distinguishable from other scales by the position of its semitones (marked with slurs).

The fingering shown is the standard one, but the scale can also be played using only the first and second fingers. To extend it, simply use your first finger on the last note instead of your fifth finger (on the right hand) and carry on in the same way as you did on the same notes an octave lower.

The encircled fingers are the important ones to remember as they function as pivots for the swinging thumb (described in exercise 3). Scales can be played in either direction, but the fingering remains the same. Remember that the left hand will play the scales an octave lower on the keyboard.

Some commonly used scales (below and opposite), include the major (5a), harmonic minor (5b), whole-tone (5c) and the blues (5d) scale. Exercises involving scales have been a staple of pianists for more than a century. French composer Camille Saint-Saëns (1835–1921), uses scales mockingly in a movement entitled 'The Pianist' from his *Carnival of the Animals*.

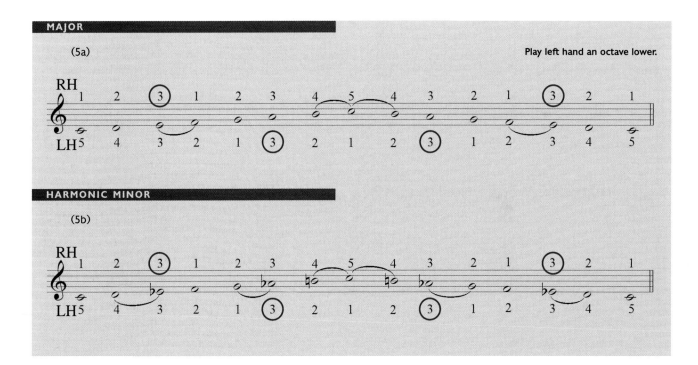

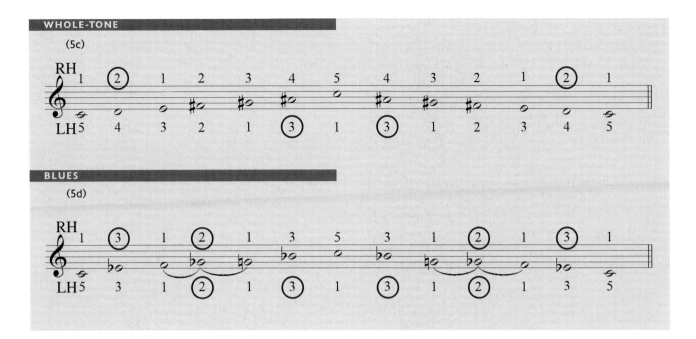

Exercise 6 – Distance of an octave

This exercise teaches the hands to recognize the distance of the octave and to keep a constant distance between first and fifth finger. The examples can be played as octaves, where two notes an octave apart are pressed simultaneously (6a), or as broken octaves, where either the top or bottom note is pressed first, then is followed by the octave (6b). Octaves are favoured by composers and you often see a concert pianist's hands flying over the keyboard as he or she plays a fiendishly difficult octave passage. This is also a lovely target-practice exercise, improving your aim on the piano. Try not to look at your hands too often, as playing must become intuitive.

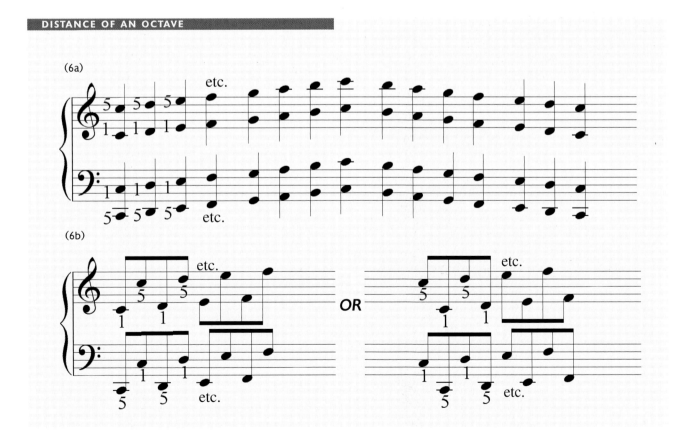

Exercise 7 – Hand formation

This is based on the previous exercise. It is a succession of chords, with the outer notes still maintaining the space of one octave apart. It teaches you to keep a constant distance between your fingers (and therefore your entire hand). If you do not keep your hand position constant, you will not be able to play the exercise, as it has a stretched-out hand position, which is difficult. However, as the strength and suppleness of your fingers improve, it should become easier to play.

This exercise is best played only on the white keys (unless you are feeling adventurous). Practise with each hand separately until you are comfortable, and then put both together. Start slowly and speed it up as you go along. The exercise can be played in both directions.

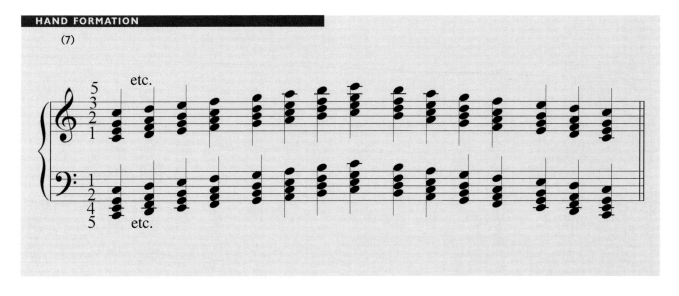

Exercise 8 – Putting it all together

This exercise contains a bit of everything and is a lot of fun to play really fast. It sounds very impressive, although it is not too difficult. The first form (8a) is a pattern of descending intervals (see p92) that requires a set pattern of fingering and teaches you to maintain your hand position while moving down the keyboard (to the left). Practise both hands separately, then together. The second form (8b) is a broken-chord version of the same notes. The movement of the hands is symmetrical from the inside outwards. Once again, note the pattern of the notes and their fingerings. Start this exercise at the top (or right) of the keyboard and play it all the way to the bottom.

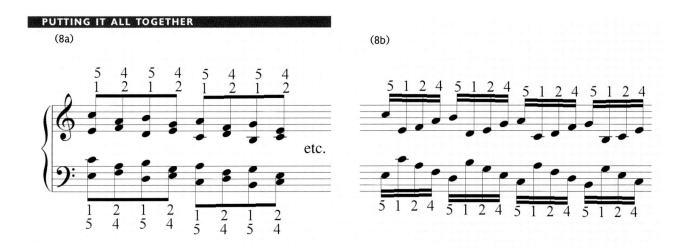

SOME TIPS FOR PRACTISING

Practising with a purpose will help you to achieve results faster than if you go about it in a disorderly and unsystematic way. But practising should never become an end in itself and you should not become discouraged if getting the hang of things takes more time than you anticipated.

All musicians have to practise. It is one aspect of making music that teaches you something about yourself. Are you patient or easily distracted? Are you hardworking or do you look for quick results? Would you prefer to do something else, anything else, rather than practise? Although it is essential if you wish to progress, practising does not have to be a chore. Approach it with a specific objective in mind and you will soon find it becomes increasingly easy to set aside time for practising. (Think of practising as exercise for your hands and create a regular work-out programme as if you were planning sessions in the gym!)

These tips will help you focus on what to do when you are practising. Follow them as far as you want to, but never forget that the reason you are practising is to learn how to make music. Make your practice sessions enjoyable. Have fun. Laugh out loud, and ignore these suggestions if they hamper your enjoyment in any way.

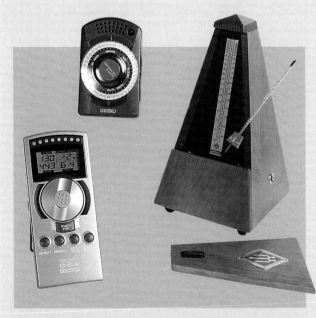

Metronomes help to establish and maintain strict rhythm.

• **Practise with each hand separately at first**, concentrating on one hand at a time. Getting a piece 'under your fingers' is the easiest way to start. Only when both hands know their separate parts well, should you proceed to put the hands together, slowing your playing down until you are comfortable. If you have good sight-reading capabilities, an initial sight-reading or a quick 'playing through' of the entire piece will help you get a feel for the music.

• **Once you have chosen your fingering, stick to it.** As strange as it may sound, your fingers remember. Changing your fingering often retards your progress when learning a new piece. Fingering marks are included in all the pieces and exercises in this book. They are not necessarily the only fingerings for the pieces, but are a good place to start until you become adept at choosing your own.

• **Start slowly.** Once your fingers and notes are secure, you can speed up your playing gradually.

• **Try not to look at your hands too often.** Your fingers should learn to be intuitive in feeling out the right distances between notes.

• **Divide the piece into sections** and concentrate on one section at a time.

• **When you make a mistake, never simply ignore it** and continue playing. Stop and play the section again. You should be able to play it perfectly at least five times before you move on to the next section.

• **Count out loud** when you first start practising a piece. This will help you concentrate more acutely on the rhythm and on staying in time. If you want something to count out the beats for you, invest in a metronome, an instrument which beats a constant pulse. It might make your playing sound a bit robotic, but it is useful to help you establish a strict rhythm. Metronomes come in both mechanical and electronic versions and the tempo can be adjusted.

• **Read through a piece** of music before you play it for the first time. Notice the details and mark anything that your eyes might miss when you are concentrating on the notes and rhythms (see p38).

• **Do not play without the sheet music** in front of you, even if you are good at memorizing music. Players who rely too much on memory are often poor sight-readers, which can inhibit their learning of new pieces.

chapter four

INTERPRETING MUSIC

THE PROCESS BY WHICH A PLAYER TURNS THE NOTES ON PAPER INTO SOUND is a highly personal one. If you compare recordings by two different artists playing the same piece, you will be amazed at how much they can differ. This aspect of music is called interpretation.

Interpreting music takes place on three levels. Firstly, you must give a clear and accurate rendition of what the composer wrote. The player is basically translating the thoughts of the composer into sound. This does not only refer to the notes themselves, but also to specific aspects, such as dynamic markings and articulation, that the composer wrote to enhance the emotional character of his music.

On a second level, interpretation means conforming to the stylistic norms and conventions associated with the music of a specific era. All musicians agree that you cannot play Bach in the same way that you play Beethoven.

Lastly, the players' own emotions dictate the subtle nuances of the music he or she plays. Every musician strives to get behind the soul of the music and be able to relate in a meaningful way with the composer.

The first two levels of interpretation can be taught or learnt from books. The third one is intuitive and accounts for the pleasure you get from listening to and appreciating music that speaks to your soul. This may sound very esoteric, but having such a goal in mind makes all the practising worthwhile.

This chapter contains a selection of musical pieces spanning 300 years. They have been chosen to give you some insight into how to go about interpreting music. Each piece comes from a specific period and some background to the era, as well as a short biography of each featured composer, are provided to help place the music in context. Each piece is accompanied by notes to aid your interpretation. If you need an explanation for something that is not covered in the playing notes, refer back to the theory in Chapter 2. As you progress, you should find that you need to refer back less and less.

Start with the first piece and work through to the last one. Some of the pieces might seem a bit difficult for beginners, but adults can usually figure most things out if shown the way, so don't get discouraged. Just relax and enjoy the music.

OPPOSITE After countless hours of practise, making music becomes magical.

Reading through a piece of music

Use the example on the opposite page to learn how to interpret music in a logical and orderly way. When you encounter an unfamiliar piece of music, first look at the top right-hand corner of the page to see who the composer is. This will help you to orientate yourself from the start to the style of the music. The example chosen is by César Franck (1822–90), a French Romantic composer.

An opus, or work number, may be written below the name of the composer (it is not in this case). This specifies the exact work and often gives a clue as to when it was written. (Usually works with smaller opus numbers come from earlier in the composer's life than those with larger opus numbers.)

The playing tips (below) highlight some of the things you need to note before you begin playing. Being aware of changes in key, tempo or time will enable you to concentrate on the notes you are playing and to play with confidence. These tips are all you need to know when it comes to the first level of interpretation. The rest of this chapter is devoted to increasing your understanding of the different styles of piano music. Different musical periods are discussed briefly, followed by music in the style of each period, accompanied by playing tips.

PLAYING NOTES

- The piece on the opposite page is quite difficult to play and is only intended to demonstrate how to interpret music.
- Does the title **A** give any clues as to its interpretation? (For instance, is it a waltz or a march?) This is the second of 'three small pieces' which is not much to go on.
- The tempo marking **B** (see p24) indicates how fast or slowly the piece should be played. Poco allegro means somewhat fast. Scan the piece for other words that might alter the tempo, including accelerando (faster) or rallentando (slower).
- Does the time signature **C** (see p19) remain constant throughout, or does it change? In this piece it remains constant.
- The key signature **D** (see p23) has four sharps (F, C, G, D), but no other changes are indicated. Accidentals **E** (see p23) indicate any notes that differ from the key signature.
- Dynamics **F** (see p24) are usually written between the two staves of the grand stave (see p22), but if each hand plays different dynamics, they are written below each stave.
- Look for words that indicate the 'character' of a piece (the way the composer wishes it to be played). The pp delicato **G** means play delicately as well as very softly (pianissimo), while dolce espr. in bar 13 means sweetly and with feeling.

Trois Petites Pièces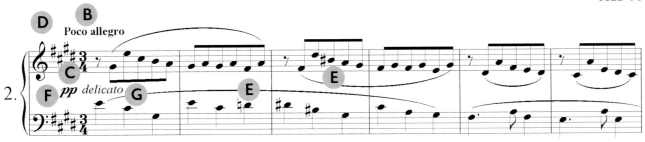

César Franck
1822–90

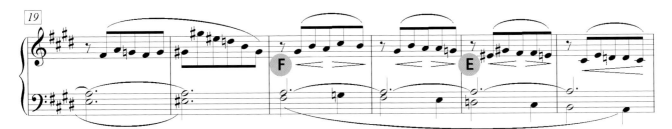

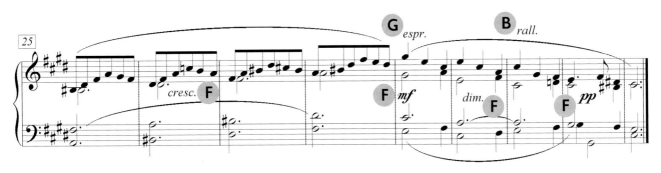

THE BAROQUE PERIOD 1600–1750

A revival in magnificent style

Baroque, from the Portuguese word *barroco* (an irregularly shaped pearl), describes the elaborate style, with its excessive ornamentation and grandiose scale, associated with the music, art and architecture of the 17th and early 18th centuries.

Artistically, the full bloom of the period is seen in the works of the Flemish painter Rubens, Italy's Caravaggio and Spain's Velásquez. Italian Giovanni Bernini, whose sculpture depicting the *Ecstasy of St Theresa* is a masterpiece of the era, also designed the majestic colonnaded piazza of St Peter's Basilica in Rome and the ornate canopy over its High Altar.

To a certain extent, the opulent Baroque style was part of the Counter Reformation, a revival of the Roman Catholic Church that followed the Protestant Reformation. Although the Church and Court remained the main sources of patronage for the arts, artists now realized that they could flourish outside these spheres.

The Baroque was greatly influenced by Italian culture. Italy had many wealthy trading cities, which supported a lively artistic life. Italy was also the cradle of the Renaissance, the great rediscovery of classical learning and art that encouraged the development of humanism and scientific inquiry

Musically, Italy was the source of new musical forms, such as the madrigal, the cantata, the oratorio, the sonata and the *dramma per musica*, which evolved into what we know as opera. Italy was also the birthplace of the violin, which evolved through the attempts of instrument makers to recreate the sound of the human voice. Composers such as Arcangelo Corelli (1653–1713) and Antonio Vivaldi (1678–1741) wrote music mainly for groups of violinists, sometimes with the addition of trumpet, oboe, bassoon or flute.

The music of Italian composers became highly popular in the cultivated circles of Europe. In 17th-century France, music revolved around the Royal Court. Both Louis XIII and Louis XIV supported musical life, in particular ballet, which was considered the highest art form. After he assumed the throne in 1661, Louis XIV built the great palace of Versailles, outside Paris. Court life featured many concerts, musical theatre, ballets and performances of religious music.

During the Baroque era the keyboard, in the form of the harpsichord and organ, became prominent. Although keyboard instruments existed during the Renaissance, most music of the time was written for church services. Two of the greatest Renaissance composers were the English organists William Byrd (1543–1623) and Orlando Gibbons (1583–1625).

The harpsichord, which produces its sound by means of a plectrum plucking strings (unlike a piano, where the strings are hammered), was well suited to the clarity and crispness of Baroque music. The range and size of the harpsichord was extended during this period, and new forms of music, such as the toccata and the cappricio, were developed to suit its capabilities.

The great Italian composer, Domenico Scarlatti (1685–1757), wrote 555 sonatas for the harpsichord, and the French composer François Couperin (1668–1733), who was also the royal organist, became renowned for his exquisite harpsichord suites.

Louis XIV's lavish palace at Versailles is one of the pinnacles of Baroque architecture.

Many musicians composed pieces especially for court dances.

⊃PLAYING NOTES

- Tempo, dynamics and articulation markings (see pp24-25) are not often seen in early music. The musicians knew how the pieces had to be played, so it was not necessary to write things down. Over the years, musicologists have pieced together evidence, but are still not entirely sure of how works by early composers should be interpreted.
- Ornaments (see p48) are smaller printed notes that embellish the melodic line. The ornament and the note it accentuates are played in the same time it would take to play the main note on its own, which receives less emphasis than the main note.

In the Lutheran churches of northern Europe, sacred music centred around chorales. These were hymns sung by the congregation or choir, not just the clergy. The church organ was an object of local pride and many German churches of this period still have beautiful organs. Cantatas, passions and oratorios, which combined chorales with the recitative-aria pattern, flourished in the Protestant churches of Germany. Among the best known are the *St Matthew Passion* and *St John Passion* by JS Bach; and Handel's oratorios, including *The Messiah* and *Judas Maccabeus*, which were performed in theatres.

The pieces included in this section are by Johann Sebastian Bach (1685–1750) and Georg Friedrich Handel (1685–1759), two musical geniuses who are often hailed as the supreme masters of the Baroque style. Musicians were often employed by the aristocracy, so much of the music composed at this time had a functional value. For example, Bach's *Goldberg Variations* for the harpsichord were written to ease a nobleman's insomnia, while many of Handel's organ concertos helped set the tone for an evening at the theatre.

By 1750 (the year Bach died), the piano was taking over from the organ and harpsichord as the most important keyboard instrument and new works were being composed for it. Today there are purists who think that as Baroque works were not conceived for the piano, they should not be played on it, but no modern pianist should be barred from exploring the wonders of early music. It is important, however, to bear in mind the instruments for which most Baroque pieces were written, and to play in a clear manner, free from dramatic and rhythmic excesses, but not in a pedantic or soulless way.

SOME COMPOSERS OF THE ERA

Johann Sebastian Bach (1685–1750)
Mass in B minor; *St Matthew Passion*; *Well-Tempered Clavier*; *Brandenburg Concertos*; *Italian Concerto*; *Toccata* and *Fugue in D minor*; *Goldberg Variations*.

Georg Friedrich Handel (1685–1759)
Water Music; *Music for the Royal Fireworks*; Concerti grossi; oratorio: *Messiah*; operas: *Julius Caesar*, *Saul*.

Domenico Scarlatti (1685–1757)
Ogni core innamorato; mass: *La Stella*; 17 sinfonias, 555 sonatas, mostly for harpsichord; opera: *Tetide in Sciro*.

François Couperin (1668–1733)
Four books (27 suites) of harpsichord pieces; *Leçons de Ténèbres*; *L'apothéose de Lully*.

Henry Purcell (1659–95)
Operas: *Dido and Aeneas*, *The Faerie Queen*; church and processional anthems including the *Bell Anthem*.

Georg Philipp Telemann (1681–1767)
Tafelmusik (125 suites played as accompaniment during banquets); many church cantatas and 55 solo concertos.

Johann Sebastian Bach
Baroque master of composition

Orphaned before he was 10, Bach was cared for by his older brother, Johann Christian. One of the most talented musicians of his day, he was soon employed as organist and konzertmeister by the Duke of Weimar. By 1718 he had moved to the court at Cöthen (while here, he composed the *Brandenburg Concertos*). In 1723 he took up the post of cantor at St Thomas's church in Leipzig, where his duties included teaching music, as well as writing works for Sunday services and church festivals. Having access to a choir inspired Bach to write on a grand scale, but eventually he felt teaching was restricting his composing and tried, unsuccessfully, to obtain another post. Troubled by cataracts, he died of a stroke after an operation to restore his sight. Bach's repertoire includes 200 cantatas, the *Christmas Oratorio*, two passions (*St John* and *St Matthew*), a *Mass in B Minor*, four orchestral suites, six *Brandenburg Concertos*, the *Goldberg Variations*, and a collection of 48 preludes and fugues published under the title *Das Wohltemperirte Klavier* (the *Well-Tempered Clavier*).

Johann Sebastian Bach
1685–1750

PLAYING NOTES

- This comes from the *Well-Tempered Clavier* and was originally written for Bach's eldest son, Wilhelm Friedemann. 'Prelude' means it is played before another piece. The BWV number refers to Bach-Werke-Verzeichnis, the catalogue of Bach's works.
- Play the piece at a moderate tempo, not too fast.
- Do not play louder than mf (mezzo forte, see p24). Keep your feet off the pedal. Using the damper pedal will smudge the music and make it muddy. Every note should be crystal-clear.
- There is a pattern that occurs twice per bar. The two bottom notes are played by the left hand and a group of three notes, played twice, is performed by the right hand. Remember to keep the fingers of your left hand down, while the right hand plays the two groups of three notes.
- To save space, from bar 6 only the chords and fingering marks are given. The pattern remains the same, except for the last three bars which are written out in full. The second half of the second-last bar can be slightly retarded. Play the last chord as a broken chord (this means you should play each note separately, starting from the bottom note).
- As there is no key signature (see p23), play each note as you see it.
- This is a beautifully serene piece. Enjoy it!

Praeludium in C

BWV 846

Johann Sebastian Bach

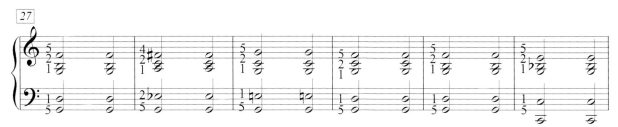

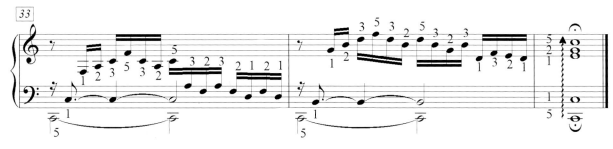

Georg Friedrich Handel
Musician in the service of royalty

Handel studied both law and music, learning the organ, violin and harpsichord, as well as composing and copying scores. By 1703 he was employed at Hamburg's opera house as a violinist and harpsichordist, and wrote the first of over 40 operas (which kept him solvent for much of his life). He spent three years in Florence, where he met Vivaldi, and began writing operas, cantatas and oratorios. Moving to London in 1712, he was working at the Court when his former master, the Elector of Hanover, who had never dismissed Handel from his service, became King George I of England. Handel's famous *Water Music* is reputed to have been written to regain the new king's favour. It must have worked, for he was appointed music director of the Royal Academy of Music. Handel visited Dublin where, in 1742, he premiered his oratorio *The Messiah* to great acclaim. It was not as well received in London, but gradually gained favour. The successful oratorio *Judas Maccabeus* was performed in 1746. Another notable work, *Music for the Royal Fireworks*, attracted a large audience when it was being rehearsed in 1749, causing a traffic jam on London Bridge.

Georg Friedrich Handel
1685–1759

PLAYING NOTES

- The gavotte was a popular French dance in the 16th century. The music is quite quick with an even time signature, often starting with an upbeat (the last bit of a bar, which is not considered bar 1). This dance is from a collection of peasant dances that were adopted by the nobility. The gavotte was a stately, but lively, dance. Play lightly, imagining ball-gowned ladies in big wigs bobbing around the dance floor.

- The piece is divided into two sections (see bar 8). The two dots next to the first double bar line mean that it should be repeated from the start. The second half is also repeated. The time signature that looks like '¢' is another way of writing 4/4 or four crotchet beats to a bar (see p19).

- Begin by playing the piece mezzo forte and when you repeat a section, play it piano. In most Baroque music, both the melody and bass-line are equally important.

- In bars 3, 13 and 15 the fingering is typically Baroque and is used to aid the phrasing. It helps to separate the little groups of two notes under the slurs. If the notes are not slurred they should be played slightly detached to promote clarity (refer to the second technical exercise on p31).

- Remember that all F's are sharpened.

Gavotte

from Keyboard Suite

Georg Friedrich Handel

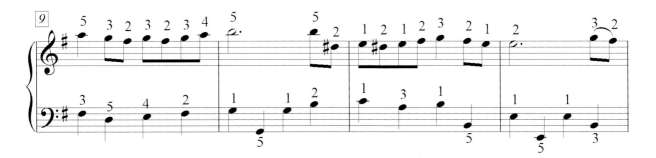

THE CLASSICAL ERA 1760–1830

Enlightenment, freedom and democracy

The 18th century was a time of enlightenment, the Age of Reason, when ordinary people became more interested in the world around them. The term 'Classical' describes a period marked by formality, elegance and grace, when musicians, painters and writers were influenced by a revival of interest in the civilization and culture of Ancient Greece and Rome.

New ideals, such as democracy and equality, which surfaced through the writings of Voltaire, Thomas Paine and Jean-Jacques Rousseau, were given impetus in the American and French revolutions. While America achieved independence from England, France underwent years of turmoil after the execution of Louis XVI in 1793, and the subsequent 'reign of terror'. Out of this came Napoleon Bonaparte, who crowned himself emperor in 1804, before embarking on a series of military campaigns which saw much of Europe fall into his hands.

For most of the 18th century, Vienna was the centre of music and culture in Europe. Three of the greatest composers of the Classical era, Mozart, Haydn and Beethoven, had strong connections with the city. Although the Austrian court was a vastly scaled-down version of its former glory, the bourgeoisie (middle class) was prospering, and soon took on the aristocracy's traditional role as patron of the arts. Musicians, no longer dependent upon royal patronage, were free to earn their living by composing and performing for anyone who hired them.

Two mainstays of Vienna's cultural life were subscription concerts (performances funded by private individuals), and salons (small gatherings in private homes). The piano became popular in the intimate surrounds of the salon, and Haydn and Mozart (see p48), were among the first to devote most of their keyboard output to it, rather than the harpsichord.

Mozart lived in Vienna from 1782, and it is here that he wrote many of his most famous works, including *Symphony No.41* 'Jupiter', and the operas *Don Giovanni*, *The Marriage of Figaro* and *The Magic Flute*. In the same year, following his marriage to Constanze Weber, Mozart initiated a series of subscription concerts in Vienna, for which many of his great piano concertos were written and performed.

Joseph Haydn (1732–1809) is less celebrated than Mozart, but his achievements make him one of the greatest figures of the Classical period. For much of his career, Haydn was the

As a boy, Mozart often played the harpsichord for members of the European aristocracy, as in this still from the movie *Amadeus*.

Napoleon conquered much of Europe during his short reign.

Kapellmeister (music director) for a Hungarian noble, Prince Paul Esterházy, and his son, Michael. After leaving their service, Haydn worked in England, where he won considerable acclaim, and in Vienna, where he briefly taught Beethoven. Haydn composed a prodigious quantity of music, and is especially known for his symphonies, string quartets and oratorios. His *Sonata in C Minor* was one of the first works to be written for the pianoforte, rather than the harpsichord, which had been the dominant keyboard instrument (together with the organ) during the Baroque period.

Another great composer with links to Vienna is Beethoven (1770–1827), whose work spans the Classical and Romantic periods (see p52). One of the first successful freelance musicians, composing for wealthy patrons rather than for the court, his style is emotional and innovative, in contrast to Mozart's elegant clarity. Beethoven's most popular works include *Piano Concerto No.5 'Emperor'*, *Symphony No.9 'Choral'* with its much-sung *Ode to Joy*, and *Piano Sonata No.23 'Appassionata'*.

By the start of the 19th century, increased prosperity meant that music was reaching a wider audience via the concert hall. This led to the growth of orchestral music, and the development of the symphony. The piano's role as a solo instrument also began to take shape. Musical instruments were becoming more affordable, and the ability to make music was being recognized as a social accomplishment.

PLAYING NOTES
- When playing Classical music, remember that the melody is more important than the bass-line, which acts as an accompaniment.
- Dynamic and rhythmic variation is still somewhat restrained.
- Signs for using the pedals were hardly ever indicated by these composers, even though pedals had begun to make an appearance. A rule of thumb is to use the pedals judiciously, if at all. (Instead of pedals, some early pianos had knobs that were operated by the player's knees.)

Wolfgang Amadeus Mozart
One of the greatest Classical composers

Born in Salzburg, Mozart's early talent prompted his father to take him on various musical tours throughout Europe. In 1772, the Archbishop of Salzburg appointed the 16-year-old as master of his court orchestra, a post he held until 1781. From then on, he lived mostly in Vienna, supporting himself by performing, composing and teaching. He initiated a series of subscription concerts, for which he wrote many piano concertos. In 1785, Mozart's opera *The Marriage of Figaro*, was performed to great acclaim in Vienna and Prague. In 1788, he composed two of his finest works, *Symphony No.40* and *Symphony No.41* ('Jupiter'), but by then his financial situation was dire. In 1791, with his health failing, he received an anonymous commission to write a requiem, but did not live to finish it. Mozart's 835 surviving works include 27 piano concertos, 23 string quartets, 35 violin sonatas and over 40 symphonies. His works were catalogued chronologically in 1862 by musicologist Ludwig von Köchel, so the 'K' or 'KV' number (*Köchel Verzeichnis*) prefixed to most of Mozart's works is an indication of when in his career it was written (although it is not always accurate).

**Wolfgang Amadeus Mozart
1756–91**

PLAYING NOTES

- This piece, called 'Little Piano Piece', comes from the London Notebook. The KV number indicates Mozart wrote it when he was very young. It was probably written for harpsichord, which explains the lack of dynamic markings. The piece can be played mezzo forte and in a lively manner.
- There are two sections, which are repeated. When repeating each section, bring the dynamic down to piano (see p24).
- The changing fingering in the right-hand part of bars 1, 7, 15, etc. facilitates the separation of repeated notes.
- The upside-down triangle ▼ is an accent (see p20). It emphasizes the note, which becomes shorter, almost staccato.
- Compare the left-hand part in bars 3-4 and 9-10. Be sure to observe the rests in the second instance.
- In bars 13, 19 and 37, three 16th-notes are grouped together with a slur and the number 3 above or below them. This is a triplet and it means that the three notes should be played in the same time it would take to play two notes of the same value, so play them in the time of one beat (an 8th note).
- Directly after the triplet in bars 13, 19 and 37 is 'tr', which means that a trill should be performed here. A trill is an ornament (see p41) and represents a rapid alternation between two adjacent notes, played like this:

Kleine Klavierstück

From the London Notebook

Wolfgang Amadeus Mozart

KV 15a

Muzio Clementi
A teacher whose lessons have endured

Clementi, one of the first piano virtuosos, was receiving organ lessons by the age of seven and was appointed as the organist at his local church, outplaying many adult rivals in the process. At the age of 14 he went to study in England, where he established his reputation by publishing six sonatas written for the piano as opposed to the harpsichord. In 1781, while on a visit to France, he had a famous piano 'duel' with Mozart, in which both composers improvised on their own compositions (the outcome was declared a tie). After travelling in Europe, Clementi settled in London in 1785, where he remained for the next 20 years, working as a soloist, conductor and composer. Many of his symphonies were unfairly compared with those of Haydn, and Clementi did not achieve much musical success in his lifetime. He continued to compose (writing more than 100 sonatas for piano alone), and expanded his interests into piano manufacturing and music publishing. Clementi was also a noted teacher. In 1817 he wrote *Gradus ad Parnassum*, a series of musical studies and exercises which influenced pianists for generations to come. They are still used today.

Muzio Clementi
1752–1832

PLAYING NOTES

- This is a waltz (*valse*), as shown by the three-beat time signature, in the form of a rondo (*rondeau*). In a rondo, an initial theme (here bars 1–8) is repeated while alternating with a series of contrasting themes (bars 17–24). Rondos were used in the final movements of sonatas, concertos and symphonies in the 18th and 19th centuries.

- The left-hand part functions as the accompaniment and should be played softer than the melody. In the left-hand part, 'sempre stacc.' in bar 7 means 'always staccato', signifying that the left-hand part should be played staccato until further notice. Both hands are written in the treble clef.

- The clear dynamic markings are easy to follow. There are crescendo (see p24) and decrescendo markings at the end of each statement of the main theme. Accentuate the high B, as it is the climax of the phrase, after which you relax.

- The key signature (see p23) indicates that all B's, E's and A's are flattened unless voided (cancelled) by a natural sign. The high A-flat at the start of the second half of each main theme (bars 5, 13, etc.) has the flat written before it to remind the player to cancel the previous A-natural.

- Pay attention to the articulation in the melody. The composer has been very specific about it.

Valse en forme de Rondeau

Muzio Clementi

THE 19TH CENTURY 1800–1900

Romanticism, nationalism and liberalism

Some of the key themes of the 19th century are the rise of Romanticism, the flourishing of nationalism and the rise of liberal ideas. The 19th century was also a time of economic expansion, as the Industrial Revolution spread from its birthplace in Britain. Cities expanded as industries flourished, and many people left their farms to seek their fortunes in the cities. After the defeat of Napoleon, the forces of conservatism and monarchical rule once more held Europe in their grip. However, by the end of the 19th century, liberal ideas, in the form of constitutional democracy and social reform, had triumphed in many states.

Romanticism, with its emphasis on emotion or intuition rather than reason, was a rejection of the restraint and rationalism that had characterized the Age of Reason. In music, art and literature, Romanticism stressed imagination, creativity and free expression. The Romantics looked back to Medieval times, influenced by tales of chivalry and epic adventures.

Tales that originated with Medieval troubadours (wandering musicians) were rich sources of inspiration. Richard Wagner's opera *Tristan und Isolde* and the *Waverley* novels from Sir Walter Scott explored these themes. Romanticism had a considerable influence on the rise of nationalism.

The roots of Romanticism lay in the late-18th century literary movement, *Sturm und Drang* (storm and stress). This was associated with the German writers Goethe and Schiller, and was concerned with the depiction of extravagant passions.

Another Romantic preoccupation was nature, which was exalted for its spiritual associations. Painters such as Turner and Constable used soft colours and flowing brushstrokes to capture the 'sublime' qualities of landscapes. In music, scenes of nature and memories of special places were evoked in works like Mendelssohn's *Italian* and *Scottish* symphonies, Beethoven's *Symphony No.6 'Pastoral'*, and the *Blue Danube* and *Tales from the Vienna Woods* by Johann Strauss II.

During the early part of the century, many nations grappled with the ideals of democracy and personal liberty, while also confronting the social and economic changes brought about by the Industrial Revolution. Factory-based industries required an urbanized workforce, and many people moved away from

In the 19th century, going to the theatre or attending a concert became staple forms of entertainment for the increasingly prosperous middle classes whose enjoyment of the arts contributed to their growth.

the land and an agrarian lifestyle. Victorian novelists such as Charles Dickens and George Eliot exposed the conditions encountered by many workers in the overcrowded cities.

Europe was rapidly changing and many Romantic composers used music to interpret the world around them. Beethoven (see p47) was the first to convey real intensity in music, using it as a way to express his inner feelings and, later, to escape the reality of his deafness. He was a brilliant pianist, and his mastery of the instrument enabled him to write ever more demanding music. Beethoven's music opened the door to the Romantic era, while remaining rooted in the form and structure of Classicism.

Hungarian composer Franz Liszt (1811–86) was an admirer of Beethoven. Liszt's piano playing created a sensation, and he is credited with the invention of the symphonic poem. Other Romantic composers include Chopin, a noted pianist whose Polish heritage is evident in his mazurkas and polonaises; Edvard Grieg, who was greatly influenced by the folk music of his native Norway; and Russian Pyotr Ilyich Tchaikovsky, whose ballet scores include *Sleeping Beauty* and *Swan Lake*.

Nationalism – the perception on the part of a group of people that they belong together because of a shared language, history or homeland – was given great impetus during the French Revolution. Nationalism flourished all over Europe, but particularly in lands ruled by foreign overlords – Poland, Italy, Ireland, Hungary and the Balkans, for instance. Romanticism and nationalism were sometimes closely linked – in 1823, the English Romantic poet, Lord George Byron, went to fight for the Greek people during their struggle against the Turks. In 1848 a wave of liberal nationalist revolutions swept over Europe, only to be crushed by the forces of kings and princes.

In music, nationalism received eloquent expression in the works of two contemporary composers, Italy's Giuseppe Verdi and Germany's Richard Wagner. Two of Verdi's best-known operas are *Aïda* and *La Traviata*, but it was *Nabucco*, with its famous Slaves' Chorus, 'Va, pensiero', that reminded his countrymen of their struggle against Austrian oppression. Wagner, by contrast, looked to Teutonic legends for his inspiration. In works like *Parsifal* and the epic Ring Cycle of operas, his development of the heroic figure, struggling against all odds, resonated with Germans battling Austro-Prussian hegemony.

Italy became a single nation in 1870, while the unification of Germany took place in 1871. Nationalism had triumphed, and the European balance of power began to shift. Old allegiances crumbled as former allies became foes, empires were carved up, and the leading nations took steps to entrench their positions. As the ideals of nationalism began to take hold, the stage was set for conflict.

SOME COMPOSERS OF THE ERA

Ludwig van Beethoven (1770–1827)
Piano Concerto No.5 'Emperor'; sonatas: *No.14 'Moonlight'*, *No.29 'Hammerklavier'*; symphonies: *No.3 'Eroica'*, *No.6 'Pastoral'*, *No.9 'Choral'*; *String Quartet in A minor*.

Felix Mendelssohn (1809–47)
Symphony No.4 'Italian'; *A Midsummer Night's Dream*; over 60 choral songs; *Elijah*; *Hebrides Overture*; 49 *Songs Without Words* (in six books) for solo piano.

Robert Schumann (1810–56)
Piano Concerto in A minor; *Dichterliebe* (Poet's Love); *Carnaval*; *Symphony No.3 'Rhenish'*; *Kreisleriana*.

Frédéric Chopin (1810–49)
Piano Sonata No.3 in B minor; solo piano works: 17 waltzes, 20 nocturnes, 15 polonaises and 58 mazurkas.

Franz Liszt (1811–86)
Hungarian Rhapsodies; *Piano Sonata in B minor*; *Piano Concertos Nos. 1 & 2*; *Mephisto Waltzes*; *Faust Symphony*.

Johannes Brahms (1833–97)
Ein Deutsches Requiem (A German Requiem); *Piano Concertos Nos. 1 & 2*; *3 Intermezzi for Piano*.

Edvard Grieg (1843–1907)
Piano Sonata in E minor; *Piano Concerto in A minor*; 10 books of *Lyric Pieces*; incidental music for *Peer Gynt*.

For a Victorian lady, playing the piano was an essential skill.

Robert Schumann
Restrained Romantic and careful critic

**Robert Schumann
1810–56**

Against his family's wishes, Schumann turned his back on his legal studies, indulging instead in his true love, music. He feverishly practised the piano in the hope of emulating the playing prowess of contemporary violinist Niccolo Paganini (1782–1840). However, Schumann ruined his career as a concert pianist after dislocating a finger on a stretching machine, and turned instead to composition and musical criticism. Throughout his life he suffered from recurring bouts of depression, and hugely creative periods would alternate with months of misery. His wife, Clara, an excellent pianist and a champion of his works, stood by him but, after trying to drown himself, he ended his days in an asylum. The selected piece comes from a happy time in Schumann's life. *Stückchen* means 'small piece' and this is a light work, originally written for his daughter Marie, together with a few other items which he eventually published in his Album for the Young (*Album für die Jugend*), which included an appendix 'Musical Rules at Home and in Life', in which he explained the joys and benefits a child obtains when he or she learns to play and appreciate good music.

PLAYING NOTES

- This piece starts with an upbeat on beats 3 and 4. The title means 'little piece from the album for the youth'.
- Above the first bar, the words 'Nicht schnell' mean 'not fast'.
- The piece is divided into two sections (indicated by the double bar line in the middle of bar 8). Only the second section is repeated.
- The lack of dynamic markings (see p24) at the beginning of the second section gives you the option of varying the dynamics with the repeat.
- Observe the long and soulful phrases, which the composer has marked with slurs.
- A trick to bear in mind is that the melody in the right hand and the lower notes of the left hand move in the same direction. This makes it quite easy to play.
- In the last bar of each section, the second finger of the left hand goes over the first, which makes the jump easier to play.
- Put your heart into this piece. After all, Schumann was a very emotional man.

Stückchen

From *Album für die Jugend*

Robert Schumann
Op.68, No.5.

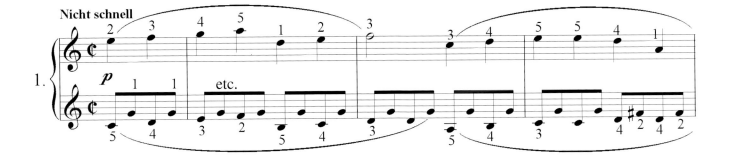

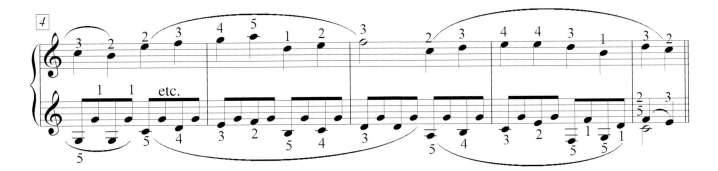

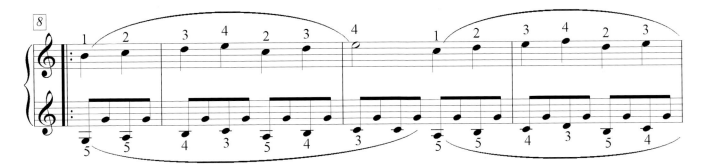

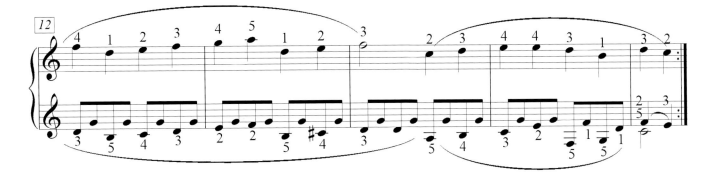

Johannes Brahms
A classical temperament in a Romantic heart

**Johannes Brahms
1833–97**

As a youth in Hamburg, Brahms made money by playing dance music for ladies of negotiable virtue and their nocturnal customers. In 1853, during a musical tour, he met the violin virtuoso Joseph Joachim, who became a significant figure in Brahms' life. Joachim introduced Brahms to Liszt, and later Schumann, who proclaimed the 20-year-old the saviour of German music (although he may have thought differently if he had known of Brahms' love for his wife, Clara). Brahms was employed as a choral conductor in Hamburg and Vienna, where he settled in 1869. He was a hesitant composer, perhaps weighed down by the early acclaim he received, only producing his *First Symphony* 14 years after he began working on it. Brahms' works are Classical in structure, despite falling into the Romantic period. His rich textures and interwoven melodies give his music an unusual emotional depth, although he had a reputation for being frank when expressing his opinions. His works include four symphonies, two piano concertos, piano quartets and quintets, a double concerto for violin and cello, a clarinet quintet (for clarinet and string quartet) and a requiem.

PLAYING NOTES

- This waltz, the second in a set of two, was not written to be danced to. Although it is a very sombre and emotional piece, the chords are beautiful to listen to.
- The piece is in two sections. After repeating the first section (ending on bar 8), play on until you reach the end of the music under the first bracket (bar 24). Repeat the second section (bars 8–19) and when you come to bar 19, ignore the first bracket and skip directly to the second one (bar 25).
- The descending two-note figure in the melody has a sighing quality and should be played that way.
- Remember that all B's are flattened unless altered by natural signs or other accidentals (see p23).
- In bar 14 cresc. means crescendo, or a gradual increase in volume (see pp24 and 92).
- At the start, the composer asks that the piece be played expressively (espressivo). While you don't know his emotional intent, if any piece moves or excites you, it has achieved its objectives. If you play this waltz with expressive pedalling, there won't be a dry eye left in the house.
- Do not worry about the strange ending, that's the way Brahms wrote it.

2 Walzer

Johannes Brahms
Op.39, No.9

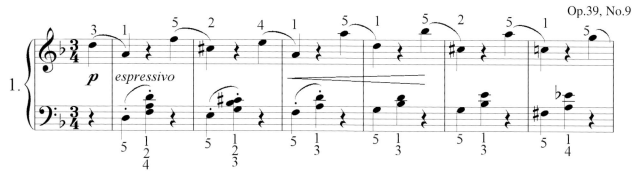

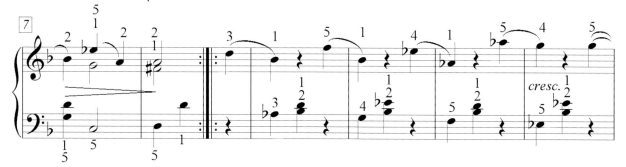

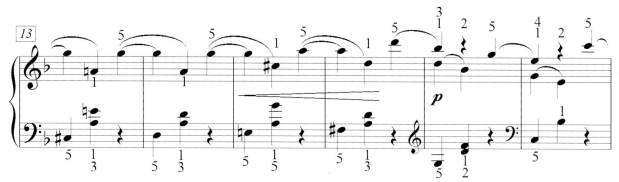

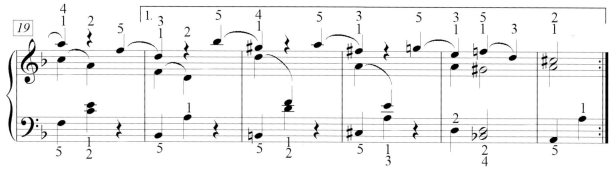

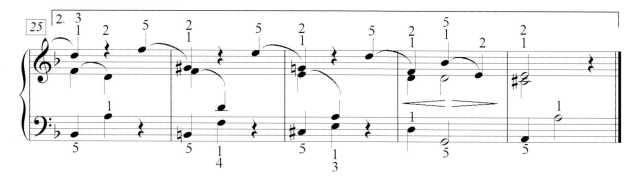

THE 20TH CENTURY 1900–2000

One hundred years of change

The 20th century was a time of unprecedented change, during which the world was transformed by technology, political turmoil, economic expansion and war. Music was no exception to this, and the century unleashed a huge amount of experimentation. New inventions – the phonograph, radio, television, the compact disc – made music more accessible, giving listeners the chance to enjoy recordings made decades earlier or to share in the excitement of a new virtuoso performer. New musical forms such as jazz flourished, but arguably pride of place belonged to the many forms of popular music – from ragtime and swing to heavy metal and techno.

First and foremost, the 20th century was defined by war and revolution. In 1914, the nations of Europe went to war. The conflict, called the Great War or World War I, soon spread over the globe. When it ended in 1918, the German, Austro-Hungarian and Ottoman empires had collapsed. New states, such as Czechoslovakia and Poland, were created out of the rubble of the old empires, and democracy replaced the rule of royal families. In 1917, revolution had toppled Russia's ruling family, and soon Communist revolutionaries known as the Bolsheviks seized power.

The end of the war brought enormous social change. Women had entered the work force in large numbers during the war, and they now demanded a more equal position in society. The post-war years were a time of economic boom, and nowhere was this more evident than in the USA, which had been untouched by the war but had (from 1917) contributed troops and equipment to the Allied war effort.

Music was central to the post-war boom. This became known as the Jazz Age because of the popularity of the new musical form. The Jazz Age was a time of celebration and merrymaking, as if the end of the war was a release from the attitudes of the previous century. Jazz itself was born at the end of the 19th century in New Orleans, Louisiana. It was a fusion of Western notions of harmony with African American spirituals (religious songs), field songs from the days of slavery and the African-derived rhythms of the blues.

Jazz also had a major impact outside the USA, with many classical composers exploring the new style. Some of the best-known jazz-influenced compositions include Shostakovich's *Jazz Suites*, Ravel's *Piano Concerto in G Major* and Gershwin's famous *Rhapsody in Blue*. For more information on the impact of jazz, see pp64–65.

The new music might have stayed in New Orleans were it not for two inventions: recorded sound and radio. Recorded sound was the brainchild of the great American inventor Thomas Alva Edison (1847–1931). Edison's invention was known as the phonograph, and later became known as the gramophone. The phonograph and its descendants allowed people to acquire sound recordings and preserve the songs and performances they liked. It was the beginning of today's multi-billion-dollar music industry.

The spread of recorded music reflected the democratic nature of the 20th century. Music and was no longer something that belonged to the nobility or the privileged middle classes. Anybody could acquire sound reproduction equipment and build up a collection of their favourite recordings. For those who lacked the means to do this, there was always the radio. Commercial radio broadcasting began in the 1920s, and radio rapidly became a tool of communication and mode of entertainment. Soon millions of people could tune in to live performances of classical music or hear the latest dance tunes from popular jazz groups.

In 1929, Hollywood embraced recorded sound. Music had always been part of the movies: in the days of silent film, a piano player usually accompanied the onscreen action. The advent of sound in movies added a new dimension to what was fast becoming the world's most popular art form.

The music on the soundtrack enhanced or heightened the experience of seeing the film. Some of the most important composers of the 20th century composed music for the movies: for example, Sergei Prokofiev and Ralph Vaughan Williams. Others, such as John Williams or Ennio Morricone, are known exclusively for their work for the screen.

Big band leader Glenn Miller was a favourite in the 1940s.

The advent of sound in movies also gave rise to a whole new genre: the musical. This was the screen equivalent of the popular stage musical. The best musicals were sparkling affairs involving attractive stars – Fred Astaire and Ginger Rogers, for example – who danced and sang their way through a light and fluffy storyline.

Musicals showcased the talents of many fine songwriters: Irving Berlin (1888–1989), one the USA's great popular composers of the 20th century, wrote or published over 1,500 songs which featured in musicals on stage and screen, including *God Bless America*, *Easter Parade* and *Alexander's Ragtime Band*.

The rise of popular music, fuelled by both Hollywood and Broadway, helped to divert attention from the economic woes caused by the Great Depression and the looming threat of war in Europe, where Fascism was on the rise in Germany and Italy.

By the late 1930s, the dominant style of jazz was big band swing, pioneered by bandleader Fletcher Henderson (1898–1952).

John Lennon (front), Paul McCartney (at the piano), George Harrison (left) and Ringo Starr, are among the world's most successful pop composers, both with The Beatles and as solo artists.

The big band sound featured elaborate arrangements written by gifted composers such as Edward 'Duke' Ellington, Benny Goodman, Tommy Dorsey and Glenn Miller. Ellington (1899–1974) a talented pianist, arranger and band leader, who wrote such classics as *Take the 'A' Train* and *Mood Indigo*, is today regarded as one of the greatest American composers. Glenn Miller (1904–44) fronted one of the most popular of the big bands, but his career was tragically cut short when his plane was lost over the English Channel in 1944.

War broke out again in 1939, with the German invasion of Poland. World War II was truly global in its scope, and few countries were spared its effects. When the war ended in 1945, much of Europe lay in ruins. Recovery and rebuilding would take many years. In the East, the dropping of atomic bombs on Hiroshima and Nagasaki ended the war with Japan, and ushered in the nuclear age.

The end of World War II heralded the onset of the Cold War, effectively a standoff between a capitalist, mainly democratic West, led by the USA, and a socialist Eastern bloc, led by the Soviet Union (later joined by China).

Despite the often-bleak international situation, punctuated by crises such as the Berlin Airlift (1948), the Korean War (1950–52), the Suez Crisis (1956) and the Cuban Missile Crisis of 1962, the Cold War era was a time of unprecedented economic prosperity and expansion for the West. New movements in the arts, such as abstract expressionist painting and existentialist philosophy, expressed the unease of the post-war mood. Jazz underwent a revolution with the advent of bebop, while popular music benefited from the huge rise in disposable income created by the post-war boom. Television, invented in the 1920s but long unaffordable, came into its own as a medium of communication and entertainment.

In the mid-1950s, popular music had its own revolution when a fusion of blues, country and hillbilly music emerged from the southern states of the USA, taking the country and eventually the world by storm. This was rock and roll, a raw and vital music of youthful rebellion and blatant sexuality. Performers such as Little Richard, Chuck Berry, Jerry Lee Lewis and Elvis Presley shocked parents and authorities with their wild performances and suggestive lyrics. Despite efforts to ban the music, it refused to go away and in time matured.

In the early 1960s, rock and roll was itself revitalized by the so-called British Invasion, led by the Beatles. The Beatles themselves soon demonstrated a mature lyrical sense and an adventurous musical ability. Their 1967 album, *Sgt Pepper's Lonely Hearts Club Band*, broke new ground in its use of different musical forms and mastery of recording technology.

Sgt Pepper was a watershed in popular music, reflecting the great social changes taking place. This was a time of youth rebellion, which erupted against the backdrop of an unpopular US war in Vietnam. Man entered space during the 1960s, and in 1969 Neil Armstrong became the first person to walk on the Moon.

By the end of the decade, pop music increasingly reflected social concerns and appealed to a restless generation in search of answers. The giant music festival held at Woodstock, in upstate New York, in 1969, brought together almost half a million young people in a celebration of the power of music to alter the world.

Since the 1960s, music has gone through many changes – the rise of punk, heavy metal, techno and the birth of hip-hop or rap. One of the most exciting developments has been the influence of 'world music' – a term for musical traditions outside the realm of Western popular music. In the 1950s, for example, jazz musicians discovered the rhythms of Brazilian *bossa nova*, while Cuban and Puerto Rican *salsa* music has brought a touch of Latin spice to the dance floor. In the 1970s, reggae music burst out of the shanty towns of Jamaica, propelling Bob Marley to fame.

Essentially, world music reflects the ways cultures influence one another – a phenonemon that goes back a long way. In the 17th century, Mozart's *Rondo alla Turca* was influenced by the sound of Turkish military bands.

Pop music is now controlled by large corporations, who spend millions of dollars to ensure an artist breaks into the hit parade. In recent years, the Internet has posed a challenge to the music scene: innovations such as MP3 files and CD burners now allow users to trade music over computer networks.

Billy Joel's song *The Piano Man* recalled his early days as a struggling musician.

Classical music of the 20th century

The complex diversity of the past 100 years is reflected in classical music. The countless '-isms' used to describe music since the late 19th century are a good barometer of the tumultuous changes that have taken place, while defying any attempts to neatly pigeonhole the era. Many 20th-century composers and performers have created their own idiom in which to work, rather than conforming to convention.

Even before the turn of the century, composers were blending elements of folk music into conventional compositions. Inspired by patriotic pride and Nationalism, this style is evident in the works of Antonin Dvořák (1841–1904), Bedrich Smetana (1824–84), Edward Elgar (1837–1934), Béla Bartók (1881–1945) and Zoltán Kodály (1882–1967).

By 1900, Impressionism was the dominant style. A term shared with painting, it describes music that is atmospheric in its harmony, instrumentation and form. The works of France's Claude Debussy (1862–1918) and Maurice Ravel (1875–1937) display a fluidity of rhythm and colour that was new to Western music at the time.

Neo-Classicism drew its inspiration from the 18th century, taking musical concepts, such as order and clarity, from that period, and using them to create a new musical idiom. Both Russian-born Igor Stravinsky (1882–1971) and Germany's Paul Hindemith (1895–1963) produced works in this style.

In contrast, Neo-Romantic composers have a predilection for big forms, sweeping musical gestures and traditional harmonic devices. The style is associated with Russian composers Serge Rachmaninoff (1873–1943) and Dmitry Shostakovich (1906–75), as well as many modern composers of film music.

In the 1920s a revolutionary musical language developed that was not centred on any key. This 'atonality' developed into serialism, where pitch, rhythm and dynamics were arranged in a row and used as the building blocks for a composition. The row could be manipulated in various ways (back-to-front, upside-down) and could be transposed. Viennese composers Arnold Schoenberg (1874–1951), Anton Webern (1883–1945) and Alban Berg (1885–1935), and Frenchman Olivier Messiaën (1908–92) are synonymous with Serialism.

Minimalism, which arose as a reaction to the complexity of Serialism, makes use of simple elements by repeating short musical figures through phasing and other variation techniques. Americans John Cage (1912–92), Steve Reich (b.1936) and Philip Glass (b.1937) are associated with this style.

Postmodernism is the newest '-ism'. Composers like John Adams (b.1947), Arvo Pärt (b.1935), John Tavener (b.1944) and Michael Nyman (b.1944), have embraced influences as diverse as Eastern music and Medieval religious texts.

SOME COMPOSERS OF THE ERA

Claude Debussy (1862–1918)
Prélude à l'après-midi d'un faune (Afternoon of the Faun); *La mer; Clair de Lune; Evening in Granada; Reflections in the Water; The Sunken Cathedral; Images* for piano.

Maurice Ravel (1875–1937)
Pavane pour une infante defunte; Jeux d'eau; Ma mere l'oye; Gaspard de la Nuit; Piano Concerto in G.

Serge Rachmaninoff (1873–1943)
Piano concertos Nos.2 and 3; *Symphony No.2 in E minor; Moments musicaux; Variations on a Theme of Corelli.*

Béla Bartók (1881–1945)
Concerto for Orchestra; Music for Strings, Percussion and Celesta; Bluebeard's Castle; Piano Concerto No.1.

Arnold Schoenberg (1874–1951)
Pierrot Lunaire; 5 Klavierstücke; Verklärte Nacht (Transfigured Night); *Kammersymphonie No.2.*

Igor Stravinsky (1882–1971)
Ballets: *The Firebird, The Rite of Spring, Petruschka, Pulcinella; Circus Polka.* Opera: *Oedipus Rex.*

Sergey Prokofiev (1891–1953)
Symphony No.1 'Classical'; Piano Concerto No.1; Piano Sonata No.8; War and Peace.

Paul Hindemith (1895–1963)
Mathis der Maler (Mathis the Artist); piano suite: *1922; Kammermusik No.1–7; Mörder; Das Nusch-Nuschi.*

Dmitry Shostakovich (1906–75)
Cello Concerto No. 1; Jazz Suites, filmscores for *Golden Mountains, The Silly Little Mouse, Encounter at the Elbe.*

John Cage (1912–92)
4'33" (Silence); *Sonatas and Interludes for Prepared Piano; Music of Changes; First Construction for 6 Players.*

Benjamin Britten (1913–76)
Peter Grimes; The Young Person's Guide to the Orchestra. Radio music for *The Rescue, King Arthur.*

Karlheinz Stockhausen (1928–)
Mikrophonie I No.15 & II No.17; Licht (Light, a cycle of seven operas); *Kontakte No.12½; Klavierstücke I–IV No.2.*

Philip Glass (1937–)
Einstein on the Beach; Akhenaten; Monster of Grace; Music with Changing Parts; Music for the film *Dracula.*

John Adams (1947–)
Grand Pianola Music; Nixon in China; Harmonium for Choir; Shaker Loops for String Orchestra; El Dorado.

Aram Ilich Khatchaturian
Mixing folk themes with classical composition

Khatchaturian's music is influenced by elements of Russian and Armenian folk music, which he absorbed from listening to his mother's singing. A latecomer to music, he rose to a high position in the Soviet musical world although, in 1948, he was censured by the government for writing 'formalist' music, instead of reflecting the optimism and simplicity of Socialist Realism. (Other Soviet composers, including Sergey Prokofiev and Dmitry Shostakovich, were similarly censured.) Khatchaturian was one of the first Russian composers to write music for films, an interest which lasted until the end of his life. Khatchaturian's music is known for the exotic beauty of his themes and the rich texture of his orchestration, which are direct expressions of his exuberant personality. His works include three symphonies, a piano concerto, a symphonic poem and the ballet *Spartacus*, which tells the story of a Roman gladiator. The featured piece was written in 1926, when Khatchaturian was 23 years old, and had recently changed his studies at Moscow University from biology to music.

Aram Ilich Khatchaturian
1903–78

PLAYING NOTES

- Andantino means a 'small andante', so play the piece slightly slower than andante. In bar 2, cantabile means to play in a singing manner, so your notes have a singing legato quality.
- In bar 14, your hands cross over and the right hand, which normally takes the higher part, plays lower than the left hand. This can be achieved by lifting the left hand slightly, allowing the right hand to move freely beneath it.
- In bar 18, the composer wants you to play notes with the left hand that are already being held by the right hand. He simply writes out the half-note value in the right hand to specify his melodic intentions. The first C in the right hand is emphasized while the subsequent C's in the left hand are played in a subdued manner (forming an accompanying pattern).
- The left-hand part in the first half of this piece is phrased with a slur (⌒) and tenuto signs (–). This means that it should be played as legato and evenly as possible.
- From bar 18 onwards, the left hand is syncopated (see p94).
- Bars 23, 24 and 28 have ornaments (see pp41 and 93).
- Don't play the eighth note in the left hand of bar 25 for too long; it makes the wide jump in the right hand more difficult.
- All B's, E's and A's are flat unless they are contradicted by accidentals.

Andantino

Aram Ilich Khatchaturian

Jazz
From New Orleans to Newport

Jazz was created largely by African Americans in and around New Orleans in the late 19th century. It has its roots in West African, Creole and Southern black music, as well as ragtime, spirituals, marching band music and the blues.

Jazz developed the melodic and harmonic elements of the blues, while adopting a radically new approach to rhythm, including ample use of syncopation (see p94). Improvisation is a cornerstone of jazz performance, with the melody often providing merely a starting point around which musicians can improvise. Many early jazz musicians could not read music, yet they were masters at picking up a theme and adapting it.

New Orleans in the 1880s was 'two cities'; affluent, French-influenced white and Creole 'downtown', east of Canal Street; and impoverished 'uptown', populated mainly by blacks, many of them former slaves. Downtown musicians were formally trained and played with dance bands and orchestras, while black musicians were mostly self-taught and their music relied more on memory and improvisation than on musical training.

In 1897 the city passed legislation that forced all brothels and prostitutes into Storeyville, centered around Basin and Canal streets. Even here segregation persisted, with uptown, or 'Back O' Town' reserved for blacks and downtown for whites. To attract customers, brothels offered musical entertainment ranging from ragtime pianists to string trios and brass bands. Music halls, saloons and cafés employed musicians from both sides of the city, creating a natural melting pot of styles and influences. Musicians of that period include King Oliver's Creole Jazz band, Ferdinand 'Jelly Roll' Morton, Papa Jack Laine's Reliance Brass Band and Nick La Rocca's Original Dixieland Jazz Band whose 1917 'Livery Stable Blues', one of the first jazz records, sold a million copies.

The fledgling recording industry did not initially see jazz as a marketable commodity, preferring to focus on the blues, but as jazz' popularity increased, it was soon heard across the USA, Latin America and Europe. This new sound captured the attention of classical composers like Igor Stravinsky, Dmitry Shostakovich, Maurice Ravel and George Gershwin, who used jazz elements in their compositions, despite the fact that the style was labelled immoral and was not universally palatable.

When the USA entered World War I, Storeyville was closed down. Some musicians moved to St Louis, Chicago, New York and Detroit, while others went to California. For jazz musicians, Chicago was the place to be in the 1920s, as its Negro population provided a ready-made audience and, with Prohibition in force, the city was home to bootleggers and mobsters whose illicit trade in alcohol ensured that clubs and nightlife flourished.

In New Orleans, jazz was played in ensemble style, but in the northern cities, innovative arrangements and the musicians' technical abilities led to improvisations that emphasized solos by different band members. Among the early soloists were saxophonist Benny Goodman, cornetist Bix Beiderbecke and trumpeter Louis 'Satchmo' Armstrong.

In 1925 Louis Armstrong recorded the first of his Hot Five band records which, along with recordings by his Hot Seven band, are regarded as jazz classics. Hot jazz is characterized by passionate, improvised solos around a melodic structure, building up to a climax. In contrast, by 1927, Bix Beiderbecke and Frank 'Tram' Trumbauer were using a linear, relaxed and lyrical style, which was dubbed 'cool' as an alternative to the extroverted, searing sound of hot jazz.

Trumpeter Louis 'Satchmo' Armstrong (2nd right) was one of the first virtuoso jazz soloists.

The advent of the big bands during the swing era of the 1930s–1950s gave jazz an air of respectability. Swing offered musicians a chance to improvise complex melodic solos. It was also robust, invigorating dance music, which was just what Americans needed after the Depression and during the war years, when dances were an important means of socializing. Popular bandleaders were Benny 'King of Swing' Goodman, Glenn Miller, Paul Whiteman, Tommy Dorsey, Duke Ellington and Count Basie. Jazz vocalists, such as Ella Fitzgerald, Bing Crosby and Frank Sinatra, also came to the fore.

In New York City, Harlem was home to a number of jazz clubs, including The Savoy and Cotton Club, where Ellington played regularly. In 1943 Ellington held the first of a series of annual concerts at Carnegie Hall, bringing jazz into what was previously the domain of classical music.

In the post-war years, jazz concerts and recordings were often broadcast on radio, exposing the style to homes across America. Jazz also began to appear on the curriculum at music schools and conservatories. The piano had initially been part of the rhythm section, but had developed into a solo instrument in the hands of pianists like the virtuoso Art Tatum, Nat 'King' Cole and Oscar Peterson, whose high standards created a competitive atmosphere in which less-talented newcomers were often challenged by established musicians.

Key innovators of Bebop, which developed in the 1940s were pianists Bud Powell, the enigmatic Thelonius Monk, saxophonist Charlie Parker and trumpeter Dizzy Gillespie. Bebop soloists improvised on chords, rather than focussing on the melody. Although bebop was initially regarded as having little commercial appeal, it became the basis of many jazz styles.

In the 1960s, hard bop grew out of bebop. Its soulful melodies were borrowed from gospel and rhythm and blues and incorporated into a sophisticated rhythm section.

In the 1950s, California was the birthplace of cool, or West Coast jazz. Continuing the tradition begun by Bix Beiderbecke and others in the 1920s, cool jazz was a reaction to swing and bebop, offering smooth harmonic tones and softer dynamics intended for listening (in performance or recordings), instead of for dancing. 'Cool' musicians include Stan Getz, Bill Evans, Dave Brubeck, Miles Davis and the Modern Jazz Quartet.

The next major style shift was free jazz, also referred to as avant garde; a wild, angry, uncompromising music played by younger players such as Ornette Coleman, John Coltrane, Cecil Taylor and McCoy Tyner, who regarded traditional jazz as museum music and wanted to express themselves more freely.

By now, jazz was competing with rock and roll, but it gained some recognition in 1964, when Thelonius Monk made the cover of *Time* magazine.

Developing parallel with free jazz was mainstream jazz, a loose style in which musicians fuse elements of classic, cool and hard bop into other musical styles. John McLaughlin has experimented with Indian music, and pianist Jacques Loussier has successfully 'jazzed up' Bach and other classical composers.

In 1954, the first Newport Jazz Festival was held in the eponymous Rhode Island (USA) town. It included a panel discussion on 'The Place of Jazz in the American Culture', setting the scene for an ongoing examination of the role of jazz that continues to engage musicians and historians to this day.

Jazz continues to evolve. Since the 1960s, new styles have proliferated, many of them an amalgamation of conventional jazz and other musical styles, including jazz-rock, fusion, soul, smooth jazz, acid jazz, funk and new swing. Contemporary jazz pianists include Herbie Hancock and Chick Corea.

SOME JAZZ PIANISTS

Count Basie *April in Paris*
Dave Brubeck *Time Out*
Bill Evans *Waltz for Debby*
Herbie Hancock *Maiden Voyage*
Keith Jarrett Trio *Standards Live*
Thelonius Monk *Brilliant Corners*
Oscar Peterson *Night Train*
Cecil Taylor *Momentum Space*
Fats Waller *The Joint is Jumpin'*

Ella Fitzgerald's fine, lyrical voice made her a huge jazz star.

When the Saints go Marching in
The legacy of the traditional negro spiritual

The history of negro spirituals is linked with slavery in the USA. Prior to 1865 (when slavery was abolished), almost all Africans who came to the New World arrived as slaves, mostly from West Africa, to work on the plantations of the South. Slaves were allowed to hold church services and these became opportunities for worship, socializing and sharing experiences. Regular services, held in churches or plantation 'praise houses', were accompanied by singing, chanting, clapping and even dancing (although this was often frowned upon). Unlike 'work songs' which dealt with daily life, the lyrics of spirituals were inspired by the Gospels and infused with the promise of freedom. References to the 'promised land', 'crossing the Jordan' (an allegory for the Ohio River, the boundary of the slave-owning South), and riding the 'gospel train', hinted at the Underground Railroad, the network by which many slaves fled to the North. After 1865, negro spirituals were often performed in fund-raising concerts for newly established black universities. Tunes were rearranged, harmonies were improved and the style became more formally structured, setting the foundation for gospel music.

Jazz performers are expected to be able to improvise as they play.

PLAYING NOTES

- This piece has a variety of elements found in the jazz style, such as syncopation (see pp64 and 94) and altered harmonies (added notes that do not form part of a traditional chord).
- There is no key signature, so play each note as it is written.
- The fingering for the left hand is mostly first and fifth fingers, so it is not provided unless this is not the case.
- It is a jazz tradition to write chords above the music so that players can improvise. Often only the chord symbols are given above the words. You may need some knowledge of jazz theory and chords before you can make head or tail of them.
- Many of the low notes in the right hand would normally be written on the bottom stave to avoid all the ledger lines. This can be confusing, as it is not clear which notes should be played with the left hand and which with the right. Use this piece as an opportunity to become more adept at reading notes on ledger lines.
- The melody is divided between the thumbs of both hands in bar 28, so treat it as a musical unity, rather than two notes.
- Remember to emphasize the syncopation in ✳ bar 29.
- In bars 3 and 5, hold the A in the right hand for its duration.

When the Saints Go Marching In

Traditional
Arranged by Philip du Toit

Scott Joplin
The original ragtime man

American composer Scott Joplin is best-known for ragtime music, which originated among black musicians in New Orleans in the late 19th century. The name comes from 'ragged time', or syncopated music in 2/4 rhythm, usually played on the piano. It was influenced by folk tradition, Creole music, minstrel shows and marching bands, and later incorporated into jazz. Joplin grew up in Sedalia, Missouri, where he played piano in social clubs such as the Black 400 and the Maple Leaf. His composition, *Maple Leaf Rag*, published in 1899, sold one million copies. In 1904 he moved to St Louis and then later to Chicago and New York, continuing to perform and compose rags and operas, often with a focus on the African American community. In 1908 he self-published a manual, *School of Ragtime*, but much of his work was in the hands of various music publishers. In 1911, composer Irving Berlin, who worked at Snyder Music, published *Alexander's Ragtime Band*, one of Joplin's most enduring tunes. The featured piece, *The Entertainer*, was used as the theme tune for the 1973 movie *The Sting*, reviving not only Joplin's popularity, but that of the whole ragtime genre.

**Scott Joplin
c.1867–1917**

PLAYING NOTES

- The *8va* and bracket in bars 1 and 2 indicate that all notes under the bracket should be played an octave higher. The same sign, accompanied by *15ma*, means the relevant notes should be played two octaves higher, while *8va basso* means to play the notes or bars an octave lower.
- This piece is full of syncopations (indicated by ✳) which should be emphasized. Syncopation (see pp64, 94) means displacing the natural beat. The usual grouping of notes is ignored and this disturbance of the normal beat adds to its effectiveness, for it surprises the hearer all the more for being unexpected.
- The symbol ♩=250 at the beginning means that the piece should be played at a speed of 250 quarter notes per minute. This is quite fast, so make sure you can play all the notes properly and slowly before speeding up.
- Remember to sharpen all Fs and Cs.

The Entertainer

Scott Joplin

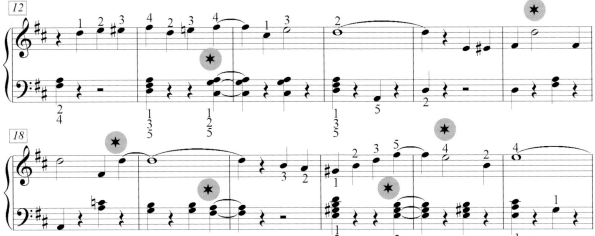

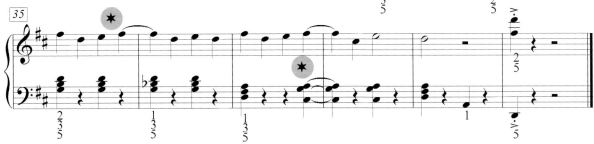

The origin of popular music
Music that moves the generations

Popular music can be defined as being written for profit and performed for public entertainment. It is almost always vocal, so lyrics are an indispensable part of the style, which usually comprises a vocal melody for a soloist or group, accompanied by drums, electric guitars and, often, an electronic keyboard. The drums and bass guitar enforce the rhythm and bass line, while the keyboard or piano is usually played in a style derived from the strumming of guitar chords, as displayed in the music of Elton John, Billy Joel, Alicia Keys and Tori Amos, for example.

Although popular songs have been around for as long as there have been singers and musicians, what we now call pop music, in its broadest sense, does not have a long history.

Rock and roll originated with the blues, which came in turn from music brought to America by slaves from West Africa and the Caribbean. In the plantations of the South, traditional songs were adapted into church music, ballads and dance tunes, forging a culture among the disenfranchised. After the Civil War ended in 1865, the blues spread from the Mississippi Delta, along the highways and railroads, to Memphis, New Orleans, St Louis, Chicago and Detroit. Over time, many styles evolved, but the blues remained rooted in African American culture. When blues vocals were combined with early pop melodies and jazz-based rhythms, the style became known as 'rhythm and blues' (or R&B, a term now used to denote a broad spectrum of black pop music).

By the 1950s, America's racial and social issues were being expressed in music. Jazz, blues, R&B and gospel, were seen as 'black' styles, while whites opted for country music or the light, bland tunes typical of artists like Pat Boone. But the generation gap was widening and teenagers were rebelling against their parents' values. Crossing the colour bar, they found expression in R&B, with its strong drum and bass beat, repetitive chord progressions, increased tempos and loud electric guitars. It wasn't long before a new style, rock and roll, was created.

The growth of rock and roll was driven by radio and television broadcasting, the relative affluence of the teenagers to whom radio stations and record company executives pitched their product, and pop's inherent ability to respond to the prevailing mood of each successive generation.

Pop music has distinctive melodies, clear syncopation and beat, repeated riffs, and danceable rhythms. Initially, rock and roll was music to dance to and, although it is not true of all rock and pop music today, the ability to dance to a song is often an important element in its success.

From the start, the singer-songwriter played a key part in the development of rock and roll. In the 1950s, Los Angeles-based Jerry Lieber and Mike Stoller began writing songs based on the black R&B sound of the time, producing hits like *There Goes My Baby* for the Drifters, and *Hound Dog*, recorded by Elvis Presley in 1956. It was the ability of writers like Lieber and Stoller, and New York's Carole King and Gerry Goffin, to bridge racial barriers and musical genres that paved the way for the birth of rock and roll as a entity in its own right.

Elvis Presley was rock and roll's first real star. A southerner who sang the blues like a black man, he united teenagers across the colour line and became an icon for his generation. Adults condemned his blatant sexuality as vulgar, but it captivated his rapidly growing fan-base. Presley's first hit for RCA, in 1956, was *Heartbreak Hotel*. This was followed, until his death in August 1977, by a string of memorable songs including *Blue Suede Shoes, Hound Dog, Love Me Tender, It's Now or Never, Suspicious Minds* and *The Wonder of You.*

Other top artists of the 1950s include Bill Haley and the Comets (*Rocking Through the Rye*), Jerry Lee Lewis (*Great Balls of Fire*). Chuck Berry (*Sweet Little Sixteen*), Britain's Cliff Richard (*Living Doll*) and, of course, Buddy Holly.

It is often said that rock and roll died with Buddy Holly in 1959 and was born again, on the other side of the Atlantic, with the Beatles in 1963. The 'British Invasion' of 1964, when the Beatles, Kinks, Rolling Stones and other UK bands broke into the American charts, underlined pop's ability to transcend national and cultural barriers and set the stage for pop music to become the global industry it is today.

Tori Amos is one of the new generation of singer-songwriters.

Playing popular music

Much popular music has its roots in folk music, which is defined by its oral and cultural traditions, story-telling role, and a melodic rather than an harmonic structure.

The pieces overleaf are examples of traditional tunes that have endured through the generations. There is no set way to play traditional pieces, so once you have learned the notes, have fun with the music.

POP AND ROCK PIANO HITS

The list of rock and pop legends is long. This 'honour roll' recalls a few songs written for piano or keyboards.

Beatles *Hey Jude, Yesterday* (Lennon/McCartney), *Something* (George Harrison), *Imagine* (John Lennon).

Elton John *Can You Feel the Love Tonight, Candle in the Wind, Your Song, Daniel, Crocodile Rock, Song for Guy.*

Billy Joel *Piano Man, The Way You Are, River of Dreams.*

Enya *Orinoco Flow, Only Time, May it Be.*

Carole King *Tapestry, You've Got a Friend, Music.*

Alicia Keys *Fallin', Girlfriend.*

Tori Amos *Winter, Cornflake Girl.*

Nina Simone *My Baby Just Cares for Me.*

Simon and Garfunkel *Sounds of Silence, The Boxer.*

Don McLean *American Pie, Vincent (Starry Starry Night).*

Stevie Wonder *You are the Sunshine of my Life.*

Jackson Browne *Doctor My Eyes, For Everyman.*

Chords

Most pop songs are published as lyrics with guitar chords, so you need to learn chords in order to play pop music on the piano. Chords are the simultaneous sounding of two or more notes. The distance between two notes is called an interval and the intervals between the composite notes of a chord distinguish it as a certain type of chord.

Intervals get their name from the way they are written on the stave. Two notes, one on a line and the other in the space to either side of that line, are a second apart. Adjacent notes on two lines or two spaces, are a third apart. This continues as far as the octave, after which intervals become compound intervals. Thus a tenth is an octave plus a third. These intervals only refer to the white keys. From this we can deduce that there are different kinds of seconds and thirds.

An easy way to determine an interval is simply to count the half tones. Adjacent notes (C–D-flat) are a minor second apart, while notes separated by one semitone (C–D) are a major second apart. In the same way, notes separated by two semitones (C–E flat) are a minor third apart, while two notes separated by three semitones (C–E) are a major third apart. Using this information, the structure of the major chord can be summarized as shown in the illustration below.

A TRIAD IS A CHORD CONSISTING OF THREE NOTES. NOTICE THE STRUCTURE OF THE INTERVALS IN THE MAJOR TRIAD.

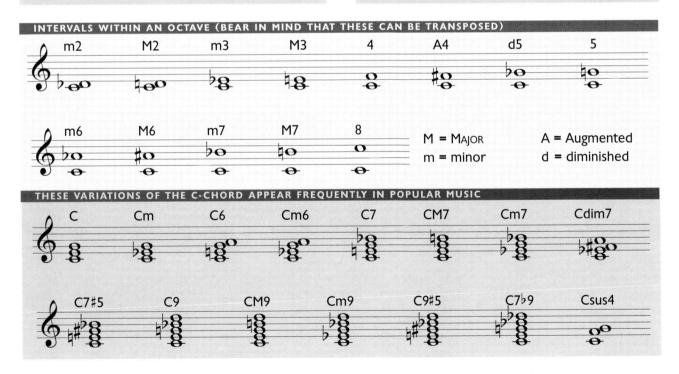

Greensleeves

Traditional

What shall we do with the drunken sailor?

English sea shanty

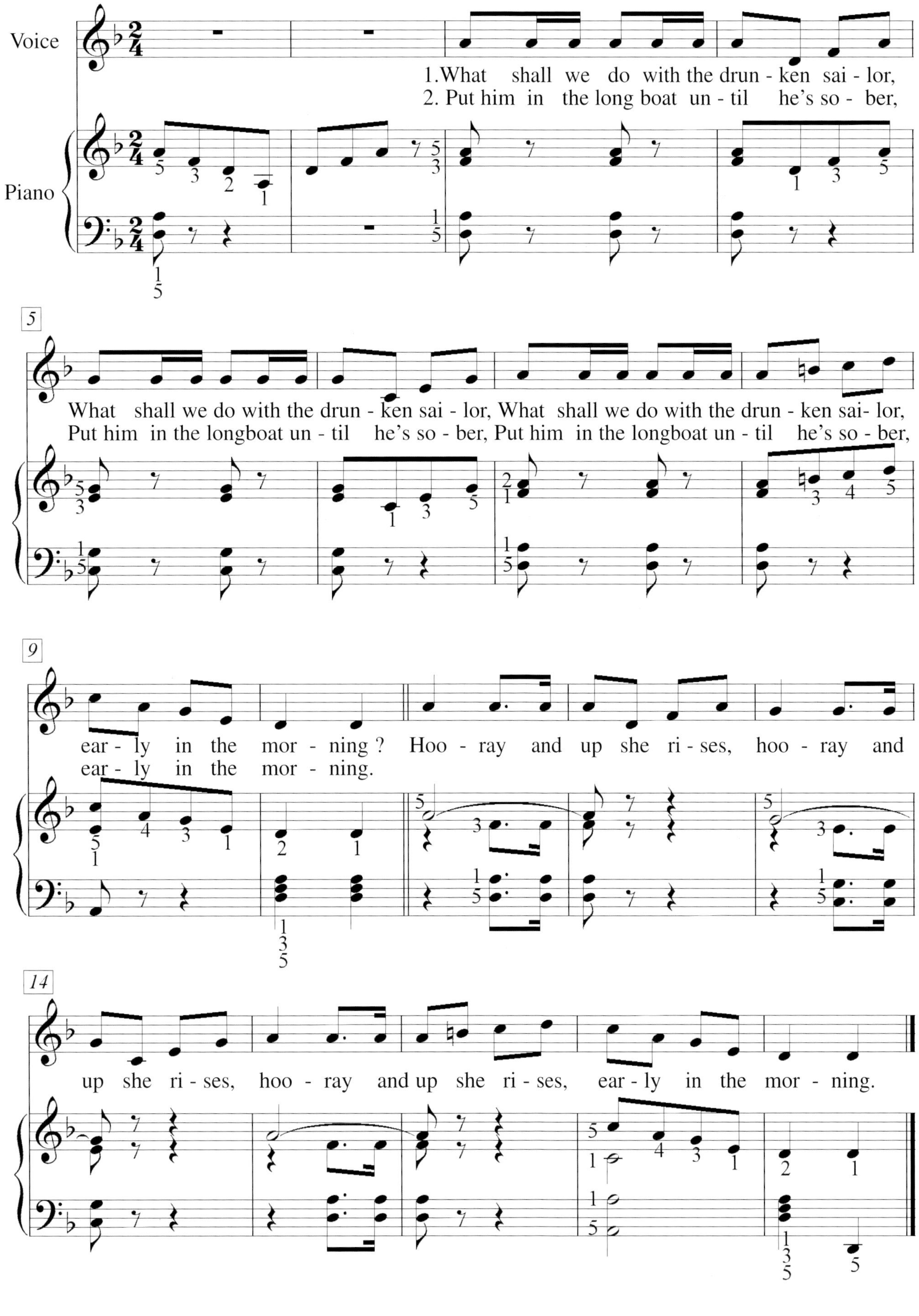

chapter five

DEVELOPING YOUR LISTENING SKILLS

MUSIC IS VERY POWERFUL AND CAN HAVE A PROFOUND EFFECT ON THE LISTENER, promoting relaxation or stimulating the senses, according to the type of music selected. But in order for music to influence you, it has to be listened to. There are two ways to listen. Passive listening occurs when the music is of secondary importance, such as the background music in shopping malls and restaurants, or while holding for a telephone call. A good example of passive listening is movie soundtracks. Although we are not always aware of the underlying music, most people would agree that removing it from movies such as *Star Wars*, *Titanic* or *Gladiator*, would greatly decrease the emotional power of the film.

Active listening takes place when the music itself is the main concern. It demands more effort and concentration on the listener's part, but the rewards are usually greater. Active listening is not only emotional, but also analytical in nature, so having a working knowledge of musical principles and of form in music makes it easier to listen to 'serious' music. Being able to distinguish a piano sonata from a piano concerto, for instance, will greatly increase your listening pleasure.

Active listening usually takes one of two forms: either listening to a recording or attending a performance. Knowing a little about sound recordings, audio equipment and concert etiquette will benefit your listening experience, as will starting your own collection of good piano recordings.

Various studies have shown that music has the capacity to influence the waves and thought processes of the brain and this has given rise to new fields of research in the health sciences. One of these is music therapy, where music is used to induce certain emotions or states of mind. Researchers have also discovered that certain types of music can help to optimize specific brain frequencies which are especially beneficial to the study of subjects like mathematics.

Music also plays an important role in cultural, traditional and religious heritage. By listening to a wide range of music, both classical and contemporary, we can further our understanding of different cultures, historical periods and music styles.

OPPOSITE Attending recitals and concerts will expose you to a wide range of musical styles.

TYPES OF MUSIC

Music written for the piano can be divided into four broad categories: orchestral music, chamber music, solo music or accompaniment for a singer or an instrument. The piano repertoire, a grand word meaning the actual music written for the instrument, is as varied as it is abundant.

Orchestral music

When played as part of an orchestra, the piano has two possible functions. Either it is just another instrument, doubling up as a second harp or giving strength to the percussion section (especially in modern orchestral music); or it features as the solo instrument in a concerto.

The concerto is a piece for a soloist accompanied by an orchestra (the instrument that takes the solo part is usually specified in the name of the work, for example Tchaikovsky's *Piano Concerto No.1*). The piano concerto has always been the domain of the virtuoso (the term for a technically brilliant player) and many composers have written concertos that can only be played by someone with overwhelming ability.

Piano concertos are usually performed in a concert hall with the pianist facing towards the right of the stage. If you get a seat on the left-hand side of the hall, you will be able to see the performer's hands doing the improbable, the impossible and the downright scary.

Chamber music

This refers to a group of soloists playing together. The number of players and the kind of instruments can vary, but they will remain a chamber group, or ensemble, as long as they do not need a conductor to keep them together. Twelve players are usually the limit. The piano features in many chamber combinations, but the most common ones are the classic piano trio (with violin and cello), the jazz piano trio (with double bass and percussion), the piano quartet (with violin, viola and cello) and the piano quintet (with string quartet).

Chamber music concerts are usually held in more intimate surroundings than a concert hall.

The 'classical' piano trio usually comprises piano, violin and cello.

Solo piano

Most piano music is written for the solo piano. The name of a piece usually indicates whether it was written in a specific musical form (such as a sonata, see below), or to convey a certain mood, or develop a specific technical ability.

Music written in a specific musical form includes the rondo (in which an initial theme is repeated while alternating with contrasting themes), and the fugue (a composition based on a theme, imitated in various voices), but the most important form is the piano sonata.

The sonata got its name from the Italian word *suonare*, which means to sound, and refers to a piece of music that is played as opposed to one that is sung (a cantata). The sonata form developed in the Baroque period (17th century), but only became standardized formally during the Classical era, in the late-18th century.

A sonata comprises three or four contrasting movements. The opening movement (called the sonata form or the first-movement form) can be further divided into three sections: the exposition, which contains the main melodies or themes; the development, which expands on them; and the recapitulation, which repeats the exposition with some minor changes.

Programme music (see p92) refers to instrumental music that is written to convey an idea, mood or impression, capture a feeling, or express a non-musical concept. Although non-musical ideas were depicted as early as the Middle Ages, programme music became important in the Romantic era of the 19th century, particularly in the works of Liszt. Examples include nocturnes (night scenes), polonaises (Polish dances) and romanze (romances). Titles like *Mazeppa*, which depicts a wild horse ride, *Schnitterliedchen* (The Reaper's Song) and *Kleiner Morgenwanderer* (A Little Morning Walk), describe the mood the composer wanted to convey and often reflect the source of his inspiration (such as babbling brooks or twittering birds).

Programme music does not include works like Beethoven's 'Moonlight' Sonata or Haydn's 'Surprise' Symphony, which were not named by the composers themselves, but by music enthusiasts who used titles to describe their own emotions on hearing the music, or to distinguish between similar works by a single composer.

Music written specifically to develop technical ability includes toccatas and études (or studies).

Even though some of these pieces sound like the technical exercises they were supposed to be, many turned out to be among the most sublime music ever written. The études by Frédéric Chopin (1810–49) are good examples of how a composer can make even exercises sound like masterpieces.

Accompaniment

The piano is generally the instrument chosen to accompany a voice or another instrument, such as a violin, flute, cello, etc. When writing music for a soloist, composers accept that he or she can only sing or play one note at a time. However, as the harmony of the music usually requires a bit more than that, the piano is ideal for 'filling in the gaps'.

When accompanying a soloist, the pianist should strive to complement the solo performance, playing in such a way that benefits the whole. This includes following the soloist's lead in all matters of tempo, phrasing, articulation and dynamics, as well as being a very good sight-reader. Even though the role of the accompaniment is of secondary importance, many composers have written accompaniments that rival the solo part in difficulty, complexity and general 'showiness'.

The solo pianist is usually a virtuoso who has spent years perfecting his art.

GOING TO CONCERTS

The development of radio and television broadcasting in the early 20th century meant that all forms of music, including classical, jazz and pop, could be communicated to a greater audience than ever before. But instead of broadening its appeal through greater exposure, classical music steadily lost ground to the popular music of the day, soon becoming so remote that many people simply stopped attending classical concerts or listening to classical music.

Eventually, dwindling attendance at classical concerts forced a change of attitude and approach by concert-hall managers and professional musicians, who suddenly found themselves without an audience. Now many established venues attempt to attract concert-goers with a less formal atmosphere and programmes featuring popular works. Efforts are being made to take music to the people by utilizing a variety of venues. In cities around the world, outdoor concerts are popular in summer, with concert-goers enjoying a picnic and drinks at interval or even while listening to the music.

The accompanist must support and complement the performance of the soloist he is accompanying.

A symphony orchestra in rehearsal. The soloist and the orchestra members must all follow the conductor's lead.

For most classical music-lovers, attending a concert is by far the best way to experience a piece of music the way the composer intended it to be heard. A live performance gives music a dimension that a recording can never quite capture, no matter how technically superior the recording process might be. Perhaps having something to watch as well as hear helps you concentrate on the music.

Although spontaneous, uninhibited behaviour is acceptable at pop concerts, a different atmosphere prevails at classical music concerts. Knowing what to do and what not to do (see p80) means you can focus on the music without worrying about when to applaud.

An exception to all the normal rules of concert behaviour is the much-loved and well-patronized Promenade Concert series, or the Proms. Initiated in the UK in 1895 by Henry Wood and taken over by the BBC in 1927, the Proms have become an enduring tradition that is replicated throughout much of the English-speaking world. A series of conventional concerts normally precedes the Last Night of the Proms (in reality, often two or even three 'Last Nights'), when anything goes. Patriotism is rampant and concert-goers wear their national colours, wave flags and throw streamers. The music is chosen for its wide appeal and the concert ends with the audience singing hearty renditions of stalwarts such as *Rule Britannia*, *Jerusalem*, and *Land of Hope and Glory*, before concluding with the national anthem.

Jazz concerts tend to be informal. Your dress should conform to the dress code of the venue where the concert is being held. In a restaurant or club, it is quite acceptable to eat, drink and even talk during the performance. However, you should not try to make your conversation heard above the entertainment, since most patrons have spent money on an entrance fee, thereby entitling them to listen to the music. It is fine to clap during a piece if the soloist has given a brilliant rendition. Clapping at the end of pieces is also good manners, even if you have to stop eating to applaud.

As you develop your enjoyment of music, you should not limit yourself to one genre or style. People who like one type of music usually enjoy other forms and it is not uncommon for music-lovers to attend a classical concert one night and a jazz or rock concert the next. By exposing yourself to a wide range of music on a regular basis, you will soon learn to distinguish the good from the mediocre or just plain bad, and you will also quickly learn which performers are grounded in a solid musical background, and which are lucky opportunists riding a wave of popularity. Once you have established your preferences, take a chance on new performers instead of just sticking to the tried and tested. You never know what talent you may be among the first to discover.

Tickets for popular performances usually sell out quickly, so advance booking is almost always necessary. In some cases, you may have to apply just to be on a waiting list for seats!

Tips for concert-goers

• Be punctual. It is especially unnerving for a soloist to see movement out of the corner of his or her eye as latecomers make their way to their seats. Most concert halls do not admit you if the performance has already started, but may allow you in at a suitable moment. If you are late, listen with your ear to the door. When the audience claps, you will have the necessary time to make a dash for your seat.

• Do not expect any sympathy from fellow concert-goers if the conductor stops the performance and glares at you as you try to silence a ringing mobile phone, beeping wristwatch or jangling jewellery. There is a composer who has written a work for mobile phones and orchestra, but it will probably not feature on the programme on that specific evening.

• What to wear is no longer an issue, unless it is a gala concert (in which case, confirm the dress code beforehand). Smart-casual clothing is always a safe option, but if you are uncertain, enquire when booking your ticket. Some older concert halls can be very hot in summer and very draughty in winter, but modern venues are normally air-conditioned.

• Do not talk during the concert. Classical music has constantly changing dynamics and you could easily be caught in mid-sentence when the music suddenly becomes softer.

Gala occasions and first nights often require formal dress.

Remember that your fellow concert-goers came to listen to the music, not your conversation.

• If you are prone to hay fever, or have a cold, have a supply of tissues and cough lozenges handy. Unwrap any sweets or lozenges beforehand. The painfully slow unwrapping of a sweet by a well-meaning concert-goer is enough to instil very violent thoughts in those around him. If you have to cough, sneeze or blow your nose, try to keep it for the noisier bits of the music, or between movements.

• Do not fall asleep. The soloist and other musicians have spent hours rehearsing the music to perfection, and to see their efforts rewarded by you nodding off is a great insult.

• The golden rule for clapping is: when in doubt, listen. There will always be people in the audience who know when to clap. In a multi-movement work, like a concerto or sonata, you should not clap between movements. However, in a longer work, like a ballet or opera, a very good performance may elicit spontaneous applause from the audience.

• If you wish to voice your appreciation, 'Bravo!', which means 'well done!' is the appropriate term.

• Do not rush out when the last applause is being given or curtain calls taken. The soloist did not practise that hard just to look at your receding back at the end of the performance.

It is possible to attend many concerts in everyday clothing.

It may look as if anything goes at the Last Night of the Proms, but the audience does observe basic concert etiquette.

LISTENING TO MUSIC AT HOME

Most music-lovers listen to music at home, while driving, or at the office. Worldwide, the growth of FM and satellite (digital) radio has resulted in a proliferation of stations dedicated to classical music, jazz and other specific musical forms, making music more portable than ever before.

Sound systems have benefited from technological advances that have put even half-decent audio equipment within reach of almost everyone. As with any other consumer commodity, price is the ultimate determinant when it comes to quality, so decide on a budget before you set off for the shops.

When it comes to hi-fi equipment, classical music has different requirements to pop music, so make sure that your system can handle the soft passages as well as the loud bits, otherwise your listening pleasure will be markedly reduced as the music fades away during the delicate passages, only to boom back when the percussion section kicks in. Take along a familiar CD when you shop, so that you can compare how different brands handle the same piece of music.

There are plenty of books and magazines on the topic of audio equipment, and a reputable dealer will be able to offer appropriate advice, but it is useful to remember a few basic points when buying a new hi-fi system:

• Shop around. Even for identical equipment, the price difference from one audio dealer to another can be quite large. Browsing through catalogues and advertisements for prices is a good place to start your investigations.

• Stick to brands with a sound reputation. Inferior products may not offer a good guarantee. The distribution network of a well-established brand means that technical help, repair and replacement parts do not take forever or cost a fortune.

• Buy from a dealer with a liberal return policy. The dimensions of your living room are not the same as those of the shop and you may have to exchange your purchase a few times until you are satisfied with the sound.

• Quality speakers amplify the defects of inferior equipment. The most important part of the process of sound reproduction is the reading of information off the CD, mini-disc, etc, so do not try to save money on your CD player if you want to get the best out of your system,

• Do not buy more equipment than you need. Why spend money on a tape deck when you only play CDs? The fewer components you purchase, the more money you can allocate to each one, so work out beforehand what your needs are and opt for the best you can afford. You can always add additional components at a later stage.

Buying pre-recorded music

Music can be bought in many different formats. The most accessible is the CD, but there is the emerging MP3 market (digital music files that can be bought on the Internet), the mini-disc and even the old-fashioned LP (long-playing record). Most reputable music stores have separate sections devoted to classical music and jazz, staffed by people who are familiar with these styles.

When buying classical music you will be confronted with many different recordings of the same piece and it is worth listening to a recording before buying it. When selecting jazz and pop CDs, the name of the artist is usually the first consideration, but with classical music, most people start with a particular piece they've heard and would like to listen to again. As your music collection grows and your taste becomes more specific, you will find that you start preferring certain orchestras and artists to others.

A comprehensive CD collection is every music-lover's dream.

Building up a music collection

Musical taste is a personal matter which constantly evolves as we are exposed to different influences and expand our own knowledge and understanding. No-one can dictate what you should listen to, but this short list of works for piano might help you get started on the road to musical discovery.

Orchestral Music

Bach, JS – *Harpsichord concerto in D minor. BWV 1052*

Mozart, WA – *Piano concerto No.17 in G. KV 453*

Beethoven, L van – *Piano concerto No.3 in C minor. Op.37*

Beethoven, L – *Piano concerto No.5 'Emperor' in E-flat. Op.73*

Chopin, F – *Piano concerto No.1 in E minor. B 47 Op.11*

Schumann, R – *Piano concerto in A minor. Op.54*

Brahms, J – *Piano concerto No.2 in B-flat. Op.83*

Tchaikovsky, PI – *Piano concerto No.1 in B-flat minor Op.23*

Saint-Saëns, C – *Piano concerto in G minor. Op.22*

Ravel, M – *Concerto for the Left Hand (1929–30)*

Rachmaninoff, S – *Piano concerto No.3 in D minor. Op.30*

Bartók, B – *Piano concerto No.1. BB 91*

Shostakovich, D – *Piano concerto No.2 in F. Op.102*

Adams, J – *Grand Pianola Music (1982)*

Chamber music

Haydn, J – *Piano trio No.28 in E-flat minor. Hob XV 31*

Mozart, WA – *Piano quartet in E-flat KV 493*

Mozart, WA – *Piano trio in G. KV 564*

Beethoven, L van – *Piano trio 'Archduke' in B-flat.Op.97*

Schubert, F – *Piano quintet 'Trout' D 667*

Schumann, R – *Fantasiestücke (trio). Op.73*

Mendelssohn, F – *Piano trio No.2 in C minor. Op.66*

Brahms, J – *Piano quintet in F minor. Op.34*

Brahms, J – *Piano trio in C minor. Op.101*

Dvořák, A – *Piano trio in B-flat Op21. B 51*

Poulenc, F – *Sextet for piano and wind instruments. Op.100*

Sonatas

Scarlatti, D – *Any of the 550-odd that he wrote*

Haydn, J – *Sonata No.47 in D. HXVI 51*

Mozart, WA – *Sonata in C minor. KV 457*

Beethoven, L – *Sonata No.8 in C minor 'Pathétique'. Op.13*

Beethoven, L van – *Sonata No.14 C-sharp minor 'Moonlight'. Op.27 No.2*

Beethoven, L van – *Sonata No.21 in C 'Waldstein'. Op.53*

Clementi, M – *Three sonatas in D, G & C. Op.21*

Brahms, J – *Sonata No.3 in F minor. Op.5*

Rachmaninoff, S – *Piano sonata No.1 in D. Op.28*

Other solo piano music

Bach, JS – *15 Inventions and 15 Sinfonias BWV 772–801*

Bach, JS – *Das Wohltemperierte Klavier BWV 846–93*

Handel, GF – *Suite in D minor. HWV 449*

Couperin, F – *Pièces de clavecin (1713)*

Mozart, WA – *Variations in C on 'Ah vous dirai-je, maman' KV 265 (300e)*

Beethoven, L van – *Bagatelle 'Für Elise' in A minor. WoO 59*

Chopin, F – *Mazurka in E minor. CT 74. Op.41 No.2*

Chopin, F – *Nocturne in G minor. CT 118. Op.37 No.1*

Chopin, F – *Polonaise in A. CT 152. Op.40 No.1*

Schumann, R – *Kinderszenen. Op.15*

Mendelssohn, F – *Lieder ohne Worte. Op.62*

Liszt, F – *Liebesträume (3 Nocturnes). LW A103 (C583–5)*

Liszt, F – *La Campanella. A15*

Debussy, C – *Children's Corner (Suite)*

Cage, J – *Music for Prepared Piano*

Stockhausen, K-H – *Klavierstücke V–X (1954–5) No.4*

Jazz

Because each jazz artist has his or her own style, it is better to concentrate on individual artists rather than to try and find a specific jazz work on record. It is also worth listening to different artists interpret the same 'standards', those key works that are an integral part of every jazz performer's repertoire.

Jazz pianists worth listening to include Oscar Peterson, Thelonius Monk, Ray Charles, Dave Brubeck, Abdullah Ibrahim ('Dollar Brand'), Herbie Hancock, Chick Corea, Bob James, Sergio Mendes, Bill Evans, Errol Garner and Keith Jarrett.

Pop and rock music

Even though the piano is not a major solo instrument in pop and rock music, many artists make good use of it and the electronic keyboard, either as the focal point of their music or as an essential element in their repertoire.

Singer-songwriters whose works include compositions with a strong piano focus include Elton John, Billy Joel, Carole King, Enya, Tori Amos and Alicia Keys (who proves the piano is compatible with R&B). Songs featuring the piano include John Lennon's *Imagine, Woman* and *Hey Jude* (with The Beatles), Simon and Garfunkel's *Bridge Over Troubled Water*, Procul Harum's *A Whiter Shade of Pale*, The Doors' *Riders on the Storm*, Deep Purple's *Child in Time* and *When a Blind Man Cries*, Cat Stevens' *Morning Has Broken*, Jackson Browne's *Late for the Sky*, Queen's *Bohemian Rhapsody*, Van Morrison's *Moondance*, The Cranberries' *Linger* and Bryan Adams' *Everything I do (I do it for You)*.

chapter six

BUYING A PIANO & FINDING A TEACHER

CLASSICAL MUSIC IS THE FOUNDATION OF ALL MUSIC THAT HAS FOLLOWED IT. Regardless of whether your preference is for Beethoven or the Beatles, you will find that every aspirant musician goes through the same basic learning curve on the way to mastering the piano, or any other instrument. Fundamental to taking your first hesitant steps along the road to musical greatness is acquiring a piano for your own use and then finding someone to teach you how to play it.

Unlike the gracious and spacious homes of previous eras, modern semis rarely have the space to accommodate a piano and, even if one can be squeezed in, the neighbours may not be too pleased to hear you practising at all hours of the day or night. Many budding pianists have to confine their practice sessions, particularly in the early days of learning, to soulless practice rooms in music schools, or to running their fingers over a paper keyboard on the dining-room table. In the early days this is perfectly acceptable, but once you reach a certain level of proficiency, there will come a time when you yearn for a piano of your own.

It is the same with teaching. As you progress, you will probably find that what you are seeking in a teacher will change. Your first teacher should be patient, encouraging and motivating, but after a while you may seek one who demands more of you, stretches you to improve month by month and offers new challenges so that you begin to master different techniques as well as expand your repertoire of pieces from different periods and in different styles.

When it comes to both buying a piano and to finding the perfect teacher, you will have to put yourself in the hands of more experienced professionals. No matter how far you are able to proceed on your own, you'll need to take their advice and guidance until you are knowledgeable enough to trust your own judgement.

OPPOSITE If you plan on buying a new piano, professional advice will help you to make the right decision when faced with an array of instruments from which to choose.

Buying a new piano

Pianos come in two shapes, upright and grand. The options for home practice are the standard upright, which measures 116–132cm (46–52in) in height, or the parlour (baby) grand piano which is 1.8–2m (6–7ft) long. A concert grand piano, by contrast, measures around 2.7m (9ft) in length.

If you intend buying a new piano, the best place to start is a reputable piano dealer or musical instrument store (try the Yellow Pages for stores in your area). Once you have looked at various models on the showroom floor and made a choice, the shop will normally allow you to 'test-drive' the piano in your home for a few days so that you can hear how it sounds in your own living room. If you are a first-time buyer and are not sure about what a good piano should sound and feel like, take along someone who can play well. Don't forget to enquire about guarantees, after-sales service and payment options (since new pianos are not exactly cheap).

Buying a used piano

This is generally the best option for beginners, who may not maintain their initial enthusiasm for playing. Used or second-hand pianos can be obtained from piano dealers and musical instrument stores. Second-hand (thrift) and antique stores may also offer used pianos at a reasonable price. Newspaper classified advertisements generally have a section devoted to second-hand musical instruments for sale.

There is always the risk that it could cost far more to get a second-hand piano in working order than buying a new one. Take along someone experienced, and check the following items before you consider buying a second-hand piano:

• Play each key individually. The keys must not stick. On release, listen to make sure that the damper has fallen back onto the string and stopped all vibrations.

• Look inside the piano to see whether the hammers strike the strings in the right place and not off-centre.

Careful and diligent craftsmanship by a well-trained piano restorer can work wonders on a dilapidated instrument.

Refurbished keys being assembled prior to fitting.

A grand piano in the process of being restrung.

• Press the right pedal to make sure it does not squeak or stick and that it effectively lifts all the dampers off the strings, allowing them to vibrate freely when they are struck.

• Press the left pedal. On an upright piano the hammers should move closer to the strings (and to the side on a grand piano), so that the hammer strikes only two strings instead of three. There should be no squeaking, sticking or rattling.

• Any sign of rust on the tuning pins or strings could seriously affect the tuning of the piano and should be avoided.

• Avoid pianos that are very badly out of tune as it can be costly to get them back into working order.

• Look for cracks in the metal plate and frame. If you spot any, find yourself another piano. Small cracks in the soundboard are not too serious but should be avoided if possible.

• Avoid pianos that are over 50 years old as you will probably not be able to get replacement parts if anything breaks. Look for the serial number on the metal plate or tuning block. A piano technician will be able to find out if parts are still available for that model.

• Finding out who the previous owner of the piano was will give some clues as to how well it may have been looked after. Pianos from schools, churches or families with young children are less desirable than those from a musician or piano student, who probably looked after the instrument well. As they tend to be used by serious musicians, second-hand grand pianos are generally in better condition than upright pianos.

• Once you have purchased a piano, whether second-hand or new, arrange for a firm of professional piano movers to transport it to your home. A piano can easily get badly damaged, even ruined, if it is moved by someone who does not know how to handle it.

Caring for your piano

When you finally have the piano at home, there are things you can do to ensure that it remains in good condition. One of the most important is that the more you play a piano, the less likely it is to go out of tune. Pianos that are left idle for months will deteriorate quite rapidly. Always have your piano serviced by a professional. The frequency with which you do this will depend on your financial status, but an annual service should be enough to lengthen the life of your piano. However, even if you play regularly and service the piano properly, you should still follow some simple recommendations unless you want your hobby to cost more than you can afford:

• Don't ever attempt to move the piano yourself. Leave it to a qualified piano technician or professional mover.

• If possible, place your piano in a room that has a stable temperature. Constant temperature fluctuations will have a negative effect on the pitch, so do not put it near draughts, air conditioners or heating sources.

• Avoid placing the piano against an exterior wall of your house, especially a wall where damp might occur.

• Water can ruin the mechanism of the piano, so don't put containers filled with liquid on top of the piano, or eat or drink anything near the keyboard. A spilled cup of tea can do an expensive amount of damage to a piano. (If you must use the top of your piano as a pot-plant stand, remove the plants to water them and ensure they are in non-drip pots!)

• When doing housework, cover the piano with a dust sheet to avoid getting dust inside the mechanism. If you are going away, or won't be using the piano for some time, cover it for the same reason.

• Clean dirty keys with a slightly damp cloth (use a bit of soap for stubborn marks), rubbing along the length of the key. Do not use oil on any part of the piano.

• If the top of one of the ivories (the keys) comes loose, fix it as soon as possible with a specialized rubber glue that you can buy from a piano dealer. Do not use any old glue since water-based glue can ruin ivory.

• If you have an upright piano against a wall you will lose a lot of the sound, so leave about 30cm (12in) behind it for the sound to rebound off the wall and upwards.

• Removing dust and insects from inside a piano should be done by a piano technician. Take care to choose someone with a good reputation and follow his or her advice. As a rule, you should not poke around or fiddle with the inside of the piano, as you could damage it without intending to.

• If your piano has real ivory keys, don't close the lid too often as ivory becomes discoloured without any sunlight.

• Placing an object on the top of your piano could cause irritating vibrations, so don't use it for ornaments.

• If you have cats, try to discourage them from sleeping on top of the piano or walking across the keyboard. It might be a cute party trick, but it doesn't do the piano any good.

In this sequence, a technician checks the alignment and operation of the entire mechanism for one key.

Printed music is the link between composer and performer, and is the means by which music endures through the years.

Buying printed music

Every music equipment shop should have printed (sheet) music for the piano. It can come as individual sheets for one particular piece, or books containing a number of pieces by one or more composer. Printed music can often be obtained from second-hand shops and garage sales. It helps to have some idea of what you are looking for when shopping for printed music. Alternatively, you can browse through a collection until you find something you like the look of:

• Look at the music and not just the cover of the book. As a beginner, if the music looks too 'black' (too difficult) on first sight, you should avoid it until you are more proficient in your playing and sight-reading capabilities.

• If you are interested in the music of a certain composer or style, then you should look for anthologies of music. (These are often graded in difficulty.)

• Do not be restrictive in the music that you buy and play. There is nothing nicer than discovering a beautiful piece of music by accident. Reading a lot of music will also improve your sight-reading capabilities.

• If the music store does not have the specific printed music you are looking for, they should be able to order it from the publisher, for which a handling fee may be charged.

• If you buy music for a solo instrument (with piano accompaniment), or for voice with piano accompaniment, make sure that you buy both the solo and the piano parts.

• If you want to play piano duets, buy music for four hands (two people playing together on the same piano), which is different to music written as a duet for two pianos. Unless you have access to two pianos you should buy the former.

• If you are seeking music that was not originally written for piano, you should look for piano transcriptions. Bear in mind though, that transcriptions of orchestral pieces are usually very difficult to play.

• When buying music for pop songs, look for those that include piano accompaniment alongside guitar chords, lyrics and vocal melody, as opposed to piano solo music.

• Buy original printed music. Playing from photocopies is a violation of copyright and deprives many hardworking musicians, editors and typesetters of their rightful income.

Learning to play in time can take time, but using a metronome or having the teacher beat out the rhythm will help you.

Taking lessons

Piano lessons will help you to move to another level of proficiency in your playing. A teacher will be able to correct your mistakes and point out areas that require more practice. A good teacher will encourage and motivate you, while challenging you to do better all the time. Many piano teachers are active professional musicians supplementing their income; some have stopped performing, while others have opted for teaching right from the start. However, there are also failed musicians who teach without any proper qualifications, so do not necessarily settle for the first teacher you find.

High schools with a music curriculum, colleges of music or tertiary music education faculties, local orchestras, performing arts councils or education authorities, should all be able to provide information on piano teachers in your area. As a beginner, you will not be able to judge your first teacher's expertise, but recommendations from experienced players will help to guide you to the right teacher:

• Make an appointment to discuss tuition. Teachers who are accustomed to giving after-school lessons to children may not be willing to accommodate adults at night or over weekends. Ask if the first lesson is free. This is a common practice which serves to establish the rapport between teacher and student. Your attitude towards your teacher is important, as you will be investing a great deal of money in lessons and have a right to choose the best teacher for yourself.

• A good musician is one who has a thorough knowledge of all aspects of music, not just a rough idea, but the best teacher is always going to be the one who meets your needs at a given moment. Be clear about what you want to achieve and establish a time-frame for progress so that you don't get discouraged if it takes a little longer than you expect before you see positive results from your lessons.

• If the teacher does not offer details of his or her qualifications and credentials, ask about them. Ask about their teaching and playing history. While public recitals and other musical activities should be taken into account, don't forget that many teachers are trained to teach, not to perform. Ask why he or she is teaching. Is he passionate about it? Does she love her instrument? A teacher is only going to inspire you to achieve your best if he or she is creative and has a flair for teaching. Bear in mind that just because someone has passed an exam does not mean that they are capable of motivating you as a student, or are even capable of playing well.

• Ask whether you can contact the teacher for advice if you are stuck while practising at home. Adults tend to be accustomed to instant responses and, unlike children, do not want to wait until the next lesson to resolve a problem.

• If you have had lessons for some time and are looking for a new teacher, you may want to ask him or her to play one or two pieces you are familiar with so that you gauge the difference in approach between your previous teacher and your prospective one. If you are looking to advance your playing in a specific direction, ensure that a new teacher will be able to meet your expectations by discussing them before signing on.

• Remember that a professional pianist who has achieved performance recognition will charge a lot more per lesson than a full-time teacher.

Achieving results is proportionate to the amount of time you are willing to spend on practising. You need to play often, do regular theory and sight-reading exercises, and not skip classes in order to progress beyond the basics.

Although the piano is an ideal solo instrument, it can be very rewarding to play with other musicians. Once you feel that your playing standard is high enough, you can begin to accompany singers or other musicians and take part in trios, quartets or other ensemble combinations. If this is your goal, you should find a teacher who teaches other instruments (such as violin or cello) as well as the piano, so that when you are ready, you will be able to play with students who are at the same level of competence as you.

Learning to play with someone else presents a new challenge.

Accent A stress on a particular beat or on certain notes, indicated by a symbol printed over the note concerned.

Accompaniment Music that is subordinate to the principal instrument, melody or voice.

Adagio (Italian, 'slowly' or 'at ease'). At a slow or relaxed pace.

Allegro (Italian, 'lively'). At a fairly fast pace.

Altered harmonies Added notes that do not form part of a traditional chord.

Andante (Italian, 'walking'). At a steady, moderate speed.

Arabesque A short piece or movement, usually for piano, with a highly ornamented or decorated melody.

Arpeggio (from Italian, *arpa* 'harp'). A chord in which notes are played in rapid succession, as if sweeping across the keys.

Arrangement A piece that has been rescored, rearranged or adapted to be performed in a different way (often for different instruments), not usually by the original composer.

Atonalism/Atonality A system where no key is dominant. It came to the fore in the early 20th century and was pioneered by composers like Arnold Schoenberg. (See also Serialism).

Bar The division of music into sections. Also, a group of beats that is repeated throughout a piece of music. The number of beats in a bar is indicated by the time signature.

Baroque Originally a 17th-century style characterized by extensive ornamentation; now any ornate, ornamented style.

Beat The basic rhythmic unit in a piece of music, usually grouped in twos, threes or fours. To indicate time by beating one's hand, a baton etc., or by the action of a metronome.

Cadenza A virtuoso solo passage in a concerto.

Chamber music Music for two to 12 solo players, with only one instrument to a part.

Chord The simultaneous sounding of a group of notes of different pitch.

Chromatic In composition, the use of notes that do not form part of the diatonic scale in which the piece is written, adding a 'colourful' quality to the harmony.

Chromatic scale A scale that progresses in semitones, using all 12 notes of an octave.

Classical Traditionally music of the 17th and 18th centuries. Also music of any period that has achieved a long-lasting status. 'Classicism' as a style emphasizes reason and restraint.

Clef (French, 'key'). A symbol at the beginning of a stave, fixing the pitch of notes according to their position on the stave.

Concerto A work for one or more solo instruments and orchestra, usually in three movements.

Concert pitch The frequency of 440 hertz (vibrations per second) assigned to the A above middle C. (See also Pitch).

Counterpoint Music that combines two or more individual melodic lines, or themes, to form an harmonious whole.

Crescendo (Italian, 'growing'). Increasing in volume.

Decrescendo Decreasing in volume.

Diatonic scale A scale of seven notes (including two semitones) and the resulting harmony, produced by playing the white keys of a keyboard instrument. The natural major and minor scales that form the basis of the key system in Western music.

Duet A work for two performers. A duo involves two pianos and a duet is two performers on one piano (four hands).

Dynamics Variations in volume, from loud to soft. Dynamic marks or markings are the directions and symbols used to indicate degrees of loudness.

Ensemble (French, 'together'). A group of soloists singing or playing together.

Etude (French, 'study'). A short instrumental piece, designed to improve or display the performer's technical ability.

Flat Indicates that the pitch is to be lowered by a semitone, shown by a symbol (♭) placed before a note or in the key signature. Playing flat means too low and out of tune.

Forte (*f*), **fortissimo** (*ff*) (Italian. Loud and very loud.)

Fugue A work in which melodic lines enter successively in imitation of one another, requiring skill at counterpoint.

Gavotte A quick dance with four beats in a bar. Also a piece of music composed in the rhythm of this dance.

Glissando The effect achieved by sliding the fingers rapidly across the piano keys so each note remains discretely audible.

Harmony Any combination of notes sounded simultaneously in a way considered pleasant, in line with the concept of tonality and the major and minor keys.

Improvisation A piece composed on the spot, without any previous preparation. An important element of jazz.

Intermezzo (Italian, 'in the middle'). A short piece of music played between the acts of an opera. A short piano piece.

Interval The difference of pitch between two notes, calculated by counting the steps on the diatonic scale between the two notes (e.g. the interval between C and G is a fifth).

Key The diatonic scale that predominates in a piece of music (e.g. a composition in the key of C major will use notes close to that scale). The main tonal centre in an extended composition (e.g. a symphony in the key of F major). See also Tonality.

Key signature The sharps or flats placed after the clef at the beginning of a stave to indicate the prevailing key.

Largo (Italian, 'broad'). A slow and measured performance.

Legato (Italian, 'bound together'). A smooth performance.

Major A diatonic scale comprising notes separated by intervals of a whole tone, except for the third and fourth notes, and seventh and eighth notes, which are separated by semitones. Relating to scales, intervals, chords and keys (e.g. a major key); the opposite of minor.

Metre (meter). Another word for time. The regular succession of rhythmic impulses, or beats, in music.

Metronome A mechanical device which indicates the exact tempo of a piece of music by producing a clicking sound from a pendulum with an adjustable period of swing.

Mezzo (Italian, 'half'). Indicating moderately; hence mezzo forte (*mf*, between loud and soft.

Minimalism A musical style in which one basic pattern is repeated again and again, providing a hypnotic quality, reminiscent of forms of Eastern music.

Minor There are two minor scales. The harmonic scale is the same ascending and descending, with intervals of a tone, except for semitones between the second and third, fifth and sixth, and seventh and eighth notes. The melodic minor scale has semitones between the second and third, and seventh and eighth notes ascending, and between the sixth and fifth, and third and second notes descending. Also relates to chords, intervals, scales and keys of a flattened nature; the opposite of major.

Movement A self-contained section of a larger work. Each movement usually has a separate tempo indication.

Neo-classical Early 20th century style based on emotional restraint, formal elegance and other attributes typical of the 18th century Classical period.

Nocturne A short lyrical composition reflecting the calm of the night; generally for solo piano or orchestra.

Notation The system or process of writing music down, using signs or symbols for individual sounds, so they can be accurately reproduced for performance.

Note A single musical sound (or tone) of specific pitch and duration. Any of a series of graphic signs representing a musical sound whose pitch is indicated by its position on the stave, and whose duration is indicated by the sign's shape.

Octave An interval of eight notes (twelve semitones) on the diatonic scale, the upper note being twice the pitch of the lower note. A series of notes extending through this interval.

Opera A dramatic work in which music forms the predominant part, consisting of arias (songs), recitatives (speech-song) and choruses, with elaborate and spectacular staging.

Opus (Latin 'work'). Opus numbers signify the chronological sequence of publication of a composer's output.

Oratorio An extended musical setting of a biblical or religious text for soloists, chorus and orchestra. Developed in Rome in the 17th century, it had a similar structure to an opera but was presented in a concert hall rather than acted out on a stage.

Ornaments Extra notes (e.g. trills, turns, etc.) added to vocal or instrumental melodies as a decoration or embellishment.

Overture A short orchestral work that introduced an opera, oratorio or ballet, and which developed into the symphony. From the 19th century onwards, overtures were often single-movement concert works written for an orchestra.

Part The music written for a particular instrument or voice in an orchestra, choir etc.

Phrase A section or group of notes, comprising a unity.

Piano (*p*), **pianissimo** (*pp*) (Italian. Quiet and very quiet.) To be played softly or very softly respectively.

Piano quintet A work for piano and string quartet, usually in several movements.

Piano trio A piece for piano plus two instruments (e.g. violin and cello, oboe and bassoon), usually in several movements.

Pitch The register ('highness' or 'lowness') of a note which determines its position on a stave; measured by the frequency of the vibrations that produce it. (See also Concert pitch.)

Polonaise A slow or stately court dance in triple time, of Polish origin. A piece of music composed in the rhythm of this dance, which found its most vigorous expression in Chopin's polonaises for piano.

Prelude An instrumental piece originally intended as an introduction to another, such as a fugue or suite, but also applied to a short, self-contained composition, usually for piano.

Presto/prestissimo (Italian, 'fast', 'very fast'). Rapidly.

Programme music Music that is inspired by non-musical ideas and seeks to convey an impression of scenes, events, people, paintings, ideas etc. (See also Symphonic poem).

Rallentando (abbr. rall.) Alternative term for Ritardando.

Recitative A form of solo singing in an opera and oratorio that adopts the patterns of ordinary speech. It is inserted between arias and choruses to convey dialogue or the narrative to the audience. It may be accompanied by the orchestra, or unaccompanied except for the occasional broken chord.

Register The range of an instrument or a singer's voice e.g. tenor, bass, soprano.

Requiem A musical setting of the Catholic mass for the dead.

Rest A measured silence.

Rhythm The organization of notes in a piece in relation to time. Rhythm is determined by the way the notes are grouped in bars, the number of beats in a bar, and the manner in which the beats are accented. (See also Metre).

Ritardando (Italian, 'slowing down'). An instruction to performers. (Often abbreviated in scores as rit.)

Romanticism A preoccupation with the expression of emotion, using nature and folk history as a source of inspiration. The Romantic movement reached its height during the 19th century in the works of Chopin, Schumann, Wagner and Verdi.

Rondo A musical form in which an initial theme is alternated with contrasting themes. Used in the final movement of sonatas and concertos in the 18th and 19th centuries.

Scale A progression of notes, ascending or descending, by determined increments. There are various types of scale, depending on the musical system being used. (See also Chromatic, Diatonic, Major, Minor, Twelve-note).

Score The written or printed version of a composition, used by conductors. It contains details of all the parts, arranged on staves down the page. Conventionally, the woodwind parts are at the top of the page and the strings are at the bottom.

Semitone Half a tone; the smallest interval conventionally used in Western Classical music. (See also Interval)

Serialism A form of atonality that involves arranging a series of pitches into a specific 'row', which is then altered in various ways, such as playing it 'back-to-front', 'upside-down' or altering it rhythmically. The early manifestation of serialism took place with the twelve-tone system of the second Viennese school (including composers Schoenberg, Berg and Webern), in which all 12 semitones in the octave had to be used at least once before a tone could be repeated. This assured that no key dominated. Later developments include total serialism, where rhythm, tempo, and even dynamics, form an integral part of the row. (See also Atonalism.)

Sharp A symbol (♯) before a note, or in a key signature, to indicate that the pitch is to be raised by a semitone. Playing or singing 'sharp' means too high, and consequently out of tune.

Solo Music sung or played by one performer.

Sonata A piece in several movements for solo piano, or piano plus one other instrument.

Sonata form The first movement of a sonata, symphony, etc., consisting of the exposition, which outlines a musical theme ('first subject') and a contrasting 'second subject'; the development, in which the themes are varied and transformed; and the recapitulation, in which the themes of the exposition are repeated in a modified form.

Stave or **staff** A grid of five parallel horizontal lines, and the corresponding spaces between them, on which notes are written. A note's position on the stave determines its relative pitch, with the point of reference indicated by the clef.

Study See Étude.

Suite A piece consisting of several contrasting dances, usually in the same key.

Symphony A large-scale instrumental work for orchestra. The classical 18th century symphony had four movements. The first was in sonata form with a vigorous tempo. The second movement was slower; the third was made up of a minuet and trio; and the last movement was fast. In the later 19th century the minuet was replaced by a vigorous scherzo.

Symphonic poem A large-scale orchestral work, usually in one movement, based on a non-musical subject. A type of programme music, it was designed to portray in music a person, event etc. (See also Programme music, Tone poem.)

Syncopation An accent (or 'off-beat') placed on a normally unaccented beat of a bar (often the second or last beat), to achieve an irregular rhythm. A constant feature of jazz.

Tempo (Italian, 'time'). The speed, or pace, at which a piece is played.

Theme A tune, partial tune or self-contained melody forming a central part of any piece of music.

Time A measure of the general movement of a piece of music, with reference to its rhythm, metre and tempo.

Toccata (Italian, 'touch'). A virtuoso show-piece to demonstrate manual dexterity, usually for a solo instrument.

Tonalism/tonality In composition, the basic principle of using a number of keys, one of which is predominant and provides the overall tonality of the music. Compare Atonalism.

Tone poem A descriptive orchestral piece in a single movement; sometimes called a symphonic poem, ballad or fantasy.

Total serialism Applying the principles of serialism to all aspects of composition, including rhythm, tempo and pitch.

Transcription The arrangement of a composition for a particular instrument(s), or for a different instrument(s).

Transposition Shifting the overall pitch of a piece so it can be performed in a higher or lower key than the original one.

Triad A chord of three different notes, usually thirds apart.

Trill A musical ornament consisting of a rapid alternation between one note and the note above or below it.

Trio Music for three voices or instruments; also the middle section of a minuet or scherzo movement in triple time.

Triple time Music with three beats to the bar, e.g. a waltz.

Triplet A group of three notes played in the same time allowed for two notes of the same duration.

Una corda Instruction in scores to play with the soft pedal depressed. (Italian. One string.)

Up-beat The unaccented beat preceding the first accented beat of a the first bar.

Variation A modification or development of a theme. Often appears as a 'theme and variations'; a form of a movement.

Vibrato (Italian, 'vibrating'.) The technique of producing a warm sound by a slight but rapid change of pitch in a voice or instrument, creating a pulsating or throbbing effect.

Virtuoso A musical master with outstanding technical skill.

Vocalize To sing without words, usually as a warm-up exercise in which a syllable or vowel sound is sung.

Waltz A dance in triple time, either slow or fast. Sometimes for solo piano (e.g. by Chopin) and not intended for dancing.

Whole-note Alternative term for a semibreve (equivalent to four crotchets).

PUBLISHER'S ACKNOWLEDGEMENTS

The author and publisher would like to thank Nicky Fransman and the staff of the Department of Music at the University of Stellenbosch, for the use of their sumptuous facilities, as well as Beulah Gericke, Frida Bekker & Yusuf Ras of the music library for their help and time; Mr Heuer of Heuer Musikhaus, Stellenbosch, for giving us free rein in his glorious music shop; models Gideon Kretschmer, Helen Mohr, Wilken Calitz, Carina du Tiot, Babette Le Roux and Greg Cox; Optical Eyes of Stellenbosch for providing props; and Editio Musica Budapest for permission to reproduce the Khatchaturian piece. The author would also like to thank Charla Schutte, Acama Fick, Catharina Struthers and Sylvia Grobbelaar for their helpful advice and knowledge.

PICTURE CREDITS

Bridgeman Art Library: p10 (left), Haydn Museum, Vienna; p40, Peter Willi; p42, Private Collection; p44, Civico Museo Bibliografico Musicale, Bologna, Italy; p47, Wallace Collection, London, UK; p50, Private Collection; p52, Christie's Images, London, UK; p56, Private Collection. **Gallo Images:** pp48, 54, 68. **Shirley de Kock Gueller:** p79. **Handrie Basson:** p37. **The Image Bank:** pp2–3, 4–5, 15, 46. **Lebrecht Music Collection:** p11 (top); p62, Suzie Maeder; pp58, 59, 64, 65, RA; p81, Richard Haughton. **Photo Access Photographic Library:** p10 (top). **Redferns Music Library:** p10 (bottom), Outline; p11 (bottom right), Harry Herd; p60, Ebet Roberts; p70, Tabatha Fireman. **Sotheby's Picture Library:** pp11 (bottom left), 41, 53.

USEFUL WEBSITES:

(The websites below were valid at the time of going to print. They offer a starting point for further investigation and no endorsement or recommendation on the part of the author or publisher should be inferred.)

abbywhiteside.org The Abby Whiteside Foundation.

amadeuspress.com Books on classical music and opera.

andante.com Weekly subscription newsletter providing the latest in classical music news, reviews and commentary.

apassion4jazz.net Styles, milestones, festivals and more.

bbc.co.uk/aboutmusic Artist profiles, news and discographies covering both classical, rock and pop music.

earfloss.com Rock and pop sheet music for piano.

history-of-rock.com The golden decade (1955–1964).

juilliard.edu/about The Juilliard School, New York.

musicroom.com The world's best music in print.

ram.ac.uk Royal Academy of Music, London.

rcm.ac.uk Royal College of Music, London.

redhotjazz.com Styles, artists, archives.

rollingstone.com Online site of the legendary magazine.

scottjoplin.org Official site of the Scott Joplin International Ragtime Foundation, Sedalia, Missouri.

sheetmusicplus.com US-based online store.

FURTHER READING:

Baker, Kenneth. The Complete Piano Player (Omnibus Edition), Music Sales Corporation, 1991.

Baker, Theodore. Baker's Biographical Dictionary of Musicians. Revised by Nicholas Slonimsky. Shirmer Books, New York, 1992.

Berlin, Edward A. King of Ragtime: Scott Joplin and His Era. Oxford, New York, 1994.

Bernstein, Seymour. 20 Lessons in Keyboard Choreography. Seymour Bernstein Music.

Cooke, Francis James. Great Pianists on Piano Playing. Dover Publications, New York, 1999.

Crombie, David. Piano, Backbeat Books, 1995.

Cummings, David. Random House Encyclopedic Dictionary of Classical Music.

Dubal, David. The Art of the Piano. Summit Books. 1989.

Elder, Dean. Pianists at Play. Khan & Averill. London 1994.

Fine, Larry, Keith Jarrett, Douglas R. Gilbert (Illustrator). The Piano Book: Buying and Owning a New or Used Piano, Brookside Press, 2001.

Gaines, James R. The Lives of the Piano. Holt, Rinehart and Winston. 1981.

Gerig, Reginald R. Famous Pianists and their Technique. Robert B. Luce, New York 1974.

Herder, Ronald (ed.). Easy Piano Classics: 104 Pieces for Early and Intermediate Players, Dover Publications, 1999.

Hill, Brad. The Complete Idiot's Guide to the Piano and Electronic Keyboards, Macmillan General Reference, 1998.

Manus, Morton, Ruby T. Palmer, Iris Manus. Alfred's Basic Adult Piano Course: Adult All-In-One, Alfred Publishing Co. Inc. 2002.

Neely, Blake, John Chappell. Piano for Dummies (with Audio CD), John Wiley & Sons, 1998.

Pinksterboer, Hugo (series editor). Rough Guide to Piano, Rough Guides, London.

Sadie, Stanley (ed.). The New Grove Dictionary of Music and Musicians. 2nd edition. Macmillan, 2001.

Online subscription version: www.grovemusic.com

Reality of Real Estate

Charles P. Nemeth

J.D., Ph.D., LL.M.

Prentice Hall
Boston   Columbus   Indianapolis   New York   San Francisco   Upper Saddle River   Amsterdam
Cape Town   Dubai   London   Madrid   Milan   Munich   Paris   Montreal   Toronto   Delhi
Mexico City   Sao Paulo   Sydney   Hong Kong   Seoul   Singapore   Taipei   Tokyo

Editor in Chief: Vernon Anthony
Acquisitions Editor: Gary Bauer
Editorial Assistant: Megan Heintz
Director of Marketing: David Gesell
Senior Marketing Manager: Leigh Ann Sims
Marketing Assistant: Les Roberts
Managing Editor: JoEllen Gohr
Production Editor: Christina Taylor
Project Manager: Laura Messerly
Operations Supervisor: Central Publishing

Art Director: Jayne Conte
Text Designer: Central Design
Cover Art: Image Source/Corbis
Cover Designer: Margaret Kenselaar
Full-Service Project Management: Mohinder Singh/ Aptara®, Inc.
Composition: Aptara®, Inc.
Printer/Binder: LSC Communications
Cover Printer: LSC Communications
Text Font: Palatino

Credits and acknowledgments borrowed from other sources and reproduced, with permission, in this textbook appear on appropriate page within text.

Library of Congress Cataloging-in-Publication Data

Nemeth, Charles P.
  Reality of real estate / Charles P. Nemeth. – 3rd ed.
    p. cm.
  Includes bibliographical references.
  ISBN-13: 978-0-13–510415-6
  ISBN-10: 0-13-510415-7
  1. Real estate business–Law and legislation–United States. 2. Real property–United States. 3. Conveyancing–United States. 4. Vendors and purchasers–United States. 5. Real estate business–United States.
  I. Title.
    KF570.N38 2011
      346.7304'37–dc22   2010009890

Prentice Hall
is an imprint of

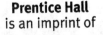

www.pearsonhighered.com

ISBN 13: 978-0-13-510415-6
ISBN 10:   0-13-510415-7

Dedication

To Mary Claire, my youngest daughter.
A lover of all beauty.

To St. Thomas Aquinas, who said:

Secondly, we may speak by buying and selling, considered as accidentally tending to the advantage of one party and to the disadvantage of the other: for instance, when a man has great need of a certain thing while another man will suffer if he be without it. In such a case the just price will depend not only on the thing sold but on the loss which the sale brings on the seller. And thus it will be lawful to sell a thing for more than it is worth in itself though the price paid be not more than it is worth to the owner.

The Summa Theologica, Volume II, Second Part, Question 77, Article 1.

Brief Contents

Contents

Preface

This is a work of both practice and theory. First and foremost, the contents serve the needs of the novice—introducing basic concepts of real estate, law and its transactional aspects. In addition, the reader is comfortably led into the world of real estate practice and its many nuances.

Chapter 1 provides an overview of the nature of real property, the various forms of real property ownership, and the duties of those practicing within the field. New information regarding partnerships, joint ventures, real estate investment trusts, and condominiums has been included.

Chapter 2 highlights the preparatory phases involving the real estate client. Primarily reviewed will be data collection techniques during the initial consultation, broker and agent disclosure, listing agreements, and file organization.

In Chapter 3, the reader is introduced to agreements or contracts of sale—all its components and clauses with a host of suggested designs. Real estate agreements set the stage for the transaction, and practitioners must be attentive to language and legal implications of clauses. Also covered are land installment contracts, options and cancellation, rescission, and release.

Chapter 4's thrust is conditional or contingent impact on contract formation and operation. Specifically reviewed will be the types of conditions most often witnessed, including financing, zoning, home inspection, and overall condition of the property. Expanded coverage of various hazardous materials has been provided and now includes Comprehensive Environmental Response, Compensation, and Liability Act (CERCLA) and underground storage tanks.

Chapter 5's content is titles. Title quality, the various means of performing searches, and title insurance are fully covered. Impediments to title thwart the transaction unless the parties agree otherwise.

Chapter 6 encompasses deeds, their parts and various styles. The type of deed chosen will depend on the needs of the parties and the state and integrity of title. Additional discussion on various deed covenants has been included.

In Chapter 7, the role and the nature of financing in the real estate transaction is covered. Mortgages and the host of documentation relevant to the award or denial are included. Types of mortgages discussed include fixed rate mortgage, governmental mortgages, and reverse, assumed and purchase money mortgages.

Chapter 8 comprehensively covers all closing and settlement processes, from the settlement sheet to the disposition of proceeds. Paralegals earn their reputation when closings are capably done and the parties to the transaction are satisfied. Chapter 8 includes a new section on software programs for closing and settlement.

Chapter 9 reviews leases for both buyers and sellers in the real estate transaction. Authorship of lease formats as well as traditional legal remedies for breach is covered.

Chapter 10 reviews the growing alternative forums available for dispute resolution in real estate cases. Highlighted is the American Arbitration Association program and the new National Association of REALTORS® (NAR) processes for the resolution of disputers.

Finally, the manual fittingly ends with a discussion of foreclosure. Added to the final chapter is a new section on bankruptcy law and the foreclosure process with an emphasis on "Chapter 7 bankruptcy."

STUDENT RESOURCES

Companion Website

Students can access a variety of study aids at www.prenhall.com/nemeth. The online Companion Website includes the following: chapter learning objectives, test-prep quiz questions for each chapter with immediate feedback, and web exercises for each chapter.

INSTRUCTOR RESOURCES

An **Instructor's Manual, PowerPoint Lecture Package, and Electronic Test Generator** are available for instructors to download from the Instructor's Resource Center. To access supplementary materials online, instructors need to request an instructor access code. Go to www.pearsonhighered.com/irc, where you can register for an instructor access code. Within 48 hours of registering you will receive a confirming e-mail including an instructor access code. Once you have received your code, locate your text in the online catalog and click on the Instructor Resources button on the left side of the catalog product page. Select a supplement and a log in page will appear. Once you have logged in, you can access instructor material for all Prentice Hall textbooks.

CourseConnect Real Estate Law Online Course

Looking for robust online course content to reinforce and enhance your student learning? We have the solution: CourseConnect! CourseConnect courses contain customizable modules of content mapped to major learning outcomes. Each learning object contains interactive tutorials, rich media, discussion questions, MP3 downloadable lectures, assessments, and interactive activities that address different learning styles. CourseConnect Courses follow a consistent 21-step instructional design process, yet each course is developed individually by instructional designers and instructors who have taught the course online. Test questions, created by assessment professionals, were developed at all levels of Bloom's Taxonomy. When you buy a CourseConnect course, you purchase a complete package that provides you with detailed documentation you can use for your accreditation reviews. CourseConnect courses can be delivered in any commercial platform such as WebCT, BlackBoard, Angel, Moodle, or eCollege platforms. For more information contact your representative or call 800-635-1579.

As always, I ask that my readers pass on any ideas or thoughts that correct my errors or misunderstandings. Your suggestions can only make this project more useful to its enlightened audience.

Charles P. Nemeth, J.D., Ph.D., LL.M.
Chair and Professor of Legal Studies, Director of the Institute for Law and Public Policy
California University of Pennsylvania
California, PA
Member of the Pennsylvania, New York, and North Carolina Bars

Acknowledgments

Every text has its own character and nuances, much the reflection of those working in unison. This text is no exception for it relies so heartily on the sweat and thought of those dedicated to task.

At this office, there is a sea of paper and books that, at first glance, seems to be in disorder. Yet upon a closer look, there is a real method, developed by those so loyal to this undertaking. My thanks are primarily given to Hope Haywood, who researches and edits most capably and masters a wealth of information and concepts.

At California University of Pennsylvania, the support continues. My staff, namely Laurie Manderino, administrative assistant extraordinaire, and Rose Mahouski, keeper of the mail and everything else, free this writer from the many tasks that sometimes interfere with creative exposition. Both the president, Angelo Armenti and the dean, Leonard Colelli, encourage this type of research with generous hearts. My graduate assistant, Chase McNutt, aided most admirably in the research effort.

Acknowledgement also goes to competing publishers who honorably share their works to bolster the value of mine, specifically: ALI-ABA, American Bar Association, Julius Blumberg Co., All-State Legal Supply, Easy Soft Inc., Argosy Legal Systems, National Association of REALTORS®, Arizona Association of Realtors, State Bar of Wisconsin, Minnesota Association of Realtors, Northeast Florida Association of REALTORS, Pennsylvania Association of REALTORS, National Arbitration and Mediation Inc., and the American Arbitration Association. These companies, boards, and associations are to be applauded, especially when one considers the growing tendency to be belligerent in the intellectual marketplace.

Aside from these players, I acknowledge, with abiding love and affection, my family, the true center of the universe and the real reason for writing anything. Thanks to Jean Marie, my loyal, completely unselfish spouse and the children she so graciously bore; Eleanor, Stephen, Anne Marie, John, Joseph, Mary Claire, and Michael Augustine.

Charles P. Nemeth, J.D., Ph.D., LL.M.
Pittsburgh, Pennsylvania

About the Author

Charles P. Nemeth, Chair and Professor of Legal Studies, Director of the Institute for Law and Public Policy, has spent the vast majority of his professional life in the study and practice of law and justice. A recognized expert on ethics and the legal system, appellate legal practice, and private-sector justice, he also is a prolific writer with forty-seven titles to his name, having published numerous texts and articles on law and justice throughout his impressive career. His most recent works include these titles: *Law & Evidence: A Primer for Criminal Justice, Criminology, Law, and Legal Studies*, 2nd ed. (Jones & Bartlett, 2010); *Homeland Security: An Introduction to Principles and Practice* (CRC Press, 2010); *Private Security and the Investigative Process*, 3rd ed. (Jones & Bartlett, 2010); *Aquinas & King: A Discourse on Civil Disobedience* (Carolina Academic Press, 2009); *Aquinas on Crime* (St. Augustine's Press, 2008); and *Aquinas in the Courtroom* (Greenwood and Praeger Publishing, 2001). In addition, the recently published are *Private Sector and Public Safety: A Community Based Approach* (Prentice Hall, 2005), *The Prevention Agency* (California University of PA Press-ILPP, 2005), and *Private Security and the Law*, 3rd ed. (Elsevier, 2005).

An educator for more than thirty years, Nemeth's distinctive career in law and justice is founded on an exemplary education, including a Master of Laws from George Washington University, a Juris Doctor from the University of Baltimore, and a Master of Arts and Ph.D. from Duquesne University. In addition, he was awarded an MS from Niagara University and received an undergraduate degree from the University of Delaware. He holds memberships in the New York, North Carolina, and Pennsylvania Bars. Dr. Nemeth came to California University to direct the university's graduate program in Criminal Justice, implement a new master's degree in Law and Public Policy, and to develop academic programs at California University of Pennsylvania's Pittsburgh Center as director of Program Development. He has also erected a think tank for legal and justice policy issues—the Institute of Law and Public Policy. His previous academic appointments include Niagara University (1977–1980), the University of Baltimore (1980–1981), Glassboro State College (1981–1986), Waynesburg College (1988–1998), and the State University of New York at Brockport (1998–2003).

He is a much sought-after legal consultant for security companies and a recognized scholar on issues involving law and morality.

The Reality of Real Estate

LEARNING OBJECTIVES

- To distinguish and differentiate the forms and types of real property interests and rights.
- To define terms unique to real estate practice.
- To describe the many methods of concurrent ownership, including tenants by the entireties, joint tenants, and tenants in common.
- To identify the peripheral rights and interests in land, including easements and rights of way.

JOB COMPETENCIES

- To identify forms of ownership in real estate transactions.
- To arrange correspondence and enter into dialogue with banks, utility companies, attorneys, and other parties in a real estate transaction regarding the nature of ownership.
- To prepare client checklist and interview sheets that gauge forms and types of property interest.

ETHICAL CONSIDERATIONS

The paralegal must be aware of the following ethical dilemmas during this phase of a real estate transaction:

- Unauthorized practice of law
- Lawyer supervision of nonlawyers
- Confidentiality issues
- Conflicts of interest

I. REAL ESTATE COMPETENCIES

Real estate professionals, title agents, and paralegals, both experienced and those in study, who are interested in the reality of real estate as a career will be impressed by its many demands and challenges.[1] Working in real estate is not an occupation for those lacking attention to detail. In fact, the duties involved in conveying, selling, and buying realty require the capability to manage many important tasks simultaneously. The coordination of buyer and seller not only demands dedication to closing the deal, but also requires that the paralegal fathom the intricate nuances of the exchange and ensure the rights of all parties. The real estate specialist, and especially paralegals, must be perfectly prepared and in a state of constant readiness as the real estate transaction unravels. The sheer volume of requirements alone calls for skill and professionalism.[2]

Today, paralegals and other practitioners who labor in real estate do so in a complex, legal, bureaucratic, and increasingly document-intensive environment. Long gone are the handshakes and oral promises of those buying and selling. Indeed, the world of real estate changes daily with electronic and computerized processes replacing the documentary patterns of yesteryear.[3]

The transaction's importance simply demands the very best of the paralegals employed in the field. In this sense, anyone desiring a career in real estate must have many skills and competencies, including the following:

- Drafting documents
- Reviewing title assessments
- Interpreting surveys
- Analyzing and preparing leases
- Inspecting property
- Assuming closing and settlement responsibilities
- Assuming postclosing responsibilities
- Recording mortgage, deed, assignment release, and other documents
- Preparing tax filings
- Securing zoning permits and applications
- Preparing legal descriptions
- Arranging for payoff of notes and release of mortgages
- Notarizing documents at closing, if qualified
- Gaining an understanding of liability and hazard insurance
- Ordering and conducting lien searches
- Assessing and analyzing means of ownership, whether sole or joint
- Assessing and analyzing types of realty
- Orchestrating multiple parties to a transaction
- Preparing client form files
- Negotiating and discussing terms of the agreement of sale
- Drafting agreement of sale
- Drafting loan commitment and attending relevant negotiations
- Drafting installment sale contracts and attending relevant negotiations
- Authoring deeds
- Reviewing titles
- Assuring compliance with governmental requirements
- Supervising closing and settlement

The preceding list is an occupational thumbnail. This multifaceted field, labeled *real estate*, calls for multifaceted people. Gone are the unregulated days when paperwork was minimal, governmental oversight was limited, and legal mandates were few. Instead, in the highly complex realty transaction, the paralegals must be eclectic; that is, they must understand a host of dimensions, from initial contract negotiations to closing on settlement day. Just as critically, the real estate specialist must be attuned to local custom and historical practice. While paraprofessionals assume a myriad of tasks, the lawyer/attorney is still the ringmaster. A recent South Carolina decision reasserts the necessity of lawyers at closing. In *Doe v. McMaster*, the Supreme Court of South

Carolina "has made it clear that the unauthorized practice of law in the context of real estate closings is an issue that is not taken lightly. Under current law, an independent attorney must properly supervise all of the steps of the transaction and be physically present at the closing. Differing opinions still exist as to the intended meaning of physical presence. Further rule additions and supreme court decisions may be necessary to clarify this complex and evolving area of the law in South Carolina."[4]

The parties—sellers of the realty (vendors) and the buyers (vendees)—do not operate on their own. They are entangled in a maze of personalities and occupational players, from listing brokers to sales agents, from mortgage loan officers to lawyers, from title agents and abstractors to title insurers, to name a few. In the final analysis, real estate comprises human interaction and documentary rigor.

To capture real estate from both a theoretical and practical perspective is what this text is all about. By titling the book *Reality of Real Estate*, the student should appreciate the text's principal content: *to understand the concepts of real estate, its pure application, and operation.*

When done, the future professional should understand not only the abstract concepts that define real estate, but also the mechanics of realty, its buying and selling, its financing and conditions, and its usage and restriction.

This is what the student will witness within: a step-by-step assessment of how realty is bought and sold; how buyers and sellers transact; and how third parties, such as real estate agents, title clerks, closing officers, bankers, and lawyers, play a crucial role in effecting closure on a proposed and agreed purchase agreement. This is the *reality* of real estate.

Any serious study of the numerous responsibilities and tasks of the real estate paralegal begins with a cursory review of just what constitutes real property.

II. BASIC PARTIES, RESOURCES, AND TERMINOLOGY

Before beginning our full-fledged examination of the reality of real estate practice, a review of the players is necessary. We will outline exactly who and what is involved in the real estate transaction. A list follows:

A. Parties

Abstractor	Specialist, lawyer, paralegal, or firm that reviews both the quality of title by the conveyancing history and existing encumbrances.
Attorney	Counsel for either buyer or seller, who advocates their respective positions relative to contract. May also act as closing agent in some jurisdictions or guarantor of title quality.
Broker	The realty representative who acts as the basis for agency in the agent/client relationship. Every agent must work under the supervision of a broker.
Mortgagee	The lender, whether bank, savings and loan, or other finance source.
Mortgagor	The person obliged to repay a mortgage that secures the home purchase, known as the borrower.
Paralegal or Legal Assistant	The eclectic player in the game of real estate. No person is entrusted with a greater range of tasks, from title search to closing, from client relations to documentary preparation.
Parties	The seller and the buyer.
Real Estate Agent	Representative of either buyer or seller, or both, depending on listing agreement.

Real Estate Sale	A conveyance of real property for a price, in money or other property, of a stipulated value by the owner to the purchaser. The transfer must be voluntary and is regulated by a contract or agreement of sale.
Recorder/Registrar of Deeds	Central depository for deed filing after closing.
Settlement Agent or Closing Officer	Person or firm entrusted with effecting formal settlement of the property on the day of closing.
Title Insurer	Licensed company issuing policies that protect buyers and banks from challenges to title.
Vendee	The buyer.
Vendor	The seller of any realty.

B. Resources

Ready access to forms, treatises, and other materials relevant to real estate practice should become a priority for real estate specialists. Recommended sources are:

- Thomas F. Bergin & Paul L. Haskell, *Preface to Estates in Land and Future Interests* (West 1966, 1984).
- Robert Bernhardt, *Real Property* (1975).
- Jerome Dasso, *Real Estate* (Prentice Hall, 2000).
- Milton R. Friedman, *Contracts and Conveyances of Real Property* (Practicing Law Inst., 1979, 1991).
- Theodore H. Gordon, *California Real Estate Law* (Regents/Prentice Hall, 1991).
- Bruce T. Harwood, *Real Estate: An Introduction to the Profession*, 6th ed. (Prentice Hall, 1992).
- Patrick K. Hetrick & Larry A. Outlaw, *North Carolina Real Estate for Brokers and Salesmen*, 4th ed. (Prentice Hall, 1994).
- Daniel F. Hinkel, *Practical Real Estate Law*, 5th ed. (Thomson West, 2008).
- H. E. Hoagland et al., *Real Estate Finance* (1977).
- William F. Hoffmeyer, *The Pennsylvania Real Estate Settlement Procedures Manual* (Chem Lane Pub. Co. of York, 1990).
- Institute for Paralegal Training, *Introduction to Real Estate Law*, Russell Bellavance, ed. (West, 1978).
- Carol K. Irvin & James D. Irvin, *Ohio Real Estate Law*, 8th ed. (South-Western Ed., 2004).
- Charles J. Jacobus & Bruce Harwood, *Real Estate Principles*, 8th ed. (Prentice Hall, 1999).
- Frank W. Kovats, *Principles and Practices of New Jersey Real Estate* (Kovko Pub., 1984, 1998).
- Charles P. Nemeth, *Pennsylvania Agreements of Sale* (George T. Bisel Company, 1996).
- Charles P. Nemeth, *Pennsylvania Real Estate Practice* (George T. Bisel Company, 1996).
- North Carolina Bar Foundation and the Real Property Section of the North Carolina Bar Association, *North Carolina Real Property Forms Book* (N.C. Bar Assoc., 1987).
- Timothy G. O'Neill, ed., *Ladner on Conveyancing in Pennsylvania* (George T. Bisel Company, 1988, 1990).
- Tim Rice, Ralph A. Palmer, & Alan Toban, *Illinois Real Estate: Principles and Practices*, 2nd ed. (South-Western Ed., 1996).
- Pennsylvania Bar Institute, *Real Estate Practice* (Penna. Bar Assoc., 1982).

- Robert E. Schreiner, *Real Estate Closings* (R. E. Schiemer, 1983).
- Lynn T. Slossberg, *The Essentials of Real Estate Law,* 2nd ed. (Thomson West, 2008).
- Herbert Thorndike Tiffany, *The Law of Real Property and Other Interests in Land* (Callaghan and Co., 1970).
- James A. Webster et al., *North Carolina Real Estate for Brokers and Salesmen,* 3rd ed. (Prentice Hall, 1986).
- I. Edward Weich, *Real Estate* (HarperCollins, 1975).

Software programs are in ready supply for those entrusted with the real estate transaction. Some of the more popular packages include the following:

- Easy HUD (2009; complete real estate transaction), Easy Soft Inc., 212 North Center Drive, North Brunswick, NJ 08902.
- Timberline Real Estate Software, 15195 NW Greenbrier Parkway, Beaverton, Oregon 97006, www.SageTimberline.com.
- AgentOffice Real Estate Software, P.O. Box 39, 412-14A Crescent, Invermere, BC V0A 1K0, www.realtystar.com.
- Property Management & Construction Software, 4660 Duke Drive, Suite 210, Mason, OH 45040, www.spectraesolutions.com.
- SettlementRoom Software, Emphasys Software, 333 North Canyons Parkway, Suite 211, Livermore, CA 94551, www.settlementroom.com.
- HomeFeedback, Showing Suite Inc., 4901 Morena Blvd., Suite 207, San Diego, CA 92117, www.homefeedback.com.
- Agent360 Realtor Software, 800-971-4360, www.agent360.net.
- Instant Realty Web site, #201-2730 Commercial Drive, Vancouver BC Canada V5N 5P4, www.interactivetools.com.
- RealtyJuggler Desktop, RealOrganized Inc., 8299 Sand Dollar Drive, Windsor, CO 80528, www.RealtyJuggler.com.

Web Exercise

Visit the HomeFeedback software program at *www.homefeedback.com.*

C. Terminology

Familiarity with the language of real estate will assist the paralegal student in understanding the work. Essential terminology is set out under Key Words at the beginning of each section.

III. THE NATURE OF REAL PROPERTY

KEY WORDS		
easements	personal property	riparian rights
fixtures	real property	
license	realty	

When compared to other forms of property, real property has a more permanent nature. **Personal property** is movable, transferable in the physical sense, and durationally limited. Personal property can be goods or services, tangible items of value for a fixed price or sum, but exists independently from their setting or location. Its place, therefore, is not fixed, like land or realty. **Real property** is a right and privilege associated with land, realty, and the fixtures thereto, with a longer or even perpetual duration. Real property is also formally bought and sold, transferred by deed, or subject to estate laws and other distribution schemes. On the other hand, personal property carries limited recognition as a perennial or perpetual interest. For example, a toaster or a basketball does not descend or transfer to others by deed. It is a fleeting, less serious form of interest, while realty is given a higher level of transactional scrutiny.

Grover C. Ladner, in his work, *Conveyancing in Pennsylvania*, a thorough treatise on the process of real property transfer, sums up the nature of real property:

> consider real property as the surface of the world and all inanimate things upon, over or beneath it or encompassed by it by nature, or affixed thereto with intent of permanency. In most instances, this means land, including the space above it, growing trees and plants upon it, buildings and other improvements upon it, and the subsoil, minerals and space below the surface.[5]

Herbert Tiffany's treatise on real property, *The Law of Real Property and Other Interests in Land*, calls the personal property "movable," while real property is "fixed in time and space":

> The fundamental distinction between land and movables, from a legal point of view, lies in the fact that "estates" exist in land, and not in movables, and that, on this doctrine of estates, there has been built up an elaborate system of rules as to the ownership of land and the creation of rights therein, which differ materially from those prevailing as to chattels.[6]

Land, that raw dirt and panorama of birds and trees and the like, is the basic genus of real property. Upon this same fertile or barren ground other forms of immovable property become just as real, such as houses, underground tanks, swimming pools, and stationary, heavily connected objects or other structures affixed to the land. Constructed homes are termed **realty**. Other objects, permanently affixed to the land and/or realty are termed **fixtures**. A fixture, even though it has personal qualities, becomes real because of its integral connection to the realty itself.

Various tests determine what constitutes a fixture as compared to personal property. Consider the comparison is a swimming pool.

1. The means and method of attachment (e.g., swimming pool dug into earth)
2. The adaptation of the object outside the real property (e.g., inground pool is not moveable, while aboveground is, ergo, "personal")
3. The intent of the party who originally affixed the object (e.g., inground pool is not temporary addition)
4. The relationship of the parties involved (e.g., owners of pool)
5. The existence of an agreement outlining the nature of the property (e.g., read agreement of sale, which may or may not include the pool).

The label "fixture" has important consequences. When real estate is bought and sold, the fixture goes with it. If it is not a fixture, being personal property instead, it remains the property of the seller.

While the land and realty constructed thereon are real property and those items of personalty so inexorably attached or fixed to the same are "fixtures" and thus real property, the concept of real property extends even farther in scope and design. Ponder the concept of an easement.

Easements are rights granted to use, yet not own, a specifically delineated piece of real property. Utility companies, needing access for wire, pole, and pipe, must acquire easement interests.

Easements afford limited usage, ownership, right-of-way access, or permission to cross or enter the land owned by another. This interest is in real, not personal, property. Tiffany explains the concept of easement as follows:

> An easement granted for a particular purpose, or arising by prescription by an exercise of the right for such a purpose, necessarily comes to an end when the purpose ceases. A way of necessity ceases with the necessity on which it is based as when the dominant owner acquires land over which he has an outlet to the highway. The right to maintain, on adjoining land, a staircase leading to one's building terminates by the destruction of the building.[7]

Easements fall into two categories.

Easements in Gross: This right usually relates to a permanent placement, such as a transmission line or pipeline, onto another property. These rights can be sold or transferred.

Appurtenant Easements: When two properties with different owners are adjacent and one has rights to use the property of the other party, the easement is designated appurtenant easement. Driveways or other access points are common examples.

An easement is an intangible right to use, yet not to own, property. As Tiffany remarks, "An easement gives no right to possess land upon which it is imposed but a right merely to the party in whom it is vested to enjoy it."[8] Easements may include natural waterways, water courses, drains, trails and paths, roadways, tunnels, party walls, supportive buildings, fences, utility lines, rights-of-way, burial rights, and access to light and air. Examples of common easements are:

- Power lines on a property.
- A common driveway that extends over two or more properties.
- A gas pipeline running through a property.
- Sewage and water access.
- County, state, and township easements that run along a road.

CASE LAW

Parties seeking to reclaim an easement will claim abandonment of the right. A Wisconsin appellate decision dealt with the logic of abandonment in the reversion of an easement.

Appeal No. 2006AP1691

Cir. Ct. No. 2004CV236

STATE OF WISCONSIN

IN COURT OF APPEALS
DISTRICT III

PAUL E. SPENCER JR.,
PLAINTIFF-RESPONDENT,

v.

JOHN KOSIR,
DEFENDANT-APPELLANT.

APPEAL from a judgment of the Circuit Court for Vilas County: NEAL A. NIELSEN III, Judge. *Affirmed.*

Before Cane, C. J., Hoover, P. J., and Peterson, J.

CANE, C. J.: John Kosir appeals a judgment establishing Paul Spencer's right to an easement across Kosir's property. Kosir argues the circuit court erred by finding the easement had not been abandoned

(continued)

and that the court erred in its determination of the location and width of the easement. We disagree with Kosir and affirm the judgment.

BACKGROUND

Kosir and Spencer own adjacent lots. Before Kosir's purchase in 1999, there were no significant improvements to either property. Spencer's property does not have access to the town road, but the deed reflects an easement across Kosir's property. Spencer only knew of the lot being visited twice. First, Spencer's mother visited the property in 1972 with her aunt, who was the recorded titleholder at that time. Second, Spencer visited the property in 2003 with his attorney.

The easement in question has been continuously recorded since 1936. The easement states "excepting and reserving in the grantors, a right of way for road purposes across the lands hereinabove described." No efforts were made to establish and use the easement until the 1990s, when Spencer's mother, who then owned the property, made a number of unsuccessful attempts to contact Kosir's predecessors in title to reach an agreement on the location of the easement road needed to comply with a DNR [Department of Natural Resources] managed forest lands agreement she entered.

In an effort to comply with the managed forest lands agreement, Spencer retained an attorney in 2003 to assist him with the easement. Kosir and Spencer subsequently met, when Kosir refused to permit a logging road on his property. In December 2004, Spencer filed this lawsuit seeking a judicial declaration confirming the existence and validity of Spencer's easement rights and a determination of an appropriate width and location of the easement.

Both Kosir and Spencer moved for summary judgment. The circuit court granted summary judgment to Spencer, establishing an easement twenty feet wide with a road no wider than twelve feet. This roadway would be located along the eastern edge of Kosir's property and adjacent to Spencer's property. The court ordered Kosir to remove all of his personal property and/or improvements from the easement within sixty days. The court's order also permits Spencer to cut down trees to clear a path for the easement. In turn, Spencer is required to compensate Kosir for the stumpage value of the harvested trees.

DISCUSSION

The grant or denial of a motion for summary judgment is a matter of law this court reviews de novo. *Torgerson v. Journal/Sentinel Inc.*, 210 Wis. 2d 524, 536, 563 N.W.2d 472 (1997). We review summary judgment without deference to the circuit court but benefiting from its analysis. *Green Spring Farms v. Kersten*, 136 Wis. 2d 304, 314-15, 401 N.W.2d 816 (1987).

Kosir argues the nonuse of the easement for roughly seventy years was sufficient to establish that the easement had been intentionally abandoned. Alternatively, Kosir argues the circuit court incorrectly expanded the purpose and scope of the easement in creating a road access. We disagree.

Kosir relies upon *Burkman v. New Lisbon*, 246 Wis. 547, 18 N.W.2d 4 (1945), to support his nonuse argument. However, this decision supports Spencer's position, and not Kosir's. In *Burkman*, the supreme court held that flowage rights acquired by prescription were lost by abandonment when the dam that created the rights was destroyed and no attempt was made to restore it. *Id.* at 557. In *Burkman*, an affirmative act, which helped persuade the court the rights were abandoned, was the fact that the dam was not rebuilt. *See id.* To reach this conclusion, the court relied on comments (c) and (d) of the RESTATEMENT OF THE LAW OF PROPERTY, VOL. V, § 504 (1940). *Id.* at 556. Comments (c) and (d) read as follows:

c. Conduct as to Use. An intentional relinquishment of an easement indicated by conduct respecting the use authorized by it constitutes an abandonment of the easement. The intention required in the abandonment of an easement is the intention not to make in the future the uses authorized by it. The benefit of an easement lies in the privilege of use of the land subject to it. *There is no abandonment unless there is a giving up of that use. The giving up must be evidenced by conduct respecting the use of such a character as to indicate an intention to give up the use for the future as well as for the present. Conduct, when inconsistent with the continuance of the use, indicates an intention to give it up.*

The conduct required for abandonment cannot consist of verbal expressions of intention. Such expressions are effective to extinguish an easement only when they comply with the requirements of a release and operate as such. Verbal expressions of an intention to abandon are relevant, however, for the purpose of giving meaning to acts which are susceptible of being interpreted as indicating an intention to give up the use authorized by an easement, but which do not give themselves conclusively demonstrate the intention which animated them.

d. Nonuse. Conduct from which an intention to abandon an easement may be inferred may consist in a failure to make the use authorized. *Nonuse does not of itself produce an abandonment no matter how long continued.* It but evidences the necessary intention. Its effectiveness as evidence is dependent upon the circumstances. Under some circumstances a relatively short period of nonuse may be sufficient to give rise to the necessary inference; under other circumstances a relatively long period may be insufficient. *The duration of the period of nonuse, though never conclusive as to the intention to abandon,* is ordinarily admissible for the purpose of showing intention in that regard. (Emphasis added.)

We agree with the circuit court that these provisions are helpful in resolving the present case. Kosir also relies on other cases involving abandonment. However, all those cases involve easements that were established and used to some extent before they were abandoned. *See Povolny v. Totzke*, 2003 Wis. App. 184, 266 Wis. 2d 852, 668 N.W.2d 834. Here, however, the easement's location was never established in the first place, let alone used. Therefore, case law that involves established easements which are later abandoned is not analogous.

We also agree with the circuit court's application of legal principles to the presented facts in this case. The court reasoned:

It is of no legal consequence that the easement road has not been constructed and used in all the years from 1936 to present. Spencer and his predecessors were under no affirmative legal obligation to construct the road when the easement was first created. It was a vacant, wooded parcel and was not occupied or used for any purpose by the owners at that time. The reservation of easement in 1936 was therefore in contemplation of a future need for legal access from the parcel to the town road. That need did not ripen until the mid-to-late 1990s when a timber harvest was contemplated by the [managed forest lands] plan for this property. At that point Spencer's mother did exercise reasonable efforts to preserve her easement claim, and Spencer himself has done so by attempting to negotiate access with Kosir and by initiating this lawsuit.

Under these circumstances, the circuit court correctly held that the easement had not been abandoned merely because it was not used for seventy years.

Kosir also contends that Spencer's and his predecessors' acquiescence in Kosir's home construction and other structures and allowing trees to grow on his property are affirmative acts establishing an intent to abandon the easement. We disagree. The affirmative act required to demonstrate an intent to abandon must be that of the easement holder. Mere acquiescence is not an affirmative act. The actions of the servient owner alone cannot establish the easement holder's intent to abandon. *See* Bruce and Ely's *the Law of Easements and Licenses in Land*, § 10:20 (West Group, 2001). The first time Spencer had reason to appreciate the extent of Kosir's improvements was in 2003, when he was attempting to enforce the easement. Furthermore, there is no evidence that Kosir's improvements are so extensive as to render Spencer's use of a roadway impossible.

Because no path was ever created or contemplated, we also reject Kosir's argument that Spencer's conduct was essentially "allowing the easement path to fall into disrepair." Furthermore, we also note that in the context of abandonment, no Wisconsin court has ever held that letting an easement fall into disrepair, by itself, is sufficient to establish abandonment. *See Povolny*, 266 Wis. 2d 852.

Alternatively, Kosir challenges the court's determination that the easement covers the eastern twenty feet of his property and limits the travel portion to no more than twelve feet in width. Kosir argues the easement should be limited to at most an eight-foot-wide walking path. We disagree.

(continued)

The easement is described as "a right of way for road purposes." The easement does not have a specified width or location. When the location of an easement is not defined, the court has the inherent power to affirmatively and specifically determine its location, after considering the rights and interests of both parties. *See Werkowski v. Waterford Homes Inc.*, 30 Wis. 2d 410, 417, 141 N.W.2d 306 (1966). We review equitable remedies for erroneous exercise of discretion. *See Mulder v. Mittelstadt*, 120 Wis. 2d 103, 115, 352 N.W.2d 223 (Ct. App. 1984). The circuit court properly exercises its discretion if it applies the appropriate law and the record shows there is a reasonable factual basis for its decision. *See Burkes v. Hales*, 165 Wis. 2d 585, 590, 478 N.W.2d 37 (Ct. App. 1991).

The court's determination of the location and width of the easement road is supported by facts in the record. The court found the easement was recorded and enforceable, entitling Spencer to "right of way for road purposes." Because the words "road purposes" specify the type of "right of way" to be granted, we reject Kosir's reading of this language as not granting a road easement. Spencer did not need to use an alternate form of access to drive vehicles to his property nor is he limited to a walking path.

The court considered Kosir's interests and located the easement on the eastern edge of Kosir's property, where it would least affect Kosir's property. The court also considered Kosir's complaints about the number of trees that would have to be cut. In response to these complaints, the court limited the width of the easement road to twelve feet and ordered Spencer to pay Kosir the stumpage value of the marketable trees harvested in order to open up the easement road. Despite his assertions to the contrary, the record establishes Kosir has to move only those structures located within the easement. The court applied the appropriate law, and the record shows a reasonable factual basis for the location and width of the easement road. *See id.* Therefore, we conclude the court properly exercised its discretion.

By the Court.—Judgment affirmed.

Easements have recently been used for tax purposes coupled with preservation programs.[9] In both historic and open land settings, such as the maintenance of a green area or forest land, owners of these parcels may grant buildings or lands to designated governmental authorities. The intent will vary but it is clear that tax law permits a sizeable deduction of the fair market value of said property. Thus, if an owner of five acres of forest land wishes to preserve it and the surrounding community wishes to foster pristine open space, the conservation easement is the mechanism to formalize these mutual desires. As in other transactions, the grantor of the easement would note its conservation purpose directly in the deed. See Figure 1–1 for sample language for the deed format.

Further down the spectrum of real property interests is the **license** or a privilege to use land for a specific purpose such as oil and gas rights, construction, mineral extraction, and similar activity. Mineral rights are also common subject matter for the license. A mineral right is a right to extract a mineral from the earth or to receive payment, in the form of royalty, for the extraction of minerals. "Mineral" may have different meanings depending on the context, and there is no universal definition. However, "mineral" generally includes:

- Fossil fuels—oil, natural gas, and coal.
- Metals and metal-bearing ores such as gold, copper, and iron.
- Nonmetallic minerals and mineable rock products such as limestone, gypsum, building stones and salt.
- May also include sand and gravel, peat, marl, and so on.

DEED OF CONSERVATION EASEMENT

THIS DEED OF CONSERVATION EASEMENT ("Conservation Easement") made this _____ day of _____, 200_, by and between _____, ("Grantor(s)"), and The State of Maryland to the use of the Department of Natural Resources ("Grantee"),

WITNESSETH

WHEREAS, by Contract of Sale approved by the Board of Public Works on February 9, 2000, the Pennsylvania Electric Company agreed to sell and the State of Maryland agreed to buy the bed of Deep Creek Lake and certain surrounding parcels of property, known collectively as Parcel 2, subject to the imposition of a conservation easement upon the State's resale of certain portions of the property;

WHEREAS, of the property purchased from Pennsylvania Electric Company, the State has determined to retain a portion of Parcel 2 contiguous to Deep Creek Lake to be reserved for public use and additional land as necessary to protect the Lake's natural, recreational, scenic, and aesthetic resources, and to delineate boundary lines, or to provide for public access to the Lake;

WHEREAS, of the remaining portions of Parcel 2, the State has determined to resell to contiguous property owners, certain parcels, subject to this Conservation Easement;

WHEREAS, Grantors herein own in fee simple real property situate, lying and being in Garrett County, Maryland, contiguous to Deep Creek Lake, thereby making them eligible to purchase a portion of Parcel Two subject to this Conservation Easement; and

WHEREAS, the within Grantors have availed themselves of the opportunity to purchase property ("Property") and are willing to grant this Conservation Easement on the Property, thereby restricting and limiting the use of the Property as hereinafter provided in this Conservation Easement for the purposes set forth below.

WHEREAS, the purpose of the Conservation Easement is to prevent development and maintain the beauty and recreational purpose and to conserve the natural and scenic qualities of the environment of Deep Creek Lake and the surrounding area;

NOW, THEREFORE, in consideration of the facts stated in the above paragraphs and the covenants, terms, conditions and restrictions (the "Terms") hereinafter set forth, the receipt and sufficiency of which are hereby acknowledged by the parties, the Grantors unconditionally and irrevocably hereby grant and convey unto the Grantee, its successors and assigns, forever and in perpetuity a Conservation Easement of the nature and character and to the extent hereinafter set forth, with respect to the Property:

ARTICLE I. DURATION OF EASEMENT

This Conservation Easement shall be perpetual. It is an easement in gross and runs with the land as an incorporeal interest in the Property, enforceable with respect to the Property by the Grantee against the Grantors and their personal representatives, heirs, successors and assigns.

ARTICLE II. PROHIBITED AND RESTRICTED ACTIVITIES

A. *Industrial or Commercial Activities on the Property*

Industrial or commercial activities are prohibited on the Property, except, with the approval of the Grantee, for activities necessary to support and gain access to lake-related, commercial and recreational uses permitted by the State of Maryland on immediately contiguous State land or on Deep Creek Lake, at the time of the proposed activity.

B. *Construction and Improvements*

No building, facility, means of access, fence or other structure shall be permitted on the Property, except: (1) pedestrian pathways or stairways constructed with wood, stone or permeable surfaces of

FIGURE 1–1
(continues)

natural materials to provide access to the lake or improvements on the Property from the contiguous property; (2) with the approval of the Grantee, utilities to serve commercial or recreational facilities on the contiguous State land; (3) structures identified on a plat of Parcel 2 as recorded among the Land Records of Garrett County, Maryland in Plat Drawer P, File 134 or in the records of the Department of Natural Resources and those structures identified on the individual plats prepared by the surveyor and recorded with each conveyance, provided that such structures were permitted by the Department or its predecessor in title prior to the Grantor's ownership of the Property; and (4) as subject to the approval of the Grantee, temporary structures with a footprint no greater than 120 square feet.

C. *Transferable, Cluster and Other Development Rights*

The Grantors hereby grant to the Grantee all transferable, cluster or other development rights under any present or future law that are now or hereafter allocated to, implied, reserved or inherent in the Property, and the parties agree that such rights are terminated and extinguished, and may not be used or transferred to any portion of the Property, or to any other property, nor used for the purpose of calculating permissible size or lot yield of the Property or any other property.

D. *Trees*

There shall be no burning, cutting, removal or destruction of trees, shrubs and other woody vegetation (collectively "Vegetation"), except: subject to the approval of the Grantee (1) Vegetation that is dead, infested or diseased; (2) Vegetation necessary to control erosion; (3) Vegetation necessary to provide reasonable access to Deep Creek Lake; and (4) Vegetation cut, maintained, or removed pursuant to a forest management plan that has been approved by the Grantee and prepared by a professional forester registered in Maryland. Trimming and maintenance of Vegetation that has been planted by the Grantor or a predecessor in title to the Grantor on the Property is permitted; provided, that the Grantor or the Grantor's predecessor provides written documentation to the Grantee of the type and location of the Vegetation prior to maintenance or trimming.

E. *Dumping, Placement or Storage of Materials*

No materials may be dumped or stored on the Property, including, but not limited to, ashes, trash, garbage, rubbish, abandoned vehicles, abandoned vessels, abandoned appliances, and abandoned machinery.

F. *Excavation of Materials*

Excavation or mining of the Property is prohibited, including, but not limited to, removal of soil or sand, except, with the approval of the Grantee, for temporary excavation: (1) to maintain access to Deep Creek Lake; or (2) to repair and extend a septic system or well that has failed on a contiguous property, so long as the failure is not due to increased use, occupancy, or size of the contiguous dwelling that the septic system or well serves, in violation of any health laws, ordinances, regulations or permits.

G. *Wetlands*

No diking, draining, filling, dredging or removal of any wetland or wetlands is permitted. "Wetland" or "wetlands" means portions of the Property defined by any State or federal laws as a wetland or wetlands at the time of the proposed activity.

H. *Signs and Billboards*

No signs, billboards, or outdoor advertising displays may be erected, displayed, placed or maintained on the Property except temporary signs not exceeding six square feet to advertise the property's sale or rental.

I. *Public Access*

This Conservation Easement does not grant the public any right to access or any right of use of the Property.

J. *Reserved Rights*

Except to the extent that prior written approval of the Grantee is required by any paragraph of this Article, all rights not prohibited by this Conservation Easement are considered to be consistent with

FIGURE 1–1
(continued)

the Terms of this Conservation Easement and require no prior notification or approval. If the Grantors have any doubt with respect to whether or not any particular use of the Property is prohibited by the Terms of this Conservation Easement, the Grantors may submit a written request to the Grantee for consideration and approval of such use.

ARTICLE III. ENFORCEMENT AND REMEDIES

A. *Remedies*

Upon any breach of the Terms of this Conservation Easement by the Grantors, the Grantee may exercise any or all of the following remedies:

1. institute suits to enjoin any breach or enforce any covenant by temporary and/or permanent injunction either prohibitive or mandatory; and

2. require that the Property be restored promptly to the condition required by this Conservation Easement.

The Grantee's remedies shall be cumulative and shall be in addition to any other rights and remedies available to the Grantee at law or equity. If the Grantors are found to have breached any of the Terms under this Conservation Easement, the Grantors shall reimburse the Grantee for any costs or expenses incurred by the Grantee, including court costs and reasonable attorney's fees.

B. *Effect of Failure to Enforce*

No failure on the part of the Grantee to enforce any Term hereof shall discharge or invalidate such Term or any other Term hereof or affect the right of the Grantee to enforce the same in the event of a subsequent breach or default.

C. *Right of Inspection*

The State of Maryland, acting by and through the Department of Natural Resources, the Grantee, their respective employees and agents, have the right, with reasonable notice to the Grantors, to enter the Property at reasonable times for the purpose of inspecting the Property to determine whether the Grantors are complying with the Terms of this Conservation Easement.

ARTICLE IV. MISCELLANEOUS

A. *Future Transfers*

By executing this Conservation Easement, the Grantors acknowledge that this Conservation Easement is permanent and is binding on their heirs, personal representatives, successors or assigns.

B. *Effect of Laws Imposing Affirmative Obligations on the Grantors*

In the event that any applicable State or federal law imposes affirmative obligations on owners of land which if complied with by the Grantors would be a violation of a Term of this Conservation Easement, the Grantors shall: (i) if said law requires a specific act without any discretion on the part of the Grantors, comply with said law and give the Grantee written notice of the Grantors' compliance as soon as reasonably possible, but in no event more than thirty (30) days from the time the Grantors begin to comply; or (ii) if said law leaves to the Grantors discretion over how to comply with said law, use the method most protective of the purpose of this Conservation Easement set forth in the recitals herein.

C. *Notices to the Grantee*

Any notices by the Grantors to the Grantee pursuant to any Term hereof shall be sent by registered or certified mail, return receipt requested, addressed to the current address of the Secretary, Department of Natural Resources, with a copy to Manager, Deep Creek Lake Natural Resources Management Area.

FIGURE 1–1
(continued)

D. *Approval of the Grantee*

In any case where the terms of this Conservation Easement require the approval of the Grantee, such approval shall be requested by written notice to the Grantee. After consultation with the Deep Creek Lake Policy Review Board, approval or disapproval shall be given promptly and in writing; in the event the request is disapproved, a statement of the reasons for the disapproval shall be given.

E. *Condemnation*

Whenever all or part of the Property is taken in the exercise of eminent domain, so as to abrogate, in whole or in part, the restrictions imposed by this Conservation Easement, or this Conservation Easement is extinguished, in whole or in part, by other judicial proceeding, the Grantors and the Grantee shall be entitled to proceeds payable in connection with the condemnation or other judicial proceedings in any amount equal to the current fair market value of their relative real estate interests. Any costs of a judicial proceeding allocated by a court to the Grantors and the Grantee shall be allocated in the same manner as the proceeds are allocated.

F. *Construction*

This Conservation Easement shall be construed pursuant to the purpose of this Conservation Easement and the purposes of Section 2-118 of the Real Property Article of the Annotated Code of Maryland, and to the laws of the State of Maryland generally.

G. *Effect of Laws and Other Restrictions on the Property*

The Terms of this Conservation Easement shall be in addition to any local, State or federal laws imposing restrictions on the Property and any real estate interests imposing restrictions on the Property.

H. *Entire Agreement and Severability of the Terms*

This instrument sets forth the entire agreement of the parties with respect to the Conservation Easement and supersedes all prior discussions, negotiations, understanding or agreements relating to the Conservation Easement. If any Term is found to be invalid, the remainder of the Terms of this Conservation Easement, and the application of such Term to persons or circumstances other than those as to which it is found to be invalid, shall not be affected thereby.

I. *Successors*

The terms "Grantors" and "Grantee" wherever used herein, and any pronouns used in place thereof, shall include, respectively, the above-named Grantors and their personal representatives, heirs, successors, and assigns and the above-named Grantee and their successors and assigns.

J. *Real Property Taxes*

Except to the extent provided for by State or local law, nothing herein contained shall relieve the Grantors of the obligation to pay taxes in connection with the ownership of the Property.

K. *Captions*

The captions in this Conservation Easement have been inserted solely for convenience of reference and are not a part of this instrument. Accordingly, the captions shall have no effect upon the construction or interpretation of the Terms of this Conservation Easement. IN WITNESS THEREOF, the Grantors have hereunto set their hands and seals in the day and year above written.

WITNESS/ATTEST: GRANTORS:

_____   _____(SEAL)

_____   _____(SEAL)

FIGURE 1–1
(continued)

STATE OF MARYLAND, _____ of _____ TO WIT:

I HEREBY CERTIFY, that on this _____ day of _____, 200__, before me the subscriber, a Notary Public of the State aforesaid, personally appeared _____, known to me (or satisfactorily proven) to be a Grantor of the foregoing Deed of Conservation Easement and acknowledged that he/she executed the same for the purposes therein contained and in my presence signed and sealed the same.

WITNESS my hand and Notarial Seal.

Notary Public

My Commission Expires: _____

(Use a separate notary for each Grantor's signature and modify the above certificate if any entity, such as a corporation, is a Grantor.)

I hereby certify that this Deed of Conservation Easement was prepared and reviewed for legal form and sufficiency by _____, an attorney admitted to practice before the Court of Appeals of Maryland.

_____
Assistant Attorney General

FIGURE 1–1
(continued)

See Figure 1–2[10] for a graphic representation.

A license allows a licensee to do something on land for an extremely limited purpose, such as mining coal or other minerals or cutting trees or farming the land. In contrast to pure ownership of land, these interests are temporary and highly restricted, though designated as real property. In general, these types of limited interests are "incidental" to the land. They are, however, not created separately as a distinct subject to property but are merely incidental to the right of ownership.[11]

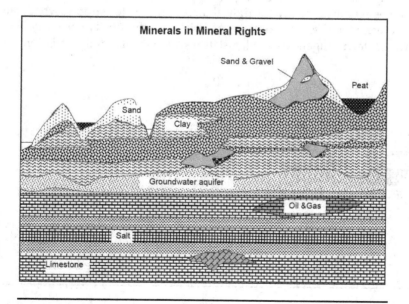

FIGURE 1–2

The grantor of the license maintains exclusive control over its lifespan. Subsequent buyers of the property have no assurances that the license right will continue. In fact, the owner may or may not extend the privilege. In this sense, as when compared to the easement, license or the privilege does not run with the land upon its alienation.

A. Riparian Rights

Since water flows on land, there are diverse interests in access and usage to that source. Exactly who has rights in water is the question of riparian law. Riparian is derived from the Latin word "ripa," which means river. See the diagram detailing Riparian Rights in Figure 1–3.

Riparian rights are rooted in both statutory and common law principles. In the most generic sense, riparian rights deal with both individual and collective rights in streams, rivers, lakes, groundwater, and wells, as well as beachfronts.[12] Riparian rights are multidimensional and include:

- Access to the water.
- The right to wharf out.
- The right to acquire accretions.
- The right to fill.
- The right to continued flow.
- The right to preservation of the view of the water.
- The right of access to the water. It is the "first and most basic right of the riparian owner," under which other riparian rights are created and protected. The right of access (1) ensures the riparian owner's "right to be and remain a riparian proprietor," (2) protects the riparian owner's ability to reach the navigable portions of adjacent waters without unreasonable impediment, (3) supports the riparian owner's right to wharf out, (4) includes the right to erect structures in aid of navigation, and (5) underlies the riparian owner's right to take title to lands that accrete beyond the mean high-water mark.

Of all these rights, questions involving the appropriation of water are very common. Appropriation determines who has the lawful right to access the water supply, what standards dictate ownership of the water, and what standards permit individual or larger usage by a community. For the most part, statewide agencies and legislatures lay out rules and regulations regarding these rights.

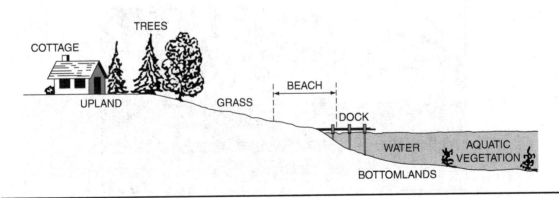

FIGURE 1–3
A diagram detailing Riparian Rights.

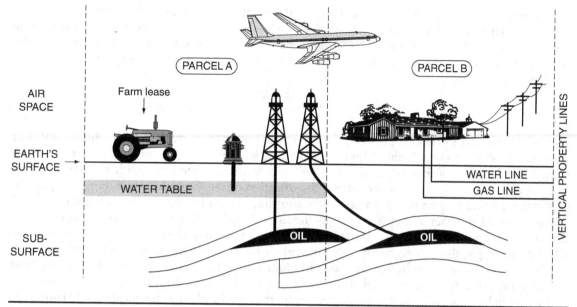

FIGURE 1–4
Graduated Interests in Land.

Web Exercise

The United States National Oceanic and Atmospheric Administration (NOAA) has developed an excellent course on the major issues involving riparian rights. Visit *www.csc.noaa.gov/ptd/module07/07.htm.*

Thus, from an interest in the land itself to an interest in the substance of that land, real property is defined as a series of interests. Bruce T. Harwood's illustration (see Figure 1–4)[13] shows the graduated interests in land from air space to the ground itself.

IV. REAL PROPERTY OWNERSHIP

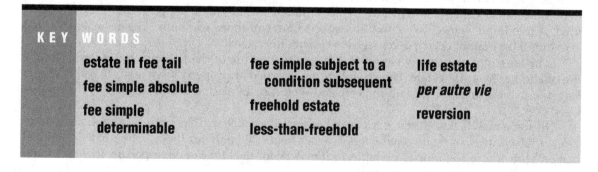

KEY WORDS

estate in fee tail	fee simple subject to a condition subsequent	life estate
fee simple absolute		*per autre vie*
fee simple determinable	freehold estate	reversion
	less-than-freehold	

How real property interests are owned constitutes a significant theoretical and practical issue. When two people desire to purchase a condominium, land, or other realty, how do they intend to own or share? Will one own a majority of the interest, or will it be equally shared? Will one owner's interest pass to the other owner or will it be inherited by the estate by and through specified beneficiaries upon the deceased owner's demise? Can one sell an interest in land without the permission of the other owners in the property?

These questions represent the enormous practical implications of how the nature of realty ownership impacts eventual transfer and alienation. The seminal questions are: Who owns the realty? How is it owned? A client's rights in a real estate transaction begin by discerning the differing forms of possessory interest and estates in land. Let us begin with the concept of freehold.

A. Freehold

For all intents and purposes, property can be owned or held in two ways: freehold estates or less-than-freehold estates. **Freehold** means "free" for whatever life the interest owner has, or by some other measure of time or duration. "Free" means that no one can invade or challenge that interest for any reason whatsoever during the duration of the freehold estate. For example, the owner can be said to own in fee simple a title affording the unlimited, unabashed use of the real property until his or her demise or until the demise of another. A freehold estate without limitation or restriction, and without a designated duration other than the life of the vested owner, is labeled fee simple absolute. A **fee simple absolute** is the most extensive interest in real property possibly possessed and controlled by the individual owner, heirs, and assignees forever without limitation or condition. Apart from this absolute right of ownership, there are distinct degrees and variations in the realty interests. For example, the **fee simple determinable** estate continues until the occurrence of a specified event or circumstance. Upon its occurrence, the estate will cease and terminate automatically with ownership rights reverting to the original grantors. Hence, a grant may indicate that property will remain in the possession of the owner as long as it is used for a specific purpose, such as a church or school. In this way, the usage of said property is restricted to the language of the grant and alienation, and when in compliance, the said property remains freely owned by the grantee. When altered, the property reverts. The interest of the grantor is designated possibility of reverter or **reversion**. The grantor's use of *until* or *as long as* signify this intent.

Fee simple subject to a condition subsequent is another freehold estate which lays out conditions that allow the possibility of a grantor reentry. To illustrate, if the grantor indicates that the property is passing *"to grantee and his or her heirs, but if the property is used for industrial purposes, the grantor may repossess"* one witnesses a condition subsequent.

When compared to the fee simple determinable, this estate may or may not remain intact. The condition subsequent expressly requires the grantor to take affirmative steps, in the event of a violation of the condition, such as reentry or repossession. It differs from a fee simple determinable in that the latter expires automatically, by operation of law, upon the happening of the event specified. A fee simple subject to a condition subsequent continues even after the occurrence of the event until the grantor acts or takes steps to reclaim the estate.

The fee simple owner owns until death, or the measure of the freehold could rest upon the life of another by a **life estate**. Hence, a deed to a particular property may read, *To Sally Seele, as long as her mother lives*. The estate thus created would be in existence only as long as the mother lives.

In some jurisdictions, estates for specified terms are deemed "periodic." As the name indicates, a life estate is an estate of which the owner holds title only for the duration of a designated person's life. It may be for one's own life, or it may be for the life of another person, in which latter case it is called an estate *per autre vie*.[14]

Hence, a life estate lasts only as long as the life measured or tied to the estate. Even so, it is still freehold, meaning full and completely owned, for this measure of time. Therefore, the freehold owner owns the property freely and unreservedly for a specified duration.

When the freehold estate limits the transfer of the estate to both the present owner and the owner's or others' issues or heirs, the estate is termed an **estate in fee tail**. If the original owners die without heirs, the estate terminates, thereby ending the estate. Legal tradition disfavors this form of freehold since the degree or circle of ownership is so narrow. Figure 1–5 encapsulates freehold forms.

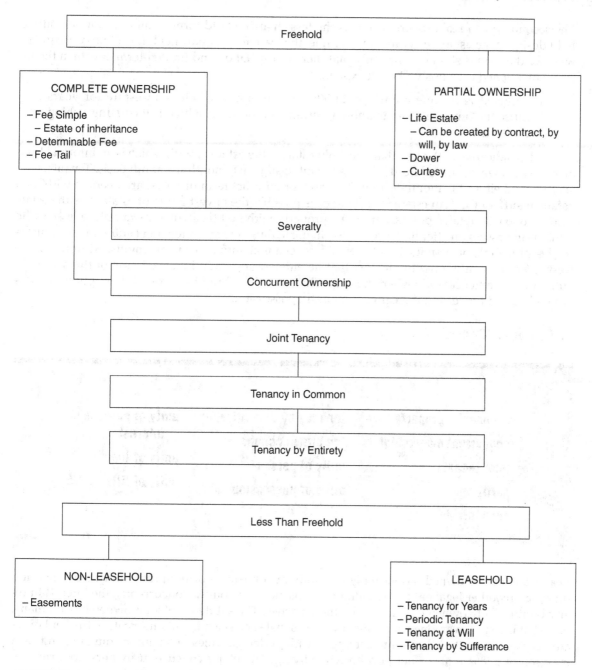

FIGURE 1–5
Flowchart of Freehold Forms of Ownership.

B. Less Than Freehold

KEY WORDS

estate at sufferance   **estate at will**   **estate for years**

The second type of real property estate is the **less-than-freehold** form. A more common nonfreehold design is the **estate for years**, for example, the lease for an apartment. It is of no consequence whether the term is short or long, only that there is a specified and limited term, less than the life estate mentioned previously. O'Neill explains:

> Whether it is for one month or 2,000 years, it is nevertheless an estate for years because the time of its end is known, certain and definite, which is its distinguishing characteristic.[15]

Also indicative of the less-than-freehold estate is the **estate at will**, which is an informal lease arrangement where the landlord allows a tenant to stay on a month-to-month basis. Tenants, who stay beyond either the month-to-month period, or an exact term of years, are deemed within an **estate at sufferance**. "An estate at sufferance is possibly the lowest grade of estate. It is the estate held by one who retains possession of real property with no title at all; for example, a lessee who remains in possession after his lease has expired. He thus becomes a tenant at sufferance so long as the lessor suffers, or permits, him to remain. A tenant at sufferance is distinguished from a mere trespasser or squatter only by the fact that he entered originally by permission of the owner."[16] Sufferance commences only when the tenant had an original right to possess, the right to possess has ended, and the tenant, thereafter, remains in possession.

C. Concurrent Ownership

KEY WORDS

community property	tenancy by the entireties	unity of purpose or interest
concurrent ownership	tenants in common	
joint tenants	unity of person	unity of time
partition	unity of possession	unity of title
survivorship		

Real estate can be owned individually or jointly by a business or nonprofit entity, trust, pension fund, or any other legal entity. When multiple parties own jointly, concurrently, the interest in realty is either fully owned or divisible by these parties. The subtleties of joint ownership are many, but what is common among concurrent owners is that each share in but one estate in the land or realty; each takes on the other's interest upon death or demise unless a tenant in common; and each may sell or alienate his or her portion while living. The major **concurrent ownership** forms are joint tenancy, tenancy by the entireties, and tenants in common.

To own concurrently, or jointly, one must have a **unity of purpose or interest** with another party or parties. At common law, joint ownership manifests a series of unities:

1. **Unity of Time:** Co-owners or tenants in land must receive their interests at the same time.
2. **Unity of Title:** Co-owners or tenants in land must acquire title from the same source.
3. **Unity of Interest:** Co-owners or tenants must have equal interest in the land, except in the case of a tenant in common.
4. **Unity of Possession:** Co-owners or tenants have an equal right to possess the whole property for possessory purposes only.
5. **Unity of Person:** Co-owners or tenants are husband and wife and viewed as the same.

How these unities play out will inevitably characterize the joint interest. In the case of a **tenancy by the entireties**, husband and wife will likely receive the realty interest at the same time, with the same deed, and by law, own and possess the property in the manner. So too with **joint tenants** and **tenants in common** whose interests will be divisible yet still owned during the same time period, possession, and extent of interest. All three concurrent forms share these unities. However, the unities mentioned are affected differently by issues of survivorship. While a husband and wife will share fully in the remaining estate by the principles of tenancy of the entirety, the joint tenant's survivors will be excluded by the remaining joint tenants. Here the unity, for purposes of inheritance, breaks down into different directions. The law does not favor joint tenancy since a right of survivorship does not extend to the heirs and descendants of a deceased joint tenant but to the remaining joint tenants. Comparatively, for tenants in common, the interest passes to heirs or other designees.

In any event, concurrent ownership is symbolized by the principles of unity or common interest. Esteemed practitioner, Frank W. Kovats, charts the many ways in which property can be owned, whether singularly or jointly (see Figure 1–6[17]).

D. Types of Joint Ownership

When the unities are satisfied, the parties may jointly own in these major ways:

- Tenants in common
- Joint tenants
- Tenancy by the entireties
- Community property

1. Tenants in Common

The tenancy in common, even though a concurrent, joint ownership form, has divisible characteristics and thereby a right of survivorship by the tenants' heirs. Hence, if A, B, and C are cotenants and if C dies, C's heirs may inherit C's divisible portion. By contrast, in a joint tenancy, C's portion would be swept up by A and B. "Tenants in common own and possess in equal shares an undivided interest in the whole property, which is an interest in fee simple that passes to statutory heirs in the event of intestacy. Accordingly, there is no right of survivorship in cotenants in common, and each tenant in common may convey, encumber or devise his undivided interest."[18]

Tenants in common may freely alienate their portion to any other party. According to *Summary of Pennsylvania Jurisprudence*: "A tenant in common cannot, however, by a conveyance of his interest in a portion of the property held in common, prejudice the rights of his cotenants, nor can he split the property into fragments so as to necessitate many separate suits for partition."[19]

2. Joint Tenants

Not favored in the law because of its survivorship impact, the joint tenancy is a second means of concurrent ownership. Evidence of ownership in land/realty will be expressed as **joint tenants** such as "Bill Rono and Allen Fono as Joint Tenants." When one or the other dies, all remaining interests descend to the surviving tenant, not to the heirs of the deceased tenant. The joint tenant owns not some discernible portion, but a unified share in the land. The joint tenant possesses four unities with all other tenants. Tiffany explains:

> The four unities, of interest, of title, of time, and of possession, characterize the tenancy. The tenants have one and the same interest, accruing by one and the same conveyance, commencing at one and the same time, and held by one and the same undivided possession.[20]

When one joint tenant dies, the other joint tenants take the deceased's portion. The deceased joint tenant's heirs have no case for distribution. The harsh **survivorship** policy of the joint tenancy

Methods of Ownership			
	Tenancy in Common	**Joint Tenancy**	**Tenancy by Entireties**
Definition	Property held by 2 or more persons, with no right of survivorship.	Property held by 2 or more individuals (not corporation), with right of survivorship.	Property held by husband and wife, with right of survivorship.
Creation	By express act; also by failure to express the tenancy.	Express intention plus 4 unities of time, title, interest and possession.	* Divorce automatically results in tenancy in common.
Possession	Equal right of possession	Equal right of possession	Equal right of possession
Title	Each co-owner has a separate legal title to his undivided interest; will be equal interests unless expressly made unequal.	One title to the whole property since each tenant is theoretically deemed owner of whole; must be equal, undivided interests.	One title in the marital unit.
Conveyance	Each co-owner's interest may be conveyed separately by its owners; purchaser becomes tenant in common.	Conveyance of 1 co-owner breaks his, tenancy; purchaser becomes tenant in common.	Cannot convey without consent of spouse.
Effect of Death	Decedent's fractional interest subject to pro-bate and included in gross estate for federal & state death taxes. The property passes by will to devisees or heirs who take as tenants common. No survivorship rights.	No probate and can't be disposed of by will; property automatically belongs to surviving co-tenants (last one holds singularly). Entire property included in decedents gross estate for federal estate tax purposes minus % attributable to survivor's contribution.	Right of survivorship, so no probate. Same death taxes as joint tenancy.
Creditor's Rights	Co-owner's fractional interest may be sold to satisfy his creditor who then becomes tenant in common.	Joint tenant's interest also subject to execution sale; joint tenancy is broken and creditor becomes tenant in common. Creditor gets nothing if debtor tenant dies before sale.	Only a creditor of both spouses can execute on property.
Presumption	Favored in doubtful cases; presumed to be equal interests.	Not favored, so must be expressly stated.	**

*Husband and wife only.
**Automatically created when names of both spouses appear on the deed.

FIGURE 1–6

has induced legislative responses and judicial restrictions on its usage. Courts will construe a deed's language to protect the interests of heirs rather than their limitations.

a. Partition Despite this presumption, joint ownership of real property is often fraught with disagreements and fractures between those who wish to own and those who wish to divide or **partition** their particular interest. At times this process can be quite litigious. Most legislators provide a statutory remedy to divide the land, which is known as "partition." Review the representative code provision from Connecticut:

> Partition of joint and common estates. Courts having jurisdiction of actions for equitable relief may, upon the complaint of any person interested, order partition of any real property held in joint tenancy, tenancy in common, coparcenary or by tenants in tail. The court may appoint a committee to partition any such property. Any decrees partitioning entailed estates shall bind the parties and all persons who thereafter claim title to the property as heirs of their bodies.[21]

Partition actions frequently emerge in divorce and separation actions when property was previously owned by the parties as joint tenants and a dispute arises as whether or not the tenancy stays joint or evolves upon marriage into a tenancy by the entireties. It is a complex question dependent on your jurisdiction.

CASE DECISION

To assess how a partition will be evaluated by a higher court, see:

THE STATE OF SOUTH CAROLINA

In the Supreme Court

Ernest Smith Jr., as Personal Representative of the Estate of Ernest J. Smith Sr., Respondent,

v.

Verne E. Cutler, as Personal Representative of the Estate of Joanne Rucker Smith, Petitioner.

ON WRIT OF CERTIORARI TO THE COURT OF APPEALS

Appeal from Orangeburg County

Olin D. Burgdorf, Master-in-Equity

Opinion No. 26085

Heard October 18, 2005—Filed December 19, 2005

REVERSED

Thomas B. Bryant, III, of Bryant Fanning & Shuler, of Orangeburg, for Petitioner.

S. Jahue Moore and M. Ronald McMahan, both of Moore, Taylor & Thomas, PA, of West Columbia, for Respondent.

(continued)

CHIEF JUSTICE TOAL: This is an action for partition of real property, brought on behalf of Ernest J. Smith Sr. (Respondent) against his wife Joanne Rucker Smith (Petitioner). The court of appeals held that Petitioner and Respondent owned the property as joint tenants with a right of survivorship and that the property was subject to partition. We reverse.

FACTUAL/PROCEDURAL BACKGROUND

On August 17, 2000, the Petitioner deeded a share in a parcel of land to her husband, Respondent. The deed, executed shortly after their marriage, granted Respondent an undivided one-half interest in the property.[1] The deed granted the property to Petitioner and Respondent "for and during their joint lives and upon the death of either of them, then to the survivor of them, his or her heirs and assigns forever in fee simple. . . ." Identical language was used in the deed's habendum clause.

Due to conflict between the families, Respondent's family instituted an action for partition. Respondent became incapacitated and Respondent's son, acting on behalf of Respondent, brought the partition action. At the time the action was instituted, Petitioner and Respondent were married and no act, such as filing for divorce, inconsistent with the intent to remain married had been taken. A successful partition action would result in a forced sale of the property which had been Petitioner's home since 1958.

The case was referred to the master-in-equity. Respondent moved for summary judgment and the motion was granted. In granting summary judgment, the master found that the deed conveyed the shared interest to the parties as joint tenants with a right of survivorship. As a result, the master relied on S.C. Code Ann. § 15-61-10 (2005) to find that the property was subject to partition.[2] The court of appeals affirmed the master's decision, holding that the deed conveyed the property to the parties as joint tenants with the right of survivorship and that the estate was subject to partition. Petitioner appealed. This Court granted certiorari to review the following issue:

Did the deed convey the shared interest in the estate to the parties as tenants in common with a right of survivorship, which is an estate that is not subject to partition?

Law/Analysis

Petitioner argues that the deed at issue creates a tenancy in common with an indestructible right of survivorship. We agree.

Although joint tenancies were favored in early common law, they have fallen into disfavor. See Harold W. Jacobs, Note, Cotenancies, Estates of in South Carolina, 11 S.C.L.Q. 520, 521-535 (1959) (explaining the movement away from construing deeds in favor of granting joint tenancies). In South Carolina, documents conveying a shared interest in property have generally been construed in favor of tenancies in common. *Herbemont v. Thomas*, 15 Chev. Eq. 21 (S.C. 1839). Courts began favoring tenancies in common over joint tenancies because the harsh results of survivorship rights often encumbered the land and defeated the intention of the grantor. *Free v. Sandifer*, 131 S.C. 232, 236, 126 S.E. 521, 522 (1925).

However, in 1953, this Court created a shared interest in property referred to as a tenancy in common with a right of survivorship. *Davis v. Davis*, 223 S.C. 182, 191-92, 75 S.E.2d 46, 50 (1953). The Court created the estate of tenancy in common with a right of survivorship because South Carolina did not permit husband and wife to hold property as tenants by the entirety.[3] *Id.* The Court in Davis opined that by adding the phrase "and the survivor of them," the parties clearly indicated that upon the death of either of them the absolute estate should vest in the survivor. *Id.* at 191, 75 S.E.2d at 50. The Court stated that while a right of survivorship is not incident to a tenancy in common, the parties may create one if they so desire. *Id.* The Court explained that:

It has been said that great care must be exercised in construing conveyances to two or more persons and to the survivor or survivors of them. If the intention was to create a tenancy in common for life, with cross remainders for life, with remainder in fee to the ultimate survivor, a joint tenancy would not accomplish the purpose because the right of survivorship may be defeated by a conveyance by any joint tenancy [sic] but the vested cross-remainders and, in general, the contingent ultimate remainders are indestructible. Thus, not all instruments which provide that the survivor of a group will ultimately take the fee in severalty contemplate a joint tenancy; the intention may be to create a true future interest by way of a remainder or an executory limitation. (Citation omitted.) (Emphasis added.)

Davis, 223 S.C. at 187, 75 S.E.2d at 48. As noted from the excerpt above, the Court held that the future interests created by a tenancy in common with a right of survivorship were indestructible – i.e., not subject to defeat by the unilateral act of one cotenant. *Id.*

In 2000, the legislature created, by statute, the estate of joint tenants with a right of survivorship. The Code directs that:

[i]n addition to any other methods for the creation of a joint tenancy in real estate which may exist by law, whenever any deed of conveyance of real estate contains the names of the grantees followed by the words "as joint tenants with rights of survivorship, and not as tenants in common" the creation of a joint tenancy with rights of survivorship in the real estate is conclusively deemed to have been created.

S.C. Code Ann. § 27-7-40 (Supp. 2004).

This Court recognizes that the two estates at issue have many similar characteristics. However, unlike a tenancy in common with a right of survivorship, a joint tenancy with a right of survivorship is capable of being defeated by the unilateral act of one joint tenant. See S.C. Code Ann. § 27-7-40(a)(v), (vii), and (viii) (depicting actions that can be taken by one joint tenant to effectively sever the joint tenancy). Further, property held in joint tenancy is subject to partition. S.C. Code Ann. § 15-61-10 (2005) (stating that all joint tenants may be compelled to partition). In contrast, a tenancy in common with a right of survivorship cannot be defeated by the act of one tenant absent the agreement of the other tenant.

We note at the outset that § 27-7-40 cited above and relied on by the court of appeals, creating a joint tenancy with a right of survivorship, was not enacted until after the deed in the current case was executed. As a result, the parties to the deed could not have intended to take advantage of the statute creating the estate of joint tenancy with a right of survivorship. However, the estate of joint tenancy still existed in South Carolina, but as previously noted, this Court construed documents in favor of tenancies.[4]

In the present case, the language of the deed clearly indicates that the parties intended to create a right of survivorship. However, the question before this Court centers on the type ownership held by both husband and wife and whether the property is subject to partition.

We hold that the use of the phrase "for and during their joint lives and upon the death of either of them, them to the survivor of them" indicates an intention of the parties to share a tenancy in common for life, with cross-remainders for life, with remainder in fee to the ultimate survivor. The deed here conveyed a true future interest in the property to the survivor of the two. This is distinct from a joint tenancy, where the full estate is vested immediately and one of the parties could end the joint tenancy. However, with a tenancy in common with a right of survivorship the property will go only to the survivor of the parties and the future interest does not vest until the death of one of the co-owners. We further hold that this conveyance does not unreasonably prevent the alienation of the property because the restriction exists only until the first tenant in common dies.

As a result, the court of appeals erred in holding that the property was subject to partition.

Conclusion

Based on the above reasoning, we reverse the court of appeals. The deed in the present case created a tenancy in common with a right of survivorship. Under Davis, the survivorship rights between tenants in common create true future interests in the entire estate that cannot be destroyed by the unilateral act of one tenant through an act such as partition.

MOORE, WALLER, BURNETT and PLEICONES, JJ., concur.

(continued)

[1] Petitioner, a woman in her seventies, and Respondent, a man in his eighties, married in June 2000. The property at issue was bought by Petitioner and owned by her most of her adult life. No other person owned an interest in the property until after the marriage when Petitioner deeded a share to Respondent. According to Petitioner's testimony, she wanted to make sure that if she were to predecease Respondent that he would get the property.

[2] S.C. Code Ann. § 15-61-10 states that "[a]ll joint tenants and tenants in common who hold, jointly or in common . . . shall be compellable to make severance and partition of such lands, tenements and hereditaments."

[3] The Married Women's Property Act was construed to abolish tenancy by the entirety. See Davis, 223 S.C. at 189, 75 S.E.2d at 49.

[4] Petitioner contends that joint tenancy has been abandoned in South Carolina. While courts have moved away from construing language in conveyances in favor of a joint tenancy, joint tenancy has not been entirely abolished. Joint tenancy was disfavored as a rule of construction, but has existed and continues to exist today. See *Herbemont v. Thomas*, 15 Chev. Eq. 21 (S.C. 1839); *Ball v. Deas*, 2 Strob. Eq. 24 (S.C. 1848) (finding that language in a deed created a joint tenancy between the parties to the deed).

The form of the partition will vary according to jurisdictional requirements. Generally, the following matter must be contained:

- The date of the decedent's death and whether he died testate or intestate, in whole or in part
- A description, giving the size and location, of the property to be partitioned, the liens and charges to which it is subject and the rents due from tenants thereof, and that the property has not been partitioned or valued for partition
- The names, addresses, and relationship of those interested in the land to be partitioned, the extent of the interest of each of such persons, and, if such interest is created by a recorded deed or will, a reference to such record
- A request for a citation upon the parties in interest who have not joined as petitioners to show cause why an inquest in partition should not be granted.

3. Tenancy by the Entireties

Husbands and wives who jointly own real estate that is the primary residence or domicile own it in only one way: tenancy by the entireties. Since common law and fortified by codification, there has been a presumption of this tenancy in marital parties. Tenancy by the entireties recognizes that marital assets are unified by and through the state of marriage. This tenancy recognizes the jointly, yet mutually concurrent, interest that spouses have. "It can exist only where the tenants are husband and wife at the time the title instrument takes effect. It is not created by a conveyance or devise to persons who subsequently marry. It is created by a deed or other instrument from a third person to the spouses and cannot at common law be created by a deed from a husband directly to his wife no matter what intention is expressed."[22]

The most important feature of tenancy by the entireties is the absolute, unequivocal right of survivorship that the remaining spouse has in the event of the other's death. When one dies, the other living spouse retains all, not some divisible portion. The realty cannot be alienated or bequested to another.

In states that follow the common law system of marital property, the parties may not convey their separate interests or demand a partition, in which the husband is entitled to sole possession and control of the property and its rents and profits. Note that property outside the primary marital home can be owned by other means.

4. Community Property

In select jurisdictions, such as California, Texas, Washington, and Louisiana, a variation of this tenancy principle has been legislated, namely the concept of community property. Instead of an automatic and complete survivorship right, mandated by the typical tenancy by the entireties, surviving spouses in community property states may not take a full and unbridled interest in the real property upon the death of the spouse.

Community property generally includes all property acquired by either spouse during the time of the marriage. In this sense, real property is community property, if acquired during a period of marriage, and not the result of gift, inheritance, or other devise. As a rule, all property, owned or acquired previous to marriage, in whatever form, remains the separate and individuated property of the spouse and is not designated community property.

Upon the death of either spouse, one-half of their community property inures to the benefit of the surviving spouse. In certain jurisdictions, all community property remains with the surviving spouse. Community property practice and procedure is highly localized and governed by statutory construction.

E. Other Forms of Ownership

KEY WORDS

condominium	joint venture	real estate investment trusts
general partnerships	limited partnerships	
joint stock association		

Aside from singular or concurrent ownership, the buyer may buy as a partnership or corporate entity. Business entities have a multitude of reasons for real estate investment, from securing office space to a long-term investment strategy. In general, real estate is owned by business entities rather than individuals. Some of the more typical arrangements for business follow.

1. General Partnership

Real estate can surely be owned by a group of individuals formed exclusively for the purpose of owning property. When two or more individuals or entities join forces to invest in real estate, a partnership is formed. There are two types of partnerships—general and limited. In the **general partnerships**, the partners are equally responsible for all aspects of the real estate activities—profit and loss, management responsibilities, and liabilities. General partners assume all the risks and the rewards of the real estate partnership. In this sense, general partners are not shielded from lawsuits and personal responsibility.[23] As each carries out his or her task in good faith, and in accordance with law and the scope of the partnership agreement, the other partners are bound to that action. The Revised Uniform Partnership Act sets out the general policy:

SECTION 301. PARTNER AGENT OF PARTNERSHIP. Subject to the effect of a statement of partnership authority under Section 303:

(1) Each partner is an agent of the partnership for the purpose of its business. An act of a partner, including the execution of an instrument in the partnership name, for apparently carrying on in the ordinary course the partnership business or business of the kind carried on by the partnership binds the partnership, unless the partner had no authority to act for the partnership in the particular matter and the person with whom the partner was dealing knew or had received a notification that the partner lacked authority.

(2) An act of a partner which is not apparently for carrying on in the ordinary course the partnership business or business of the kind carried on by the partnership binds the partnership only if the act was authorized by the other partners.[24]

Without express direction within the four corners of the partnership agreement, a partner's share in the business will be deemed equally or proportionately divisible as outlined in the Uniform Partnership Act.

Yet, even with the cautions mentioned above, the general partnership remains an excellent vehicle for the real estate investor. Before making the choice of the general partnership, consider these issues:

- There are few legal requirements to creating a partnership. As mentioned, a partnership agreement is not necessary, although it is advised. Also, no filings with the secretary of state are required for formation.
- Partners may pool their resources and talents. This allows all partners to share control and participate equally in management of the partnership.
- A general partnership has flow-through taxation, meaning that the partnership does not pay taxes. Instead, the individual partners are taxed on the income they receive from the partnership.
- Profits and losses are divided among partners in any manner they choose.
- There are no fees associated with creating a general partnership.
- Under a general partnership, assets of any of the partners can be used to cover the business's liabilities, regardless of which partner incurred the liability.
- Partners have unlimited liability in a partnership form of business.

Web Exercise

Visit RUPA—the Revised Uniform Partnership Act at *www.law.upenn.edu/bll/archives/ulc/fnact99/1990s/upa97fa.htm.*

Also, there is no standardized form which lays out the necessary provisions for a meaningful partnership.

2. Limited Partnership

Limited partnerships are special partnerships created by statute. A limited partnership must have one or more general partners who are typically subject to the same rules as partners of a general partnership. Additionally, a limited partnership must have one or more limited partners who have a restricted role in the operation of the enterprise. Limited partners can invest cash, property, or services in the entity with the expectation that the investment will pay a meaningful return. The limited partner's risk is directly tied to the amount of the investment itself.[25]

> An obligation of a partnership incurred while the partnership is a limited liability partnership, whether arising in contract, tort, or otherwise, is solely the obligation of the partnership. A partner is not personally liable, directly or indirectly, by way of contribution or otherwise, for such an obligation solely by reason of being or so acting as a partner. This subsection applies notwithstanding anything inconsistent in the partnership agreement that existed immediately before the vote required to become a limited liability partnership under Section 1001(b).[26]

As a result, the limited partner has less at risk than the general partner, whose responsibility extends to the full allocation of profit as well as loss. Limited partners, however, cannot engage in the management or control of the business.

General partners assume losses and liabilities of the partnership business while the limited partners bear limited liability based on their proportionate interest in the overall partnership. The avoidance should not be construed in any negative light, but viewed as a vehicle for investment in the American economy and engines for economic growth. Limited partners are significant contributors to the American economy especially in the area of real estate development. Limited partnerships have some unique and very favorable characteristics such as the following:

- A limited partnership is an entity distinct from its partners.
- It must contain both general partners and limited partners.
- A person can serve as a general and limited partner.
- The partnership agreement governs relations among the partners and between the partners and the partnership.
- It achieves both limited liability and partnership principles.
- No fiduciary duty exists with the limited partnership or to any other partner solely by reason of being a limited partner.
- A limited partnership has the power to sue, be sued, and defend in its own name and to maintain an action against a partner for harm caused to the limited partnership by a breach of the partnership agreement or violation of a duty to the partnership.

3. Joint Venture

In addition, certain types of real estate transactions are by **joint venture**, which is a limited ownership interest for investment purposes. A joint venture (also known as a joint adventure, coadventure, business consortium, syndicate, group, pool, joint enterprise, joint undertaking, or joint speculation) is an unincorporated association created by the co-owners of a business venture, usually to carry out a particular venture, as contrasted with a partnership's operation of a business. (See Figure 1–7 for an example of a joint venture agreement.)

Joint ventures frequently display an inordinate riskiness. Since profit is the primary motive, the conduct of the venture partners may be less attentive to law and ethics than in the corporate setting. A frequently seen venture involves exploration for oil and gas reserves. Advise clients of the pitfalls.[27]

In some circles, the joint venture is labeled a **joint stock association**. The association displays all the qualities of a corporation yet it is not incorporated. It issues shares, carries out the business of the association with annual meetings and typical protocols, though it remains unincorporated. Georgia defines the joint stock association as:

> "Joint stock association" includes any association of the kind commonly known as a joint stock association or joint stock company and any unincorporated association, trust, or enterprise having members or having outstanding shares of stock or other evidences of financial and beneficial interest therein, whether formed by agreement or under statutory authority or otherwise, but does not include a corporation, partnership, or nonprofit organization. A joint stock association as defined in this paragraph may be one formed under the laws of this state, including a trust created pursuant to Article 3 of Chapter 12 of Title 53, or one formed under or pursuant to the laws of any other state or jurisdiction.[28]

JOINT VENTURE AGREEMENT

THIS JOINT VENTURE AGREEMENT (the "Agreement"), made and entered into as of this _(1)_ day of _____(2)_____, 19_(3)_, by and between _____(4)_____ of _____(5)_____ (hereinafter "_____") and _____(6)_____ of _____(7)_____ (hereinafter "_____").

ARTICLE I
GENERAL PROVISIONS

1.01 Business Purpose. The business of the Joint Venture shall be as follows: (Describe Business Purpose)

1.02 Term of the Agreement. This Joint Venture shall commence on the date first above written and shall continue in existence until terminated, liquidated, or dissolved by law or as hereinafter provided.

ARTICLE II
GENERAL DEFINITIONS

The following comprise the general definitions of terms utilized in this Agreement:

2.01 Affiliate. An Affiliate of an entity is a person that, directly or indirectly through one or more intermediaries, controls, is controlled by or is under common control of such entity.

2.02 Capital Contribution(s). The capital contribution to the Joint Venture actually made by the parties, including property, cash and any additional capital contributions made.

2.03 Profits and Losses. Any income or loss of the Partnership for federal income tax purposes determined by the Partnership's fiscal year, including, without limitation, each item of Partnership income, gain, loss or deduction.

ARTICLE III
OBLIGATIONS OF THE JOINT VENTURES

_____(8)_____ is responsible for all operations and decisions of the Joint Venture and will be compensated for providing various services.

ARTICLE IV
ALLOCATIONS

4.01 Profits and Losses. Commencing on the date hereof and ending on the termination ofthe business of the Joint Venture, all profits, losses and other allocations to the JointVenture shall be allocated as follows at the conclusion of each fiscal year:

_____........ _(9)_%
_____........ (10)_%

ARTICLE V
RIGHTS AND DUTIES OF THE JOINT VENTURES

5.01 Business of the Joint Venture. _____(11)_____ shall have full, exclusive and complete authority and discretion in the management and control of the business of the Joint Venture for the purposes herein stated and shall make all decisions affecting the business of the Joint Venture. At such, any action taken shall constitute the act of, and serve to bind, the Joint Venture. _____(12)_____ shall manage and control the affairs of the Joint Venture to the best of its ability and shall use its best efforts to carry out the business of the Joint Venture. _____(13)_____ shall not participate in or have any control over the Joint Venture business nor shall it have any authority or right to act for or bind the Joint Venture.

ARTICLE VI
AGREEMENTS WITH THIRD PARTIES AND WITH AFFILIATES OF THE JOINT VENTURES

6.01 Validity of Transactions. Affiliates of the parties to this Agreement may be engaged to perform services for the Joint Venture. The validity of any transaction, agreement or payment involving the

FIGURE 1–7
(continues)

Joint Venture and any Affiliates of the parties to this Agreement otherwise permitted by the terms of this Agreement shall not be affected by reason of the relationship between them and such Affiliates or the approval of said transactions, agreement or payment.

6.02 Other Business of the Parties to this Agreement. The parties to this Agreement and their respective Affiliates may have interests in businesses other than the Joint Venture business. The Joint Venture shall not have the right to the income or proceeds derived from such other business interests and, even if they are competitive with the Partnership business, such business interests shall not be deemed wrongful or improper.

ARTICLE VII
PAYMENT OF EXPENSES

All expenses of the Joint Venture shall be paid by _____(14)_____ and shall be reimbursed by the Joint Venture.

ARTICLE VIII
INDEMNIFICATION OF THE JOINT VENTURES

The parties to this Agreement shall have no liability to the other for any loss suffered which arises out of any action or inaction if, in good faith, it is determined that such course of conduct was in the best interests of the Joint Venture and such course of conduct did not constitute negligence or misconduct. The parties to this Agreement shall each be indemnified by the other against losses, judgments, liabilities, expenses and amounts paid in settlement of any claims sustained by it in connection with the Joint Venture.

ARTICLE IX
DISSOLUTION

9.01 Events of the Joint Ventures. The Joint Venture shall be dissolved upon the happening of any of the following events:

(a) The adjudication of bankruptcy, filing of a petition pursuant to a Chapter of the Federal Bankruptcy Act, withdrawal, removal or insolvency of either of the parties.

(b) The sale or other disposition, not including an exchange of all, or substantially all, of the Joint Venture assets.

(c) Mutual agreement of the parties.

ARTICLE X
MISCELLANEOUS PROVISIONS

10.01 Books and Records. The Joint Venture shall keep adequate books and records at its place of business, setting forth a true and accurate account of all business transactions arising out of and in connection with the conduct of the Joint Venture.

10.02 Validity. In the event that any provision of this Agreement shall be held to be invalid, the same shall not affect in any respect whatsoever the validity of the remainder of this Agreement.

10.03 Integrated Agreement. This Agreement constitutes the entire understanding and agreement among the parties hereto with respect to the subject matter hereof, and there are no agreements, understandings, restrictions or warranties among the parties other than those set forth herein provided for.

10.04 Headings. The headings, titles and subtitles used in this Agreement are for ease of reference only and shall not control or affect the meaning or construction of any provision hereof.

10.05 Notices. Except as may be otherwise specifically provided in this Agreement, all notices required or permitted here under shall be in writing and shall be deemed to be delivered when deposited

FIGURE 1–7
(continued)

in the United States mail, postage prepaid, certified or registered mail, return receipt requested, addressed to the parties at their respective addresses set forth in this Agreement or at such other addresses as may be subsequently specified by written notice.

10.06 Applicable Law and Venue. This Agreement shall be construed and enforced under the laws of the State of _____(15)_____.

10.07 Other Instruments. The parties hereto covenant and agree that they will execute each such other and further instruments and documents as are or may become reasonably necessary or convenient to effectuate and carry out the purposes of this Agreement. IN WITNESS WHEREOF, the parties hereto have executed this Agreement as of the day and year first above written. Signed, sealed and delivered in the presence of:

_____(16)_____   _____(17)_____
_____(16)_____   _____(16)_____
_____(18)_____

FIGURE 1–7
(continued)

4. Real Estate Investment Trusts

Another investment model is the **Real Estate Investment Trusts** (REITs). The REITs exist when a fractional, divisible investment in a bevy of real estate properties is allotted based on the amount of investment. REITs invest in blocks of real estate venture and issue shares proportionate to the investment. It is a sort of mutual fund for real estate investors. REITs may be public or private in design and some REITs are actually traded on the various exchanges. A REIT is a company that buys, develops, manages, and sells real estate assets. REITs allow participants to invest in a portfolio of real estate properties. REITs usually qualify as pass-through entities, companies who are able to distribute the majority of income cash flows to investors without traditional taxation at the personal level. There are three basic forms of REITs generally seen in the marketplace.[29]

- **Equity REITs:**   Equity REITs invest in and own properties and derive income principally from their properties' rents.
- **Mortgage REITs:**   Mortgage REITs deal in investment and ownership of property mortgages. This type of REIT loans money for mortgages. Revenue is generated from the interest paid on these mortgages.
- **Hybrid REITs:**   Hybrid REITs dabble in both the equity and mortgage sides of the business.

Web Exercise

Visit the Investor's Guide to REITs at *www.reit.com/Portals/0/PDF/2009Kekst.pdf.*

5. Condominiums

"The owner of a condominium has a fee simple interest but does not have an exclusive interest in the common areas of the property."[30] Literally defined, a **condominium** is an interest in real property consisting of an undivided interest in common in a portion of a parcel of real property, together with a separate interest in space.[31] Most individuals think of condominiums as large, apartment-style complexes. Under the condominium arrangement, the owner buys the exclusive right to occupy space where a unit is located. He or she also receives an undivided interest in the land and common areas (e.g., lobby, hallways, elevators, structure of the building, recreation facilities).[32] Cooperative or concurrent ownership, especially in the condominium market, constitutes a significant market for the paralegal. Ads in newspapers and other popularly read publications grandiosely describe the positive values of time sharing, joint ownership, vacation sharing, and other parceled interests in real property. The reasons for the attraction to condominiums are many, but none more compelling than the allowance for fee simple absolute ownership without fee simple obligation. The burdens of repair, maintenance of common areas and other drudgeries of home ownership are replaced by or delegated to an association—a collective of owners—who wish to avoid these recurring responsibilities. Some individuals dub a condominium as a freehold with lease characteristics.

Foundationally, the owner of a condominium unit has a fee simple interest but does not have an exclusive interest in the common areas of the property.[33] Literally defined, a condominium is an interest in real property consisting of an undivided interest in common, in a portion of a parcel of real property together with a separate interest in space.[34] Most individuals think of condominiums as large properties, apartment type complexes that are being converted. "Under the condominium arrangement, the individual owner buys the exclusive right to occupy space where his unit is located. If his unit is located in a multistory building with other units above or below him, his exclusive right is to airspace his unit occupies. The apartment owner also receives an undivided interest in the land and common areas, such as the lobby, hallways, elevators, structure of the building, and, the recreation facilities."[35] The maintenance and day-to-day oversight of the property is entrusted to an "association, which is all of the unit owners acting as a group to manage and maintain the condominium property. Through its bylaws and rules, the association's board of directors governs condominium administration. The board's powers include handling condominium revenues and expenditures as well as levying and collecting assessments for expenses."[36] Problems with fraud and corruption have been common within the association framework, and states are increasingly regulated in their conduct.[37]

In essence, the condominium owner is like a tenant in common owning one piece of an entire tract yet having the same interests that other individuals have on a fractionalized basis. Condominiums ownership shares these characteristics:

1. A master deed which identifies the property
2. Common areas of usage
3. A fractionalized or prorated formula of undivided interest in the entire property
4. An association or group of unit owners with corresponding bylaws
5. Maintenance agreement regarding all common areas, which usually include exterior walls, girders, roof, public halls, and major systems
6. A group of directors or other body of individuals who perform a governing function
7. Participation dues and other fees
8. Certain restrictions and guidelines on occupancy[38]
9. Some restrictions on alienability or preemptive transfer regulation[39]

Condominiums are also not limited to residential purposes and have included medical and legal offices, and even industrial buildings and complexes. Document preparation for either the establishment or subsequent ownership of a condominium is often handled by a paralegal. Skills of draftsmanship and document organization are necessary for preparing the following:

- Master deed
- Bylaws
- Collection of blueprints and subdivision plans
- Disclosure statements

Much of how property is owned depends upon the nature of the real estate, the needs of the buyers and sellers, and the purposes of the transaction.

CHAPTER ONE **SUMMARY**

Chapter One discussed the following topics:

- Various competencies that must be mastered by a real estate paralegal
- Basic parties, resources, and terminology in the real estate field
- The nature of real property and how it differs from personal property
- Fixtures, easements, and licenses
- The various types of real property ownership: specifically, fee simple, life, freehold, and fee tail estates
- The various types of less-than-freehold estates
- Joint ownership and the various unities that must be fulfilled for such an estate to exist
- Concurrent ownership and its various forms and requirements
- Types of joint ownership and the general requirements for each
- The nature of partnerships, limited partnerships, joint ventures, real estate investment trusts, and condominiums

REVIEW **QUESTIONS**

1. How is real property distinguishable from personal property?
2. Define what a fixture is and how it differs from personal property.
3. Discuss the nature of less-than-freehold estates, including the differences in its various forms.
4. What is tenancy by the entireties?
5. Define and give various examples of an easement.
6. Does concurrent ownership require unity of time, title, interest, and possession? Why or why not?
7. What is the role of the paralegal in a real estate transaction?
8. What estate conveys only partial ownership? Explain.
9. Name and discuss which estate is characterized by a wrongful possession.
10. A reversion exists in what type of estate? How does this differ from other estates?

DISCUSSION **QUESTION**

John and Bob want to own property together. Upon their deaths, both want the property to pass down to their respective families. Discuss the various types of ownership relative to their situation, giving a recommendation as to the best form of ownership for their case.

EXERCISE 1

Write a one page essay explaining the similarities and differences of a joint venture and a real estate investment trust. Include when they are most beneficial to the investor.

THE CASE OF JOHN WHITE AND MARTHA SMITH

John White and Martha Smith are brother and sister who are in the market to purchase a vacation home in the mountains of North Carolina. John is a widow with no children. His only living blood relative is Martha, his sister. Martha is married with two children. Upon John's demise, he wishes his share in the vacation home to revert to Martha or her heirs. Upon Martha's demise, she wishes her share in the home to revert to her husband or children. Additional information for John and Martha is provided following. Use the information given here to complete the end of chapter exercises throughout the text. If required information is not provided, create fictional data as needed.

> John White
> D.O.B: 6/15/53
> Occupation: Police Officer
> Annual Income: $73,452
> Address: 143 Sunny Way
> Anytown, OH 00000
> Phone: 555-222-0000
> Current residence is owned outright, no outstanding debt on home. His home is valued at $142,500.

> Martha Smith
> D.O.B: 1/20/55
> Occupation: Homemaker
> Annual Income: $0
> Husband's Annual Income: $137,000
> Address: 275 Ocean Drive
> Mytown, MD 00000
> Phone: 555-111-0000
> Current residence is owned by Martha and her husband, Robert. Two years are left on their mortgage, with an outstanding balance of $27,000. Their current home is valued at $350,000.
> Children: Two daughters, Amy and Jennifer

Assignment for the Case of John and Martha

Review John and Martha's case information. Suggest the best option for ownership in their situation. Include in your discussion why other forms of ownership were not chosen.

REFERENCES

1. Lesley G. Cox, *Providing Cost-Effective Legal Services through the Effective Use of Paralegals*, 28 MONTANA LAWYER 26 (2002). *See* the National Federation of Paralegal Association's real estate task list at www.paralegals.org/displaycommon.cfm?an=1&subarticlenbr=293%20, last visited on August 24, 2009; the American Bar Association's utilization rules of paralegals in general and in particular real estate at www.abanet.org/legalservices/paralegals/downloads/modelguidelines.pdf; *see also* Shari Snell Faulkner, *How to Effectively Use a Paralegal in a Probate Manner*, 17 UTAH BAR J. 42 (2004); Janet Kennedy Dawson, *Updates on North Carolina Real Estate Law: The Role of Laypersons in the Closing of Residential Real Estate Transactions: North Carolina's New Approach*, 7 N.C. BANKING INST. 277 (2003); Michael C. Ksiazek, *The Model Rules of Professional Conduct and the Unauthorized Practice of Law: Justification for Restricting Conveyancing to Attorneys*, 37 SUFFOLK U. L. REV. 169 (2004); Richard C. Grant, *Board Certification Specialty Areas: Real Estate*, 77 FLA. BAR J. 57 (2003); Forrest S. Mosten, *Unbundle Your Practice: Increase Profits by Coaching Clients*, 16 UTAH BAR J. 26 (2003); Michael Madison, *The Real Properties of Contract Law*, 82 B.U. L. REV. 405 (2002).

2. *See* U.S. CENSUS BUREAU, U.S. DEPT. OF COMMERCE, STATISTICAL ABSTRACT OF THE UNITED STATES 430 tbl. 684, 507 tbl. 787, 507 tbl. 788 (120th ed. 2000) (illustrating the increase of

establishments, employees, revenues, and earnings in the real estate brokerage industry during the 1990s); *see also* BUSINESS STATISTICS OF THE UNITED STATES 260 tbl. 20-1 (Linz Audain & Cornella J. Strawser eds., 6th ed. 2000) (illustrating the real estate industry's increased payroll during the 1990s).

3. Raymond T. Nimmer, *Symposium on Approaching E-Commerce Through Uniform Legislation: Understanding the Uniform Computer Information Transactions Act and the Uniform Electronic Transactions Act: Through the Looking Glass: What Courts and UCITA Say about the Scope of Contract Law in the Information Age*, 38 DUQ. L. REV. 255 (2000).

4. Tara Austin, *Legal Professionalism: Doe v. McMaster and the Lawyer's Role in Real Estate Transactions*, 55 S.C.L. REV. 591 (2004).

5. TIMOTHY G. O'NEILL, LADNER ON CONVEYANCING IN PENNSYLVANIA (1988).

6. HERBERT THORNDIKE TIFFANY, THE LAW OF REAL PROPERTY AND OTHER INTERESTS IN LAND 4 (1970).

7. TIFFANY, *supra* note 6, at 350.

8. *Id*. at 320.

9. Conservation easements have been addressed by the National Commission on Uniform State Laws at www.cals.ncsu.edu/wq/lpn/PDFDocuments/uniform.pdf.

10. STATE OF MICHIGAN, DEPARTMENT OF ENVIRONMENTAL QUALITY, MINERAL RIGHTS BROCHURE at www.deq.state.mi.us/documents/deq-ogs-land-oilandgas-mineral-rights.pdf.

11. TIFFANY, *supra* note 6, at 350.

12. DANIEL F. HINKEL, PRACTICAL REAL ESTATE LAW, 5th ed., 4 (2008).

13. BRUCE T. HARWOOD, REAL ESTATE: AN INTRODUCTION TO THE PROFESSION, 6th ed., 65 (1978, 1992).

14. O'NEILL, *supra* note 5, at §1.03.

15. *Id*. at §1.04(a).

16. *Id*. at §1.04(c).

17. Adapted from FRANK KOVATS, PRINCIPLES AND PRACTICES OF NEW JERSEY REAL ESTATE, 13th ed., 67 (1984, 1998).

18. SUMMARY OF PENNSYLVANIA JURISPRUDENCE 2d, § 6:2.

19. *Id*. at § 6:38.

20. TIFFANY, *supra* note 6, at 159.

21. CONN. GEN. STAT. §52-495 (2009).

22. *Id*. at 165-66.

23. FILLMORE W. GALATY, WELLINGTON J. ALLAWAY, & ROBERT C. KYLE, MODERN REAL ESTATE PRACTICE 406 (2002).

24. NATIONAL CONFERENCE OF COMMISSIONERS ON UNIFORM STATE LAWS, UNIFORM PARTNERSHIP ACT (1997).

25. *See Id*. at § 306.

26. *Id*.

27. Elizabeth Cosenza, *Co-Invest at Your Own Risk: An Exploration of Potential Remedial Theories for Breaches of Rights of First Refusal in the Venture Capital Context*, 55 AM. U.L. REV. 87 (2005); *See also* Robert W. Hillman, *Law, Culture, and the Lore of Partnership: Of Entrepreneurs, Accountability, and the Evolving Status of Partners*, 40 WAKE FOREST L. REV. 793 (2005).

28. GA. CODE § 14-3-1101.

29. Su Han Chan, John Erickson, and Ko Wang, Real Estate Investment Trusts: Structure, Performance, and Investment Opportunities (Financial Management Association Survey and Synthesis Series) (2002).

30. Institute of Continuing Legal Education, 1 Michigan Basic Practice Handbook, 5th ed., 93 (1986, 2001).

31. Tiffany, *supra* note 6, at 184.

32. Harwood, *supra* note 13, at 172.

33. Michigan Handbook, *supra* note 29, at 93.

34. Tiffany, *supra* note 6, at 184.

35. Harwood, *supra* note 13, at 172.

36. Mark R. Hinkston, *Wisconsin's Revised Condominium Ownership Act*, Wis. Law., Sept. 2004, at 10.

37. *For example*, see Wis. Stat. § 703.15.

38. Preston Tower Condominium Association v. S. B. Realty Inc., 685 S.W. 2d 98 (Tex. App. 1985).

39. Cambridge Co. v. East Slope Investment Corp., 700 P. 2d 537 (Colo. 1985).

The Real Estate Transaction: Listings, Disclosure, and Agency

LEARNING OBJECTIVES

- To discuss the various types of listing agreements.
- To assess the broker-client relationship and its forms.
- To recognize the importance of seller disclosure, types of misrepresentation, and the role of consumer protection in the real estate industry.
- To demonstrate the procedure used during the initial client interview.
- To use appropriate listing agreements, dual agency, and other agreements of representation.

JOB COMPETENCIES

- To identify and prepare various types of listing agreements.
- To demonstrate effective communication with brokers and clients regarding the various types of listing agreements and broker relationships.
- To identify various disclosure and consumer protection requirements and help, under the supervision of an attorney, to ensure that they are adhered to.
- To employ interview skills and collect necessary information from a buyer or seller in a real estate transaction.

ETHICAL CONSIDERATIONS

The paralegal must be aware of the following ethical dilemmas during this phase of a real estate transaction:

- Unauthorized practice of law
- Lawyer supervision of nonlawyers
- Confidentiality issues
- Conflicts of interest
- Partnerships between lawyers and nonlawyers
- Communications with persons outside of law firm

I. LISTINGS

Sellers and buyers deal in real property that is presently offered, on the market, or "listed." To "list" implies an offer to sell. These types of agreements cover the numerous forms of property interests, whether commercial, apartment complexes, industrial locations, or single-family residences.

Listings are generated or held by real estate brokers or agents. The **broker**, a licensed, state-approved professional is directly responsible for a real estate office operation. **Real estate agents** work under the supervision of the broker. A broker can be an agent, and an agent can be a broker. But a real estate agent cannot operate his or her own agency because any agency depends on finding a real estate office to generate sales activity. Both brokers and agents have a contractual understanding that specifies how commissions are computed and split and how expenses are to be allotted. Brokers and agents author listing agreements, whereby a seller engages them to sell the realty in question. In some states, buyer agency relationships are possible.[1]

Web Exercise

U.S. Legal publishes listing agreements for all fifty states. See *www.uslegalforms.com/realestate*.

CASE LAW

If there is anything true about the broker-client relationship, it is the unswerving obligation of loyalty. One of the perennial ethical tussles involving broker representation has to do with dual agency—or representing both the buyer and the seller simultaneously. See how an Oklahoma Court deals with the dilemma.

Snider v. Oklahoma Real Estate Commission

1999 OK 55

987 P.2d 1204

70 OBJ 1834

Case Number: 88917

Decided: 06/01/1999

Mandate Issued: 09/17/1999

Supreme Court of Oklahoma

  Cite as: 1999 OK 55, 987 P.2d 1204

  KENNETH W. SNIDER,

  APPELLANT,

v.

STATE OF OKLAHOMA ex rel. OKLAHOMA REAL ESTATE COMMISSION,

  APPELLEE.

ON CERTIORARI TO THE COURT OF CIVIL APPEALS, DIVISION I

(continues)

The Real Estate Commission reprimanded and fined Kenneth W. Snider, the appellant, $200 for false and misleading statements in an advertising brochure, which the Commission found to be in violation of 59 O.S.1991, § 858–312(2). Snider appealed the Commission's order to the district court, which affirmed the order. Snider then further appealed the judgment of the district court, and the Court of Civil Appeals affirmed.

CERTIORARI PREVIOUSLY GRANTED;

OPINION OF THE COURT OF CIVIL APPEALS VACATED;

JUDGMENT OF THE DISTRICT COURT REVERSED.

Vickie L. Cook, Woodward, Oklahoma, For Appellant,

Philip Holmes, Brent W. Pitt, PHILIP HOLMES INC., Oklahoma City, Oklahoma, For Appellee.

Alma Wilson, Justice:

The appellant, Kenneth W. Snider, seeks review of the judgment of the district court, which affirmed an order of the Oklahoma Real Estate Commission. The Commission reprimanded Snider and assessed a $200 fine for false and misleading statements in an advertising brochure, in violation of 59 O.S.1991, § 858–312(2) and Oklahoma Real Estate Commission Rule 605:10–9-4(a)(5). The Administrative Procedures Act provides a standard of review for this Court in reviewing orders of state agencies. The appellant claims that his substantial rights were prejudiced because the agency's findings, inferences, and conclusions were clearly erroneous in view of the evidence, and were arbitrary and capricious. We agree and accordingly vacate the decision of the Court of Civil Appeals, reverse the judgment of the district court, and set aside the order of the Real Estate Commission.

I. FACTS

The Oklahoma Real Estate Commission on June 6, 1995, sent Snider a letter accusing him of violating Commission Rule 605:10–9-4(a)(5) by using a booklet in his advertising, entitled "The Buyer's Agent" published by The Buyer's Agent Inc. The Commission questioned the assertions in the booklet that buyers' agents saved buyers thousands of dollars. The Commission also questioned the statement on the inside back cover of the booklet that read, "Beware of any agent who mentions the words "dual agent," "assigned agent," "contract broker" [etc.]." The Commission informed Snider that dual agency is permissible in Oklahoma with the knowledge and consent of all parties involved. The Commission cited Rule 605:10–15-2, that an agent can work for a buyer and seller at the same time. Subsection (a) of that Rule provides:

"After July 1, 1990, in every real estate sales transaction involving a licensee, as agent or principal, the licensee must clearly disclose to the buyer and seller the agency relationship(s). The disclosure must be made prior to the buyer and seller entering into a binding agreement with each other; and when a binding agreement is signed, the prior agency disclosure must be confirmed in a separate provision, incorporated in or attached to that agreement."

Snider responded on June 9, 1995, that he was referring the matter to the legal counsel for The Buyer's Agent Inc. Counsel responded in a letter to the Commission dated June 12, 1995, that the company kept meticulous records of documented savings, and explained how this was done. Counsel's letter quoted in full the statement on the back cover of the booklet: "Beware of any agent who mentions the words "dual agent," "assigned agent," "contract broker," "facilitator," "transaction broker," or "designated agent." These are all methods of conducting real estate transactions which give the buyers less than full representation." Counsel replied that the statement was not misleading but entirely true. The letter continued that whether or not dual agency was permissible, dual agents attempt to represent both buyers and sellers and therefore cannot legally fully represent the interests of a home buyer. Counsel asserted that the statement was enlightening to home buyers. Counsel admonished that the duty of real estate commissions is to protect the public, not Realtors or former Commissioners, and that Counsel could not understand the Commission's statement in the letter to Snider. Counsel cautioned the Commission that this country gave everyone, including the company and its franchisees, the right to express an opinion and to make a truthful statement, whether or not such statement was unpopular.

She also related that she was forwarding all communications to the Federal Trade Commission because it was conducting a study of the harassment of buyer brokers in their advertising.

At the August 9, 1995, Federal Trade Commission meeting, the Commission voted to open a formal investigation. The Commission sent a letter to Snider advising him of the formal investigation, and that the decision was based on information indicating that his advertising could be misleading, inaccurate, and could misrepresent services provided by real estate agents. On November 1, 1995, the executive director of the Commission sent a letter to Snider's attorney listing the representations in the booklet that the Commission considered false or misleading. Nothing on the list mentioned the dual agent warning from the booklet. A preliminary investigation was held and parts of the booklet were cited, which the case examiner concluded may have been in violation of the Oklahoma Real Estate License Code. One of the references states, "Page 14 [of the booklet] contains a warning to buyers against the use of other types of licensees." After the report of the case examiner was presented to the Commission, it voted to set a formal hearing, and subsequently gave notice to Snider.

The formal hearing before a hearing examiner was held on May 7, 1996. The examiner in his report to the Commission recited the allegations, including the falsity of the booklet's reports of savings by clients using The Buyer's Agent in purchasing homes. But Snider had presented signed statements from the actual buyers whose savings were documented in the booklet. They affirmed that they had saved the amounts advertised. Also before the hearing examiner was the allegation that the statements in the booklet contrasting tasks done by "traditional agents" with tasks "always performed" by The Buyer's Agent were false and misleading. The hearing examiner noted that the State did not present evidence to indicate that these statements were false or misleading. Finally, the hearing examiner quoted the dual agent statement from the booklet and concluded, "The last sentence is false and misleading on its face in that it indicates that the "agents" referred to always give buyers less than full representation." The hearing examiner concluded that Snider had violated 59 O.S.1991, § 858–312(2) and Oklahoma Real Estate Commission Rule 605:10–9-4(a)(5). The hearing examiner recommended that Snider be formally reprimanded and fined $200.

Snider filed with the Commission a written exception to the final order. Snider asserted that at the beginning of the May 7, 1996, hearing, the hearing examiner announced the issues that were to be discussed and decided on that day based upon the complaint filed earlier. The issue of whether the statement from the booklet was misleading and false was not one of the issues the hearing examiner announced would be discussed. Snider added that no evidence was presented to show that the statement was misleading or false, and he affirmatively asserted that the statement was true. Nevertheless, the Commission followed the recommendations of the hearing examiner and on July 10, 1996, ordered that Snider be formally reprimanded and fined $200.

Snider appealed to the district court, which stated in its order, "That the primary basis upon which the finding was made did not deal with the dual agency question at all, but dealt with the advertised thousands of dollars saved to purchasers." The court found that the publication included advertising that was misleading or could be misleading to the general public, and that there was no basis in law upon which the court could set aside the findings and order of the Commission. It therefore affirmed the July 10, 1996, order. Snider then appealed, and the Court of Civil Appeals affirmed the order. We have previously granted certiorari.

Both the appellate courts and the district courts review the entire record made before an administrative agency acting in its adjudicatory capacity to determine whether the findings and conclusions in the agency order are supported by substantial evidence and by applicable law. If the order is supported by substantial evidence, it will be affirmed.

In contrast to the requirement that an order be supported by substantial evidence to be affirmed, no evidence supported the order of the Commission, which adopted the report of the hearing examiner that the last sentence of the booklet was misleading. The district court was also in error by rejecting the alleged misleading statement concerning dual agency as a basis for Snider's discipline and finding

(continued)

statements from the booklet regarding savings by clients of The Buyers Agent Inc., to be misleading. The hearing examiner received evidence on those savings and based on that evidence, did not find the statements concerning savings to be misleading.

The Commission argues, "Whether the advertisement of Mr. Snider stating that other agents provide less than full representation is misleading is a question to be determined by the Commissioners in the exercise of their expertise." The Commission's brief cites *City of Hugo v. State ex rel. Public Employees Relations Board*, 1994 OK 134, 886 P.2d 485, concerning the great weight to be accorded the expertise of an administrative agency, and the presumption of validity attaching to the exercise of expertise. The Commission, however, gives no reason why its expertise in real estate matters should be upheld when its finding is supported by merely a bald statement that the advertising is false and misleading on its face. The Commission's full finding on the issue reads: "That Respondent Kenneth W. Snider made false and misleading statements in an advertisement in that he stated that certain agents always provide less than full representation to buyers." No further explanation is given, and no reasons cited for finding the language to be false and misleading. We are not required to rubber-stamp an adjudicatory order of an administrative agency, nor do we accept the premise that the Commission's expertise is necessary to determine whether the statement in the advertisement for which Snider was disciplined is false and misleading.

A review of the entire booklet from which the statement found false and misleading is taken reveals one premise. That premise is stated on page two of the booklet, and is that traditional real estate firms represent the seller, and that when they try to represent the seller and the buyer, they cannot meaningfully represent both. Page four of the booklet states that "By law, selling agents must negotiate in the best interest of their clients, not withhold information from them, and must present their property in a favorable manner." It uses the illustration that one would not go to court using the same attorney who represents the opposing side. The booklet explains its reasons for these statements and the advantage to a buyer who is represented by an agent. The information in the booklet continuously refers to the law of agency. Agency law is not an area in which the Oklahoma Real Estate Commission can claim expertise superior to the courts of Oklahoma.

The challenged sentence is the last statement in the booklet, which was attached as an exhibit to the appellant's brief to the trial court. The entire booklet was also copied and attached as an exhibit in the Record of Proceedings before the Real Estate Commission. The booklet clearly expresses that an agent for the seller in a real estate transaction, or a dual agent representing both the seller and the buyer cannot fully represent the buyer. That conclusion is neither false nor misleading, and is in fact, the law of the State of Oklahoma. It is true that a real estate agent may legally represent both the buyer and seller in a real estate transaction so long as both parties know of the dual representation and give their assent. The reason assent is necessary is the dangers involved for the parties in dual representation. The very purpose of the rule is shown by *Skirvin v. Gardner*, 36 Okla. 613, 129 P. 729 (1913). The facts reveal that the plaintiff was going to purchase a farm for $13,000. When the defendants, a firm of real estate brokers, learned of the negotiations, they persuaded the plaintiff that they could obtain the farm for the plaintiff at the same price but would split the $600 commission with the plaintiff once the sale was complete. The real estate firm then persuaded the seller to sell through the agency of the firm. But when the sale was complete, the real estate firm refused to split the commission with the plaintiff. The trial court dismissed the petition. Upon appeal, the Court found this to be a fraudulent scheme, whose sole object was to take undue advantage of the seller, who was entitled to the unswerving loyalty and honesty of the agent. The Court held that where a petition shows that an agent, or broker, is obtaining commissions from more than one party, it must affirmatively appear that each party knew of this relationship and assented to it. The Court reasoned that permitting an agent of a vendor to become interested as the agent of a purchaser in the subject matter caused a dangerous conflict between duty and self-interest.

Where an agent undertakes to act for both parties to a contract, and the nature of his duties requires the exercise of discretion, the dual representation is contrary to public policy, and the contract is voidable upon the application of either party. The exception to this rule is where the parties have knowledge of the dual agency. Dual agents attempt to serve parties with conflicting interests. That is why the law requires that dual agents obtain the informed consent of the parties. In *Hunter Realty Co. v.*

Spencer, 21 Okla. 155, 95 P. 757 (1908), one of the partners in the real estate business attempted to represent three parties in a "triangular transaction." Two of the parties sued, and the district court canceled the deeds and gave other relief to remedy the wrong. In affirming the district court, the Court held that the entire transaction, independent of the question whether any of the parties were injured, was against public policy and voidable in equity at the suit of any of the parties. The Court cited with approval cases and authorities holding that the essence of an agent's contract is that he will use his best skill and judgment in promoting the interest of his employer, which he cannot do where he acts for two persons whose interest are essentially adverse, and when he acts without their assent or knowledge as their mutual agent, he commits a fraud on his principals.

The statutes provide for sanctions for a real estate agent who acts as a dual agent without disclosing that fact. Title 59 O.S.Supp.1998, § 858–312(3) provides that the Real Estate Commission may impose sanctions pursuant to 59 O.S.Supp. 1998, § 858–209, against any real estate licensee who acts for more than one party in a transaction without the knowledge of all parties for whom the licensee acts. In this manner, the legislature has also recognized the dangers involved in dual agency.

In the traditional, historical relationship a real estate agent was the agent of the seller, and this agency did not extend to the buyer, even though both parties received and relied on information from the agent. The buyer was not represented. The problem with the traditional relationship is that unsophisticated buyers negotiate with brokers who have little or no duty to protect buyers' interests.

With residential real estate transactions, "it is a widely accepted rule of agency law that a real estate broker operating under an exclusive listing contract with the seller of the property stands in an agency relationship to the seller." The Supreme Court of Colorado observed that the prevailing perception of the broker as an agent of the seller is firmly embedded in the real estate business, and therefore a written agreement is necessary to establish an agency relationship between a purchaser and a real estate broker or salesperson. One government survey has shown that over 70% of all buyers surveyed believed that the cooperating broker was acting as their agent. This misunderstanding by buyers of whether or not they were being represented by the real estate agent with which they were dealing was apparently significant enough that the Oklahoma Real Estate Commission believed the promulgation of a rule was necessary. Oklahoma Real Estate Commission Rule 605:10–15-2 (1996) provides that in every real estate sales transaction involving a licensee as an agent or principal, the licensee must clearly disclose to the buyer and seller the agency relationship or relationships.

We find that the statement in the booklet for which the appellant was sanctioned is neither false nor misleading. Sellers' agents and dual agents do not and cannot by law give a buyer the same degree of loyalty as an agent who acts on behalf of a buyer. Sellers' agents owe their allegiance to the seller. Dual agency invites a conflict of interest. A buyer who relies on the seller's agent or on dual agency does not receive the same degree of legal protection as that afforded by an agent acting solely on behalf of the buyer. Accordingly, we find that the order of the Oklahoma Real Estate Commission is clearly erroneous, contrary to its own rule, and without evidentiary support and must be set aside.

II. LISTING AGREEMENTS

KEY WORDS

exclusive agency	exclusive listing	listing
exclusive agency agreement	exclusive right to sell	net listing
	flat fee listing	open listing

During the preliminary stage of the real estate transaction, sellers may seek out the real estate attorney for legal assistance and advice. While the owner selling is still seen with regularity, the incredible complexity of the modern real estate transactions, the legal nuances, and potential liabilities for disclosure necessitate the hiring of a broker/agent as well as legal counsel.[2]

The relationship of a broker/agent with either buyer or seller is contractual by design. The contract form is defined as a listing. The **listing** gives a right, under agreed terms and conditions, to the broker/agent to sell a property. The style, extent of agency, and other interpretive qualities of listing agreements vary enormously.

For example, the real estate agent may wish to be the exclusive agent of the seller. In an **exclusive agency agreement**, the owner agrees to appoint the broker as the sole, exclusive agent and grants the broker the **exclusive right to sell** or exchange the property in question. On the other hand, an **open listing** allows more brokers to market simultaneously.[3]

A. Exclusive Listing Agreement

The preferred listing among real estate professionals is the **exclusive listing**—a listing that precludes other competing brokers and agents from marketing such property. The listing is sometimes referred to as the **exclusive right to sell**. Exclusive listings encompass sellers and broker/agents. Exclusive listings insure that the broker will garner a commission no matter who produces a buyer. Naturally, broker/agents prefer this listing agreement over all others. Figure 2–1 represents the usual exclusive listing agreement.

A closer examination of the agreement is worthwhile. The first clause of the agreement deals with the length of time for which the agreement will be in effect. However, the seller may ultimately terminate the contract for legal cause. Usually the reason behind such a move is the seller's dissatisfaction with the performance of the agency.

The next few clauses discuss in detail the broker's commission. These clauses simply state what the broker's commission is and designate any commissions payable to other brokers/agents involved in the sale. The clarity of the listing provision on commissions is a critical drafting issue. Kathleen H. Dooley writes:

> The bulk of litigation arises from disagreements between the broker and the seller as to when the broker is entitled to a commission. Typically such disputes occur when, subsequent to a broker's procuring a buyer for the seller's property, the seller is unable to complete the transaction. In most jurisdictions, the rule is that absent an express agreement, a broker earns his commission when he produces a buyer who is ready, willing, and able to purchase the property on the seller's terms.[4]

That defensibility of commissions extends even beyond a breached contract or agreement.[5] Further discussion of the broker's commission is found in Chapter 3.

The final clause on the front of the form notifies the seller that the real estate company is a member of the local Multiple Listing Service (MLS) and that the property for sale will be submitted to the MLS along with asking price and ultimate sale price. The only time the sale price will not be made public is when there is a properly executed agreement of sale. This exception is necessary to prevent prospective buyers from having the unfair advantage of knowing what price the seller would have accepted in the event that a deal falls through.

The majority of the clauses on the backside of the form deal with discrimination issues, and state that discrimination may trigger regulatory sanction and civil penalty under cited codification. There have been many cases where persons would not sell their home to a certain buyer because they were not the "right" person. There have also been occasions when real estate companies have received telephone calls and walk-ins inquiring about a specific property in a certain area. These inquiries turn out to be nothing but tests by official or unofficial parties regarding the efficacy of the nondiscrimination policies. For a standard format from Colorado, see Figure 2–2.

EXCLUSIVE LISTING AGREEMENT

DATE

Agreement between _____ , BROKER and,

,Seller in consideration of BROKER listing and endeavoring to procure a purchaser or tenant
for the property known as _____ SELLER grants BROKER the sole exclusive right to sell or
exchange the property for $ _____ or to lease the property for $ _____ . The term of this listing shall be
from _____ until midnight _____ .

Authorization to affix a lockbox to the property for use by all Multiple Listing Service Members is _____ is not
_____ granted.

Authorization to post 'For Sale' sign on property is _____ is not _____ granted.

SELLER agrees to pay BROKER a commission if this property, or any portion is sold, leased or exchanged by BROKER, other cooperating agent, SELLER or any other person during the term of this Agreement. Commission shall be due and payable at the closing
of title or upon execution of lease by landlord and tenant and payment of 1st month's rent.

Sale Commission _____

Rental Commission _____

AS SELLER. YOU HAVE THE RIGHT TO INDIVIDUALLY REACH AN AGREEMENT ON ANY FEE, COMMISSION, OR OTHER VALU-
ABLE CONSIDERATION WITH ANY BROKER. NO FEE, COMMISSION OR OTHER CONSIDERATION HAS BEEN FIXED BY ANY GOV-
ERNMENTAL AUTHORITY OR BY ANY TRADE ASSOCIATION OR MULTIPLE LISTING SERVICE. Nothing herein is intended to prohibit an individual broker from independently establishing a policy regarding the amount of fee, commission or other valuable consideration to be charged in transaction by the broker.

BROKER offers the following commission to Sub-Agents _____ Buyer-Agents: _____ . SELLER and BROKER understand that if
a purchaser has been obtained by a Buyer-Agent who has an Exclusive Buyer Agency Agreement with that purchaser, in that case
the Buyer-Agent is representing the purchaser and has no relationship, fiduciary or otherwise, with the SELLER or BROKER,
regardless of participation in brokerage fees.

BROKER offers the following commission to Transaction Brokers:

SELLER guarantees that if property is sold and closed he will have sufficient funds to satisfy all liens and encumbrances and pay
brokerage commission as set forth in Agreement.

BROKER shall be entitled to a commission if the property is sold, leased or exchanged within _____ months after the end
of the term of the listing or any extension thereof to a buyer who was introduced to the property during the term of the listing.
However, SELLER shall not be obligated to pay such commission if a valid listing agreement is entered into during the term of said
protection period with another licensed real estate broker and the sale, lease or exchange of property is made during the term of
said protection period.

BROKER shall be entitled to the following commission: _____ if the property is sold no later than _____ to a tenant
obtained by BROKER. If a valid listing agreement is entered into with another licensed real estate broker, SELLER agrees to advise
broker of aforementioned arrangement.

SELLER agrees to refer to BROKER every prospective buyer who directly contacts SELLER during the term of this Agreement.

SELLER represents that he/they is the sole owner of the property and has the legal right to sell, lease, or exchange the property
and has no binding listing agreement with any other broker at the start of the period of this listing. SELLER states that the property
information which has been filled in on the profile sheet for this listing is correct to the best of his knowledge, and SELLER will
indemnify BROKER against loss resulting from reliance upon such information.

SELLER acknowledges that he has received the Consumer Information Statement on New Jersey Real Estate Relationships.
"I _____ as an
     Name of Licensee

authorized representative of _____ intend, as of this time,
      Name of Brokerage Firm

to work with you, the SELLER, as a _____ * (Indicate one of the following: sellers (landlord) agent only,
seller's (landlord's) agent and disclosed dual agent if the opportunity arises, transaction broker).

FIGURE 2–1
(continues)

SELLER acknowledges that he has read and received a copy of this Listing Agreement and that he has also read and understands the SELLER's responsibilities under New Jersey's Law Against Discrimination (N.J.S.A. 10:5-1 et seq., as amended and supplemented) set forth on the reverse side of this Agreement.

BROKER will list property in the following Multiple Listing Services (MLS): _____ whose member participants will act as cooperating agents of BROKER in the sale of the premises.

		L.S.
_____	_____	_____
Listing Office	Date Signed	SELLER/Authorize Representative

		L.S
By: _____	_____	_____
Broker/Authorized Representative	Date Signed	SELLER/Authorized Representative

_____	_____
Mailing Address	Mailing Address

_____
Telephone Number

FIGURE 2–1

Web Exercise

Visit the Pennsylvania Code for explicit instructions on what needs to be included in the exclusive listing at *www.pacode.com/secure/data/049/chapter35/s35.332.html*.

B. Open Listing

An **open listing** is a listing given to a number of brokers at the same time, while the owner still reserves the right to sell the property. If the owner does sell the property, the owner is under no obligation to pay a commission.[6] Brokers do not favor this arrangement because any agent may collect the full commission despite another broker's listing and the obvious labor which goes uncompensated. According to Billie J. Ellis Jr., under this arrangement, the seller can retain several brokers simultaneously, and the principal will not be obligated to pay any broker a commission if the seller is the procuring cause of the "transaction."[7] See Figure 2–3 for an example of an open listing agreement.

Web Exercise

Compare and contrast Figure 2–3 with the Open Listing provided by Colorado Department of Regulatory Agencies at *www.dora.state.co.us/Real-estate/contracts/2006Contracts*.

NONDISCRIMINATION. The parties agree not to discriminate unlawfully against any prospective buyer because of the race, creed, color, sex, sexual orientation, marital status, familial status, physical or mental disability, handicap, religion, national origin or ancestry of such person.

FIGURE 2–2
Non-Discrimination Clause.

OPEN LISTING AGREEMENT

AGREEMENT made _____, _____, between _____, of _____, _____, Pennsylvania, hereinafter referred to as "Owner," and _____, of _____, _____, Pennsylvania, hereinafter referred to as "Broker."

Seller grants to Broker the nonexclusive right to act as Seller's agent to acquire a purchaser for Seller's property, further described in Paragraph 1 below. The Seller reserves the right to enter into listing contracts with other brokers and reserves the right to sell the property personally, with no responsibility for compensation to Broker, unless Seller sells to a buyer obtained by the Broker.

- PROPERTY. The property to be sold pursuant to this listing is situated at _____, _____, _____ County, Pennsylvania, hereinafter referred to as "Property" and more thoroughly described as: _____.

- TERMS OF SALE OF PROPERTY. The selling price of the Property shall be $ _____. All those expenses, costs, and other charges with respect to the Property will be paid by the Owner during escrow. Any decrease in the selling price shall be approved by the Seller only. The selling price shall be payable in lawful money of the United States.

- TERM. This listing shall commence on _____, _____, and terminate on _____, _____, unless extended by addendum.

- COMPENSATION. The Owner shall pay to Broker, in lawful money of the United States, as his commission _____% of the selling price. The Broker's commission shall be earned, due, and payable ONLY in the event the Owner enters into a sales agreement with the purchasers through the efforts of the Broker.

IN WITNESS WHEREOF, the parties have executed this agreement the day and year first above written.

_____
Owner

_____
Broker

FIGURE 2–3

C. Flat Fee Listing

Another type of listing agreement is the **flat fee listing**, where broker and agent agree to a predetermined commission, despite the amount of the sale price. Since real estate commissions are tied to the sales price, the seller's effort to reduce the amount owed is not a warmly received gesture. Most brokers and agents do not like predetermined commissions. Some companies have flourished nationally by offering a flat rate fee. Since costs are low and services are widely curtailed, both the broker and buyer incur far less risk. The fees will vary from $199 to approximately $2,000.

The lower the fee, the more work will be assumed by the sellers. The higher the fee, the more energetic the broker/agent will be. At a minimum, the seller has his or her house listed in the MLS. See Figure 2–4 for an example of this type of agreement.

D. Net Listing Agreement

In the **net listing** a broker or an agent earns a commission only on the part of the sales price that is in excess of a stated price. Here the broker/agent is rewarded for an aggressive sales price. Be wary of exaggerated appraisals in this listing format. See Figure 2–5 for an example of a net listing agreement.

E. Exclusive Agency

When a seller grants an **exclusive agency**, the agent retains all rights with the exception of the seller selling. In essence, the exclusive agency undermines the sales incentive of the broker/agent since their legs, so to speak, will be cut from under them. If the seller finds a buyer, this ruins the commission of the broker/agent. Other real estate agents and brokers who affect a sale will not

---

FLAT FEE LISTING AGREEMENT

AGREEMENT made _____, _____, between , of _____, _____, Pennsylvania, hereinafter referred to as "Owner," and _____, of _____, _____, Pennsylvania, hereinafter referred to as "Broker."

- PROPERTY. The property to be sold pursuant to this listing is situated at _____, _____, _____ County, Pennsylvania, hereinafter referred to as "Property", and more thoroughly described as: _____

- TERMS OF SALE OF PROPERTY. The selling price of the Property shall be $ _____. The Owner shall pay all those expenses, costs, and other charges with respect to the Property which must be paid by the Owner during escrow. The sale price shall not be changed unless approved by the Owner in writing. The selling price shall be payable in lawful money of the United States.

- TERM. This listing shall commence on _____, _____, and terminate on _____, _____, unless extended by addendum.

- COMPENSATION. The Owner shall pay to Broker, in lawful money of the United States, as his commission a flat fee of _____ ($ _____) Dollars. The Broker's commission shall be earned, due, and payable in the event the Owner enters into a sales agreement with the purchasers through the efforts of the Broker.

IN WITNESS WHEREOF, the parties have executed this agreement the day and year first above written.

_____   _____
Owner   Broker

FIGURE 2–4

thwart the listing agent's commission. Some consider the exclusive agency to be counterproductive and an unhealthy alliance. Throughout the arrangement, listing broker/agents are always unsure of the seller motivation, and hence much less inclined to invest money, time, and energy into the sale of a home. Figures 2–6[8] and 2–7[9] lay out one method of attaining an exclusive agency—an exclusive-right–to-sell listing contract coupled with an exclusive brokerage listing addendum.

NET LISTING AGREEMENT

AGREEMENT made _____, _____, between _____, of _____, Pennsylvania, hereinafter referred to as "Owner," and _____, of _____, _____, Pennsylvania, hereinafter referred to as Broker."

- PROPERTY. The property to be sold pursuant to this listing is situated at _____ County, Pennsylvania, hereinafter referred to as "Property," and more thoroughly described as: _____.

- TERMS OF SALE OF PROPERTY. The selling price of the Property shall be at least $ _____ net to the Owner and all those expenses, costs, and other charges with respect to the Property which must be paid by the Owner during escrow. Subject to this minimum, the selling price shall be determined, fixed, and approved in writing by the Broker, at his discretion. The selling price shall be payable in lawful money of the United States.

- TERM. This listing shall commence on _____, _____, and terminate on _____, _____, unless extended by addendum.

- COMPENSATION. The Owner shall pay to Broker, in lawful money of the United States, as his commission _____% of that portion of the selling price in excess of the sum of $ _____net to the Owner and all such expenses, cost, and other charges which must be paid by the Owner as set forth in Paragraph 2. The Broker's commission shall be earned, due, and payable in the event the Owner enters into a sales agreement with the purchasers through the efforts of the Broker.

IN WITNESS WHEREOF, the parties have executed this agreement the day and year first above written.

Owner: _____   Broker: _____

FIGURE 2–5

The printed portions of this form, except differentiated additions, have been approved by the Colorado Real Estate Commission. (LC50-5-09) (Mandatory 7-09)

THIS IS A BINDING CONTRACT. THIS FORM HAS IMPORTANT LEGAL CONSEQUENCES AND THE PARTIES SHOULD CONSULT LEGAL AND TAX OR OTHER COUNSEL BEFORE SIGNING.

Compensation charged by real estate brokerage firms is not set by law. Such charges are established by each real estate brokerage firm.

DIFFERENT BROKERAGE RELATIONSHIPS ARE AVAILABLE WHICH INCLUDE BUYER AGENCY, SELLER AGENCY OR TRANSACTION-BROKERAGE.

EXCLUSIVE RIGHT-TO-SELL LISTING CONTRACT

SELLER AGENCY   TRANSACTION-BROKERAGE

Date: _____

1.   AGREEMENT. Seller and Brokerage Firm enter into this exclusive, irrevocable contract (Seller Listing Contract) as of the date set forth above.

2.   BROKER AND BROKERAGE FIRM.
    2.1.   Multiple-Person Firm. If this box is checked, the individual designated by Brokerage Firm to serve as the broker of Seller and to perform the services for Seller required by this Seller Listing Contract is called Broker. If more than one individual is so designated, then references in this Seller Listing Contract to Broker shall include all persons so designated, including substitute or additional brokers. The brokerage relationship exists only with Broker and does not extend to the employing broker, Brokerage Firm or to any other brokers employed or engaged by Brokerage Firm who are not so designated.
    2.2.   One-Person Firm. If this box is checked, Broker is a real estate brokerage firm with only one licensed natural person. References in this Seller Listing Contract to Broker or Brokerage Firm mean both the licensed natural person and brokerage firm who shall serve as the broker of Seller and perform the services for Seller required by this Seller Listing Contract.

3.   DEFINED TERMS.
    3.1.   Seller: _____

    3.2.   Brokerage Firm: _____

    3.3.   Broker: _____

    3.4.   Property. The Property is the following legally described real estate in the County of _____, Colorado:

known as No. _____

| Street Address | City | State | Zip |

together with the interests, easements, rights, benefits, improvements and attached fixtures appurtenant thereto, and all interest of Seller in vacated streets and alleys adjacent thereto, except as herein excluded.
    3.5.   Sale.
        3.5.1. A Sale is the voluntary transfer or exchange of any interest in the Property or the voluntary creation of the obligation to convey any interest in the Property, including a contract or lease. It also includes an agreement to transfer any ownership interest in an entity which owns the Property.
        3.5.2. If this box is checked, Seller authorizes Broker to negotiate leasing the Property. Lease of the Property or Lease means any lease of an interest in the Property.
    3.6.   Listing Period. The Listing Period of this Seller Listing Contract shall begin on _____, and shall continue through the earlier of (1) completion of the Sale of the Property or (2) _____. Broker shall continue to assist in the completion of any transaction for which compensation is payable to Brokerage Firm under § 7 of this Seller Listing Contract.
    3.7.   Applicability of Terms. A check or similar mark in a box means that such provision is applicable. The abbreviation "N/A" or the word "Deleted" means not applicable. The abbreviation "MEC" (mutual execution of this contract) means the latest date upon which both parties have signed this Seller Listing Contract.
    3.8.   Day; Computation of Period of Days, Deadline.
        3.8.1.   Day. As used in this Seller Listing Contract, the term "day" shall mean the entire day ending at 11:59 p.m., United States Mountain Time (Standard or Daylight Savings as applicable).

FIGURE 2–6
(continues)

3.8.2. Computation of Period of Days, Deadline. In computing a period of days, when the ending date is not specified, the first day is excluded and the last day is included, e.g., three days after MEC. If any deadline falls on a Saturday, Sunday or federal or Colorado state holiday (Holiday), such deadline **Shall** **Shall Not** be extended to the next day that is not a Saturday, Sunday or Holiday. Should neither box be checked, the deadline shall not be extended.

4. BROKERAGE RELATIONSHIP.

4.1. If the Seller Agency box at the top of page 1 is checked, Broker shall represent Seller as a Seller's limited agent (Seller's Agent). If the Transaction-Brokerage box at the top of page 1 is checked, Broker shall act as a Transaction-Broker.

4.2. In-Company Transaction – Different Brokers. When Seller and buyer in a transaction are working with different brokers, those brokers continue to conduct themselves consistent with the brokerage relationships they have established. Seller acknowledges that Brokerage Firm is allowed to offer and pay compensation to brokers within Brokerage Firm working with a buyer.

4.3. In-Company Transaction – One Broker. If Seller and buyer are both working with the same broker, Broker shall function as:

4.3.1. Seller's Agent. If the Seller Agency box at the top of page 1 is checked, the parties agree the following applies:

4.3.1.1. Seller Agency Only. Unless the box in § 4.3.1.2 **(Seller Agency Unless Brokerage Relationship with Both)** is checked, Broker shall represent Seller as Seller's Agent and shall treat the buyer as a customer. A customer is a party to a transaction with whom Broker has no brokerage relationship. Broker shall disclose to such customer Broker's relationship with Seller.

4.3.1.2. Seller Agency Unless Brokerage Relationship with Both. If this box is checked, Broker shall represent Seller as Seller's Agent and shall treat the buyer as a customer, unless Broker currently has or enters into an agency or Transaction-Brokerage relationship with the buyer, in which case Broker shall act as a Transaction-Broker.

4.3.2. Transaction-Broker. If the Transaction-Brokerage box at the top of page 1 is checked, or in the event neither box is checked, Broker shall work with Seller as a Transaction-Broker. A Transaction-Broker shall perform the duties described in § 5 and facilitate sales transactions without being an advocate or agent for either party. If Seller and buyer are working with the same broker, Broker shall continue to function as a Transaction-Broker.

5. BROKERAGE DUTIES. Brokerage Firm, acting through Broker, as either a Transaction-Broker or a Seller's Agent, shall perform the following **Uniform Duties** when working with Seller:

5.1. Broker shall exercise reasonable skill and care for Seller, including, but not limited to the following:

5.1.1. Performing the terms of any written or oral agreement with Seller;

5.1.2. Presenting all offers to and from Seller in a timely manner regardless of whether the Property is subject to a contract for Sale;

5.1.3. Disclosing to Seller adverse material facts actually known by Broker;

5.1.4. Advising Seller regarding the transaction and advising Seller to obtain expert advice as to material matters about which Broker knows but the specifics of which are beyond the expertise of Broker;

5.1.5. Accounting in a timely manner for all money and property received; and

5.1.6. Keeping Seller fully informed regarding the transaction.

5.2. Broker shall not disclose the following information without the informed consent of Seller:

5.2.1. That Seller is willing to accept less than the asking price for the Property;

5.2.2. What the motivating factors are for Seller to sell the Property;

5.2.3. That Seller will agree to financing terms other than those offered;

5.2.4. Any material information about Seller unless disclosure is required by law or failure to disclose such information would constitute fraud or dishonest dealing; or

5.2.5. Any facts or suspicions regarding circumstances that could psychologically impact or stigmatize the Property.

5.3. Seller consents to Broker's disclosure of Seller's confidential information to the supervising broker or designee for the purpose of proper supervision, provided such supervising broker or designee shall not further disclose such information without consent of Seller, or use such information to the detriment of Seller.

5.4. Brokerage Firm may have agreements with other sellers to market and sell their property. Broker may show alternative properties not owned by Seller to other prospective buyers and list competing properties for sale.

5.5. Broker shall not be obligated to seek additional offers to purchase the Property while the Property is subject to a contract for Sale.

5.6. Broker has no duty to conduct an independent inspection of the Property for the benefit of a buyer and has no duty to independently verify the accuracy or completeness of statements made by Seller or independent inspectors. Broker has no duty to conduct an independent investigation of a buyer's financial condition or to verify the accuracy or completeness of any statement made by a buyer.

5.7. Seller understands that Seller shall not be liable for Broker's acts or omissions that have not been approved, directed, or ratified by Seller.

5.8. When asked, Broker **Shall** **Shall Not** disclose to prospective buyers and cooperating brokers the existence of offers on the Property and whether the offers were obtained by Broker, a broker within Brokerage Firm or by another broker.

6. ADDITIONAL DUTIES OF SELLER'S AGENT. If the Seller Agency box at the top of page 1 is checked, Broker is Seller's Agent, with the following additional duties:

6.1. Promoting the interests of Seller with the utmost good faith, loyalty and fidelity.

6.2. Seeking a price and terms that are set forth in this Seller Listing Contract.

6.3. Counseling Seller as to any material benefits or risks of a transaction that are actually known by Broker.

7. COMPENSATION TO BROKERAGE FIRM; COMPENSATION TO COOPERATIVE BROKER. Seller agrees that any Brokerage Firm compensation that is conditioned upon the Sale of the Property shall be earned by Brokerage Firm as set forth herein without any discount or allowance for any efforts made by Seller or by any other person in connection with the Sale of the Property.

7.1. Amount. In consideration of the services to be performed by Broker, Seller agrees to pay Brokerage Firm as follows:

7.1.1. Sale Commission. (1) _____% of the gross purchase price or (2) _____, in U.S. dollars.

FIGURE 2–6
(continued)

123 **7.1.2.** **Lease Commission.** If the box in § 3.5.2 is checked, Brokerage Firm shall be paid a fee equal to (1) _____% of the
124 gross rent under the lease, or (2) _____, in U.S. dollars, payable as follows: _____.
125 **7.2.** **When Earned.** Such commission shall be earned upon the occurrence of any of the following:
126 **7.2.1.** Any Sale of the Property within the Listing Period by Seller, by Broker or by any other person;
127 **7.2.2.** Broker finding a buyer who is ready, willing and able to complete the transaction as specified herein by Seller; or
128 **7.2.3.** Any Sale (or Lease if § 3.5.2 is checked) of the Property within _____ calendar days subsequent to the expiration of the
129 Listing Period (Holdover Period) to anyone with whom Broker negotiated and whose name was submitted, in writing, to Seller by Broker
130 during the Listing Period (including any extensions thereof). However, Seller **Shall** **Shall Not** owe the commission to Brokerage Firm
131 under this § 7.2.3 if a commission is earned by another licensed real estate brokerage firm acting pursuant to an exclusive agreement entered
132 into during the Holdover Period. If no box is checked above in this § 7.2.3, then (**Shall Not**) shall apply and Seller shall not owe the
133 commission to Brokerage Firm.
134 **7.3.** **When Applicable and Payable.** The commission obligation shall apply to a Sale made during the Listing Period or any extension
135 of such original or extended term. The commission described in § 7.1.1 shall be payable at the time of the closing of the Sale, or, if there is no
136 closing (due to the refusal or neglect of Seller) then on the contracted date of closing, as contemplated by § 7.2.1 or § 7.2.3, or upon fulfillment
137 of § 7.2.2 where the offer made by such buyer is not accepted by Seller.
138 **7.4.** **Other Compensation.** _____
139 **7.5.** **Cooperative Broker Compensation.** Broker shall seek assistance from, and Brokerage Firm offers compensation to, outside
140 brokerage firms, whose brokers are acting as:
141 **Buyer Agents:** _____% of the gross sales price or _____, in U.S. dollars.
142 **Transaction-Brokers:** _____% of the gross sales price or _____, in U.S. dollars.
143

144 **8.** **LIMITATION ON THIRD-PARTY COMPENSATION.** Neither Broker nor the Brokerage Firm, except as set forth in § 7, shall accept
145 compensation from any other person or entity in connection with the Property without the written consent of Seller. Additionally, neither
146 Broker nor Brokerage Firm shall assess or receive mark-ups or other compensation for services performed by any third party or affiliated
147 business entity unless Seller signs a separate written consent.
148

149 **9.** **OTHER BROKERS' ASSISTANCE, MULTIPLE LISTING SERVICES (MLS) AND MARKETING.** Seller has been advised by
150 Broker of the advantages and disadvantages of various marketing methods, including advertising and the use of MLS and various methods of
151 making the Property accessible by other brokerage firms (e.g., using lock boxes, by-appointment-only showings, etc.), and whether some
152 methods may limit the ability of another broker to show the Property. After having been so advised, Seller has chosen the following (check all
153 that apply):
154 **9.1.** **MLS/Information Exchange.**
155 **9.1.1.** The Property **Shall** **Shall Not** be submitted to one or more multiple listing services and **Shall** **Shall Not** be
156 submitted to one or more property information exchanges. If submitted, Seller authorizes Broker to provide timely notice of any status change
157 to such multiple listing services and information exchanges. Upon transfer of deed from Seller to buyer, Seller authorizes Broker to provide
158 sales information to such multiple listing services and information exchanges.
159 **9.1.2.** Seller authorizes the use of electronic and all other marketing methods except: _____.
160 **9.1.3.** Seller further authorizes use of the data by multiple listing services and property information exchanges, if any.
161 **9.1.4.** The Property Address **Shall** **Shall Not** be displayed on the Internet.
162 **9.1.5.** The Property Listing **Shall** **Shall Not** be displayed on the Internet.
163 **9.2.** **Property Access.** Access to the Property may be by:
164 Lock Box
165 _____
166 Other instructions: _____
167 **9.3.** **Broker Marketing.** The following specific marketing tasks shall be performed by Broker:
168
169
170 **9.4.** **Brokerage Services.** The Broker shall provide brokerage services to Seller.
171

172 **10.** **SELLER'S OBLIGATIONS TO BROKER; DISCLOSURES AND CONSENT.**
173 **10.1.** **Negotiations and Communication.** Seller agrees to conduct all negotiations for the Sale of the Property only through Broker, and
174 to refer to Broker all communications received in any form from real estate brokers, prospective buyers, tenants or any other source during the
175 Listing Period of this Seller Listing Contract.
176 **10.2.** **Advertising.** Seller agrees that any advertising of the Property by Seller (e.g., Internet, print and signage) shall first be approved by
177 Broker.
178 **10.3.** **No Existing Listing Agreement.** Seller represents that Seller **Is** **Is Not** currently a party to any listing agreement with any
179 other broker to sell the Property.
180 **10.4.** **Ownership of Materials and Consent.** Seller represents that all materials (including all photographs, renderings, images or other
181 creative items) supplied to Broker by or on behalf of Seller are owned by Seller, except as Seller has disclosed in writing to Broker. Seller is
182 authorized to and grants to Broker, Brokerage Firm and any multiple listing service (that Broker submits the Property to) a nonexclusive
183 irrevocable, royalty-free license to use such material for marketing of the Property, reporting as required and the publishing, display and
184 reproduction of such material, compilation and data. This license shall survive the termination of this Seller Listing Contract.
185 **10.5.** **Colorado Foreclosure Protection Act.** The Colorado Foreclosure Protection Act (Act) generally requires that (1) the Property is
186 residential, (2) any loan secured by the Property is at least thirty days delinquent or in default, (3) Buyer does not reside in the Property for at
187 least one year and (4) Buyer is subject to the Act. If all requirements 1, 2, 3 and 4 are met and the Act otherwise applies, then a contract,
188 between Buyer and Seller for the sale of the Property, that complies with the provisions of the Act is required. Therefore, if the Act applies,
189 Seller agrees that Broker is **not** authorized to prepare such a contract for the sale of the Property. It is recommended that an attorney prepare the
190 required documents.

LC50-5-09. **EXCLUSIVE RIGHT-TO-SELL LISTING CONTRACT**   Page 3 of 6

FIGURE 2–6
(continued)

191
192 **11. PRICE AND TERMS.** The following Price and Terms are acceptable to Seller:
193   **11.1.**   **Price.** U.S. $ _____
194   **11.2.**   **Terms.**   **Cash**   **Conventional**   **FHA**   **VA**
195   **Other:** _____
196   **11.3.**   **Loan Discount Points.** _____
197   **11.4.**   **Buyer's Closing Costs (FHA/VA).** Seller shall pay closing costs and fees, not to exceed $ _____ , that Buyer is not
198 allowed by law to pay, for tax service and _____.
199   **11.5.**   **Earnest Money.** Minimum amount of earnest money deposit U.S. $ _____ in the form of _____.
200   **11.6.**   **Seller Proceeds.** Seller will receive net proceeds of closing as indicated: **Cashier's Check** at Seller's expense;   **Funds**
201 **Electronically Transferred (Wire Transfer)** to an account specified by Seller, at Seller's expense; or   **Closing Company's Trust Account**
202 **Check**.
203   **11.7.**   **Advisory: Tax Withholding.** The Internal Revenue Service and the Colorado Department of Revenue may require closing
204 company to withhold a substantial portion of the proceeds of this Sale when Seller either (1) is a foreign person or (2) will not be a Colorado
205 resident after closing. Seller should inquire of Seller's tax advisor to determine if withholding applies or if an exemption exists.
206
207 **12. DEPOSITS.** Brokerage Firm is authorized to accept earnest money deposits received by Broker pursuant to a proposed Sale contract.
208 Brokerage Firm is authorized to deliver the earnest money deposit to the closing agent, if any, at or before the closing of the Sale contract.
209
210 **13. INCLUSIONS AND EXCLUSIONS.**
211   **13.1.**   **Inclusions.** The Purchase Price includes the following items (Inclusions):
212   **13.1.1. Fixtures.** If attached to the Property on the date of this Seller Listing Contract, lighting, heating, plumbing, ventilating, and
213 air conditioning fixtures, TV antennas, inside telephone, network and coaxial (cable) wiring and connecting blocks/jacks, plants, mirrors, floor
214 coverings, intercom systems, built-in kitchen appliances, sprinkler systems and controls, built-in vacuum systems (including accessories),
215 garage door openers including _____ remote controls; and
216
217
218   **13.1.2. Personal Property.** If on the Property whether attached or not on the date of this Seller Listing Contract: storm
219 windows, storm doors, window and porch shades, awnings, blinds, screens, window coverings, curtain rods, drapery rods, fireplace inserts,
220 fireplace screens, fireplace grates, heating stoves, storage sheds, and all keys. If checked, the following are included: **Water Softeners**
221   **Smoke/Fire Detectors**   **Security Systems**   **Satellite Systems** (including satellite dishes); and
222
223
224   The Personal Property to be conveyed at closing shall be conveyed by Seller free and clear of all taxes (except personal property taxes for
225 the year of closing), liens and encumbrances, except _____.
226 Conveyance shall be by bill of sale or other applicable legal instrument.
227   **13.1.3. Trade Fixtures.** The following trade fixtures: _____
228   The Trade Fixtures to be conveyed at closing shall be conveyed by Seller, free and clear of all taxes (except personal property taxes for the
229 year of closing), liens and encumbrances, except _____.
230 Conveyance shall be by bill of sale or other applicable legal instrument.
231   **13.1.4. Parking and Storage Facilities.**   **Use Only**   **Ownership** of the following parking facilities: _____;
232 and   **Use Only**   **Ownership** of the following storage facilities: _____.
233   **13.1.5. Water Rights.** The following legally described water rights:
234
235
236   Any water rights shall be conveyed by _____ deed or other applicable legal instrument. The Well Permit # is _____.
237   **13.1.6. Growing Crops.** The following growing crops:
238
239
240   **13.2.**   **Exclusions.** The following are excluded (Exclusions): _____
241
242 **14. TITLE AND ENCUMBRANCES.** Seller represents to Broker that title to the Property is solely in Seller's name. Seller shall deliver to
243 Broker true copies of all relevant title materials, leases, improvement location certificates and surveys in Seller's possession and shall disclose
244 to Broker all easements, liens and other encumbrances, if any, on the Property, of which Seller has knowledge. Seller authorizes the holder of
245 any obligation secured by an encumbrance on the Property to disclose to Broker the amount owing on said encumbrance and the terms thereof.
246 In case of Sale, Seller agrees to convey, by a _____ deed, only that title Seller has in the Property. Property shall be
247 conveyed free and clear of all taxes, except the general taxes for the year of closing.
248   All monetary encumbrances (such as mortgages, deeds of trust, liens, financing statements) shall be paid by Seller and released except as
249 Seller and buyer may otherwise agree. Existing monetary encumbrances are as follows: _____.
250   The Property is subject to the following leases and tenancies: _____.
251   If the Property has been or will be subject to any governmental liens for special improvements installed at the time of signing a Sale
252 contract, Seller shall be responsible for payment of same, unless otherwise agreed. Brokerage Firm may terminate this Seller Listing Contract
253 upon written notice to Seller that title is not satisfactory to Brokerage Firm.
254
255 **15. EVIDENCE OF TITLE.** Seller agrees to furnish buyer, at Seller's expense, a current commitment and an owner's title insurance policy
256 in an amount equal to the Purchase Price in the form specified in the Sale contract, or if this box is checked,   **An Abstract of Title** certified
257 to a current date.
258

FIGURE 2–6
(continued)

259 **16. ASSOCIATION ASSESSMENTS.** Seller represents that the amount of the regular owners' association assessment is currently payable at
260 $ _____ per _____ and that there are no unpaid regular or special assessments against the Property except the current regular
261 assessments and except _____. Seller agrees to promptly request the owners' association to deliver to buyer before date of
262 closing a current statement of assessments against the Property.

264 **17. POSSESSION.** Possession of the Property shall be delivered to buyer as follows: _____,
265 subject to leases and tenancies as described in § 14.

267 **18. MATERIAL DEFECTS, DISCLOSURES AND INSPECTION.**
268 **18.1. Broker's Obligations.** Colorado law requires a broker to disclose to any prospective buyer all adverse material facts actually
269 known by such broker including but not limited to adverse material facts pertaining to the title to the Property and the physical condition of the
270 Property, any material defects in the Property, and any environmental hazards affecting the Property which are required by law to be disclosed.
271 These types of disclosures may include such matters as structural defects, soil conditions, violations of health, zoning or building laws, and
272 nonconforming uses and zoning variances. Seller agrees that any buyer may have the Property and Inclusions inspected and authorizes Broker
273 to disclose any facts actually known by Broker about the Property.
274 **18.2. Seller's Obligations.**
275 **18.2.1. Seller's Property Disclosure Form.** A seller is not required by law to provide a written disclosure of adverse matters
276 regarding the Property. However, disclosure of known material latent (not obvious) defects is required by law. Seller **Agrees Does Not**
277 **Agree** to provide a Seller's Property Disclosure form completed to the best of Seller's current, actual knowledge.
278 **18.2.2. Lead-Based Paint.** Unless exempt, if the improvements on the Property include one or more residential dwellings for
279 which a building permit was issued prior to January 1, 1978, a completed Lead-Based Paint Disclosure (Sales) form must be signed by Seller
280 and the real estate licensees, and given to any potential buyer in a timely manner.
281 **18.2.3. Carbon Monoxide Alarms.** Note: If the improvements on the Property have a fuel-fired heater or appliance, a
282 fireplace, or an attached garage and one or more rooms lawfully used for sleeping purposes (Bedroom), Seller understands that Colorado law
283 requires that Seller assure the Property has an operational carbon monoxide alarm installed within fifteen feet of the entrance to each Bedroom
284 or in a location as required by the applicable building code, prior to offering the Property for sale or lease.

286 **18.3. Right of Broker to Terminate.** Although Broker has no obligation to investigate or inspect the Property, and no duty to verify
287 statements made, Broker shall have the right to terminate this Seller Listing Contract if the physical condition of the Property, Inclusions, any
288 proposed or existing transportation project, road, street or highway, or any other activity, odor or noise (whether on or off the Property) and its
289 effect or expected effect on the Property or its occupants, or if any facts or suspicions regarding circumstances that could psychologically
290 impact or stigmatize the Property are unsatisfactory to Broker.

292 **19. FORFEITURE OF PAYMENTS.** In the event of a forfeiture of payments made by a buyer, the sums received shall be divided between
293 Brokerage Firm and Seller, one-half thereof to Brokerage Firm but not to exceed the Brokerage Firm compensation agreed upon herein, and the
294 balance to Seller. Any forfeiture of payment under this section shall not reduce any Brokerage Firm compensation owed, earned and payable
295 under § 7.

297 **20. COST OF SERVICES AND REIMBURSEMENT.** Unless otherwise agreed upon in writing, Brokerage Firm shall bear all expenses
298 incurred by Brokerage Firm, if any, to market the Property and to compensate cooperating brokerage firms, if any. Neither Broker nor
299 Brokerage Firm shall obtain or order any other products or services unless Seller agrees in writing to pay for them promptly when due
300 (examples: surveys, radon tests, soil tests, title reports, engineering studies). Unless otherwise agreed, neither Broker nor Brokerage Firm shall
301 be obligated to advance funds for the benefit of Seller in order to complete a closing. Seller shall reimburse Brokerage Firm for payments made
302 by Brokerage Firm for such products or services authorized by Seller.

304 **21. DISCLOSURE OF SETTLEMENT COSTS.** Seller acknowledges that costs, quality, and extent of service vary between different
305 settlement service providers (e.g., attorneys, lenders, inspectors and title companies).

307 **22. MAINTENANCE OF THE PROPERTY.** Neither Broker nor Brokerage Firm shall be responsible for maintenance of the Property nor
308 shall they be liable for damage of any kind occurring to the Property, unless such damage shall be caused by their negligence or intentional
309 misconduct.

311 **23. NONDISCRIMINATION.** The parties agree not to discriminate unlawfully against any prospective buyer because of the race, creed,
312 color, sex, sexual orientation, marital status, familial status, physical or mental disability, handicap, religion, national origin or ancestry of such
313 person.

315 **24. RECOMMENDATION OF LEGAL AND TAX COUNSEL.** By signing this document, Seller acknowledges that Broker has advised
316 that this document has important legal consequences and has recommended consultation with legal and tax or other counsel before signing this
317 Seller Listing Contract.

319 **25. MEDIATION.** If a dispute arises relating to this Seller Listing Contract, prior to or after closing, and is not resolved, the parties shall first
320 proceed in good faith to submit the matter to mediation. Mediation is a process in which the parties meet with an impartial person who helps to
321 resolve the dispute informally and confidentially. Mediators cannot impose binding decisions. The parties to the dispute must agree, in writing,
322 before any settlement is binding. The parties will jointly appoint an acceptable mediator and will share equally in the cost of such mediation.
323 The mediation, unless otherwise agreed, shall terminate in the event the entire dispute is not resolved within 30 calendar days of the date written
324 notice requesting mediation is delivered by one party to the other at the party's last known address.

FIGURE 2–6
(continued)

326 **26. ATTORNEY FEES.** In the event of any arbitration or litigation relating to this Seller Listing Contract, the arbitrator or court shall award
327 to the prevailing party all reasonable costs and expenses, including attorney and legal fees.
328
329 **27. ADDITIONAL PROVISIONS.** (The following additional provisions have not been approved by the Colorado Real Estate Commission.)
330
331
332
333 **28. ATTACHMENTS.** The following are a part of this Seller Listing Contract:
334
335
336
337 **29. NO OTHER PARTY OR INTENDED BENEFICIARIES.** Nothing in this Seller Listing Contract shall be deemed to inure to the
338 benefit of any person other than Seller, Broker and Brokerage Firm.
339
340 **30. NOTICE, DELIVERY AND CHOICE OF LAW.**
341   **30.1. Physical Delivery.** All notices must be in writing, except as provided in § 30.2. Any document, including a signed document or
342 notice, delivered to the other party to this Seller Listing Contract, is effective upon physical receipt. Delivery to Seller shall be effective when
343 physically received by Seller, any signator on behalf of Seller, any named individual of Seller or representative of Seller.
344   **30.2. Electronic Delivery.** As an alternative to physical delivery, any document, including any signed document or written notice may
345 be delivered in electronic form only by the following indicated methods: **Facsimile   Email   Internet   No Electronic Delivery**.
346 Documents with original signatures shall be provided upon request of any party.
347   **30.3. Choice of Law.** This Seller Listing Contract and all disputes arising hereunder shall be governed by and construed in accordance
348 with the laws of the State of Colorado that would be applicable to Colorado residents who sign a contract in this state for property located in
349 Colorado.
350
351 **31. MODIFICATION OF THIS LISTING CONTRACT.** No subsequent modification of any of the terms of this Seller Listing Contract
352 shall be valid, binding upon the parties, or enforceable unless made in writing and signed by the parties.
353
354 **32. COUNTERPARTS.** If more than one person is named as a Seller herein, this Seller Listing Contract may be executed by each Seller,
355 separately, and when so executed, such copies taken together with one executed by Broker on behalf of Brokerage Firm shall be deemed to be a
356 full and complete contract between the parties.
357
358 **33. ENTIRE AGREEMENT.** This agreement constitutes the entire contract between the parties, and any prior agreements, whether oral or
359 written, have been merged and integrated into this Seller Listing Contract.
360
361 **34. COPY OF CONTRACT.** Seller acknowledges receipt of a copy of this Seller Listing Contract signed by Broker, including all
362 attachments.
363
364 Brokerage Firm authorizes Broker to execute this Seller Listing Contract on behalf of Brokerage Firm.
365

Date: _____   Date: _____

Seller's Name: _____   Broker's Name: _____

Seller's Signature   Broker's Signature

Address: _____   Address: _____

_____   _____

Phone No.: _____   Phone No.: _____

Fax No.: _____   Fax No.: _____

Email Address: _____   Email Address: _____

    Brokerage Firm's Name: _____

    Address: _____

    _____

    Phone No.: _____

    Fax No.: _____

    Email Address: _____

366

FIGURE 2–6
(continued)

1 The printed portions of this form, except differentiated additions, have been approved by the Colorado Real Estate Commission.
2 (EBA53-5-09) (Mandatory 7-09)

4 **THIS FORM HAS IMPORTANT LEGAL CONSEQUENCES AND THE PARTIES SHOULD CONSULT LEGAL AND TAX OR**
5 **OTHER COUNSEL BEFORE SIGNING.**

EXCLUSIVE BROKERAGE LISTING ADDENDUM
TO
EXCLUSIVE RIGHT-TO-SELL LISTING CONTRACT

11 Date: _____

13 **A.   ADDENDUM TO EXCLUSIVE RIGHT-TO-SELL LISTING CONTRACT.** This Exclusive Brokerage Listing Addendum
14 (Addendum) is made part of that Exclusive Right-To-Sell Listing Contract dated _____, (Seller Listing Contract),
15 between Seller and Brokerage Firm named below, for the property

16 known as No. _____.
17 Street Address   City   State   Zip
18 This Addendum shall control in the event of any conflict with the Seller Listing Contract to which it is attached.

20 **B.   PROVISIONS AMENDED.** The following provisions of the Seller Listing Contract are changed to read:

22 **1.   AGREEMENT.** Seller and Brokerage Firm enter into this exclusive, irrevocable contract (Seller Listing Contract) as of the date set
23 forth above. However, this Seller Listing Contract does not apply to a Sale of the Property to a buyer procured solely by Seller without the
24 assistance of Broker or any other person (Seller Sale).

26 **7.   COMPENSATION TO BROKERAGE FIRM; COMPENSATION TO COOPERATIVE BROKER.** Other than a Seller Sale,
27 Seller agrees that any Brokerage Firm compensation that is conditioned upon the Sale of the Property shall be earned by Brokerage Firm as
28 set forth herein without any discount or allowance for any efforts made by Seller or by any other person in connection with the Sale of the
29 Property.
30   **7.1.   Amount.** In consideration of the services to be performed by Broker, Seller agrees to pay Brokerage Firm as follows:
31   **7.1.1.   Sale Commission.** (1) _____% of the gross purchase price, or (2) _____,
32 in U.S. dollars.
33   **7.1.2.   Lease Commission.** If the box in § 3.5.2 is checked, Brokerage Firm shall be paid a fee equal to (1) _____% of
34 the gross rent under the lease, or (2) _____, in U.S. dollars, payable as follows: _____.
35   **7.2.   When Earned.** Such commission shall be earned upon the occurrence of any of the following:
36   **7.2.1.**   Any Sale of the Property, except a Seller Sale, within the Listing Period, by Broker or by any other person;
37   **7.2.2.**   Broker finding a buyer who is ready, willing and able to complete the transaction as specified herein by Seller; or
38   **7.2.3.**   Any Sale of the Property, except a Seller Sale, within _____ calendar days subsequent to the expiration of the
39 Listing Period (Holdover Period) to anyone with whom Broker negotiated and whose name was submitted, in writing, to Seller by Broker
40 during the Listing Period (including any extensions thereof). However, Seller   **Shall**   **Shall Not** owe commission to Brokerage Firm
41 under this § 7.2.3 if a commission is earned by another licensed real estate brokerage firm acting pursuant to an exclusive agreement entered
42 into during the Holdover Period.
43   **7.3.   When Applicable and Payable.** The commission obligation shall apply to a Sale, other than a Seller Sale, made during the
44 Listing Period or any extension of such original or extended term. The commission described in § 7.1.1 shall be payable at the time of the
45 closing of the Sale as contemplated by § 7.2.1 or § 7.2.3, or upon fulfillment of § 7.2.2 where either the offer made by such buyer is defeated
46 by Seller or by the refusal or neglect of Seller to consummate the Sale as agreed upon.
47   **7.4.   Other Compensation.** _____.

49 **10.   SELLER'S OBLIGATIONS TO BROKER; DISCLOSURES AND CONSENT.**
50   **10.1.   Negotiations and Communication.** Other than a Seller Sale, Seller agrees to conduct all negotiations for the Sale of the
51 Property only through Broker, and to refer to Broker all communications received in any form from real estate brokers, during the Listing
52 Period of this Seller Listing Contract.

54 **C.   ADDITIONAL AMENDMENTS:**

59 Brokerage Firm authorizes Broker to execute this Addendum on behalf of Brokerage Firm.

FIGURE 2–7
(continues)

Date: _____   Date: _____

Seller's Name: _____   Broker's Name: _____

_____   _____
Seller's Signature   Broker's Signature

                    Brokerage Firm's Name: _____

61

FIGURE 2–7
(continued)

Realizing the seriousness and legal complications of a listing, the terms, breadth, and powers of the document must be seriously weighed. Considering the primordial importance a home has for the average person, the generosity of realty commissions, and the emotional nature of buying and selling for the average person, the practitioner must employ clear and precise language in the listing agreement.

III. DISCLOSURE AND CONSUMER PROTECTION

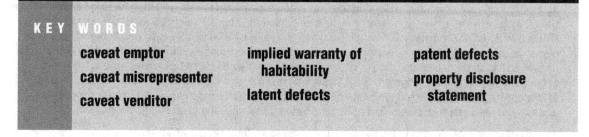

KEY WORDS

caveat emptor	implied warranty of habitability	patent defects
caveat misrepresenter		property disclosure statement
caveat venditor	latent defects	

After the preliminary steps of identifying broker/agents and the corresponding compensatory arrangement, the paralegal and supervising attorney need to collect, verify, and corroborate the integrity of their information. Each party to the process must relate accurate and reliable information about the property itself, its condition, and its legal status. Figure 2–8,[11] The Real Estate Interview Guide for Seller, is just the tool to gather this sort of data.

Here, one can be assured that the seller is satisfied with their representation and the terms under which they wish the sale to proceed. Here too, the seller affirms the condition of the property and discloses known defects in good faith. The rules of disclosure demand honesty and fair dealing in the assertion. Simultaneously, the listing agent is obliged to collect and portray accurate information regarding the property listed on the market, and sellers are duty-bound to disclose those **patent** and **latent defects** of which they are aware or which could be easily discovered. Agents and brokers bear a similar duty and cannot hide behind a real or feigned wall of ignorance about the condition of the property. Each must act in good faith and have an affirmative obligation to disclose what a reasonable person knows or can easily discern. Today, the thrust and burden rest with those that market the property. Gone are the days when the seller could simply remain silent.

In earlier days, the doctrine of **caveat emptor** ("let the buyer beware") applied. It was the buyer's responsibility to discover defects, either latent (hidden) or those obvious to the naked eye. Caveat emptor made sellers silent, or at least allowed them to feel right about their silence. In short, here's a house—take it as it is!

CASE LAW

Caveat emptor has long been part of the legal landscape in the American experience when the U.S. Supreme Court affirmed its black letter status in 1817.

Laidlaw v. Organ

15 U.S. (2 Wheat.) 178

Syllabus

The vendee of merchandise is not bound to communicate to the vendor intelligence of extrinsic circumstances exclusively within the knowledge of the vendee which may affect the price of the same.

It would be difficult circumscribe the contrary doctrine within proper limits when the means of intelligence are equally accessible to both. But at the same time, each party must take care not to say anything tending to impose upon the other.

(continues)

The defendant in error filed his petition or libel in the court below, stating that on 18 February, 1815, he purchased of the plaintiffs in error one hundred and eleven hogsheads of tobacco, as appeared by the copy of a bill of parcels annexed, and that the same were delivered to him by the said Laidlaw & Co., and that he was in the lawful and quiet possession of the said tobacco, when, on the 20th day of the said month, the said Laidlaw & Co., by force and of their own wrong, took possession of the same and unlawfully withheld the same from the petitioner notwithstanding he was at all times, and still was, ready to do and perform all things on his part stipulated to be done and performed in relation to said purchase, and had actually tendered to the said Laidlaw & Co. bills of exchange for the amount of the purchase money, agreeably to the said contract, to his damage, &c. Wherefore the petition prayed that the said Laidlaw & Co. might be cited to appear and answer to his plaint and that judgment might be rendered against them for his damages, &c. And inasmuch as the petitioner did verily believe that the said one hundred and eleven hogsheads of tobacco would be removed, concealed, or disposed of by the said Laidlaw & Co., he prayed that a writ of sequestration might issue and that the same might be sequestered in the hands of the marshal to abide the judgment of the court, and that the said one hundred and eleven hogsheads of tobacco might be finally adjudged to the petitioner, together with his damages, &c., and costs of suit, and that the petitioner might have such other and further relief as to the court should seem meet, &c.

The bill of parcels referred to in the petition was in the following words and figures, to-wit:

"Mr. Organ bought of Peter Laidlaw & Co. 111 hhds. Tobacco, weighing 120,715 pounds n't.—fr. $7,544.69."

"New Orleans, 18 February, 1815"

On 21 February, 1815, a citation to the said Laidlaw & Co. was issued, and a writ of sequestration, by order of the court, to the marshal, commanding him to sequester 111 hogsheads of tobacco in their possession, and the same so sequestered to take into his (the marshal's) possession, and safely keep, until the further order of the court; which was duly executed by the marshal. And on 2 March, 1815, counsel having been heard in the case, it was ordered that the petitioner enter into a bond or stipulation, with sufficient sureties in the sum of $1,000, to the said Laidlaw & Co., to indemnify them for the damages which they might sustain in consequence of prosecuting the writ of sequestration granted in the case.

On 22 March, 1815, the plaintiffs in error filed their answer stating that they had no property in the said tobacco claimed by the said petitioner or ownership whatever in the same, nor had they at any time previous to the bringing of said suit, but disclaimed all right, title, interest, and claim to the said tobacco, the subject of the suit. And on the same day, Messrs. Boorman & Johnston filed their bill of interpleader or intervention stating that the petitioner having brought his suit and filed his petition, claiming of the said Laidlaw & Co. 111 hogsheads of tobacco, for which he had obtained a writ of sequestration when, in truth, the said tobacco belonged to the said Boorman & Johnston, and was not the property of the said Laidlaw & Co., and praying that they, the said Boorman & Johnston, might be admitted to defend their right, title, and claim, to the said tobacco against the claim and pretensions of the petitioner, the justice of whose claim, under the sale as stated in his petition, was wholly denied, and that the said tobacco might be restored to them, &c.

On 20 April, 1815, the cause was tried by a jury, who returned the following verdict, to-wit: "The jury finds for the plaintiff for the tobacco named in the petition, without damages, payable as per contract." Whereupon the court rendered judgment

"That the plaintiff recover of the said defendants the said 111 hogsheads of tobacco, mentioned in the plaintiff's petition, and sequestered in this suit, with his costs of suit to be taxed, and ordered that the marshal deliver the said tobacco to the said plaintiff and that he have execution for his costs aforesaid upon the said plaintiff's depositing in this court his bills of exchange for the amount of the purchase money endorsed, &c., for the use of the defendants, agreeably to the verdict of the jury."

On 29 April, 1815, the plaintiffs in error filed the following bill of exceptions, to-wit:

"Be it remembered that on 20 April in the year of our Lord, 1815, the above cause came on for trial before a jury duly sworn and empanelled, the said Peter Laidlaw & Co. having filed a disclaimer, and Boorman and Johnston of the City of New York, having filed their claim.

Real Estate Interview Guide - Seller(s)

(Where space is found insufficient, use blank sheet and refer to question number)

File No. _____ Date of Interview _____ Interviewed by _____

Person(s) Present _____ Time _____ to _____

Referred by _____

☐ New Client ☐ Former Client ☐ Send a "Thank You" Letter

CLIENT

1. **CLIENT #1:**
   Full formal name _____

   Name to be referred to as _____

   a. Age _____ Birthdate _____ Soc. Sec. _____

   b. Variances in spelling _____

   c. Other names used (include maiden name) _____

   d. _____ State _____ Zip _____
   Municipality/Township/Boro/City/Town *(also Circle one)*

   e. Telephone: Home (___) _____ Listed ☐ Y ☐ N Business (___) _____

   Fax No.: Home (___) _____ Business (___) _____

   f. Citizenship _____

   g. Present mailing address (if different from "d") _____

2. **CLIENT #2:**
   Full formal name _____

   Name to be referred to as _____

   a. Age _____ Birthdate _____ Soc. Sec. _____

   b. Variances in spelling _____

   c. Other names used (include maiden name) _____

   d. Residence (if different from client #1) _____

   e. Telephone: Home (___) _____ Listed ☐ Y ☐ N Business (___) _____

   Fax no.: Home (___) _____ Business (___) _____

   f. Citizenship _____

1410S - Real Estate Interview Guide To Be Used for a Seller
Rev. 1/98   P 3/98

©1998 by ALL-STATE LEGAL®
A Division of ALL-STATE International, Inc.
www.aslegal.com   800.222.0510   Page 1

FIGURE 2–8
(continues)

PERSONAL DATA:

3. Date and place of present marriage _____

4. Previous Matrimonial Information

    a. Name of former spouse; date and location of this marriage: _____

    b. If prior spouse has died ___Yes ___No (go to #4c below).

        (1) Date and location of death: _____

        (2) Death certificate attached ___ Yes ___ No

        (3) Was estate probated in New Jersey ___ Yes ___No

        (4) Name and address of attorney who probated estate:

    c. If prior marriage ended in divorce:

        (1) Date _____

        (2) Judgment of divorce attached: ___ Yes ___ No (detail below)

            (i) If in New Jersey, County Judgment filed in: _____

            (ii) If another state or country, name, address and telephone number of attorney representing you: _____

            _____

5. Judgments or bankruptcies by any party _____

_____

_____

6. EMPLOYMENT INFORMATION:

    a. Employer of client #1: _____ (can we contact ___ Yes ___ No)

        Name: _____

        Address_____

        Telephone no._____ Fax no. _____

    b. Employer of client #2: _____ (can we contact ___ Yes ___ No)

        Name:_____

        Address_____

        Telephone no._____ Fax no. _____

1410S - Real Estate Interview Guide To Be Used for a Seller
Rev. 1/98   P 3/98

©1998 by ALL-STATE LEGAL®
A Division of ALL-STATE International, Inc.
www.aslegal.com   800.222.0510   Page 2

FIGURE 2–8
(continued)

7. OTHER PARTIES:

Full formal name _____

Name to be referred to as _____

a. Age _____ Birthdate _____ Soc. Sec. _____

b. Variances in spelling _____

c. Other names used (include maiden name) _____

d. Residence _____

e. Telephone: Home (_____) _____ Business (_____) _____

   Fax no.: Home (_____) _____ Fax no. Business (_____) _____

f. Person to contact _____

g. Attorney Name, Address, Tel. no. & Fax no. _____

_____

8. BROKERS:

a. Selling broker & firm _____

Address _____

Telephone: Home (_____) _____ Office (_____) _____

Fax no.: Home (_____) _____ Office (_____) _____

b. Listing broker _____

Address _____

Telephone: (_____) _____ Fax (_____) _____

c. Realtor's Commission _____

9. PROPERTY:

a. Address _____

_____

b. Tax Reference: Block _____ Lot _____ Qualifier No. _____ Annual Taxes $ _____

c. General description (include underground leaks if present) _____

_____

d. Present use _____

1410S - Real Estate Interview Guide To Be Used for a Seller
Rev. 1/98   P 3/98

FIGURE 2–8
(continued)

e. Zoning designation _____

f. Age of buildings and general physical condition _____

_____

_____

g. Changes to property lines (explain): _____

h. Fuel used: ☐ gas ☐ oil ☐ electric ☐ _____

i. Water: ☐ city ☐ private ☐ well ☐ _____

j. Sewerage: ☐ sewer ☐ septic ☐ _____

Any problems with above: _____

k. Recent (within last four months) or anticipated improvements or change in use and when _____

_____

l. Present and anticipated municipal assessments _____

_____

m. Does the town require a Certificate of Occupancy? _____

n. Is the property in a flood zone? _____

o. Present Tenants (list names, apartments, security deposits, lease terms and copies of leases and what appliances belong to each tenant):

_____

_____

_____

_____

_____

p. Are any guarantees transferable to the Buyers? _____

_____

q. Back Title (include details and copies of deed and title insurance) _____

_____

r. Name and Address of Title Company _____

_____

FIGURE 2–8
(continued)

s. Date of most recent survey and whether or not there have been changes to the property (obtain copies)

____

Surveyor name and address ______________________________

____

t. Is the property subject to any easements or restrictions? ______________________________

____

u. Eligibility of Buyers or Sellers for tax deductions (include details as to status claimed, such as veteran, senior citizen, disabled or surviving spouse)

____

____

____

v. Part of original property sold ___ Yes ___ No; if yes, detail:

____

____

____

10. MORTGAGE(S)

a. Present Mortgage(s): (names and addresses of holders, date payment due, where payment is due, account numbers, payment amount and type of mortgage) ______________________________

____

____

b. Problems regarding the Seller's buying or renting a new home (include new address, if known) ______________________________

____

____

11. CONTRACT DATA

a. Status of negotiations ______________________________

b. Desired closing date: ______________ ☐ Sellers ______________ ☐ Buyers ______________

c. Price $ ______________ Deposit $ ______________ Down payment $ ______________

d. Financing arrangements of Buyers and related contractual provisions ______________________________

____

1410S - Real Estate Interview Guide To Be Used for a Seller
Rev. 1/98 P 3/98

 Page 5

FIGURE 2–8
(continued)

Name and address of lending institution _____

Mortgage Amount _____ Interest Rate _____ Term: _____

e. Inspections desired (termite, structural, etc.) (If previous termite treatment, state date) _____

Date when all inspections are to be completed _____

Radon test: _____

Previously conducted __Yes __No If yes, has copy been provided to Buyer as per NJSA 26:2D-73 __Yes __No

f. Contractual provisions to be included or excluded from contract _____

_____

_____

_____

g. Items included or excluded from sale: _____

_____

Included	Excluded		Included	Excluded	
☐	☐	Air conditioner	☐	☐	Mirrors
☐	☐	Awnings	☐	☐	Refrigerator
☐	☐	Built-in cabinets and bookshelves	☐	☐	Smoke and fire alarms
☐	☐	Burglar alarm	☐	☐	Storm windows and doors
☐	☐	Carpeting	☐	☐	Trash cans
☐	☐	Chandelier	☐	☐	TV antenna and attachments
☐	☐	Dishwasher	☐	☐	Washing machine
☐	☐	Dryer	☐	☐	Water softener
☐	☐	Fireplace equipment	☐	☐	Window and door screens
☐	☐	Lighting fixtures	☐	☐	Window shades, curtains, draperies, rods, valances and supporting fixtures
☐	☐	Mats and matting in hall			

h. Are there any problems with above (specify) _____

_____

_____

FIGURE 2–8
(continued)

12. ☐ Copies needed (check if provided):   ☐ Latest property tax bill   ☐ Deed
                                                    ☐ Title Policy   ☐ Survey

13. Closing costs _____

14. Notes regarding explanations to client(s) _____

_____

_____

_____

_____

15. **ADDITIONAL INFORMATION**
(Details if Basement Flooding)

_____

_____

_____

_____

_____

_____

_____

_____

_____

_____

_____

_____

_____

_____

_____

_____

_____

_____

(Use back of form for additional information)

1410S - Real Estate Interview Guide To Be Used for a Seller
Rev. 1/98   P 3/98

©1998 by ALL-STATE LEGAL®
A Division of ALL-STATE International, Inc.
www.aslegal.com   800.222.0510   Page 7

FIGURE 2–8
(continued)

From a consumer's perspective, it was and still is a harsh reality.[12]

Web Exercise

For an interesting case where buyer alleges fraud due to the haunted house condition of a home to be purchased, listen to the audio file as to case argument at *www.audiocasefiles.com/acf_cases/8932-stambovsky-v-ackley*.

It is no longer safe to assume that a buyer will dutifully investigate the premises and be obliged to take the property as is. Buyers are now increasingly caricatured as unsophisticated and in need of legislative or judicial protections.

Frona M. Powell writes:

> Under the traditional doctrine of caveat emptor, courts protected sellers by requiring purchasers to protect their own interests by making an independent investigation of any assertions concerning the property. Today, the trend is toward placing the burden on the vendors to verify their facts before making representations and to grant the purchasers relief even though their failure to investigate constitutes negligence. Nevertheless, some courts continue to distinguish between fraudulent and nonfraudulent misrepresentation in determining what effect to give to a recipient's fault in not discovering the misrepresentation.[13]

For some theorists, the seller has the upper hand in the transaction.

> [The seller] . . . quite often possesses superior knowledge of the condition of the property and could be aware of defects not readily observable to even the most cautious buyer.[14]

For many years, the buyer's protection largely depended upon whether the seller's representations were innocent, ignorant, or malevolent or whether the buyer could have discovered the defect through the exercise of reasonable diligence. Seller had no liability for defects if his representations were the result of innocent ignorance. Liability attached to the sellers only when their representations were the result of fraudulent intent. When defects to the home are known by the seller, the question of disclosure varies according to jurisdiction, but the movement leans to an affirmative obligation. Increasingly, courts find that sellers have an obligation to disclose latent defects in the premises conveyed. To fail to disclose may give rise to an action in fraud and misrepresentation. At the same time, buyers have an obligation to investigate. The doctrine of caveat emptor still exists, though in a much softer form than its common-law counterpart. While the seller has more pressure applied to his obligation to know and disclose, the buyer must be vigilant and ferret out the obvious. And this obligation becomes more demanding upon the buyer when it can be shown the seller mistakenly represented, or negligently failed in some fashion rather than engaged in intentional falsehood. "Therefore, negligent misrepresentation claims will be barred in whole (contributory negligence) or in part (comparative negligence), if the purchaser failed to investigate the premises. The purchaser's duty to investigate is especially strong in three situations: (1) when the defect is obvious; (2) when the realtor is not the purchaser's agent; and (3) when the realtor's representation is vague."[15]

In truth, caveat emptor is being replaced with a new doctrine: **caveat venditor** ("let the seller beware").[16] Virtually, every jurisdiction has now backed away from an exclusive and strict application of the doctrine of caveat emptor due to harsh results.

CASE LAW

Caveat venditor expressly replaces caveat emptor in this Iowa Supreme Court decision. It is a rich opinion that traces and tracks the common law, modern statutory constructions, and the public policy implications of both theories.

IN THE SUPREME COURT OF IOWA

No. 103 / 05–1996

Filed February 1, 2008

ROBERT M. SPEIGHT and **BEVERLY E. SPEIGHT**,

Appellants,

vs.

WALTERS DEVELOPMENT COMPANY, LTD.,

Appellee.

On review from the Iowa Court of Appeals.

Appeal from the Iowa District Court for Polk County, Robert A. Hutchison, Judge.

Third-party purchasers of home appeal from summary judgment for builder in suit for breach of implied warranty of workmanlike construction. **DECISION OF COURT OF APPEALS VACATED; JUDGMENT OF DISTRICT COURT REVERSED; CASE REMANDED.**

Harley C. Erbe of Erbe Law Firm, West Des Moines, for appellants.

Brian P. Rickert and Michael J. Green of Brown, Winick, Graves, Gross, Baskerville & Schoenebaum, P.L.C., Des Moines, for appellee.

LARSON, Justice.

The plaintiffs, Robert and Beverly Speight, appeal from a summary judgment entered against them in their suit for breach of implied warranty of workmanlike construction against the builder of their home. The court of appeals affirmed. Both the district court and the court of appeals expressly declined to recognize an implied-warranty claim in favor of third-party purchasers, deferring for such a decision to this court. We now extend our common law of implied warranty to cover such parties and therefore vacate the decision of the court of appeals, reverse the judgment of the district court, and remand for further proceedings.

I. Facts and Prior Proceedings.

The Speights are the present owners of a home in Clive, Iowa, which was custom-built in 1995 by the defendant, Walters Development Company, Ltd. It was built for use by the original buyers, named Roche. The Roches sold the home to people named Rogers, who in turn sold it to the Speights on August 1, 2000. Sometime after purchasing the home, the Speights noticed water damage and mold. A building inspector determined that the damage was the result of a defectively constructed roof and defective rain gutters. Nothing in the record indicates that any of the owners between the original builder and the Speights had actual or imputed knowledge of these defects.

The Speights filed suit against Walters on May 23, 2005, alleging a breach of implied warranty of workmanlike construction and general negligence in construction of the home. Both the Speights and Walters moved for summary judgment, raising the issue of whether the Speights, as remote purchasers, could pursue a claim for breach of an implied warranty of workmanlike construction. Walters also raised the issue of whether the plaintiffs' claim for breach of implied warranty was barred by Iowa Code section 614.1(4) (2005), the applicable statute of limitations. The district court concluded that, under the present state of the law, the Speights could not maintain an implied-warranty claim, and in any event, such claim would be barred by the statute of limitations. The district court also concluded that the Speights could not bring a general negligence claim because they did not assert an accompanying claim for personal injury—a ruling the plaintiffs do not challenge on appeal.

II. The Implied-Warranty Claim.

The implied warranty of workmanlike construction is a judicially created doctrine implemented to protect an innocent home buyer by holding the experienced builder accountable for the quality of construction.

(continued)

See 17 Richard A. Lord, *Williston on Contracts* § 50:30 (4th ed. 2007) [hereinafter Lord]. Home buyers are generally in an inferior position when purchasing a home from a builder-vendor because of the buyer's lack of expertise in quality home construction and the fact that many defects in construction are latent. These defects, even if the home were inspected by a professional, would not be discoverable. *See* Sean M. O'Brien, Note, *Caveat Venditor: A Case for Granting Subsequent Purchasers a Cause of Action Against Builder-Vendors for Latent Defects in the Home*, 20 J. Corp. L. 525, 529 (Spring 1995).

The implied warranty of workmanlike construction addresses the inequities between the buyer and the builder-vendor by requiring that a building be constructed "in a reasonably good and workmanlike manner and . . . be reasonably fit for the intended purpose." *Kirk v. Ridgway*, 373 N.W.2d 491, 492 (Iowa 1985). In *Kirk* this court applied the doctrine of implied warranty of workmanlike construction to the sale of a home by the builder to the first owner. 373 N.W.2d at 496. In doing so, we noted that interest in consumer protection had increased, and the complexity of homes had increased, making it difficult for a buyer to discover defects in the construction. *Id.* at 493–94. In *Kirk* we rejected the application of the doctrine of *caveat emptor* under which "it has been observed, courts considered purchasing as a game of chance." *Id.* at 493 (citing Roberts, *The Case of the Unwary Home Buyer: The Housing Merchant Did It*, 52 Cornell L.Q. 835, 836 (1967)). We noted that home buyers are ill-equipped to discover defects in homes, which are increasingly complex, and therefore must rely on the skill and judgment of the vendor. *Id.* at 494.

In *Kirk* we held that, in order to sustain a claim that a builder-vendor has breached the implied warranty of workmanlike construction, the buyer must show:

(1) [t]hat the house was constructed to be occupied by the [buyer] as a home;

(2) that the house was zpurchased from a builder-vendor, who had constructed it for the purpose of sale;

(3) that when sold, the house was not reasonably fit for its intended purpose or had not been constructed in a good and workmanlike manner;

(4) that, at the time of purchase, the buyer was unaware of the defect and had no reasonable means of discovering it; and

(5) that by reason of the defective condition the buyer suffered damages.

Id. at 496; *see also Flom v. Stahly*, 569 N.W.2d 135, 142 (Iowa 1997). In *Kirk* we defined a "builder" as

> "a general building contractor who controls and directs the construction of a building, has ultimate responsibility for completion of the whole contract and for putting the structure into permanent form thus, necessarily excluding merchants, material men, artisans, laborers, subcontractors, and employees of a general contractor."

373 N.W.2d at 496 (quoting *Jeanguneat v. Jackie Hames Constr. Co.*, 576 P.2d 761, 762 (Okla. 1978)).

The plaintiffs ask this court to take the cause of action recognized in *Kirk* one step further by applying it to the case of a subsequent purchaser. Jurisdictions outside of Iowa are split on this issue.

Many jurisdictions do not permit subsequent purchasers to recover for a breach of the implied warranty of workmanlike construction.[1] This holding stems from the lack of a contractual relationship between the

---

[1] *See, e.g., Lee v. Clark & Assocs. Real Estate, Inc.*, 512 So. 2d 42 (Ala. 1987); *Aas v. Super. Ct.*, 12 P.3d 1125 (Cal. 2000) (superseded by statute on other grounds); *Cosmopolitan Homes, Inc. v. Weller*, 663 P.2d 1041 (Colo. 1983); *Coburn v. Lenox Homes, Inc.*, 378 A.2d 599 (Conn. 1977); *Council of Unit Owners of Sea Colony East, Phases III, IV, VI & VII v. Carl M. Freeman Assocs., Inc.*, 1989 WL 48568 (Del. Super. 1989); *Drexel Props., Inc. v. Bay Colony Club Condo., Inc.*, 406 So. 2d 515 (Fla. Dist. Ct. App. 1981), *disapproved of on other grounds by Casa Clara Condo. Ass'n, Inc. v. Charley Toppino & Sons, Inc.*, 620 So. 2d 1244 (Fla. 1993); *Dunant v. Wilmock, Inc.*, 335 S.E.2d 162 (Ga. Ct. App. 1985); *Miles v. Love*, 573 P.2d 622 (Kan. Ct. App. 1977); *Real Estate Mktg., Inc. v. Franz*, 885 S.W.2d 921 (Ky. 1994); *Tereault v. Palmer*, 413 N.W.2d 283 (Minn. Ct. App. 1987); *John H. Armbruster & Co. v. Hayden Co.—Builder Developer, Inc.*, 622 S.W.2d 704 (Mo. Ct. App. 1981); *Butler v. Caldwell & Cook, Inc.*, 505 N.Y.S.2d 288 (N.Y. App. Div. 1986); *Brown v. Fowler*, 279 N.W.2d 907 (S.D. 1979); *Briggs v. Riversound Ltd. P'ship*, 942 S.W.2d 529 (Tenn. Ct. App. 1996); *Schafir v. Harrigan*, 879 P.2d 1384 (Utah Ct. App. 1994); *Northridge Co. v. W.R. Grace & Co.*, 471 N.W.2d 179 (Wis. 1991).

subsequent purchaser and the builder-vendor. Michael A. DiSabatino, J.D., Annotation, *Liability of Builder of Residence for Latent Defects Therein as Running to Subsequent Purchasers from Original Vendee*, 10 A.L.R.4th 385, 388 (1981) [hereinafter DiSabatino]. The implied warranty of workmanlike construction is contractual in nature, and because privity is traditionally required in order to maintain a contract action, some courts have concluded that the lack of privity between the subsequent purchaser and the builder-vendor prevents the subsequent purchaser's implied-warranty claim. O'Brien, 20 J. Corp. L. at 537; *see also* Mary Dee Pridgen, *Consumer Protection and the Law* § 18:19 (2006) [hereinafter Pridgen] (discussing the holding in *Crowder v. Vandendeale*, 564 S.W.2d 879, 881 (Mo. 1978)); 2 James Acret, *Construction Law Digests* § 14:12 (2007) [hereinafter Acret] ("The implied warranty of habitability arises out of a contract between the builder and the initial buyer. There is no hint in the case law that it arises out of the general duty to build a reasonably fit house, by reason of which the builder would be liable to remote purchasers, that is, the general public, having no privity with it." (discussing the holding in *Foxcroft Townhome Owners Ass'n v. Hoffman Rosner Corp.*, 449 N.E.2d 125 (Ill. 1983))). Further, because there is a lack of privity between the subsequent purchaser and the builder-vendor, there is no reliance by the subsequent purchaser on any representations made by the builder-vendor regarding the quality of construction. See Pridgen, § 18:19. Finally, some courts have concluded that the justifications for eliminating the privity requirement in products liability cases do not exist in the sale of real estate. See DiSabatino, 10 A.L.R.4th at 397–98 ("The court reasoned that a house which is not the product of a mass marketing scheme or which is not designed as a temporary dwelling differs from the usual item to which the principles of strict liability have generally been applied, in that it is not an item which generally changes owners or occupants frequently." (discussing *Coburn v. Lenox Homes, Inc.*, 378 A.2d 599 (Conn. 1977))).

Other jurisdictions do permit subsequent purchasers to recover for a breach of the implied warranty of workmanlike construction.[2] The purpose of the implied warranty of workmanlike construction is to ensure that innocent home buyers are protected from latent defects. This principle is " 'equally applicable to subsequent purchasers' " who are in no better position to discover those defects than the original purchaser. Acret, § 14:12 (discussing and quoting the holding in *Lempke v. Dagenais*, 547 A.2d 290 (N.H. 1988)); *see also* Pridgen, § 18:19 (" 'The purpose of a warranty is to protect innocent purchasers and hold builders accountable for their work. With that object in mind, any reasoning which would arbitrarily interpose a first buyer as an obstruction to someone equally as deserving of recovery is incomprehensible.' " (quoting *Moxley v. Laramie Builders, Inc.*, 600 P.2d 733, 736 (Wyo. 1979))). Thus, the public policy justifications for eliminating the doctrine of caveat emptor for original purchasers of new homes similarly support allowing subsequent purchasers to recover on a theory of a breach of the implied warranty of workmanlike construction. *See* O'Brien, 20 J. Corp. L. at 531–32 ("[B]y definition, latent defects are not discoverable by reasonable inspection. Thus, home buyers are left with the choice of relying on a builder-vendor's expertise, or not buying a home at all. As one court stated, '(t)o apply the rule of caveat emptor to an inexperienced buyer, and in favor of a builder(-vendor) who is daily engaged in the business of building and selling houses is manifestly a denial of justice.' " (Internal citations omitted.)). Further, the purpose of the implied warranty of workmanlike construction is to ensure the home " 'will be fit for habitation,' a matter that 'depends upon the quality of the dwelling delivered' not the status of the buyer." Pridgen, § 18:19 (quoting *Tusch Enters. v. Coffin*, 740 P.2d 1022 (Idaho 1987)).

The lack of privity between the subsequent purchaser and the builder-vendor is not an impediment, in these jurisdictions, to allowing a subsequent purchaser to recover on an implied-warranty claim.

---

[2]*See, e.g., Richards v. Powercraft Homes, Inc.*, 678 P.2d 427 (Ariz. 1984); *Blagg v. Fred Hunt Co.*, 612 S.W.2d 321 (Ark. 1981); *Tusch Enters. v. Coffin*, 740 P.2d 1022 (Idaho 1987); *Redarowicz v. Ohlendorf*, 441 N.E.2d 324 (Ill. 1982); *Barnes v. Mac Brown & Co.*, 342 N.E.2d 619 (Ind. 1976); *Degeneres v. Burgess*, 486 So. 2d 769 (La. Ct. App. 1986); *Dunelawn Owners' Ass'n v. Gendreau*, 750 A.2d 591 (Me. 2000) (citing 33 M.R.S.A. § 1604–113(f)); *Keyes v. Guy Bailey Homes, Inc.*, 439 So. 2d 670 (Miss. 1983); *Moglia v. McNeil Co.*, 700 N.W.2d 608 (Neb. 2005); *Lempke v. Dagenais*, 547 A.2d 290 (N.H. 1988); *Hermes v. Staiano*, 437 A.2d 925 (N.J. 1981); *Gaito v. Auman*, 327 S.E.2d 870 (N.C. 1985); *Baddour v. Fox*, 2004 WL 1327925 (Ohio Ct. App. 2004); *Elden v. Simmons*, 631 P.2d 739 (Okla. 1981); *Nichols v. R.R. Beaufort & Assocs., Inc.*, 727 A.2d 174 (R.I. 1999); *Terlinde v. Neely*, 271 S.E.2d 768 (S.C. 1980); *Gupta v. Ritter Homes, Inc.*, 646 S.W.2d 168 (Tex. 1983), *overruled in relevant part in Amstadt v. U.S. Brass Corp.*, 919 S.W.2d 644 (Tex. 1996); *Sewell v. Gregory*, 371 S.E.2d 82 (W. Va. 1988); *Moxley v. Laramie Builders, Inc.*, 600 P.2d 733 (Wyo. 1979).

(continued)

Though the implied warranty of workmanlike construction " 'has roots in the execution of the contract for sale,' " it exists independently of the contract by its very nature. O'Brien, 20 J. Corp. L. at 538 (citations omitted). Additionally, requiring privity to sue for a breach of an implied warranty has been disfavored in products liability cases in some jurisdictions. Many jurisdictions find similar justifications for extinguishing the privity requirement in the purchase of a home. See O'Brien, § 50:30 ("[T]he builder was in the same position as a manufacturer who sells an article which, if defective, will be imminently dangerous to persons who come in contact with it, 'and liability is not limited to those with whom the manufacturer contracts.' " (quoting *Leigh v. Wadsworth*, 361 P.2d 849 (Okla. 1961))). From a practical perspective, these jurisdictions note that many latent defects "are often not discoverable for some time after completion of the house. By the time the defects come to light, the original purchasers may have sold the home. For that reason, subsequent purchasers need protection for faulty construction." Pridgen, § 18:19. Additionally, the reality is that our society is increasingly mobile, and as a result, a home's ownership is likely to change hands a number of times. See O'Brien, 20 J. Corp. L. at 526 (noting that, at the time the note was written, "[n]early four million single-family used homes [were] sold in the United States every year"). A blanket rule prohibiting subsequent purchasers from recovering for a breach of the implied warranty of workmanlike construction would do injustice to those who purchase a home from a previous buyer shortly after the home was constructed when the subsequent purchaser later discovers that the home was defectively constructed. See id. at 538. Finally, one author posits that the doctrine of assignment allows for the transfer to the subsequent purchaser of the original purchaser's right to sue for breach of the implied warranty of workmanlike construction. Id. at 538–40.

We believe that Iowa law should follow the modern trend allowing a subsequent purchaser to recover against a builder-vendor for a breach of the implied warranty of workmanlike construction. As in many jurisdictions, this court has eliminated the privity requirement in products liability cases raising a breach-of-implied-warranty claim. *See State Farm Mut. Auto. Ins. Co. v. Anderson-Weber, Inc.*, 110 N.W.2d 449, 456 (Iowa 1961). As the court discussed in *State Farm*, the privity requirement was eliminated in other jurisdictions to " 'ameliorate the harsh doctrine of *caveat emptor*,' " and because " 'the [implied warranty] obligations on the part of the seller were imposed by operation of law, and did not depend for their existence upon express agreement of the parties,' " privity was not necessary. *Id.* at 454 (quoting *Henningsen v. Bloomfield Motors, Inc.*, 161 A.2d 69 (N.J. 1960)). The same is true in a case such as the present one in which a home buyer raises an implied-warranty claim. Further, the implied warranty of workmanlike construction is a judicial creation and does not, in itself, arise from the language of any contract between the builder-vendor and the original purchaser. Thus, it is not extinguished upon the original purchaser's sale of the home to a subsequent purchaser. The builder-vendor warrants that the home was constructed in a workmanlike manner, not that it is fit for any particular purpose the original owner intended. As such, there is no contractual justification for limiting recovery to the original purchaser.

Additionally, the public policy justifications supporting our decision to recede from the doctrine of *caveat emptor* in the sale of new homes by builder-vendors equally apply to the sale of used homes to subsequent purchasers. As discussed above, latent defects are, by definition, undiscoverable by reasonable inspection. Thus, the subsequent purchaser is in no better position to discover those defects than the original purchaser. It is inequitable to allow an original purchaser to recover while, simultaneously, prohibiting a subsequent purchaser from recovering for latent defects in homes that are the same age.

Walters contends that allowing the recovery the Speights seek would lead to increased costs for builders, increased claims, and increased home prices. However, builder-vendors are currently required to build a home in a good and workmanlike manner. The implied warranty of workmanlike construction reasonably puts the risk of shoddy construction on the builder-vendor. The builder-vendor's risk is not increased by allowing subsequent purchasers to recover for the same latent defects for which an original purchaser could recover. As discussed more fully below, the statute of limitations and statute of repose are the same for original purchasers and subsequent purchasers, thus eliminating any increased time period within which a builder-vendor is subject to suit.

Walters argues that allowing subsequent purchasers to recover for a breach of the implied warranty of workmanlike construction would subject builder-vendors to unlimited liability; however, we are not persuaded. Iowa Code section 614.1(11) provides a safety net—a statute of repose for potential plaintiffs seeking to recover for breach of an implied warranty on an improvement to real property. A statute of repose works to " 'terminate[] any right of action after a specified time has elapsed, regardless of whether or not there has as yet been an injury.' " *Bob McKiness Excavating & Grading, Inc. v. Morton*, 507 N.W.2d 405, 408 (Iowa 1993) (quoting *Hanson v. Williams County*, 389 N.W.2d 319, 321 (N.D. 1986)). Section 614.1(11) applies to an action for breach of the implied warranty of workmanlike construction in the purchase of a building. *See id.* at 409. That section provides

> an action arising out of the unsafe or defective condition of an improvement to real property based on tort and implied warranty . . . and founded on injury to property, real or personal, or injury to the person or wrongful death, shall not be brought more than fifteen years after the date on which occurred the act or omission of the defendant alleged in the action to have been the cause of the injury or death.

Iowa Code § 614.1(11). Pursuant to section 614.1(11), the period of repose begins to run on the date of the act or omission causing the injury. In cases involving the construction of a building, such as this home, that period begins upon completion of the construction of the building. *See Bob McKiness Excavating & Grading, Inc.*, 507 N.W.2d at 409. As a result, builder-vendors are not liable on an implied-warranty claim after the statute of repose has run, regardless of who owns the home. In summary, we adopt what we view to be the emerging and better view that subsequent purchasers may recover for breach of implied warranty of workmanlike construction against a builder-vendor as recognized in *Kirk* for first-party purchasers. Subsequent purchasers, of course, may not be afforded greater rights of recovery than the original purchasers.

III. The Statute of Limitations.

The defendant contends that, even if we recognize a cause of action under these circumstances, it would be barred by the statute of limitations under Iowa Code section 614.1(4). The district court and the court of appeals agreed and concluded that this suit was time-barred. We disagree.

Under Iowa Code section 614.1,

> [a]ctions may be brought within the times herein limited, respectively, *after their causes accrue*, and not afterwards, except when otherwise specially declared:
>
> . . . .
>
> 4. *Unwritten contracts—injuries to property—fraud— other actions.* Those founded on unwritten contracts, those brought for injuries to property, or for relief on the ground of fraud in cases heretofore solely cognizable in a court of chancery, and all other actions not otherwise provided for in this respect, within five years . . . .

(Emphasis added.)

The question in this case is when the plaintiffs' cause of action accrued. The defendant argues, and the district court held, that the cause of action accrued in 1995, when the house was sold by the defendant to the original purchasers. The Speights filed this suit in 2005, which was well beyond the five-year statute of limitations, according to the defendant. The defendant's time-bar argument relies on Iowa Code section 554.2725(2), under which all actions for breach of implied warranty accrue at the time of delivery, not at the time the damage is discovered. The Speights counter that their claim is not based on the sale of goods and, therefore, section 554.2725(2), which is part of the Uniform Commercial Code (UCC), does not apply. We agree with the Speights' position. Article 2 of the UCC applies only to transactions involving the sale of goods. Iowa Code § 554.2102. Goods are "all things . . . which are movable at the time of identification to the contract for sale." *Id.* § 554.2105(1). Clearly, the construction of a home is not a transaction for the sale of goods to which the UCC applies. Therefore, the limitation provided in section 554.2725(2) does not apply to cases such as the present one. We made that clear in *Brown v. Ellison*, 304 N.W.2d 197 (Iowa 1981), in which we distinguished cases involving breach of implied warranties of workmanship from those under the UCC.

> We hold that the discovery rule is applicable to cases arising from express and implied warranties. This holding, of course, does not apply to situations in which statutes expressly provide that a cause of action accrues when the breach occurs, regardless of the aggrieved

(continued)

party's lack of knowledge of the breach. *See, e.g.*, Iowa Uniform Commercial Code, § 554.2725 . . . . The trial court was, therefore, correct in applying the discovery rule.

Brown, 304 N.W.2d at 201.

We reject the defendant's argument that the plaintiffs' cause of action accrued in 1995 when the house was originally sold. Under the discovery rule, a cause of action does not accrue until the injured party has actual or imputed knowledge of the facts that would support a cause of action. We have said:

> "Knowledge is imputed to a claimant when he gains information sufficient to alert a reasonable person of the need to investigate. As of that date he is on inquiry notice of all facts that would have been disclosed by a reasonably diligent investigation."

Perkins v. HEA of Iowa, Inc., 651 N.W.2d 40, 44 (Iowa 2002) (quoting *Ranney v. Parawax Co.*, 582 N.W.2d 152, 155 (Iowa 1998)). The Speights' suit was filed on May 23, 2005, which was within five years of their purchase of the home. It cannot, therefore, be credibly argued that the plaintiffs had knowledge—either actual or imputed—of the defect more than five years before their suit was filed because they did not even own the property at that time.

We adopt and apply the doctrine of implied warranty of workmanlike construction to subsequent, as well as initial, purchasers. We conclude as a matter of law that the plaintiffs could not have gained actual or imputed knowledge of the defect in their home more than five years prior to commencing this action, and their suit is therefore not time-barred under Iowa Code section 614.1(4). We vacate the decision of the court of appeals, reverse the judgment of the district court, and remand for further proceedings.

DECISION OF COURT OF APPEALS VACATED; JUDGMENT OF DISTRICT COURT REVERSED; CASE REMANDED.

All justices concur except Appel, J., who takes no part.

Some have suggested the traditional test of caveat emptor be supplanted by **caveat misrepresenter**. Five types of misrepresentations have been recognized by courts:

1. fraudulent
2. reckless
3. negligent
4. innocent
5. silent[17]

All of these tests impose a burden on sellers to disclose.

The liability imposed depends on the mentality of those making the representations. Unsophisticated sellers are clearly not held to the same standard as brokers and agents. "Real estate agents can no longer hide behind the shield of caveat emptor when they make material misrepresentations to purchasers. Even in jurisdictions not recognizing innocent misrepresentations, real estate agents expose themselves to considerable liability when making representations to purchasers. Any material misstatements about the property will likely constitute reckless or negligent misrepresentations, and any material nondisclosure of property defects will likely constitute silent misrepresentations."[18]

This trend toward buyer protection has been even more aggressively applied in **latent defect** cases that involve new housing construction. Caveat venditor is based on a premise that a sound price calls for a sound article; and that when one sells an article, the seller implies that it has value.[19] In this sense, the seller by selling a house implies warranty of its fitness as a house.[20] Certain U.S. jurisdictions refer to this as an **implied warranty of habitability**, with courts sometimes interchanging the word "habitability" with "fitness, workmanlike construction, quality, or suitability."[21] The theory recognizes that ordinary home purchasers are generally forced to rely upon a builder-vendor's skill and experience when purchasing new homes. In effect, courts invoking the doctrine conclude that implied in the sale of a home is a guarantee that the home was built in a workmanlike manner and is suitable for habitation.[22]

With these issues in mind, it is no wonder that property owners and the agents who represent them are cautious about what they say.[23] As the proconsumer, probuyer standards multiply, automatic disclosure rules multiply simultaneously.

Web Exercise

Implied Warranty of Habitability: Texas has adopted various provisions that relate to new constructions. Visit Texas Statutes, Title 16, Chapter 430 at *www.statutes.legis.state.tx.us/Index.aspx.*

Both sellers and agents prepare a **property disclosure statement** for use in multilist programs. See Figure 2–9[24] for a complete series of disclosures relative to major home systems.

Agents and brokers usually reference this disclosure statement in their listing agreement.

The property disclosure statement is the seller's report on the current condition of their home, with representations on occupancy, soil and boundaries, roof, pests, structural quality, plumbing, basement and garage, additions, heating, air conditioning, electric system, appliances, and environmental concerns contained therein.

IV. BROKER/AGENT DISCLOSURE

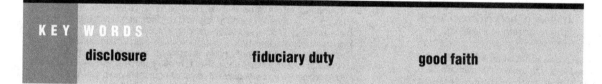

KEY WORDS		
disclosure	fiduciary duty	good faith

Brokers and agents are held to even higher standards relative to **disclosure**[25] because of their experience, training, fiduciary responsibilities, and contractual **good faith.** Courts often speak of "broker expertise," acknowledging that brokers have risen to an advantageous position in the real estate market. Unlike buyers, brokers are involved in countless real estate transactions each year and, therefore, conduct numerous inspections of property every year. Buyers rely on brokers precisely because of this experience and training. Buyers perceive that the licensing requirements of brokers and their constant involvement with residential real property must breed in them "expertise." Indeed, it is this expertise that buyers solicit when contacting a real estate broker.[26] But this general rule is peppered with exceptions and technical difficulties. Too often buyers are afforded less protection than sellers. Argued from another slant, it is the seller's commission that tends to predispose the agency. Commissions are what real estate agents think of first, though this economic incentive, intentionally or inadvertently, affects the purity of representation. Hence, many states now mandate "choice" of representations. Gretchen Coles describes the process as a sort of "Miranda warning":

> A Miranda-style warning for potential buyers—an ironically true portrayal of the current world of real estate. Every day thousands of consumers are faced with a confusing real estate disclosure and they are forced to make complex choices about their representation. In the past it was simple—brokers represented sellers. As real estate practice changed, and courts across the country expanded broker's duties to include duties to buyers, legislatures responded with added disclosure requirements and codified arrangements of agency relationships for brokers. Instead of correcting the true problem of confusion by buyers, these disclosures and arrangements only added complexity for brokers and consumers.[27]

Web Exercise

Visit a statutory authority on broker/agent fiduciary duty at *www.ct.gov/dcp/lib/dcp/dcp_regulations/ 20–325d_real_estate_brokers_and_salesmen_(1).pdf.*

RESIDENTIAL SELLER ADVISORY

Document updated:
February 2008

WHEN IN DOUBT – DISCLOSE!

Sellers are obligated by law to disclose all known material (important) facts about the property to the buyer. Arizona law requires that you disclose material facts about the property whether or not you are asked by the buyer or a real estate agent, or when asked to complete a disclosure form. There are also some very specific seller disclosures that you are required by statute to make. For example, sellers are required to disclose information on lead based paint in homes built prior to 1978, and if the property is in the vicinity of a military or public airport. **You may also be required to complete and record an Affidavit of Disclosure if you are selling property in an unincorporated area of a county.**

> *"...you have a duty to disclose the information, regardless of whether or not you consider the information material."*

If the buyer asks you about an aspect of the property, you have a duty to disclose the information, regardless of whether or not you consider the information material. You also have a legal duty to disclose facts when disclosure is necessary to prevent a previous statement from being misleading or misrepresented: for example, if something changes. However, a seller does not generally have a legal obligation to correct defects in the property, as long as the defects are disclosed. Any correction of the defects is a matter of contract negotiation between you and the buyer.

If you do not make the legally required disclosures, you may be subject to civil liability. Under certain circumstances, nondisclosure of a fact is the same as saying that the fact does not exist. Therefore, nondisclosure may be given the same legal effect as fraud.

The Arizona Association of REALTORS® Residential Seller's Property Disclosure Statement ("SPDS") is designed to assist you in making these legally required disclosures and to avoid inadvertent nondisclosures of material facts.

You should complete the SPDS by answering all questions as truthfully and as thoroughly as possible. Attach copies of any available invoices, warranties, inspection reports, and leases, to insure that you are disclosing accurate information. Also, use the blank lines to explain your answers. If you do not have the personal knowledge to answer a question, it is important not to guess — use the blank lines to explain the situation.

The SPDS is divided into six general sections:

(1) **Ownership and Property:** This section asks for general information about the property, such as location, ownership and occupancy. Any seller, whether or not that seller has actually lived in the property, should be able to answer most, if not all, of the questions in this section.

(2) **Building and Safety Information:** This section asks for information regarding the physical aspects of the property. You should disclose any past or present problems with the property and any work or improvements made to the property. You are also asked specifically to disclose any knowledge of past or current presence of termites or other wood destroying organisms on the property, and whether scorpions or other possible "pests" have ever been present on the property. Although many sellers will answer affirmatively to these questions, they were necessitated by lawsuits involving the alleged non-disclosure of these natural inhabitants.

(3) **Utilities:** You are asked whether the property currently receives the listed utilities, and if so, to identify the provider. The water source and any known information about drinking water problems should also be disclosed.

(4) **Environmental Information:** A variety of environmental information is requested. In addition to questions regarding environmental hazards, you are asked to disclose any issues relating to soil settlement/expansion, drainage/grade, or erosion; noise from the surrounding area including airport and traffic noise; and any odors or other nuisances. As a result of recent lawsuits and potential health concerns, you are asked specifically if you are aware of any past or present mold growth on the property. Mold spores are everywhere and when mold spores drop in places where there is water damage or excessive moisture, or where there has been flooding, mold will grow. Thus, you are asked to disclose any conditions conducive to mold growth, such as past or present dampness/moisture, flooding, and water damage or water leaks of any kind.

(5) **Sewer/Waste Water Treatment:** There are many questions dealing with the topic of sewer or wastewater treatment as a result of claims involving alleged misrepresentations that the property was connected to a sewer, when in fact it was not. You are asked if the entire property is connected to a sewer and if so, whether the sewer connection has been professionally verified. If the property is served by an on-site wastewater treatment facility, i.e., a septic or alternative wastewater system, a variety of additional information is required.

(6) **Other Conditions and Factors – Additional Explanations:** These blank lines provide space for you to disclose any other important information concerning the property that might affect the buyer's decision-making process, the value of the property, or its use, and to make any other necessary explanations.

Please note: By law, sellers are not obligated to disclose that the property is or has been: (1) the site of a natural death, suicide, homicide, or any other crime classified as a felony; (2) owned or occupied by a person exposed to HIV, or diagnosed as having AIDS or any other disease not known to be transmitted through common occupancy of real estate; or (3) located in the vicinity of a sex offender. However, the law does not protect a seller who makes an intentional misrepresentation. For example, if you are asked whether there has been a death on the property and you know that there was such a death, you should not answer "no" or "I don't know"; instead you should either answer truthfully or respond that you are not legally required to answer the question.

FIGURE 2–9
(continues)

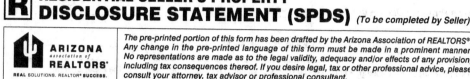

Page 1 of 6

RESIDENTIAL SELLER'S PROPERTY
DISCLOSURE STATEMENT (SPDS) *(To be completed by Seller)*

Document updated:
February 2008

The pre-printed portion of this form has been drafted by the Arizona Association of REALTORS®. Any change in the pre-printed language of this form must be made in a prominent manner. No representations are made as to the legal validity, adequacy and/or effects of any provision, including tax consequences thereof. If you desire legal, tax or other professional advice, please consult your attorney, tax advisor or professional consultant.

MESSAGE TO THE SELLER:

Sellers are obligated by law to disclose all known material (important) facts about the Property to the Buyer. The SPDS is designed to assist you in making these disclosures. If you know something important about the Property that is not addressed on the SPDS, add that information to the form. Prospective Buyers may rely on the information you provide.

INSTRUCTIONS: (1) Complete this form yourself. (2) Answer all questions truthfully and as fully as possible. (3) Attach all available supporting documentation. (4) Use explanation lines as necessary. (5) If you do not have the personal knowledge to answer a question, use the explanation lines to explain. *By signing below you acknowledge that the failure to disclose known material information about the Property may result in liability.*

MESSAGE TO THE BUYER:

Although Sellers are obligated to disclose all known material (important) facts about the Property, there are likely facts about the Property that the Sellers do not know. Therefore, it is important that you take an active role in obtaining information about the Property.

INSTRUCTIONS: (1) Review this form and any attachments carefully. (2) Verify all important information. (3) Ask about any incomplete or inadequate responses. (4) Inquire about any concerns not addressed on the SPDS. (5) Review all other applicable documents, such as CC&R's, association bylaws, surveys, rules, and the title report or commitment. (6) Obtain professional inspections of the Property. (7) Investigate the surrounding area.

THE FOLLOWING ARE REPRESENTATIONS OF THE SELLER(S) AND ARE NOT VERIFIED BY THE BROKER(S) OR AGENT(S).

OWNERSHIP AND PROPERTY

1. As used herein, "Property" shall mean the real property and all fixtures and improvements thereon and appurtenances incidental thereto,
2. plus fixtures and personal property described in the Contract.

3. **PROPERTY ADDRESS:** _____
   (STREET ADDRESS)　　　　　　(CITY)　　　　(STATE)　　(ZIP)

4. Is the Property located in an unincorporated area of the county? ☐ **Yes** ☐ **No** If yes, and five or fewer parcels of land other than subdivided
5. **land are being transferred, the Seller must furnish the Buyer with a written Affidavit of Disclosure in the form required by law.**

6. **LEGAL OWNER(S) OF PROPERTY:** _____ Date Purchased: _____

7. Is the legal owner(s) of the Property a foreign person or a non-resident alien pursuant to the Foreign Investment in Real Property
8. Tax Act (FIRPTA)? ☐ **Yes** ☐ **No** **If yes, consult a tax advisor; mandatory withholding may apply.**

9. Is the property located in a community defined by the fair housing laws as housing for older persons? ☐ **Yes** ☐ **No**
10. Explain: _____

11. Approximate year built: _____. **If Property was built prior to 1978, Seller must furnish the Buyer with a lead-based paint disclosure form.**

12. **NOTICE TO BUYER: IF THE PROPERTY IS IN A SUBDIVISION, A SUBDIVISION PUBLIC REPORT, WHICH CONTAINS A VARIETY OF INFOR-**
13. **MATION ABOUT THE SUBDIVISION AT THE TIME THE SUBDIVISION WAS APPROVED, MAY BE AVAILABLE BY CONTACTING THE**
14. **ARIZONA DEPARTMENT OF REAL ESTATE OR THE HOMEBUILDER. THE PUBLIC REPORT INFORMATION MAY BE OUTDATED.**

15. The Property is currently: ☐ **Owner-occupied** ☐ **Leased** ☐ **Estate** ☐ **Foreclosure** ☐ **Vacant** If vacant, how long?_____
16. If a rental property, how long? _____ Expiration date of current lease: _____ (Attach a copy of the lease if available.)
17. If any refundable deposits or prepaid rents are being held, by whom and how much? Explain: _____
18. _____

	YES	NO	
19.	☐	☐	Have you entered into any agreement to transfer your interest in the Property in any way, including rental renewals
20.			or options to purchase? Explain: _____
21.	☐	☐	Are you aware if there are any association(s) governing this Property?
22.			If yes, provide contact(s) information: Name: _____ Phone #: _____
23.			If yes, are there any fees? How much? $_____ How often? _____
24.	☐	☐	Are you aware of any transfer fees or other fees due upon transfer of the Property? Explain: _____
25.			_____

>>

Initials>

BUYER	BUYER

FIGURE 2–9
(continued)

Residential Seller's Property Disclosure Statement (SPDS) >>

	YES	NO	
26.	☐	☐	Are you aware of any proposed or existing association assessment(s)? Explain: _____
27.			_____
28.	☐	☐	Are you aware of any pending or anticipated disputes or litigation regarding the Property or the association(s)?
29.			Explain: _____
30.	☐	☐	Are you aware of any of the following recorded against the Property? (Check all that apply):
31.			☐ Judgment liens ☐ Tax liens ☐ Other non-consensual liens
32.			Explain: _____
33.	☐	☐	Are you aware of any assessments affecting this Property? (Check all that apply)
34.			☐ Paving ☐ Sewer ☐ Water ☐ Electric ☐ Other
35.			Explain: _____
36.	☐	☐	Are you aware of any title issues affecting this Property? (Check all that apply):
37.			☐ Recorded easements ☐ Use restrictions ☐ Lot line disputes ☐ Encroachments
38.			☐ Unrecorded easements ☐ Use permits ☐ Other _____
39.			Explain: _____
40.	☐	☐	Are you aware of any public or private use paths or roadways on or across this Property?
41.			Explain: _____
42.	☐	☐	Are you aware of any problems with legal or physical access to the Property? Explain: _____
43.			The road/street access to the Property is maintained by the ☐ **County** ☐ **City** ☐ **Homeowners' Association** ☐ **Privately**
44.	☐	☐	If privately maintained, is there a recorded road maintenance agreement? Explain: _____
45.	☐	☐	Are you aware of any violation(s) of any of the following? (Check all that apply)
46.			☐ Zoning ☐ Building Codes ☐ Utility Service ☐ Sanitary health regulations
47.			☐ Covenants, Conditions, Restrictions (CC&R's) ☐ Other _____ (Attach a copy of notice(s) of violation if available.)
48.			Explain: _____
49.			_____
50.	☐	☐	Are you aware of any homeowner's insurance claims having been filed against the Property?
51.			Explain: _____

52. NOTICE TO BUYER: YOUR CLAIMS HISTORY, YOUR CREDIT REPORT, THE PROPERTY'S CLAIMS HISTORY
53. AND OTHER FACTORS MAY AFFECT THE INSURABILITY OF THE PROPERTY AND AT WHAT COST. UNDER
54. ARIZONA LAW, YOUR INSURANCE COMPANY MAY CANCEL YOUR HOMEOWNER'S INSURANCE WITHIN 60
55. DAYS AFTER THE EFFECTIVE DATE. CONTACT YOUR INSURANCE COMPANY.

BUILDING AND SAFETY INFORMATION

	YES	NO	
56.			**STRUCTURAL:**
57.	☐	☐	Are you aware of any past or present roof leaks? Explain: _____
58.			_____
59.	☐	☐	Are you aware of any other past or present roof problems? Explain: _____
60.			_____
61.	☐	☐	Are you aware of any roof repairs? Explain: _____
62.			_____
63.	☐	☐	Is there a roof warranty? (Attach a copy of warranty if available.)
64.	☐	☐	If yes, is the roof warranty transferable? Cost to transfer _____
65.			**NOTICE TO BUYER: CONTACT A PROFESSIONAL TO VERIFY THE CONDITION OF THE ROOF.**
66.	☐	☐	Are you aware of any interior wall/ceiling/door/window/floor problems? Explain: _____
67.			_____
68.	☐	☐	Are you aware of any cracks or settling involving the foundation, exterior walls or slab? Explain: _____
69.			_____
70.	☐	☐	Are you aware of any chimney or fireplace problems, if applicable? Explain: _____
71.			_____

>>

Initials> | BUYER | BUYER |

FIGURE 2-9
(continued)

Residential Seller's Property Disclosure Statement (SPDS) >>

	YES	NO	
72.	☐	☐	Are you aware of any damage to any structure on the Property by any of the following? (Check all that apply):
73.			☐ Flood ☐ Fire ☐ Wind ☐ Expansive soil(s) ☐ Water ☐ Hail ☐ Other _____
74.			Explain: _____

75. **WOOD INFESTATION:**
76. Are you aware of any of the following:

	YES	NO	
77.	☐	☐	Past presence of termites or other wood destroying organisms on the Property?
78.	☐	☐	Current presence of termites or other wood destroying organisms on the Property?
79.	☐	☐	Past or present damage to the Property by termites or other wood destroying organisms?
80.			Explain: _____
81.			_____
82.	☐	☐	Are you aware of past or present treatment of the Property for termites or other wood destroying organisms?
83.			If yes, date last treatment was performed: _____
84.			Name of treatment provider: _____
85.	☐	☐	Is there a treatment warranty? (Attach a copy of warranty if available.)
86.	☐	☐	If yes, is the treatment warranty transferrable?

87. **NOTICE TO BUYER: CONTACT STATE OF ARIZONA STRUCTURAL PEST CONTROL COMMISSION**
88. **FOR PAST TERMITE REPORTS OR TREATMENT HISTORY.**

89. **HEATING & COOLING:**
90. Heating: Type(s) _____
91. Cooling: Type(s) _____

	YES	NO	
92.	☐	☐	Are you aware of any past or present problems with the heating or cooling system(s)?
93.			Explain: _____

94. **PLUMBING:**

	YES	NO	
95.	☐	☐	Are you aware of the type of water pipes, such as galvanized, copper, PVC, CPVC or polybutylene?
96.			If yes, identify: _____
97.	☐	☐	Are you aware of any past or present plumbing problems? Explain: _____
98.			_____
99.	☐	☐	Are you aware of any water pressure problems? Explain: _____
100.			Type of water heater(s): ☐ **Gas** ☐ **Electric** ☐ **Solar** Approx. age(s): _____
101.	☐	☐	Are you aware of any past or present water heater problems? Explain: _____
102.			_____
103.	☐	☐	Is there a landscape watering system? If yes, type: ☐ **automatic timer** ☐ **manual** ☐ **both**
104.	☐	☐	If yes, are you aware of any past or present problems with the landscape watering system?
105.			Explain: _____
106.	☐	☐	Are there any water treatment systems? (Check all that apply):
107.			☐ water filtration ☐ reverse osmosis ☐ water softener ☐ Other _____
108.			Is water treatment system(s) ☐ **owned** ☐ **leased (Attach a copy of lease if available.)**
109.	☐	☐	Are you aware of any past or present problems with the water treatment system(s)?
110.			Explain: _____

111. **SWIMMING POOL/SPA/HOT TUB/SAUNA/WATER FEATURE:**

	YES	NO	
112.	☐	☐	Does the Property contain any of the following? (Check all that apply):
113.			☐ Swimming pool ☐ Spa ☐ Hot tub ☐ Sauna ☐ Water feature
114.	☐	☐	If yes, are either of the following heated? ☐ **Swimming pool** ☐ **Spa** If yes, type of heat: _____
115.	☐	☐	Are you aware of any past or present problems relating to the swimming pool, spa, hot tub, sauna or water feature?
116.			Explain: _____

>>

Residential Seller's Property Disclosure Statement (SPDS)
Updated: February 2008 • Copyright © 2008 Arizona Association of REALTORS®.
All rights reserved.

Initials> _____
BUYER | BUYER

Page 3 of 6

FIGURE 2–9
(continued)

Residential Seller's Property Disclosure Statement (SPDS) >>

	YES	NO	
117.			**ELECTRICAL AND OTHER RELATED SYSTEMS:**
118.	☐	☐	Are you aware of any past or present problems with the electrical system? Explain: _____
119.			_____
120.	☐	☐	Is there a security system? If yes, is it (Check all that apply):
121.			☐ **Leased (Attach copy of lease if available)** ☐ **Owned** ☐ **Monitored** ☐ **Other** _____
122.	☐	☐	Are you aware of any past or present problems with the security system? Explain: _____
123.			_____
124.	☐	☐	Does the Property contain any of the following systems or detectors?(Check all that apply):
125.			☐ Smoke/fire detection ☐ Fire suppression (sprinklers) ☐ Carbon monoxide detector
126.			If yes, are you aware of any past or present problems with the above systems? Explain: _____
127.			_____
128.			**MISCELLANEOUS:**
129.	☐	☐	Are you aware of or have you observed any of the following on the Property? (Check all that apply):
130.			☐ Scorpions ☐ Rabid animals ☐ Bee swarms ☐ Rodents ☐ Reptiles ☐ Other: _____
131.			Explain: _____
132.			How often is the Property serviced or treated for pests, reptiles, insects or animals? _____
133.			Name of service provider: _____ Date of last service: _____
134.	☐	☐	Are you aware of any work done on the Property, such as building, plumbing, electrical or other improvements?
135.			**(If no, skip to line 144.)**
136.			Explain: _____
137.	☐	☐	Are you aware of any rooms added to the Property or converted to bedrooms?
138.	☐	☐	Were permits for the work required? Explain: _____
139.	☐	☐	If yes, were permits for the work obtained? Explain: _____
140.	☐	☐	Was the work performed by a person licensed to perform the work? Explain: _____
141.	☐	☐	Was approval for the work required by any association governing the property? Explain: _____
142.			If yes, was approval granted by the association? Explain: _____
143.	☐	☐	Was the work completed? Explain: _____
144.	☐	☐	Are there any security bars or other obstructions to door or window openings? Explain: _____
145.	☐	☐	Are you aware of any past or present problems with any built-in appliances? Explain: _____
146.			_____
147.	☐	☐	Are there any leased propane tanks, equipment or other systems on the Property? Explain: _____
148.			_____

UTILITIES

149.			**DOES THE PROPERTY CURRENTLY RECEIVE THE FOLLOWING SERVICES?**	**PROVIDER**
	YES	NO		
150.	☐	☐	Electricity:	_____
151.	☐	☐	Fuel: ☐ **Natural gas** ☐ **Propane** ☐ **Oil**	_____
152.	☐	☐	Cable:	_____
153.	☐	☐	Telephone:	_____
154.	☐	☐	Garbage Collection:	_____
155.	☐	☐	Fire:	_____
156.	☐	☐	Irrigation:	_____
157.	☐	☐	Water **Source:** ☐ **Public** ☐ **Private water co.** ☐ **Private well** ☐ **Shared well** ☐ **Hauled water**	
158.			**If water source is a private or shared well, complete and attach DOMESTIC WATER WELL/WATER USE ADDENDUM.**	
159.			If source is public, a private water company, or hauled water, Provider is: _____	
160.			**NOTICE TO BUYER: IF THE PROPERTY IS SERVED BY A WELL, PRIVATE WATER COMPANY OR A**	
161.			**MUNICIPAL WATER PROVIDER, THE ARIZONA DEPARTMENT OF WATER RESOURCES MAY NOT**	
162.			**HAVE MADE A WATER SUPPLY DETERMINATION. FOR MORE INFORMATION ABOUT WATER SUPPLY,**	
163.			**CONTACT THE WATER PROVIDER.**	

>>

FIGURE 2–9
(continued)

Residential Seller's Property Disclosure Statement (SPDS) >>

	YES	NO	
164.	☐	☐	Are you aware of any past or present drinking water problems? Explain: _____
165.			_____
166.	☐	☐	Are there any alternate power systems serving the Property? If yes, indicate type (Check all that apply):
167.			☐ Solar ☐ Wind ☐ Generator ☐ Other _____
168.			If yes, are you aware of any past or present problems with the alternate power system(s)? Explain: _____
169.			_____

ENVIRONMENTAL INFORMATION

	YES	NO	
170.	☐	☐	Are you aware of any past or present issues or problems with any of the following on the Property? (Check all that apply):
171.			☐ Soil settlement/expansion ☐ Drainage/grade ☐ Erosion ☐ Fissures ☐ Dampness/moisture ☐ Other
172.			Explain: _____
173.	☐	☐	Are you aware of any past or present issues or problems in close proximity to the Property related to any of
174.			the following? (Check all that apply):
175.			☐ Soil settlement/expansion ☐ Drainage/grade ☐ Erosion ☐ Fissures ☐ Other _____
176.			Explain: _____

177.
178. **NOTICE TO BUYER: THE ARIZONA DEPARTMENT OF REAL ESTATE PROVIDES EARTH FISSURE MAPS TO**
179. **ANY MEMBER OF THE PUBLIC IN PRINTED OR ELECTRONIC FORMAT UPON REQUEST AND ON ITS WEBSITE AT www.azre.gov.**

	YES	NO	
180.	☐	☐	Are you aware if the Property is subject to any present or proposed effects of any of the following? (Check all that apply):
181.			☐ Airport noise ☐ Traffic noise ☐ Rail line noise ☐ Neighborhood noise ☐ Landfill ☐ Toxic waste disposal
182.			☐ Odors ☐ Nuisances ☐ Sand/gravel operations ☐ Other _____
183.			Explain: _____
184.	☐	☐	Are you aware if the Property is located in the vicinity of an airport (military, public, or private)?
185.			Explain: _____

186.
187. **NOTICE TO SELLER AND BUYER: PURSUANT TO ARIZONA LAW A SELLER SHALL PROVIDE A WRITTEN**
188. **DISCLOSURE TO THE BUYER IF THE PROPERTY IS LOCATED IN TERRITORY IN THE VICINITY OF A MILITARY**
189. **AIRPORT OR ANCILLARY MILITARY FACILITY AS DELINEATED ON A MAP PREPARED BY THE STATE LAND**
190. **DEPARTMENT. THE DEPARTMENT OF REAL ESTATE ALSO IS OBLIGATED TO RECORD A DOCUMENT AT THE**
191. **COUNTY RECORDER'S OFFICE DISCLOSING IF THE PROPERTY IS UNDER RESTRICTED AIR SPACE AND TO**
     MAINTAIN THE STATE LAND DEPARTMENT MILITARY AIRPORT MAP ON ITS WEBSITE AT www.azre.gov.

	YES	NO	
192.	☐	☐	Are you aware of the presence of any of the following on the Property, past or present? (Check all that apply):
193.			☐ Asbestos ☐ Radon gas ☐ Lead-based paint ☐ Pesticides ☐ Underground storage tanks ☐ Fuel/chemical storage
194.			Explain: _____
195.	☐	☐	Are you aware if the Property is located within any of the following? (Check all that apply):
196.			☐ Superfund/ WQARF/ CERCLA ☐ Wetlands area
197.	☐	☐	Are you aware of any open mine shafts/tunnels or abandoned wells on the Property?
198.			If yes, describe location: _____
199.	☐	☐	Are you aware if any portion of the Property is in a flood plain/way? Explain: _____
200.			_____
201.	☐	☐	Are you aware of any portion of the Property ever having been flooded? Explain: _____
202.			_____
203.	☐	☐	Are you aware of any water damage or water leaks of any kind on the Property? Explain: _____
204.			_____
205.	☐	☐	Are you aware of any past or present mold growth on the Property? If yes, explain: _____
206.			_____

>>

FIGURE 2–9
(continued)

Residential Seller's Property Disclosure Statement (SPDS) >>

SEWER/WASTEWATER TREATMENT

	YES	NO	
207.	☐	☐	Is the entire Property connected to a sewer? Explain: _____
208.	☐	☐	If yes, has a professional verified the sewer connection? If yes, how and when: _____
209.			**NOTICE TO BUYER: CONTACT A PROFESSIONAL TO CONDUCT A SEWER VERIFICATION TEST.**
210.			Type of sewer: ☐ Public ☐ Private ☐ Planned and approved sewer system, but not connected
211.			Name of Provider _____
212.	☐	☐	Are you aware of any past or present problems with the sewer? Explain: _____
213.	☐	☐	Is the Property served by an On-Site Wastewater Treatment Facility? **(If no, skip to line 226.)**
214.			If yes, the Facility is: ☐ **Conventional septic system** ☐ **Alternative system; type:** _____
215.	☐	☐	If the Facility is an alternative system, is it currently being serviced under a maintenance contract?
216.			If yes, name of contractor: _____ Phone #: _____
217.			Approximate year Facility installed: _____ (Attach copy of permit if available.)
218.	☐	☐	Are you aware of any repairs or alterations made to this Facility since original installation?
219.			Explain: _____
220.			_____
221.			Approximate date of last Facility inspection and/or pumping of septic tank: _____
222.	☐	☐	Are you aware of any past or present problems with the Facility? Explain: _____
223.			
224.			**NOTICE TO SELLER AND BUYER: THE ARIZONA DEPARTMENT OF ENVIRONMENTAL QUALITY REQUIRES A**
225.			**PRE-TRANSFER INSPECTION OF ON-SITE WASTEWATER TREATMENT FACILITIES ON RE-SALE PROPERTIES.**

OTHER CONDITIONS AND FACTORS

226. What other material (important) information are you aware of concerning the Property that might affect the buyer's decision-making
227. process, the value of the Property, or its use? Explain: _____
228. _____
229. _____

ADDITIONAL EXPLANATIONS

230. _____
231. _____
232. _____

233. **SELLER CERTIFICATION:** Seller certifies that the information contained herein is true and complete to the best of Seller's
234. knowledge as of the date signed. Seller agrees that any changes in the information contained herein will be disclosed in writing by Seller
235. to Buyer prior to Close of Escrow, including any information that may be revealed by subsequent inspections.

236. _____ _____ ^ SELLER'S SIGNATURE _____
    ^ SELLER'S SIGNATURE   MO/DA/YR   ^ SELLER'S SIGNATURE   MO/DA/YR

237. Reviewed and updated: Initials: _____ / _____ _____
    SELLER   SELLER   MO/DA/YR

238. **BUYER'S ACKNOWLEDGMENT:** Buyer acknowledges that the information contained herein is based only on the Seller's actual
239. knowledge and is not a warranty of any kind. Buyer acknowledges Buyer's obligation to investigate any material (important) facts in
240. regard to the Property. Buyer is encouraged to obtain Property inspections by professional independent third parties and to
241. consider obtaining a home warranty protection plan.

242. **NOTICE:** Buyer acknowledges that by law, Sellers, Lessors and Brokers are not obligated to disclose that the Property is or has been: (1) the site
243. of a natural death, suicide, homicide, or any other crime classified as a felony; (2) owned or occupied by a person exposed to HIV, diagnosed as
244. having AIDS or any other disease not known to be transmitted through common occupancy of real estate; or (3) located in the vicinity of a sex offender.

245. **By signing below, Buyer acknowledges receipt only of this SPDS. If Buyer disapproves of any items provided herein, Buyer**
246. **shall deliver to Seller written notice of the items disapproved as provided in the Contract.**

247. _____ _____ ^ BUYER'S SIGNATURE _____
    ^ BUYER'S SIGNATURE   MO/DA/YR   ^ BUYER'S SIGNATURE   MO/DA/YR

FIGURE 2–9
(continued)

In general, brokers and agents owe a **fiduciary duty** to the individuals they represent.[28] The term *fiduciary* comes from the Latin words "fides" and "fidelis"—faith, loyalty, and faithfulness to client and cause. As a fiduciary, a real estate broker's loyalty lies with the party he or she represents. The same is true for the agents and subagents working simultaneously on the case. Fiduciary duty encompasses the following qualities:

- Loyalty
- Obedience
- Disclosure
- Confidentiality
- Reasonable care and diligence
- Accounting

In loyalty, the broker and/or agent acts solely in the best interests of the principal, excluding all other interests, including that of the broker. What is required under the fiduciary duty will also depend on the part represented. The interests of buyers and sellers call for distinct and different loyalties and corresponding professional behaviors.

Seller's Agent	Exclusive Buyer's Agent
Must do everything possible to gain an advantage for the seller.	Must do everything possible to gain an advantage for the buyer.

The next quality, obedience, means that lawful requests and instructions need proper and professional attention.

Seller's Agent	Exclusive Buyer's Agent
Must obey all lawful instructions of the seller; is not obligated to obey instructions from the buyer.	Must obey all lawful instructions of the buyer; is not obligated to obey instructions from the seller.

As to **disclosure**, the fiduciary obligation demands that the agent relay facts or conditions that affect the value of the property. Such disclosure implies that the broker/agent will not reveal facts that are speculative or could force a lower valuation of his or her client's property. On the other hand, if representing a buyer, the broker agent has an affirmative obligation to educate the buyer on all aspects of the home, the community, and the risk to be undertaken.

Seller's Agent	Exclusive Buyer's Agent
Must reveal any known material defects in the property.	Must tell buyer everything they can find out about the seller, including the motivation for selling and any reasons the seller may have for wanting a quick sale.
Must NOT reveal information about traffic problems, poor school system, declining property values, etc., since these items might make the property less desirable to buyers.	Must tell buyer everything they can find out about the property, including traffic problems, poor school system, high crime rates, etc.

Confidentiality requirements mandate respect for a client's privacy and overall position. A broker/agent should never divulge what he thinks his client will do, nor expressly betray the conversations of his client.

Sellers Agent	Exclusive Buyer's Agent
Must tell the seller everything they can find out about the buyer, including all financial details they can obtain. divorce, etc.	Must keep all information about the buyer confidential, including the buyer's ability or willingness to pay more for the property than they are offering as well as the buyer's motivation for buying.

A broker is rightfully expected to use reasonable care and diligence in carrying out his or her affairs and being possessive of a superior skill level than the parties to the transactions triggers the highest demands for professional behavior.

Seller's Agent	Exclusive Buyer's Agent
Must be prepared through education and study to competently represent the seller in all matters.	Must be prepared through education and study to competently represent the buyer in all matters.

All monies, deposits, and proceeds must be properly accounted for and to fail in this area is to breach the fiduciary obligation.

Seller's Agent	Exclusive Buyer's Agent
Must account to seller for any money or documents entrusted to him or her.	Must account to buyer for any money or documents entrusted to him or her.

The fiduciary duty compels the broker to relay facts that might impact his principal that involve the agency agreement itself.[29] The broker has a duty to the seller to disclose any relationship he has with the buyer, including a familial, personal, or business relationship. The broker has a duty to disclose the actual value of the listed property, particularly when the broker is the purchaser of the property.[30]

CASE LAW

Broker Fiduciary Duty

COURT OF APPEAL, FOURTH APPELLATE DISTRICT

DIVISION ONE

STATE OF CALIFORNIA

ROBERT T. FIELD et al.,   D023751

Plaintiffs and Respondents,

v.   (Super. Ct. No. EC005873)

CENTURY 21 KLOWDEN-FORNESS
REALTY et al.,

Defendants and Appellants.

In this decision, we hold the two-year statute of limitations established by Civil Code section 2079.4 does not apply to claims for a breach of fiduciary duty brought against real estate brokers by purchasers whom they exclusively represent.

Real estate broker Century 21 Klowden-Forness Realty and its agent Shirley Hays (collectively Century 21) appeal a judgment awarding damages to Robert and Betty Field, whom Century 21 exclusively represented in their purchase of a rural residential property. Century 21 does not claim the evidence of breach is insufficient, but challenges the trial court's failure to find the Fields' action time-barred under section 2079.4.

For the following reasons, we conclude actions by buyers against brokers who exclusively represent them in real estate purchase transactions are not limited by the two-year time bar of section 2079.4 which, by its terms, is limited to claims for breaches of duty imposed by sections 2079 through 2079.24. (Tit. 6, ch. 3, art. 2.) We reject the argument that because a portion of the buyers' claims were based on their broker's failure to determine the extent of an easement was substantially more burdensome than represented and the acreage of the property was not accurate, that their action is one for breach of the duties imposed on sellers' brokers by section 2079.

We conclude the fiduciary duty of a broker, who contracts to exclusively represent a purchaser of real property to investigate for its client, is independent of the separate obligation imposed on a seller's broker to conduct a reasonable visual inspection of the marketed property for a buyer's protection, as announced in *Easton v. Strassburger* (1984) 152 Cal.App.3d 90 and incorporated into section 2079.

We also reject Century 21's claim the trial court erred in refusing to give comparative negligence instructions, BAJI No. 12.53 (pertaining to the effect of an independent investigation by the plaintiff), and BAJI No. 6.37.2 which would have advised jurors that one who acts as a professional need not be perfect. Thus, we affirm the judgment.

FACTUAL AND PROCEDURAL BACKGROUND

A.

In September 1992, the buyers, the Fields, sued their real estate agent Century 21 and others for negligence and negligent misrepresentation arising from their 1988 purchase of a rural residence. They alleged Century 21 breached its statutory duty by failing to conduct a reasonably competent and diligent visual inspection on their behalf as required by section 2079, and also had falsely represented the residence's physical condition. After demurrers challenged the section 2079 allegations as barred by the special two-year limitations period enacted in section 2079.4, they were eliminated from superseding pleadings.

The Fields' third amended complaint alleged negligence, negligent misrepresentation, and breach of fiduciary duty, citing Century 21's failure to inspect related title documents and to determine the scope of an easement in favor of Otay Water District. This pleading alleged defendants falsely represented Otay had an easement only for use of the driveway, although in fact the easement prevented the Fields from exclusively using a major portion of their property.

Although the conduct was no longer alleged as a section 2079 violation, Century 21 continued to contend the claims were time-barred by section 2079.4 for all allegations based on a failure to inspect.

B.

Trial established the Otay Water District easement was more extensive than what had been represented to the Fields, i.e., the easement was substantially more intrusive, covered more area and included the right to "spill" water onto the Fields' land, including some area occupied by the residence. Further, the acreage of the property was less than represented. Although buyers' agent was aware an

(continued)

easement existed, she neither verified the extent of the easement or the represented acreage of the property, nor did she advise the Fields to do so. Rather, the conduct of the agent implied both the acreage and the extent of easement were as erroneously represented. Further, an addition to the house violated setback requirements and Century 21 did not inquire whether permits or variances had been obtained for the addition or advise the Fields to do so. Although the septic system was inadequate and not in code compliance and the house suffered from various physical defects, Century 21 did not recommend inspection of the septic system for code compliance or alert the buyers to signs of obvious physical defects.

Not only did the Fields' real estate agent not inspect the preliminary title report in a timely manner, she did not even receive it from the title company until after escrow closed. Both the plaintiffs' and defendants' experts agreed the buyers' representative had breached her fiduciary relationship with the Fields by not reviewing the preliminary title report before the close of escrow to verify, among other things, the scope of the easement revealed in the transfer disclosure statement. The real estate agent testified she did not recall asking anyone about the easement, did not explain the Fields could have the title company come out and mark the easement, did not recall verifying the acreage information presented in the multiple listing service, and did not recall checking the preliminary title report for acreage information. Plaintiffs' expert testified the agent fell below the standard of care by, among other things, failing to advise the Fields that, since the property was in a rural area, they should consult with the title officer to review the title report before the close of escrow and to explain and plot the easement, and by failing to investigate the status of permits for the room addition or advise the Fields to do so.

The case was submitted to the jury with instructions regarding negligence, and negligent misrepresentation based on fiduciary or confidential relationship.

The court denied motions for new trial or judgment notwithstanding the verdict which were based on the two-year-from-date-of-possession limitations of section 2079.4.

DISCUSSION

I

SECTION 2079.4 STATUTE OF LIMITATIONS

Section 2079 requires sellers' real estate brokers, and their cooperating brokers, to conduct a "reasonably competent and diligent visual inspection of the property", and to disclose all material facts such an investigation would reveal to a prospective buyer. Section 2079.4 establishes a statute of limitations for breaches of those duties imposed by section 2079 of two years from the date of possession.

Section 2079 was enacted to codify and focus the holding in *Easton v. Strassburger, supra,* 152 Cal.App.3d 90. In Easton, the court recognized that case law imposed a duty on sellers' brokers to disclose material facts actually known to the broker. Easton expanded the holdings of former decisions to include a requirement that sellers' brokers must diligently inspect residential property and disclose material facts they obtain from that investigation. Further, the case held sellers' brokers are chargeable with knowledge they should have known had they conducted an adequate investigation. (*Id.* at p. 99.)

Section 2079 statutorily limits the duty of inspection recognized in Easton to one requiring only a visual inspection. (See *Wilson v. Century 21 Great Western Realty* (1993) 15 Cal.App.4th 298, 308.) Further, the statutory scheme expressly states a selling broker has no obligation to purchasers to investigate public records or permits pertaining to title or use of the property. That is, section 2079.3 states the inspection required under section 2079 "does not include or involve an inspection of areas that are reasonably and normally inaccessible to such an inspection, nor an affirmative inspection of areas off the site of the subject property or public records or permits concerning the title or use of the property. . . ." (Italics added.)

The statutory scheme includes an expression of legislative intent. "It is the intent of the Legislature to codify and make precise the holding of *Easton v. Strassburger,* 152 Cal.App.3d 90. It is not the intent of the Legislature to modify or restrict existing duties owed by real estate licensees." (§ 2079.12, subd. (b), italics added.) The statute also provides: "[n]othing in this section is intended to affect the court's ability to interpret sections 2079 to 2079.6, inclusive." (§2079.12, subd. (a)(4).)

While the statute of limitations for the duty delineated in section 2079 is two years from the date of possession (§ 2079.4), the statute of limitations for actions involving a fiduciary obligation is normally triggered on the date the plaintiff discovers, or should have discovered, the negligence. (See *Lee v. Escrow Consultants Inc.* (1989) 210 Cal.App.3d 915, 921; *Neel v. Magana, Olney, Levy, Cathcart & Gelfand* (1971) 6 Cal.3d 176, 186–190; see generally, 3 Witkin, Cal. Procedure (4th ed. 1996) Actions, § 463, p. 583; § 619, pp. 795–796.)

As we will explain, an examination of the law existing before Easton and the enactment of section 2079 shows the fiduciary duty owed by brokers to their own clients is substantially more extensive than the nonfiduciary duty codified in section 2079. Moreover, since the triggering event for the statute of limitations applicable to fiduciaries is more flexible than the two-year-from-possession limitation set forth in section 2079.4, to apply section 2079.4 to fiduciary duties of a buyer's broker would, contrary to the legislature's express statement of intent, restrict the ability of buyers to obtain redress for duties owed by their own real estate licensees which existed before section 2079.4 was enacted.

Under the common law, unchanged by Easton and section 2079, a broker's fiduciary duty to his client requires the highest good faith and undivided service and loyalty. (*Stiefel v. McKee* (1969) 1 Cal.App.3d 263, 266; *Timmsen v. Forest E. Olsen Inc.* (1970) 6 Cal.App.3d 860, 871; *Ford v. Cournale* (1973) 36 Cal.App.3d 172, 180.)

"The broker as a fiduciary has a duty to learn the material facts that may affect the principal's decision. He is hired for his professional knowledge and skill; he is expected to perform the necessary research and investigation in order to know those important matters that will affect the principal's decision, and he has a duty to counsel and advise the principal regarding the propriety and ramifications of the decision. The agent's duty to disclose material information to the principal includes the duty to disclose reasonably obtainable material information. [¶] . . . [¶] The facts that a broker must learn, and the advice and counsel required of the broker, depend on the facts of each transaction, the knowledge and the experience of the principal, the questions asked by the principal, and the nature of the property and the terms of sale. The broker must place himself in the position of the principal and ask himself the type of information required for the principal to make a well-informed decision. This obligation requires investigation of facts not known to the agent and disclosure of all material facts that might reasonably be discovered." (Miller & Starr, Real Estate Law 2d, Agency, §3.17, pp. 94, 96–97, 99.)

Thus, depending on the circumstances, a broker's fiduciary duty may be much broader than the duty to visually inspect and may include a duty to inspect public records or permits concerning title or use of the property, a duty which is expressly excluded from section 2079.

For example, in *Salahutdin v. Valley of California Inc.* (1994) 24 Cal.App.4th 555, 562, the buyer's broker was found liable for damages resulting from a failure to tell the buyer he had not verified the accuracy of the acreage and boundary information obtained from the seller, although the broker knew this information was material to the buyer's decision to purchase. (*Id.* at p. 563.)

It is for this reason that brokers and agents need to prepare disclosure documentation and make good faith attempts to discern and disclose defects judiciously. While broker diligence does not negate a buyer's or seller's responsibilities, it is clear that the appellate courts are advancing greater broker responsibility.[31] In *Easton v. Strassburger*,[32] a California appellate court did so by finding that both buyers and brokers have a duty to inspect the property involved in a transaction. The buyer, however, lacks the expertise to detect and discover hidden-but-discoverable defects. The broker, having superior knowledge, skills, and experience, should be able to discern defects. Brokers and agents have a duty to make "reasonably competent and diligent inspections."[33] If the defect is manifest or it is blatantly plain to the naked eye, the obligation to disclose cannot be insisted upon. A buyer who fails to detect "manifest defects" upon an inspection of the property[34,35] would be and should be solely responsible.

The concerns over broker liability relative to housing defects, whether latent or obvious, are escalating. Buyers sue brokers for various reasons. Unwary purchasers, lured to the sale by the broker's assurances of affordability and security, now sue the broker when forced to lose their homes as victims of creative financing. Disgruntled home buyers sue the seller—and the seller's broker—for complaints that range from defects in title to leaking roofs and rusty plumbing.[36,37] Modern judicial reasoning reflects a general trend toward the expansion of sale-related liability. However, this expansionism is not without limitation. In *Bortz v. Noon*, the Pennsylvania Supreme Court upheld causes of action based on intentional misrepresentation but balked at "negligent" representation.[38]

Thus, there is a growing call for mandatory house inspections as a mechanism to alleviate the pent-up pressure inherent in a realty transaction, as well as other legislative responses regarding disclosure in the real estate transaction. A Florida commentator poses this dilemma:

> The homebuyer purchases an economic headache; the homeseller risks post-sale liabil-
> ity; the broker walks a legal tightrope, where high visibility and perpetual solvency can
> lead to actions filed by both buyers and sellers.[39]

Hence, states repeatedly seek ways for protection in each agency, whether buyer or seller, but the conflicts are extraordinary. While consumers have benefited from the wider array of agency relationships made available over the past few decades, examining choice alone does not paint a full or accurate picture of the protection provided to consumers. In fact, the degree of choice does not necessarily even correlate with the level of consumer protection a given statute provides.[40] What is patently clear is the need for disclosure, the emphasis on garnering reliable information on the state and condition of the property bought or sold, and communicating that information to buyers and sellers.

The issue of fiduciary obligation courses its way through many disciplinary cases involving real estate brokers and agents. The temptation to serve multiple masters, to place a client at a disadvantage to ensure closing, and the press and pressure of commission-based selling can sometimes tip the ethical wagon in usually very decent individuals. The mighty often fall.

The bases for discipline, most of which arise from breaches in the fiduciary realm, are diverse:

1. Failure to act in the best interests of a client
2. Deliberately misleading a client as to the market value of the property
3. Failing to advertise the property as obligated by the listing agreement
4. Deliberately misrepresenting to prospective purchasers or their agents the condition of the property or the availability of access to show the property
5. Purchasing or transferring of the property through an intermediary in order to conceal the purchase by the licensee
6. Inducing a seller to list the property through false representations
7. Inducing a seller through false representations or false promises to transfer the property to the licensee
8. Taking unfair advantage of a client's or customer's age, disability, or lack of understanding of the English language
9. Engaging in conduct with the public or other real estate licensees in the practice of real estate in a manner that is abusive, harassing, or lewd
10. Representing oneself as a sponsoring broker or managing broker without providing the actual supervision and management of the real estate business

11. Failing to reasonably safeguard confidential information or improperly using confidential information

12. Obstructing an inspection, audit, investigation, examination, or a disciplinary proceeding

In the rough and tumble of real estate, it is always better to maintain one's ethical compass, for doing so not only assures personal integrity but guarantees and long and illustrious career.

V. INITIAL CLIENT CONSULTATION

Now that a property is formally listed, listing agreements are prepared and executed, and appropriate disclosure statements are authored and verified, sellers await the buyer's offer to purchase. When an offer to buy—usually titled *Agreement of Sale, Contract for Purchase of Real Estate,* or *Agreement to Purchase Realty*—arrives, a close and diligent inspection of the document is required.

CHAPTER TWO **SUMMARY**

Chapter Two discussed the following topics:

- The difference between brokers and agents
- The various types of listing agreements
- The function of a multiple listing service
- The doctrine of caveat emptor
- Misrepresentation in the real estate transaction
- Broker/agent disclosure, good faith, and fiduciary duty
- Client consultation and information gathering

REVIEW **QUESTIONS**

1. What are the functions of a real estate agent and broker? How do their functions differ?
2. Discuss the various buyer agency relationships.
3. Define the purpose of an exclusive listing agreement.
4. Does an open listing differ from a multiple listing service? Why or why not?
5. What is the difference between an exclusive agency agreement and an exclusive listing agreement?
6. What is the doctrine of caveat emptor?
7. What are the five types of misrepresentations that have been recognized by the courts?
8. Discuss an implied warranty of habitability.
9. What is the function of a property disclosure statement?
10. What is a fiduciary duty?

DISCUSSION **QUESTION**

Discuss broker and agent disclosure, the fiduciary duty that a broker owes to the principal, and the good faith effort to disclose.

EXERCISE 1

Complete an exclusive listing agreement and an open listing agreement using the following fact patterns. Be sure to complete both agreements using one fact pattern for each agreement.

Fact Pattern A

Current Owner—John and Jody Smith

Broker—Lisa Charles of All County Realty

Property Address—123 First Street, Mytown, US

Selling Price—$125,000

Beginning date of listing—July 1, 2009

Ending date of listing—October 30, 2009

Broker Commission—7%

The owners are not willing to lease the property and do not want a For Sale sign posted on the property. They are willing to grant a 6.5% commission to any agent or broker other than their own who sells the property.

Fact Pattern B

Current Owner—Mrs. Edwin Jones

Broker—Lisa Charles of All County Realty

Property Address—50 Railroad Lane, Mytown, US

Selling Price—$55,900

Beginning date of listing—July 18, 2009

Ending date of listing—November 15, 2009

Broker Commission—7.25%

The owner is not willing to lease the property and requests that a For Sale sign be placed on the property. She is willing to grant a 7% commission to any agent or broker other than her own who sells the property.

EXERCISE 2

Complete a property disclosure statement by using the following fact pattern. Hypothetical information may be inserted where needed.

The property for sale is located at 123 First Street, Mytown, U.S., in Brown School District. It is a residential home with four bedrooms. Three of the bedrooms are 12' by 12'. The master bedroom is 12' by 15', with direct access to a master bath. All four bedrooms are on the second floor, which also includes a second full bath. The first floor includes a 12' by 10' kitchen, a 12' by 12' dining room, and a 24' by 12' family room with a large fireplace. There is also a half bath or powder room and a laundry room on the first floor.

The property was constructed of brick in 1915 in a Victorian style, with a large wraparound porch. The property includes .75 acres of fenced land and a three-car detached garage.

The property has gas-forced central air and heat and is serviced by public water and sewer.

Assignment for the Case of John and Martha

John and Martha have decided on a property to purchase. Complete an Initial Interview (Buyer) for John and Martha. Reference this interview sheet throughout the remainder of the exercises as needed. Additional information needed to complete the interview is as follows:

> Seller: Estate of Susan Right, by the estate's executor Lillian Jones, her daughter.
> Address of Property: #3 Big Mountain Lake Estates
> Big Mountain Township
> Big Mountain, NC 00000
> Purchase Price: $83,500

All furniture, window coverings, large kitchen appliances, air-conditioning units, carpeting and floor covering, and light fixtures are to be included in the sale of the home.

REFERENCES

1. James T. Baldwin, *Bortz v. Noon: The Supreme Court of Pennsylvania Creates Unfortunate Precedent for All Parties Involved in Residential Real Estate Transactions*, 10 WIDENER J. PUB. L. 83 (2000).

2. Ann Morales Olazabal, *Redefining Realtor Relationships and Responsibilities: The Failure of State Regulatory Responses*, 40 HARV. J. ON LEGIS. (2003); *see also* Ann Morales Olzabal, *Redefining Realtor Relationships: The Failure of State Regulatory Responses*, 43 HARV. J. LEGIS 65 (2003).

3. KATHRYN J. HAUPT & DAVID ROCKWELL, PRINCIPLES OF CALIFORNIA REAL ESTATE, 12th ed., 130 (Rockwell Publishing, 2006).

4. Kathleen H. Dooley, *Real Property—Brokerage Commission—Threshold Standard for Imposing Seller Liability for a Brokerage Commission in a Failed Transaction Is a Determination That the Seller Breached the Sales Contract*, 18 SETON HALL L. REV. 183, 184–85 (1988); *see also* D. Barlow Burke Jr., LAW OF REAL ESTATE BROKERS 2nd ed., 3.5, at 3:69–3:70 (1992 & Supp. 2001); Arthur R. Gaudio, REAL ESTATE BROKERAGE LAW 153, at 218 (1987 & Supp. 2001). (It is unrealistic to believe that most sellers, no matter how vigilant and resourceful, would be able to protect themselves by investigating the buyer's financial ability.)

5. D. W. McLauchlan, *Forfeiture of Deposits: Punishing the Contract Breaker*, 2002 N.Z. LAW REVIEW 1 (2002).

6. Mary Long, Esq., *Legal Reports: Real Estate License Necessary to Recover Commissions: Superior Court Reviews Licensing and Registration Act*, 2 LAWYERS J. 2 (2000).

7. Billie J. Ellis Jr., *Preparing the Listing Agreement between Owner and Broker (with Form)*, 2 PRAC. REAL EST. L. 51, 55 (1986); Listing agreements are increasingly subject to statutory and code oversight. *See* the Pennsylvania example at www.pacode.com/secure/data/049/chapter35/s35.332.html.

8. Colorado Real Estate Commission, 1900 Grant Street, Suite 600, Denver, CO 80203—Form LC50–5-09.

9. Colorado Real Estate Commission, 1900 Grant Street, Suite 600, Denver, CO 80203—Form EBA53–5-09.

10. Florida Association of Realtors, 7025 Augusta National Dr., Orlando, FL 32822–5017—Form EBLA-3.

11. All-State Legal, Form 1410S—Real Estate Interview Guide—Seller(s).

12. Aimee Bader, *Caveat Emptor Eroding in Maryland*, MD. B. BUL., Aug. 2005.

13. Frona M. Powell, *Relief for Innocent Misrepresentation: A Retreat from the Traditional Doctrine of Caveat Emptor*, 19 REAL EST. L.J. 130, 131 (1990).

14. James P. Cooksey, *Caveat Venditor in Real Estate Sales*, LX (9) FLA. B.J. 31 (Oct. 1986).

15. Clearance E. Hagglund, *Caveat Emptor: Realty Purchaser's Duty to Investigate*, 20 REAL EST. L.J. 373 (1992).

16. *See* Lauren Rubenstein Reskin, *Let the Seller Beware in Real Property Sales*, A.B.A. J. 108 (March 1, 1986).

17. Claren E. Huggland et al., *Caveat Misrepresenter: The Real Estate Agents Liability to the Purchaser*, 5 HOFSTRA PROPERTY L.J. 383 (1993).

18. *Id.* at 403.

19. *See* Humber v. Morton, 426 S.W.2d 554, 557 (Tex. 1968).

20. *Id.*

21. *See* Jane P. Mallor, *Extension of the Implied Warranty of Habitability to Purchasers of New Homes*, 20 AM. BUS. L.J. 361, 361 (1982).

22. Sean M. O'Brien, *Caveat Venditor: A Case for Granting Subsequent Purchasers a Cause of Action Against Builder-Vendors for Latent Defects in the Home*, 20 J. CORP. L. 526, 529 (Sp. 1995).

23. BARBARA NICHOLS, THE NO LAWSUIT GUIDE TO REAL ESTATE TRANSACTION (2007); BARLOW BURKE, LAW OF REAL ESTATE BROKERS (2007).

24. Arizona Association of Realtors, 255 East Osborn Road, Suite 200, Phoenix, AZ 85012—Seller's Property Disclosure Statement (SPDS).

25. *See, for example,* Robert S. Hulett, *New Real Estate Legislation Includes Sweeping Changes*, IND. LAW. 13 (June 23, 1999) (discussing discomfort and confusion experienced by agents and buyers regarding duties under subagency practice); J. Clark Pendergrass, Note, *The Real Estate Consumer's Agency and Disclosure Act: The Case Against Dual Agency*, 48 A.L.A. L. REV. 277, 277 (1996). (Confusion among home buyers and sellers as to the real estate broker's role in residential real estate transactions is a problem common to Alabama and the nation.); Roy T. Black, *Proposed Alternatives to Traditional Real Property Agency: Restructuring the Brokerage Relationship*, 22 REAL EST. L.J. 201, 205 (1994) (coining the term *accidental agency* for the situation where unintending seller's agents or subagents are deemed by the buyer and/or the court to be the buyer's agent); Guy P. Wolf & Marianne M. Jennings, *Seller/Broker Liability in Multiple Listing Service Real Estate Sales: A Case for Uniform Disclosure*, 20 REAL EST. L.J. 22, 31 (1991) ("even experienced real estate brokers are not fully aware of the agency relationships created in real estate transactions...nor can they be certain of the extent of their duties and liabilities."); Matthew M. Collette, Note, *Sub-agency in Residential Real Estate Brokerage: A Proposal to End the Struggle with Reality*, 61 S. CAL. L. REV. 399, 403 (1988) (describing the traditional subagency relationship as "counterintuitive in light of actual experience."); Joseph M. Grohman, *A Reassessment of the Selling Broker's Agency Relationship with the Purchaser*, 61 ST. JOHN'S L. REV. 560, 581–84 (1987); Paula C. Murray, *The Real Estate Broker and the Buyer: Negligence and the Duty to Investigate*, 32 VILL. L. REV. 939, 947–48 (1987); La. Reg'l Off., Fed. Trade Comm'n, Residential Real Estate Brokerage Industry 7, 9 (Dec. 1983) [FTC REPORT].

26. Kevin C. Culum, *Hidden-But-Discoverable Defects: Resolving the Conflicts Between Real Estate Buyers and Brokers*, 50 MONTANA L. REV. 331, 342 (1989).

27. Gretchen D. Coles, *The Pennsylvania Real Estate Licensing Act: The "Miranda Warning" of Real Estate*, 107 Dick. L. Rev. 119 (2002).

28. Royce de Rohan Barondes & Carlos V. Slawson Jr., *Examining Compliance with Fiduciary Duties: A Study of Real Estate Agents*, 84 OR. L. REV. 681–724 (2005).

29. *See* Molly Moore Romero, *Theories of Real Estate Broker Liability: Arizona's Emerging Malpractice Doctrine*, 20 ARIZ. L. REV. 767, 774 (1978); *see also* Craig W. Dallon, *Theories of Real Estate Broker Liability and the Effect of the 'As Is' Clause*, 54 FL. L. REV. 395 (2002).

30. Paula C. Murray, *The Real Estate Broker and the Buyer: Negligence and the Duty to Investigate*, 32 VILL. L. REV. 939, 945–946 (1987).

31. Ronald Benton Brown & Thomas H. Thurlow III, *Buyers Beware: Statutes Shield Real Estate Brokers and Sellers Who Do Not Disclose That Properties Are Psychologically Tainted*, 49 OKLA. L. REV. 625 (1996).

32. 152 CAL. APP. 3d 90, 199 CAL. RPTR. 383 (1984).

33. *Id.* at 99, 199 CAL RPTR. at 388.

34. *Id.* at 103, 199 CAL. RPTR. at 391.

35. Kevin C. Culum, *Hidden-But-Discoverable Defects: Resolving the Conflicts Between Real Estate Buyers and Brokers*, 50 MON. L. REV. 331, 339 (1989).

36. *See* Murray, *Am I My Brother's Keeper? Real Estate Broker Liability for Sellers' Misrepresentations*, 46 TEX. B.J. 1374 (1983); Fossey and Roston, *The Broker's Liability in a Real Estate Transaction: Bad News and Good News for Defense Attorneys*, 12 U.C.L.A–ALASKA L. REV. 37 (1982).

37. Gary S. Gaffney, *Real Estate Broker Liability in Florida: Is Mandatory Housing Inspection in Florida's Future?* 11 NOVA L. REV. 825, 827 (1987).

38. James T. Baldwin, *Bortz v. Noon: The Supreme Court of Pennsylvania Creates Unfortunate Precedent for All Parties Involved in Residential Real Estate Transactions*, 10 WIDENER J. PUB. L. 83 (2000).

39. GAFFNEY, *supra* note 37, at n. 164.

40. Ann Morales Olazabal, *Redefining Realtor Relationships and Responsibilities: The Failure of State Regulatory Responses*, 40 HARV. J. ON LEGIS. 65 (2003).

Agreements of Sale

LEARNING OBJECTIVES

- To describe the elements, clauses, and provisions of a typical real estate sales agreement.
- To assess whether or not an agreement of sale is legally valid and enforceable.
- To identify the unique terminology contained in agreements of sale.
- To differentiate between a land installment contract and an option to purchase and their respective purposes.
- To discuss cancellation, rescission, and release.
- To create legally enforceable agreements of sale and other real estate documentation.

JOB COMPETENCIES

- To acquire local, preprinted agreements of sale.
- To assist the attorney in the preparation of the agreement of sale.
- To verify information relative to mortgaging, conditions, contingencies, financing, and zoning arrangements to ensure an enforceable contract.
- To create a tickler system or file, which ensures that all rights and obligations under the agreement of sale are being honored.
- To recognize and create, under the supervision of an attorney, the elements, clauses, and provisions of a typical real estate sales agreement.
- To create, under the supervision of an attorney, the conditions and contingencies that affect the enforceability of real estate contracts.

ETHICAL CONSIDERATIONS

The paralegal must be aware of the following ethical dilemmas during this phase of a real estate transaction:

- Unauthorized practice of law
- Lawyer supervision of nonlawyers
- Confidentiality issues

I. INTRODUCTION

Sales **agreements** or **contracts of sale** are the cornerstone of the real estate transaction. Without an agreement or **contract**, banks will not accept an application for a loan, lawyers hesitate to represent clients, buyers will not be obligated to buy, and sellers will not be obligated to sell. The agreement "is an instrument that should delineate the rights and obligations of each party, both purchaser and seller, regarding the transfer and grant of real property. In some jurisdictions, the signing of the document provides for an equitable transfer of ownership with settlement merely being the consummation of that agreement."[1]

No agreement of sale is enforceable unless it is in writing and executed, as prescribed by the **Statute of Frauds**. The Statute of Frauds is rooted in common law tradition. Its intent is not to refuse recognition of oral real estate contracts, rather to refuse a remedy by a party advocating a claim based upon an oral assertion. The prevention of fraud is its primary aim.

The object of the statute is to prevent the assertion of verbal understandings in the creation of interests or estates in land and to obviate the opportunity for fraud and perjury. It is not a mere rule of evidence but a declaration of public policy. It does not absolutely invalidate an oral contract relating to land but is intended to guard against fraud and perjury by giving a waivable defense to the party entitled to claim its protection. Specific evidence that would make rescission of an oral contract inequitable and unjust will take the contract out of the Statute of Frauds.[2]

Every agreement of sale should contain these components:

1. Introduction: outline of parties
2. Legal Description of the property
3. Personal Property: exclusions and inclusions
4. Terms and Conditions of Payment: consideration clause
5. Condition of Title: encumbrance clause
6. Fixture clause
7. Time of Possession and Place of Settlement
8. Realty Transfer Tax clause
9. Inspection clause
10. Apportionment and Pro Rata clause
11. Fire and Loss Provision
12. Assessment clause
13. Conditions and Contingencies
14. Title Insurance
15. Integration of Terms
16. Brokerage clause
17. Signatures/Execution
18. Time Is of the Essence

A full discussion of these and other terms and conditions as well as a simultaneous inspection of a variety of agreement formats follows.

II. AGREEMENT FORMS AND DRAFTING TECHNIQUES

The form and substance of agreements of sale varies enormously—from those generated by software firms, to those authored by local realty boards and associations, to those crafted by esoteric law firms involved in sophisticated transactions. Many agreements are prepublished and standardized. Standardization attempts give consistency to real estate practice, comply with statutory and case authorities, and lend a uniform quality to an often complex undertaking.

CASE LAW

NUMBER 13-06-00690-CV

COURT OF APPEALS

THIRTEENTH DISTRICT OF TEXAS

CORPUS CHRISTI - EDINBURG

ERA REALTY GROUP, INC.,   **Appellant,**

v.

ADVOCATES FOR CHILDREN AND FAMILIES, INC.,   **Appellee.**

On appeal from the 267th District Court of Victoria County, Texas.

OPINION

**Before Chief Justice Valdez and Justices Garza and Benavides
Opinion by Chief Justice Valdez**

Appellant, ERA Realty Group, Inc. ("ERA"), appeals from a summary judgment favoring appellee, Advocates for Children and Families, Inc. ("Advocates"). ERA sued

Advocates over an alleged breach of a real estate representation agreement. Advocates moved for summary judgment and sought attorney's fees. The trial court granted summary judgment in favor of Advocates and awarded it $15,000 in attorney's fees. By three issues, ERA contends that the trial court: (1) erred in granting summary judgment; (2) was biased and unobjective; and (3) lacked sufficient evidence to award attorney's fees. We affirm.

I. BACKGROUND

On March 23, 2005, ERA and Advocates entered into a residential buyer/tenant representation agreement (the "agreement"). The agreement was a standardized pre-printed form that contained blanks that were completed by ERA in typeface print.[1] By the agreement's terms, Advocates granted ERA the exclusive right to act as Advocates' real estate agent for the purpose of buying or leasing property in Calhoun or Victoria Counties from March 23, 2005 through September 30, 2005.[2] The agreement contained the following real estate commission terms:

> Commission: The parties agree that [ERA] will receive a commission calculated as follows: (1) 6.00 % of the gross sales price if [Advocates] agrees to purchase property in the market area, and (2) if [Advocates] agrees to lease property in the market a fee equal to *(check only one box)* ☐ ___ % of one month's rent or ☐ 6 __ % of all rents to be paid over the term of the lease.

As to the lease provisions, neither box was checked but the number "6" is typed into the final blank space.

Advocates entered into a twelve year lease with College Church of Christ in Victoria County on July 8, 2005, without ERA's participation. ERA subsequently learned of Advocates' lease and filed a breach of contract suit seeking its purported commission and

---

[1] Advocates made some handwritten interlineations to the agreement.

[2] By handwritten interlineation, the agreement included the buying or leasing of property in Victoria County after June 30, 2005.

attorney's fees. *See* TEX. CIV. PRAC. & REM. CODE ANN. § 38.001(8) (Vernon 1997). Advocates answered by generally denying ERA's allegations.

On May 11, 2006, Advocates moved for traditional summary judgment on the grounds that the agreement between the parties did not create a duty for Advocates to pay ERA a commission when Advocates leased property. *See* TEX. R. CIV. P. 166a(c). The rationale for Advocates' argument was that the terms of the agreement did not obligate Advocates to pay a commission to ERA on a lease because an appropriate box was not checked. Advocates also sought attorney's fees from ERA.[3] Advocates offered the agreement and an affidavit executed by Joyce Hyak, an Advocates' representative, as summary judgment evidence.

ERA responded to Advocates' summary judgment motion by arguing that the contract evidenced an intent to pay ERA commission on a lease because the number "6" was typed into an appropriate blank, even though no box was checked. Attached to ERA's response was an affidavit of Tom Tucker, ERA's owner, and portions of the transcript of Hyak's deposition testimony.

The trial court granted Advocates a summary judgment without providing a rationale. It also awarded Advocates $15,000 in attorney's fees. No findings of fact or conclusions of law were requested. This appeal ensued.

II. SUMMARY JUDGMENT

By its first issue, ERA contends that the trial court erred in granting summary judgment because the agreement, when read in its entirety, evidences an intent by both parties to pay lease commissions.

---

[3] Advocates supplemented its summary judgment motion to include a request for attorney's fees. Advocates argued that the agreement's terms provide for attorney's fees. The relevant provision reads, "If [Advocates] or [ERA] is a prevailing party in any legal proceeding brought as a result of a dispute under this agreement or any transaction related to this agreement, such party will be entitled to recover from the non-prevailing party all costs of such proceeding and reasonable attorney's fees."

A.   Standard of Review

We analyze a traditional motion for summary judgment under a well-established standard of review. The movant bears the burden to show that there is no genuine issue of material fact, and that it is entitled to judgment as a matter of law. TEX. R. CIV. P. 166a(c). We review the motion and the evidence de novo, taking as true all evidence favorable to the nonmovant, indulging every reasonable inference, and resolving any doubts in the nonmovant's favor. *Valence Operating Co. v. Dorsett*, 164 S.W.3d 656, 661 (Tex. 2005). When, as here, the trial court does not specify the grounds on which the judgment is based, we will affirm the judgment if it is correct on any legal theory expressly placed at issue and supported by the evidence. *See* TEX. R. CIV. P. 166a(c) (stating that issues must be "expressly set out in the motion or in an answer or any other response"); *Dow Chem. Co. v. Francis*, 46 S.W.3d 237, 242 (Tex. 2001) (per curiam) (holding that when the grounds for the ruling are not specified, we are to affirm "if any of the theories advanced are meritorious").

B.   Applicable Law

The primary goal in interpreting a contract is to give effect to the written expression of the parties' intent. *See Balandran v. Safeco Ins. Co.*, 972 S.W.2d 738, 741 (Tex. 1998). To determine the parties' intent, courts must consider the entire writing in an effort to harmonize all the provisions of the instrument. *See Preston Ridge Fin. Servs. Corp. v. Tyler*, 796 S.W.2d 772, 775 (Tex. App.–Dallas 1990, writ denied) (citing *Coker v. Coker*, 650 S.W.2d 391, 393 (Tex. 1983)). Parol evidence is not admissible to render a contract ambiguous; however, "the contract may be read in light of the surrounding circumstances to determine whether an ambiguity exists." *Balandran*, 972 S.W.2d at 741; *see also Nat'l Union Fire Ins. Co. v. CBI Indus., Inc.*, 907 S.W.2d 517, 520 (Tex. 1995).

Not every difference in the interpretation of a contract creates an ambiguity. *See Forbau v. Aetna Life Ins. Co.*, 876 S.W.2d 132, 134 (Tex. 1994). The mere disagreement over the meaning of a particular provision in a contract does not make it ambiguous. *GTE Mobilnet of S. Tex. Ltd. P'ship v. Telecell Cellular, Inc.*, 955 S.W.2d 286, 289 n.1 (Tex. App.–Houston [1st Dist.] 1997, pet. denied). In order for an ambiguity to exist when the parties advance conflicting interpretations, both interpretations must be reasonable. *See Columbia Gas Transmission Corp. v. New Ulm Gas, Ltd.*, 940 S.W.2d 587, 589 (Tex. 1996).

If a contract is found ambiguous, it must be construed strictly against the author and in a manner so as to reach a reasonable result that is consistent with the intent of the parties. *See, e.g., Gonzalez v. Mission Am. Ins. Co.*, 795 S.W.2d 734, 737 (Tex. 1990 (providing that an insurance company has the duty to make its policy clear and unambiguous because the terms, language, and conditions of the insurance policy are selected by the insurance company itself); *Republic Nat'l Bank v. Nw. Nat'l Bank*, 578 S.W.2d 109, 115 (Tex. 1978).

C.   Analysis

The beginning of the agreement evidences an intent by the parties to have ERA represent Advocates in the purchase or lease of appropriate real estate. The provision contains a commission calculation if Advocates purchases property and also a commission calculation if Advocates leases property. No lease calculation is selected, although the number "6" is typed before the phrase, "% of all rents to be paid over the term of the lease." Clearly, the instruction to "check only one box" was not followed because no box is checked. The agreement, therefore, can be read in one of two ways: (1) as providing for a lease commission because the number "6" is typed, or (2) as making no provision for a lease commission because no box is checked.

ERA argues that the number "6" is a specific provision that conflicts with the "general provision" reading "check only one box." *See generally Ostrowski v. Ivanhoe Prop. Owners Improvement Ass'n*, 38 S.W.3d 248, 254 (Tex. App.–Texarkana 2001, pet. denied) (providing that a general rule of construction is that when there is a conflict between two provisions, the specific provision controls over the general provision.). We disagree. What ERA considers a "general provision" is in fact an instruction that ERA did not follow. The omission of a check and the number "6" in the lease provision, are properly characterized as scrivener errors rather than what ERA terms "specific provisions."

Because an ambiguity exists and ERA completed the form, we strictly construe the agreement against ERA. *See Gonzalez*, 795 S.W.2d at 737. We hold that the agreement made no provision for a commission when Advocates leased property because no commission calculation was selected. ERA's first issue is overruled.

III. TRIAL COURT'S BIAS

By its second issue, ERA contends that it was the victim of a biased judge. ERA points to two statements made by the trial court at the summary judgment hearing, which it contends is evidence that the trial court favored non-profit causes to ERA's detriment. ERA relies on *Sicott v. Oglesby*, 721 S.W.2d 290, 293 (Tex. 1986) and *Pitt v. Bradford Farms*, 843 S.W.2d 705, 708 (Tex. App.–Corpus Christi 1992, no writ) to support its position. Neither case cited by ERA is applicable, however, because each deals with allegations of judicial misconduct by a judge who presided over a jury trial. Instead, this case was decided by the trial court on Advocates' motion for summary judgment and without the aid of a jury. We note that the summary judgment granted in Advocates' favor has already been sustained on the merits. Furthermore, an independent review of the record does not evidence any bias on the trial court's part. ERA's second issue is overruled.

IV. ATTORNEY'S FEES

By its third issue, ERA argues that the trial court lacked sufficient evidence to award Advocates $15,000 in attorney's fees. ERA points to the affidavit submitted by Terry Carroll Jr., an attorney representing Advocates, which states the following:

> I am a licensed attorney practicing in Victoria County, Texas[.] I have practiced in that county since 1990, and I am familiar with the rates charged by attorneys in that county for legal services of the type provided to Defendant in this matter. I am one of the attorneys representing Defendant [Advocates] in [this lawsuit,] I have been designated an expert witness on attorney's fees in this matter[,] and I am familiar with the pleadings, correspondence, discovery, and other actions. I have also considered the nature of the dispute and the complexity of the legal issues.
>
> Based on the above-cited information, I state that the reasonable amount of attorney's fees for the services provided to Defendant in this matter through the completion of the hearing scheduled for July 31, 2006 is $15,000.

ERA did not object to Carroll's affidavit. On appeal, ERA argues that the affidavit is legally insufficient because it is conclusory. We disagree.

Generally, the testimony of an interested witness, such as a party to the suit, though not contradicted, does no more than raise a fact issue to be determined by the factfinder. *Ragsdale v. Progressive Voters League*, 801 S.W.2d 880, 882 (Tex. 1990) (per curiam). Where the testimony of an interested witness, however, is not contradicted by any other witness, or attendant circumstances, and the same is clear, direct and positive, and free from contradiction, inaccuracies, and circumstances tending to cast suspicion thereon, it is taken as true, as a matter of law. *Id.* This is especially true where the opposing party had the means and opportunity to disprove the testimony or evidence and failed to do so. *Id.* at 882. This exception to the general rule regarding interested witness testimony, however, does not mean in every case in which a party offers uncontradicted testimony, such testimony mandates an award of the entire amount sought. *Ragsdale*, 801 S.W.2d at 882; *Welch v. Hrabar*, 110 S.W.3d 601, 602 (Tex. App.–Houston [14th Dist.] 2003, pet. denied); *Hanssen v. Our Redeemer Lutheran Church*, 938 S.W.2d 85, 91 (Tex.

App.–Dallas 1996, writ denied). Even though the evidence might be uncontradicted, if the offered evidence is unreasonable, incredible, or its belief is questionable either from another witness or attendant circumstances, then such evidence would only raise a fact issue to be determined by the trier of fact. *Ragsdale*, 801 S.W.2d at 881-82; *Welch*, 110 S.W.3d at 602; *Hanssen*, 938 S.W.2d at 91.

Based on our review, Carroll's affidavit is legally sufficient to support the trial court's award of attorney's fees. Carroll testified that he is a duly licensed attorney, he is familiar with the usual and customary attorney's fees in Victoria County, he has personal knowledge of the services rendered to Advocates on this matter, and those services were reasonable and necessary. *See Columbia Rio Grande Regional Hosp. v. Stover*, 17 S.W.3d 387, 397 (Tex. App.–Corpus Christi 2000, no pet.) (finding a similar affidavit sufficient to support an award of attorney's fees). Accordingly, we conclude Carroll's affidavit was legally sufficient to support the trial court's judgment for attorney's fees. *See Tex. Commerce Bank v. New*, 3 S.W.3d 515, 517-18 (Tex. 1999); *see also Cap Rock Elec. Coop. v. Tex. Utils. Elec. Co.*, 874 S.W.2d 92, 101-02 (Tex. App.–El Paso 1994, no writ) (uncontested affidavit establishing prima facie case for attorney's fees legally sufficient to support fee award). ERA's third issue is overruled.

V. Conclusion

The trial court's judgment is affirmed.

ROGELIO VALDEZ,
Chief Justice

Opinion delivered and filed this
the 5th day of June, 2008.

Given the litigiousness in real estate, any effort that sets out forms and conditions according to guidelines, accepted customs, and practices is welcome. Standardized forms represent convenience and ease when compared to starting from scratch. Despite this advantage, standardization has its downside. Not all clients need every provision included in a standard document. Nor do all standard forms meet every need. By way of illustration, some buyers may wish the increased protection of an appliance guarantee on the washer and dryer. Other buyers may not need this protection. For the most part, standard forms only mention the working condition of fundamental systems like electricity, water, and heat. They usually contain the essentials, not the particulars suited to a particular client. Donald C. Taylor urges paralegals to be aware of the standard forms' flaws:

> In the majority of residential real estate transactions, the property is being sold and purchased through a real estate broker. In most situations the real estate broker will prepare the agreement of sale. Even so, there are still quite a few things you . . . should check or change.[3]

To Taylor and others, the drafting of a real estate agreement is more than filling in spaces. One must also be prepared for the "homegrown" varieties of agreements—a practice not recommended. Even so, as a paralegal you will see them. Such agreements should be scrutinized closely by both you and your supervising attorney. Realtors in some jurisdictions may prepare contracts without the aid of counsel. In other jurisdictions, licensed real estate brokers or agents may prepare some types of agreements of sale without being guilty of the unauthorized practice of law. In some states, contracts prepared by brokers and agents must contain certain language stating that the contract will become legally binding within a certain period of time and that within that time frame the buyer or seller should have the contract reviewed by an attorney to determine its legality.[4,5] Professional organizations at the state and national level post and publish all sorts of forms for the real estate practitioner. Some are free and some are fee-based. The National Association of Realtors (NAR) leads the way on the design and promulgation of suggested formats. See Figure 3–1.[6]

Furthermore, commercial publishers such as All-State Legal, Blumberg-Excelsior, and Easy Soft, vigorously produce standard documents. Finally, legal form books and practice series are filled with standard forms.

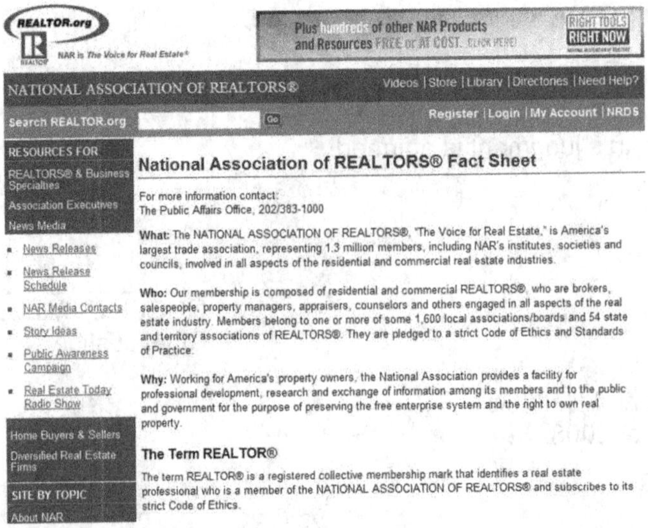

FIGURE 3–1
National Association of Realtor's Fact Sheet.

III. AGREEMENT OF SALE COMPONENTS

While there are hundreds of standard forms published by the Board of Realtors, local bar associations, and commercial carriers, they all share similar features and components listed on the following pages:

- Name and address of parties
- Agent, if any, and agent's authority in writing
- Name to appear in deed
- Source and nature of seller's title
- Title to be conveyed
- Insurance
- Defects
- Description of land and buildings
- Consideration
- Insurance
- Title insurance
- Municipal improvements
- Statement of zoning classification and legality of use
- Fixtures and personal property
- Date and conditions of possession
- Waste
- Apportionment and allotment of charges
- Pro rata as of closing
- Time of essence clause
- Contingencies
- Financing
- Deed
- Acknowledging and recording

IV. DRAFTSMANSHIP, LANGUAGE, AND THE AGREEMENT OF SALE

KEY WORDS

assignment	prorations
binder	risk of loss
default	time is of the essence
escrow	title insurance
flood insurance	transfer taxes
homeowner's insurance	zoning classification
legal description	

How a purchase agreement is drafted depends on many factors including but not limited to jurisdictional demands, type of transaction, financing, and particular interests of the buyer and the seller. Indeed, the agreement largely reflects the interests of the party represented. Hence, for sellers, the contract takes on its own identity by favoring the needs and desires of the selling party. Contrarily, buyers will push the terms of contract to their own end. As both parties negotiate, the agreement will eventually reflect these competing desires. Two checklists that outline the respective needs of buyers and sellers are at Figure 3–2 and Figure 3–3.

CHECKLIST FOR PREPARATION AND/OR REVIEW OF THE AGREEMENT OF SALE WHEN REPRESENTING BUYER

I. Seller

- List Seller's name, address and telephone numbers.
- Ascertain legal status of seller(s).
- If corporation, ascertain the state of incorporation.
- If partnership, is it general, limited, or limited liability, and list names of the individuals?
- If husband and wife, do they both approve of the sale?
- If single person: Was the single person married at the time title was acquired? Was the single person married at any time thereafter the title was acquired? How was the marriage terminated?
- If executor or administrator, obtain proof of authority to sell?

II. Buyer

- List Buyer(s) name, address and telephone numbers.
- Ascertain manner in which buyer(s) will take and hold title:
  As a partnership in the partnership name
  As a partnership in the individual names of the partners and their spouses, as joint tenants with rights of survivorship, tenants in common, or otherwise
  As husband and wife as tenants by the entireties
  As a single person(s)
- Ascertain purpose for property purchase:
  buyer's residence
  speculation
  subdivision
  commercial development
  other: _____.

III. The Property

- List location: street, lot number, township, city, county, state.
- Any deed reference or boundaries necessary and describe.
- If a metes and bounds description is available, insert in the agreement of sale.
- If any personal property is to be sold with the land, add an addendum to the agreement, entitle it "Inventory," and list each item.

IV. The Purchase Price and Financing

- List the total purchase price.
- Determine the amount of the down payment and due date(s).
- Ascertain manner in which payment of purchase price is to be made at time of final settlement:
  Assumption of existing mortgage
  Purchase money mortgage
  Cash if no financial arrangements are made with a lending institution

---

FIGURE 3–2
(continues)

- Mortgage contingency clause. If buyer must obtain a loan commitment for financing the property, indicate the specifics in the mortgage contingency clause
- Determine who is to retain down payment until final closing: the broker, buyer, seller or attorney

V. General Considerations

- Determine settlement date on or before X date.
- Determine from seller (or seller's attorney) exactly what personal property owned by seller is included in the sale, then list each item and the purchase price.
- Determine the amount of insurance seller is presently carrying on the property and insert in the agreement of sale.
- Make sure there is only one remedy in agreement of sale in case of default by the buyer.
- Obtain statement as to what use property is zoned for.
- Seller will convey to buyer good and marketable title.
- There is no pending or threatened condemnation.
- Make sure there are no deed restrictions affecting any portion of the property or any special conditions, exceptions, covenants or reservations.
- Seller has complied with all laws, ordinances, etc., relating to the property.
- The question of discrimination in housing practice forever needs to concern agents.
- There is available water, sewer and electricity.
- There are no notices of any violation by any governmental unit or agency and that if there are, seller will correct said violations at seller's cost and expense prior to settlement.
- Is any requisite approval of subdivision planning required? If so, note the dates for the necessary approval.
- Approval of leases, if any. Are they assignable?
- Approval or appraisal of property by lending institution, F.H.A or V.A.
- Termite clause. Add clause which benefits the buyer.
- Rezoning or issuance of permits consonant with use of land.
- Fuel oil to be included in sale and purchase price.
- Is contract assignable by buyer(s)?
- Notice provisions. Does notice have to be received or is mailing adequate?
- Is the successors and assigns clause in the contract?
- Entire agreement clause: If contained, no spoken evidence is allowed.
- Severability clause to prevent failure of entire agreement if one provision is invalid.
- Time of essence, should state that time is of the essence of the contract. If silent, performance within a reasonable time will suffice.
- Has buyer placed any time limit within which seller must accept the contract?
- Is the signature page acceptable for proper execution?
- Is the agreement of sale dated?
- Were any amendments or modifications to the agreement of sale made? If so, were they made to suffice legally?
- Real Estate Commissioners: Are the commissions conditioned on the closing of the transaction if not already determined by listing contract?
- Is the responsible party to the contract listed as to be the one responsible to pay any real estate commissions?
- Is there representation and warranty by both parties that no other brokers are involved in the transaction?
- Are the breaches of the contract and what constitutes the breaches clearly stated and the remedies to the seller clearly stated?
- Are any surveys to be obtained? If so, by whom? Who is responsible for the costs and expenses of the surveys?
- Is the "not to be recorded clause" in the agreement?
- Special considerations and clauses:_____

FIGURE 3–2
(continued)

**CHECKLIST FOR PREPARATION AND/OR REVIEW OF THE AGREEMENT
OF SALE WHEN REPRESENTING SELLER**

I. Seller

- List seller(s)' name, address and telephone numbers.
- Ascertain legal status of seller(s):
- If corporation, the state of incorporation
- sign a conveyance of the property, i.e., general or limited.
- If partnership holding title in the individual names of one or more of the partners, list names of the partners and whether they approve of the sale.
- If husband and wife, do both approve of the sale? If single person: Was the single person married at the time title was acquired or at any time thereafter and how the marriage was terminated.
- If a surviving joint tenant, how and when was the joint tenancy terminated?
- If an executor or administrator, proof of authority to sell.

II. Buyer

- List buyer's name, address and telephone numbers.
- The manner in which the buyer(s) will take and hold title:
  As a partnership in the partnership name
  As a partnership in the individual names of the partners or the individual names of the partners and their spouses as joint tenants with right of survivorship, tenants in common, or otherwise
  As husband and wife as tenants by the entireties
  As a single person(s).

III. The Property

- Location: street, lot number, ward, township, city, county, state
- Inventory or description of any personal property to be sold with the land and attach as an addendum to the agreement of sale.

IV. The Purchase Price and Financing

- The total purchase price
- The manner in which the purchase price is to be paid
- The down payment or other deposit at signing of the agreement of sale and due date
- Assumption of existing mortgage
- Purchase money mortgage
- Cash (no financial arrangements with a lending institution)
- Assumption of existing encumbrances on property
- The manner in which payment of the purchase price, if payable in installments, is to be secured.

V. General Considerations

- Delivery of vacant property to buyer at time of final settlement
- Approval of leases, if existing and assignment of lease
- Buyer's obtaining a loan or commitment for loans on the property (the mortgage contingency)
- Termite inspection. Insert pro-seller
- Certification of zoning classification
- Settlement date
- Name and location of broker handling settlement, if any
- Broker's commission specified
- Other: _____

FIGURE 3–3

For the most part, agreements of sale are composed with remarkable similarity. Yet, despite this, there are a host of nuances and differences. In the analysis within, the reader is exposed to three distinct yet similar formats, styles, and drafting approaches all of which illustrate these core elements of the agreement of sale. The examples are:

1. Contract for Sale of Real Estate (Julius Blumberg Inc.) Figure 3–4[7]
2. Contract for Sale of Real Estate (Easy Soft Inc.) Figure 3–5[8]
3. Purchase and Sale Agreement and Deposit Receipt (Northeast Florida Association of REALTORS® (NFAR)) Figure 3–6[9]

---

922   Contract for sale of real estate,
      long form, plain language, 5-86.

© 1984 Julius Blumberg, Inc., Publisher, NYC 10013

Consult your Lawyer before signing this contract — it has important legal consequences.

CONTRACT FOR SALE OF REAL ESTATE

Seller

This Contract is made and dated   19
Between:

*Address:
include
no., street,
municipality,
county,
state
and zip.*

(from now on called "the Seller")

And

Buyer

*Address:
include
no., street,
municipality,
county,
state
and zip.*

(from now on called "the Buyer")

The words "Seller" and "Buyer" include all sellers and all buyers under this Contract.

Table of Contents

1. Sale and Purchase
2. Property
3. Purchase Price and Payment
4. Deposit in Escrow
5. Acceptable Funds
6. Contingent Events
   (a) Mortgage Financing
   (b) Present Mortgage Assumable
   (c) Termite Inspection
   (d) Building Inspections
   (e) Roll-Back Taxes
7. Condition of Property at Time of Contract
8. Condition of Property at Closing
9. Casualty Damage
10. Assessments for Municipal Improvements
11. Compliance with Laws
12. Statements of Seller
13. Transfer of Ownership
    (a) Utility Company Easements
    (b) Restrictive Covenants
    (c) Tenancies
    (d) Other Exceptions
14. Transfer of Possession
15. Closing of Title
16. Deed and Realty Transfer Fee
17. Affidavit of Title
18. Corporate Seller
19. Payment of Liens
20. Adjustment of Property Expenses
21. Broker
22. Cancellation of Contract
23. Notices
24. No Assignment
25. Certification of Non-Foreign Status
26. Full Agreement
27. Changes in Contract
28. Contract Binding on Successors

The Seller and the Buyer agree as follows:

Sale and Purchase

1. The Seller shall sell and the Buyer shall buy the Property under the terms of this Contract.

Property

2. The word "Property" as used in this Contract includes (a) through (d) below:

FIGURE 3–4

(continues)

Land (a) All of the land located in the   of
County of   and State of New Jersey, specifically
described as follows:

☐ **This Contract was prepared by**

. . . .
Print or type name.

. . . .
Signature

Street address

Municipal tax map designation: Lot No.   Block No.

Buildings and (b) All buildings, driveways and other improvements on the land.
Other Improvements

All Other Rights (c) All other rights of the Seller with regard to the land.

Fixtures and (d) All fixtures, equipment, and personal property attached to or otherwise
Personal Property used with the land, buildings and improvements, when present at the time of
the signing of this Contract, unless specifically excluded below. These are
delete fully paid for and owned by the Seller. They include the following: plumbing,
items heating, electric, and cooking fixtures, electric dishwasher, garbage disposal
not unit, hot water heater, water conditioner, lighting fixtures, TV antenna,
included wall-to-wall carpeting, radiator covers, fireplace equipment, smoke and
burglar alarms, wall shelves, built-in cabinets and bookshelves, attached
mirrors, built-in air conditioners, window shades and blinds, rods and
valances, curtains and draperies, storm windows and doors, window and
door screens, awnings, shrubbery, pool equipment, garage door openers, gas
barbeque grills and tool shed.

The following are excluded from this sale: furniture, household furnishings,
refrigerator, freezer, clothes washer, clothes dryer, window air-conditioners,
snow blower, lawn mower, and tools.

Purchase *Check the* 3. The purchase price is
Price and *paragraphs which*   Dollars ($)
Payment *apply and*
complete the and is payable by the Buyer to the Seller as follows:
blanks.

Preliminary Deposit ☐ (a) Deposit previously paid . . . . $

Deposit ☐ (b) Deposit paid on the signing of this
Contract, by check subject to collection . . . . $

FIGURE 3–4
(continued)

Mortgage Money

☐ (c) Money borrowed from an established lender
as a first mortgage loan
on the Property in the principal amount of ...... $
This amount shall be paid to the Seller at the closing.

Assumption of Mortgage

☐ (d) By the Buyer assuming the payment at the
closing of the mortgage now on the Property which is
held by
and has an approximate unpaid balance of ...... $
This mortgage shall be in good standing
at the closing. It is payable with interest
at the yearly rate of   % in monthly installments
of $ The entire unpaid amount of the
principal is payable on   19

Note and Mortgage to Seller

☐ (e) By a note and mortgage from the Buyer to the
Seller in the principal amount of .... $
This amount shall be payable with interest at the
yearly rate of   % by monthly installments
of $ It shall be due in full
in   years with full prepayment rights
and   day default period. The Buyer shall pay
for a policy of title insurance protecting the Seller's
interest in the Mortgage. The Buyer shall not claim a
credit against the principal or interest payable on the
Mortgage for taxes paid. The Note, Mortgage and
Mortgagor's Affidavit of Title to be signed by the
Buyer at the closing shall be prepared on standard
law forms generally available in New Jersey. These
forms shall be prepared by the attorney for the Seller
at a cost to the Buyer of $ plus
costs of recording, credit report on Buyer and
mortgagee policy of title insurance.

Remainder of Purchase Price

☐ (f) Remainder of purchase price at closing, subject
to adjustments provided for in this Contract ..... $_____

Total Purchase Price .... $

Deposit in Escrow

4. In this Contract, escrow is the delivery of the deposit to a third party to
be held in trust until certain conditions are met.

The deposit shall be held in escrow by the Seller's attorney until (a) the
closing of title, at which time the deposit shall be paid to the Seller, or (b) the
exercise of a permitted right of cancellation under this Contract, in which
event the deposit shall be returned to the Buyer.

Acceptable Funds

5. All moneys to be paid by the Buyer to the Seller at the closing (both the
Buyer's funds and the lender's funds) shall be in the form of any one or more
of the following: (a) cash (but not over 2% of the purchase price), (b) bank
check, (c) cashier's check, and (d) certified check. All checks must be payable
to the order of the Seller or to the order of the Buyer. If payable to the order
of the Buyer the check must be endorsed by the Buyer to the order of the
Seller in the presence of the Seller or the Seller's attorney.

Contingent Events
*Check the events
which apply and complete
the blanks.*

6. The Buyer's obligation to complete this Contract depends on the
occurrence of the following events:

Mortgage Financing

☐ (a) The receipt by the Buyer of the written commitment of an established mortgage lender to make a first mortgage loan on the Property. The
Buyer shall promptly apply for this loan and make a good faith effort to
obtain it. The written commitment must be received by the Buyer by
                    19   The terms of the commitment must be at least as
favorable to the Buyer as the following:

FIGURE 3–4
(continued)

- Principal amount of mortgage loan ....$
- Type of mortgage (□ conventional, □ FHA,
    □ VA, □ other.....................)
- Annual interest rate ....   %
- Length of mortgage ....   years
    with monthly payments based on   year
    payment schedule
- "Points" if any to be paid: by Buyer ....
                                by Seller ....

The Seller and the Buyer may later agree to extend the date for obtaining the commitment. The Buyer may accept a commitment on less favorable terms or agree to buy the Property without this mortgage loan. If none of these events occurs and the Buyer does not receive the written commitment by the above date, either party may cancel this Contract.

**Present
Mortgage
Assumable**

☐ (b) The receipt by the Buyer of the holder's written confirmation that the present mortgage on the Property may be assumed by the Buyer. The Buyer shall promptly ask the holder for this confirmation. It must be received by the Buyer by   19   Either party may cancel this Contract if the holder of the mortgage does not permit the Buyer to assume the mortgage.

**Termite
Inspection**

☐ (c) The Buyer shall order an inspection of the Property by an established termite and pest control company. The inspection must be made by   19   The Buyer shall pay for the inspection. The Seller shall make the Property available for inspection on reasonable notice. The Buyer shall give a copy of the written inspection report to the Seller within 5   days after the Buyer receives it. The report shall include an estimate of the cost to eliminate any infestation found. If damage from infestation is found, the Buyer shall give the Seller the estimate of an established contractor of the cost of repairing the damage.

The inspection report may reveal the presence of termites or other wood-destroying insects. If so, the Seller shall hire an established and recognized termite and pest control company to:

- chemically treat the building in a safe manner,
- eliminate the infestation, and
- issue a one-year guarantee to the Buyer.

The inspection report may reveal damage caused by past or present infestation. If so, the Seller shall hire an established contractor to repair all damage.

All extermination and repair work shall be completed at the Seller's expense before the closing. However, if the estimated cost exceeds $750.00   either party may cancel this Contract within 10   days after the receipt of the inspection report by the Seller.

If the Buyer does not (1) have the Property inspected within the time allowed or (2) give a copy of the written inspection report to the Seller within the time allowed, the Buyer gives up the right to cancel the Contract under this termite inspection clause.

**Building
Inspections**

☐ (d) The Buyer shall order a structural, mechanical, plumbing, heating, and electrical inspection of the Property by an established inspector. The Buyer may also order inspections of the septic or other sewage disposal system, the water system for potability and pressure, and any environmental inspections. The inspections must be made by   19   The Buyer shall pay for the inspections. The Seller shall make the Property available for the inspections on reasonable notice. If the report of any of the inspections is not satisfactory to the Buyer, the Buyer may cancel this Contract within 10   days after the inspections. The Buyer shall include a copy of the inspection report with the notice of cancellation.

FIGURE 3–4
(continued)

If the Buyer does not (1) have the Property inspected within the time allowed or (2) cancel the Contract within the time allowed, the Buyer gives up the right to cancel the Contract under this building inspection clause.

Roll-Back Taxes

☐ (e) The receipt by the Buyer of written confirmation by the appropriate municipal official that (1) the Property is not assessed under the Farmland Assessment Act of 1964 and (2) no part of the Property is subject to roll-back taxes because of a change from agricultural or horticultural use. The Buyer shall promptly request this confirmation. It must be received by the Buyer by   19   If not, either party may cancel this Contract within 10   days after this time period expires.

Condition of Property at Time of Contract

7. The Buyer has inspected the Property or has had the Property inspected by others. Except for any rights of inspection reserved in this Contract, the Buyer accepts the Property "as is." The Seller makes no statement or promise about the condition or value of the Property.

Condition of Property at Closing

8. The Seller shall transfer the Property to the Buyer in its present condition except for normal wear caused by reasonable use between now and the closing. The grounds shall be maintained. The buildings shall be vacant and in broom-clean condition. All debris and the Seller's personal property not included in the sale shall be removed. The walks and driveway shall be free of snow and ice. The Buyer may inspect the Property within 7 days before the closing on reasonable notice to the Seller.

Casualty Damage

9. The Seller is responsible for any damage to the Property except for normal usage until the closing. If the Property is damaged by fire, vandalism, storm, flood, or any other casualty between now and the closing, the parties shall obtain an estimate, from an established contractor of their choice, of the cost of repairing the damage. If the estimated cost is less than 5%   of the purchase price, the Seller shall (a) repair the damage before the closing at the Seller's expense or (b) deduct the estimated cost from the purchase price. If the estimated cost is more than 5%   of the purchase price, the Buyer may (a) cancel this Contract, (b) require the Seller to repair the damage before the closing, or (c) proceed with the purchase, in which case the estimated cost of repair shall be deducted from the purchase price.

Assessments for Municipal Improvements

10. Municipalities may make local improvements such as street repairs or the installation of sewer systems. The cost is charged against the real estate receiving the benefit of the improvement. This charge, known as an assessment, is in addition to real estate taxes.

If a municipal improvement to the Property has been completed before the date of this Contract, the Seller shall pay the assessment at or before the closing. If the assessment has not yet been confirmed, the Buyer shall obtain an estimate from the appropriate municipal official. The Buyer's attorney shall withold this amount at the closing from the amount due to the Seller. The Buyer's attorney shall pay the assessment from this amount when the bill is received. The Buyer's attorney shall return any money remaining to the Seller.

If a municipal improvement to the Property has not been completed before the date of this Contract, the Buyer shall pay the assessment as it becomes due.

Compliance with Laws

11. (a) The Seller shall obtain at the Seller's expense before the closing any certificate of occupancy or other permit if it is required by the municipality. The Seller shall make any repairs required for the issuance of the certificate.

(b) If the Property has 3 or more units of living space, the Seller shall give to the Buyer before the closing proof of compliance with the New Jersey Hotel and Multiple Dwelling Act.

Statements of Seller

12. The Seller states to the best of Seller's knowledge:

(a) The Property is legally zoned for a   family house.

FIGURE 3–4
(continued)

(b) The Seller has not received notice that any building or improvement is in violation of any housing, building, safety, health, environmental, or fire law, ordinance or regulation.

(c) The Property is not in a Federal or State flood hazard area.

(d) All buildings, driveways and other improvements are inside the boundary lines of the Property. There are no improvements on adjoining lands which extend onto the Property.

The Buyer may learn before the closing that any of these statements is not accurate and the Buyer may decide not to accept the Property under such circumstances. In that case the Buyer's only remedy is to cancel this Contract. However, before canceling this Contract because a survey of the Property shows that statement (d) above is not accurate, the Buyer shall give the Seller at least 10 days to correct any defects.

Transfer of Ownership

13. The Seller shall transfer ownership of the Property to the Buyer at the closing, free of all claims and rights of others, except the following:

Utility Company Easements

(a) The rights of telephone, electric and gas, water, and sewer utility companies to maintain poles, wires, pipes, mains and cables over, along, and under the street next to the Property, the part of the Property next to the street, or any such utility services running to any improvement on the Property.

Restrictive Covenants

(b) Limitations on the use of the Property known as restrictive covenants, provided that they (1) are not now violated, (2) do not contain a clause under which the Property would be forfeited if they were violated, and (3) do not materially restrict the normal use and enjoyment of the Property.

Tenancies

(c) The rights of any tenants described in the following Section 14.

Other Exceptions

(d)

In addition, the Buyer must be able to obtain title insurance on the Property from a title insurance company authorized to do business in New Jersey, subject only to the exceptions set forth in this Section 13 and in the following Section 14.

The Buyer shall accept the transfer of ownership of the Property as it is described in this Section 13. However, the Seller may not be able to transfer the quality of ownership described in this Section 13 because of another exception, (not the result of the Seller's willful default) which the Buyer learns of before the closing and will not accept. In that case the Buyer's only remedy is to cancel this Contract after giving the Buyer at least 10 days to remove the exception.

Transfer of Possession

14. The Seller shall transfer possession and keys of the Property to the Buyer at the closing, free of all rights of tenants except the following:

Tenancies

Attach copy of leases

Name of Tenant	Area Rented	Lease or Month-to-Month	Monthly Rent	Security Deposit

These tenancies are not in violation of any laws. No tenant has any rights in the Property by way of option to buy, right of first refusal, pre-paid rental, or otherwise. At the closing the Seller shall give the Buyer any security deposits and interest earned as required by law.

FIGURE 3–4
(continued)

**Closing
of Title**

15. The closing of title (also referred to in this Contract as "the closing") is the meeting at which the Seller transfers the Seller's ownership of the Property by deed to the Buyer and the Buyer pays the balance of the purchase price to the Seller. The closing shall take place at the office of

at   .M. on   19   This is the estimated date. Either party may set a definite date by giving at least 10 days notice to the other party stating that time is of the essence. This notice cannot be given before the estimated date.

**Deed and
Realty Transfer Fee**

16. At the closing, the Seller shall transfer ownership of the Property to the Buyer by a Deed of Bargain and Sale with Covenant as to Grantor's Acts. This Deed contains a covenant, defined by law, that the Seller has not encumbered the Property. The Deed shall be in proper form for recording. The Seller shall pay the Realty Transfer Fee required by law. This sum shall be deducted from the amount payable to the Seller at the closing. If requested by the Buyer the Seller shall give a Bill of Sale covering any personal property included in this sale.

**Affidavit
of Title**

17. At the closing, the Seller shall give to the Buyer a sworn statement known as an Affidavit of Title. This affidavit shall contain information about the Seller reasonably necessary to clarify the Seller's ownership of the Property, such as (a) the Seller's marital history, (b) rights of tenants, and (c) claims on record against persons having the same or similar name as the Seller.

**Corporate
Seller**

18. If the Seller is a corporation, the officers signing this Contract are properly authorized to bind the Corporation to this sale. At the closing it shall give the Buyer a written certification signed and sealed by its secretary or assistant secretary. The certification shall include a true copy of a resolution properly adopted by the Board of Directors (a) approving this sale and (b) authorizing the signing of this Contract and the Deed, Affidavit of Title, and other closing documents by specified officers. The certification shall also state whether this sale (a) represents all or substantially all of the assets of the corporation and (b) is not in the regular course of its business. If both conditions are present, the secretary shall give the Buyer proof that the sale has been properly authorized and approved by the shareholders.

**Payment
of Liens**

19. A lien is the legal claim of another against real estate for (a) the payment of money owed or (b) the performance of an obligation. Examples of liens are real estate taxes, court judgments, and mortgages. The Seller shall pay all liens against the property in full before or at the closing. Provided that the proceeds of sale exceed the liens, the Seller or the Buyer shall have the right to direct that any liens be paid and satisfied from the proceeds of sale at the closing. If necessary for this purpose, all or a portion of the proceeds of sale may be deposited in the trust account of the Buyer's attorney and disbursed accordingly.

**Adjustment
of Property
Expenses**

20. The parties shall apportion the following expenses relating to the Property as of the closing date according to the period of their ownership: (a) municipal real estate taxes, (b) water and sewer charges, (c) rents as and when collected, (d) interest and tax and insurance escrow on existing mortgage if assumed by the Buyer, (e) premiums on insurance policy if assumed by the Buyer, and (f) fuel oil in the tank at the price paid by the Seller.
The parties shall not apportion the homestead rebate.

Broker

21. *Check the box which applies:*

☐ The Seller and the Buyer recognize

as the Broker who brought about this sale. The Seller shall pay to the Broker a commission of   when title closes and the Buyer pays the balance of the purchase price to the Seller.

☐ No broker was responsible for bringing about this sale.

FIGURE 3–4
(continued)

Cancellation of Contract

22. In this Contract, the parties have the right to cancel this Contract under certain circumstances. In order to cancel, a party must give written notice to the other. If this Contract is so cancelled, the deposit shall be promptly returned to the Buyer. The Seller and the Buyer shall then be released from all further liability to each other. However, if this Contract is cancelled by the Buyer because of the inability of the Seller to transfer the quality of ownership described in Section 13, the Seller shall in addition pay the Buyer for reasonable costs of search and survey.

Notices

23. All notices given under this Contract must be in writing. They may be given by:
(a) personal delivery to the other party or to the attorney for the other party, or
(b) certified mail, return receipt requested, addressed to the other party at the address written at the beginning of this Contract or to the attorney for the other party.
Each party must accept and claim the notices given by the other.

No Assignment

24. The Buyer may not transfer the Buyer's rights under this Contract to another without the written consent of the Seller.

Certification of Non-Foreign Status

25. The Seller shall provide the Buyer at or before the closing with a Certification of Non-Foreign Status under IRC § 1445.

Full Agreement

26. This Contract is the full agreement of the Buyer and the Seller. Neither party has made any other agreement or promise that is not included in this Contract.

Changes in Contract

27. The parties may not change this Contract unless the change is in writing and signed by both parties. The parties authorize their attorneys to agree in writing to any changes in dates and time periods provided for in this Contract.

Contract Binding on Successors

28. This Contract is binding on the Seller and the Buyer and all those who lawfully succeed to their rights or take their places.

Signatures

The Seller and the Buyer agree to the terms of this Contract by signing below. If a party is a corporation this Contract is signed by its proper corporate officers and its corporate seal is affixed.

Witnessed or attested by:

_____	_____ (SEAL)	_____ (SEAL)
As to Seller	Seller	Seller
_____	_____ (SEAL)	_____ (SEAL)
As to Buyer	Buyer	Buyer

CERTIFICATE OF ACKNOWLEDGMENT BY INDIVIDUAL

State of New Jersey, County of
I am a
an officer authorized to take acknowledgments and proofs in this State. I sign this acknowledgment below to certify that it was made before me.

On _____ , 19 _____ . _____

appeared before me in person. *(If more than one person appears, the words "this person" shall include all persons named who appeared before the officer and made this acknowledgment).* I am satisfied that this person is the person named in and who signed this Document. This person acknowledged signing, sealing and delivering this Document as this person's act and deed for the uses and purposes expressed in this Document.

_____
Officer's signature. Print, stamp or type name and title directly beneath.

FIGURE 3–4
(continued)

CORPORATE PROOF BY THE SUBSCRIBING WITNESS

State of New Jersey, County of
   I am a
an officer authorized to take acknowledgments and proofs in this State.

   On _____ , 19 _____ , _____

_____
(from now on called the "Witness") appeared before me in person. The Witness was duly sworn by me according to law under oath and stated and proved to my satisfaction that:

   1. The Witness is the _____ Secretary of the Corporation named in this Document.

   2. _____ the officer who signed this Document, is the _____ President
of the Corporation (from now on called the "Corporate Officer").

   3. The making, signing, sealing, and delivery of this Document have been duly authorized by a proper resolution of the Board of Directors of the Corporation.

   4. The Witness knows the corporate seal of the Corporation. The seal affixed to this Document is the corporate seal of the Corporation. The seal was affixed to this Document by the Corporate Officer. The Corporate Officer signed and delivered this Document as and for the voluntary act and deed of the Corporation. All this was done in the presence of the Witness who signed this Document as attesting witness. The Witness signs this proof to attest to the truth of these facts.

Sworn to and signed before me on the date written above.

_____
                            Witness: sign above and print or type name below.

_____
Officer's signature. Print, stamp or type name and title directly beneath.

CONTRACT FOR SALE *to*	*Record and return to:*

FIGURE 3–4
(continued)

Prepared by: (Print signer's name below signature)

_____

CONTRACT FOR SALE OF REAL ESTATE

This Contract for Sale is made on

BETWEEN

whose address is   ,   ,   referred to as the Seller, **AND**

whose address is   ,   ,   referred to as the Buyer.

The words "Buyer" and "Seller" include all Buyers and all Sellers listed above.

1. Purchase Agreement. The Seller agrees to sell and the Buyer agrees to buy the property described in this contract.

2. Property. The property to be sold consists of (a) the land and all the buildings, other improvements and fixtures on the land; (b) all of the Seller's rights relating to the land; and (c) all personal property specifically included in this contract. The real property to be sold is commonly known as   ,   ,   in the   of   in the County of   , and State of   . It is shown on the municipal tax map as lot   in block   . This property is more fully described in the attached Schedule A.

FIGURE 3–5
(continues)

3. Purchase Price. The purchase price is   .

4. Payment of Purchase Price. The Buyer will pay the purchase price as follows:

Previously paid by the Buyer (initial deposit)
Upon signing of this contract (balance of deposit)
Amount of mortgage (paragraph 6)
By assuming the obligation to pay the present mortgage according to its
terms, this mortgage shall be in good standing at the closing. Either party
may cancel this contract if the Lender does not permit the Buyer to assume
the mortgage (estimated balance due)
By the Seller taking back a note and mortgage for   years at   %
interest with monthly payments based on a   year payment schedule.
The Buyer will pay the Seller's attorney   for the preparation of the
necessary documents.
The Buyer will also pay all recording costs and provide the
Seller with an adequate affidavit of title
Balance to be paid at closing of title, in cash or by certified
or bank cashier's check subject to adjustment at closing

5. Deposit Moneys. All deposit moneys will be held in trust by   until   .

6. Mortgage Contingency. The Buyer agrees to make a good faith effort to obtain a first mortgage
loan upon the terms listed below. The Buyer has until   , to obtain a commitment from a
lender for this mortgage loan or to agree to buy the property without this loan. If this is not done before
this deadline, and any agreed upon extensions, either party may cancel this contract.

Type of Mortgage: conventional,   FHA,   VA,   other   .
Amount of Loan: . Interest Rate: %
Length of Mortgage: years with monthly payments based on a   year payment schedule.
Points: The Buyer agrees to pay   points for a total of   .
        The Seller agrees to pay   points for a total of   .

7. Time and Place of Closing. The closing date cannot be made final at this time. The Buyer and
Seller agree to make   the estimated date for the closing. Both parties will fully cooperate so the
closing can take place on or before the estimated date. The closing will be held at   .

8. Transfer of Ownership. At the closing, the Seller will transfer ownership of the property to the
Buyer. The Seller will give the Buyer a properly executed deed and an adequate affidavit of title. If the
Seller is a corporation, it will also deliver a corporate resolution authorizing the sale.

9. Type of Deed. A deed is a written document used to transfer ownership of property. In this sale, the
Seller agrees to provide and the Buyer agrees to accept a deed known as   .

10. Personal Property and Fixtures. Many items of property become so attached to a building or
other real property that they become a part of it. These items are called fixtures. They include such
items as fireplaces, patios and built-in shelving. All fixtures are INCLUDED in this sale unless they are
listed below as being EXCLUDED.

    (a) The following items are INCLUDED in this sale: gas and electric fixtures, chandeliers, wall-
to-wall carpeting, linoleum, mats and matting in halls, screens, shades, awnings, trash cans, storm
windows and doors, TV antenna, water pump, sump pump, water softeners,
    (b) The following items are EXCLUDED from this sale:

11. Physical Condition of the Property. This property is being sold "as is". The Seller does not make
any claims of promises about the condition or value of any of the property included in this sale. The

FIGURE 3–5
(continued)

Buyer has inspected the property and relies on this inspection and any rights which may be provided for elsewhere in this contract. The Seller agrees to maintain the grounds, buildings and improvements subject to ordinary wear and tear.

12. Inspection of the Property. The Seller agrees to permit the Buyer to inspect the property at any reasonable time before the closing. The Seller will permit access for all inspections provided for in this contract.

13. Building and Zoning Laws. The Buyer intends to use the property as a   family home. The Seller states that this use does not violate any applicable zoning ordinance, building code or other law. The Seller will obtain and pay for all inspections required by law. This includes any municipal "certificate of occupancy". If the Seller fails to correct any violations of law, at the Seller s own expense, the Buyer may cancel this contract.

14. Flood Area. The federal and state governments have designated certain areas as "flood areas". This means they are more likely to have floods than other areas. If this property is in a flood area the Buyer may cancel this contract within 30 days of the signing of this contract by all parties.

15. Property Lines. The Seller states that all buildings, driveways and other improvements on the property are within its boundary lines. Also, no improvements on adjoining properties extend across the boundary lines of this property.

16. Ownership. The Seller agrees to transfer and the Buyer agrees to accept ownership of the property free of all claims and rights of others. Except for:

(a) the rights of utility companies to maintain pipes, poles, cables and wires over, on and under the street, the part of the property next to the street or running to any house or other improvement on the property;

(b) recorded agreements which limit the use of the property, unless the agreements: (1) are presently violated; (2) provide that the property would be forfeited if they were violated; or (3) unreasonably limit the normal use of the property;

(c) all items included in Schedule A as part of the description of the property.

In addition to the above, the ownership of the Buyer must be insurable at regular rates by any title insurance company authorized to do business in New Jersey subject only to the above exceptions.

17. Correcting Defects. If the property does not comply with paragraphs 15 or 16 of this contract the Seller will be notified and given 30 days to make it comply. If the property still does not comply after that date the Buyer may cancel this contract or give the Seller more time to comply.

18. Termite Inspection. The Buyer is permitted to have the property inspected by a reputable termite inspection company to determine if there is any damage or infestation caused by termites or other wood-destroying insects. If the Buyer chooses to have this inspection, the inspection must be completed and the Seller notified of the results within 10 days of the signing of this contract by all parties. The   will pay for this inspection. If infestation or damage is found, the Seller will be given 10 days to agree to exterminate all infestation and repair all damage before the closing. If the Seller refuses or fails (within the 10-day period) to agree to exterminate all infestation and repair all damage before the closing, the Buyer may cancel this contract.

19 Risk of Loss. The Seller is responsible for any damage to the property, except for normal wear and tear until the closing. If there is damage, the Buyer can proceed with the closing and either:

(a) require that the Seller repair the damage before the closing; or
(b) deduct from the purchase price a fair and reasonable estimate of the cost to repair the property.

FIGURE 3–5
(continued)

In addition the Buyer may cancel this contract if the estimated cost of repair is more than.

20. Cancellation of Contract. If this contract is legally and rightfully canceled, the Buyer can get back the deposit and the parties will be free of liability t o each other. However, if the contract is canceled in accordance with paragraph 13, 14, 17, 18 or 19 of this Contract, the Seller will pay the Buyer for all title and survey costs.

21. Assessments for Municipal Improvements. Certain municipal improvements such as sidewalks and sewers may result in the municipality charging property owners to pay for the improvement. All unpaid charges (assessments) against the property for work completed before the closing will be paid by the Seller at or before the closing. If the improvement is not completed before the closing, then only the Buyer will be responsible. If the improvement is completed. but the amount of the charge (assessment) is not determined, the Seller will pay an estimated amount at the closing. When the amount of the charge is finally determined, the Seller will pay any deficiency to the Buyer (if the estimate proves to have been too low), or the Buyer will return any excess to the Seller (if the estimate proves to have been too high).

22. Adjustments at Closing. The Buyer and Seller agree to adjust the following expenses as of the closing date: rents, municipal water charges, sewer charges, taxes, interest on any mortgage to be assumed and insurance premiums. If the property is heated by fuel oil, the Buyer will buy the fuel oil in the tank at the closing date. The price will be the current price at that time as calculated by the supplier. The Buyer or the Seller may require that any person with a claim or right affecting the property be paid off from the proceeds of this sale.

23. Possession. At the closing the Buyer will be given possession of the property. No tenant will have any right to the property unless otherwise agreed in this contract.

24. Complete Agreement. This contract is the entire and only agreement between the Buyer and the Seller. This contract replaces and cancels any previous agreements between the Buyer and the Seller. This contract can only be changed by an agreement in writing signed by both Buyer and Seller. The Seller states that the Seller has not made any other contract to sell the property to anyone else. The Seller's agreement to pay the Broker (if any) is contained on the back of this page.

25. Parties Liable. This contract is binding upon all parties who sign it and all who succeed to their rights and responsibilities.

26. Notices. All notices under this contract must be in writing. The notices must be delivered personally or mailed by certified mail, return receipt requested, to the other party at the address written in this contract, or to that party's attorney.

SIGNED AND AGREED TO BY:

Witnessed or Attested by: Date Signed:

                                                       (Seal)

_____
                                BUYER

                                                         (Seal)

_____
As to Buyer(s)   BUYER

                                                         (Seal)

_____
                                  SELLER

                                                         (Seal)

_____
As to Seller(s)   SELLER

FIGURE 3–5
(continued)

STATE OF New Jersey, COUNTY OF Middlesex SS:

I CERTIFY that on

personally came before me and acknowledged under oath, to my satisfaction, that this person (or if more than one, each person):

    (a) is named in and personally signed this document; and
    (b) signed, sealed and delivered this document as his or her act and deed.

_____

STATE OF New Jersey, COUNTY OF Middlesex SS:

I CERTIFY that on   ,

personally came before me, and this person acknowledged under oath, to my satisfaction, that:

    (a) this person is the   secretary of   the corporation named in this document;
    (b) this person is the attesting witness to the signing of this document by the proper corporate officer who is   the   President of the corporation;
    (c) this document was signed and delivered by the corporation as its voluntary act duly authorized by proper resolution of its Board of Directors;
    (d) this person knows the proper seal of the corporation which was affixed to this document; and
    (e) this person signed this proof to attest to the truth of these facts.

Signed and sworn to before me on

_____

CONTRACT
 FOR SALE OF REAL ESTATE
 Between
           Seller,
 And
           Buyer.
	Dated:
	 Record and return to:
	 John Public Esq.
	 123 Pin Oak Drive
	 New Brunswick, New Jersey 09989

Broker's Commission The Seller agrees to pay   as commission (fee) of   % of the purchase price. This commission is not earned until the title is transferred and the purchase price is paid. This commission will be paid at the closing. This agreement takes the place of any prior agreement regarding the payment of commissions.

Dated

_____   _____
Broker   Seller

FIGURE 3–5
(continued)

PURCHASE AND SALE AGREEMENT AND DEPOSIT RECEIPT

COPYRIGHTED BY AND SUGGESTED FOR USE BY THE MEMBERS OF

THE NORTHEAST FLORIDA ASSOCIATION OF REALTORS®, INC.

REALTOR®   REALTOR®

1 **PARTIES**_____ ("BUYER/PURCHASER"),

2 and_____ ("SELLER"),
3 which terms may be singular or plural and include the successors, personal representatives and assigns of
4 SELLER and BUYER, hereby agree that SELLER will sell and BUYER will buy the following property
5 ("Property"), upon the following terms and conditions if completed or marked. In any conflict of terms or
6 conditions, that which is added will supersede that which is printed or marked. The Property is in
7 _____ County, Florida and is described as follows (if lengthy, attach legal
8 description):_____
9 _____
10 _____
11 **ADDRESS:** _____ Zip: _____
12 It is understood that the Property will be conveyed by statutory general warranty deed, trustee's, personal
13 representative's or guardian's deed as appropriate to the status of the SELLER (unless otherwise required
14 herein), subject to current taxes, existing zoning (unless specified otherwise in paragraph 12), covenants,
15 restrictions, and easements of record.

16 1.   TOTAL PURCHASE PRICE to be paid by BUYER is payable as follows:
17   (A) Binder deposit, which will remain a binder until closing, unless sooner
18   disbursed, according to the provisions of this Agreement..........................$_____

19   (B) Additional binder deposit due within _____ days after acceptance of this
20   Agreement..$_____

21   (C) Balance due at closing (not including BUYER's closing costs, prepaid
22   items or prorations) by cashiers, official or certified check or wire transfer.... $_____

23   (D) Proceeds of new note and mortgage to be executed by BUYER to any
24   lender other than SELLER.. $_____

25   (E) **TOTAL PURCHASE PRICE** .... $_____

26 2. [ ] **FINANCING:** If BUYER does not obtain the required financing but otherwise complies with the terms
27   hereof, the binder deposit, less sale and loan processing costs incurred, will be returned to BUYER.
28   (A) **APPLICATION:** Within _____days of the date of acceptance of this Agreement, BUYER will make
29   application for financing, pay lender for appraisal and credit reports, instruct lender to order same
30   without delay, and timely furnish any and all credit, employment, financial and other information
31   required by lender. Unless the mortgage loan is approved within _____ days (30 days if blank) of
32   date of acceptance of this Agreement (the Financing Contingency Period) without contingencies,
33   except those pertaining to the Property which are required for closing, such as marketable title, wood-
34   destroying organism inspection and survey as required by this Agreement, SELLER or BUYER will
35   have right to terminate this Agreement. If within 5 days after expiration of the Financing Contingency
36   Period (unless the Financing Contingency Period is extended in writing by the parties) neither the
37   BUYER nor SELLER has terminated this Agreement by written notice to the other party, this
38   Agreement shall no longer be subject to a financing contingency and neither party will have the right to
39   terminate under this provision and all time periods for closing and delivery of title insurance
40   commitment and survey shall run from the end of the five (5) day period.
41   1. [ ] **FHA:**"It is expressly agreed that, notwithstanding any other provisions of this Contract, the
42   PURCHASER shall not be obligated to complete the purchase of the Property described herein or to
43   incur any penalty by forfeiture of earnest money deposits or otherwise unless the PURCHASER has
44   been given in accordance with HUD/FHA or VA requirements a written statement by the Federal
45   Housing Commissioner, Department of Veteran Affairs, or a Direct Endorsement lender setting forth
46   the appraised value of the Property of not less than $ _____. The PURCHASER shall
47   have the privilege and option of proceeding with consummation of the Contract without regard to the
48   amount of the appraised valuation. The appraised valuation is arrived at to determine the maximum
49   mortgage the Department of Housing and Urban Development will insure. HUD does not warrant the
50   value nor the condition of the Property. The PURCHASER should satisfy himself/herself that the
51   price and condition of the Property are acceptable."
52   2. [ ] **VA:** It is expressly agreed that, notwithstanding any other provisions of this Agreement, the
53   BUYER shall not incur penalty by forfeiture of earnest money or otherwise be obligated to complete
54   the purchase of the Property described herein, if the Agreement purchase price or cost exceeds the
55   reasonable value of the Property established by the Veterans Administration. The BUYER shall,
56   however, have the privilege and option of proceeding with the consummation of the Agreement
57   without regard to the amount of reasonable value established by the VA.
58   3. [ ] **OTHER FINANCING:** [ ] **MORTGAGE ASSUMPTION** [ ] **SELLER FINANCING.** If marked
59   see Addendum attached hereto and made a part of.
60 3. **LOSS OR DAMAGE:** If the Property is damaged by any casualty prior to closing, and cost of restoration
61   does not exceed 3% of the purchase price of the Property, cost of restoration will be an obligation of
62   SELLER and closing will proceed pursuant to the terms of this Agreement with cost thereof escrowed at
63   closing. In the event the cost of repair or restoration exceeds 3% of the purchase price of the Property and
64   SELLER declines to repair or restore, BUYER may either take the Property as is, together with either the
65   said 3% or any insurance proceeds payable by virtue of such loss or damage, or terminate this Agreement.

FIGURE 3–6
(continues)

66 **4. PRORATIONS:** All taxes, rentals, condominium, association fees and interest on assumed mortgages will
67 be prorated through day before closing based on the most recent information available to the closing
68 attorney/settlement agent using the gross tax amount for tax prorations. Any proration based on an
69 estimate shall be reprorated at the request of either party upon receipt of the actual tax bill.
70 **PROPERTY TAX DISCLOSURE SUMMARY:** BUYER SHOULD NOT RELY UPON SELLER'S CURRENT
71 PROPERTY TAXES AS THE AMOUNT OF PROPERTY TAXES THAT THE BUYER MAY BE
72 OBLIGATED TO PAY IN THE YEAR SUBSEQUENT TO PURCHASE. A CHANGE OF OWNERSHIP OR
73 PROPERTY IMPROVEMENTS TRIGGERS REASSESSMENTS OF THE PROPERTY THAT COULD
74 RESULT IN HIGHER PROPERTY TAXES. IF YOU HAVE ANY QUESTIONS CONCERNING
75 VALUATION, CONTACT THE COUNTY PROPERTY APPRAISER'S OFFICE FOR INFORMATION.

76 **5. BUYER WILL PAY:**
77 (A) CLOSING COSTS: [ ] Recording fees [ ] Note stamps [ ] Intangible tax [ ] Credit report (s)
78 [ ] Mortgage transfer and assumption charges [ ] VA funding fee [ ] Mortgage origination fee
79 [ ] Mortgage insurance premium [ ] Closing attorney/settlement fee [ ] BUYER's Courier fees
80 [ ] Transaction/Professional service fee [ ] Mortgage discount [ ] Wood-destroying organism report
81 [ ] Appraisal fee [ ] Survey [ ] Tax service [ ] Doc prep fee [ ] Processing fee [ ] Home warranty
82 [ ] _____ Title insurance policy [ ] Title search and exam fee [ ] Title insurance
83 endorsements [ ] Underwriting Fee [ ] Flood Certification Fees [ ] Other _____

84 (B) All other charges required by lender, unless prohibited by law or regulation.
85 (C) Homeowners association transfer and statement fees.
86 (D) PREPAIDS: Prepaid hazard insurance, taxes, interest and mortgage insurance premiums, required by
87 the lender.

88 **6. SELLER WILL PAY:**
89 (A) CLOSING COSTS: [ ] Deed stamps [ ] _____ Title insurance policy
90 [ ] Title search and exam fee [ ] Closing attorney/settlement fee [ ] SELLER's Courier fees
91 [ ] Transaction/Professional service fee [ ] Underwriting Fee [ ] Flood Certification Fees
92 [ ] Real estate brokerage fee [ ] Mortgage discount not to exceed_____ [ ] Satisfaction of
93 mortgage and recording fee [ ] Survey [ ] Doc Prep fee [ ] Processing fee [ ] Repairs or
94 replacements, in addition to those in paragraph 15 (C), not to exceed $_____
95 [ ] For VA sale only, wood-destroying organism report [ ] Appraisal fee [ ] Tax service
96 [ ] Title insurance endorsements [ ] Home warranty [ ] Other _____
97 _____
98 (B) All other charges required by lender which BUYER is prohibited from paying by law or regulation.
99 (C) All mortgage payments, condominium or homeowners association fees and assessments, and
100 government special assessments due and payable shall be paid current at SELLER's expense at the
101 time of closing.
102 (D) If SELLER is a "foreign person" as defined by the Foreign Investment in Real Property Tax Act, the
103 parties shall comply with the Act.

104 **7. NON-DEFAULT PAYMENT OF EXPENSES:**
105 (A) If BUYER fails to perform, but is not in default, all loan and sale processing and closing costs incurred,
106 whether the same were to be paid by SELLER or BUYER, will be the responsibility of BUYER, with
107 costs deducted from the binder deposit. This will include but not be limited to the transaction not closing
108 because SELLER elects not to make the mortgage to BUYER or because BUYER does not obtain the
109 required financing as provided in this Agreement or BUYER invokes BUYER's right to terminate under
110 any other contingency in this agreement.
111 (B) If SELLER fails to perform, but is not in default, all loan and sale processing and closing costs incurred,
112 whether the same were to be paid by SELLER or BUYER will be the responsibility of SELLER, and
113 BUYER will be entitled to the return of the binder deposit. This will include, but not be limited to the
114 transaction not closing because SELLER is unable or unwilling to complete the transaction for a
115 qualified BUYER, or because the Property does not appraise for an amount sufficient to enable the
116 lender to make the required loan, or because SELLER elects not to pay for the amount in excess of the
117 amounts in paragraphs 3, 6, 15 (with respect to repairs and/or treatment), or because the zoning is not
118 as required in paragraph 12, or because SELLER cannot deliver a marketable title.
119 **8. DEFAULT:** If BUYER defaults under this Agreement, all deposit(s) paid and agreed to be paid, after
120 deduction of unpaid closing costs incurred, will be retained by SELLER as agreed upon liquidated
121 damages, consideration for the execution of this Agreement and in full settlement of any claims,
122 whereupon BUYER and SELLER will be relieved of all obligations to each other under this Agreement. If
123 SELLER defaults under this Agreement, BUYER shall seek specific performance or receive the
124 return of BUYER's deposit(s) without thereby waiving any action for damages resulting from SELLER's
125 default. Binder deposit(s) retained by SELLER as liquidated damages will be distributed pursuant to the
126 terms of the listing agreement.

127 **9. BINDER DISPUTE/WAIVER OF JURY TRIAL:**
128 (A) In the event of a dispute between BUYER and SELLER as to entitlement to the binder deposit(s), the
129 holder of the binder deposit(s) may file an interpleader action in accordance with applicable law to
130 determine entitlement to the binder deposit(s) and interpleader's attorney's fees and costs, or the
131 broker holding the binder deposit(s) may request the issuance of an escrow disbursement order from
132 the Florida Real Estate Commission and, in either event, BUYER and SELLER agree to be bound
133 hereby.
134 (B) All controversies and claims between BUYER, SELLER or Broker, directly or indirectly, arising out of
135 or relating to this agreement or this transaction will be determined by non-jury trial. BUYER, SELLER
136 and Broker, jointly and severally, knowingly, voluntarily and intentionally waive any and all rights to a
137 trial by jury in any litigation, action or proceeding involving BUYER, SELLER or Broker, whether arising
138 directly or indirectly from this Agreement or this transaction or relating thereto. Each party will be liable
139 for their own costs and attorney's fees except for interpleader attorney's fees and cost.

FIGURE 3–6
(continued)

140 10. **TITLE EVIDENCE:** Within [ ] _____ days after date of acceptance or [ ] _____ days after date of
141   Loan Approval without contingencies other than those commonly found in institutional loan approvals,
142   SELLER will deliver to BUYER or closing agent: [ ] Title insurance commitment for an owner's
143   policy in the amount of the purchase price [ ] Title insurance commitment for mortgage policy in the
144   amount of the new mortgage. Any expense of curing title defects such as but not limited to legal fees,
145   discharge of liens and recording fees will be paid by SELLER.

146 11. **SURVEY:** Within [ ] _____ days after date of acceptance or [ ] _____ days after date of Loan
147   Approval without contingencies other than those commonly found in institutional loan approvals, SELLER
148   will deliver to BUYER or closing agent: [ ] A new staked survey dated within 3 months of closing showing
149   all improvements now existing hereon and certified to BUYER, lender, and the title insurer. [ ] A copy of
150   a previously made survey of the Property showing all improvements now existing thereon. [ ] No survey
151   is required. If a flood elevation certification is required, BUYER shall pay for it.

152 12. [ ] **ZONING and RESTRICTIONS:** Unless the Property is zoned _____ and can be
153   legally used for _____
154   or if there is notice of proposed zoning changes or deed or other restrictions that could prevent such use
155   at the time of closing, BUYER will have the right to terminate this Agreement. SELLER warrants and
156   represents that there is ingress and egress to and from the Property sufficient for its intended use as
157   described herein. BUYER will have 10 days from date of acceptance to verify the existing zoning and
158   current proposed changes and deliver written notice of objections to SELLER or be deemed to have
159   waived objections.

160 13. **TITLE EXAMINATION AND TIME FOR CLOSING:**
161   (A) If title evidence and survey, as specified above, show SELLER is vested with a marketable title, the
162   transaction will be closed and the deed and other closing papers delivered on or before
163   [ ] _____ [ ] _____ days after date of acceptance
164   [ ] _____ days after date of Loan Approval and satisfaction of conditions in paragraph 18,
165   if any, unless extended by other conditions of the Agreement. Marketable title means title which a
166   Florida title insurer will insure as marketable at its regular rates and subject only to matters to be cured
167   at closing and the usual exceptions such as survey, current taxes, zoning ordinances, covenants,
168   restrictions and easements of record. If on the date of closing hazard insurance underwriting is
169   suspended, BUYER may postpone the closing for up to five (5) days after suspension is lifted.
170   (B) If title evidence or survey reveal any defects which render the title unmarketable, BUYER or closing
171   agent will have seven (7) days from receipt of title commitment and survey to notify SELLER of such
172   title defects. SELLER agrees to use reasonable diligence to cure such defects at SELLER's expense
173   and will have 30 days to do so, in which event this transaction will be closed within ten days after
174   delivery to BUYER of evidence that such defects have been cured. SELLER agrees to pay for and
175   discharge all due and delinquent taxes, liens and other encumbrances, unless otherwise agreed. If
176   SELLER is unable to convey to BUYER a marketable title, BUYER will have the right to terminate this
177   Agreement, at the same time returning to SELLER all title evidence and surveys received from
178   SELLER, or BUYER will have the right to accept such title as SELLER may be able to convey, and to
179   close this transaction upon the terms stated herein, which election will be exercised within ten (10)
180   days from notice of SELLER's inability to cure.

181 14. **PROPERTY DISCLOSURE:** SELLER does hereby represent that SELLER has legal authority and
182   capacity to convey the Property with all improvements. SELLER represents that SELLER has no
183   knowledge of facts materially affecting the value of the Property other than those which BUYER can
184   readily observe **except:** _____.
185   SELLER further represents that the Property is not now and will not be prior to closing subject to a
186   municipal or county code enforcement proceeding and that no citation has been issued **except:** _____
187   _____ (If the Property is or becomes subject
188   to such a proceeding prior to closing, SELLER shall comply with Florida Statutes 125.69 and 162.06;
189   notwithstanding anything contained within said Statutes, SELLER shall be responsible for compliance with
190   applicable code and all orders issued in such proceeding unless otherwise agreed herein.)
191   (A) **Energy Efficiency:** In accordance with Florida Statute 553.996, notice is hereby given that the
192   BUYER of real property with a building for occupancy located thereon may have the building's
193   energy-efficiency rating determined. BUYER acknowledges receipt of the energy efficiency rating
194   information brochure prepared by the State of Florida at the time of or prior to BUYER signing this
195   Agreement.
196   (B) **Radon Gas Disclosure:** Radon gas is a naturally occurring radioactive gas that, when it has
197   accumulated in a building in sufficient quantities, may present health risks to persons who are
198   exposed to it over time. Levels of radon that exceed federal and state guidelines have been found in
199   buildings in Florida. Additional information regarding radon testing may be obtained from your county
200   public health unit.
201   (C) **Flood Zone:** BUYER is advised to verify with the lender and appropriate government agencies
202   whether flood insurance is required and what restrictions apply to improving the Property and
203   rebuilding in the event of casualty.
204   (D) **Mold Disclosure:** Mold is naturally occurring. The presence of mold in a home or building may cause
205   health problems and damage to Property. If BUYER is concerned or desires additional information
206   BUYER should seek appropriate professional advice.
207   (E) **Other:** BUYER should exercise due diligence with respect to information regarding neighborhood
208   crimes, sexual offenders/predators and any other matters BUYER deems relevant to the purchase of
209   the Property.

FIGURE 3–6
(continued)

210 15. **MAINTENANCE, INSPECTION AND REPAIR:** SELLER will maintain the Property in its present condition
211 until closing, except for normal wear and tear and any repairs required by this Agreement.

212 (A) **Professional Inspections:** BUYER may, at BUYER's expense, have the Property inspected as
213 described below by a professional inspector who specializes in home inspections and holds an
214 occupational license for such purpose or holds a Florida license to build, repair or maintain the items
215 inspected. **It is agreed that the costs of inspections below or any other inspections requested by**
216 **the BUYER are exempt from the terms in Paragraph 7 of this Purchase and Sale Agreement**
217 **and will be paid by the BUYER regardless of the outcome of this Agreement.** If the professional
218 inspection is not done within the time required, BUYER waives the right to have the inspection and
219 accepts the Property in its "AS IS" condition, except as provided in paragraph 15(C) below. BUYER
220 will be responsible for repair of all damages to the Property resulting from inspections and return the
221 Property to its pre-inspection condition.

222 (1) Within <u>ten (10) days</u> after acceptance of this Agreement, BUYER, may have the Property
223 inspected to determine if:

224 (a) all major appliances; heating, cooling, mechanical, electrical and plumbing systems; and pool
225 equipment (if any) are in working condition, except _____;

226 (b) the main structure and the roof and pool (if any) are structurally sound and water tight;

227 (c) the roof on the main structure has a remaining economic life of two (2) years or any longer
228 period required by lender. "Working Condition" means operating in the manner in which the item
229 was designed to operate. <u>The Professional Inspection is not intended to discover or note</u>
230 <u>cosmetic conditions and SELLER is not obliged to cure cosmetic conditions or to bring any item</u>
231 <u>into compliance with current building codes unless necessary to put an item in working condition.</u>
232 "Cosmetic Condition" means visible aesthetic imperfections which do not affect the working
233 condition of the item, such as, but not limited to, tears, worn spots and discoloration of floor
234 coverings, wallpapers, or window treatments, nail holes, scratches, dents, scrapes, chips and
235 caulking in bathroom ceiling, walls, flooring, tile, fixtures or mirrors, and minor cracks in windows,
236 driveways, sidewalks, pool decks, garage floors and patio floors. <u>Fogged windows are deemed</u>
237 **<u>not</u>** <u>to be a cosmetic condition.</u>

238 BUYER must, within <u>fifteen (15) days</u> after acceptance of this Agreement, deliver to SELLER
239 written notice of any items which are not in the condition required and a copy of the inspector's
240 written report, if any.

241 (2) **Walk-Through Inspection:** BUYER may, no later than <u>two (2) days</u> prior to closing, walk through
242 the Property solely to verify that SELLER has made repairs required under this Agreement and
243 has maintained the Property. No other issues may be raised as a result of the walk-through
244 inspection, unless the issue was not visible during the inspection.

245 (3) **Access and Utilities:** SELLER will make the Property available for inspections during the time
246 provided in paragraph 15, and, if not, the time for inspections will be extended by the time access
247 was denied. If utilities are not active at the time the inspections or appraisal are to be made,
248 SELLER will pay to have the utilities activated for these purposes.

249 (4) **Broker's Notice:** Neither the Listing Broker nor Selling Broker warrant the condition, size or
250 square footage of the Property and neither is liable to either party in any manner whatsoever for
251 any claim, loss or damage regarding same. Therefore, BUYER and SELLER release and hold
252 harmless said Brokers and their licensees from any claim, loss or damage arising out of or
253 occurring with respect to the condition, size or square footage of the Property. Broker shall not be
254 liable for the performance by any provider of services or products recommended by Broker. Such
255 recommendations are made as a courtesy only and the parties are free to select their own
256 providers.

257 (5) **Buyer's Responsibility:** Repairs or replacements to the Property after closing or BUYER's
258 occupancy, whichever occurs first, will be BUYER's responsibility unless otherwise agreed in
259 writing.

260 (B) **Repair:** SELLER is obligated only to make repairs and replacements identified in the BUYER's written
261 notice described in paragraph 15 (A) and then only as is necessary to bring those items to the
262 condition required, unless otherwise set forth in this Agreement. SELLER's obligation to pay for
263 repairs and replacements are limited to the amount shown in paragraph 6(A) of this Agreement.
264 SELLER, within <u>ten (10) days</u> after receiving BUYER's written notice of repairs and BUYER's loan
265 approval, if applicable, will have repairs made in a workmanlike manner by an appropriately licensed
266 person. If such costs exceed the amount specified in paragraph 6(A) and SELLER declines to pay
267 the excess, BUYER may cancel this Agreement within <u>five (5) days</u> after receipt of SELLER's notice
268 of SELLER's refusal to pay by giving written notice to the SELLER, or be deemed to have elected to
269 proceed with the transaction, in which event, BUYER will receive credit at closing of an amount equal
270 to the total of the SELLER's repair limit in paragraph 6(A), if allowed by lender. If prohibited by lender,
271 SELLER will accomplish the required repairs and BUYER will pay excess amount to SELLER at
272 closing. To secure the BUYER's obligation to pay the excess to SELLER, BUYER shall deposit an
273 additional binder ("Excess Binder") with the Broker in the amount which, when added to the amount to
274 be paid by SELLER, will equal cost of the repairs. The Excess Binder will not be refunded to BUYER
275 unless SELLER is unable or unwilling to perform its obligations hereunder.

FIGURE 3–6
(continued)

276   (C) **Wood-Destroying Organisms:** "Wood-Destroying Organisms (WDO)" means arthropod or plant life,
277   which may damage a structure. Within twenty (20) days of acceptance of this Agreement BUYER, at
278   BUYER's expense (unless VA), may have the Property inspected by a Florida certified pest control
279   firm and notify SELLER as to whether there is any visible active wood-destroying organism infestation
280   or visible existing damage to the improvements from wood-destroying organisms by furnishing a copy
281   of firm's written report to SELLER. SELLER will, within ten (10) days after receiving firm's written
282   WDO report and BUYER's loan approval, if applicable, have repairs made in a workman like manner
283   by an appropriately licensed person. SELLER will pay costs of treatment and repair, by appropriately
284   licensed persons, of all wood destroying organism report damage up to one percent (1.0%) of the
285   purchase price. If such costs exceed the amount agreed to be paid by SELLER and SELLER declines
286   to pay the excess, BUYER will have the option of (a) terminating this Agreement, or (b) proceeding
287   with this transaction, in which event SELLER will bear costs equal to one percent (1.0%) of the
288   purchase price. SELLER is not obligated to treat the Property if there is evidence of previous
289   infestation but no visible live infestation and SELLER provides written proof to Buyer of previous
290   treatment of the Property for such infestation by a Florida certified pest control firm or transfers a
291   current bond or service agreement for such infestation to Buyer at Closing. BUYER will pay for any
292   reinspection fees required by BUYER's lender unless prohibited by law or regulation.

293 16. **OCCUPANCY:** [   ] SELLER represents that there are no parties in occupancy other than SELLER.
294   BUYER will be given occupancy at closing unless otherwise specified herein, _____
295   _____ .
296   If occupancy is to be delivered before or after closing, the parties shall execute a separate agreement
297   prepared by legal counsel at BUYER's expense. Property will be swept clean and all personal property not
298   included in sale will be removed by time of BUYER'S occupancy.
299   [   ] BUYER understands that Property is available for rent or rented and the tenant may continue in
300   possession following closing unless otherwise agreed in writing. All deposits will be transferred to BUYER
301   at closing.

302 17. **PERSONAL PROPERTY:** Included in the purchase price is all fixed equipment such as, but not limited
303   to, automatic garage door opener & controls, drapery hardware, attached lighting fixtures, mailbox, all
304   ceiling fans, fence, plants and shrubbery as now installed on the Property, and these additional items:
305   _____
306   _____
307   _____
308   _____
309   Items specifically excluded from this Agreement: _____
310   _____
311   _____

312 18. **ADDITIONAL TERMS, CONDITIONS, OR ADDENDA:**_____
313   _____
314   _____
315   _____
316   _____
317   _____

318 19. **COMPLETE AGREEMENT/MISCELLANEOUS:** BUYER and SELLER acknowledge receipt of a copy of
319   this Agreement. The parties agree that the terms of this Agreement constitute the entire agreement
320   between them and they have not received or relied on any representations by Broker or any printed
321   material regarding the Property including, but not limited to, the listing information sheet, that are not
322   expressed in this Agreement. **No prior or present agreements or representations will bind BUYER,**
323   **SELLER or Broker unless incorporated into this Agreement.** Modifications of this Agreement will not
324   be binding unless in writing, signed and delivered by the party to be bound. Headings are for reference
325   only and shall not be deemed to control interpretations. Signatures, initials and modifications
326   communicated by facsimile will be considered as original. If any provision of this Agreement is or
327   becomes invalid or unenforceable, all remaining provisions will continue to be fully effective. This
328   Agreement will not be recorded in any public records. **If not understood, parties should seek**
329   **competent legal advice.** Any time periods herein, other than the time of acceptance, which end on a
330   Saturday, Sunday, or State holiday shall extend to the next day which is not a Saturday, Sunday or State
331   holiday. TIME IS OF THE ESSENCE IN THIS AGREEMENT. In the performance of the terms and
332   conditions of this Agreement each party will deal fairly and in good faith with the other. Other than fact of
333   acceptance of this Agreement, notice to the Broker for a party shall be deemed notice to that party. All
334   assignable repair and treatment contracts and warranties are deemed assigned by SELLER to BUYER
335   at closing unless otherwise stated herein. SELLER agrees to sign all documents necessary to
336   accomplish same, at BUYER's expense, if any.

337 20. **BUYER'S AND SELLER'S NOTICES:** BUYER and SELLER represent that they have not entered into
338   any other agreements with real estate brokers other than those named below with regard to the Property.
339   SELLER and BUYER give Broker authorization to advise surrounding neighbors who will be the new
340   owner of this Property. "Broker", as used in this Agreement, is intended to refer to persons licensed to
341   sell real property in the State of Florida.

342 21. **HOMEOWNER'S ASSOCIATION DISCLOSURE:** If applicable, see homeowners association disclosure
343   summary attached hereto and incorporated herein by this reference. Buyer shall not sign this Agreement
344   until Buyer has received and read the disclosure summary.

FIGURE 3–6
(continued)

345 **22. ACCEPTANCE:** IF THIS OFFER IS NOT SIGNED BY AND DELIVERED TO ALL PARTIES OR FACT
346 OF ACCEPTANCE COMMUNICATED IN WRITING (INCLUDING FAX) BETWEEN THE PARTIES ON
347 OR BEFORE _____:01 [ ] A.M. [ ] P.M. Date _____, this offer will terminate.

348 **23. ESCROW DISCLOSURE:** The Parties agree that Broker may place escrow funds in an interest bearing
349 account pursuant to the rules and regulations of the Florida Real Estate Commission and retain any
350 interest earned as the cost associated with maintenance of said escrow.

351 **24. SOCIAL SECURITY/ TAX I.D. NUMBER:** Parties agree to provide their respective Social Security or Tax
352 I.D. number to closing attorney/ settlement agent upon request.

353 _____   _____   _____   _____
354 BUYER   DATE   SELLER   DATE

355 _____   _____   _____   _____
356 BUYER   DATE   SELLER   DATE

357 Broker joins in this Agreement to evidence Broker's consent to be bound by the provisions of paragraph 9
358 above. Broker, by signature below, acknowledges receipt of $ _____ [ ] cash [ ] check
359 as binder deposit which is the amount specified in paragraph 1(A) of this Agreement. It will be deposited and
360 held in escrow pending disbursement according to terms hereof, together with all additional binder deposits
361 escrowed by terms of this Agreement.

362 _____   _____   _____
363 Company   By   Title

364 **BROKER'S FEE:** SELLER agrees to pay listing Broker named below according to the terms of an existing
365 listing agreement or as mutually agreed in this Agreement. (If there is no listing agreement, SELLER agrees to
366 pay Selling Broker _____% of gross purchase price or $_____.)

367 Listing Broker agrees to pay Selling Broker a commission of _____% of the gross purchase price or
368 $_____.If the transaction does not close due to SELLER's refusal or failure to perform, SELLER
369 will pay the full fee to listing Broker on demand. In any litigation arising out of this Agreement concerning the
370 Broker's fee, each party will be liable for their own costs and attorney's fees. If there is no separate listing
371 agreement in effect and, if BUYER fails to perform and deposit(s) is retained, 50% thereof, after deduction of
372 costs, will be paid to SELLER and balance will be paid to Broker as full consideration of Broker's services, but
373 the amount paid to Broker will not exceed the Broker's fee provided above.

374 _____   _____   _____
375 Firm Name of Listing Broker   Firm Name of Selling Broker   Seller

376 By:_____   By: _____   _____
377   Authorized Licensee   Authorized Licensee   Seller

FIGURE 3–6
(continued)

Review the agreements closely and highlight the similarities in clauses and terms. Highlight the differences between clauses and terms as well. A closer look at the elements and the components of these agreements follow.

A. Identification of Real Estate Agents/Firms

Just who the real estate agents will be during the transaction is usually noted somewhere on the agreement of sale. Generally speaking, the agent is the firm and its broker who list the property or who represents the buyer in an agency capacity. A sales agent may be distinct from the listing broker. If the buyer wishes to be represented by an agent who will act exclusively in the buyer's interest, it is required that the buyer's agent notify the seller's agent of this before showing the property. This notification advises the seller and his agent that the buyer's agent will not be acting in the same capacity as the seller's agent.

(hereinafter "Blumberg") takes an unusual approach to a sale, recognizing in Clause 21, the possibility that an agent may not be responsible for the sale of a piece of property. (hereinafter "Easy Soft") does not address the issue of brokers and commission in their contract, leaving that to an external agreement. (hereinafter NFAR) includes spaces to positively identify the broker's relationship to seller and buyer at the end of the contract.

Web Exercise

Most state realtor associations now publish forms and agreements for those laboring in real estate. Visit *www.nh-commercial-realestate.com/Properties/Properties/Forms_files/page10_2.pdf.*

B. Identification Information

The parties or principals to the agreement, their addresses, and, in some cases, their Social Security numbers are listed under the introductory paragraph. The names must be spelled without errors, and addresses must be complete, with the street and house number listed. If the address is a rural delivery, the route and box number must be stated. If either of the parties has a post office box number that must be included; the city, county, state, and zip code must be inscribed as well.

The Blumberg, Easy Soft, and NFAR forms list buyer and seller, along with their respective addresses at the beginning of the form.

C. Legal Description

The agreement represents the full and comprehensive vision of what is to be conveyed, thus the agreement must sufficiently describe the realty subject to the agreement. "Following the introduction comes the description. . . . The description must be definite enough to identify the property,[10] but if it names a definite object it satisfies the statute of frauds, for parol evidence is then admissible to identify the property in more detail or to locate it on the ground.[11] An agreement to sell real estate cannot be specifically enforced unless it identifies the land in terms sufficient to enable a surveyor to determine its location and boundaries by metes and bounds or by adjoiners."[12] In most areas of the country, a short **legal description** of the property is all that is necessary.

All that certain lot or piece of ground within the buildings and improvements thereon erected, situated in the township of _____, county of _____, state of _____, and known as _____ Street, as more particularly described in the deed to be delivered at settlement as hereafter provided.

It is extremely important to have correct and complete information. All information must be carefully checked against records in current deed books.

The Blumberg form is quite specific about the description of the "property" being sold. Aside from leaving over an entire page for the property description, the "property" also includes buildings and improvements, other rights, fixtures, and personal property. The Easy Soft form takes a similar track, but leaves much less space for a property description, and is more restrictive in the recital of personalty and fixtures included in "property," leaving that designation up to the buyer and seller. The NFAR form is basically a mirror image of the Easy Soft format.

D. Terms and Conditions of Payment

The underlying consideration that supports the real estate contract must be clearly delineated. All three agreements typify a payment/purchase clause, leaving spaces for a first and any additional deposits, amount of mortgage, and balance due at closing. When there is a cash deposit, assure that an official receipt, issued by the receiving party, is given to the prospective buyer. The cash deposit is then transferred to the selling agent's office. If the deposit is made by check, it should be made payable to the real estate company that represents the seller. The deposit, along with the agreement of sale and any other attached documents, should be handed over to the seller's agent. How the initial deposit is termed is a matter of local custom. This package should be accompanied by a cover letter.

The real estate agents who represent the buyer and seller should make sure that any monies due are paid before the due date to ensure the validity of the agreement. Additional payments may be made by cash, check, or note. The balance of the purchase price is due on the day of settlement and is paid to the seller. All parties must be present, and final payment must be made for the transaction to be complete and valid.

E. Property Settlement Contingency

Any agreement may contain a provision that allows the buyers to sell their present home before the final settlement is made. The language may state:

This agreement is subject to the settlement of buyer's property located at _____ on or before _____.

Although none of the agreements contain this contingency, ample space is given for the addition of such a clause.

F. Performance Data

Every agreement of sale should keep the parties on a timely path to closing. The date when a mortgage commitment is to be received, as well as the date for approval by the seller and the completion date of other contingencies, is fully discussed in several clauses of all three contracts. For example, the Blumberg agreement mentions the financing commitment date in Clause 6(a) and the closing date in Clause 15. Other deadlines are mentioned throughout in the appropriate clauses.

G. Settlement Adjustment/Terms

The question of pro rata tax payments (that is, the amount of real estate taxes divided upon recording to the time of possession in the taxing year), payments to **escrow** accounts to cover insurance or other costs, and credits for payments in advance or arrears is addressed in the adjustment section of the agreement. Blumberg's form addresses settlement adjustments in several places. Prorated expenses are discussed in Clause 20, "Adjustment of Property Expenses." Realty transfer fees are addressed in Clause 16. Easy Soft includes all settlement adjustments in one paragraph, Clause 22, "Adjustments at Closing." Prorations, settlement costs, and tax withholdings are thoroughly addressed in Clause 4 of the NFAR form. The clause sets forth the specific responsibilities of the buyer and seller, the prorated items, and the tax obligations of the buyer and seller.

The amount of **transfer taxes**, that sum usually imposed by cities, countries, or states upon formal conveyance, will usually be divided equally between the buyer and seller, although this is not set in stone and local customs must be taken into consideration. If agreed, one party may take on the responsibility of paying all of the transfer tax.

Taxes, rents on water and sewage, homeowner association fees, and so forth will be prorated. The transfer of leases and security deposits is not automatic in the case of a rental property. This needs to be negotiated between the buyer and seller. Although the seller will be reimbursed for heating and/or cooking fuels, the basis of calculation of the reimbursement needs to be negotiated. Depending on the current practice in a region, this may include coal and firewood. Preprinted forms may or may not include these items in the sale price. The broker needs to inform the seller to pay strict attention to these items because it can mean the difference between hundreds, or even thousands of dollars. All of this must be agreed upon before the settlement date, or difficulties may arise that can result in a delay of the settlement. John H. Scheid states:

> Adjustment provisions usually pertain to such items as utility bills, taxes, rents, service contract charges, etc. In order to compel proration of an item, it must have been provided for in the written contract. Where, with no fault on buyer's part, there has been a delay in the closing, thus preventing him from entering into possession, the buyer is entitled to have the taxes prorated as of the actual date of the closing rather than the time specified in the contract.[13]

H. Financing or Other Contingency

Most agreements have a financing or other contingency. A contingency awaits a certain fulfillment such as the award of mortgage financing or grant of a zoning permit.

The typical conditional or contingent situations in real estate practice are:

- Whether the agreement has effect if mortgage financing is not obtainable.
- Whether the agreement has effect if alternative mortgage financing is available other than that stated in the contract.
- Whether failure to acquire certification for septic systems will void a contract.
- Whether failure to be granted zoning will serve as an excusable condition or failure to meet a contingent requirement under a contract.
- Whether a political subdivision permitted development of land in a certain way or right as envisioned under the original contract.
- Whether the condition of water and soil meets regulatory guidelines.
- Whether there is evidence of termite and insect infestation.
- Whether there is evidence of environmental contamination or toxic pollution.

A contract with a contingency or a condition is little more than a conditional contract which lacks enforceability until the condition is met. Conditions and contingencies in real estate law have triggered a formidable body of case law.

In *Hodorowicz v. Szulc,* buyers' and sellers' contract provided that the buyers had to sell a house by a specific date which was set forth in the contract.[14] The court found the contract void for failure to meet a condition. Purchasers were to have a mortgage commitment within 60 days of the signing of the contract. When no commitment occurred within the 60-day period, the court held that these purchasers were under no obligation to perform under a contract that was void and nonexistent.

An Illinois case, *Dodson v. Nink,*[15] declared a contract of sale null and void since purchasers would accept a VA loan, but not agree to be responsible for any repair costs. In upholding the condition, the court strictly interpreted the contract.

The Delaware Supreme Court's respected Honorable Andrew D. Christie skillfully decided a similar case, *E. I. Dupont et al. v. Crompton-Townsend Inc.*[16] When purchasers decided not to approve the survey, sellers balked and said the problems could have been corrected. In fact, their objections to the survey were trivial. Judge Christie characterized the contract as "not a sale as to the purchase of a survey and to the terms on which a sale would take place if all the parties at a future date decided to agree to convert the conditional sales agreement into a binding contract by approving the survey."[17] Judge Christie, in strictly construing the contract, choosing not to infer or surmise the purchasers' motivations, held that the conditional language of the contract was unambiguous.

Both case law and scholarly legal analysis support the fundamental contention that a condition precedent, neither met nor waived, cannot lead to an obligation of contractual performance.

Financing contingencies are the most frequently witnessed conditional terms in the agreement of sale. "The standard provisions concerning mortgage contingencies allowing the purchaser to rescind the contract if the purchaser is not able to obtain certain mortgage results in many pitfalls. When does a purchaser have a firm commitment for a mortgage? Most contracts specify that the purchaser must apply for a mortgage, in compliance with the terms of the contract, within a certain number of days, such as five banking days, after the signing of the contract."[18]

The Blumberg agreement includes a standard mortgage clause, including the date by which the commitment is to be received and the type of mortgage product the buyer will accept, including the amount to be financed, the type of mortgage, interest rate, length of mortgage, and any points payable. The clause also states that if the mortgage offered to the buyer is not as designated, either party can cancel the contract—if the buyer does not choose to accept the funding. The Easy Soft agreement includes the same types of provisions.

The NFAR financing contingency appears at Clause 2 and includes a few differences. It allows either a set or specified number of days to apply for the mortgage and receive the commitment. It includes no mention of interest rate, terms, and so forth. The seller and their attorney and paralegal should pay close attention to the financing commitment date so they may assure mortgage approval by the set date. This is necessary because banks and other lenders are not bound by the agreement. If there is any chance that the financing date will not be adhered to, it may be changed prior to the settlement date, if mutually agreeable.

The seller and seller's agent should pay close attention to the dates set and memorialize any changes in an addendum document to be signed and dated by both parties.

I. Miscellaneous Conditions and Contingencies

Aside from financing, the paralegal will be exposed to a host of other possible contingencies during the life of an agreement. The scope and coverage of conditional and contingent language will mirror the issue in the agreement. Conditions are generally memorialized in an addendum or additional clause. Examples are:

Home Inspection: Form 13–13

Swimming Pools: Form 13–14

Water and Septic: Form 13–15

Radon: Form 13–16

UFFI: Form 13–17

Wood Infestation: Form 13–18

Zoning: Form 13–19

J. Special Clauses

The seller's property disclosure statement should be included as a special clause. The statement should be read and signed or initialed by the buyer along with other clauses such as: the inspection addendum, the purchase agreement, well inspection and water potability test (if applicable), wood boring/destroying insect reports, and a joint driveway agreement, if applicable. These are only a few examples of clauses that may be attached to the agreement.

Another way of incorporating certain conditions or terms is by way of addendum.

K. Notice and Disclosure

As a general rule, notice of a failed condition eliminates questions about the goodwill of the party not meeting the condition. State and federal law mandate various disclosures as to material or latent defects. Notices are discussed under Clause 23 of the Blumberg contract. The contract states that all notices must be in writing, delivered personally or by certified mail, and each party must accept the notices of the other. The Easy Soft notices Clause 26, which is identical except for the omission of any discussion of acceptance. The NFAR contract is also similar. But it provides that, if the buyer does not deliver written notice to the seller of a contingency, the contingency will be null and void.

Mandatory disclosure to the contract's parties may be a contractual obligation. The Blumberg form skirts over the issue of any environmental hazards in Clause 12(b), as does Easy Soft, stating at Clause 11 that the property is being sold "as is," as does the Blumberg form at Clause 7. The NFAR agreement takes a protectionist track and includes a statement that the seller denies any knowledge of any material defects. This disclosure also puts the buyer on notice that any finding on energy efficiency, radon gas, and flood zone is the buyer's responsibility.

L. Zoning Classification

How a property is zoned is inexorably tied to usage and purpose. Eliminate any real or potential confusion on zoning. Blumberg includes zoning information in Clause 12, "Statements of Seller," only addressing the current **zoning classification**. The Easy Soft agreement is a little more thorough. At Clause 13, it states that the intended use of the property does not violate any zoning ordinance, building code, or other law. It also provides that if a "certificate of occupancy" is required, the seller will obtain it along with any inspections required by law. The NFAR agreement includes a zoning clause at Clause 12, "Zoning and Restrictions," and gives the buyer ten days to verify the existing zoning designation. If the zoning designation is not as stated, the buyer has the option to cancel the contract.

Even though the standardized form may mention that the property or each parcel of such property is zoned solely for single-family dwellings, it is necessary to determine whether the zoning classification is correct. There have been many instances when a property's zoning classification has changed from residential to commercial and then back to residential again. The paralegal, under direction of an attorney, should investigate this matter to assure that the correct classification is listed on the agreement. Otherwise court action may result.

M. Deposits

Buyer's deposit on a prospective home is guided by the explicit language of contract. Clause 4 of the Blumberg agreement thoroughly discusses deposits, who will hold deposits in escrow, and when the funds will be released. Easy Soft only mentions where the funds will be held and the release date in Clause 5. Clause 1 of the NFAR agreement designates deposits. Deposits are usually paid to the seller's agent, the agent depositing the funds in an escrow account. Some agents disregard the law and commingle funds. When the transaction is finalized at settlement, the seller's agent hands over the deposit monies to the settlement officer. The settlement officer, who is often an attorney or paralegal, then records the transaction on the settlement sheet.

If a dispute between the buyer and seller emerges, the contract may give instructions on disbursements of deposits. If the agreement is silent, the agent for the seller retains the deposit funds in the escrow account until a written settlement or court order is produced.

N. Municipal Assessments

Sewage, sidewalk, or road assessments or other specified levies are treated in the contract. Clause 10 of the Blumberg agreement and Easy Soft's Clause 21 address the possibility of an assessment, and designate the party who will carry the responsibility for payment for any improvements, but they make no mention of the seller's knowledge of any pending assessments. The NFAR form makes no mention of municipal assessments.

O. Title and Costs

Any legitimate agreement of sale will deal with the question and quality of title and the costs associated with delivery of good title. The Blumberg agreement states at Clauses 13 and 16, "Seller shall transfer ownership of the Property to the Buyer at the closing, free of all claims, and rights of others . . . by Deed of Bargain and Sale with Covenant as to Grantor's Acts." Exceptions to this transfer are building restrictions, ordinances, easements, legitimate rights-of-way, privileges, and rights of public services companies. The preceding must be properly described in the deed. The NFAR agreement Clause 10 is similar, while the Easy Soft agreement leaves the deed designation up to the seller and buyer in Clauses 8 and 9.

According to Section 13(B) of the NFAR agreement, if no good or marketable title can be produced, the buyer may either cancel the transaction or accept the defective title and close the transaction. The Blumberg and Easy Soft agreements are similar, stating the same thing, although not as plainly. They mention "above exceptions" instead of just a "good and marketable title." There are times when the deed is lost or one never existed. When this occurs, the court can intervene and order that a deed be produced to enable the seller to sell the property.

P. Title Insurance

When the title to the property has been determined to be good and marketable, a title **insurance** policy, issued by a title insurer, insures against any subsequent challenge to title. It may only be necessary to take out this type of insurance to cover the lending institutions for the amount of the mortgage. This decision is made solely by the buyer and the lending institution. The Blumberg agreement requires the buyer to obtain title insurance, as does the Easy Soft agreement. The NFAR agreement is more specific in Clause 10, which sets out the title insurance process and states which party has the responsibility for title insurance costs.

Q. Flood and Hazard Insurance

Flood insurance needs to be acquired only if the dwelling is in a flood zone—an area of land with a history of flooding or governmentally designated as such. If the property is in a flood zone, it is mandatory to obtain this type of insurance because a lender will not approve a mortgage without it.

Homeowner's insurance, also called fire insurance with extended coverage or hazard insurance, is a necessity for any homeowner mortgage or financing. The lender usually requires that only the amount of the mortgage be covered by this type of insurance. When the agreement of sale is signed, the buyer will ask his or her insurance company for a **binder**, or proof of insurance. This binder will be followed by the policy, which will be presented at the settlement.

R. Closing Costs

Agreements will portray responsibility for closing or settlement costs. Clauses 5 and 6 of the NFAR agreement provide an itemized listing of the major closing costs that the buyer or seller will be responsible for at settlement. The other two agreements make no mention of an estimate of closing costs. This will advise the buyer how much money, in addition to the mortgage amount, will be needed at the time of settlement.

S. Survey

Surveys are not universally required within the real estate transaction, though questions of boundary and zoning are frequent concerns for buyers and sellers. Banks and mortgage entities generally require a survey that is less than two years old.[19]

The NFAR is the only agreement to address surveys. Clause 11 states that the buyer has the right, prior to closing, to have the property surveyed. Any surveys required by the buyer or the buyer's agent are to be paid for by the buyer.

CASE DECISION

As banks and finance companies package their products and services, delivering not only the financing but also the title services, closing and settlement as well as surveys. Consumers have been suspicious of the pricing and the incentive to foster higher costs on buyers and sellers. Read a recent administrative ruling from Michigan on whether a bank could also own a company that performed the land surveys.

March 8, 1999

STATE OF MICHIGAN

DEPARTMENT OF CONSUMER AND INDUSTRY SERVICES

FINANCIAL INSTITUTIONS BUREAU

IN THE MATTER OF CITIZENS FIRST SAVINGS BANK INVESTING IN A SUBSIDIARY WHICH WILL ENGAGE IN THE BUSINESS OF PERFORMING REAL ESTATE SURVEYS PURSUANT TO SECTION 401(2) OF MICHIGAN'S SAVINGS BANK ACT, AS AMENDED

BACKGROUND

Davidson, Staiger and Hill, P.C., counsel for Citizens First Savings Bank (Citizens), Port Huron, Michigan, a state-chartered savings bank, has asked the Financial Institutions Bureau to confirm that Citizens is authorized, pursuant to Section 401(1) of the Savings Bank Act (Act), as amended, to use a subsidiary to conduct real estate surveys in support of Citizens' real estate mortgage business. Alternatively, the Bureau has been asked to issue a declaratory ruling or order pursuant to Section 401(2) permitting Citizens' subsidiary to engage in performing real estate surveys in support of Citizens' real estate mortgage business.

Counsel represents the surveys will be conducted by licensed surveyors who will be either employees of the subsidiary or independent contractors. The surveys will be done in support of Citizen's real estate mortgage loans. A survey is defined as a document that shows the exact boundaries of a property, including lot lines and placement of improvements on the property and is said to look much like a map of the property. A survey is an important element of the real estate mortgage underwriting process.

Because of the broad applicability of the issue, it is the Bureau's position that a declaratory ruling is more appropriate than an order as a vehicle for a decision issued pursuant to Section 401(2) of the Act.

ISSUE PRESENTED

May a Michigan state-chartered savings bank own and operate a subsidiary that performs real estate surveys in support of the savings bank's real estate mortgage business?

ANALYSIS

Applicable Statues:

Section 401 of the Savings Bank Act (MCL 487.3401; MSA 23.710(3401) states in part:

"Except as otherwise provided by this act, a savings bank may engage in the business of banking and exercise all powers incidental to the business of banking or which further or facilitate the purposes of a savings bank."

Section 401(1)(p), *supra*, states that a savings bank is authorized:

"To conduct its business through subsidiaries, at the same location or a location different from the savings bank. . . ."

Section 401(2), *supra*, states:

"The commissioner may promulgate rules under Section 208, or issue declaratory rulings, or issue orders, permitting savings banks to exercise powers not authorized by this act. It is intended that this subsection shall vest in the commissioner the discretion and authority to authorize savings banks to exercise all powers appropriate and necessary to compete with other depository financial institutions and other providers of financial services. In the exercise of the discretion permitted by this subsection, the commissioner shall consider the ability of savings banks to exercise any additional power in a safe and sound manner, the authority of state and national banks, associations, and state and federal credit unions, operating under state or federal law or regulation, the powers of other competing entities providing financial services in this state, and any specific limitations on powers contained in this act or in any other state law. On at least a quarterly basis, the commissioner shall give notice to all savings banks of rules promulgated, or declaratory rulings or determinations, or orders, issued under this subsection."

Section 201(2) of the Act (MCL 487.3201(2); MSA 23.710(3201)(2)), provides:

"The commissioner shall maximize the capacity of savings banks in this state to offer convenient and efficient financial services, to promote home ownership and economic development, and to ensure that savings banks remain competitive with other types of financial institutions and providers of financial services."

Discussion:

Section 201 of the Act requires the commissioner to consider the evolution of the financial marketplace and, if justified, act favorably on matters that promote competition among financial institutions.

Section 401 of the Act defines the corporate powers of a savings bank by providing the initial parameters for the operation of a savings bank. A savings bank is authorized to engage in the business of banking and exercise those powers contained in the Act as well as engage in a business that is incidental to the business of banking or which furthers or facilitates the purposes of a savings bank. Section 401 also provides a list of additional specific corporate powers authorized to a state-chartered savings bank. More specifically, Section 401(2) authorizes the commissioner to issue a declaratory ruling permitting a savings bank to exercise powers not authorized by the Act.

Section 401(2) of the Act requires the commissioner to consider four factors in exercising the discretion to authorize savings banks to exercise a new power.

First, the commissioner must consider a savings bank's ability to exercise the new power in a safe and sound manner. Bank ownership of a subsidiary that conducts real estate surveys represents very little risk. The investment would be nominal. Possible risks might involve clerical errors and property misidentification. Risks of this nature are the type commonly taken by savings banks in their traditional activities. Adequate insurance coverage combined with proper policies and procedures will mitigate most survey risks.

Second, the commissioner must consider the authority of state and national banks, associations, and state and federal credit unions to exercise the power. On September 22, 1988, the Comptroller of the Currency issued Interpretive Letter 450. This Interpretive Letter concluded:

"The most restrictive test of bank powers, that applied in *Arnold Tours Inc. v. Camp*, 472 F.2d 427 (1st Cir. 1972), permits national banks to engage in an activity that is 'convenient or useful in the performance of one of the bank's established activities pursuant to its express powers . . . ' since surveys, title searches, and title opinions are a necessary part of the real estate lending process, it would be convenient or useful for banks to be able to perform these tasks themselves. Surveying, performing title searches, and arriving at legal title opinions are at least as integral to the process of real estate lending as is the previously-authorized sale of title insurance. National banks may, therefore, perform surveys and title searches, and produce title opinions, in connection with their real estate mortgage business."

While national banks have been authorized by the Comptroller of the Currency to perform real estate surveys, no state banks, associations, or state or federal credit unions have received such authority.

Third, the commissioner must consider powers of competing entities providing financial services in Michigan. This requirement is met given the authority of national banks to engage in performing real estate surveys.

Fourth, the commissioner must determine whether there are any specific limitations on savings bank powers contained in the Act or in any other state law. The Act does not prohibit a state-chartered savings bank from engaging in the proposed activity. Further, no other Michigan law prohibits a savings bank from engaging in the proposed activity directly or through a wholly-owned subsidiary.

FINDINGS OF FACT AND OR LAW

Real estate lending and activities incidental thereto are normally associated with the operation of a savings bank. A survey is one of the principal documents obtained as part of the real estate mortgage underwriting process. Performing real estate surveys furthers and facilitates the business of a savings bank while introducing manageable safety and soundness concerns. Owning a subsidiary that performs real estate surveys in conjunction with a savings bank's mortgage lending business presents no more risk than if the activity is done by the savings bank itself. The risk is manageable through proper policies and procedures and appropriate insurance.

A savings bank is authorized to conduct its business through subsidiaries. National banks are authorized to perform surveys in connection with their real estate mortgage business.

DECLARATORY RULING

Finally, neither the Act nor any other state law prohibits a savings bank or its subsidiary from performing real estate surveys.

Consistent with the spirit and intent of sections 201 and 401(2) of the Act, the commissioner finds that a Michigan state-chartered savings bank may own and operate a subsidiary that performs real estate surveys.

Patrick M. McQueen, Commissioner

Financial Institutions Bureau

Department of Consumer and Industry Services

Date: March 8, 1999

T. Prepossession Inspection

Under most American jurisdictions, an inspection right exists for the benefit of the purchaser. Usually, one week to 24 hours before closing, purchasers have a right to inspect the premises and its major systems to determine operability, to verify habitability, and to ensure that all terms and conditions of the contract are being met. Under traditional custom and usage in the industry, the house should substantially be in the same condition as the date of sale and turned over in broom-swept condition.

When defects to the home are known by the seller, the question of disclosure varies according to jurisdiction. Increasingly, courts find that sellers have an obligation to disclose latent defects in the premises conveyed. The failure to disclose may give rise to action in fraud and misrepresentation. At the same time, buyers have an obligation to investigate. The doctrine of *caveat emptor* still exists, though in a much softer form than its common law counterpart.[20]

A walk-through inspection on the day before closing or some other mutually agreeable time is for the purpose of assuring that repairs regarding wood-destroying organisms or repairs necessary to bring warranted items up to the warranted condition have been completed. This clause is a common provision. The Blumberg agreement states in Clause 8 that the property will be transferred in its present condition, buildings will be vacant and in "broom-clean" condition, and all personalty not included in the sale shall be removed. The clause also allows the buyer to inspect the property within seven days before closing, provided that the seller is given ample notice of the time. The Easy Soft agreement is basically the same, Clauses 11 and 12, but makes no promises about the cleanliness of the property.

If there are items to be included with the sale of the property or something on the premises is changed or damaged, it should be noted during the inspection. The changes should then be addressed at settlement where price adjustments can be made.

The Blumberg and NFAR agreements provide the buyer with the right to have the property and all warranted items inspected within a certain number of days before the effective date of the agreement. Otherwise, the right is waived. (See Clauses 6(c), 6(d), and 7 of the Blumberg agreement and Clause 15(A)(1) and (2) of the NFAR agreement.) The Easy Soft agreement allows only a walk-through and termite inspection within ten days of the signing of the contract. This section also states that if any requested/required tests are not performed by a certain date then the buyer gives up the right to run the tests and must purchase the property as is. At times, an appraiser from the lending institution will also act as their inspector. In those instances, the appraiser will order repairs and/or adjustments to the property within 24 hours or the mortgage will not be available at settlement. Unless the inspectors are fully licensed to act in that capacity, the inspectors will be disqualified because they are not qualified to render opinions on construction, engineering, environmental matters, plumbing, wiring, septic systems, wells, and so forth. Only licensed inspectors should be allowed to inspect the property.

It is also imperative that the seller be sure that the real and personal property remain safe and in good working order while the agreement is executory. If anything should happen to the personal property between the signing of the agreement and the settlement date, the seller is responsible for repairs or replacement. It is well to include a clause to this effect in the agreement.

U. Personal Property and Fixtures

Personal property is automatically distinct and separable from the real estate purchase price unless the agreement lists it as an inclusion. If the seller disagrees, the seller must strike it from the printed form and initial.

Be sure that all of the personal property that is to be included in the settlement is agreed upon by both the buyer and seller and listed in a clause attached to the agreement of sale. Include in this list such things as appliances, air-conditioning, garage door openers, light fixtures, shrubbery, and so forth. Traditional fixtures, as noted in Chapter 1, are considered to be a part of the realty and are automatically conveyed.

Clause 2(d) of the Blumberg agreement, Clause 10 of the Easy Soft agreement, and Clause 17 of the NFAR agreement address all personal property and fixtures that are to be included in the sale. Each of these agreements leave ample space for the designation of items not originally listed. There is also space to designate items specifically excluded from the sale. The only difference evident is the length of the list of personalty included in the original contract. (See Blumberg's Clause 2(d) for the most complete list.) If the seller wishes a listed item not to be included in the sale, that item can be crossed out and initialed by the buyer and seller or can be designated in an addendum if space is not provided on the contract.

V. Risk of Loss

Who bears the responsibility for losses in the event of fire, hazard, or other catastrophe—the buyer or the seller? All three agreements state that the seller will bear the **risk of loss** from fire and/or other casualties until the time of settlement. The only differences are the threshold damage amounts for cancellation of the contract and the time allowed for repairs. The buyer and the buyer's agent should make sure that the seller has valid fire/casualty insurance on the property and that it will remain valid until the settlement.

The seller is liable for the risk of loss where:

1. Contract specifically provides for such risk allocation.
2. Seller does not have marketable title at the time of the loss, the argument being that it is unfair to put risk of loss on the buyer when the seller is in no position to perform the seller's own contract obligations.
3. Seller delays closing and loss occurs during delay.
4. Loss is due to seller's carelessness.[21]

W. Default/Time Is of the Essence

The contract should be clear as to the rights of the parties in the event of a **default** by the seller. It is extremely important that the seller's lawyer advises him/her of the consequences of a default.[22] In most cases in which the buyer defaults, the contract is clear that the deposit is forfeited. Most contracts, however, are not clear in specifying whether the real estate broker is then entitled to any commission. Of course, anything changing the rights of the real estate broker has to be agreed to by the real estate broker.

The NFAR agreement lists the remedies exercisable in the event of default (Clause 8). Additional terms are set forth regarding the resolution of disputes, other than default, through mediation, arbitration, and legal proceedings. The Blumberg and Easy Soft agreements do not specifically mention default but do list certain remedies in the event of cancellation or inability to complete contract performance (see Blumberg's clauses 4, 13, and 22 and Easy Soft's clauses 13, 14, 17, 18, 19, and 20).

"**Time is of the essence**" is most frequently a requirement in the following circumstances:

1. Bank application: Has the purchaser made the application to the lender for financing?
2. Mortgage commitment: Has the purchaser received a commitment from the lender regarding financing within the specific time periods?
3. Earnest money deposit: Has the purchaser made the necessary earnest money deposit payments on a schedule or as otherwise noted?
4. Certificates: Have the buyer and seller acquired and provided evidence of certificates for water, soil, and percolation?
5. Purchaser's failure to sell residence: If the contract is conditional on the purchaser selling a residence within a certain time frame, has that period been met?[23]

Unfortunately, for buyers and sellers in real estate, there has been much judicial intervention in the interpretation of a standardized contract. The crux of the matter in determining "time is of the essence" is as follows:

- What are the reasonable expectations in the industry's definition of time?
- What are the circumstances behind the transaction?
- What are the parties' purposes in making the contract?
- What is the significance of timely performance?
- How reasonable is the date set for performance?
- Does the contract possess a "time is of the essence" designation?
- Is the bank or other agency whose subject matter deals with a condition or other contingency cooperating with the buyer?
- Does the lender or bank or other agency refuse to provide information necessary to effect the contract?
- Does the person who has a benefit of a condition promptly repudiate the contract after a failure of condition?
- Does the doctrine of waiver and estoppel play a role in the interpretation of "time is of the essence"?

In the absence of a contract's expressly stated dates, the modern penchant has been to be more flexible or to tolerate delays. While historically time frames were strictly construed, jurisdictional differences now abound.

Web Exercise

Review a recent opinion issued by a Connecticut office on how to interpret "time is of the essence" at *www.cga.ct.gov/2002/olrdata/ins/rpt/2002-R-1013.htm.*

Paralegals handling real estate contracts that include a "time is of the essence" clause, should adhere to time frames religiously.

X. Recording of the Agreement

On rare occasions, a buyer will try to have the agreement of sale recorded in a county office. When this occurs, a buyer is usually trying to intimidate or annoy the seller. In turn, the seller may threaten the buyer with a breach of agreement suit. Such cases usually do not come to the settlement table. The three form agreements do not mention the permissibility of recording the agreement.

Y. Assignment

This provision attempts to regulate an **assignment** of a party's contractual interest. An assignment constitutes a sell, alienation, or transfer of the party's interests in the agreement of sale. As a rule, the law does not favor assignments in real estate contracts. The binding effect is largely dependent on the nature of the transaction. If a buyer enters into the transaction with a small down payment and a large mortgage commitment, the mortgage commitment is withdrawn upon the buyer's death because it is not transferable.

The Blumberg agreement in clauses 24 and 28 mention assignability, but only with the written consent of the seller. These clauses also make the contract binding on the heirs, administrators, and so forth, of the buyer, seller, and broker.

Z. Entire Agreement or Integration Clause

That the "four corners" of the document contain the parties' understanding is elementary law. That agents, lawyers, and practitioners wish to deny this legal maxim is unfortunately true. In essence, they would like to alter the terms of the agreement by introducing a term or condition that is not contained in the written agreement. Since contracts are restrictive instruments, integration clauses make irrelevant any extrinsic evidence concerning the contract. Such evidence will be inadmissible in court for purposes of contract interpretation. The integration clause recites the basic rules of contractual integration in relation to the agreement.

All three agreements permit written changes to the contract if signed by both parties or their agents/attorneys. Clause 19 of the NFAR agreement additionally states that changes to the contract are not valid unless signed by and delivered to the other party. The contract also gives priority to hand or typewritten terms in or attached to the contract. They will control over the form language. Signatures, initials, and modifications by facsimile will be accepted as original.

AA. Signature/Witness/Date of Execution

A contract is not binding unless fully executed. While witnesses are a debatable legal requirement, they add credibility to the parties' intentions. The date of the contract is relevant since the time requirements for applying for mortgages, zoning certificates, and other issues become important from this date forward.[24]

The Blumberg and Easy Soft forms allow for buyer and seller inscriptions at the end of the contract, with both agreements providing additional space for notarization. The Blumberg form provides space for corporate inscription. The NFAR provides basic signature lines.

BB. Unique Clauses

1. Broker's Clause

The broker's main desire is to bring the buyer and seller to an effective closing. He or she serves as a fiduciary—an agent owing unbridled and unfailing loyalty to those represented. His or her business interests and commission are guided by the agreement of sale.

The Blumberg and Easy Soft agreements only contain basic broker information such as their name and commission, while the clause below the signature line of the NFAR agreement designates the listing and the selling broker and their firms and addresses their agency relationships with the buyer and seller. There is also space to designate the commission that will be due to the listing and selling brokers.

Not every broker charges the same commission rate. If they did, there might be evidence of price fixing. Brokers and agents, while trying to get a reasonable commission, should not refuse to negotiate. If the seller is unreasonable in negotiating a fair commission rate, the broker may be better off refusing the listing.

2. Sewage Facility Notice

Some agreements of sale contain provisions regarding sewage and water. If there is a community sewage system, few impediments outside of outstanding fees or assessments are likely. If a septic tank and drain field have been in use for many years, problems are very predictable. Permit problems and frequent changes in rules and regulations involving septic systems cause havoc in the realty marketplace. Even professionals often have difficulty keeping abreast of all the modifications. It is best to leave worries to a reputable septic specialist who can take care of all aspects of the system from obtaining the permit to getting the design approved, to performing required maintenance.

Web Exercise

Read Steiner v. Thexton—a recent California Appeals Court finding. Why does the arrangement lack enforceability? Why does the court conclude that the agreement lacks the requisite form for enforcement? See *www.courtinfo.ca.gov/opinions/revpub/C054605.DOC.*

V. MISCELLANEOUS AGREEMENTS TO PURCHASE REAL ESTATE

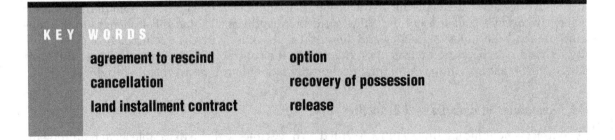

KEY WORDS

agreement to rescind	option
cancellation	recovery of possession
land installment contract	release

The standard real estate agreement is only one way of initiating a real estate transaction. In good or bad housing markets, both buyers and sellers create alternative instruments to foster transactions. The second way will be briefly assessed here: the land installment contract and the option.

A. Land Installment Contract

A **land installment contract** is, in reality, a contract for a deed or a right to purchase land under certain terms and conditions that include the payment of the purchase price in installments. The technique may be helpful to buyers who are unable to garner sufficient funds or financing to make the purchase. However, no title is conveyed to the buyer until all of the installment payments have been made. Land installment contracts have generally been defined by statute or codification, such as this Ohio design:

For an example of a land installment contract see Figure 3–7.

5313.01 Land installment contract definitions.

As used in Chapter 5313 of the Revised Code:

(A) "Land installment contract" means an executory agreement which by its terms is not required to be fully performed by one or more of the parties to the agreement within one year of the date of the agreement and under which the vendor agrees to convey title in real property located in this state to the vendee and the vendee agrees to pay the purchase price in installment payments, while the vendor retains title to the property as security for the vendee's obligation. Option contracts for the purchase of real property are not land installment contracts.[25]

Land installment contracts are curious exchanges and can be onerously applied against a hopeful buyer. The seller retains the title to the property during the life of the installment contract. This type of arrangement can prove to be beneficial for both the buyer and seller under certain limited conditions. But, it has significant pitfalls. Particularly, the buyer cannot be sure that the seller will be able to hand over the title after the installment payments have been completed. Litigation concerning the land, tax liens, bankruptcy, and the seller's death are but a few of those pitfalls. The seller's remedies for a buyer's failure to pay the installments may include retention of previously paid installments and **recovery of possession**. Other causes of action resulting from the buyer's breach of contract may be rather illusory in view of the buyer's default.

Land installment contracts should contain the following provisions:

1. The full names and then current mailing addresses of all the parties to the contract
2. The date when the contract was signed by each party
3. A legal description of the property conveyed
4. The contract price of the property conveyed
5. Any charges or fees for services that are includable in the contract separate from the contract price
6. The amount of the vendee's down payment
7. The principal balance owed
8. The amount and due date of each installment payment
9. The interest rate on the unpaid balance and the method of computing the rate
10. A statement of any encumbrances against the property conveyed
11. A statement requiring the vendor to deliver a general warranty deed on completion of the contract, or another deed that is available when the vendor is legally unable to deliver a general warranty deed
12. A provision that the vendor provide evidence of title in accordance with the prevailing custom in the area in which the property is located
13. A provision that, if the vendor defaults on any mortgage on the property, the vendee can pay on that mortgage and receive credit on the land installment contract
14. A provision that the vendor shall cause a copy of the contract to be recorded
15. A requirement that the vendee be responsible for the payment of taxes, assessments, and other charges against the property from the date of the contract, unless agreed to the contrary
16. A statement of any pending order of any public agency against the property.

LAND INSTALLMENT CONTRACT

On this _____ day of _____, 20___, the following named Buyer and Seller, enter into this Land Installment Contract:

Full Name(s) and Addresses of Buyers: _____
_____ (hereinafter "Buyer")

Full Name(s) and Mailing Addresses of Seller(s): _____
_____ (hereinafter "Seller")

for the purpose of the sale and purchase of the property located at _____, in the Township of _____, County of _____, City of _____, State of _____ and more particularly described as follows:

(insert legal description)

Seller agrees to sell and Buyer agrees to purchase the Property, and in accordance with the following terms and conditions:

1. **Purchase Price.** The total purchase price shall be the sum of _____ Dollars ($_____), payable to the Seller as follows:

   _____ Dollars ($_____) payable upon the execution of this Contract, with the balance of _____ Dollars ($_____) to be paid in accordance with Paragraph 2 of this contract.

2. **Monthly Installment Payments.** Buyer shall make monthly installment payments of interest and principal in the amount of _____Dollars ($_____), due and payable on the _____ day of every month, beginning _____, 20___, and continuing the _____ day of every month thereafter, until the principal balance and accrued interest is paid in full.

   The interest rate included with each monthly installment payment shall be _____ percent (___%) per annum. In addition, there shall be a late charge in the amount of percent _____ (___%) of the monthly installment payment then due and payable for any payment that is not received by Seller within _____ (_____) days after the due date. All payments shall be directed to Seller at the address above unless Buyer is notified in writing otherwise.

3. **Prepayment.** Buyer may prepay all or part of the balance of the principal and interest at any time and without penalty and without notice. Such prepayment shall not include any unearned interest.

4. **Possession**. Buyer shall be entitled to possession of the Property on and after _____ day of _____, 20___,

5. **Evidence of Title.** Seller shall provide to Buyer, within _____ (___) business days after the execution of this Contract, evidence of title to the Property. Such evidence shall show marketable title to the Property, free and clear of all encumbrances, except for the restrictions and easements of record as of the execution date of this Contract and except for taxes, assessments, and other governmental charges against the Property that are not delinquent and which will be the responsibility of Buyer after Buyer takes possession.

6. **Taxes and Assessments**. Buyer shall pay all real estate taxes and assessments that accrue against the Property that are due after the date Buyer takes possession, as stated above in Paragraph 4 above, and then for each and every installment thereafter. In the event Buyer fails to pay any taxes or assessments when due, Seller shall have the right, but not the obligation, to pay such delinquent taxes or assessments and Buyer shall immediately reimburse Seller for such payments, with the same late charge stated in Paragraph 2 above applying to such payments.

FIGURE 3–7
(continues)

7. **Insurance**. Buyer agrees to maintain and pay for comprehensive homeowner's insurance on the Property and improvements in the amount not less than the purchase price stated in paragraph 1 above and comprehensive liability coverage insurance in the amount of not less than _____ Dollars ($_____). Buyer shall provide to Seller proof of payment, as well as a copy of the policies.

8. **Utilities**. As of the date Buyer is entitled to take possession, Buyer shall pay for all utilities used in connection with the use of the Property, including but not limited to telephone, electric, gas, water, cable, and sewage.

9. **Delivery of Deed.** Upon full payment of the Purchase Price and all other amounts owed to Seller under this Contract, Seller shall execute and deliver to Buyer a good and marketable general warranty deed conveying the Property to Buyer, free of all encumbrances and restrictions, except for the following encumbrances:

10. **Recording**. As soon as practical after the effective date of this Contract, Seller shall cause a copy of this Contract to be recorded in the appropriate office of the county wherein the Property is located. Seller shall provide Buyer with evidence of such recording.

11. **Default**. If any installment is not made within thirty (30) days of the due date specified herein, Seller shall give Buyer written notice of the failure to make the required payment. Thereafter, if such payment is not made to Seller within sixty (60) days of receipt by Buyer of such notice of non-payment, Seller may declare a default. In the event Seller declares a default, Seller shall be released from any and all obligation to convey the Property and Buyer shall forfeit all rights thereto. In the event of such a default, Buyer hereby agrees that the Property and all improvements made by Buyer shall automatically become Seller's, and that all previous payments shall be considered as compensation for the use and occupying of the Property and shall be retained by Seller.

12. **Assignment**. Buyer shall not assign any interest in this Contract without the prior express written consent of the Seller.

13. **Annual Statement**. Seller shall provide Buyer with an annual statement by no later than January 31 of each year during the term of this Contract, which shall state: the total amount of payments made during the previous calendar year; the amounts credited to principal and interest for such payments made during the previous calendar year; and the remaining balance due under this Contract.

14. **Maintenance and Improvements**. Buyer shall maintain the Property at Buyer's own expense. Buyer shall not have the right to improve or alter the Property without Seller's prior consent. Buyer shall not use inferior materials for improvements and shall obtain any and required permits and licenses at Buyer's own cost.

15. **Entire Agreement**. This Contract is binding upon the Parties and their respective heirs, executors, administrators, successors, and assigns. No prior stipulation, agreement, or understanding, verbal or otherwise of the Parties or their agents, shall be valid or enforceable unless set forth in this Contract. This Contract constitutes the entire agreement and understanding of the Parties, superseding any prior oral or written agreements with respect hereto. No amendment, addition, or waiver shall be valid unless in writing signed by all of the Parties.

FIGURE 3–7
(continued)

In the event the buyer cannot come up with the money during the designated period, the seller needs to give notice that the terms of the installment contract have not been met and the contract has no further enforceability. The notice:

- Reasonably identifies the contract and describes the property covered by it.
- Specifies the terms and conditions of the contract which have not been complied with.
- Notifies the vendee that the contract will stand forfeited unless the vendee performs as per the terms and conditions of the contract within ten days of the completed service of notice and notifies the vendee to leave the premises.

OPTION AGREEMENT TO PURCHASE REAL ESTATE

This Option is given this day _____ of _____, 20___, by _____ _____ ("Owner"), residing at _____ _____, to _____ ("Buyer"), currently residing at _____.

Owner, in consideration of _____Dollars ($_____), paid by Buyer, receipt of which is hereby acknowledged, grants to Buyer the exclusive right and option to purchase the Property located at _____ , in accordance with the Real Estate Sales Contract, which is attached to and made part of this Option.

The term of this Option shall commence on date stated above and shall continue until _____ ___.m. on the _____day of _____, 20___.

Buyer may exercise this Option by signing the Exercise Provision on the bottom of this agreement and delivering a copy to Owner, prior to the expiration of the Option Period stated above. If this Option is exercised, Owner and Buyer shall sign the attached Real Estate Sales Contract and shall be bound by its terms and conditions.

In the event Buyer does not exercise this Option, Owner shall retain the amount paid as consideration for this Option. In the event Buyer does decide to exercise this Option, the amount paid as consideration for this Option shall be applied to the purchase price for the Property.

This Option and, if this Option is exercised, the attached Real Estate Sales Contract shall be binding upon and shall inure to the benefit of the Parties and their respective heirs, successors, or assigns.

Buyer:_____ Owner:_____

Buyer:_____ Owner:_____

Exercise of Option

By Signing below and delivering a copy of such to Owner as specified above, Buyer is hereby exercises the above Option.

Buyer:_____ Date:_____

Buyer:_____ Date:_____

FIGURE 3–8

B. Options

An **option** is a right to purchase property at a later date. It is not an obligation to do so. An option to purchase does not bind the buyer to buy until it is exercised by the buyer.[26] Like any other contract, an option must be supported by an offer and acceptance as well as sufficient consideration before it becomes an option agreement. "The option agreement is a unilateral one, binding upon the option or from the date of execution of the instrument. However, it does not become a contract between the parties creating an absolute covenant to convey on the one side and to purchase on the other until exercised by the optionee."[27]

For an example of an option agreement see Figure 3–8.

C. Cancellation

A change of heart that results from buyer's remorse or an extraordinary circumstance, such as a loss of job or a tragedy, will sometimes cause buyers to seek **cancellation**. If buyers want to be released from their contractual obligations, request the seller to cancel with consideration. In other words, buyers might agree to forfeit earnest money or pay other funds for a release from the contractual obligation. See Figure 3–9 for a cancellation of agreement format.

CANCELLATION OF AGREEMENT

THIS AGREEMENT entered in this _____ day of _____, _____, by and between _____, as parties of the first part, and _____, parties of the second part.

WITNESSETH:

That, whereas an Agreement has therefore been entered into between the parties of this Agreement, whereas the parties of the first part agreed to sell to the parties of the second part the property at: _____

AND, WHEREAS, it has been agreed between the respective parties hereto, that the Agreement so pending is to cease and any existing rights by and between the respective parties pertaining to said Agreement of Sale are to be canceled:

NOW THEREFORE, it is agreed that in consideration of the payment by the parties of the second part to the parties of the first part, the sum of _____ dollars and other good and valuable consideration, the parties of the first part do hereby jointly and severally release that parties of the second part from their obligation and liability arising by virtue of any contract between the parties hereto, whether verbally or in writing, and any and all claims and demands of every kind in character whatsoever of the parties of the first part against the parties of the second part.

In consideration of the Release by the parties of the first part of any liability or claim against the parties of the second part, the parties of the second part do hereby release the parties of the first part, Sales Agreement dated _____, and any and all claims or demands of any kind or character whatsoever that the parties of the second part may have against the parties of the first part.

In consideration of the payment made by the parties of the second part to the party of the first part, and the mutual release of liability between the parties hereto, any and all contract of every kind and character whatsoever now existing between the said parties, and any and all claims, demands or liability of any kind and character whatsoever that parties of the second part may have, are discharged.

_____   _____
Witness:

FIGURE 3–9

D. Rescission

To cancel is to extinguish; to rescind is to annul, avoid, or withdraw from the contract.[28] In most cases, an **agreement to rescind** is presented to the seller for agreement and signature simply because the buyer had a change of heart and does not wish to finalize the purchase. Buyers and sellers may also rescind for a failure to meet a condition or by mutual agreement.

Web Exercise

Find out about the particulars of your state requirements regarding the format of recession at *www.findlegalforms.com/forms/mutual-rescission-of-contract*.

AGREEMENT TO RESCIND

THIS AGREEMENT made this _____ day of _____ A.D. ____ between _____, Seller and _____ Buyer.

WITNESSETH:

WHEREAS under date of _____ A.D. _____ Seller and Buyer entered into an agreement for the sale of premises known as _____; and

WHEREAS the parties have mutually agreed to rescind the said agreement,

NOW, THEREFORE, it is mutually agreed between the parties as follows:
1. The aforementioned Agreement of Sale is hereby rescinded, canceled and rendered null and void.
2. The original and all executed copies of the said Agreement shall be returned to Seller.
3. The parties do hereby release each other of and from all claims, demands, action, causes of action, whatsoever in law or equity, which either may have against the other by virtue of the execution of the said Agreement of Sale.
4. Any money deposited by Buyer under the said Agreement shall be returned to Buyer.

IN WITNESS WHEREOF the parties have executed this Agreement the day and year first above written, intending to be legally bound hereby.

WITNESS:
_____   _____

FIGURE 3–10

It is highly unlikely that the seller may benefit from a request to rescind, though in a hot realty market a better offer may be on the horizon. If the parties cannot mutually agree to a rescission, the objecting party may balk. In this case, the first move the seller should make is to refuse to sign the agreement and to point out to the buyer's agent that the buyer is expected to comply with the terms and conditions of the agreement of sale. The seller should also state that in case of noncompliance the seller has the right to file suit in a court of law against the buyer.

In certain cases, a lawsuit will be inevitable. At other times, the buyer and seller will resolve the matter themselves. This may involve the buyer's decision to forfeit any down payment as well as paying additional funds to the seller for nonperformance. The matter may be settled by the buyer and seller or their agents or intermediaries.

See Figure 3–10 for an agreement to rescind.

E. Releases

Even if the parties agree to cancel or rescind, releases should be executed. Releases formalize the end to an agreement or contract. At times, **release** language is within the cancellation or rescission agreements. To remove any doubt about intent and to be capable of a full defense in the event of litigation, the parties should memorialize their action by executing a mutual release from their respective obligations under the purchase agreement.

For a release, see Figure 3–11.

MUTUAL RELEASE

Whereas the undersigned parties hereto entered into an Agreement of Sale for a piece of real estate situated at:_____

Whereas the parties hereto agree that it is in the best interest of all that the aforesaid Real Estate Agreement dated _____, be canceled and rescinded.

Now therefore, in consideration of _____ and intending to be legally bound by their signatures hereto, the parties hereto hereby release and exonerate each other from any and all obligations under the aforesaid Agreement of Sale.

WITNESS our hands and seals this _____ day of _____, _____

_____   _____
Witness: **Seller**

_____   _____
Witness: **Seller**

_____   _____
Witness: **Buyer**

_____   _____
Witness: **Buyer**

_____   _____

FIGURE 3–11

CHAPTER THREE **SUMMARY**

Chapter Three discussed the following topics:

- Contents and necessity of an agreement of sale
- The Statute of Frauds and contract enforceability
- Various forms of agreements of sale
- Land installment contracts and options to purchase
- Cancellation, rescission, and releases in relation to the agreement of sale

REVIEW **QUESTIONS**

1. The Statute of Frauds requires writings in transactions involving the transfer of real property. Prove true or false.
2. In a standard agreement of sale, three parties have an interest in the content of the agreement. Name them.

3. When interpreting a sales agreement, the parties must be attentive to specific time lines. The broad standard "time is of the essence" controls the parties' conduct. Give four examples of timely action under most real estate contracts.

4. What types of disagreements typically result from the interpretation of real estate contracts?

5. How are changes normally made to an executed agreement of sale?

6. Under what circumstances is the language "time is of the essence" normally seen?

7. What is the difference between a land installment contract and an option contract?

8. Define the terms cancellation, rescission, and release as they relate to agreements of sale.

9. What clauses must exist for an agreement of sale to be valid and enforceable?

10. Name three clauses that are not mandatory and only need to be included under certain circumstances.

DISCUSSION **QUESTION**

Discuss cancellation, rescission, and release. When are these appropriate measures to end an agreement of sale? How do they differ, and how are they similar?

EXERCISE 1

Complete an agreement of sale using the following fact patterns.

Owners—John and Jody Smith

Purchasers—Bob and Sally Johnson

Sellers Property Address—123 First Street, Mytown, US

Purchasers Address—9876 Pike Drive, Mytown, US

Selling Price—$125,000

Deposit Amount—$25,000 paid at signing of agreement on July 24, 2009, balance due at closing

Mortgage Amount—$100,000

Maximum acceptable interest rate—7%

Mortgage Term—30 years

Settlement within ninety days of the signing of the agreement

Mortgage application must be made within four business days, with a commitment from the bank within sixty days.

All kitchen appliances, draperies, and furniture are excluded from the sale, except for one John Deere riding mower.

EXERCISE 2

Bob and Sally Johnson were unable to obtain a mortgage commitment according to the contingencies listed in the agreement of sale. According to the agreement, Bob and Sally can cancel the agreement without penalty with a return of deposit monies. Draft a cancellation and release for the transaction.

EXERCISE 3

Bob and Sally Johnson found a similar property for rent with an option to purchase. Draft an option to purchase using the following facts.

Owner—Ralph Owens

Property Address—487 Rolling Run Road, Mytown, US

Purchase Price—$100,000

Time limit to exercise option—3 years

Payments as follows: 10% at signing of contract, balance due on exercise of option

Mortgage must be in the amount of $90,000, for thirty years at a rate no more than 7%.

EXERCISE 4

Ethical Parameters of Paralegal Practice in the World of Real Estate.

Read the Supreme Court of Georgia's Advisory Opinion on the role of paralegals in real estate closings? Does the conclusion reached by the court resolve the difficulty? How does the term "close" impact its decision making?

> Formal Advisory Opinion No. 86–5
> State Bar of Georgia
> Issued by the Supreme Court of Georgia
> On May 12, 1989
> Formal Advisory Opinion No. 86–5

Ethical Propriety of Lawyer's Delegating to Nonlawyers the Closing of Real Estate Transactions.

The closing of real estate transaction constitutes the practice of law as defined by O.C.G.A § 15-19-50. Accordingly, it would be ethically improper for lawyers to permit nonlawyers to close real estate transactions. Certain tasks can be delegated to nonlawyers, subject to the type of supervision and control outlined in State Bar Advisory Opinion No. 21. The lawyer cannot, however, delegate to a nonlawyer the responsibility to "close" the real estate transaction without the participation of an attorney.

Correspondent asks whether it is ethically permissible for a lawyer to delegate to a nonlawyer the closing of real estate transactions. This question involves, among other things, an interpretation of Standard 24, Rule 3-103 (Canon III), EC 3-1, EC 3-2, EC 3-6, DR 3-101 (A), DR 3-102 (A), and DR 3-103. With the exception of Standard 24, all of the foregoing Ethical Considerations and Directory Rules are cited and quoted in State Bar Advisory Opinion No. 21 (attached hereto).

Standard 24 provides as follows:

> A lawyer shall not aid a nonlawyer in the unauthorized practice of law. A violation of this Standard may be punished by a public reprimand.

As the role of nonlawyers (particularly paralegals and legal secretaries) in the closing of real estate transactions has expanded in recent years, questions have arisen as to the scope of duties which can be delegated to nonlawyers. A general discussion of duties which may ethically be delegated to nonlawyers can be found in State Bar Advisory Opinion Nos. 19 and 21. In short, those advisory opinions stress that

> Avoidance of charges that the paralegal is engaging in the unauthorized practice of law may be achieved only by strict observance of the direction found in EC 3-6, quoted above, indicating that delegation of activities which ordinarily comprise the practice of law is proper only if the lawyer maintains a direct relationship with the client involved, supervises and directs the work delegated to the paralegal and assumes complete ultimate professional responsibility for the work product produced by the paralegal. Supervision of the work of the paralegal by the attorney must be direct and constant to avoid any charges of aiding the unauthorized practice of law. *State Bar Advisory Opinion No. 21.*

The question to be addressed in this opinion is whether the closing of a real estate transaction constitutes "the practice of law." This in turn depends upon what it means to "close" a real estate transaction. If the "closing" is defined as the entire series of events through which title to the land is conveyed from one party to another party, it would be ethically improper for a nonlawyer to "close" a real estate transaction.

O.C.G.A. § 15-19-50 states that the "practice of law" includes "conveyancing," "the giving of any legal advice," and "any action taken for others in any matter connected with the law." In *Georgia Bar Association v. Lawyers Title Insurance Corporation*, 222 Ga. 657 (1966), the Georgia Supreme Court characterizes the "closing of real estate transactions between applicants for title insurance and third persons" as the rendering of legal services and advice. Moreover, to the extent that any legal advice is given during any part of the closing, this would constitute "the practice of law" by definition and could not be ethically delegated to nonlawyers.

In light of all of the foregoing, it appears that the closing of real estate transactions constitutes the practice of law as defined by O.C.G.A. 15-19-50. Accordingly, pursuant to Standard 24, Canon III, and the Ethical Considerations and Disciplinary Rules cited above, it would be ethically improper for a lawyer to aid nonlawyers to "close" real estate transactions. This does not mean that certain tasks cannot be delegated to nonlawyers, subject to the type of supervision and control outlined in State Bar Advisory Opinion No. 21. The lawyer cannot, however, delegate to a nonlawyer the responsibility to "close" the real estate transaction without the participation of an attorney.

Assignment for the Case of John and Martha

Prepare an agreement of sale for John and Martha.

REFERENCES

1. CHARLES P. NEMETH, THE PARALEGAL RESOURCE MANUAL, 2nd ed., 498 (1995).
2. TIMOTHY G. O'NEILL, LADNER ON CONVEYANCING IN PENNSYLVANIA,' 6.03 (1988).
3. Donald C. Taylor, *Some Agreement of Sale Basics (with Forms)*, PRAC. REAL EST. LAW. May 1988, at 69.
4. Michael L. Closen & Trevor J. Orsinger, *Family Ties That Bind, and Disqualify: Toward Elimination of Family-Based Conflicts of Interest in the Provision of Notarial Services*, 36 VAL. U. L. REV. 505 (2002).
5. George H. Hathaway, *Plain Language: Clarity Awards for Fall 1999*, 78 MI. BAR. J. 988 (1999).
6. National Association of Realtors, *National Association of REALTORS® Fact Sheet* at www.realtor.org/press_room/public_affairs/narfactsheet.
7. Blumberg Excelsior, 62 White Street, New York, NY 10013, Form 922.
8. Easy Soft Inc., 212 North Center Drive, North Brunswick NJ 08902, www.easysoft-usa.com, Contract for Sale of Real Estate.
9. Northeast Florida Association of REALTORS®, PASA 10-04.
10. Pierro v. Pierro, 438 Pa. 119 (1970); C. B. Howard & Co. v. Innes, 253 Pa. 593 (1916).
11. Feld v. Shapiro, 87 Pa. Super. 557 (1926).
12. O'NEILL, *supra* note 2, at § 6.05.
13. John H. Scheid, *Buying Blackacre: Form Contracts and Prudent Provisions*, 23 J. MARSHALL L. REV. 15, 52–53 (1989).
14. Hodorowicz v. Szulc, 16 ILL. APP. 2d 317, 147 N.E. 2d 887, 889 (1958). *See also* Goldberg v. Abastasi, 272 MD. 61, 321 A. 2d 155 (1974).
15. Dodson v. Nink, 72 ILL. APP. 3d 51, 390 N.E. 2d 546.

16. E. I. Du Pont et al. v. Crompton Townsend Inc., No. C.A. 1284, (Superior Court of Del., New Castle County, 1976); *see also* Forrest Creek v. McLean Savings, 831 F. 2d 1238 (4th Cir. 1987). For a precise, rigid application of conditional principles, *see also* Ditman v. Huyer, No. 990 (Ct. of Common Pleas of Greene County, Pa., November 3, 1988).

17. E. I. Du Pont et al. v. Crompton Townsend Inc., No. C.A. 1284 at 26, (Superior Court of Del., New Castle County, 1976).

18. Taylor, *supra* note 3, at 79–80.

19. Stephen V. Estopinal, A Guide to Understanding Land Surveys, 3rd ed. (2008).

20. Therefore, negligent misrepresentation claims will be barred in whole (contributory negligence) or in part (comparative negligence), if the purchaser failed to investigate the premises. The purchaser's duty to investigate is especially strong in three situations: (1) when the defect is obvious; (2) when the realtor is not the purchaser's agent; and (3) when the realtor's representation is vague. Clearance E. Hagglund, *Caveat Emptor: Realty Purchaser's Duty to Investigate*, 20 Real Est. L. J. 373 (1992).

21. Scheid, *supra* note 13, at 47.

22. Taylor, *supra* note 3, at 72.

23. Nemeth, *supra* note 1, at 506.

24. *Id*. at 506.

25. Ohio Rev. Code § 5313.01 (2009).

26. Alan Tonnon, Washington Real Estate Law 253 (2005); *See also* Steven D. Fisher, The Complete Guide to Real Estate Options (2007).

27. Summa. Pa. Jur. 2d, § 8.19.

28. For an excellent summary of the bases for rescission, *see* marydrury.com/index.php?option=com_content&view=article&id=16&Itemid=5.

Conditions, Contingencies, and Other Qualifications

LEARNING OBJECTIVES

- To identify conditions and contingencies that affect the enforceability of real estate contracts.
- To explain the importance of verifying information relative to mortgaging, conditions, and zoning.
- To list the environmental and hazardous conditions that can affect a real estate purchase.
- To compose necessary addenda reflecting various conditions and contingencies or insert required conditional clauses into an agreement of sale.

JOB COMPETENCIES

- To compose, under the supervision of an attorney, various addenda to the agreement of sale.
- To identify and interpret information regarding mortgage financing, zoning, hazardous materials, and inspections.

ETHICAL CONSIDERATIONS

The paralegal must be aware of the following ethical dilemmas during this phase of a real estate transaction:

- Unauthorized practice of law
- Lawyer supervision of nonlawyers
- Confidentiality issues

I. QUALIFYING THE AGREEMENT OF SALE

It is essential for the paralegal to understand that few real estate agreements of sale are fulfilled without conditional terms. A **condition** is a set of events, an occurrence, or other state that must be achieved before a contract comes to fruition. If the condition is not met or fulfilled, one's obligation to perform is excused. "A contract for the sale of land may stipulate that a party thereto is entitled to rescind and be excused from performance of it upon the happening or failure of a certain future event or circumstance. If the agreement specifies the failures of conditions that shall be grounds for rescission or nonenforcement, the contract governs the rights of the parties in this respect, and a court cannot ignore, but is bound to give effect to, such conditions, unless of course, they have been altered or waived by the parties."[1]

In real estate practice, conditions are sometimes labeled **contingencies**, for example, "The agreement is contingent upon buyer selling a current home." Conditions may deal with a variety of subjects, including financing, zoning, termites, well capacity, quality of construction, or other structural questions. Real estate transfers are frequently conditioned or contingent upon some event or circumstance. Conditions, as noted above, may either be **precedent** or **subsequent**. In short, the condition, until fulfilled or met, creates an estate in expectancy. A contingency awaits fulfillment, such as the award of mortgage financing or grant of a zoning permit.

The typical conditional or contingent situations in real estate practice are:

■ Whether the agreement has effect if mortgage financing is not obtainable.

■ Whether the agreement has effect if alternative mortgage financing is available other than that stated in the contract.

■ Whether failure to acquire certification for septic systems will void a contract.

■ Whether failure to be granted zoning or failure to meet a contingent requirement under a contract will serve as an excusable condition.

■ Whether a political subdivision permitted development of land in a certain way or right as envisioned under the original contract.

■ Whether the condition of water and soil meets regulatory guidelines.

- Whether there is evidence of termite and insect infestation.
- Whether there is evidence of environmental contamination or toxic pollution.

A contract with a contingency or a condition is little more than a conditional contract which lacks enforceability until the condition is fulfilled. Some label the underlying contract as one in expectancy—one that is at best illusory because it lacks legal force. Professor Milton Friedman of the Practicing Law Institute, in his treatise, *Contract and Conveyance of Real Property,* notes:

> The contract may also be conditional upon the buyers' obtaining a mortgage to finance the purchase, or a license or other permit to use the premises for some designed purpose. In these situations the condition precedent is not to the existence of a contract . . . but performance of the conditions is a condition precedent to further obligations under the contract. If there is no such performance, the Buyer is entitled to refund his down payment.[2]

Conditions and contingencies in real estate law have triggered a formidable body of case law.

In *Hodorowicz v. Szulc,* a contract for the sale of real estate provided that the buyers had to sell their present home by a specific date. Finding a void contract for failure to meet a condition, since the buyer's home did not sell, the court noted:

> It is also equally plain that before that contingency happened under the very terms of the contract, by lapse of time, the sellers had acquired an additional right to terminate it at their will and it therefore ceased to be binding upon the sellers and the purchasers could not have enforced it against the sellers anytime thereafter. When in May of 1955 the contingency happened and the property previously owned by the purchasers had been sold, the contract had already lost its binding power upon the sellers and there was therefore never a mutually binding and enforceable contract and agreement in effect between the parties.[3]

The same result could occur within a mortgage contingency. When purchasers were to have a mortgage commitment within sixty days of the signing of the contract, and the commitment was not forthcoming, an unenforceable contract was the result. In essence, when the commitment did not materialize within the designated sixty-day period, the purchasers were under no obligation to perform by reason of a contract that became void and nonexistent once the condition could not be met.

An Illinois case, *Dodson v. Nink,*[4] declared a contract of sale null and void because purchasers would accept a VA loan, but they would not agree to be responsible for any repair costs. In upholding the condition, the court strictly interpreted the contract holding:

> Our holding merely gives effect to the agreement of the parties at the time the contract was entered into. When plaintiff contracted to purchase . . . , she did not agree . . . to repair the house to complete a sale. . . . We therefore conclude that the contingencies in both contracts did not occur, and that both contracts became void and unenforceable pursuant to their own terms. Plaintiff was thus entitled to the return of her earnest money.[5]

The Delaware Supreme Court's respected the Honorable Andrew D. Christie skillfully decided a similar case, *E. I. Du Pont et al. v. Crompton-Townsend Inc.*[6] in a survey dispute. Assessing the conditional clause on a survey in a standard real estate contract, Judge Christie used the following language:

> Boundary lines for said subdivision to be subject to written approval of both the sellers and purchasers. Should written approval not be obtained from either party on or before July 30, 1976, then this contract shall be declared null and void and all monies on deposit refunded to Purchasers.[7]

When purchasers decided not to approve the survey, sellers balked and took the position that the problems could have been corrected. In fact, their objections to the survey were trivial. Judge

Christie characterized the contract as "not a sale as to the purchase of a survey and to the terms on which a sale would take place if all the parties at a future date decided to agree to convert the conditional sales agreement into a binding contract by approving the survey."[8] Judge Christie, in strictly construing the contract and choosing not to infer or surmise the purchasers' motivations, held that the conditional language of the contract was unambiguous.

Both case law and scholarly legal analysis support the fundamental contention that a condition precedent, neither met nor waived, cannot lead to an obligation of contractual performance.

In *Pena v. Security Title Company*,[9] the parties entered into a binding contract for real estate with the conditional language "subject to buyer securing a loan of approximately $12,000." When purchasers' loan application was rejected by the bank, the court construed the language as creating a conditional duty under the contract and,

> (that) the provision constituted a condition and unless such a loan was obtained, neither the bargain and sale terms nor the forfeiture provisions would become effective.[10]

Pena referred extensively to *Hodorowicz v. Szulc*,[11] a case in which there were no written extensions, modifications, or waivers. The *Hodorowicz* court reviewed the issues by discussing first whether there was a contract at all because the condition was not met.

> [I]t becomes necessary for us to determine whether there was ever a binding and enforceable contract between the parties. If there was not, obviously there could be no breach and the statement of claim never stated a cause of action. It is clear that this contract was not enforceable at the time it was executed because of the condition contained in the clause stated in the contract . . . and that it only could become effective and enforceable, by either party, upon the happening of that contingency.[12]

A review of case law unanimously supports the principle that a mortgage contingency is a condition precedent. In *Fischer v. Kennedy*,[13] the failure to acquire mortgage financing resulted in a contract being declared null and void. In *Roberts v. Maxwell*,[14] a purchaser's failure to procure a GI loan was held a condition precedent releasing purchaser from further obligation on the contract.

CASE LAW

SUPERIOR COURT OF NEW JERSEY

APPELLATE DIVISION

DOCKET NO. A-3529-03T33529-03T2

CHARLES B. DAVIS and BARBARA DAVIS,

Plaintiffs-Appellants

v.

EILEEN STRAZZA, NONA BERNESBY and CHRISTOPHER BERNESBY,

Defendants-Respondents,

and

MORRIS LEO GREB and NANCY FEINBERG,

Defendants.

(continued)

Argued September 19, 2005 - Decided

Before Judges Alley, Fisher, C. S., and Yannotti.

On appeal from the Superior Court of New Jersey, Law Division, Essex County, Docket No. L-11159-01.

Charles B. Davis, appellant, argued the cause pro se.

Noel E. Schablik argued the cause for respondents (Mr. Schablik and John T. Knapp, on the brief).

The opinion of the court was delivered by

YANNOTTI, J. A. D.

Plaintiffs Charles B. Davis and Barbara Davis appeal from an order entered May 24, 2002 denying their motion for partial summary judgment and an order entered November 22, 2002 granting summary judgment in favor of defendants Eileen Strazza, Nora Bernesby and Christopher Bernesby. We affirm.

The facts relevant to the issues raised on this appeal are essentially undisputed. On May 31, 2001, plaintiffs and defendants entered into a contract under which plaintiffs agreed to sell and defendants agreed to buy certain real property in South Orange, New Jersey. The contract provided in pertinent part that:

[t]his agreement is contingent upon the purchaser obtaining a conventional mortgage at a prevailing rate of interest for 30 years with monthly payments based upon a 30 year payment schedule. The purchaser agrees to make immediate written application for such financing and to pay applicable original fees or points. If a written mortgage commitment is not received in thirty (30) days, or any agreed upon extensions, either party may cancel this contract.

The agreement required defendants to make a deposit of $25,000, which would be held in the trust account of defendants' attorney until closing of title. In addition, the agreement provided that, if the contract is "legally and rightfully" cancelled, the deposit would be returned to defendants and the parties will be free of liability to each other. The contract established a closing date of August 10, 2001. Pursuant to the terms of the agreement, defendants deposited $25,000 in the trust account of their attorney.

Defendants applied for mortgage financing and, on June 18, 2001, New Century Mortgage Company issued a written mortgage commitment. The first page of the commitment stated that the loan would be funded if defendants meet all of the terms and conditions in the commitment, "and any and all attached riders indicated, which comprise an integral part of this commitment." The attached rider consisted of three pages setting forth certain terms and conditions, including the requirement that defendants verify the funds available for closing and provide an executed HUD-1, or equivalent closing statement, respecting the sale of any property that is a source of such funds. The Bernesbys owned property in West Orange, New Jersey, and Strazza owned property in Montclair, New Jersey. The sale of both properties was necessary to provide funds to close.

On June 21, 2001, defendants' attorney provided a copy of the first page of the mortgage commitment to plaintiff's attorney. Defendants undertook to have plaintiffs' home inspected and, on August 1, 2001, requested that the closing date be extended to September 28, 2001. Plaintiffs in turn demanded $1,000 to extend the closing date and also sought agreement by defendants to a liquidated damages clause.

On August 6, 2001, before defendants had responded to plaintiffs' demands, New Century advised defendants by letter that the mortgage commitment was cancelled because it was unable to verify account balances. The letter stated that properties "required to be sold will not be sold" and sufficient assets were not available for closing. By letter dated August 7, 2001, defendants advised plaintiffs that their mortgage application had been denied and they were terminating the contract. Plaintiffs refused to consent to the termination of the agreement. Efforts to resolve the matter failed, and plaintiffs filed this action, in which they asserted claims against defendants for breach of contract, negligent misrepresentation and fraud.

On April 2, 2002, plaintiffs filed a motion for partial summary judgment on liability. Defendants filed a cross-motion for summary judgment. The judge denied the motions without prejudice by order entered

May 24, 2002. In a decision set forth on the record, the judge determined that because the contract was contingent upon the defendants' obtaining a 30-year conventional mortgage and because the defendants did not obtain such a mortgage, they had the right to cancel the contract and to the return of their deposit with interest. The judge added, however, that before the matter could be resolved, it was essential for the court to know what steps defendants had taken to sell their homes. The judge said that if defendants acted in good faith, in endeavoring to comply with the condition of the mortgage commitment, defendants would be entitled to prevail.

Defendants again moved on September 23, 2002 for summary judgment. Plaintiffs filed a cross-motion for reconsideration of the judge's May 24, 2002 order and renewed their earlier motion for partial summary judgment. Based on the submissions, which detailed defendants' efforts to sell their properties, the judge found that defendants acted in good faith in endeavoring to comply with the condition imposed in the mortgage commitment. The judge therefore entered an order on November 22, 2002 denying plaintiffs' motions, granting summary judgment in favor of defendants and ordering the return to defendants of their deposit monies plus interest. This appeal followed.

Plaintiffs argue that defendants were obligated to close under the terms of the agreement, and since they failed to do so, they were in breach of the contract. They also contend that there were genuine issues of material fact concerning defendants' efforts to sell their properties, and therefore summary judgment was inappropriate. We disagree.

In *Farrell v. Janik*, 225 N.J. Super. 282 (Law Div. 1988), the parties entered into a contract for the sale of certain property. The agreement provided, among other things, that the contract was contingent upon the buyer's obtaining "a firm written commitment" for a conventional mortgage in the amount of $185,000. *Id.* at 285. The contract also stated that, if the mortgage commitment was not obtained by October 2, 1986, the agreement "shall be null and void." *Ibid.* The mortgage contingency date later was extended to October 20, 1986. The buyers applied for a mortgage and were informed that they would not qualify for a $185,000 loan but would probably qualify for a loan in the amount of $162,000. *Ibid.* On September 30, 1986, buyers and sellers received the mortgage commitment letter, which stated that the loan was only for $162,000. The commitment letter also stated that, prior to or simultaneous with the closing, the buyers must obtain a fully executed contract for the sale of their home at a minimum price of $275,000. *Id.* at 286. The realtor who appraised the home believed that such a price was unattainable and concluded that the contract had been nullified. *Ibid.* Asserting that they had not received a "firm written commitment" for a mortgage, buyers sought the return of their deposit monies and the sellers asserted that the buyers had breached the contract by failing to close. *Ibid.*

The judge in *Farrell* stated that a mortgage contingency clause "informs the sellers in clear and unmistakable language that the buyers do not possess sufficient funds to consummate the purchase without a loan." *Id.* at 287. The judge noted that the sellers knew or should have known that "what the buyers wanted and needed was a loan that was subject to no conditions or only conditions that were within their sole control." *Ibid.* The judge added:

A mortgage-loan-contingency clause certainly requires the buyers to use their best efforts to comply with any and all conditions imposed by the lending institution as a pre-condition for obtaining the loan. Thus, if a condition of the loan is obtaining employment verification, the buyer must execute and submit an authorization to secure the necessary documents from his employer. Or, if a condition is the issuance of a satisfactory termite inspection report, the buyer must order and pay for such an inspection. But a condition that the buyers sell their home at a minimum price is not within the buyers' sole control but is subject to the vagaries of market conditions and can be satisfied only if another person offers to purchase at the minimum price. *[Ibid.]*

The court concluded that because the buyers did not obtain the required mortgage loan by October 20, 1986, the contract became null and void, according to the expressed terms of the agreement. *Id.* at 288.

Our decision in *McKenna v. Rosen*, 239 N.J. Super. 191 (App. Div. 1990), involved a similar factual scenario. There, plaintiffs entered into a contract to purchase from defendants certain real property.

(continued)

The contract was contingent upon the purchasers obtaining a "firm written commitment" for a 30-year conventional mortgage, at prevailing rates of interest. *Id.* at 192. The agreement provided that, if the mortgage commitment was not obtained by a specified date, the agreement "shall be null and void unless purchasers immediately waive benefit of the mortgage contingency clause in writing, and consider the clause as having been fully satisfied." *Id.* at 193. When received, the commitment included a condition that the buyers provide evidence of the sale of the buyer's previous residence with net proceeds of at least $90,000. *Ibid.* Because the buyers' home had been on the market for several months and had not been sold, they informed the sellers that they would not be able to accept the condition and they were terminating the agreement. *Ibid.* The sellers maintained that the buyers could not terminate if the commitment was conditional and they refused to refund the deposit monies. *Ibid.*

We held in *McKenna* that, because the buyers had not obtained a firm commitment for a mortgage loan, they were entitled to cancel the contract and a refund of their deposit. *Id.* at 194-96. We endorsed the reasoning of the Law Division judge in *Farrell. Id.* at 193. We stated that if a mortgage commitment includes conditions over which the borrowers have no control, the commitment is less than "firm." *Id.* at 194–95. A contract requiring buyers to obtain a "firm commitment" is one in which the buyers intend to be bound "only if they could secure a mortgage commitment with contingencies they had the power to fulfill." *Id.* at 196. We applied general principles of contract interpretation, noting that a contract must be construed "as a whole" and the language of the agreement must be "given its ordinary, reasonable meaning absent anything to show that it was used in a different sense." *Ibid.* We added:

The interpretation which we give to the contract here, as in *Farrell,* is one which realistically allows for a determination of whether a mortgage commitment is firm. A purchaser has secured a firm commitment if any contingency is within his power alone to fulfill. If the fulfillment of the contingency is not within the sole control of the purchaser, the language of the contingent commitment should be interpreted to relieve him of his obligation under the realty contract. In such a case, the purchaser clearly bargained for the right to void the land purchase contract when the contingency could not be met. . . . [*Ibid.*]

We are satisfied that in this case the judge correctly applied the principles set forth in *Farrell* and *McKenna* in granting summary judgment in favor of defendants. The contract at issue here was expressly contingent upon defendants obtaining mortgage financing. The agreement required defendants to immediately apply for the mortgage. It also provided that either the buyers or the sellers could cancel the contract if a written mortgage commitment was not received within 30 days of the signing of the agreement. Although defendants received a written mortgage commitment, it was conditioned on, among other things, the sale of their properties. *Farrell* and *McKenna* make clear that, because fulfillment of such a condition is not within the sole power of the purchasers, the mortgage commitment was not firm and did not satisfy the contract's mortgage contingency clause. In these circumstances, defendants were not obligated to perform and had the right to cancel the contract.

Plaintiffs argue that defendants were required to terminate the agreement by June 30, 2001 and, having failed to do so, defendants were precluded from canceling the agreement thereafter. We disagree. As we stated previously, the contract gave the parties the right to terminate in the event the buyers did not obtain the mortgage commitment within 30 days of the date of the agreement. Although defendants received the mortgage commitment within the required time frame, the commitment was subject to a contingency that plainly was beyond their sole ability to fulfill. *McKenna, supra,* 239 *N.J. Super.* at 196. Because the buyers had not obtained a firm mortgage commitment within the time frame specified by the agreement, defendants had the right to cancel. However, the contract did not expressly require that they do so within the 30-day period for obtaining the commitment. Thus, we are satisfied that the agreement did not foreclose defendants from canceling the agreement after June 30, 2001.

We are convinced that such a conclusion accords with the apparent intention of the parties to this agreement. As we pointed out in *McKenna,* when a contract for the sale of realty is made contingent upon the purchaser obtaining firm mortgage financing, it is illogical to assume that the purchaser agreed to be bound to accept a mortgage commitment subject to a contingency that is beyond the purchaser's sole control. *Ibid.* In the absence of some language indicating a contrary intention by the parties, the agreement must be construed to relieve the purchaser of his or her obligations under the contract if the purchaser receives a mortgage commitment with such conditions. *Ibid.* Unless the contract provides otherwise, we must assume that the purchaser bargained for the right to void the agreement in these circumstances. *Ibid.*

Plaintiffs argue that the decision granting summary judgment in favor of defendants is inconsistent with our decision in *Malus v. Hager*, 312 N.J. Super. 483 (App. Div. 1998). In our view, the motion judge correctly found that the *Malus* case was not controlling. In *Malus*, the parties entered into a contract for the sale of property which provided that buyers' obligation to perform was contingent upon the buyer obtaining a mortgage. The agreement stated that, in the event buyers failed to obtain the mortgage within a specified period of time, the buyers or the sellers may void the contract within ten days thereafter. The agreement further stated that if the buyers or sellers do not void the agreement within this specified time period, the buyers and sellers waive their rights to void the contract under this provision. *Id.* at 484-85. The buyers applied for a mortgage loan and received a mortgage commitment within the required time frame. Under the commitment, the bank retained the right to cancel in the event the buyers' financial condition or employment status changed adversely. *Id.* at 485. When one of the buyers became unemployed, the bank declined to make the loan. The sellers refused to return the deposit monies and the buyers sued. *Ibid.*

We held in *Malus* that the sellers were entitled to retain the deposit monies. We refused to interpret the mortgage contingency clause to encompass not only the receipt of a mortgage commitment, but also the availability at closing of mortgage proceeds necessary to complete the purchase. We said that were we to interpret the clause in that manner, the parties would be left in "an intolerable state of limbo until the closing is finally consummated." *Id.* at 486. We added, "[c]onfusion and uncertainty can only result from extending, as a matter of law, the mortgage contingency clause to the date of closing." *Ibid.*

We are convinced that plaintiffs' reliance upon *Malus* is misplaced. In *Malus*, the mortgage contingency clause provided that the purchaser and seller could *only* void the contract if they acted within ten days of the period specified in the contract for obtaining the mortgage commitment. The agreement expressly provided that if the parties did not act within that time frame, they waived their rights to void the contract under that section of the agreement. *Id.* at 485. Here, by contrast, the agreement did not specify when the parties were required to cancel. It also did not contain a waiver of rights provision. Therefore, we are convinced that the *Malus* decision is not controlling here.

Plaintiffs additionally argue that the judge erred in granting summary judgment because there was a genuine issue of material fact as to whether defendants acted in good faith in endeavoring to sell their properties. We are satisfied, however, that the evidence before the trial court was so "one-sided" that this factual issue could be resolved as a matter of law. *Brill v. Guardian Life Ins. Co. of Am.*, 142 N.J. 520, 540 (1995)(quoting *Anderson v. Liberty Lobby Inc.*, 477 U. S. 242, 252, 106 S. Ct. 2505, 2512, 91 L. Ed.2d 202, 214 (1986)).

With regard to the West Orange property, the record shows that during contract negotiations, the Bernesbys reduced their sale price. They also agreed to treat termite infestation, repair any termite damage and make certain repairs. When the Bernesbys refused to make certain other repairs, the prospective purchasers cancelled the contract. Concerning the Montclair property, the record shows that Strazza listed the house for sale at a reduced price because it was in substantial disrepair. Strazza intended to sell the property "as is," with the exception of termite treatment. The prospective purchasers executed the contract for sale but, following the home inspection, demanded that Strazza make certain repairs. Before Strazza responded to the demand, the purchasers cancelled the contract.

In our view, based on the evidence before her, the judge properly determined that that there was no genuine issue of material fact and defendants were entitled to judgment as a matter of law. *R.* 4:46-2(c). As the judge found, the evidence was insufficient to support a finding by a trier of fact that defendants acted in bad faith in endeavoring to sell their properties. Accordingly, the judge did not err in granting summary judgment in favor of defendants.

Affirmed.

Before a buyer proceeds to closing, conditions must be satisfied, met, or waived. The conditions are posed as if a question must be answered.

- Will the agreement have effect if mortgage financing is not obtainable?
- Will the agreement have effect if alternative mortgage financing is available other than the type stated in the contract?
- Will the failure to acquire certification for septic systems void a contract?
- Will the failure to be granted zoning variance serve as an excusable condition or failure to meet a contingent requirement under a contract?
- Will a political subdivision permit development of land in a certain way or right as envisioned under the original contract?
- Are the water and soil in good condition?
- Is the purchase contingent upon the resolution of underlying or aligned civil litigation?[15]
- Is there termite or other wood destroying insect infestation?[16]

At common law, these types of contingencies are termed ***conditions precedent***, meaning the agreement is not enforceable until the stated condition is satisfied, removed, or rectified. "Words which apparently impose a condition precedent may be construed as creating a vested interest postponing merely the enjoyment of possession."[17]

Web Exercise

Visit the Pennsylvania Association of Realtors web location for an assessment of the new contingency clause for financing at *www.parealtor.org/content/MortgageContingencyClause.htm*.

To illustrate the effect of a condition precedent on a contract, assume that the parties to the real estate agreement made the contract subject to the buyer being satisfied with the survey. An acceptable survey is a condition precedent to performance in the following contract language:

> Boundary lines for said subdivision to be subject to written approval of both the sellers and purchasers. Should written approval not be obtained from either party on or before July 30, 1976, then this contract shall be declared null and void and all monies on deposit refunded to Purchasers.[18]

Until the survey is acceptable, the contract is ". . . not a sale as to the purchase of a survey and to the terms on which a sale would take place if all the parties at a future date decided to agree to convert the conditional sales agreement into a binding contract by approving the survey;"[19] until the survey is satisfactory, the condition controls the contract. Hence, the parties to the real estate agreement made the contract subject to the buyer being satisfied with a survey. Thus, an acceptable survey is a precedent of performance, as the contract stated.

Most standardized contracts published by Boards of Realtors include explicit conditions that can be either excluded or included. Even so, litigation on the nature of these conditions and those obligated to fulfill them is rampant. When drafting, paralegals must stay close to the language of the contract in whole and avoid the emotional rationales of "fairness" often propounded by disgruntled parties. If the seller is repulsed by conditions or contingencies, reject them as contractually posed. Flawed arguments by disgruntled sellers are discovered in many appellate cases, none more compelling than *Hodorowicz v. Szulc*.[20] In sum, conditions not met kill contracts. At best, a conditional contract is an agreement in expectancy.

An examination of the most often seen conditions and contingencies in real estate practice is a crucial requirement for the professional paralegal and real estate practitioner. Realize that conditional language can be fully integrated into the underlying contract by an existing clause or provision or incorporated by an attached addendum or endorsement. The **endorsement** format is basically generic, calling upon the paralegal to fill in the modification or change. The **addendum** expressly lists those conditions and contingencies the buyer wishes to exercise. The addendum design may encompass more than one condition. See Figure 4–1.

ADDENDUM TO AGREEMENT OF PURCHASE AND SALE

RIGHT OF INSPECTION; CONDITION OF PREMISES; LIMITATION OF REMEDIES; SETTLEMENT AS FINAL

This is an Addendum to an Agreement of Purchase and Sale (the "Agreement") dated as of _____ between _____ as Seller and _____, as Purchaser with respect to the property known as _____. In the event of any conflict between the provisions of this Addendum and the provisions of the Agreement, the provisions of this Addendum shall be controlling.

1. RIGHT OF INSPECTION. Purchaser shall have the right to inspect the premises and fixtures, appliances and personal property (collectively "Contents") or have the premises inspected by experts selected by Purchaser (as described in and to meet the time limits stated in Paragraph 3, below). Such inspections may include, but shall not be limited to inspection to determine:

    a.   The existence of any defect, whether structural or otherwise, latent or apparent;
    b.   The existence of infestation or damage by or as a result of termites, fungi, dry rot, or other wood destroying insects, pests or conditions;
    c.   The presence of urea formaldehyde foam insulation.

All such inspections shall be at the sole cost and expense of Purchaser.

2. CONDITION OF PREMISES. The premises and the Contents being sold and purchased are not new. Purchaser understands and acknowledges that neither the Seller nor any agent of the Seller has made any representation concerning the premises or the Contents except as specifically set forth below (specify for each item: the name of the person who made the representation; by whom that person is employed; the date the representation was made): (if none, please enter "none" and initial)

_____ Seller's Initials

_____ Purchaser's Initials

Seller has no knowledge of any latent defect in the premises or the contents except: (if none, please enter "none" and initial)
_____ Seller's Initials

_____ Purchaser's Initials

Purchaser is buying the premises and the contents in their present condition, "as is," and not in reliance on any representation or statement of seller or any other person unless such representation or statement appears on this Addendum.

FIGURE 4–1

MORGAGE CONTINGENCY CLAUSE

MORTGAGE CONTINGENCY CLAUSE

This contract is subject to the condition that purchaser be able to procure within _____ days a firm commitment for a loan to be secured by a mortgage or trust deed on the real estate in the amount of $_____, or such lesser sum as purchaser accepts, with interest not to exceed _____% a year to be amortized over _____ years, the commission and service charges for such loan not to exceed _____%. After making every reasonable effort, if purchaser is unable to procure such commitment within the time specified herein and so notified seller thereof within that time, this contract shall become null and void and all earnest money shall be returned to purchaser: provided that if seller, at his option, within a like period of time following purchaser's notice, procures for purchaser such a commitment or notifies purchaser that seller will accept a purchase money mortgage upon the same terms, this contract shall remain in full force and effect.

FIGURE 4–2

II. CONDITIONS RELATING TO FINANCING

The majority of real estate contracts contain some conditional language relative to the acquisition of financing. In essence, the sale is conditional upon the buyer securing the funds necessary to close the transaction. "Such clauses create a condition precedent to the contract and are for the sole benefit of the purchaser. . . . When these conditions are met and the mortgage cannot be obtained, the contract may be terminated and the down payment recovered."[21] There are various ways in which such a condition can be expressed.

First, the basic agreement of sale may contain the condition within its form contents. Consider the language in Figure 4–2, a typical **mortgage contingency clause** in a standing contract.

Within this conditional framework, the buyer must act in good faith in seeking financing according to rate and term. "But even where the parties' agreement of sale does not specify the steps to be taken, a good-faith effort requires more than an oral inquiry regarding a loan application. The vendee must request financing in a manner that would cause a lender to seriously evaluate the request and formally respond thereto."[22]

All that buyers are obligated to do in the course of meeting the standards of the mortgage contingency clause is to apply for a mortgage within the time, the agreement designates, to make honest representation to the lender, and to make a good faith effort to acquire financing. The purchaser is required to make a "genuine effort" to obtain a mortgage and to act in good faith. When these conditions are met and the mortgage cannot be obtained, the contract may be terminated and the down payment recovered.[23]

III. HOME INSPECTIONS

Increasingly included in the real estate transaction is the buyer's desire for a **home inspection**. The inspection accomplishes two purposes: first, the buyer is apprised of the home's condition, especially as to the major systems and structure; second, any faults may serve as a failed condition precedent allowing withdrawal from the transaction.

Web Exercise

For a sample inspection report, visit *www.accuratebuilding.com/services/inspections/home_inspection_sample_report.html*.

Most transactions with inspection rights rely on the addendum or **rider** document, if a clause is not already included in the sales agreement. Figure 4–3 allows an inspection exercisable within a

ADDENDUM TO AGREEMENT OF PURCHASE AND SALE

The undersigned parties to an Agreement of Purchase and Sale dated _____ between _____ as Seller(s) and _____ as Buyer(s) on property known as _____ hereby mutually agree to amend such contract as follows:

CONDITION OF PREMISES: It is understood that the property being sold is not new, and Buyer hereby acknowledges that there has been no representation by the Seller or any agent of the Seller regarding the condition of premises or of any of the appliances that may be contained therein unless specifically set forth in said Agreement of Purchase and Sale. Buyer is further informed that Seller is unaware of any latent defects in the property, or any component thereof, including but not limited to the presence of urea formaldehyde insulation, plumbing, heating, air conditioning, and electrical systems, fixtures and appliances, roof, sewers, septic systems, soil conditions, foundation, structural conditions, and pool and related equipment, if applicable, unless otherwise mentioned in this agreement.

RIGHT OF INSPECTION: Buyer is hereby granted the right to inspect the premises, or to obtain inspection reports of qualified experts at his own expense. Should such reports reveal latent defects not discoverable by ordinary inspection, requested repairs, if any, must be submitted in writing to Seller or Seller's Agent not later than _____ ( ) days after Buyer executes this inspection addendum.

LIMITATION OF REMEDIES: Upon receipt of such notice, Seller may:
a. Treat the condition and repair the damage at Seller's own cost and expense, in which event Buyer shall consummate this transaction pursuant to the terms of the Agreement;
b. Advise Buyer of the cost of the necessary repairs and, subject to the Agreement of Buyer, the amount to be credited to Buyer at settlement; or
c. Terminate the Agreement and refund to the Buyer all sums paid by Buyer to Seller hereunder.
Seller shall advise Buyer of Seller's intent to exercise any such option within ten (10) days of receipt of written notice of the defect.

Regardless of which alternative Seller chooses, Buyer shall have the option to proceed with the settlement, taking the property subject to such condition and damage as may exist and subject to the further terms and conditions of the Agreement (including the original purchase price), provided that written notice of such intention is delivered to Seller or Seller's Agent within thirty (30) days after date Buyer executes this Inspection Addendum.

SETTLEMENT AS FINAL: Anything contained in the Agreement or the Addendum to the contrary notwithstanding, Buyer and Seller agree that delivery of the Deed at the settlement and acceptance thereof by Buyer shall constitute an acknowledgment by Buyer that the premises and the Contents were in satisfactory condition at the time of closing, and that Seller shall have no liability with respect thereto. This provision shall survive delivery of the Deed.

For purposes of this Inspection Addendum to Agreement, "TIME IS OF THE ESSENCE."

_____	_____	_____
Witness	Date	Purchaser
_____	_____	_____
Witness	Date	Purchaser
_____	_____	_____
Witness	Date	Purchaser

FIGURE 4–3

time frame. Additionally, how those repairs, if any, are to be remedied is narrowly construed within the additional provisions.

Defining a **major defect** exactly is a critical issue for the drafter. Buyers have no right to repair because of trivial imperfections. Usually, a small sum of money, $1,000 or so, is the benchmark for what means "major." From this measure, the addendum should limit the subject matter for inspection to include major systems or foundations.

Even home inspections do not assume a perfect abode. Arizona State University Professor, Marianne Jennings, dwells upon the supernatural defects in housing in a most humorous series of questions. In other words, avoid the house that fails to answer these questions:

Jennings' Psychological Questions for Buyers Concerned about Prior Property Use and History

1. Why do neighborhood children with garlic around their necks race by this house screaming?
2. Why have seventeen families lived in this house in the past eighteen months?
3. Why is this 4,200-square-foot Aspen property selling for $12,000?
4. Why do the neighbors giggle each time I come to see the house?
5. Why are there potholes in the ground-level living room?
6. Is there anything significant about the number of gun racks in the house?
7. Why do you keep referring to your "former client"?
8. Why do you keep saying, "talk to the neighbors"?
9. How long did Janet Leigh live here?
10. How often do those uranium tailings float through the air, creating that radioactive pink haze?[24]

Now, for more serious, reality-based examples.

A. Swimming Pool

In properties having pools, additional risks and burdens are encountered. A pool in poor shape is a liability, not an asset. Not only does the physical condition of the pool need to be considered, but the water supply, filter system, and fence and gate must also be inspected.

Place the inspection clause in Figure 4–4 within the agreement of sale.

This agreement is conditioned and contingent upon Buyer obtaining a satisfactory inspection report issued by a reputable swimming pool inspector/installer indicating that the swimming pool is free from material defects and in good working order and condition. Buyer shall have _____ days from the date of this agreement to complete said inspection, the cost of which will be borne by _____.

In the event that said report discloses material defects, then Seller shall bear the cost and expense of remedying same. In the event that the estimated cost of repairs exceeds $_____, then at Seller's sole option, Seller may terminate this agreement, whereupon all hand money paid on account of the purchase price shall be returned to Buyer and there shall be no further liability on the part of either party to the other.

FIGURE 4–4
Swimming Pool Inspection Clause.

This Agreement is conditioned and contingent upon buyer obtaining a satisfactory inspection report issued by a reputable well driller and water testing laboratory indicating that the existing well produces a minimum sustained flow of _____ gallons per minute and that the water produced is bacteriologically and otherwise suitable for human consumption. Buyer shall have _____ days from the date of this agreement to complete said inspection, the cost of which shall be borne by _____.

In the event that said well inspection fails to meet the foregoing standards as to either quality or quantity, then buyer, at their sole option, may accept the inspection report as indicated, or may terminate this agreement, whereupon all hand money paid on account of the purchase price shall be returned to buyer and there shall be no further liability on the part of either party to the other.

FIGURE 4–5
Well Inspection Clause.

B. Well, Water, and Septic

Given the extraordinary environmental controls over water and wells and the growing concern over bacteriological quality, it is good practice to receive assurance for these systems.

A well that produces insufficient flow is an expensive proposition. Include a well inspection clause, as in Figure 4–5, within the agreement of sale.

Aside from water potability, the buyer of property lacking public sewers has to weigh septic considerations. Leakage, inefficient reception, and waste management can be determined by qualified septic inspectors.

Of course, buyers may choose to waive the said testing in a formal sense. For a testing waiver, see Figure 4–6.

IV. HAZARDOUS MATERIALS

Real estate litigiousness has been clearly generated by **hazardous material** or environmental risk cases of which all paralegals should be aware. Purchasers, wary of environmental problems, are opting for conditional contract language or addenda.

A. The Comprehensive Environmental Response, Compensation, and Liability Act[25]

Commercial realty owners are frequently faced with environmental concerns in the sale. Known as *brownfields*, these locations, if containing designated waste materials, need to be mitigated as a condition of sale.[26] The **Comprehensive Environmental Response, Compensation, and Liability Act (CERCLA)** publishes lists of hazardous materials that need to be dealt with before transfer. Figure 4–7 is a partial list posted in 2007.

Web Exercise

Become familiar with the terms of CERCLA by visiting *www.law.cornell.edu/uscode/uscode42/usc_sec_42_00009601—000-.html*.

B. Radon

Radon is the latest environmental concern. "Radon is a naturally occurring radioactive gas that is odorless, tasteless, and invisible. Radon enters a structure through openings or cracks in the structure. Radon may also enter a structure through the water supply and through certain materials, including brick and concrete, used in the construction process. Radon presents a health risk

TO THE RHODE ISLAND DEPARTMENT OF ENVIRONMENTAL MANAGEMENT:

We, _____, the owner and seller, and _____, the buyers of the property identified as
Street: _____ Pole No. _____
City or Town: _____
Assessor's Plat Number: _____   Assessor's Lot Number: _____
Recorded Plat Number: _____   Recorded Lot Number: _____
Subdivision: _____   Subdivision Lot Number: _____
Seller's deed recorded in Book _____ at Page: _____

Legal description and/or copy of deed of area to be certified is enclosed _____

Anticipated date of conveyance: _____

We hereby individually and collectively waive all requirements under Title 23, Chapter 19.5, of the Rhode Island General Laws of 1956, as amended.

Signed _____ (Seller)   Signed _____ (Buyer)

Home address: _____   Home address: _____
Business address: _____   Business address: _____
City or town: _____   City or town: _____

State of Rhode Island
County of
On this date the above signatories personally appeared before me and on oath deposed and said that all statement herein are correct and true to their knowledge and belief.

Subscribed and sworn to before me in [city/town], Rhode Island on this _____ day of _____, ___, 2001.

_____

Notary Public

Printed Name: _____

My commission expires: _____

FIGURE 4–6
Water Inspection Waiver.

when it becomes concentrated in the structure. According to health professionals, prolonged exposure (about 20 years) to the decay products of radon, referred to as radon progeny or radon daughters, may lead to the development of lung cancer."[27] See Figure 4–8[28] for a map of the radon zones in the U.S.

Brokers and agents may also incur liability over levels of radon. Thus, real estate brokers face potential liability for nondisclosure, misdisclosure, or negligent disclosure of defects in homes they broker.[29]

2007 RANK	SUBSTANCE NAME	TOTAL POINTS	2005 RANK	CAS #
1	ARSENIC	1672.58	1	007440-38-2
2	LEAD	1534.07	2	007439-92-1
3	MERCURY	1504.69	3	007439-97-6
4	VINYL CHLORIDE	1387.75	4	000075-01-4
5	POLYCHLORINATED BIPHENYLS	1365.78	5	001336-36-3
6	BENZENE	1355.96	6	000071-43-2
7	CADMIUM	1324.22	8	007440-43-9
8	POLYCYCLIC AROMATIC HYDROCARBONS	1316.98	7	130498-29-2
9	BENZO(A)PYRENE	1312.45	9	000050-32-8
10	BENZO(B)FLUORANTHENE	1266.55	10	000205-99-2
11	CHLOROFORM	1223.03	11	000067-66-3
12	DDT, P,P'-	1193.36	12	000050-29-3
13	AROCLOR 1254	1182.63	13	011097-69-1
14	AROCLOR 1260	1177.77	14	011096-82-5
15	DIBENZO(A,H)ANTHRACENE	1165.88	15	000053-70-3
16	TRICHLOROETHYLENE	1154.73	16	000079-01-6
17	DIELDRIN	1150.91	17	000060-57-1
18	CHROMIUM, HEXAVALENT	1149.98	18	018540-29-9
19	PHOSPHORUS, WHITE	1144.77	19	007723-14-0
20	CHLORDANE	1133.21	21	000057-74-9
21	DDE, P,P'-	1132.49	20	000072-55-9
22	HEXACHLOROBUTADIENE	1129.63	22	000087-68-3
23	COAL TAR CREOSOTE	1124.32	23	008001-58-9
24	ALDRIN	1117.22	25	000309-00-2
25	DDD, P,P'-	1114.83	24	000072-54-8
26	BENZIDINE	1114.24	26	000092-87-5
27	AROCLOR 1248	1112.20	27	012672-29-6
28	CYANIDE	1099.48	28	000057-12-5
29	AROCLOR 1242	1093.14	29	053469-21-9
30	AROCLOR	1091.52	62	012767-79-2
31	TOXAPHENE	1086.65	30	008001-35-2
32	HEXACHLOROCYCLOHEXANE, GAMMA-	1081.63	32	000058-89-9

FIGURE 4–7

CERCLA's List of Hazardous Materials that must be addressed before a property transfer.

(continues)

33	TETRACHLOROETHYLENE	1080.43	31	000127-18-4
34	HEPTACHLOR	1072.67	33	000076-44-8
35	1,2-DIBROMOETHANE	1064.06	34	000106-93-4
36	HEXACHLOROCYCLOHEXANE, BETA-	1060.22	37	000319-85-7
37	ACROLEIN	1059.07	36	000107-02-8
38	DISULFOTON	1058.85	35	000298-04-4
39	BENZO(A)ANTHRACENE	1057.96	38	000056-55-3
40	3,3'-DICHLOROBENZIDINE	1051.61	39	000091-94-1
41	ENDRIN	1048.57	41	000072-20-8
42	BERYLLIUM	1046.12	40	007440-41-7
43	HEXACHLOROCYCLOHEXANE, DELTA-	1038.27	42	000319-86-8
44	1,2-DIBROMO-3-CHLOROPROPANE	1035.55	43	000096-12-8
45	PENTACHLOROPHENOL	1028.01	45	000087-86-5
46	HEPTACHLOR EPOXIDE	1027.12	44	001024-57-3
47	CARBON TETRACHLORIDE	1023.32	46	000056-23-5
48	AROCLOR 1221	1018.41	47	011104-28-2
49	COBALT	1015.57	50	007440-48-4
50	DDT, O,P'-	1014.71	49	000789-02-6
51	AROCLOR 1016	1014.33	48	012674-11-2
52	DI-N-BUTYL PHTHALATE	1007.49	52	000084-74-2
53	NICKEL	1005.40	55	007440-02-0
54	ENDOSULFAN	1004.65	54	000115-29-7
55	ENDOSULFAN SULFATE	1003.56	53	001031-07-8
56	DIAZINON	1002.08	57	000333-41-5
57	ENDOSULFAN, ALPHA	1001.30	58	000959-98-8
58	XYLENES, TOTAL	996.07	59	001330-20-7
59	CIS-CHLORDANE	995.08	51	005103-71-9
60	DIBROMOCHLOROPROPANE	994.87	60	067708-83-2
61	METHOXYCHLOR	994.47	61	000072-43-5
62	BENZO(K)FLUORANTHENE	981.26	63	000207-08-9
63	ENDRIN KETONE	978.99	64	053494-70-5
64	TRANS-CHLORDANE	973.99	56	005103-74-2
65	CHROMIUM(VI) OXIDE	969.58	66	001333-82-0
66	METHANE	959.78	67	000074-82-8
67	ENDOSULFAN, BETA	959.19	65	033213-65-9

FIGURE 4–7
(continued)

68	AROCLOR 1232	955.64	68	011141-16-5
69	ENDRIN ALDEHYDE	954.86	69	007421-93-4
70	BENZOFLUORANTHENE	951.48	70	056832-73-6
71	TOLUENE	947.50	71	000108-88-3
72	2-HEXANONE	942.02	72	000591-78-6
73	2,3,7,8-TETRACHLORODIBENZO-P-DIOXIN	938.11	73	001746-01-6
74	ZINC	932.89	74	007440-66-6
75	DIMETHYLARSINIC ACID	922.06	75	000075-60-5
76	DI(2-ETHYLHEXYL)PHTHALATE	919.02	76	000117-81-7
77	CHROMIUM	908.52	77	007440-47-3
78	NAPHTHALENE	896.67	78	000091-20-3
79	1,1-DICHLOROETHENE	891.19	79	000075-35-4
80	METHYLENE CHLORIDE	888.96	81	000075-09-2
81	AROCLOR 1240	888.11	80	071328-89-7
82	2,4,6-TRINITROTOLUENE	883.59	82	000118-96-7
83	BROMODICHLOROETHANE	870.00	83	000683-53-4
84	HYDRAZINE	864.41	85	000302-01-2
85	1,2-DICHLOROETHANE	863.99	84	000107-06-2
86	2,4,6-TRICHLOROPHENOL	863.71	86	000088-06-2
87	2,4-DINITROPHENOL	860.45	87	000051-28-5
88	BIS(2-CHLOROETHYL) ETHER	859.88	88	000111-44-4
89	THIOCYANATE	849.21	89	000302-04-5
90	ASBESTOS	841.54	90	001332-21-4
91	CHLORINE	840.37	92	007782-50-5
92	CYCLOTRIMETHYLENETRINITRAMINE (RDX)	840.28	91	000121-82-4
93	HEXACHLOROBENZENE	838.34	93	000118-74-1
94	2,4-DINITROTOLUENE	837.88	96	000121-14-2
95	RADIUM-226	835.93	94	013982-63-3
96	ETHION	834.03	97	000563-12-2
97	1,1,1-TRICHLOROETHANE	833.81	95	000071-55-6
98	URANIUM	833.41	98	007440-61-1
99	ETHYLBENZENE	832.13	99	000100-41-4
100	RADIUM	828.07	100	007440-14-4
101	THORIUM	825.17	101	007440-29-1

FIGURE 4–7
(continued)

102	4,6-DINITRO-O-CRESOL	822.78	102	000534-52-1
103	1,3,5-TRINITROBENZENE	820.17	103	000099-35-4
104	CHLOROBENZENE	819.69	105	000108-90-7
105	RADON	817.89	104	010043-92-2
106	RADIUM-228	816.76	106	015262-20-1
107	THORIUM-230	814.72	107	014269-63-7
107	URANIUM-235	814.72	107	015117-96-1
109	BARIUM	813.46	109	007440-39-3
110	FLUORANTHENE	812.40	113	000206-44-0
111	URANIUM-234	812.11	110	013966-29-5
112	N-NITROSODI-N-PROPYLAMINE	811.05	111	000621-64-7
113	THORIUM-228	810.36	112	014274-82-9
114	RADON-222	809.78	114	014859-67-7
115	HEXACHLOROCYCLOHEXANE, ALPHA-	809.56	116	000319-84-6
116	1,2,3-TRICHLOROBENZENE	808.41	143	000087-61-6
117	MANGANESE	807.90	115	007439-96-5
118	COAL TARS	807.07	117	008007-45-2
119	CHRYSOTILE ASBESTOS	806.68	119	012001-29-5
119	STRONTIUM-90	806.68	119	010098-97-2
121	PLUTONIUM-239	806.67	118	015117-48-3
122	POLONIUM-210	806.39	122	013981-52-7
123	METHYLMERCURY	806.39	121	022967-92-6
124	PLUTONIUM-238	806.01	123	013981-16-3
125	LEAD-210	805.90	124	014255-04-0
126	PLUTONIUM	805.23	125	007440-07-5
127	CHLORPYRIFOS	804.93	125	002921-88-2
128	COPPER	804.86	133	007440-50-8
129	AMERICIUM-241	804.55	128	086954-36-1
130	RADON-220	804.54	127	022481-48-7
131	AMOSITE ASBESTOS	804.07	129	012172-73-5
132	IODINE-131	803.48	130	010043-66-0
133	HYDROGEN CYANIDE	803.08	132	000074-90-8
134	TRIBUTYLTIN	802.61	131	000688-73-3
135	GUTHION	802.32	134	000086-50-0
136	NEPTUNIUM-237	802.13	135	013994-20-2

FIGURE 4–7
(continued)

137	CHRYSENE	802.10	139	000218-01-9
138	CHLORDECONE	801.64	136	000143-50-0
138	IODINE-129	801.64	136	015046-84-1
138	PLUTONIUM-240	801.64	136	014119-33-6
141	S,S,S-TRIBUTYL PHOSPHOROTRITHIOATE	797.88	140	000078-48-8
142	BROMINE	789.15	142	007726-95-6
143	POLYBROMINATED BIPHENYLS	789.11	141	067774-32-7
144	DICOFOL	787.56	144	000115-32-2
145	PARATHION	784.14	145	000056-38-2
146	1,1,2,2-TETRACHLOROETHANE	782.15	146	000079-34-5
147	SELENIUM	778.98	147	007782-49-2
148	HEXACHLOROCYCLOHEXANE, TECHNICAL GRADE	774.91	148	000608-73-1
149	TRICHLOROFLUOROETHANE	770.74	149	027154-33-2
150	TRIFLURALIN	770.12	150	001582-09-8
151	DDD, O,P'-	768.73	151	000053-19-0
152	4,4'-METHYLENEBIS(2-CHLOROANILINE)	766.66	152	000101-14-4
153	HEXACHLORODIBENZO-P-DIOXIN	760.42	153	034465-46-8
154	HEPTACHLORODIBENZO-P-DIOXIN	754.47	154	037871-00-4
155	PENTACHLOROBENZENE	753.58	155	000608-93-5
156	1,3-BUTADIENE	747.31	201	000106-99-0
157	AMMONIA	745.55	156	007664-41-7
158	2-METHYLNAPHTHALENE	743.24	157	000091-57-6
159	1,4-DICHLOROBENZENE	737.32	159	000106-46-7
160	1,1-DICHLOROETHANE	736.23	158	000075-34-3
161	ACENAPHTHENE	731.25	160	000083-32-9
162	1,2,3,4,6,7,8,9-OCTACHLORODI-BENZOFURAN	726.14	161	039001-02-0
163	1,1,2-TRICHLOROETHANE	724.96	162	000079-00-5
164	TRICHLOROETHANE	723.32	163	025323-89-1
165	HEXACHLOROCYCLOPENTADIENE	719.01	164	000077-47-4
166	HEPTACHLORODIBENZOFURAN	718.58	165	038998-75-3
167	1,2-DIPHENYLHYDRAZINE	713.90	166	000122-66-7
168	2,3,4,7,8-PENTACHLORODIBENZOFURAN	710.71	167	057117-31-4
169	TETRACHLOROBIPHENYL	709.21	168	026914-33-0

FIGURE 4–7
(continued)

170	CRESOL, PARA-	707.83	169	000106-44-5
171	OXYCHLORDANE	706.32	170	027304-13-8
172	1,2-DICHLOROBENZENE	704.91	171	000095-50-1
173	1,2-DICHLOROETHENE, TRANS-	704.04	178	000156-60-5
174	INDENO(1,2,3-CD)PYRENE	703.30	180	000193-39-5
175	GAMMA-CHLORDENE	702.59	172	056641-38-4
176	CARBON DISULFIDE	702.55	174	000075-15-0
177	TETRACHLOROPHENOL	702.54	173	025167-83-3
178	AMERICIUM	701.62	175	007440-35-9
178	URANIUM-233	701.62	175	013968-55-3
180	PALLADIUM	700.66	177	007440-05-3
181	HEXACHLORODIBENZOFURAN	700.56	179	055684-94-1
182	PHENOL	696.96	183	000108-95-2
183	CHLOROETHANE	693.90	182	000075-00-3
184	ACETONE	693.31	181	000067-64-1
185	P-XYLENE	690.20	185	000106-42-3
186	DIBENZOFURAN	689.19	187	000132-64-9
187	ALUMINUM	688.13	186	007429-90-5
188	2,4-DIMETHYLPHENOL	685.76	189	000105-67-9
189	CARBON MONOXIDE	684.49	188	000630-08-0
190	TETRACHLOROETHANE	677.97	190	025322-20-7
191	HYDROGEN SULFIDE	676.51	193	007783-06-4
192	PENTACHLORODIBENZOFURAN	673.21	192	030402-15-4
193	CHLOROMETHANE	670.19	191	000074-87-3
194	BIS(2-METHOXYETHYL) PHTHALATE	666.08	194	034006-76-3
195	BUTYL BENZYL PHTHALATE	659.38	195	000085-68-7
196	CRESOL, ORTHO-	658.66	196	000095-48-7
197	HEXACHLOROETHANE	653.10	199	000067-72-1
198	VANADIUM	651.70	198	007440-62-2
199	N-NITROSODIMETHYLAMINE	650.71	200	000062-75-9
200	1,2,4-TRICHLOROBENZENE	647.30	203	000120-82-1
201	BROMOFORM	643.53	202	000075-25-2
202	TETRACHLORODIBENZO-P-DIOXIN	635.74	204	041903-57-5
203	1,3-DICHLOROBENZENE	631.41	205	000541-73-1
204	PENTACHLORODIBENZO-P-DIOXIN	625.12	207	036088-22-9
205	N-NITROSODIPHENYLAMINE	624.79	208	000086-30-6

FIGURE 4–7
(continued)

206	1,2-DICHLOROETHYLENE	622.49	206	000540-59-0
207	2,3,7,8-TETRACHLORODIBENZOFURAN	622.15	210	051207-31-9
208	2-BUTANONE	620.01	209	000078-93-3
209	2,4-DICHLOROPHENOL	616.45	212	000120-83-2
210	1,4-DIOXANE	616.29	215	000123-91-1
211	FLUORINE	613.28	214	007782-41-4
212	NITRITE	612.64	216	014797-65-0
213	CESIUM-137	612.50	217	010045-97-3
214	SILVER	612.19	213	007440-22-4
215	CHROMIUM TRIOXIDE	610.85	218	007738-94-5
216	NITRATE	610.66	219	014797-55-8
217	POTASSIUM-40	608.91	220	013966-00-2
218	DINITROTOLUENE	607.65	221	025321-14-6
219	ANTIMONY	605.37	222	007440-36-0
220	COAL TAR PITCH	605.33	224	065996-93-2
221	THORIUM-227	605.32	223	015623-47-9
222	2,4,5-TRICHLOROPHENOL	604.83	225	000095-95-4
223	ARSENIC ACID	604.45	226	007778-39-4
224	ARSENIC TRIOXIDE	604.36	227	001327-53-3
225	PHORATE	603.10	228	000298-02-2
226	BENZOPYRENE	603.00	230	073467-76-2
227	CRESOLS	602.74	229	001319-77-3
228	CHLORDANE, TECHNICAL	602.62	231	012789-03-6
229	DIMETHOATE	602.61	232	000060-51-5
230	ACTINIUM-227	602.57	233	014952-40-0
230	STROBANE	602.57	233	008001-50-1
232	4-AMINOBIPHENYL	602.51	235	000092-67-1
232	PYRETHRUM	602.51	235	008003-34-7
234	ARSINE	602.42	237	007784-42-1
235	NALED	602.32	238	000300-76-5
236	DIBENZOFURANS, CHLORINATED	602.13	239	042934-53-2
236	ETHOPROP	602.13	239	013194-48-4
238	ALPHA-CHLORDENE	601.94	241	056534-02-2
238	CARBOPHENOTHION	601.94	241	000786-19-6
240	DICHLORVOS	601.64	243	000062-73-7
241	CALCIUM ARSENATE	601.45	244	007778-44-1

FIGURE 4–7
(continued)

241	MERCURIC CHLORIDE	601.45	244	007487-94-7
241	SODIUM ARSENITE	601.45	244	007784-46-5
244	FORMALDEHYDE	599.64	247	000050-00-0
245	2-CHLOROPHENOL	599.62	248	000095-57-8
246	PHENANTHRENE	597.68	249	000085-01-8
247	HYDROGEN FLUORIDE	588.03	250	007664-39-3
248	2,4-D ACID	584.47	251	000094-75-7
249	DIBROMOCHLOROMETHANE	580.59	252	000124-48-1
250	DIURON	579.16	253	000330-54-1
251	BUTYLATE	578.43	254	002008-41-5
252	DIMETHYL FORMAMIDE	578.23	255	000068-12-2
253	PYRENE	577.95	256	000129-00-0
254	DICHLOROBENZENE	577.70	211	025321-22-6
255	ETHYL ETHER	572.47	257	000060-29-7
256	DICHLOROETHANE	570.46	258	001300-21-6
257	4-NITROPHENOL	567.79	259	000100-02-7
258	1,3-DICHLOROPROPENE, CIS-	561.82	184	010061-01-5
259	PHOSPHINE	559.74	260	007803-51-2
260	TRICHLOROBENZENE	557.96	261	012002-48-1
261	2,6-DINITROTOLUENE	555.20	262	000606-20-2
262	FLUORIDE ION	549.64	263	016984-48-8
263	1,2,3,4,6,7,8-HEPTACHLORODIBENZO-P-DIOXIN	547.90	264	035822-46-9
264	METHYL PARATHION	545.83	265	000298-00-0
265	PENTAERYTHRITOL TETRANITRATE	545.59	266	000078-11-5
266	1,3-DICHLOROPROPENE, TRANS-	543.37	267	010061-02-6
267	BIS(2-ETHYLHEXYL)ADIPATE	540.20	268	000103-23-1
268	CARBAZOLE	534.52	269	000086-74-8
269	METHYL ISOBUTYL KETONE	533.24	271	000108-10-1
270	1,2-DICHLOROETHENE, CIS-	533.15	270	000156-59-2
271	STYRENE	532.70	272	000100-42-5
272	CARBARYL	530.98	273	000063-25-2
273	1,2,3,4,6,7,8-HEPTACHLORO-DIBENZOFURAN	529.45	274	067562-39-4
274	ACRYLONITRILE	528.28	275	000107-13-1
275	1-METHYLNAPHTHALENE	526.51	NEW	

FIGURE 4–7
(continued)

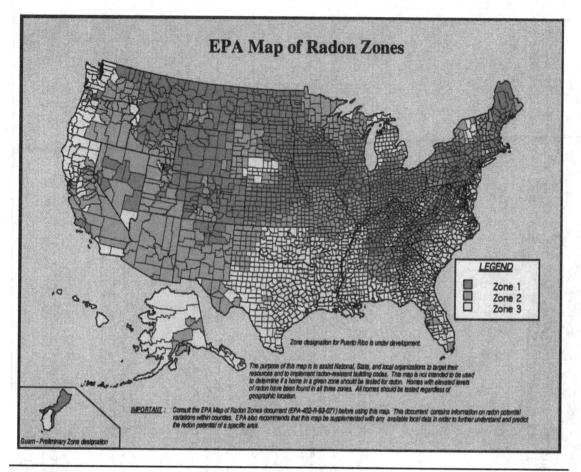

FIGURE 4–8

Any radon clause must specify an acceptable radon level before the contract continues. Follow-up tests are also recommended. "The most popular short-term screening device is the charcoal canister. The actual test takes about three to seven days, and the parties should allow a week for the laboratory to analyze the canister. The Environment Protection Agency (EPA) protocols do not recognize the validity of 'grab samples,' which are nothing more than a sample of air taken from the structure."[30]

See the press release from the surgeon general at Figure 4–9.[31]

For a radon contingency clause that calculates acceptable radon levels, see Figure 4–10.

In addition, traditional common law theories include negligence, strict liability, fraud, negligence *per se*, and misrepresentation. Statutory claims could be based on consumer protection or antifraud laws. Aggrieved parties do not have to search far to find a potentially useful theory on which to base a liability claim.[32]

C. Urea Formaldehyde Foam Insulation

Foam insulation, the manufacture of which contains formaldehyde, is another lightning rod in an age of environmental worry. This insulation is termed **Urea Formaldehyde Foam Insulation (UFFI)**. The material has been discovered behind paneling, fascia, vinyl siding, and around plumbing and rafters. Within closed quarters, fumes are emitted that are allegedly harmful. The UFFI materials are a modern construction application, so be sure to inform clients regarding this

HHS - Office of the Surgeon General, Surgeon General Releases National Health Advisory On Radon

U.S. Department of **Health & Human Services** www.hhs.gov

Office of the Surgeon General

Search [ ] go
This Site All HHS Sites

Font Size – + **Print** **Download Reader**

News Release

FOR IMMEDIATE RELEASE
Thursday, January 13, 2005

Contact: HHS Press Office
(202) 690-6343

Surgeon General Releases National Health Advisory On Radon

U.S. Surgeon General Richard H. Carmona warned the American public about the risks of breathing indoor radon by issuing a national health advisory today. The advisory is meant to urge Americans to prevent this silent radioactive gas from seeping into their homes and building up to dangerous levels. Dr. Carmona issued the advisory during a two-day Surgeon General's Workshop on Healthy Indoor Environment.

"Indoor radon is the second-leading cause of lung cancer in the United States and breathing it over prolonged periods can present a significant health risk to families all over the county," Dr. Carmona said. "It's important to know that this threat is completely preventable. Radon can be detected with a simple test and fixed through well-established venting techniques."

Radon is an invisible, odorless and tasteless gas, with no immediate health symptoms, that comes from the breakdown of uranium inside the earth. Simple test kits can reveal the amount of radon in any building. Those with high levels can be fixed with simple and affordable venting techniques. According to U.S. Environmental Protection Agency (EPA) estimates, one in every 15 homes nationwide have a high radon level at or above the recommended radon action level of 4 picoCuries (pCi/L) per liter of air.

National Health Advisory on Radon

Radon gas in the indoor air of America's homes poses a serious health risk. More than 20,000 Americans die of radon-related lung cancer every year. Millions of homes have an elevated radon level. If you also smoke, your risk of lung cancer is much higher. Test your home for radon every two years, and retest any time you move, make structural changes to your home, or occupy a previously unused level of a house. If you have a radon level of 4 pCi/L or more, take steps to remedy the problem as soon as possible.

"Americans need to know about the risks of indoor radon and have the information and tools they need to take action. That's why EPA is actively promoting the Surgeon General's advice urging all Americans to get their homes tested for radon. If families do find elevated levels in their homes, they can take inexpensive steps that will reduce exposure to this risk," said

http://www.surgeongeneral.gov/pressreleases/sg01132005.html (1 of 2)7/31/2009 11:10:37 AM

FIGURE 4–9
(continues)

Jeffrey R. Holmstead, Assistant Administrator, Office of Air and Radiation, U.S. Environmental Protection Agency (EPA).

"Based on national averages, we can expect that many of the homes owned or financed by federal government programs would have potentially elevated radon levels. The federal government has an opportunity to lead by example on this public health risk. We can accomplish this by using the outreach and awareness avenues we have, such as EPA's Web site, to share information and encourage action on radon to reduce risks," said Edwin Piñero, Federal Environmental Executive, Office of the Federal Environmental Executive (OFEE).

A national Public Service Announcement (PSA) that was released to television stations across America in January, National Radon Action Month, is reinforcing this recently updated health advisory. In the television spot, the camera scans a neighborhood with rooftop banners that remind the occupants of the importance to test their homes for radon. The television PSA can be viewed at: http://www.epa.gov/radon/rnpsa.html.

For more information about radon go to EPA's Web site www.epa.gov/radon; or call your state radon office; or call a national toll-free hotline at 1-800-SOS-RADON (1-800-767-7236).

The Surgeon General's Workshop on Healthy Indoor Environment is bringing together the best scientific minds in the nation to discuss the continuing problem of unhealthful buildings. Indoor environments are structures including workplaces, schools, offices, houses and apartment buildings, and vehicles. According to a recent study, Americans spend between 85 and 95 percent of their time indoors.

In just the past 25 years, the percentage of health evaluations that the National Institute for Occupational Safety and Health at the Centers for Disease Control and Prevention (CDC) has conducted related to indoor-air quality has increased from 0.5 percent of all evaluations in 1978, to 52 percent of all evaluations since 1990. This means that in those years, the evaluations related to air quality concerns have increased from one of every 200 evaluations to one of every two.

The problem is also adversely affecting our children's health as millions of homes and apartments and one in five schools in America have indoor air quality problems. This can trigger various allergies and asthma. Asthma alone accounts for 14 million missed school days each year. The rate of asthma in young children has risen by 160 percent in the past 15 years, and today one out of every 13 school-age children has asthma. Dr. Carmona is especially focusing on how unhealthy indoor environment affects children, as he promotes 2005 as The Year of the Healthy Child.

#

Note: All HHS press releases, fact sheets and other press materials are available at http://www.hhs.gov/news.

Last revised: January 4, 2007

Accessibility | Privacy Policy | Freedom of Information Act | Disclaimers
The White House | USA.gov | Helping America's Youth
Office of Public Health and Science, U.S. Department of Health and Human Services

FIGURE 4-9
(continued)

RADON INSPECTION CONTINGENCY

Buyer, at Buyer's expense, has the option to obtain, from a certified inspector, a radon test of the Property, and will deliver a copy of the test report to Seller within DAYS (15 days if not specified) of the execution of this Agreement.

   1. If the test report reveals the presence of radon below 0.02 working levels (4 picocuries/liter), Buyer accepts the Property and agrees to the RELEASE set forth in paragraph ____of this Agreement.
   2. If the test report reveals the presence of radon at or exceeding 0.02 working levels (4 picocuries/liter), Buyer will, within ___ DAYS of receipt of the test results:

Option 1

a. Accept the Property in writing and agree to the RELEASE set forth in paragraph ____ of this Agreement, OR
b. Terminate this Agreement in writing, in which case all deposit monies paid on account of purchase price will be returned promptly to Buyer and this Agreement will be VOID, OR
c. Submit a written, corrective proposal to Seller. The corrective proposal will include, but not be limited to, the name of the certified mitigation company; provisions for payment, including retests; and a projected completion date for corrective measures.
(1) Within _____ DAYS of receiving the corrective proposal, Seller will:
   (a) Agree to the terms of the corrective proposal in writing, in which case Buyer accepts the Property and agrees to the RELEASE set forth in paragraph ___ of this Agreement, OR
   (b) Not agree to the terms of the corrective proposal.
(2) Should Seller not agree to the terms of the corrective proposal or if Seller **fails to respond within the time given**, Buyer will, within _____ DAYS, elect to:
   (a) Accept the Property in writing and agree to the RELEASE set forth in paragraph ____of this Agreement, OR
   (b) Terminate this Agreement in writing, in which case all deposit monies paid on account of purchase price will be returned promptly to Buyer and this Agreement will be VOID.

Option 2

a. Accept the Property in writing and agree to the RELEASE set forth in paragraph _____ of this Agreement, OR
b. Submit a written, corrective proposal to Seller. The corrective proposal will include, but not be limited to, the name of the certified mitigation company; provisions for payment, including retests; and a projected completion date for corrective measures. Seller will pay a maximum of $ toward the total cost of remediation and retests, which will be completed by settlement.
(1) If the total cost of remediation and retests EXCEEDS the amount specified in paragraph 11(B) (Option 2) b, Seller will, within 5 DAYS of receipt of the cost of remediation, notify Buyer in writing of Seller's choice to:
   (a) Pay for the total cost of remediation and retests, in which case Buyer accepts the Property and agrees to the RELEASE set forth in paragraph ____ of this Agreement, OR
   (b) Contribute toward the total cost of remediation and retests only the amount specified in paragraph _____ (Option 2) b.
(2) If Seller chooses not to pay for the total cost of remediation and retests, or if Seller **fails to choose either option within the time given**, Buyer will, within _____ DAYS, notify Seller in writing of Buyer's choice to:
   (a) Pay the difference between Seller's contribution to remediation and retests and the actual cost thereof, in which case Buyer accepts the Property and agrees to the RELEASE set forth in paragraph ____ of this Agreement, OR
   (b) Terminate this Agreement, in which case all deposit monies paid on account of purchase price will be returned promptly to Buyer and this Agreement will be VOID.

FIGURE 4–10

environmentally sensitive substance in homes built after 1950. There are some remedial and mitigation steps that have proven useful for homeowners, namely:

- Purchasing pressed wood products labeled as low-emitting or products made from phenol formaldehyde, such as oriented strand board or softwood plywood.
- Increasing ventilation after bringing new sources of formaldehyde into your home.
- Using alternate products such as lumber, metal, or solid wood furniture.
- Avoiding the use of foamed-in-place insulation containing formaldehyde, especially urea-formaldehyde foam insulation.
- Enclosing unfinished pressed wood surfaces of furniture, cabinets, or shelving with laminate or water-based sealant.
- Washing durable-press fabrics before use.
- Ensuring combustion sources are properly adjusted.

- Avoiding smoking indoors.
- Maintaining moderate temperatures and low (30% to 50%) relative humidity levels.

See Figure 4–11 for a traditional UFFI addendum.

MASSACHUSETTS DEPARTMENT OF PUBLIC HEALTH
UFFI DISCLOSURE

The dwelling located at _____
(Number and Street)

MA
_____
(City/Town)   (State)   (Zip Code)

contains urea formaldehyde foam insulation (UFFI). The Commonwealth of Massachusetts has established a program to promote a healthier living environment by identifying the presence of formaldehyde emissions from UFFI in residential dwellings and by facilitating the removal of UFFI from those dwellings where either the formaldehyde level in the air is greater than 0.10 parts per million (ppm), or where an occupant of the dwelling has suffered adverse health effects from the presence of UFFI. Any seller or landlord of a residential dwelling containing UFFI has an affirmative obligation to determine the presence of UFFI and to disclose both its presence and the formaldehyde levels in the dwelling to buyers, tenants, or prospective tenants.

UFFI is located in this dwelling in the following places (where checked):

_____ exterior walls (which) _____
_____ interior walls (which) _____
_____ floor/ceiling space (where) _____
_____ attic
_____ other _____

The date the UFFI was installed is _____

The air in this dwelling has been tested in accordance with procedures established by the Massachusetts Department of Public Health. A copy of the laboratory report is attached. The test results were as follows:

Locations (rooms)	Formaldehyde Level measured in parts per million (ppm)
1._____	1._____
2._____	2._____
3._____	3._____
4._____	4._____
5._____	5._____

FIGURE 4–11
(continues)

By law, no real estate agent, broker or salesperson, and no bank, lending institution or mortgagee doing business in Massachusetts may discriminate in any manner against a dwelling containing UFFI, or against its owner, when the formaldehyde level in the air of the dwelling is 0.10 ppm or below.

I/we attest that all the information provided by me/us in this Disclosure is true and accurate to the best of my/our knowledge.

Date:_____   Signature of the Seller(s) or Landlord:

_____
_____
_____

For Buyer(s):
I/we received this UFFI Disclosure and accompanying UFFI Information Sheet before giving a deposit on, or signing an offer to Purchase or a Purchase and Sale Agreement for, the dwelling referred to in this Disclosure.

Date:_____   Signature of Buyer(s):

_____
_____
_____

For Tenant (s):

Prospective tenant (s): I/we received this UFFI Disclosure and accompanying UFFI Information Sheet before entering into a lease or rental agreement for the dwelling referred to in this Disclosure.

Date:_____   Signature of Prospective Tenant(s):

_____
_____
_____

Existing Tenant(s): I/we received this UFFI Disclosure and accompanying UFFI Information Sheet on or before February 1, 1987.

Date:_____   Signature of Existing Tenant(s):

_____
_____
_____

For additional information please read the Massachusetts Department of Public Health's UFFI Information Sheet, which by Law must be distributed to you with this Disclosure. You may also call the Department of Public Health's at (617) 983-6762.

FIGURE 4–11
(continued)

To the best of Seller's knowledge and without any independent investigator or inquiry by Seller, no hazardous waste, toxic waste or solid waste substances have been treated, stored, released or disposed of on the Property, no condition on the Property that could give rise to environmental liability, no asbestos containing material is located on the Property and the Property does not now contain or has it in the past contained an underground storage tank, as that term is defined in Minnesota Statute §116.46, Subd. 8 except as herein noted:

FIGURE 4–12
Underground Storage Tank Inspection Clause.

D. Underground Storage Tanks

The problem with rusting and leaking **underground storage tanks (UST)** presents another conditional challenge for the property buyer and seller. Underground storage tanks, for most homeowners, have long exposure to home heating oil. In commercial properties, the tanks have held every imaginable substance—both toxic and nontoxic alike. Buyers do not wish to assume the responsibility of correcting tank deficiencies. Hence, a conditional addendum is very often witnessed concerning underground storage tanks. So pressing is this issue that the EPA has erected an entire office dedicated to underground storage containers—the Office of Underground Storage Tanks.

Web Exercise

You can search where there are problem areas in the world of USTs at *www.epa.gov/OUST/wheruliv.htm*. The National Association of Realtors also publishes a guidebook and manual on the complicated dimensions of the UST at *www.realtor.org/library/library/fg715*.

Storage tank addendums with conditional language reflect the unique qualities of the substance stored and the sophistication of the parties to the transaction. Figure 4–12 comprises the more common language.

V. PEST INFESTATION

Wood-boring insects, from termites to carpenter ants, undermine structural integrity.[33] Houses built with crawl spaces, constructed primarily of wood, and located in humid, water-based areas are highly prone to infestation. It is a sound practice for the paralegal to include a pest infestation clause in the agreement or attach by addendum.

Web Exercise

Read the EPA's comprehensive guide to pest and pesticides at *www.epa.gov/oppfead1/Publications/ Cit_Guide/citguide.pdf*.

The wood infestation addendum to the agreement of sale in Figure 4–13 treats the subject comprehensively. Of practical import is Section B, providing the buyer and seller remedies in the event qualifying insects are discovered.

For new construction under FHA and VA guidelines, the builder, abiding by Mortgagee Letter 99–03 issued by the U.S. Department of Housing and Urban Development, must guarantee against termite infestation. Required forms are HUD–NPCA–99–A, Subterranean Termite Treatment Builders Certification and Guarantee (Figure 4–14) and HUD–NPCA–99–B, New Construction Subterranean Termite Soil Treatment Record (Figure 4–15). NPCA–99–B must only be used in

CALIFORNIA ASSOCIATION OF REALTORS®

WOOD DESTROYING PEST INSPECTION AND ALLOCATION OF COST ADDENDUM
(C.A.R. Form WPA, Revised 10/02)

This is an addendum to the ☐ California Residential Purchase Agreement or ☐ Other _____
_____ ("Agreement"), dated _____ ,
on property known as _____ ("Property"),
between _____ ("Buyer")
and _____ ("Seller").

THE FOLLOWING SHALL REPLACE THE WOOD DESTROYING PEST INSPECTION PARAGRAPH (4A in the California Residential Purchase Agreement (RPA-CA)) and shall supersede any conflicting terms in any previously-generated agreement:

WOOD DESTROYING PESTS

A. ☐ Buyer ☐ Seller shall pay for a Pest Control Report for wood destroying pests and organisms only ("Report"). The Report shall be prepared by _____ , a registered structural pest control company, who shall separate the Report into sections for evident infestation or infection (Section 1) and for conditions likely to lead to infestation or infection (Section 2). The Report shall cover the main building and attached structures and, if checked: ☐ detached garages and carports, ☐ detached decks, ☐ the following other structures on the Property: _____ .
The Report shall not include roof coverings. If the Property is a unit in a condominium or other common interest subdivision, the Report shall include only the separate interest and any exclusive-use areas being transferred, and shall not include common areas. Water tests of shower pans on upper level units may not be performed unless the owners of property below the shower consent. If Buyer requests inspection of inaccessible areas, Buyer shall pay for the cost of entry, inspection and closing for those areas, unless otherwise agreed. A written Pest Control Certification shall be issued prior to Close Of Escrow, unless otherwise agreed, only if no infestation or infection is found or if required corrective work is completed.

B. **(Section 1)** ☐ Buyer ☐ Seller shall pay for work recommended to correct "Section 1" conditions described in the Report and the cost of inspection, entry and closing of those inaccessible areas where active infestation or infection is discovered.
(Section 2) ☐ Buyer ☐ Seller shall pay for work recommended to correct "Section 2" conditions described in the Report if requested by Buyer.

By signing below, the undersigned acknowledge that each has read, understands and has received a copy of this Addendum.

Date _____   Date _____

Buyer _____   Seller _____

Buyer _____   Seller _____

SURE TRAC
The System for Success™

Published by the
California Association of REALTORS®

Reviewed by _____ Date _____

EQUAL HOUSING OPPORTUNITY

WPA REVISED 10/02 (PAGE 1 OF 1)
WOOD DESTROYING PEST INSPECTION AND ALLOCATION OF COST ADDENDUM (WPA PAGE 1 OF 1)

FIGURE 4–13

conjunction with NPCA–99–A if the area is treated with soil termiticide. These forms were mandatory and effective from July 1, 1999.

If there is existing construction in an affected area, Form HUD–NPCA–1, Wood Destroying Insect Infestation Report or a similar state mandated form is required. See Figure 4–16.

This form is valid for ninety days from the date of the inspection. These forms can be obtained from the National Pest Control Association, 8100 Oak Street, Dunn Loring, Virginia 22027, through their Web site www.pestworld.org, or by calling (703) 573–8330. They are also available online from the U.S. Department of Housing & Urban Development Resources page at www.hud.gov/offices/adm/hudc lips/forms.

Subterranean Termite Protection Builder's Guarantee
This form is completed by the builder.

OMB Approval No. 2502-0525
(exp. 02/29/2012)

Public reporting burden for this collection of information is estimated to average 5 minutes per response, including the time for reviewing instructions, searching existing data sources, gathering and maintaining the data needed, and completing and reviewing the collection of information. This information is required to obtain benefits. HUD may not collect this information, and you are not required to complete this form, unless it displays a currently valid OMB control number. Section 24 CFR 200.926d(b)(3) requires that the sites for HUD insured structures must be free of termite hazards. This information collection requires a licensed Pest Control company to provide the builder a record of specific treatment information in those cases when if any method other than use of pressure treated lumber is used for prevention of subterranean termite infestation. When applicable, form HUD-NPMA-99-B must accompany the form HUD-NPMA-99-A. Builders, pest control companies, mortgage lenders, homebuyers, and HUD as a record of treatment for specific homes will use the information collected. The information is not considered confidential, therefore no assurance of confidentiality is provided.

This form is submitted for proposed (new) construction cases when prevention of subterranean termite infestation is specified by the builder or required by the lender, the architect, FHA or VA.

This form is to be completed by the builder. This guarantee is issued by the builder to the buyer. This guarantee is not to be considered as a waiver of, or in place of, any legal rights or remedies that the buyer may have against the builder.

FHA/VA Case No.: _____

Location of Structure(s) (Street Address, or Legal Description, City, State and Zip): _____

_____

_____

Buyer's Name: _____

Builder is to check and complete either box 1 or box 2.

1. ☐ Pest Control Company Applied Treatment (See HUD-NPMA 99B for treatment information)

The undersigned builder hereby certifies that a State licensed or otherwise authorized pest control company (where required by State law) was contracted to treat the property at the location referenced above to prevent subterranean termites. The builder further certifies that the contract with the pest control company required the treatment materials and methods used to be in conformance with all applicable State and Federal requirements. All work required by the contract has been completed unless noted on HUD-NPMA 99B. Where not prohibited by applicable State requirements, the buyer, for an additional fee payable to the pest control company, may extend the protection against subterranean termites. Contact the pest control company listed on the attachment for further information.

The builder hereby guarantees that, if subterranean termite infestation should occur within one year from the date of closing, the builder will ensure that a licensed or otherwise State authorized pest control company will treat as necessary to control infestations in the structure. This further treatment will be without cost to the buyer. If permitted by State law, the buyer may contract directly, at the buyer's expense, with a pest control company to inspect the property on a periodic basis and use EPA registered products to control any infestation. The builder will not be responsible for guaranteeing such contracted work. The builder further agrees to repair all damage by subterranean termites within the one-year builder's warranty period. This guarantee does not apply to additions or alterations that are made by the buyer, which affects the original structure or treatment. Examples include, but are not limited to, landscape and mulch alterations, which disturb the treated area and create new subterranean termite hazards, or interfere with the control measures. If within the guarantee period the builder questions the validity of a claim by the buyer, the claim will be investigated by an unbiased expert mutually agreeable to the buyer and builder. The report of the expert will be accepted as the basis for disposition of the case. The non-prevailing party will pay the cost of any inspections made to investigate the claim. For further information, contact your State structural pest control regulatory agency. **All service must be in compliance with the International Residential Code.**

Type of Service:: ☐ Termite Bait System ☐ Field Applied Wood Treatment ☐ Soil Treatment ☐ Installed Physical Barrier System

2. ☐ Builder Installed Subterranean Termite Prevention using Pressure Treated Lumber

The builder certifies that subterranean termite prevention was installed using pressure treated lumber only and certifies that use of the pressure treated lumber is in compliance with applicable building codes and HUD requirements including Mortgagee Letter 2001-04. **Note: Using pressure treated sills as a sole method of termite prevention is NOT acceptable and violates the requirements of Mortgagee Letter 2001-04.**

_____   _____
Initial of Builder   Date

Attachments: _____

Builder's Company Name: _____ Phone No: _____

Builder's Signature: _____ Date: _____

Consumer Maintenance Advisory regarding integrated Pest Management for Prevention of Wood Destroying insects. Information regarding prevention of wood destroying insect infestation is helpful to any property owner interested in protecting the structure from infestation. Any structure can be attacked by wood destroying insects. Periodic maintenance should include measures to minimize possibilities of infestation in and around a structure. Factors which may lead to infestation from wood destroying insects include foam insulation at foundation, earth-wood contact, faulty grade, firewood against structure, insufficient ventilation, moisture, wood debris in crawl space, wood mulch, tree branches touching structures, landscape timbers, and wood rot. Should these or other such conditions exist, corrective measure should be taken by the owner in order to reduce the chances of infestations by wood destroying insects, and the need for treatment.

An original and one copy of this guarantee are to be prepared by the builder and sent to the lender. The lender provides one copy to the buyer at closing and includes a copy in the VA loan package or HUD insurance case binder. The builder sends one copy to the licensed pest control company which performed the treatment.

Attached is a copy of the state authorized pest control company's New Construction Subterranean Termite Service Record, HUD-NPMA-99-B.

Warning: HUD will prosecute false claims and statements. Conviction may result in criminal and/or civil penalties. (18 U.S.C. 1001, 1010, 1012;31 U.S.C. 3729,3802)

form **HUD-NPMA-99-A** (8/2008)

FIGURE 4–14

New Construction Subterranean Termite
Service Record

OMB Approval No. 2502-0525
(exp. 02/29/2012)

This form is completed by the licensed Pest Control Company

Public reporting burden for this collection of information is estimated to average 15 minutes per response, including the time for reviewing instructions, searching existing data sources, gathering and maintaining the data needed, and completing and reviewing the collection of information. This information iis required to obtain benefits. HUD may not collect this information, and you are not required to complete this form, unless it displays a currently valid OMB control number.

Section 24 CFR 200.926d(b)(3) requires that the sites for HUD insured structures must be free of termite hazards. This information collection requires the builder to certify that an authorized Pest Control company performed all required treatment for termites, and that the builder guarantees the treated area against infestation for one year. Builders, pest control companies, mortgage lenders, homebuyers, and HUD as a record of treatment for specific homes will use the information collected. The information is not considered confidential, therefore, no assurance of confidentiality is provided.

This report is submitted for informational purposes to the builder on proposed (new) construction cases when treatment for prevention of subterranean termite infestation is specified by the builder, architect, or required by the lender, architect, FHA, or VA.

All contracts for services are between the Pest Control company and builder, unless stated otherwise.

Section 1: General Information (Pest Control Company Information)

Company Name: _____

Company Address _____ City _____ State _____ Zip _____

Company Business License No. _____ Company Phone No. _____

FHA/VA Case No. (if any) _____

Section 2: Builder Information

Company Name _____ Phone No. _____

Section 3: Property Information

Location of Structure (s) Treated (Street Address or Legal Description, City, State and Zip) _____

Section 4: Service Information

Date(s) of Service(s) _____

Type of Construction (More than one box may be checked) ☐ Slab ☐ Basement ☐ Crawl ☐ Other _____

Check all that apply:

☐ A. Soil Applied Liquid Termiticide
Brand Name of Termiticide: _____ EPA Registration No. _____
Approx. Dilution (%): _____ Approx. Total Gallons Mix Applied: _____ Treatment completed on exterior: ☐ Yes ☐ No

☐ B. Wood Applied Liquid Termiticide
Brand Name of Termiticide: _____ EPA Registration No. _____
Approx. Dilution (%): _____ Approx. Total Gallons Mix Applied: _____

☐ C. Bait system Installed
Name of System _____ EPA Registration No. _____ Number of Stations installed _____

☐ D. Physical Barrier System Installed
Name of System _____ Attach installation information (required)

Service Agreement Available? ☐ Yes ☐ No
Note: Some state laws require service agreements to be issued. This form does not preempt state law.

Attachments (List) _____

Comments _____

Name of Applicator(s) _____ Certification No. (if required by State law) _____

The applicator has used a product in accordance with the product label and state requirements. All materials and methods used comply with state and federal regulations.

Authorized Signature _____ Date _____

Warning: HUD will prosecute false claims and statements. Conviction may result in criminal and/or civil penalties. (18 U.S.C. 1001, 1010. 1012; 31 U.S.C. 3729, 3802)

form **HUD-NPMA-99-B** (08/2008)

FIGURE 4–15

OFFICIAL SOUTH CAROLINA WOOD INFESTATION REPORT

THIS REPORT VALID FOR 45 DAYS ONLY. THIS REPORT MAY **NOT** BE USED IN A REAL ESTATE CLOSING AFTER 45 DAYS. THIS REPORT IS **NOT** TO BE CONSTRUED AS A GUARANTEE OR WARRANTY AGAINST FUTURE INFESTATION OR DAMAGE. IT IS RECOMMENDED BY THE DEPARTMENT OF PESTICIDE REGULATION, REGULATORY AND PUBLIC SERVICE PROGRAMS, AND THE SOUTH CAROLINA PEST CONTROL ASSOCIATION THAT THE **PURCHASER** OF THE STRUCTURE, RATHER THAN THE SELLER, OBTAIN THIS WOOD INFESTATION REPORT.

Date_____   File No._____

    This is to report that a qualified inspector employed by the below named firm has carefully inspected readily accessible areas, including attics and crawl spaces which permit entry, of the property located at the below address for termites, other wood-destroying insects, and fungi. The inspection for fungi and fungi damage commonly called water damaged wood, rot or decay is limited to the area below the first main floor of the structure as defined by DPRPN-198. This report specifically excludes hidden areas and areas not readily accessible, readily accessible, and the undersigned pest control operator disclaims that he has made any inspections of such hidden areas or of such areas not readily accessible.

    The inspection described has been made **on the basis of visible evidence, and special attention was given to those accessible areas which experience has shown to be particularly susceptible to attack by wood-destroying insects. Probing and/or sounding of those areas and other visible and accessible wood members showing evidence of infestation was performed. This report is submitted without warranty, guarantee, or representation as to concealed evidence of infestation or damage or as to future infestation.**

    If there is evidence of active infestation or past infestation of termites and/or other wood-destroying insects or fungi, it must be assumed that there is some damage to the building caused by this infestation; however, any visible damage to a wood member in accessible areas has been reported. The below-named firm's inspectors are not engineers or builders, and you may wish to call a qualified engineer or expert in the building trade to provide their opinion as to whether there is structural damage to this property.

LOCATION AND DESCRIPTION OF PROPERTY INSPECTED: _____

_____

TYPE OF TRANSACTION: FHA _____   VA _____   CONVENTIONAL _____   LOAN ASSUMPTION _____   CASH SALE _____

	Check Only Appropriate Items	
IF ANY OF THE FOLLOWING ITEMS ARE MARKED YES, DESCRIBE ON REVERSE:	YES	NO
WERE ANY AREAS OF THE PROPERTY OBSTRUCTED OR INACCESSIBLE?	[ ]	[ ]
INFESTATION:		
1. There is visible evidence of active: (A) subterranean termites.	[ ]	[ ]
(B) other wood-destroying insects.	[ ]	[ ]
2. There is visible evidence of a previous infestation of:		
(A) subterranean termites	[ ]	[ ]
(B) other wood-destroying insects.	[ ]	[ ]
3. There is visible evidence of prior subterranean termite treatment	[ ]	[ ]
4. There is evidence below the first main floor of the presence of:		
(A) active wood-destroying fungi (wood moisture content 28% or above)	[ ]	[ ]
(B) wood-destroying fungi is present but not active (less than 28% wood moisture content).	[ ]	[ ]
5. There is evidence of the presence of excessive moisture conditions below the first main floor (20% or above wood moisture content, standing water, etc.)	[ ]	[ ]

DAMAGE: Termite, other wood-destroying insects and fungi (Note: reporting of fungi damage to wood, commonly called water damage, decay or rot, is limited to the area below the first main floor of the structure as defined by DPRPN-198.)

	YES	NO
At the time of our inspection, there were visibly damaged wooden members (e.g. insect damage to columns, sills, joists, plates, door jambs, headers, exterior stairs, porches, or fungi damage below the first main floor) If the answer is "YES," specify causes and location(s) on back.	[ ]	[ ]

DAMAGE OBSERVED (IF ANY)

Check Appropriate Block Below

A. Will be or has been corrected by this company   [ ]

B. Will be or has been corrected by another company (see attached contract)   [ ]

C. Will not be corrected by this company; recommend that structure be thoroughly and completely evaluated by a qualified building expert licensed or registered with the S.C. Department of Labor, Licensing, and Regulations, Residential Builder's Commission and that needed repairs be made.   [ ]

D. In our opinion there is insufficient visible damage to recommend repair.
(Explanation on the reverse side why repair was not recommended.)   [ ]

TREATMENT

Check Appropriate Block Below

1. The property described was treated by us for the prevention or control of

_____   _____   [ ]
                                               (date of treatment)

A waiver has been issued and is attached to this form   [ ]

The present treatment warranty will expire on _____

and may be renewed initially at $ _____ by the owner.

2. The property described has not been treated by us and is not now under contract with our firm   [ ]

SEE OTHER SIDE OF THIS REPORT FOR ADDITIONAL CONDITIONS GOVERNING THIS REPORT.

CL-100 Approved *by* the South Carolina Pest Control Association, Inc., and the Division of Regulatory and Public Service Programs of Clemson University. Revised 3/99 Supersedes earlier versions.

(OVER)

FIGURE 4–16
(continues)

CONDITIONS GOVERNING THIS REPORT
Please read carefully.

This report is based on the observations and opinions of our inspector. It must be noted that all buildings have some wood members which are not visible or accessible for inspection. It is not always possible to determine the presence of infestation without extensive probing and in some cases actual dismantling of parts of the structure being inspected.

All inspections and reports will be made on the basis of what is visible, and we will not render opinions covering areas that are enclosed or not readily accessible, areas of finished rooms, areas concealed by wall coverings, floor coverings, insulation, furniture, equipment, stored articles, or any portion of the structure in which inspection would necessitate tearing out or marring finished work. We do not move furniture, appliances, equipment, etc. Plumbing leaks may not be apparent at the time of inspection. If evidence of such leaks is disclosed, liability for the correction of such leaks is specifically denied. No opinion can be rendered as to infestation or damage on that portion of sheathing, siding or other susceptible material which continues below soil grade.

The areas of the substructure and attic that are accessible and open for inspection have been inspected. The substructure is defined as that portion of the building below the first main floor living space.

Detached garages, sheds, lean-tos, fences, or other buildings on the property are not included in this inspection report unless specifically noted.

The company, upon specific request and agreement as to additional charge, will open any inaccessible, concealed, or enclosed area and inspect same and make a report thereon.

REMARKS
THIS SPACE IS TO BE USED TO DETAIL ANY "YES" ANSWERS FROM THE FRONT OF THIS FORM. INCLUDE ITEM NUMBER WITH EACH EXPLANATION. CLARIFICATION AND EXPLANATION OF OTHER ITEMS MAY ALSO BE INCLUDED.

_____
_____
_____
_____
_____
_____
_____
_____
_____
_____
_____
_____
_____
_____
_____
_____
_____
_____
_____
_____
_____

Neither I nor the company for which I am acting have had, presently have, or contemplate having any interest in this property. I do further state that neither I nor the company for which I am acting is associated in any way with any party to this transaction.

LICENSE NUMBER OF PERSON SIGNING THIS

Firm: _____

_____

BY: _____

(MUST BE CERTIFIED IN CATEGORY)

ADDRESS: _____

Business License Number _____

OF FIRM: _____

ACKNOWLEDGMENT:

PURCHASER ACKNOWLEDGES THAT A COPY OF THIS REPORT HAS BEEN REVIEWED AND RECEIVED.

_____   _____
DATE ACKNOWLEDGED   PURCHASER'S SIGNATURE

FIGURE 4–16
(continued)

Web Exercise

Visit the consumer information sheet published by the State of North Carolina at *www.ncagr.gov/SPCAP/ structural/pubs/consumer/wdirmemo.htm*.

VI. ZONING

In certain jurisdictions, the zoning classification of any property, except for single-family dwellings, must be included in any sales agreement or sales contract. Failure to do so will render the sales agreement or contract null and void and allow the buyer the return of a deposit without any necessity for court action.[34]

For instance, a buyer may contract for the express purpose of using a property both as a residence and for commercial purposes. The buyer is obligated to seek zoning approval or **zoning variance** in good faith. "Absent language in the contract to the contrary, this duty is satisfactorily fulfilled where the buyer has properly brought the matter before the governmental authority in question and secured a decision; appeal of an adverse determination or the institution of legal action seeking to compel the granting of the desired approval is not necessary. Once the authority has declared its resolution of the matter, no further action by the purchaser is required, even where the agreement in question is worded so strongly as to obligate him or her to use all due diligence and do everything required to obtain the approval."[35]

A zoning addendum encompassing the good faith standard may also be used. See Figure 4–17.

ENDORSEMENT TO AGREEMENT OF SALE

Date _____

Re property: _____

Sellers: _____ Buyers: _____

Date of Agreement: _____ Settlement Date: _____ Sale Price: _____

It is understood and agreed that the above agreement of sale shall be endorsed as follows:

Seller agrees to seek a variance from the present zoning classification of R–2 to a zoning classification of C–2. This agreement is contingent on a successful variance appeal.

All other terms and conditions of the said agreement shall remain unchanged and in full force and effect.

_____   _____
Witness: Buyer   Agent
_____   Seller _____
                                                              Seller _____
_____
Witness: Buyer

FIGURE 4–17

SALE OF BUYER'S PROPERTY

This contract is contingent on the closing of buyer's property located at:
_____. If buyer's property does not close within
_____ days from the effective date of this contract, this contract will be considered null and void
and buyer's deposit will be refunded.

FIGURE 4–18

VII. BUYER'S SALE OF PRESENT HOME

Sometimes buyers cannot close the transaction unless their present home is sold. Usually, the proceeds from that home are necessary for the purchase of the new residence. To accomplish this, the paralegal can include either a conditional clause within the agreement of sale or a conditional or contingent addendum setting forth the proper intent. In the former, insert language such as in Figure 4–18.

Generally, this type of clause allows the seller to continue to offer the subject residence for sale. In the event a new offer is made, seller can accept only by "wiping out" the condition imposed. By **wipeout**, the seller advises the buyers of the legitimate offer and, at the same time, affords sellers the option of waiving the condition. See Figure 4–19.

Although courts on occasion have held that similar contract conditions were for the benefit of both parties, the standard provisions that relate to the ability of the purchaser to sell his present house in contracts for the sale of property allow the purchaser, not the seller, to rescind the contract if he is not able to sell the house. The seller, however, is not completely at the mercy of the buyer in this instance. A contract of sale that is conditioned on the purchaser's ability to sell the purchaser's house requires the purchaser to make reasonable efforts to sell the house.[36]

Another term applied to this form of condition is the right of first refusal. See the contingency addendum, in Figure 4–20, for securing buyer's and seller's rights when a second offer occurs.

VIII. NOTICE TO TERMINATE

Whenever a condition or contingency fails to be met, the party claiming said condition is under an affirmative obligation to give a **notice to terminate** the agreement indicating the refusal to follow through on the terms of contract. Of course, this type of refusal is perfectly defensible

---

It is further understood and agreed that this agreement is subject to and contingent upon the sale and closing of buyer's real property, known and numbered as _____. Seller shall have the right to continue to offer their property for sale. (Should the seller receive another acceptable bona fide written offer, then buyer shall be given written notice of such offer by registered mail. In the event buyers fail to waive the within condition in writing within 48 hours from date of receipt as evidenced by date of return receipt, then this agreement shall be terminated and all deposits be returned to buyers.)

FIGURE 4–19
Wipeout clause.

RIGHT OF FIRST REFUSAL

SELLER: _____   _____

BUYER: _____   _____

PROPERTY: _____

DATE: _____

1. This sale is subject to the buyer obtaining a Purchase and Sale Agreement on the buyer's home at _____,on or before, _____, and further subject to the buyer's buyer obtaining a mortgage commitment on said property on or before _____.

    If a fully executed Purchase and Sale Agreement is not obtained on said property by the above date, then either buyer or seller shall have the option of voiding this Agreement, and all obligations of all parties hereunder shall cease, at which time the buyer's deposit will be returned in full.

2. The Seller hereby reserves the right to continue to offer for sale and show the property at _____. In the event that a second buyer makes a written offer with terms that are acceptable to the Seller, the above named Buyer(s) shall be notified immediately, and will have a _____ hour period of time within which to decide whether to proceed with purchase, regardless of whether or not their home is under agreement, or to withdraw from the Agreement and receive a refund of their deposit in full. In the event of a co-broke situation, a notification to the cooperating agency will be deemed to be notification as required herein. If the above named Buyer(s) agrees to proceed with the purchase, written evidence of necessary interim financing is to be given with seven (7) bank business days. This Right of First Refusal shall remain in effect for 30 days, and may only be extended upon mutual agreement of the parties named herein.

3. If the Buyer(s) named herein accepts a deposit on his property at _____ contingent upon the sale of any other property, this Agreement shall be rendered null and void, and all parties discharged and the Buyer's deposit will be returned in full.

4. The Buyer(s) hereunder agrees to provide _____ with a copy of the executed Purchase and Sale Agreement for the property named in #1 above within five (5) days after the Agreement is executed by all parties. The Buyer(s) waives all rights with regard to this contingency upon providing the Purchase and Sale Agreement within the five (5) day period. However, the Purchase and Sale Agreement between the named parties shall still be subject to the Buyer's buyer obtaining a mortgage commitment on the subject property as stated in #1 above.

Seller:_____   Buyer:_____

Seller:_____   Buyer:_____

FIGURE 4–20

Reproduced with permission of the Northeast Florida Association of Realtors.

since the seller or buyer is obliged to satisfy the condition. Either party might send a letter or utilize a preprinted form, such as that posted by the State of Colorado which lays out the basis for termination.

See Figure 4–21.

THIS FORM HAS IMPORTANT LEGAL CONSEQUENCES AND THE PARTIES SHOULD CONSULT LEGAL AND TAX OR OTHER COUNSEL BEFORE SIGNING.

NOTICE TO TERMINATE

Date: _____

This Notice terminates the Contract dated _____ between _____ (Seller) and

_____ (Buyer) relating to the sale and purchase of the Property known as: _____

_____. Terms used herein shall have the same meaning as in the Contract.

BUYER'S NOTIFICATION OF UNSATISFACTORY CONDITION.
Buyer notifies Seller that the Contract is terminated (§ 25 Contract) because the following are unsatisfactory to Buyer:

☐ **Assumption Balance** (§ 4.6)	☐ **Objection to Title** (subject to correction § 8.5)
☐ **New Loan** (§ 5.2)	☐ **Property or Inclusions Inspection** (§ 10.2.1)
☐ **Appraisal Condition** (§ 6.2)	☐ **Insurability** (§ 10.5)
☐ **CIC Documents** (§ 7.4.5)	☐ **Methamphetamine Laboratory** (§ 11)
☐ **Survey** (§ 8.3.2)	☐ **Causes of Loss, Insurance** (§ 19.1)
☐ **Special Taxing Districts** (§ 8.4)	
☐ **Other:** _____	

SELLER'S NOTIFICATION OF UNSATISFACTORY CONDITION.
Seller notifies Buyer that the Contract is terminated (§ 25 Contract) because the following are unsatisfactory to Seller:

☐ **Credit Information and Buyer's New Senior Loan** (§ 5.3)
☐ **Release of Liability and Loan Transfer Approval** (§ 5.4)
☐ **Property Approval** (§ 6.1)
☐ **Other:** _____

Terminating Party: ☐ Buyer   ☐ Seller

Date: _____   Date: _____

_____   _____
Signature   Signature

FIGURE 4–21

CHAPTER FOUR **SUMMARY**

Chapter Four discussed the following topics:

- The nature of contingencies and conditions in the agreement of sale
- The impact that conditions and contingencies have on the agreement of sale
- Various conditions and contingencies that exist in agreement of sale language

REVIEW **QUESTIONS**

1. A conditional contract, or a contract with a contingency, is unenforceable until the condition or contingency is met or removed. True or False? Explain.
2. Name three of the more common contingencies in a real estate contract.
3. If buyers cannot get mortgage financing as outlined in the mortgage/financing clause of a contract, what are the possible results?
4. Explain the difference between a condition and a contingency.
5. What is the purpose of an addendum?
6. In a home inspection addendum, what clauses are normally seen?
7. What hazardous materials are commonly mentioned in contingency language?
8. Contingency language never contains remedial language. True or False? Explain.
9. What is a right of first refusal?
10. Under what condition is a notice to terminate utilized?

DISCUSSION **QUESTION**

Most agreements of sale have conditional requirements. If a home inspection proved that major defects exist in the structure, what impact does it have on the agreement? What remedial action may be taken?

EXERCISE 1

Draft a mortgage contingency clause using the following fact patterns:

Time to receive mortgage commitment—90 days

Minimum amount of acceptable mortgage—$90,000

Maximum interest rate—7%

Term—30 years

EXERCISE 2

Draft a right of first refusal addendum using the following information:

Buyer is still trying to sell current home, and seller wishes the option of soliciting other buyers for the home. Buyer and seller have agreed to extend the date of the agreement of sale until December 12, 2009. All notices must be delivered within two days. If buyer receives a notice from the seller of an offer, the buyer will have 48 hours to remove the contingency and deliver a second deposit of $5,000 to the seller within 72 hours.

EXERCISE 3

Draft an endorsement to the agreement of sale to make the agreement contingent on the seller successfully changing the present residential zoning classification to a zoning classification of light commercial. This will affect none of the other terms or conditions in the agreement.

Assignment for the Case of John and Martha

Draft the following addenda to the agreement of sale:

- Mortgage financing
- Home inspection
- Pest inspection
- Hazardous materials

REFERENCES

1. SUMMA PA JUR. 2d, §8:45.
2. MILTON R. FRIEDMAN, CONTRACT AND CONVEYANCE OF REAL PROPERTY 123 (1979).
3. Hodorowicz v. Szulc, 16 ILL. APP. 2d 317, 147 N.E. 2d 887, 889 (1958). *See also* Goldberg v. Abastasi, 272 MD. 61, 321 A. 2d 155 (1974).
4. Dodson v. Nink, 72 ILL. APP. 3d 51, 390 N.E. 2d 546.
5. *Id.* N.E. 2d at 550.
6. E. I. Du Pont et al. v. Crompton Townsend Inc., No. C.A. 1284, (Superior Court of Del., New Castle County, 1976); *see also* Forrest Creek v. McLean Savings, 831 F. 2d 1238 (4th Cir. 1987). For a precise, rigid application of conditional principles, *see* Ditman v. Huyer, No. 990 (Ct. of Common Pleas of Greene County, PA, November 3, 1988).
7. *Id.* at 26.
8. *Id.*
9. Pena v. Security Title Company, 267 S.W.2d 847 (Tex. Civ. App. 1954).
10. *Id.* at 848.
11. Hodorowicz , *supra* note 3, at 887 (1958).
12. *Id.* at 888-89.
13. Fischer v. Kennedy, 106 CONN. 484, 138 A. 503 (1927).
14. Roberts v. Maxwell, 94 GA. APP. 406, 94 S.E. 2d 764 (1959).
15. *See Vendor-Purchaser: Purchase Option Contingent Upon Resolution of Litigation in Favor of Seller*, REAL EST. L. REP., Nov. 1990, at 7.
16. CHARLES P. NEMETH, THE PARALEGAL RESOURCE MANUAL, 2nd ed., 504 (1995).
17. HERBERT THORNDIKE TIFFANY, THE LAW OF REAL PROPERTY AND OTHER INTERESTS IN LAND 74 (1970).
18. Du Pont, *supra* note 6, at 26.
19. *Id.*
20. Hodorowicz, *supra* note 3, at 887; *see also* Carsek Corp v. Stephen Schifter Inc., 431 PA 550, 246 A2d. 365 (1968).
21. John M. Payne, *From the Courts—Mortgage Contingency Clauses*, 19 REAL EST. L.J. 249, 250 (1991); *see also* Robert L. Tucker, *Disappearing Ink: The Emerging Duty to Remove Invalid Policy Provisions*, 42 AKRON L. REV. 519 (2009).

22. SUMMA, *supra* note 1, at §8:50.

23. Payne, *supra* note 21, at 250.

24. Marianne Jennings, *Buying Property from the Addams Family*, 22 REAL EST. L.J., 43, 53–54 (1993).

25. 42 U.S.C. ch. 103 - *Comprehensive Environmental Response, Compensation, and Liability Act*.

26. 42 U.S.C. §9607; *See also* United States Department of Energy, Public Involvement News at www.bechteljacobs.com/pdf/news/PubInvNews200610.pdf.

27. Kevin L. Shepherd, *Drafting Radon Contingency Clauses (with Form)*, 6 PRAC. REAL EST. LAW 43, 44 (1990).

28. U.S. Environmental Protection Agency Web site, *EPA Map of Radon Zones* at www.epa. gov/radon/images/zonemapcolor_800.jpg.

29. Paul. A Locke & Patricia I. Elliott, *Caveat Broker: What Can Real Estate Licenses Do about Their Potentially Expanding Liability for Failure to Disclose Radon Risks in Home Purchases and Sale Transactions?* 25 COLUM. J. ENVTL. L. 71 (2000).

30. Shepherd, *supra* note 27, at 48.

31. U.S. Department of Health and Human Services, Office of the Surgeon General, Press Release of January 13, 2005, *Surgeon General Releases National Health Advisory on Radon* at www.surgeongeneral.gov/pressreleases/sg01132005.html.

32. Locke & Elliott, *supra* note 29.

33. Gene Marsh, *The Liability of Home Inspectors in Residential Real Estate Sales*, 59 AL. L. REV. 107 (2007); Locke & Elliott, *supra* note 29.

34. TIMOTHY G. O'NEILL, LADNER ON CONVEYANCING IN PENNSYLVANIA, 6.05 (1988).

35. SUMMA PA JUR, *supra* note 1, at §8:53.

36. Despite the rule against perpetuities, buyer's right of first refusal, exercisable over 25 years was upheld in Mizell v. Greensboro, (412 S.E.2d 904)(N.C. App. 1992); *see also Vendor/Purchaser: Right of First Refusal for 25 Years*, REAL EST. L. REP. 3 (Aug. 1992).

Title Abstraction

LEARNING OBJECTIVES

- To describe the various techniques of title abstraction and search.
- To distinguish a conveyance search from an encumbrance search.
- To recognize the many impediments to a transfer or conveyance of title.
- To compose a title report.
- To illustrate the steps involved in the issuance of title insurance.

JOB COMPETENCIES

- To perform a title search.
- To compose a title report in conjunction with an attorney.
- To acquire title insurance.
- To cite and list those defects in title that would restrict the transfer of property.

ETHICAL CONSIDERATIONS

The paralegal must be aware of the following ethical dilemmas during this phase of a real estate transaction:

- Unauthorized practice of law
- Lawyer supervision of nonlawyers
- Confidentiality issues
- Conflicts of interest
- Partnerships between lawyers and nonlawyers
- Communications with persons outside of law firm

I. INTRODUCTION

KEY WORDS

conveyancer	special warranty deed
judgment	title
lien	title company
owner's policy	title examinations
quitclaim deed	title insurance
sheriff's deed	

Buyers expect not only the transfer of property, but also assurances on the quality of transfer. The term **"title"** implies a right, a condition, and a quality of what is conveyed. "Good title" comes free and clear of encumbrances and impediments and with full and free usage. Title less than good is burdened with some type of difficulty such as a **lien** or a chink in the chain of ownership. In either case, the giver or alienator of title gives assurances in a series of ways. For example, some sellers may wish to convey property without guarantees while others give every imaginable assurance as to the quality of said title. In the former instance, such as a sheriff's sale or foreclosure, the buyer gets a title riddled with potential problems. A foreclosed property, by nature, suffers from creditor flaws.[1] In the latter case, the seller warrants that the title flows free and clear of any defects, and in the event a defect or impediment occurs, the seller promises to fix the issue.

When such assurances are given, the seller transfers with a general or **special warranty deed** which includes the following language:

> In the event the Seller is unable to give a good and marketable title or such as will be insured by a reputable title company, subject as aforesaid, Buyer shall have the option of taking such title as the Seller can give without abatement of price or of being repaid all monies paid by the Buyer to the Seller on account of the purchase price and the Seller will reimburse the Buyer for any costs incurred by the Buyer for those items specified in Paragraph 12(b) items (i), (ii), (iii) and in Paragraph 12(c); and in the latter event there shall be no further liability or objection on either of the parties hereto and this Agreement shall become NULL AND VOID.

Between these two extremes exists a continuum of guarantee, of promise and quality in any title transfer. In most cases, buyers demand a good, marketable **title**. In select cases, given the price and circumstance of sale a **quitclaim deed** or **Sheriff's deed** whereby no assurances are communicated, may make better sense. But, precisely what is a good, marketable title? To some theorists, good title means:

> The premises are to be conveyed free and clear of all liens, encumbrances, and easements excepting, however, mortgage encumbrances as herein before set forth [only if buyer is to take subject to an existing mortgage], ordinances, easements of roads and following items, none of which prevent the use of the premises as presently improved, as a single-family dwelling, none of which have been violated and none of which impose a financial burden on the buyer: existing building restrictions; privileges or rights of public service companies within the right of way of public roads or

within ten feet of the perimeter of the real property subject to this agreement; agreements or like matters of record, otherwise *the title to the above-described real estate shall be good and marketable* and as such as will the insured by the title company at regular rates.[2]

Put another way, good title is exactly what it implies—a title devoid of defects such as competing claims to ownership, encumbrances, liens, **judgments**, or debts. When good title is passed, the buyer gets a clean slate. So to represent that the title is good, the seller must demonstrate:

- That the property is rightfully and lawfully owned by the seller.
- That the property is free from liens and other encumbrances.
- That the seller has present and rightful possession.
- That the property is insurable.

Good title expressly promises a host of things but at its heart the seller assures the buyer that the title and exchange is unfettered and free in every way. Title, in order to be free and clear must have:

- No adverse or secondary conveyances.
- No other unsatisfied mortgages.
- No restrictions markedly influencing the use of property.
- No outstanding judgments.
- No inconsistencies with legal descriptions of the property as represented in past surveys.
- No outstanding liens filed by municipalities for sewer charges, refuse collection, or other assessment.
- No outstanding state, local, or federal tax liens.[3]

Since most buyers insist on a good title, the seller represents these qualities in title. These representations are only as dependable as the proof of their accuracy. Bare assertions and representations cannot be relied upon at face value for these claims, if unchecked and unverified are at best laymen's claims to the quality of title. Buyers need more than the oral assurance of the seller. Instead, buyers must corroborate these representations through the examination and analysis of title. Proof and confirmation about the quality of title is the stuff of title examination and abstraction. **Title examinations** verify the condition of title and here is where paralegals earn their keep by conducting close reviews of the history and present condition of a designated title. Title searches are mandatory confirmations which give assurances to buyers.

Title searches are conducted each and every day in public offices, such as the Recorder of Deeds or other locations. Paralegals search a bevy of primary materials to discover the quality of title, from deed books, judgment records, and tax rolls which are fully open to the public. On any given day, one will witness numerous people rummaging through these dusty books and stacks, catalogued by the recorder. The task of a title examiner is multifaceted and multidimensional for there are a host of parties and players interested in the final product regarding title. The paralegal-examiner must wear many hats, including:

- Prepare lists of all legal instruments applying to a specific piece of land and the buildings on it.
- Examine documentation such as mortgages, liens, judgments, easements, plat books, maps, contracts, and agreements in order to verify factors such as properties' legal descriptions, ownership, or restrictions.

- Read search requests in order to ascertain types of title evidence required and to obtain descriptions of properties and names of involved parties.

- Copy or summarize recorded documents, such as mortgages, trust deeds, and contracts that affect property titles.

- Examine individual titles in order to determine if restrictions, such as delinquent taxes, will affect titles and limit property use.

- Prepare reports describing any title encumbrances encountered during searching activities, and outlining actions needed to clear titles.

- Verify accuracy and completeness of land-related documents accepted for registration; prepare rejection notices when documents are not acceptable.

- Confer with realtors, lending institution personnel, buyers, sellers, contractors, surveyors, and courthouse personnel in order to exchange title-related information or to resolve problems.

- Enter into recordkeeping systems appropriate data needed to create new title records or update existing ones.

- Direct activities of workers who search records and examine titles, assigning, scheduling, and evaluating work, and providing technical guidance as necessary.

Web Exercise

Discover a typical county Recorder of Deeds protocol at *www.co.berks.pa.us/recorder/.*

Most individuals hire an attorney, title abstractor, or paralegal skilled in the nuances of title examination to insure good title. During simpler times, a **conveyancer** conducted the examination. Conveyancers were professionals whose task was to orchestrate the sale and transfer of property. Conveyancers authored documents for transferring the ownership of real property. Ladner notes the dramatic, historic role conveyancers played in the real estate industry.

[A] Remarkable change has occurred in the business of conveyancing, especially in and near the larger cities, mainly attributable to the modern tendency to specialization in all business. In the real estate business, one of the results has been the formation of corporations making a specialty of searching and insuring titles, called title insurance companies. Over a century ago, a conveyancer . . . besides drawing the necessary papers, always made the title searches, the correctness of which he certified by signing the abstract or brief of title. However, there was no guarantee other than the personal integrity and reputation of the individual conveyancer. But in those days that was no small thing. The conveyancers, inheritors of the traditions of the English solicitors, were a splendid group of men, proud of their calling and jealous of their unblemished reputations. They were well grounded in the law and their opinions on real estate law often were sought as eagerly as a lawyer's. Indeed, the examinations necessary to gain admission to their conveyancers' associations were considered to be more difficult than the lawyers' examination for admission to the bar.[4]

While conveyancers still are prominent figures in England and other Commonwealth nations, the shift away from conveyancers in the American experience, has been slow but sure over the last hundred years. "Conveyancers have seen their responsibilities entrusted to title agents and abstractors who work for title companies that issue title insurance policies. Title companies and their agents research the quality of title and do it more expeditiously and perhaps better"[5] than the homeowner, paralegal, or attorney who irregularly examines title. Title companies have flourished because of the need for title assurance and because of their narrow competence.

The **title company** affirms whether the title is good and marketable by identifying problems in the chain of ownership, locating easements and rights-of-way, and deciphering legal property descriptions for compatibility with physical surveys when it conducts title searches. **Title insurance** underwriters agree to indemnify owners and/or lenders in the event of an actual future loss caused by a covered defect in the title. Title insurance underwriting is different from casualty insurance companies, however, in that title companies put a large amount of their earned premium into risk elimination efforts to minimize the risk of a future loss. Of course, title insurance companies assume risks as well and provide financial indemnity to policyholders in the event of a loss, but they are able to take additional steps to eliminate the risk by searching the title to determine what needs to be done to convey clear title to a purchaser.

Web Exercise

Test your title knowledge in the interactive game posted by the American Land Title Association at *www.alta.org/lti/triumph.cfm*.

There are two major types of policies. One insures title for a purchaser or owner (**Owner's Policy**) and remains in effect as long as the owner or the owner's heirs own the property. Owner's Title Insurance, referred to as an Owner's Policy, is usually issued in the amount of the real estate purchase. Paid only once, the policy protects the buyer from designated title challenges such as:

- Errors or omissions in deeds
- Mistakes in examining records
- Forgery
- Undisclosed heirs

Title policies insure against these and other challenges to title. The implications of error or impediments can be quite draconian.

CASE DECISION

A case that highlights the impact of title defect resulting from a failure to record manifest the importance of being insured in the transaction.

FILED

Mar 19 2009, 9:41 am

CLERK
of the supreme court,
court of appeals and
tax court

FOR PUBLICATION

ATTORNEYS FOR APPELLANT:

JAMES J. NAGY
Munster, Indiana

ATTORNEYS FOR APPELLEE:

SCOTT J. FANDRE
CARL A. GRECI
WENDY K. WALKER-DYES
Baker & Daniels LLP
South Bend, Indiana

IN THE
COURT OF APPEALS OF INDIANA

ATUL KUMAR,	)
	)
Appellant-Defendant,	)
	)
vs.	) No. 45A03-0803-CV-91
	)
BAY BRIDGE, LLC, an Indiana	)
Limited Liability Company,	)
	)
Appellee-Plaintiff.	)

APPEAL FROM THE LAKE SUPERIOR COURT
The Honorable Gerald N. Svetanoff
Cause No. 45D04-0701-PL-00006

March 19, 2009

OPINION – FOR PUBLICATION

MATHIAS, Judge

Bay Bridge LLC ("Bay Bridge") filed a complaint in Lake Superior Court to quiet title to a parcel of real estate commonly known as 149th and Colfax, Cedar Lake, Indiana ("the real estate") and named Atul Kumar ("Kumar") as a defendant. Kumar had purchased the real estate at a tax sale but failed to record his deed. The trial court granted Bay Bridge's motion for summary judgment. Kumar appeals

(continued)

and raises several issues. However, we address only the following dispositive issue: whether Bay Bridge was a bona fide purchaser of the real estate at issue.[1] We affirm.

Facts and Procedural History

On September 25, 2001, Kumar purchased the real estate at a tax sale. The record owner of the real estate, INB National Bank Trust No. 26, had not paid the property taxes in 1999 and in years prior. Although the tax sale notices were returned as undeliverable, on January 27, 2003, the Lake Circuit Court issued a tax deed to Kumar. Kumar failed to record the deed at that time.

On December 13, 2004, Bank One Trust Company (the successor-in-interest to INB National Bank) conveyed the property to Bay Bridge. Bay Bridge recorded the trustee's deed shortly thererafter. Bay Bridge later discovered that Kumar claimed an interest in the real estate. On January 16, 2007, Bay Bridge filed a complaint to quiet title to the real estate in Lake Superior Court and named Kumar as a defendant.[2] On February 6, 2007, Kumar recorded his tax deed.

Both parties filed motions for summary judgment. Bay Bridge argued that Kumar's tax deed was void and/or that it was a bona fide purchaser of the property. In his motion, Kumar challenged the jurisdiction of the Lake Superior Court, argued that Bank One Trust could not convey property they did not own, and that adequate notice of the tax sale was provided to the record owner of the real estate.

After a hearing, the trial court issued an order granting Bay Bridge's motion for summary judgment. The court specifically found that "the notice provided to Bay Bridge's predecessor in interest in the property, INB Trust No. 26 is insufficient to satisfy due process. As such the tax sale and the Tax Deed conveying the Property to Kumar was void." Appellant's App. p. 9. The trial court did not address whether Bay Bridge was a bona fide purchaser. Kumar appeals. Additional facts will be provided as necessary.

Standard of Review

A trial court should grant a motion for summary judgment only when the evidence shows that "there is no genuine issue as to any material fact and that the moving party is entitled to a judgment as a matter of law." Ind. Trial Rule 56(C). The trial court's grant of a motion for summary judgment comes to us cloaked with a presumption of validity. Rodriguez v. Tech Credit Union Corp., 824 N.E.2d 442, 446 (Ind. Ct. App. 2005). However, we review a trial court's grant of summary judgment de novo, construing all facts and making all reasonable inferences from the facts in favor of the non-moving party. Progressive Ins. Co. v. Bullock, 841 N.E.2d 238, 240 (Ind. Ct. App. 2006), trans. denied. We examine only those materials designated to the trial court on the motion for summary judgment. Trietsch v. Circle Design Group, Inc., 868 N.E.2d 812, 817 (Ind. Ct. App. 2007). We may affirm the trial court's grant of summary judgment upon any basis that the record supports. Rodriguez, 824 N.E.2d at 446. Our standard of review is not altered by the fact that the parties filed cross motions for summary judgment. Pond v. McNellis, 845 N.E.2d 1043, 1053 (Ind. Ct. App. 2006), trans. denied.

The trial court made findings and conclusions in support of its entry of summary judgment. "Although we are not bound by the trial court's findings and conclusions, they aid our review by providing reasons for the trial court's decision." See GDC Environmental Servs. Inc., v. Ransbottom Landfill, 740 N.E.2d 1254, 1257 (Ind. Ct. App. 2000). "If the trial court's entry of summary judgment can be sustained on any theory or basis in the record, we must affirm." Id.

Discussion and Decision

First, we observe that Kumar correctly noted in his summary judgment motion that Bay Bridge's challenge to his tax deed should have been filed in Lake Circuit Court. Indiana Code section 6-1.1-24-4.7(f) provides: "The court that enters judgment under this section shall retain exclusive continuing supervisory jurisdiction

---

[1]Kumar raises several issues that arise from the trial court's conclusion that his tax deed was void because the notice provided to Bay Bridge's predecessor in interest was insufficient to satisfy due process. We need not address those issues given our resolution of the issue noted above.

[2]While Bay Bridge was aware of Kumar's claimed interest in the real state at issue before its complaint to quiet title was filed, the record does not disclose when Bay Bridge discovered that Kumar had a tax deed to the property.

over all matters and claims relating to the tax sale." See also Star Financial Bank v. Shelton, 691 N.E.2d 1338, 1341 (Ind. Ct. App. 1998). However, by failing to object at his first opportunity, i.e. when he filed his answer, Kumar waived his claim of procedural error. See Packard v. Shoopman, 852 N.E.2d 927, 929-30 (Ind. 2006).

Therefore, we turn our attention to Bay Bridge's claim that it was entitled to summary judgment on its complaint to quiet title because the undisputed facts establish that Bay Bridge is a bona fide purchaser for value. See Appellant's App. p. 99; Appellee's Br. at 28. The trial court entered findings of fact and conclusions of law with regard to whether Kumar's tax deed was void, but did not issue any findings with regard to Bay Bridge's bona fide purchaser argument. However, as set forth supra, we may affirm the trial court's grant of summary judgment upon any basis that the record supports. Rodriguez, 824 N.E.2d at 446.

Indiana Code section 32-21-4-1 provides that a conveyance, mortgage of land, a lease for more than three years, or any interest in the land must be recorded in the recorder's office of the county where the land is situated. Further,

> A conveyance, mortgage, or lease takes priority according to the time of its filing. The conveyance, mortgage, or lease is fraudulent and void as against any subsequent purchaser, lessee, or mortgagee in good faith and for a valuable consideration if the purchaser's, lessee's, or mortgagee's deed, mortgage, or lease is first recorded.

"The purpose of the recording statute is to provide protection to subsequent purchasers, lessees, and mortgagees." Meyer v. Marine Builders, Inc., 797 N.E.2d 760, 774 (Ind. Ct. App. 2003).

Consistent with the recording statute, Indiana has long recognized the bona fide purchaser doctrine. "[T]o qualify as a bona fide purchaser, one has to purchase in good faith, for a valuable consideration, and without notice of the outstanding rights of others." Keybank Nat'l Ass'n v. NBD Bank, 699 N.E.2d 322, 327 (Ind. Ct. App. 1998). "The theory behind the bona fide purchaser defense is that every reasonable effort should be made to protect a purchaser of legal title for a valuable consideration without notice of a legal defect." S & S Enterprises v. Marathon Ashland Petroleum, LLC, 799 N.E.2d 18, 23 (Ind. Ct. App. 2003).

"The law recognizes both constructive and actual notice." Bank of New York v. Nally, 820 N.E.2d 644, 648 (Ind. 2005). A "purchaser of real estate is presumed to have examined the records of such deeds as constitute the chain of title thereto under which he claims, and is charged with notice, actual or constructive, of all facts recited in such records showing encumbrances, or the non-payment of purchase-money." Id. (citation omitted). "A record outside the chain of title does not provide notice to bona fide purchasers for value." Id. at 648-49 (quoting Szakaly v. Smith, 544 N.E.2d 490, 492 (Ind. 1989)).

Kumar failed to record his tax deed as required by Indiana Code section 32-21-4-1, and it remained unrecorded until after Bay Bridge filed its complaint to quiet title. Therefore, Bay Bridge did not have constructive notice of Kumar's interest in the real estate at issue.[3] See Keybank, 669 N.E.2d at 327 ("Constructive notice is provided when a deed or mortgage is properly acknowledged and placed on the record as required by statute[.]").

---

[3] We are unpersuaded by Kumar's argument that Bay Bridge had constructive notice of the tax sale because the records of the tax sale were available in the Lake County Court Clerk's office. Kumar essentially dismisses the fact that his failure to record his tax deed for over four years has resulted in the litigation at issue. Kumar inaccurately states, "[w]hile it may have ameliorated the situation somewhat if Kumar had recorded his Tax Deed before Bay Bridge became involved, this should not affect the outcome of this matter." Reply Br. of Appellant at 25. "A person charged with the duty of searching the records of a particular tract of property is not on notice of any adverse claims which do not appear in the chain of title; because, otherwise, the recording statute would prove a snare, instead of a protection." Keybank, 699 N.E.2d at 327. Moreover, "an otherwise valid instrument which is . . . recorded out of the chain of title does not operate as constructive notice[.]" Id.

(continued)

With regard to actual notice, prior to purchasing the property, Bay Bridge requested a title search, which "found of record no lis pendens, no certificate of tax sale, no tax deed, nor any other record interest of Atul Kumar in the property purchased by Bay Bridge." Appellant's App. p. 80. Moreover, Kumar did not designate any evidence to the trial court which would establish that Bay Bridge had actual notice of his claimed interest in the property. See id. ("Notice is actual when notice [has] been directly and personally given to the person to be notified. Additionally, actual notice may be implied or inferred from the fact that the person charged had means of obtaining knowledge which he did not use.").

From our review of the record before us, we conclude that Bay Bridge designated evidence establishing that it was a bona fide purchaser for value, and Kumar failed to designate any evidence that would create a genuine issue of material fact on this issue. Therefore, the trial court properly granted Bay Bridge's motion for summary judgment on its complaint to quiet title.

Affirmed.

BAKER, C.J., and BROWN, J., concur.

The Owner's Policy generally consists of a property description, the coverage agreed to, and any conditions or exceptions the policy will not extend to. The policy may also have a series of endorsements that either guarantee defense or exclude insurance from a particular issue such as zoning or water rights. The content of a policy depends upon the parties' desires and intents and the condition of title itself. See the American Land Title Association's format for an owner's policy at Figure 5–1.

HOMEOWNER'S POLICY OF TITLE INSURANCE

For a one-to-four family residence

Issued By

BLANK TITLE INSURANCE COMPANY

OWNER'S INFORMATION SHEET

Your Title Insurance Policy is a legal contract between You and Us.

It applies only to a one-to-four family residence and only if each insured named in Schedule A is a Natural Person. If the Land described in Schedule A of the Policy is not an improved residential lot on which there is located a one-to-four family residence, or if each insured named in Schedule A is not a Natural Person, contact Us immediately.

The Policy insures You against actual loss resulting from certain Covered Risks. These Covered Risks are listed beginning on page of the Policy. The Policy is limited by:

- Provisions of Schedule A
- Exceptions in Schedule B
- Our Duty To Defend Against Legal Actions On Page _____
- Exclusions on page ___
- Conditions on pages ___ and ___.

You should keep the Policy even if You transfer Your Title to the Land. It may protect against claims made against You by someone else after You transfer Your Title.

FIGURE 5–1
(continues)

IF YOU WANT TO MAKE A CLAIM, SEE SECTION 3 UNDER CONDITIONS ON PAGE __.

The premium for this Policy is paid once. No additional premium is owed for the Policy.

This sheet is not Your insurance Policy. It is only a brief outline of some of the important Policy features. The Policy explains in detail Your rights and obligations and Our rights and obligations. Since the Policy–and not this sheet–is the legal document,

YOU SHOULD READ THE POLICY VERY CAREFULLY.

If You have any questions about Your Policy, contact:

BLANK TITLE INSURANCE COMPANY

_____

_____

HOMEOWNER'S POLICY OF TITLE INSURANCE

For a one-to-four family residence

Issued By

BLANK TITLE INSURANCE COMPANY

TABLE OF CONTENTS

FIGURE 5–1
(continued)

HOMEOWNER'S POLICY OF TITLE INSURANCE

For a one-to-four family residence

Issued By

BLANK TITLE INSURANCE COMPANY

As soon as You Know of anything that might be covered by this Policy, You must notify Us promptly in writing at the address shown in Section 3 of the Conditions.

OWNER'S COVERAGE STATEMENT

This Policy insures You against actual loss, including any costs, attorneys' fees and expenses provided under this Policy. The loss must result from one or more of the Covered Risks set forth below. This Policy covers only Land that is an improved residential lot on which there is located a one-to-four family residence and only when each insured named in Schedule A is a Natural Person.

Your insurance is effective on the Policy Date. This Policy covers Your actual loss from any risk described under Covered Risks if the event creating the risk exists on the Policy Date or, to the extent expressly stated in Covered Risks, after the Policy Date.

Your insurance is limited by all of the following:

- The Policy Amount
- For Covered Risk 16, 18, 19 and 21, Your Deductible Amount and Our Maximum Dollar Limit of Liability shown in Schedule A
- The Exceptions in Schedule B
- Our Duty To Defend Against Legal Actions
- The Exclusions on page
- The Conditions on pages   and   .

COVERED RISKS

The Covered Risks are:

1. Someone else owns an interest in Your Title.

2. Someone else has rights affecting Your Title because of leases, contracts, or options.

3. Someone else claims to have rights affecting Your Title because of forgery or impersonation.

4. Someone else has an Easement on the Land.

5. Someone else has a right to limit Your use of the Land.

6. Your Title is defective. Some of these defects are:

   a. Someone else's failure to have authorized a transfer or conveyance of your Title.
   b. Someone else's failure to create a valid document by electronic means.
   c. A document upon which Your Title is based is invalid because it was not properly signed, sealed, acknowledged, delivered or recorded.
   d. A document upon which Your Title is based was signed using a falsified, expired, or otherwise invalid power of attorney.
   e. A document upon which Your Title is based was not properly filed, recorded, or indexed in the Public Records.
   f. A defective judicial or administrative proceeding.

7. Any of Covered Risks 1 through 6 occurring after the Policy Date.

8. Someone else has a lien on Your Title, including a:

   a. lien of real estate taxes or assessments imposed on Your Title by a governmental authority that are due or payable, but unpaid;

FIGURE 5–1

(continued)

b. Mortgage;

c. judgment, state or federal tax lien;

d. charge by a homeowner's or condominium association; or

e. lien, occurring before or after the Policy Date, for labor and material furnished before the Policy Date.

9. Someone else has an encumbrance on Your Title.

10. Someone else claims to have rights affecting Your Title because of fraud, duress, incompetency or incapacity.

11. You do not have actual vehicular and pedestrian access to and from the Land, based upon a legal right.

12. You are forced to correct or remove an existing violation of any covenant, condition or restriction affecting the Land, even if the covenant, condition or restriction is excepted in Schedule B. However, You are not covered for any violation that relates to:

    a. any obligation to perform maintenance or repair on the Land; or

    b. environmental protection of any kind, including hazardous or toxic conditions or substances unless there is a notice recorded in the Public Records, describing any part of the Land, claiming a violation exists. Our liability for this Covered Risk is limited to the extent of the violation stated in that notice.

13. Your Title is lost or taken because of a violation of any covenant, condition or restriction, which occurred before You acquired Your Title, even if the covenant, condition or restriction is excepted in Schedule B.

14. The violation or enforcement of those portions of any law or government regulation concerning:

    a. building;

    b. zoning;

    c. land use;

    d. improvements on the Land;

    e. land division; or

    f. environmental protection,

    if there is a notice recorded in the Public Records, describing any part of the Land, claiming a violation exists or declaring the intention to enforce the law or regulation. Our liability for this Covered Risk is limited to the extent of the violation or enforcement stated in that notice.

15. An enforcement action based on the exercise of a governmental police power not covered by Covered Risk 14 if there is a notice recorded in the Public Records, describing any part of the Land, of the enforcement action or intention to bring an enforcement action. Our liability for this Covered Risk is limited to the extent of the enforcement action stated in that notice.

16. Because of an existing violation of a subdivision law or regulation affecting the Land:

    a. You are unable to obtain a building permit;

    b. You are required to correct or remove the violation; or

    c. someone else has a legal right to, and does, refuse to perform a contract to purchase the Land, lease it or make a Mortgage loan on it.

The amount of Your insurance for this Covered Risk is subject to Your Deductible Amount and Our Maximum Dollar Limit of Liability shown in Schedule A.

17. You lose Your Title to any part of the Land because of the right to take the Land by condemning it, if:

    a. there is a notice of the exercise of the right recorded in the Public Records and the notice describes any part of the Land; or

    b. the taking happened before the Policy Date and is binding on You if You bought the Land without Knowing of the taking.

FIGURE 5–1

(continued)

18. You are forced to remove or remedy Your existing structures, or any part of them - other than boundary walls or fences - because any portion was built without obtaining a building permit from the proper government office. The amount of Your insurance for this Covered Risk is subject to Your Deductible Amount and Our Maximum Dollar Limit of Liability shown in Schedule A.

19. You are forced to remove or remedy Your existing structures, or any part of them, because they violate an existing zoning law or zoning regulation. If You are required to remedy any portion of Your existing structures, the amount of Your insurance for this Covered Risk is subject to Your Deductible Amount and Our Maximum Dollar Limit of Liability shown in Schedule A.

20. You cannot use the Land because use as a single-family residence violates an existing zoning law or zoning regulation.

21. You are forced to remove Your existing structures because they encroach onto Your neighbor's land. If the encroaching structures are boundary walls or fences, the amount of Your insurance for this Covered Risk is subject to Your Deductible Amount and Our Maximum Dollar Limit of Liability shown in Schedule A.

22. Someone else has a legal right to, and does, refuse to perform a contract to purchase the Land, lease it or make a Mortgage loan on it because Your neighbor's existing structures encroach onto the Land.

23. You are forced to remove Your existing structures which encroach onto an Easement or over a building set-back line, even if the Easement or building set-back line is excepted in Schedule B.

24. Your existing structures are damaged because of the exercise of a right to maintain or use any Easement affecting the Land, even if the Easement is excepted in Schedule B.

25. Your existing improvements (or a replacement or modification made to them after the Policy Date), including lawns, shrubbery or trees, are damaged because of the future exercise of a right to use the surface of the Land for the extraction or development of minerals, water or any other substance, even if those rights are excepted or reserved from the description of the Land or excepted in Schedule B.

26. Someone else tries to enforce a discriminatory covenant, condition or restriction that they claim affects Your Title which is based upon race, color, religion, sex, handicap, familial status, or national origin.

27. A taxing authority assesses supplemental real estate taxes not previously assessed against the Land for any period before the Policy Date because of construction or a change of ownership or use that occurred before the Policy Date.

28. Your neighbor builds any structures after the Policy Date – other than boundary walls or fences – which encroach onto the Land.

29. Your Title is unmarketable, which allows someone else to refuse to perform a contract to purchase the Land, lease it or make a Mortgage loan on it.

30. Someone else owns an interest in Your Title because a court order invalidates a prior transfer of the title under federal bankruptcy, state insolvency, or similar creditors' rights laws.

31. The residence with the address shown in Schedule A is not located on the Land at the Policy Date.

32. The map, if any, attached to this Policy does not show the correct location of the Land according to the Public Records.

OUR DUTY TO DEFEND AGAINST LEGAL ACTIONS

We will defend Your Title in any legal action only as to that part of the action which is based on a Covered Risk and which is not excepted or excluded from coverage in this Policy. We will pay the costs, attorneys' fees, and expenses We incur in that defense.

We will not pay for any part of the legal action which is not based on a Covered Risk or which is excepted or excluded from coverage in this Policy.

FIGURE 5–1
(continued)

We can end Our duty to defend Your Title under Section 4 of the Conditions.

THIS POLICY IS NOT COMPLETE WITHOUT SCHEDULES A AND B.

[Witness clause optional]

BLANK TITLE INSURANCE COMPANY

BY: _____

                PRESIDENT

BY: _____

                SECRETARY

EXCLUSIONS

In addition to the Exceptions in Schedule B, You are not insured against loss, costs, attorneys' fees, and expenses resulting from:

1. Governmental police power, and the existence or violation of those portions of any law or government regulation concerning:

    a. building;

    b. zoning;

    c. land use;

    d. improvements on the Land;

    e. land division; and

    f. environmental protection.

    This Exclusion does not limit the coverage described in Covered Risk 8.a., 14, 15, 16, 18, 19, 20, 23 or 27.

2. The failure of Your existing structures, or any part of them, to be constructed in accordance with applicable building codes. This Exclusion does not limit the coverage described in Covered Risk 14 or 15.

3. The right to take the Land by condemning it. This Exclusion does not limit the coverage described in Covered Risk 17.

4. Risks:

    a. that are created, allowed, or agreed to by You, whether or not they are recorded in the Public Records;

    b. that are Known to You at the Policy Date, but not to Us, unless they are recorded in the Public Records at the Policy Date;

    c. that result in no loss to You; or

    d. that first occur after the Policy Date - this does not limit the coverage described in Covered Risk 7, 8.e., 25, 26, 27 or 28.

5. Failure to pay value for Your Title.

6. Lack of a right:

    a. to any land outside the area specifically described and referred to in paragraph 3 of Schedule A; and

    b. in streets, alleys, or waterways that touch the Land.

    This Exclusion does not limit the coverage described in Covered Risk 11 or 21.

FIGURE 5–1

(continued)

HOMEOWNER'S POLICY OF TITLE INSURANCE

For a one-to-four family residence

Issued By

BLANK TITLE INSURANCE COMPANY

CONDITIONS

1. DEFINITIONS

   a. Easement - the right of someone else to use the Land for a special purpose.
   b. Known - things about which You have actual knowledge. The words "Know" and "Knowing" have the same meaning as Known.
   c. Land - the land or condominium unit described in paragraph 3 of Schedule A and any improvements on the Land which are real property.
   d. Mortgage - a mortgage, deed of trust, trust deed or other security instrument.
   e. Natural Person - a human being, not a commercial or legal organization or entity. Natural Person includes a trustee of a Trust even if the trustee is not a human being.
   f. Policy Date - the date and time shown in Schedule A. If the insured named in Schedule A first acquires the interest shown in Schedule A by an instrument recorded in the Public Records later than the date and time shown in Schedule A, the Policy Date is the date and time the instrument is recorded.
   g. Public Records - records that give constructive notice of matters affecting Your Title, according to the state statutes where the Land is located.
   h. Title - the ownership of Your interest in the Land, as shown in Schedule A.
   i. Trust - a living trust established by a human being for estate planning.
   j. We/Our/Us - Blank Title Insurance Company.
   k. You/Your - the insured named in Schedule A and also those identified in Section 2.b. of these Conditions.

2. CONTINUATION OF COVERAGE

   a. This Policy insures You forever, even after You no longer have Your Title. You cannot assign this Policy to anyone else.
   b. This Policy also insures:
      (1) anyone who inherits Your Title because of Your death;
      (2) Your spouse who receives Your Title because of dissolution of Your marriage;
      (3) the trustee or successor trustee of a Trust to whom You transfer Your Title after the Policy Date; or
      (4) the beneficiaries of Your Trust upon Your death.
   c. We may assert against the insureds identified in Section 2.b. any rights and defenses that We have against any previous insured under this Policy.

3. HOW TO MAKE A CLAIM

   a. Prompt Notice Of Your Claim
      (1) As soon as You Know of anything that might be covered by this Policy, You must notify Us promptly in writing.
      (2) Send Your notice to **Blank Title Insurance Company,** Attention: Claims Department. Please include the Policy number shown in Schedule A, and the county and state where the Land is located. Please enclose a copy of Your policy, if available.
      (3) If You do not give Us prompt notice, Your coverage will be reduced or ended, but only to the extent Your failure affects Our ability to resolve the claim or defend You.

FIGURE 5–1
(continued)

b. Proof Of Your Loss

    (1) We may require You to give Us a written statement signed by You describing Your loss which includes:
        (a) the basis of Your claim;
        (b) the Covered Risks which resulted in Your loss;
        (c) the dollar amount of Your loss; and
        (d) the method You used to compute the amount of Your loss.
    (2) We may require You to make available to Us records, checks, letters, contracts, insurance policies and other papers which relate to Your claim. We may make copies of these papers.
    (3) We may require You to answer questions about Your claim under oath.
    (4) If you fail or refuse to give Us a statement of loss, answer Our questions under oath, or make available to Us the papers We request, Your coverage will be reduced or ended, but only to the extent Your failure or refusal affects Our ability to resolve the claim or defend You.

4. OUR CHOICES WHEN WE LEARN OF A CLAIM

a. After We receive Your notice, or otherwise learn, of a claim that is covered by this Policy, Our choices include one or more of the following:
    (1) Pay the claim;
    (2) Negotiate a settlement;
    (3) Bring or defend a legal action related to the claim;
    (4) Pay You the amount required by this Policy;
    (5) End the coverage of this Policy for the claim by paying You Your actual loss resulting from the Covered Risk, and those costs, attorneys' fees and expenses incurred up to that time which We are obligated to pay;
    (6) End the coverage described in Covered Risk 16, 18, 19 or 21 by paying You the amount of Your insurance then in force for the particular Covered Risk, and those costs, attorneys' fees and expenses incurred up to that time which We are obligated to pay;
    (7) End all coverage of this Policy by paying You the Policy Amount then in force, and those costs, attorneys' fees and expenses incurred up to that time which We are obligated to pay;
    (8) Take other appropriate action.
b. When We choose the options in Sections 4.a. (5), (6) or (7), all Our obligations for the claim end, including Our obligation to defend, or continue to defend, any legal action.
c. Even if We do not think that the Policy covers the claim, We may choose one or more of the options above. By doing so, We do not give up any rights.

5. HANDLING A CLAIM OR LEGAL ACTION

a. You must cooperate with Us in handling any claim or legal action and give Us all relevant information.
b. If You fail or refuse to cooperate with Us, Your coverage will be reduced or ended, but only to the extent Your failure or refusal affects Our ability to resolve the claim or defend You.
c. We are required to repay You only for those settlement costs, attorneys' fees and expenses that We approve in advance.
d. We have the right to choose the attorney when We bring or defend a legal action on Your behalf. We can appeal any decision to the highest level. We do not have to pay Your claim until the legal action is finally decided.
e. Whether or not We agree there is coverage, We can bring or defend a legal action, or take other appropriate action under this Policy. By doing so, We do not give up any rights.

FIGURE 5–1
(continued)

6. LIMITATION OF OUR LIABILITY

a. After subtracting Your Deductible Amount if it applies, We will pay no more than the least of:
   (1) Your actual loss;
   (2) Our Maximum Dollar Limit of Liability then in force for the particular Covered Risk, for claims covered only under Covered Risk 16, 18, 19 or 21; or
   (3) the Policy Amount then in force.

   and any costs, attorneys' fees and expenses that We are obligated to pay under this Policy.

b. If We pursue Our rights under Sections 4.a.(3) and 5.e. of these Conditions and are unsuccessful in establishing the Title, as insured:
   (1) the Policy Amount then in force will be increased by 10% of the Policy Amount shown in Schedule A, and
   (2) You shall have the right to have the actual loss determined on either the date the claim was made by You or the date it is settled and paid.

c. (1) If We remove the cause of the claim with reasonable diligence after receiving notice of it, all Our obligations for the claim end, including any obligation for loss You had while We were removing the cause of the claim.
   (2) Regardless of 6.c.(1) above, if You cannot use the Land because of a claim covered by this Policy:
      (a) You may rent a reasonably equivalent substitute residence and We will repay You for the actual rent You pay, until the earlier of:
         (i) the cause of the claim is removed; or
         (ii) We pay You the amount required by this Policy. If Your claim is covered only under Covered Risk 16, 18, 19 or 21, that payment is the amount of Your insurance then in force for the particular Covered Risk.
      (b) We will pay reasonable costs You pay to relocate any personal property You have the right to remove from the Land, including transportation of that personal property for up to twenty-five (25) miles from the Land, and repair of any damage to that personal property because of the relocation. The amount We will pay You under this paragraph is limited to the value of the personal property before You relocate it.

d. All payments We make under this Policy reduce the Policy Amount then in force, except for costs, attorneys' fees and expenses. All payments We make for claims which are covered only under Covered Risk 16, 18, 19 or 21 also reduce Our Maximum Dollar Limit of Liability for the particular Covered Risk, except for costs, attorneys' fees and expenses.

e. If We issue, or have issued, a Policy to the owner of a Mortgage that is on Your Title and We have not given You any coverage against the Mortgage, then:
   (1) We have the right to pay any amount due You under this Policy to the owner of the Mortgage, and any amount paid shall be treated as a payment to You under this Policy, including under Section 4.a. of these Conditions;
   (2) Any amount paid to the owner of the Mortgage shall be subtracted from the Policy Amount then in force; and
   (3) If Your claim is covered only under Covered Risk 16, 18, 19 or 21, any amount paid to the owner of the Mortgage shall also be subtracted from Our Maximum Dollar Limit of Liability for the particular Covered Risk.

f. If You do anything to affect any right of recovery You may have against someone else, We can subtract from Our liability the amount by which You reduced the value of that right.

FIGURE 5–1
(continued)

7. <u>TRANSFER OF YOUR RIGHTS TO US</u>

   a. When We settle Your claim, We have all the rights and remedies You have against any person or property related to the claim. You must not do anything to affect these rights and remedies. When We ask, You must execute documents to evidence the transfer to Us of these rights and remedies. You must let Us use Your name in enforcing these rights and remedies.

   b. We will not be liable to You if We do not pursue these rights and remedies or if We do not recover any amount that might be recoverable.

   c. We will pay any money We collect from enforcing these rights and remedies in the following order:

      (1) to Us for the costs, attorneys' fees and expenses We paid to enforce these rights and remedies;

      (2) to You for Your loss that You have not already collected;

      (3) to Us for any money We paid out under this Policy on account of Your claim; and

      (4) to You whatever is left.

   d. If You have rights and remedies under contracts (such as indemnities, guaranties, bonds or other policies of insurance) to recover all or part of Your loss, then We have all of those rights and remedies, even if those contracts provide that those obligated have all of Your rights and remedies under this Policy.

8. <u>THIS POLICY IS THE ENTIRE CONTRACT</u>

This Policy, with any endorsements, is the entire contract between You and Us. To determine the meaning of any part of this Policy, You must read the entire Policy and any endorsements. Any changes to this Policy must be agreed to in writing by Us. Any claim You make against Us must be made under this Policy and is subject to its terms.

9. <u>INCREASED POLICY AMOUNT</u>

The Policy Amount then in force will increase by ten percent (10%) of the Policy Amount shown in Schedule A each year for the first five years following the Policy Date shown in Schedule A, up to one hundred fifty percent (150%) of the Policy Amount shown in Schedule A. The increase each year will happen on the anniversary of the Policy Date shown in Schedule A.

10. <u>SEVERABILITY</u>

If any part of this Policy is held to be legally unenforceable, both You and We can still enforce the rest of this Policy.

11. <u>ARBITRATION</u>

   a. If permitted in the state where the Land is located, You or We may demand arbitration.

   b. The law used in the arbitration is the law of the state where the Land is located.

   c. The arbitration shall be under the Title Insurance Arbitration Rules of the American Land Title Association ("Rules"). You can get a copy of the Rules from Us.

   d. Except as provided in the Rules, You cannot join or consolidate Your claim or controversy with claims or controversies of other persons.

   e. The arbitration shall be binding on both You and Us. The arbitration shall decide any matter in dispute between You and Us.

   f. The arbitration award may be entered as a judgment in the proper court.

12. <u>CHOICE OF LAW</u>

The law of the state where the Land is located shall apply to this policy.

FIGURE 5–1
(continued)

HOMEOWNER'S POLICY OF TITLE INSURANCE

For a one-to-four family residence

Issued By

BLANK TITLE INSURANCE COMPANY

SCHEDULE A

Our name and address is: Blank Title Insurance Company

(Company Name)
(Company Address)

Policy No.: [Premium: $_____] Policy Amount: $ Policy Date [and Time]:

Deductible Amounts and Maximum Dollar Limits of Liability
For Covered Risk 16, 18, 19 and 21:

	Your Deductible Amount	Our Maximum Dollar Limit of Liability
Covered Risk 16:	% of Policy Amount Shown in Schedule A or $ (whichever is less)	$
Covered Risk 18:	% of Policy Amount Shown in Schedule A or $ (whichever is less)	$
Covered Risk 19:	% of Policy Amount Shown in Schedule A or $ (whichever is less)	$
Covered Risk 21:	% of Policy Amount Shown in Schedule A or $ (whichever is less)	$

Street Address of the Land:

1. Name of Insured:

2. Your interest in the Land covered by this Policy is:

3. The Land referred to in this Policy is described as:

FIGURE 5–1
(continued)

HOMEOWNER'S POLICY OF TITLE INSURANCE
For a one-to-four family residence
Issued By
BLANK TITLE INSURANCE COMPANY
SCHEDULE B
EXCEPTIONS

In addition to the Exclusions, You are not insured against loss, costs, attorneys' fees, and expenses resulting from:

The second one insures title to a lender (Mortgagee Policy) and remains in effect as long as the lender or their assignees own the loan. Here the lender receives assurances that its investment in title will be defended in the even of challenge. While the policy gives some piece of mind to lenders, it is always striking to see what policies except or refuse to extend protection to. The standard Lender policy will have a series of exceptions as evidenced by a stated Schedule. See Figure _____

EXCEPTIONS FROM COVERAGE AND
AFFIRMATIVE INSURANCES

Except to the extent of the affirmative insurance set forth below, this policy does not insure against loss or damage (and the Company will not pay costs, attorneys' fees, or expenses) which arise by reason of:

1. Those taxes and special assessments that become due or payable subsequent to Date of Policy. (This does not modify or limit the coverage provided in Covered Risk 11(b).)
2. Covenants, conditions, or restrictions, if any, appearing in the Public Records; however, this policy insures against loss or damage arising from:
   (a) the violation of those covenants, conditions, or restrictions on or prior to Date of Policy;
   (b) a forfeiture or reversion of Title from a future violation of those covenants, conditions, or restrictions, including those relating to environmental protection; and
   (c) provisions in those covenants, conditions, or restrictions, including those relating to environmental protection, under which the lien of the Insured Mortgage can be extinguished, subordinated, or impaired.
   As used in paragraph 2(a), the words "covenants, conditions, or restrictions" do not refer to or include any covenant, condition, or restriction (a) relating to obligations of any type to perform maintenance, repair or remediation on the Land, or (b) pertaining to environmental protection of any kind or nature, including hazardous or toxic matters, conditions, or substances, except to the extent that a notice of a violation or alleged violation affecting the Land has been recorded or filed in the Public Records at Date of Policy and is not referenced in an addendum attached to this policy.
3. Any easements or servitudes appearing in the Public Records; however, this policy insures against loss or damage arising from (a) the encroachment, at Date of Policy, of the improvements on any easement, and (b) any interference with or damage to existing improvements, including lawns, shrubbery, and trees, resulting from the use of the easements for the purposes granted or reserved.
4. Any lease, grant, exception, or reservation of minerals or mineral rights appearing in the Public Records; however, this policy insures against loss or damage arising from (a) any affect on or impairment of the use of the Land for residential one-to-four family dwelling purposes by reason of such lease, grant, exception or reservation of minerals or mineral rights, and (b) any damage to existing improvements, including lawns, shrubbery, and trees, resulting from the future exercise of any right to use the surface of the Land for the extraction or development of the minerals or mineral rights so leased, granted, excepted, or reserved. Nothing herein shall insure against loss or damage resulting from subsidence.

FIGURE 5–1
(continued)

Other policies can insure minerals, leasehold interests, airspace, easements, and other interests as approved.[6] In short, title companies tell buyers what they are buying and the seller what they are selling and provide varying levels of protection in the event of challenge. In the final analysis, a title company's level of insurance largely depends upon the quality of title. Discovering what that quality is remains a crucial paralegal responsibility.

II. TITLE ABSTRACTION

KEY WORDS

abstract of title   marketable title

free and clear   title defects

impediments

Only by abstracting a title can a paralegal indicate a title's quality. By an **abstract of title**, we mean the tracing of all previous owners in an unbroken chain of title and the identification of any liabilities, encumbrances, or liens that saddle the property in question. The paralegal essentially searches the history of the property. Abstraction requires the practitioner to be technically proficient, intellectually ordered, and have an eye for detail. The attorney and practitioner have to ensure the alienation and transfer of a good and marketable title. If it is not, documents, which highlight legal inadequacies, must be prepared.

Searching a title is a sometimes simple, sometimes complicated history of the ownership of a specific piece of land or realty, often extending back as far as the original owners of the land during America's colonial period.

A title in trouble has defects and impediments such as:

- Unsatisfied mortgages (satisfied mortgage needs documentation)
- Unsatisfied liens
- Judgments of courts of local or federal jurisdiction
- Federal tax claims
- Estate tax claims
- Corporate taxes
- Welfare liens
- Sales and use taxes
- Unemployment compensation contributions
- Personal income tax claims
- Use tax claims
- Inheritance and estate tax claims
- Real estate tax claims
- Municipal claims for services
- Municipal assessments
- Rights-of-way
- Building and use restrictions
- Easements

- Ground rents
- Leases
- Water rents
- *Lis Pendens* (notice of pending legal action)[7]

Defects in title can also result from technical errors, improper party designees, a lack of competency in the parties, or other public policy issues. **Title defects** are not strictly questions involving cost or economic burden but also include these issues:

- Mistakes in the interpretation of wills or other legal documents
- Impersonation of the owner
- Forged deeds, mortgage releases, and so on
- Instruments executed under expired powers of attorney
- Deeds delivered after death of seller or buyer
- Undisclosed or missing heirs
- Wills not probated
- Deeds or mortgages by those mentally incompetent or of minor age
- Birth or adoption of children after date of will
- Mistakes in the public records
- Falsified records
- Name confusion
- Transfer of title through foreclosure sale where requirements of foreclosure statute have not been adhered to

If no defects or **impediments** are found, the title is "**free and clear.**" If defects are identified, they must be corrected or resolved. Defects or impediments to a title result in the examiner's objections thereto. If the buyer wishes to go ahead despite the defects, the buyer should draft an addendum reflecting the fact that the seller has no liability for any defects of title. Minor, hypertechnical errors are curable and in certain jurisdictions, such as Rhode Island, serve as no basis for any serious impediment. A title is not defective or unmarketable by reason of:

1. Minor errors in area as referenced in the description; inaccuracies of distances between bounds; the omission of a bound or a repetition of a bound or incorrect bounds or courses or bearings in a description, where it can be readily discerned from a general review of the descriptions in the chain of title that the omissions or errors are clearly occasioned by mistake; or

2. The omission of, or an erroneous reference to, either the date or the record reference (but not both) to a mortgage in the case of an amendment, assignment, modifications, subordination, partial release, or discharge of such mortgage.

3. With respect to a lot on a recorded plat, minor inconsistencies in references to the name of the recorded plat, especially if the references to the book and page number where the plat map is recorded and/or the plat card number are correct.[8]

A good and marketable title frees itself from defects.

A marketable title, which a vendor of realty is ordinarily obligated to furnish to his or her purchaser, is one that is free from liens and encumbrances and which a reasonable purchaser, well informed as to the facts and their legal bearings, willing and ready to perform his or her contract, would, in the exercise of that prudence which business persons ordinarily bring to bear upon such transactions, be willing to accept and ought to accept. In other words, a marketable title is a title free from all reasonable doubt, though not necessarily from all possible doubt.[9]

Web Exercise

For an erudite review of how to resolve common title problems, see *www.texascbar.org/content/ legal_library/real_estate/downloads/titleproblems.pdf.*

A. Search Methods

Now that a good title has been adequately defined, some discussion of how to search titles is necessary. Title searches fall into two basic categories: conveyance and encumbrance. In the former, the paralegal traces the history of ownership and transfer. This is sometimes referred to as a "bring down," where the chain of title is assessed according to these elements:

1. Names of grantors and marital status
2. Names of grantees and marital status
3. Date of deed
4. Verification of the description of property on the deed
5. Tax stamps as required
6. Transfer stamps as required
7. Form and type of acknowledgment
8. Deed book volume and page references
9. Dates of recordation
10. Easements and restrictions
11. Any unusual features
12. Comparison of preceding deed
13. List of any defects or encumbrances throughout history[10]

Web Exercise

Searches can now be done electronically in many American jurisdictions. Visit Cook County, Illinois, at *www.ccrd.info/CCRD/il031/index.jsp.*

The second method looks to encumbrances, from mortgages to judgments, from tax liens to estate debts. A more focused view of both methods follows:

1. Conveyance Searches

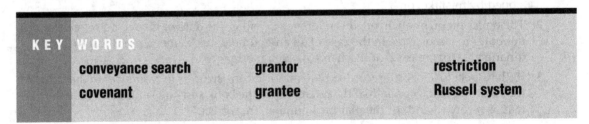

KEY WORDS

conveyance search	grantor	restriction
covenant	grantee	Russell system

The primary technique in the **conveyance search** is to look at the **grantor** (seller) and **grantee** (buyer) index, or, in the alternative, the grantee/grantor index. These are generally interchangeable sources in most jurisdictions. Grantor and grantee indexes are located at the office of the Recorder of Deeds or other governmental office. Deeds are indexed twice, in both the grantor and the grantee indexes. Ladner's treatise on conveyances explains this method thoroughly, though the student is cautioned that local differences abound.

The grantor index is a series of books (each series covering deeds recorded during one or more designated years), one book for each letter of the alphabet, one book for corporations, and one book for each of several names or parts of names (such as "Smith," "Mc," etc.) that are numerous. Each book is divided into twenty-six subdivisions, each subdivision being lettered, in alphabetical order beginning with "A." The first letter of the grantor's surname determines the book in which his name is to be found, and the first letter of his Christian name determines the subdivision of the book. Thus, the name Andrew Gallagher would be found in the index book for "G," in the subdivision "A." In the subdivision will be found the name of every grantor (for the period covered by the book) whose last name begins with "G" and whose first name begins with "A." The searcher must look through those names until he comes to the one he seeks.

    The first column shows the date (month and day) when the deed was recorded. At the top of the page is the year and, in Philadelphia, the initials of the Recorder of Deeds (now Commissioner of Records) at that time. Then follows the book number and page where the deed is recorded (i.e., copied), the surname and first name of the grantor, and finally the name of the grantee. The arrangement of the grantee *(ad sectum)* index is virtually the same except that the grantee's name is the one that is indexed and appears before the name of the grantor . . . .[11]

Mortgage and judgment books follow exactly the same method of grantor/grantee indexes.

    Thus, the indices refer to specific deed volumes and pages. In fact, look closely at the most recent deed to which you have access. It will refer to a former deed book that traces the previous recording. In other words, if you have the most recent deed, you can start your trek back in time. For two checklists that aid the paralegal employing the grantor/grantee method, see Figures 5–2 and 5–3.[12]

    A slightly more complicated conveyancing approach is the **Russell system**. The method is summarized as follows:

This system is based on the fact that most last names contain one or more of the letters, L, M, N, R, and T. Under this system a corporation is searched by means of the first word in the name of the corporation in most cases, except where the first word is an article or a proper name. The corporation index is located at the end of the particular volume or volumes if there is more than one volume for a particular last name letter.

    To search an individual's name, for example "John Smith," one would go first to the index for the volume for the letter "S." Then the volume containing the first names beginning with "J" would be consulted. On the inside front cover of each volume is a key or chart. From left to right at the top are the initials of the first name. Vertically at the left are listed the key letters of the surname. Since the name "Smith" contains the key letters "M" and "T," one would look for the key letters "MT" in the "J" column, which will show a page reference in the particular volume. Each such major page reference is subdivided, commencing with Subpage 1 and continuing as needed.

    Generally, on the first page of each major page number, there will be an initial list of the most common names. Thus, since Smith is a common name, there would be in this initial list a reference to the name "Smith," with particular subpages where all the transactions under the name "Smith" are located. The purpose of this is to make the search somewhat easier by locating the same last names in groups. The actual index entries are made chronologically, so that all the subpages under the major page headings, or at least those subpages devoted to the particular name, must be checked. Generally, the name being searched will be located in the left-hand column of the index page. Other columns will give book and page references to the documents desired and the recording date of the instrument or judgment. Also, very often one column will indicate the nature of the paper, such as a deed, lease or agreement, and the location of the property in question. In addition, the other parties involved in a transaction are also listed in a separate column. For example, if one is searching the grantor, there will be a column listing the grantee.[13]

TITLE EXAMINATION ABSTRACT OF CONVEYANCE

City/County: _____

Deed Book: _____

Dated: _____

Acknowledged: _____

Recorded: _____

Consideration: $_____

Grantor(s): _____

Covenants: G/W _____ M/E _____ S/W: _____

Signed and Sealed: _____

Grantee(s): _____

CONVEYS: (Note estate, if it is less than entire fee.)

_____

Page: _____

FIGURE 5–2

Conveyance searches focus on the content of deeds. Within the language of deed documents are **restrictions**, **covenants**, and other impacts that affect good, marketable title. Some of the areas to emphasize are:

- Encroachments
- Defective deed language
- Easements
- Mineral rights
- Well rights
- Estate and heir claims
- Use restrictions
- Restrictive covenants
- Leases
- Oil and gas rights
- Rights-of-way
- Privileges

TITLE SEARCH

File No. ______________

1. Client: ____________________

2. Current Owners (as title is vested): ____________________

3. Brief Property Description: ____

4. County taxes paid through: ______________

City or Town of ______________ Taxes paid through: ______________

See attached tax sheet for listing information.

5. Res. Cov.: Book __________ Page __________ Date of Recording __________

Amended: Book __________ Page __________ Date of Recording __________
Amended: Book __________ Page __________ Date of Recording __________
Set back: ________________________________
Set front: ________________________________
Set side: ________________________________
Set rear: ________________________________
Set Utility Easements: ______________________
Set: ____________________________________

6. Map Information: __________

Book/Cabinet: __________ Page/Slide: __________
Set Back: ________________________________
Front: __________________________________
Rear: __________________________________
Side: __________________________________
Easements: ______________________________
Does survey match plat? __________

7. Means of Access: ________________________

8. U.C.C.s: (only HHG or fixture filings)—None

FIGURE 5–3

2. Encumbrance Searches

KEY WORD

encumbrance search **judgment** **mechanic's lien**

While conveyance searches deal with rights and restrictions in the use and ownership of real property and the language of deeds and ownership, **encumbrance searches** cover external interests or claims exerted against the real property. For example, when creditor A sues in small claims court for $5,000 of goods and receives a **judgment**, in the absence of other available assets to execute upon, a judgment can be recorded against a debtor's or defendant's home. This judgment is called an *encumbrance*.

Encumbrance searches look for defects or impediments based on these categories:

- Mortgages
- Judgments of the state supreme court (or other court)
- Federal court judgments and federal liens
- Judgments of the criminal courts and road damages awards
- Judgments, mechanics' liens, and possible revival of liens of debts of decedents
- Municipal liens and taxes
- Pending actions affecting the title
- Federal tax liens
- Sheriff's sales
- Liens of debts of or claims against decedent
- If any corporation has been in title, a search should be ordered to determine what, if any, taxes are due by the corporation, assessed for the period during which it held title, are still unpaid
- Obtain affidavit and receipts and so forth, to protect against possible unfiled tax, municipal and mechanics' liens and liens for inheritance and federal estate taxes.[14]

Some particularized attention of these encumbrances follows:

a. Mortgages   The most commonly encountered encumbrance is a mortgage, whether a first or second, equity loans, or lines of credit. Unsatisfied mortgages are plainly impediments to free alienation. Utilize the *Direct Mortgage Index,* usually located in the office of the Recorder of Deeds to identify claims. If a mortgage has been paid, prepare and submit to the lender a mortgage satisfaction piece.

b. Federal Taxes   The local prothonotary or Recorder of Deeds office will have an index of federal lien notices. Additionally, any lawsuits filed in conjunction with these taxes will be docketed at the U.S. district court.

c. Local Taxes   Depending on your county, there may or may not be access to delinquent tax rolls or the lien list. Check with the recorder, prothonotary, or responsible tax authority. Pay close attention to water bureau fees or other special assessments, occupational privilege, or property tax liens. Tax certifications symbolizing timely payment are generally submitted at closing. Before initiating a closing, the paralegal or other practitioner will verify tax payment status and the existence of ongoing tax liens with local officials.

d. Judgments   Local and state rules govern the method of recording judgments. Actions in the courts of common pleas or other general trial courts are the most likely location for filed and recorded judgments. The prothonotary's office actually compiles and maintains a judgment index. Such an entry may appear as follows:

Defendant	Plaintiff	Court	Term	No.	Atty.	Date	Amount
Gallagher Andrew J.	Robinson	1	J.58	1478	Smith	06/09/58	$2,000

If the judgment has been paid, released, or otherwise satisfied, the fact and date of it would be noted or impressed in some fashion.

Please be aware that the judgment index can be unreliable. This author conducted a recent search, finding $68,000 of hospital bills, with a judgment applied against specific real property still appearing, yet satisfied twenty years earlier. Any existing and unremoved judgments should cause the preparation of a release. See Form 8–3 in Chapter 8, Closing and Settlement.

e. Mechanic's Liens Perusal of the judgment index may also reveal filed **mechanic's liens**. "A mechanic's lien against property to be conveyed may constitute such an encumbrance entitling a buyer under a contract for purchase free and clear of encumbrances to cancel the transaction."[15] Disgruntled and unpaid contractors usually trigger mechanic's liens. But watch out for the rights of suppliers, who can do the same.[16]

CASE DECISION

For a case fraught with impediments and defects in the real estate transfer, read Hahn.

Hahn v. Love (Tex.App.- Houston [1st Dist.] Nov. 6, 2008)(Keyes)

REVERSE TC JUDGMENT AND REMAND CASE TO TC FOR FURTHER PROCEEDINGS:

Opinion by Justice Keyes

Before Chief Justice Radack, Justices Keyes and Higley

01-07-00096-CV Allon R. Hahn, Individually and d/b/a *Hahn's Gulf Service v. Bertrand Love*

Appeal from 157th District Court of Harris County

Trial Court Judge: Hon. Ronald L. Wilson

OPINION

Appellee Bertrand R. Love, the purchaser of a property located in Harris County, Texas, intervened in a lawsuit between appellant, Allon R. Hahn, individually and d/b/a Hahn's Gulf Service (collectively, "Hahn"), and Mid-Town Roofing and Construction Inc. ("Mid-Town"), seeking to enjoin Hahn from carrying out an execution sale on the property to satisfy a judgment lien against a third-party, O'Neal Session, and to remove Hahn's claims as a cloud on the title. The trial court granted Love's motion for summary judgment, removing Hahn's claims as a cloud on Love's title and dismissing Hahn's counterclaims for fraudulent transfer and constructive trust against Love. Hahn appeals, contending in five issues that (1) a general warranty deed transferring the property from Session to Mid-Town, dated April 2002, after the expiration of Hahn's judgment lien, and recorded January 2004, two days prior to revival of the judgment, is void as a matter of law because the description of the land is legally inadequate; (2) Hahn's second abstract of judgment, filed in March 2004, after his revival of the judgment, attached to the property because no prior valid deed transferred the property from Session; (3) genuine issues of material fact exist as to whether Session fraudulently conveyed the property to Mid-Town and as to Love's good faith and notice of the alleged fraudulent transfer when he purchased the property in April 2004, hence as to Love's entitlement to summary judgment on Hahn's fraudulent transfer claims against him and on Love's suit to remove the cloud from his title; (4) a legal basis for a constructive trust exists against Love; and (5) the trial court erred in permitting Love to file his motion for summary judgment after the deadline in the docket control order had passed.

We reverse and remand.

Background

On October 20, 1988, Hahn won a judgment against O'Neal Session, C. J. Foreman, and Roofs by C. J., jointly and severally, for $77,136.05 plus interest. On April 16, 1992, Hahn filed an abstract

---

(continued)

of judgment, but the defendants in the 1988 judgment had no assets to seize at that time. Then, in August 2001, the property that is the subject of this suit was conveyed to O'Neal Session. (1) Hahn's judgment lien automatically attached to the property by virtue of a properly recorded and indexed abstract of judgment. (2) Hahn's judgment lien expired on April 16, 2002, however, and his judgment against Session, Foreman, and Roofs by C. J. became dormant. (3) On April 26, 2002, ten days after Hahn's judgment lien expired, Session purportedly conveyed the property to Mid-Town, an entity that Hahn contends is owned and operated by members of Session's immediate family, specifically Pamela Session and Toshoner Session Egans. This transfer was not recorded until January 2004.

In August 2003, after the purported execution of the 2002 deed conveying the property to Mid-Town, O'Neal Session and his wife Myria entered into a contract to sell the property to Walter Strickland for $350,000. Real estate broker Herman Gary was involved in this deal on behalf of Strickland, the purchaser. The deal to sell the property to Strickland fell through on December 2, 2003, when Fidelity National Title Company sent the title commitment to Session and Strickland and requested payoff of Hahn's judgment lien and the Sessions refused to pay the amount of the judgment lien from the proceeds.

On December 10, 2003, Hahn filed a motion to revive his judgment against Session and sent notice of the hearing to the Sessions.

On January 7, the Sessions and Strickland signed another earnest money contract to convey the property to Strickland for $450,000 and delivered the contract to American Title for closing. This time, Gary acted as broker on behalf of the Sessions.

On January 21, 2004, a General Warranty Deed reflecting the conveyance of the property from Session to Mid-Town on April 26, 2002 was recorded (the "2002 deed"). That deed lacked a metes-and-bounds description of the property.

Two days later, on January 23, 2004, following a hearing, Hahn obtained an order for the revival of his 1988 judgment against O'Neal Session, C.J. Foreman, and Roofs by C.J. (4) Hahn's lawyer testified by affidavit:

I filed the motion to revive the judgment and served scire facias on Mr. O'Neal Session by Certified Mail, Return Receipt Requested . . . . On the date of the hearing before Judge Ken Wise, Mr. Session, Pamela Session, and [her lawyer] appeared and asked the Judge for more time to respond to the motion. They did not announce that two days before they [had] recorded a deed of the subject property from the Sessions to Mid-Town dated almost two years earlier.

On March 1, 2004, Hahn filed for record a second abstract of judgment, again listing O'Neal Session, C. J. Foreman, and Roofs by C. J. as the judgment debtors and creating a judgment lien against their real property.

On March 3, 2004, two days after Hahn refiled his abstract of judgment against O'Neal Session, Session filed a correction deed to clarify the April 26, 2002 conveyance of the property from himself to Mid-Town.

The correction deed added a metes and bounds description of the property. In support of his motion for summary judgment, Love testified by affidavit that "shortly before April 14, 2004" he received a telephone call from Gary, the real estate broker who had initially represented Strickland and then the Sessions in the two attempted 2003 sales of the property by the Sessions to Strickland. Gary indicated that the property was available for purchase and that Love "would have to act relatively fast because the initial purchaser under a contract could not qualify to close and the contract was about to expire." Love further testified by affidavit that, "[a]ccording to Mr. Gary, if [the contract expired] then the property would go back on the market." Love testified by affidavit that, based on the success of his past dealings with Gary, he was interested in the investment opportunity and that he proceeded to purchase the property. Love sent a cashier's check for $448,587.13 to American Title Company, and Gary took the necessary closing documents for Love to sign in New Orleans, Louisiana.

A few days later, on April 14, 2004, the transaction closed, and Mid-Town executed a deed that conveyed the property to Love. This deed was recorded on April 16, 2004.

In August 2004, Hahn attempted to proceed with an execution sale of the property to satisfy his judgment against Session. Mid-Town sued Hahn, seeking a temporary restraining order and a temporary and permanent injunction prohibiting the execution sale of the property. Love intervened in the suit, seeking an injunction prohibiting the sale of the property and seeking to remove the cloud from his title.

Hahn filed counterclaims against Mid-Town and Love and a third-party action against Session, his wife Myria Mae Session, and other members of the Session family, Pamela Session and Toshoner Session Egans, seeking a declaratory judgment that he had a valid lien against the property. Specifically, Hahn asked for a judgment declaring (1) that the conveyances of the property from Session to Mid-Town and from Mid-Town to Love were both void as fraudulent conveyances under Chapter 24 of the Texas Business and Commerce Code; (2) that the March 1, 2004 judgment lien attached to the property because the 2002 deed was void for lack of a sufficient legal description at the time the second abstract of judgment was filed for record; and (3) that the April 14, 2004, conveyance of the property from Mid-Town to Love was subject to Hahn's judgment lien and to the imposition of a constructive trust because Love was not a bona fide purchaser for value, in good faith, and without notice of Hahn's interest in the property. Hahn also sought an execution sale to satisfy the judgment lien and a money judgment for assets that had been fraudulently transferred.

On July 11, 2005, Love filed a motion for summary judgment, which he supplemented on May 12, 2006. On June 2, 2006, Love filed an amended motion for summary judgment, requesting that the trial court remove Hahn's claims as a cloud on Love's title to the property and that Hahn take nothing against him. Love contended that "no judgment lien existed that attached to the Property at the time Love acquired it" or thereafter. Rather, he contended that he took the property by a general warranty deed from Mid-Town, which had taken the property in 2002 by a valid general warranty deed unencumbered by Hahn's judgment lien, which had expired, and, therefore, the cloud on his title should be removed and he should be dismissed from the suit. Love also claimed that he was entitled as a matter of law to summary judgment on Hahn's fraudulent transfer claims and to removal of the cloud from his title because he was a bona fide purchaser of the property for value, in good faith, and without notice under section 24.009(a) of the Texas Business and Commerce Code (5) and under section 13.001 of the Property Code. (6) Therefore, Hahn was entitled to take nothing from him with respect to those claims.

Love's motion for summary judgment was filed as both a traditional and no-evidence motion for summary judgment. The trial court granted Love's motion for summary judgment on July 6, 2006. On January 12, 2007, the trial court severed the claims between Hahn and Love from the rest of the case, making the summary judgment in Love's favor final and appealable. This appeal of the trial court's July 2006 court order granting Love's motion for summary judgment followed.

Standard of Review

We review de novo the trial court's grant of summary judgment. *Provident Life & Accident Ins. Co. v. Knott*, 128 S.W.3d 211, 215 (Tex. 2003). We must make inferences, resolve doubts, and view the evidence in the light most favorable to the nonmovant. *Rhône-Poulenc Inc. v. Steel*, 997 S.W.2d 217, 223 (Tex. 1999). Love's motion for summary judgment contained both traditional and no-evidence grounds for summary judgment. See Tex. R. Civ. P. 166a(c), (i). A traditional summary judgment under Rule of Civil Procedure 166a(c) is properly granted only when the movant establishes that there are no genuine issues of material fact and that he is entitled to judgment as a matter of law. Tex. R. Civ. P. 166a(c); Knott, 128 S.W.3d at 215-16. Summary judgment is proper on claims for which the movant is the defendant only when the movant negates at least one element of each of the plaintiff's causes of action or when the movant conclusively establishes each element of an affirmative defense. *Science Spectrum Inc. v. Martinez*, 941 S.W.2d 910, 911 (Tex. 1997); see also *Rhone-Poulenc Inc. v. Steel*, 997 S.W.2d 217, 223 (Tex. 1999). If the movant conclusively negates an element of each of the plaintiff's causes of action or conclusively establishes its own cause of action the burden shifts to the nonmovant to respond with evidence raising a genuine issue of material fact that would preclude

(continued)

summary judgment. See Rhone-Poulenc, 997 S.W.2d at 222-23. In deciding whether there is a disputed material fact precluding summary judgment, evidence favorable to the nonmovant will be taken as true, every reasonable inference must be indulged in favor of the nonmovant, and any doubts must be resolved in favor of the nonmovant. Knott, 128 S.W.3d at 215.

A no-evidence summary judgment motion asserts that no evidence exists as to at least one essential element of the nonmovant's claims on which the nonmovant would have the burden of proof at trial. *Bendigo v. City of Houston*, 178 S.W.3d 112, 114 (Tex. App.–Houston [1st Dist.] 2005, no pet.) (citing *Jackson v. Fiesta Mart Inc.*, 979 S.W.2d 68, 70-71 (Tex. App.–Austin 1998, no pet.)). The trial court must grant the motion unless the nonmovant produces summary judgment evidence that raises a genuine issue of material fact. Tex. R. Civ. P. 166a(i); *Southwest Elec. Power Co. v. Grant*, 73 S.W.3d 211, 215 (Tex. 2002). The movant "must be specific in challenging the evidentiary support for an element of a claim or defense; paragraph (i) does not authorize conclusory motions or general no-evidence challenges to an opponent's case." Tex. R. Civ. P. 166a(i), 1997 cmt.; *Mott v. Red's Safe and Lock Servs. Inc.*, 249 S.W.3d 90, 97 (Tex. App.–Houston [1st Dist.] 2007, no pet.). Moreover, "[p]aragraph (i) does not apply to ordinary motions for summary judgment under paragraphs (a) or (b), in which the movant must prove that it is entitled to summary judgment by establishing each element of its claim or defense as a matter of law." Tex. R. Civ. P. 166a(i), 1997 cmt.; *Brown v. Hearthwood II Owner's Ass'n. Inc.*, 201 S.W.3d 153, 157-58 & n.7 (Tex. App.–Houston [14th Dist.] 2006, pet. denied).

In his amended motion for summary judgment, Love failed to identify any specific element of any of Hahn's claims on which Hahn had the burden of proof and had produced no evidence. Therefore, we dismiss Love's no-evidence motion for summary judgment as conclusory and address only his traditional motion for summary judgment. See Tex. R. Civ. P. 166a(i), 1997 cmt.; Brown, 201 S.W.3d at 157-58 & n.7. When, as here, a trial court's order granting summary judgment does not specify the grounds relied upon, we affirm the summary judgment if any of the summary judgment grounds is meritorious. FM Props. *Operating Co. v. City of Austin*, 22 S.W.3d 868, 872-73 (Tex. 2000).

Love's Right to Summary Judgment on Hahn's Claims Under the Fraudulent Transfer Act and Love's Suit to Remove the Cloud from His Title.

In his second and third issues, Hahn argues that Love was not entitled to summary judgment because Love did not prove as a matter of law either (1) that the conveyances of the property to Mid-Town and to Love were not fraudulent or (2) that Love himself was a bona fide purchaser of the property for value without notice and in good faith. We address these issues together with respect to both Hahn's fraudulent transfer claims and Love's suit to remove the cloud from his title.

1. Hahn's Claims Under the Fraudulent Transfer Act

Love was awarded summary judgment on Hahn's claims against him under the Fraudulent Transfer Act on the ground that he was entitled to the bona fide purchaser defense in the Act set out at section 24.009(a) of the Business and Commerce Code. See Tex. Bus. & Com. Code Ann. § 24.009(a) (Vernon 2002). Section 24.009(a) states that a "transfer or obligation is not voidable under Section 24.005(a)(1) of this code against a person who took in good faith and for a reasonably equivalent value or against any subsequent transferee or obligee." *Id.*

Fraudulent Transfer

A fraudulent transfer is a transfer by a debtor with the intent to hinder, delay, or defraud his creditors by placing the debtor's property beyond the creditor's reach. Tex. Bus. & Com. Code Ann. § 24.005(a)(1) (Vernon 2002) ("A transfer made or obligation incurred by a debtor is fraudulent as to a creditor, whether the creditor's claim arose before or within a reasonable time after the transfer was made or the obligation was incurred, if the debtor made the transfer or incurred the obligation . . . with actual intent to hinder, delay, or defraud any creditor of the debtor."); *Nobles v. Marcus*, 533 S.W.2d 923, 925 (Tex. 1976).

The actual intent to defraud is shown, among other things, by evidence that the transfer was made to an insider, including a relative; the transfer was concealed; the debtor was sued or threatened with suit before the transfer and the value of the consideration received by the debtor was reasonably equivalent to the value of the asset transferred; the debtor was insolvent; and the transfer occurred shortly before or after a substantial debt was incurred. Tex. Bus. & Com. Code Ann. § 24.005(b) (Vernon 2002). A transfer to an insider is one of the factors in proving actual intent to defraud under the Fraudulent Transfer Act. See Tex. Bus. & Com. Code Ann. § 24.005(b)(1) (listing factors). (7)

The facts and circumstances set out in section 24.005(b) that may be considered in determining fraudulent intent are nonexclusive and are considered mere "badges of fraud." *Flores v. Robinson Roofing & Const. Co. Inc.*, 161 S.W.3d 750, 755 (Tex. App.–Fort Worth 2005, pet. denied). Therefore, because "'fraudulent intent is only to be deduced from facts and circumstances which the law considers as mere badges of fraud, and not fraud per se, these must be submitted to the trier of fact, which draws the inference as to the fairness or fraudulent character of the transaction.'" *Id.* (quoting *Coleman Cattle Co. Inc. v. Carpentier*, 10 S.W.3d 430, 433 (Tex. App.–Beaumont 2000, no pet.); see also *Quinn v. Dupree*, 157 Tex. 441, 303 S.W.3d 769, 774 (1957). Thus, "[t]he question of whether a debtor conveyed property with the intent to defraud creditors is 'ordinarily a question for the jury or the court passing on the fact'" Flores, 161 S.W.3d at 755 (quoting *Spoljaric v. Percival Tours Inc.*, 708 S.W.2d 432, 434 (Tex. 1986)); see also *Equitable Trust Co. v. Roland*, 644 S.W.3d 46, 51 (Tex. App.–San Antonio 1982, writ ref'd n.r.e.) (pointing out that trial court's decision to grant instructed verdict on fraudulent conveyance issues "was in contradiction of the general rule that the existence of a fraudulent conveyance is a question for the trier of the facts"). (8) "Intent is a fact question uniquely within the realm of the trier of fact because it so depends upon the credibility of the witnesses and the weight to be given to their testimony." Flores, 161 S.W.3d at 755.

If intent to defraud is proved, a creditor may obtain "avoidance of the transfer or obligation to the extent necessary to satisfy the creditor's claim," "an attachment or other provisional remedy," "an injunction against further disposition by the debtor or a transferee, or both, of the asset transferred," or "any other relief the circumstances may require." Tex. Bus. & Com. Code Ann. § 24.008(a) (Vernon 2002). Also, "If a creditor has obtained a judgment on a claim against the debtor, the creditor, if the court so orders, may levy execution on the asset transferred or its proceeds." *Id.* § 24.008(b).

Bona Fide Purchaser Defense

The remedies provided creditors by the Act are, however, subject to the limitation in Section 24.009 of the Business and Commerce Code, providing for a bona fide purchaser defense. Specifically, section 24.009(a) of the Act states that a "transfer or obligation is not voidable under Section 24.005(a)(1) of this code against a person who took in good faith and for a reasonably equivalent value or against any subsequent transferee or obligee." *Id.* § 24.009(a) (Vernon 2002). Good faith is thus an affirmative defense to a fraudulent transfer claim. Flores, 161 S.W.3d at 756. A person who invokes that affirmative defense "carries the burden of establishing good faith and the reasonable equivalence of the consideration obtained." *Id.* (quoting Uniform Fraudulent Transfer Act § 8 cmt. 1, 7A II U.L.A. 352 (1999)). Thus, in seeking summary judgment on his bona fide purchaser affirmative defense, Love had the burden to prove as a matter of law that he took the property in good faith. See Flores, 161 S.W.3d at 756; Rhone-Poulenc, 997 S.W.2d at 223. (9) To defeat summary judgment based on such proof, Hahn had to raise a material fact issue on Love's good faith. See Rhone-Poulenc, 997 S.W.2d at 222-23.

A transferee who takes property with knowledge of such facts as would excite the suspicions of a person of ordinary prudence and put him on inquiry of the fraudulent nature of an alleged transfer does not take the property in good faith and is not a bona fide purchaser. See *Wright v. Lynn*, 16 Tex. 34, 1856 WL 4851, at *5 (Tex. 1856) (holding that lack of good faith is proved by any "competent means, which affords any fair presumption or inferences as to the real object and intention of the parties, tending to show knowledge of "the fraudulent acts and intentions of the [transferor]"); *First S. Props. Inc. v. Gregory*, 538 S.W.2d 454, 457-58 (Tex. Civ. App. 1976) (holding that transferee without actual or constructive notice of circumstances tending to show fraudulent intent of transferor is bona

(continued)

fide purchaser); see also Flores, 161 S.W.3d at 756 (defining good faith as lack of awareness of transferor's intent). Notice of fraudulent intent can be either actual or constructive. See *Madison v. Gordon*, 39 S.W.3d 604, 606 (Tex. 2001); First S. Props., 538 S.W.2d at 457-58. Actual notice results from personal information or knowledge; constructive notice is notice the law imputes to a person not having personal information or knowledge. Madison, 39 S.W.3d at 606; see *Carr v. Hunt*, 651 S.W.2d 875, 880 (Tex. App.–Dallas 1983, writ ref'd n.r.e.) (finding no notice of actual knowledge of fraudulent acts or facts that would have put purchaser of property on further inquiry as to possible claims of fraud). The question of whether a party has notice is a "question of fact which is foreclosed by the judgment of the trier of the facts; it becomes a question of law only when there is no room for ordinary minds to differ as to the proper conclusion to be drawn from the evidence." *O'Ferral v. Coolidge*, 228 S.W.2d 146, 148 (Tex. 1950). Thus a transferor's notice of fraudulent intent is a question of fact that generally goes to the jury. See Wright, 1856 WL 4851, at *5 (because proof positive of actual knowledge of purchaser of property and fraudulent acts of vendor could seldom be obtained, evidence conducing to prove fraudulent intent should have been permitted to go to jury to decide whether assignment was fraudulent and whether purchaser "was party to and affected by the attempted fraud of his vendor"); see also *Hardy Road 13.4 Joint Venture v. Med. Ctr. Bank*, 867 S.W.2d 889, 893 (Tex. App.–Houston [1st Dist.] 1993, writ denied) (noting that whether or not party had notice of title issues is generally fact issue and thus is inappropriate for resolution by summary judgment).

Application of the Law

The evidence shows that this case is no exception to the rule that fraudulent transfer and bona fide purchaser status are generally questions for the trier of fact that are inappropriate for summary judgment.

Love stated in his motion for summary judgment and in his affidavit that he purchased the property for nearly $450,000. Hahn does not dispute Love's summary judgment evidence that Love paid a reasonably equivalent value for the property. However, Love also had to prove that he was a purchaser in good faith as a matter of law and was, therefore, entitled to summary judgment on Hahn's claims.

Love argues that the alleged legal sufficiency of the 2002 deed proves that Mid-Town became the true owner of the property in 2002, when there was no judgment lien against Session attached to the property. Therefore, Love argues that the property was clear of Hahn's lien when Session sold it to his predecessor, Mid-Town, which validly conveyed it to him in April 2004. (10) The lien Hahn filed on the revived judgment in March 2004 was invalid because Session had sold the property when there was no judgment lien encumbering it, and therefore Love was not on notice of a valid lien. Love also states that he did not have actual or constructive knowledge of any intent to defraud in the transfer of the property from Session to Mid-Town or from Mid-Town to himself.

The only evidence Love presented to prove his lack of notice of Hahn's claim was his own affidavit. In his affidavit, Love testified that at the time he purchased the property he did not know O'Neal Session, Pamela Session, Toshoner Session Egans, or Hahn and did not know anything about Mid-Town except that it was the owner of the property. Love testified, "Shortly before April 14, 2004, I received a telephone call from Herman Gary. Herman Gary is a local realtor in Houston who I have known for several years. In the past I have invested in real estate in Houston and have utilized Mr. Gary on several occasions." Gary stated "that the property in question in this lawsuit was available for purchase and that it represented a good perspective [sic] investment," and he "indicated that I would have to act relatively fast because the initial purchaser under a contract could not qualify to close and the contract was about to expire." Love averred that he "purchased the property in good faith, for a valuable consideration and had no knowledge of any claim by Hahn whatsoever."

However, in tension with his claim in his affidavit that he "had no knowledge of any claim by Hahn whatsoever," Love also pled in his motion for summary judgment that Hahn had alleged that "Love's father was a close personal friend of Herman Gary, the real estate broker, that Love had known Gary for 20 years and that Gary brought him many deals," that he, Love, "had loaned Gary and Strickland [the initial intended buyer of the property] money on prior occasions" and that "Strickland bought other property from Love on prior occasions." Love stated that because of the success of his past dealings with Gary, he was interested in the investment opportunity and proceeded to purchase the property by sending a cashier's check for $448,587.13 to American Title Company–the same title company for the attempted sale of the property to Strickland as well as to Love–and that Gary took the necessary closing documents for Love to sign in New Orleans, Louisiana. (11)

The Texas Rules of Civil Procedure provide that a summary judgment "may be based on uncontroverted testimonial evidence of an interested witness... if the evidence is clear, positive and direct, otherwise credible and free from contradictions and inconsistencies, and could have been readily controverted." Tex. R. Civ. P. 166a(c). Love's testimony is "clear, positive and direct," but it is not "otherwise credible and free from contradictions and inconsistences" with regard to Love's claimed lack of "knowledge of any claim by Hahn whatsoever." Rather, Love acknowledged that he had past real estate deals with Gary, a realtor whom he had known for "several" years, and he acknowledged in his motion for summary judgment that Hahn had claimed that Love "had loaned Gary and Strickland (the initial intended buyer of the property) money on prior occasions," and that "Strickland bought other property from Love on prior occasions," while he also stated in his affidavit in support of that motion that he knew from Gary that he had "to act relatively fast because the initial purchaser under a contract could not qualify to close and the contract was about to expire."

In addition to Love's own averrals regarding his relationship with both Gary and Strickland, Hahn produced evidence of numerous facts raising an inference of fraudulent conveyance and of Love's actual or constructive knowledge of fraudulent intent in the transfers of the property, including the following:

- The 2002 deed from O'Neal Session to Mid-Town, an alleged insider corporation controlled by Session's daughter and/or granddaughter occurred immediately after Hahn's original judgment lien on the property expired, yet it was not recorded until 2004, well after the second judgment lien on the property naming O'Neal Session as the debtor had attached.
- After the purported execution of the 2002 deed, O'Neal Session and his wife Myria—not Mid-Town—executed an earnest money contract on or about August 29, 2003, to convey the property to Strickland; Gary was the realtor who represented Strickland. O'Neal and Myria delivered the contract to Fidelity National Title Company. Fidelity asked for a judgment payoff for Hahn's outstanding judgment lien. O'Neal and Myria announced withdrawal and cancellation of the contract for sale to Strickland on December 2, 2003.
- Hahn filed a motion to revive his judgment and lien a week later on December 10, 2003 and served scire facias on O'Neal Session.
- About January 7, 2004, O'Neal and Myria signed another earnest money contract for conveyance of the property to Strickland for $405,000. This time Gary was the realtor for O'Neal and Myria Session.
- On January 21, 2004, two days before the hearing on revival of the judgment, Pamela Session, recorded the 2002 deed conveying the Property to Mid-Town, with its allegedly defective legal description.
- On January 23, 2004, Hahn's judgment was revived, and he filed an abstract of judgment listing O'Neal Session as the debtor on March 1, 2004.
- O'Neal and Myria Session filed a correction deed in the transfer of the property from them to Mid-Town on March 15, 2004.
- On April 14, 2004, Mid-Town conveyed the property to Love by general warranty deed pursuant to an earnest money contract that identified the sellers of the property as O'Neal and Myria. This time Gary served as the broker for Love, who, by his own admission, had known Gary and Strickland well for a long time and had done deals with them. No distribution of the proceeds of the sale was made to Hahn, despite his judgment lien against Session.

Hahn points out that Gary, the broker who acted as Love's agent for the purchase of the property, had previously acted in the first abortive attempted sale of the property to Strickland in 2003 as the broker for Strickland and in the second abortive sale in January 2004 as the broker for both Strickland and the judgment debtor Session. The summary judgment record also reflects that both attempted sales

(*continued*)

by Session to Strickland in 2003 took place after the property was purportedly conveyed from Session to Mid-Town in 2002, and both attempted sales took place before the purported 2002 deed was recorded. It further reflects that the 2002 deed was recorded after Session received notice of Hahn's suit to revive his judgment lien and that, similarly, the correction deed was filed after Hahn's abstract of judgment lien against Session had been refiled in March 2002.

Gary as the broker for Love, Strickland, and Session in the three transactions necessarily had notice of each of these facts, as well as of both attempts by Session to sell the property to Strickland after the property was purportedly conveyed to Mid-Town in 2002, and, therefore, of Hahn's interest in the property. These facts, as well as Love's own statements and his adoption of the facts stated in Hahn's pleadings, are inconsistent with Love's claim that he had "no knowledge of any claim by Hahn whatsoever," since he acknowledged that he knew about a prior contract for the sale of the property that had not gone through—namely, the prior contract between Session and Strickland, the "initial purchaser"—and that he had known both the broker Gary and Strickland for years and had done real estate deals with them and loaned them money. (12)

The close nature of Love's long-standing business relationship with Gary and Strickland and the nature of Gary's obligations to Love as his broker raise fact questions as to whether Love had either actual or constructive notice that the Sessions' conveyance of the property to Mid-Town was fraudulent and that Mid-Town might not have a clear title to the property. See *Janes v. CPR Corp.*, 623 S.W.2d 733, 740 (Tex. App.–Houston [1st Dist.] 1981, no writ) ("A broker is a fiduciary required to exercise fidelity in good faith toward his principal in all matters within the scope of his employment. . . . This requirement not only forbids conduct on the part of the broker which is fraudulent or adverse to his client's interest, but also imposes upon him the positive duty of communicating all information he may possess or acquire which is, or may be, material to his employer's advantage.").

Because there are fact questions both as to whether the transfer of the property to Love was fraudulent and as to Love's actual or constructive notice of facts and circumstances indicating the intent to defraud for purposes of the Fraudulent Transfer Act, we hold that Love failed to establish his entitlement to summary judgment on his bona fide purchaser affirmative defense under section 24.009(a) of the Texas Business and Commerce Code. We sustain Hahn's second and third issues insofar as they relate to Hahn's fraudulent transfer claims.

2. Love's Right to Summary Judgment on his Suit to Remove Cloud on Title Hahn also contends that material fact issues precluded summary judgment on Love's suit to remove the cloud on his title based on Love's claim to be a bona fide purchaser without notice of a valid claim against the property.

A bona fide purchaser is protected under Texas law against an interest in property, such as Hahn's judgment creditor's lien, unless the instrument was on file at the time of the purchase. Specifically, section 13.001 of the Texas Property Code states:

(a) A conveyance of real property or an interest in real property or a mortgage or deed of trust is void as to a creditor or to a subsequent purchaser for a valuable consideration without notice unless the instrument has been acknowledged, sworn to, or proved and filed for record as required by law.

(b) The unrecorded instrument is binding on a party to the instrument, on the party's heirs, and on a subsequent purchaser who does not pay a valuable consideration or who has notice of the instrument.

Tex. Prop. Code Ann. § 13.001(a), (b) (Vernon 2004).

"A cloud on title exists when an outstanding claim or encumbrance is shown, which on its face, if valid, would affect or impair the title of the owner of the property." *Angell v. Bailey*, 225 S.W.3d 834, 838 n.6 (Tex. App.–El Paso 2007, no pet.). "Any deed, contract, judgment or other instrument not void on its face that purports to convey an interest in or make any charge upon the land of a true owner, the invalidity of which would require proof, is a cloud upon the legal title of the owner." *Johnson v. Williams*, No. 01-05-00445-CV, 2006 WL 1653656, at *4 (Tex. App.–Houston [1st Dist.] June 15, 2006, pet. denied) (memo. op.) (quoting *Best Inv. Co. v. Parkhill*, 429 S.W.2d 531, 534 (Tex. Civ. App.–Corpus Christi 1968, writ dism'd w.o.j.)); In re Stroud Oil Props. Inc., 110 S.W.3d 18, 26 (Tex. App.–Waco 2002, no pet.).

The principal issue in a suit to remove a cloud from a title, or a suit to quiet title, is the existence of a cloud that equity will remove. Johnson, 2006 WL 1653656, at *4; Bell, 606 S.W.2d at 952-53. An action to remove a cloud from title exists "to enable the holder of the feeblest equity to remove from his way to legal title any unlawful hindrance having the appearance of better right." Bell, 606 S.W.2d at 952 (quoting *Thomson v. Locke*, 1 S.W. 112, 115 (Tex. 1886)). In a suit to remove a cloud from his title, the plaintiff has the burden of supplying the proof necessary to establish his superior equity and right to relief. See *Bell v. Ott*, 606 S.W.2d 942, 952 (Tex. App.–Waco 1980, writ ref'd n.r.e.). That is, the plaintiff must prove, as a matter of law, right, title, or ownership in himself with sufficient certainty to enable the court to see that he has a right of ownership and that the alleged adverse claim is a cloud on the title that equity will remove. See Johnson, 2005 WL 1653656, at *4; *Wright v. Matthews*, 26 S.W.3d 575, 578 (Tex. App.–Beaumont 2000, pet. denied) (citing *Ellison v. Butler*, 443 S.W.2d 886, 888-89 (Tex. App.–Corpus Christi 1969, no writ)).

Love argues that he is entitled to summary judgment removing the cloud from his title because he has proved as a matter of law that there was no lien on the property when it was validly conveyed to his transferor Midtown by general warranty deed in 2002 and, therefore, the property was free of Hahn's lien when Love purchased the property from Mid-Town in April 2004. Thus, Love had no notice of a valid lien on the property.

Love's argument is without merit. Hahn's lien was an "instrument not void on its face that purport[ed] to . . . make [a] charge upon the land of a true owner, the invalidity of which would require proof." Johnson, 2005 WL 1653656, at *4; In re Stroud Oil Props., 110 S.W.3d at 26. It was, therefore, by definition, a cloud upon Love's legal title. See Johnson, 2005 WL 1653656, at *4; In re Stroud Oil Props., 110 S.W.3d at 26. The Texas Supreme Court has held that "a purchaser is bound by every recital, reference and reservation contained in or fairly disclosed by any instrument which forms an essential link in the chain of title under which he claims." *Westland Oil Dev. Corp. v. Gulf Oil Corp.*, 637 S.W.2d 903, 908 (Tex. 1982).

The Westland Oil court stated: The rationale for the rule is that any description, recital of fact, or reference to other documents puts the purchaser upon inquiry, and he is bound to follow up this inquiry, step by step, from one discovery to another and from one instrument to another, until the whole series of title deeds is exhausted and a complete knowledge of all the matters referred to and affecting the estate is obtained. *Id.* (quoting *Loomis v. Cobb*, 159 S.W. 305, 307 (Tex. Civ. App.–El Paso 1913, writ ref'd)).

Here, a title search of the property would have indicated the nature of the conveyance from the Sessions to Mid-Town. See *First S. Props. Inc. v. Vallone*, 533 S.W.2d 339, 340 (Tex. 1976) (outlining appellant's title search as including "a courthouse search of the grantor-grantee indices, deed of trust records, lis pendens records, abstract of judgment records, mechanic's and materialman's lien records, and the federal bankruptcy records, and a search of indices to the same records at [a Houston title company]"). The chain of title clearly reflected the Sessions' conveyance of the property to Mid-Town in 2002—a conveyance that several title searches indicated was of questionable validity because the 2002 deed did not contain a metes and bounds description of the property. And it clearly indicated the filing of the correction deed on March 3, 2004, two days after Hahn's judgment lien against O'Neal Session was refiled. Moreover, previous title searches had returned information regarding Hahn's interest in O'Neal Session's property. These facts also raise a fact question as to whether Love had, or should have had, notice of Hahn's interest in the property. See *Martin v. Cadle Co.*, 133 S.W.3d 897, 905 (Tex. App.–Dallas 2004, pet. denied) (holding that party "cannot be considered innocent purchasers without notice because, although they submitted affidavit testimony stating they purchased the property in good faith, they are charged with knowledge of all facts appearing in the chain of title to the property" and holding that suspicious circumstances in timing of transfer "put them on notice of the defects within their chain of title").

(*continued*)

Moreover, as shown above, Hahn produced summary judgment evidence, in addition to the information a title search would have shown, sufficient to raise material fact questions of facts and circumstances giving rise to the inference of fraud and of Love's actual or constructive notice of those facts. Accordingly, we hold that the trial court erred in granting Love summary judgment on his suit to remove the cloud from his title. See Tex. R. Civ. P. 166a(c); Knott, 128 S.W.3d at 215-16 (holding that summary judgment is properly granted only when there are no genuine issues of material fact).

We sustain Hahn's first, second, and third issues insofar as they relate to Love's suit to remove the cloud from his title. (13)

Love's Right to Summary Judgment on Hahn's Counter-Claim for a Constructive Trust

In his fourth issue, Hahn claims that a legal basis exists for imposing a constructive trust against Love. To be entitled to summary judgment on Hahn's counter-claim that a constructive trust should be imposed on the property, Love was required to prove as a matter of law that Hahn failed to meet at least one of the requirements for imposing a constructive trust. Science Spectrum Inc., 941 S.W.2d at 911. In deciding whether there is a disputed material fact precluding summary judgment, evidence favorable to the nonmovant, Hahn, must be taken as true, every reasonable inference must be indulged in favor of the nonmovant, and any doubts must be resolved in favor of the nonmovant. Knott, 128 S.W.3d at 215.

A constructive trust is an equitable remedy created by the courts to prevent unjust enrichment—a breach of duty or an actual or constructive fraud must be present in order to impose a constructive cause. See *Medford v. Medford*, 68 S.W.3d 242, 248 (Tex. App.–Fort Worth 2002, no pet.). To establish that a constructive trust exists, the proponent must prove (1) breach of a special trust, fiduciary relationship, or actual fraud; (2) unjust enrichment of the wrongdoer; and (3) tracing to an identifiable res. *Hubbard v. Shankle*, 138 S.W.3d 474, 485 (Tex. App.–Fort Worth 2004, pet. denied) (citing *Mowbray v. Avery*, 76 S.W.3d 663, 681 n.27 (Tex. App.–Corpus Christi 2002, pet. denied)).

Love argues in his motion for summary judgment that Hahn presented no evidence of any prior relationship between Hahn and Love and that strict proof of a prior confidential relationship between the parties is required. He cites *Hamblet v. Coveney* to support his contention. See 714 S.W.2d 126, 128 (Tex. App.–Houston [1st Dist.] 1986, writ ref'd n.r.e.). In Hamblet, this Court stated, "Before a constructive trust can be imposed, there must be strict proof of a prior confidential relationship and unfair conduct or unjust enrichment on the part of the wrongdoer." *Id*. However, Hamblet was not a case that involved actual fraud, and, therefore, it is distinguishable from the present case. See *id*. at 132.

The Texas Supreme Court has held, "Actual fraud, as well as breach of a confidential relationship, justifies the imposition of a constructive trust." *Meadows v. Bierschwale*, 516 S.W.2d 125, 128 (Tex. 1974). The appellant in Meadows made an argument similar to Love's, namely, that a constructive trust was appropriate only when a breach of a fiduciary relationship was involved. *Id*. The Meadows Court stated that the appellant's argument might have been the result of confusion arising from a previous case that had held that a fiduciary relationship must have arisen before and apart from the agreement made the basis of the suit. *Id*. at 129 (quoting *Consolidated Gas & Equip. Co. v. Thompson*, 405 S.W.2d 333, 336 (Tex. 1966)). The Meadows Court went on to state that the language in its previous case "must be viewed in the context of the fact situation that gave rise to it." *Id*.

Here, Hahn has alleged that Love, the Sessions, Gary, and Mid-Town were involved in an actual fraud. There are genuine issues of material fact as to whether an actual fraud took place and whether Love was unjustly enriched in his dealings with the Sessions and Mid-Town, as discussed above; furthermore, the property in question is an identifiable res. See Meadows, 516 S.W.2d at 129; Hubbard, 138 S.W.3d at 485. We conclude that summary judgment on this issue was not proper because Love failed to prove that Hahn failed to meet at least one of the requirements for imposing a constructive trust as a matter of law. See Science Spectrum Inc., 941 S.W.2d at 911.

We sustain Hahn's fourth issue. (14)

Conclusion

We reverse the order of the trial court and remand the cause for proceedings consistent with this opinion.

Evelyn V. Keyes

Justice

Panel consists of Chief Justice Radack and Justices Keyes and Higley.

1. The property consists of two lots in the City of Houston in Harris County, Texas, located at 1615 and 1621 Wheeler Street ("the property").

2. See Tex. Prop. Code Ann. §§ 52.001-.004 (Vernon 2007 & Supp. 2008); *Wilson v. Dvorak*, 228 S.W.3d 228, 233-34 (Tex. App.–San Antonio 2007, no pet.) (outlining process for creating judgment lien and stating, "When properly recorded and indexed, an abstract of judgment creates a judgment lien that is superior to the rights of subsequent purchasers and lien holders.").

3. See Tex. Prop. Code Ann. § 52.006 (Vernon Supp. 2008) (governing length of time judgment lien is valid); Tex. Civ. Prac. & Rem. Code Ann. § 34.001 (Vernon 2008) (governing length of time judgment is active and providing for renewal of judgment with writ of execution issued within ten years of previous writ).

4. See Tex. Civ. Prac. & Rem. Code Ann. § 34.006 (Vernon 1997) ("A dormant judgment may be revived by scire facias or by an action of debt brought not later than the second anniversary of the date that the judgment becomes dormant.").

5. See Tex. Bus. & Com. Code Ann. § 24.009 (Vernon 2002).

6. See Tex. Prop. Code Ann. § 13.001 (Vernon 2004).

7. The Fraudulent Transfer Act states:

An "Insider" includes:

(A) if the debtor is an individual:

(i) a relative of the debtor or a general partner of the debtor;

(ii) a partnership in which the debtor is a general partner;

(iii) a general partner in a partnership described in subparagraph (ii) of this paragraph; or

(iv) a corporation of which the debtor is a director, officer, or person in control.

. . .

(D) an affiliate, or an insider of an affiliate as if the affiliate were the debtor; and

(E) a managing agent of the debtor.

Tex. Bus. & Com. Code Ann. § 24.002(7).

8. When a transferee is an insider and knows the transferor is insolvent at the time of the transfer he cannot be a good faith transferee. Flores, 161 S.W.3d at 756; *Putman v. Stephenson*, 805 S.W.2d 16, 20 (Tex. App.–Dallas, 1991, no writ). Nor is insider status limited to the four subjects listed in section 24.002(7); rather, the list is provided "for purposes of exemplification." Putman, 805 S.W.2d at 18. In general, an "insider" is "an entity whose close relationship with the debtor subjects any transactions made between the debtor and the insider to heavy scrutiny." *Tel. Equip. Network Inc. v. TA/Westchase Place Ltd.*, 80 S.W.3d 601, 609 (Tex. App.–Houston [1st Dist.] 2002, no pet.). In determining insider status, courts are to consider (1) the closeness of the relationship between the transferee and the debtor and (2) whether the transactions were at arm's length. *Id.* (citing In re Holloway, 955 F.2d 1008, 1010 (5th Cir. 1992)). However, it is not necessary to prove that a transferee is an insider in order to

(*continued*)

prove the transferee's knowledge of the transferor's fraudulent intent. See Tex. Bus. & Com. Code Ann. § 24.005(b); Wright, 1856 WL 4851, at *5; Flores, 161 S.W.3d at 754 (listing, from Tex. Bus. & Com. Code Ann. § 24.005(b), "facts and circumstances, known as badges of fraud, that may be considered in determining fraudulent intent" and opining that if "'fraudulent intent is only to be deduced from facts and circumstances which the law considers as mere badges of fraud and not fraud per se, these must be submitted to the trier of fact, which draws the inference as to the fairness or fraudulent character of the transaction.'") (quoting Coleman Cattle Co., 10 S.W.3d 430, 434 (Tex. App.–Beaumont 2000, no pet.)).

9. In supplemental briefing, Love argues that Hahn bears the burden to prove that Love was not a good faith purchaser for value, and, in support, he cites *Rucker v. Steelman*. See 619 S.W.2d 5, 7 (Tex. App.–Houston [1st Dist.] 1981, writ ref'd n.r.e.) ("A creditor seeking to defeat a prior conveyance of a judgment debtor must prove fraudulent intent on the part of the debtor at the time of the execution of the conveyance and then, if a valuable consideration is shown to have been paid for the property, the creditor must further prove that at the time of such payment the party taking the conveyance had notice of the debtor's fraud"). However, Rucker was a suit to remove cloud on title in which the creditor was the plaintiff attempting to show that he was entitled to have a cloud on his title removed. *Id.* In a suit to remove cloud on title, the burden of proof is on the person seeking to remove the cloud from his title. If the cloud is a fraudulent transfer, the person asserting fraudulent transfer must prove fraudulent intent and notice on the part of the transferee. *Id.* Here, however, Love, the purchaser, not Hahn, the creditor, sought summary judgment on his own suit to remove the cloud from his title and on his affirmative defense that he was not subject to Hahn's fraudulent transfer claims because he was a bona fide purchaser under the Texas Uniform Fraudulent Transfer Act. See Tex. Bus. & Com. Code Ann. §§ 24.001-.013 (Vernon 2002 & Supp. 2008). The TUFTA treats good faith raised by the party claiming to be a bona fide purchaser as an affirmative defense and places the burden of proving the defense on the party asserting it—in this case, on Love. See *Flores v. Robinson Roofing & Const. Co.*, 161 S.W.3d 750, 756 (Tex. App.–Fort Worth 2005, pet. denied) (holding that burden of proving good faith rests on party invoking defense and that it is not appropriate basis for no-evidence summary judgment). Therefore, we analyze this potential ground for support of the trial court's granting of summary judgment under Love's traditional motion for summary judgment because it is not an appropriate basis to grant a no-evidence summary judgment.

10. See Tex. Prop. Code Ann. § 52.001 (Vernon Supp. 2008) (stating that procedures for establishing judgment lien apply to "a first or subsequent abstract of judgment" that is properly recorded and indexed). The parties agree that the second abstract of judgment is not retroactive. However, the Fraudulent Transfer Act provides relief for creditors when "the creditor's claim arose before or within a reasonable time after the transfer was made." Tex. Bus. & Com. Code Ann. § 24.005(a) (Vernon 2002) (emphasis added).

11. In his motion for summary judgment, Love stated:

Hahn alleges that the sale to Love was a sale to an insider. The basis for this allegation is that Love's father was a close personal friend of Herman Gary, the real estate broker, that Love had known Gary for 20 years and that Gary brought him many deals. Hahn also claims Love is an insider because he had loaned Gary and Strickland (the initial intended buyer of the property) money on prior occasions. Hahn alleges that Strickland bought other property from Love on prior occasions. For purposes of the Fraudulent Transfer Act, "insider" is defined in § 24.002(7) of the Tex. Bus. & Com. Code and none of the definitions or categories of insiders include the relationships or facts claimed by Hahn. As a matter of law, the claim that Love is an insider fails.

It is clear that Love purchased in good faith and for a reasonably equivalent value and, therefore, no action lies against him under the Fraudulent Conveyance Act. Moreover, the transfer that Hahn seeks to set aside is not even one from the debtor. The debtor was O'Neal Session, the grantor in Love's deed was Mid-Town.

12. See *Natividad v. Alexser Inc.*, 875 S.W.2d 695, 699 (Tex. 1994) (in evaluating motion for summary judgment on pleadings, court assumes that all allegations and facts in nonmovant's pleadings are true and indulges all inferences in nonmovant's pleadings in light most favorable to nonmovant); Emerald

Oil and Gas L.C. ex rel. *Saglio P'ship Ltd. v. Exxon Corp.*, 228 S.W.3d 166, 169 (Tex. App.–Corpus Christi 2005, no pet.) (same); see also *Beta Supply Inc. v. G.E.A. Power Cooling Sys. Inc.*, 748 S.W.2d 541, 542 (Tex. App.–Houston [1st Dist.] 1988, writ denied) ("assertions of fact, not pled in the alternative, in the live pleadings of a party are regarded as formal judicial admissions").

13. Because the sufficiency of the legal description in the purported 2002 deed is not material to the proof of Love's right to removal of the cloud from his title, we do not address Hahn's first issue, arguing that Love did not prove his entitlement to have the cloud removed from his title because the description of the land in the general warranty deed dated April 26, 2002, by which Session purported to convey the property to Mid-Town, was legally insufficient, and, therefore, the deed was void as a matter of law.

14. Because we reverse the order of the trial court granting Love's motion for summary judgment and remand this cause to the trial court, we do not need to address Hahn's fifth issue regarding whether it was error for the trial court to overrule Hahn's objection to Love's motion for summary judgment, which was filed after the deadline set out in the trial court's docket control order. See Tex. R. App. P. 47.1.

Other issues emerge as well during title analysis, including:

- Forgeries
- Missed mortgages
- Unrecorded or missed easements that interfere with the use of the property
- Clerical mistakes
- Missing heirs
- Defective deeds
- Fabricated deeds
- Wills not probated at the time of closing
- Confusion as to similar names
- Invalid divorces or marriages
- Lack of legal access to and from the land
- Deeds by minors or those of an unsound mind
- Conveyances under duress [17]

Discussed later are the release and waiver documents necessary to eliminate these types of liens. See Chapter 8, Closing and Settlement.

In sum, a good and marketable title is not feasible unless these encumbrances are eliminated:

- The amount required to pay any judgments of record, including cost of satisfaction
- The amount required to pay off any mortgages of record, including costs of satisfaction
- The amount of delinquent sewage bills, if any
- The amount of delinquent water bills, if any
- The amount required to pay any unfiled municipal claims
- The amount required to pay unpaid taxes and lien costs, if any
- The amount of taxes for the year in which the closing is held
- If there are any unfiled mechanic's liens that might have priority over the mortgage to be recorded, when the closing is held on behalf of a bank or savings and loan institution (seller's affidavit can cover this) [18]

Use Title Abstract Worksheets to track your progress. See Figure 5–4.[19]

DATASEARCH
PEOPLE.PARTNERS.PIONEERS

TITLE ABSTRACT WORKSHEET

Copy Costs: $_____ Report Fee: $_____

DSI Report Number: _____

Address:_____ **Verified with County?** Yes   No

County: _____ **County Land Records Thru Date:** ____/____/____

Judgment Records Thru Date: ____/____/____

DEED INFO

Deed Type (Circle One): Quit Claim - Tax - Sheriff - Trustee - Warranty - Probate/Estate - Other

Current Owner:_____

_____

Prior Owner):_____

Dated: ____/____/____ **Recorded:** ____/____/____ **BK:**_____ **PG:**_____ **Instr:**_____

Tenancy: T/E - T/C - J/T - Sole - H/W   **(Circle if Applies)** Survivorship - No Survivorship - Life Estate/Interest

% of Interest: _____   First Right of Refusal - Missing Interest

---

TAX INFO

Taxed (Circle One): Annual - Biannual - Quarterly - Winter/Summer - Other _____

Tax / Parcel Number: _____ **Map:** _____ **District:** _____

Year/Period	Amount	Status (Circle)	Due	Paid	Thru
_____	$_____	Paid - Due - Open - Del	___/___/___	___/___/___	___/___/___
_____	$_____	Paid - Due - Open - Del	___/___/___	___/___/___	___/___/___
_____	$_____	Paid - Due - Open - Del	___/___/___	___/___/___	___/___/___
_____	$_____	Paid - Due - Open - Del	___/___/___	___/___/___	___/___/___

Delinquent Tax Year(s): _____ **Amount(s):** _____

Other Tax Type	Amount	Status (Circle)	Notes
_____	$_____	Paid - Due - Open - Del	_____
_____	$_____	Paid - Due - Open - Del	_____

Did you search for Tax Sales? Yes   No   **Did you search for delinquent taxes?** Yes   No

Manufactured Home? Yes   No   **If Yes**, taxed as   Real / Personal Property.

Assessed Value: Land:_____ **Improvements:**_____ **Total:** _____

ENCUMBRANCES

Type: _____ **Dated:** ____/____/____ **Recorded:** ____/____/____

BK:_____ **PG:**_____ **Instr:**_____ **Amount: $** _____

To: _____

Trustee: _____

Signed: All Parties on Deed - Prior Owner - Other:_____

Assignment: _____

Notice of Default/Foreclosure? Yes   No   Circle if applicable: Equity Line - Line of Credit - Open Ended

ARE THERE ADDITIONAL ENCUMBRANCES? YES _____ (SEE ADDITIONAL SHEET)   NO _____

LIENS

ARE THERE JUDGMENTS? YES _____ (SEE ADDITIONAL SHEET)   NO - JUDGMENTS ARE CLEAR ____

ESTATE/PROBATE INFORMATION: YES _____ (SEE ADDITIONAL SHEET) NO _____

OUT CONVEYANCES: YES _____ (SEE ADDITIONAL SHEET)   NO _____

Page _____ **of** _____

FIGURE 5–4
(continues)

DATASEARCH
PEOPLE.PARTNERS.PIONEERS

DSI Report Number: _____

ADDITIONAL ENCUMBRANCE INFORMATION

Type: _____ Dated: ____/____/____ Recorded: ____/____/____

BK:_____ PG:_____ Instr:_____ Amount: $ _____

To: _____

Trustee: _____

Signed: All Parties on Deed - Prior Owner - Other:_____

Assignment: _____

Notice of Default/Foreclosure? Yes   No   Circle if applicable: Equity Line - Line of Credit - Open Ended

Type: _____ Dated: ____/____/____ Recorded: ____/____/____

BK:_____ PG:_____ Instr:_____ Amount: $ _____

To: _____

Trustee: _____

Signed: All Parties on Deed - Prior Owner - Other:_____

Assignment: _____

Notice of Default/Foreclosure? Yes   No   Circle if applicable: Equity Line - Line of Credit - Open Ended

Type: _____ Dated: ____/____/____ Recorded: ____/____/____

BK:_____ PG:_____ Instr:_____ Amount: $ _____

To: _____

Trustee: _____

Signed: All Parties on Deed - Prior Owner - Other:_____

Assignment: _____

Notice of Default/Foreclosure? Yes   No   Circle if applicable: Equity Line - Line of Credit - Open Ended

Type: _____ Dated: ____/____/____ Recorded: ____/____/____

BK:_____ PG:_____ Instr:_____ Amount: $ _____

To: _____

Trustee: _____

Signed: All Parties on Deed - Prior Owner - Other:_____

Assignment: _____

Notice of Default/Foreclosure? Yes   No   Circle if applicable: Equity Line - Line of Credit - Open Ended

Notes:

ARE THERE ADDITIONAL ENCUMBRANCES? YES _____ (SEE ADDITIONAL SHEET)   NO _____

Page _____ of _____

FIGURE 5–4
(continued)

DATASEARCH
PEOPLE.PARTNERS.PIONEERS

DSI Report Number: _____

JUDGMENT / LIEN INFORMATION

Type: _____ Dated: ____/____/____ Recorded: ____/____/____

Docket:_____ Page:_____ Case #:_____ Amount: $ _____

Plaintiff:_____

Attorney:_____

Defendant:_____

Address: _____ Other Info:_____

Court Filed In:_____ Pending: Yes No

Type: _____ Dated: ____/____/____ Recorded: ____/____/____

Docket:_____ Page:_____ Case #:_____ Amount: $ _____

Plaintiff:_____

Attorney:_____

Defendant:_____

Address: _____ Other Info:_____

Court Filed In:_____ Pending: Yes No

Type: _____ Dated: ____/____/____ Recorded: ____/____/____

Docket:_____ Page:_____ Case #:_____ Amount: $ _____

Plaintiff:_____

Attorney:_____

Defendant:_____

Address: _____ Other Info:_____

Court Filed In:_____ Pending: Yes No

Type: _____ Dated: ____/____/____ Recorded: ____/____/____

Docket:_____ Page:_____ Case #:_____ Amount: $ _____

Plaintiff:_____

Attorney:_____

Defendant:_____

Address: _____ Other Info:_____

Court Filed In:_____ Pending: Yes No

Notes:

ARE THERE ADDITIONAL JUDGEMENTS / LIENS? YES _____ (SEE ADDITIONAL SHEET) NO _____

Page _____ **of** _____

Web: www.data-search.com • E-Mail: titles@data-search.com • Voice: (800) 817-7730 • Fax: (800) 270-6619

FIGURE 5–4
(continued)

DATASEARCH
PEOPLE.PARTNERS.PIONEERS

DSI Report Number: _____

PROBATE / ESTATE INFORMATION

Decedent:_____ Date of Death:____/____/____ Estate Closed: Yes No

Died Intestate - No Will Found: _____ Executor of Estate:_____

Book: _____ Page: _____ Dated: ____/____/____ Recorded: ____/____/____

Heir / Devisee	Relation	Heir / Devisee	Relation
_____	_____	_____	_____
_____	_____	_____	_____
_____	_____	_____	_____

Notes:_____

_____

_____

Decedent:_____ Date of Death:____/____/____ Estate Closed: Yes No

Died Intestate - No Will Found: _____ Executor of Estate:_____

Book: _____ Page: _____ Dated: ____/____/____ Recorded: ____/____/____

Heir / Devisee	Relation	Heir / Devisee	Relation
_____	_____	_____	_____
_____	_____	_____	_____
_____	_____	_____	_____

Notes:_____

_____

_____

OUT SALES / OUT CONVEYANCES

Book:_____ Page:_____ Instr#:_____ Dated: ____/____/____ Recorded: ____/____/____

From: _____

To:_____

Description of Parcel conveyed: _____

Book:_____ Page:_____ Instr#:_____ Dated: ____/____/____ Recorded: ____/____/____

From: _____

To:_____

Description of Parcel conveyed: _____

Book:_____ Page:_____ Instr#:_____ Dated: ____/____/____ Recorded: ____/____/____

From: _____

To:_____

Description of Parcel conveyed: _____

Page _____ of _____

Web: www.data-search.com • E-Mail: titles@data-search.com • Voice: (800) 817-7730 • Fax: (800) 270-6619

FIGURE 5–4

(continued)

DATASEARCH
PEOPLE.PARTNERS.PIONEERS

DSI Report Number: _____

CHAIN OF TITLE

Deed Type (Circle One): Quit Claim - Tax - Sheriff - Trustee - Warranty - Probate/Estate - Other

Book:_____ Page:_____ Instr#:_____ Dated: ____/____/____ Recorded: ____/____/____

Grantee: _____

Grantor:_____

Legal Description same as current deed: Yes   No   If no, explain:_____

All interests accounted for: Yes No   If no, explain: _____

Notes:_____

_____

Deed Type (Circle One): Quit Claim - Tax - Sheriff - Trustee - Warranty - Probate/Estate - Other

Book:_____ Page:_____ Instr#:_____ Dated: ____/____/____ Recorded: ____/____/____

Grantee: _____

Grantor:_____

Legal Description same as current deed: Yes   No   If no, explain:_____

All interests accounted for: Yes No   If no, explain: _____

Notes:_____

_____

Deed Type (Circle One): Quit Claim - Tax - Sheriff - Trustee - Warranty - Probate/Estate - Other

Book:_____ Page:_____ Instr#:_____ Dated: ____/____/____ Recorded: ____/____/____

Grantee: _____

Grantor:_____

Legal Description same as current deed: Yes   No   If no, explain:_____

All interests accounted for: Yes No   If no, explain: _____

Notes:_____

_____

Deed Type (Circle One): Quit Claim - Tax - Sheriff - Trustee - Warranty - Probate/Estate - Other

Book:_____ Page:_____ Instr#:_____ Dated: ____/____/____ Recorded: ____/____/____

Grantee: _____

Grantor:_____

Legal Description same as current deed: Yes   No   If no, explain:_____

All interests accounted for: Yes No   If no, explain: _____

Notes:_____

_____

Page _____ of _____

Web: www.data-search.com • E-Mail: titles@data-search.com • Voice: (800) 817-7730 • Fax: (800) 270-6619

FIGURE 5–4
(continued)

III. TITLE INSURANCE

The majority of residential transactions call for the purchase of title insurance. Certainly, it is rare to find a lender who does not demand a title policy. Buyers find comfort in a title policy as well. The **title insurance policy** generates confidence in those investing in real estate, granting an assurance of title quality, promising to defend against competing and hostile claims, and warranting to its purchaser that this title is worthy of protection.

Forms and other procedures are fairly standardized and mirror the recommendations of the American Land Title Association (ALTA). ALTA policy forms generally include coverage against the unmarketability of title, against the lack of a legal (not necessarily actual) right of access to and from the land, and assurance that the company will pay for counsel to represent the insured as to any claim based on a matter covered by the policy. In addition to the ALTA policies, endorsements are frequently added to expand, constrict, or otherwise modify the policy coverage. Some of them occur with such frequency and are so prevalent nationwide that ALTA has created standardized ones (often available only to lenders) to give affirmative coverage as to situations in truth-in-lending matter, zooming classifications, condominium and planned unit development status, variable rate loans, environmental liens, and other matters of importance to purchasers and lenders.[20]

The title evaluation is for the most part delivered by title agents/abstractors working for title companies or attorneys or paralegals who are on a title company's approved list. Rates for title insurance are based on direct title company issuance, usually the highest rate, or the much more economical approved attorney system. A review of the title insurance regimen is within.

A. The Application Process

The title insurance process commences by application. Questions cover owner and insured mortgage holder and a legal property description. It is best to attach the deed. See Figure 5–5.

B. Binder

If the title company wishes to pursue coverage, it issues a **binder**. The binder indicates a conditional willingness to insure dependent upon the investigation of title. Even when coverage is granted, various exceptions and exemptions appear on the policy's schedule.[21] Sometimes referred to as a **title commitment**, the binder expressly defines what the company will insure and what the company excludes. A title commitment is a promise to issue an insurance policy on a piece of property. The title commitment is organized into five main parts:

1. Party to be insured—generally, the lender and the owner
2. The amount of the insurance—usually the loan amount for the mortgagee and the sales price for the owner
3. What is being insured—the legal description of the property

Application for Title Insurance

_____ Purchase _____ Refinance Loan Amount: $_____   Purchase Price: $_____

Property Address: _____

_____

Legal Description: _____

_____

Borrowers Information: (name) _____

Co-Borrowers Information: (name) _____

Current address: _____

_____

Sellers Information: (name) _____

Current address: _____

_____

Seller 1 S.S. # _____   Seller 2 S. S. # _____

Mortgage Broker:_____   Fax Number:_____
Listing Real Estate Office:_____   Cell Phone: _____
Contact Person:_____   Email Address: _____
Contact Person:_____   Fax Number: _____
Phone Number:_____   Lender: _____
Phone Number:_____   Phone Number:_____
Special Instructions:

_____

_____

_____

_____

_____

_____

FIGURE 5–5

4. What conditions need resolution to insure marketeable title, such as:

   ■ Proof of taxes paid

   ■ Lien affidavit, also known as sellers'/owners' affidavit, to be signed at closing

   ■ Cancellation of any open mortgages, judgments, or liens

   ■ Survey of the property by a licensed surveyor

The title binder will also list those things it will not insure against. These are often referred to as "exceptions" or "exclusions." More typical examples of these exceptions are:

   ■ Servitudes/Easements—the right, usually granted to a utility company, to make limited use of a portion of the property.

   ■ Restrictions/Covenants—rules and regulations, usually established by the developer of the subdivision.

   ■ Oil, gas, and mineral titles.

   ■ Miscellaneous exceptions.

Web Exercise

A sample title commitment is at *www.mbaa.org/files/Conferences/2006/Document_Custody_Conference/ ALTACommitmentForms.pdf*

C. Owner's Affidavit

To assure the integrity of seller's representation, the title company requests the present owner to complete an **affidavit of title** attending the various issues outlined in Figure 5–6.[22]

D. Purchaser's Affidavit

Similarly, the buyer must affirm or deny various items listed on the title affidavit. Title insurers essentially agree that purchaser's representations are reliable. Stated another way, if any clauses are falsely answered, the title company can avoid coverage on part or all of the policy. See Figure 5–7.[23]

E. Title Abstractor's Report of Title

Once conditionally bound, the title abstractor conducts a title examination. From notes and rough drafts, the abstractor may issue a precursory report that preliminarily indicates the quality of the title. More often, once the search process is concluded, the examiner will complete a certificate or final **report of title**. See Figure 5–8.

The report identifies deeds, judgments, and mortgages, as well as any other identifiable liens. Another legal property description is attached. The abstractor or attorney should summarize any and all objections.

F. Attorney's Certificate or Final Report of Title

Some title insurers wait until all available information is collected and analyzed before a final report, in certificate form, is issued. The final certificate irrevocably states:

> I hereby certify that I have searched all the records which could affect title to the realty described in the attached report of title, commitment or interim binder from the date thereof as to the date of this final certificate, and I find that the following instruments affecting title thereto have been recorded subsequent to the date of said report (if so applicable).

No policy will even be issued if the following steps are not taken:

1. Required removal of exceptions is completed.

2. Obtain affidavits or other proof necessary to remove exceptions.

Affidavit of Title

STATE OF NEW JERSEY COUNTY OF   SS:

say(s) under oath:

1. **Representations**.   If only one person signs this Affidavit, the words "we," "us" and "our" shall mean "I," "me" and "my." The statements in this Affidavit are true to the best of our knowledge, information and belief.

2. **Name, Age and Residence.**   We have never changed our names or used any other names. We are citizens of the United States and at least 18 years old. After today, we will live at

3. **Ownership and Possession.**   We are the only owners of Property located at
                                                                                             called "this Property."
                                                                                             called the "Buyers."
We now sell this Property to
We are in sole possession of this Property. There are no tenants or other occupants of this Property. We have owned this Property since   . Since then no one has questioned our ownership or right to possession. We have never owned any Property which is next to this Property. Except for our agreement with the Buyers, we have not signed any contracts to sell this Property. We have not given anyone else any rights concerning the purchase or lease of this Property.

4. **Improvements.**   No additions, alterations or improvements are now being made or have been made to this Property since   . We have always obtained all necessary permits and Certificates of Occupancy. All charges for municipal improvements such as sewers, sidewalks, curbs or similar improvements benefiting this Property have been paid in full. No building, addition, extension or alteration on this Property has been made or worked on within the past 90 days. We are not aware that anyone has filed or intends to file a mechanic's lien, Notice of Unpaid Balance and Right to File Lien Claim, construction lien or building contract relating to this Property. No one has notified us that money is due and owing for construction, alteration or repair work on this Property.

5. **Liens or Encumbrances.**   We have not allowed any interests (legal rights) to be created which affect our ownership or use of this Property. No other persons have legal rights in this Property, except the rights of utility companies to use this Property along the road or for the purpose of serving this Property. There are no pending lawsuits or judgments against us or other legal obligations which may be enforced against this Property. No bankruptcy or insolvency proceedings have been started by or against us. We have never been declared bankrupt. No one has any security interest in any personal Property or fixtures included in this sale. All liens (legal claims, such as judgments) listed on the attached judgment or lien search are not against us, but against others with similar names.

6. **Marital/Civil Union History.**   (Check where appropriate)
   ☐ We are not married or civil union partners.
   ☐ We are married to each other or are civil union partners. We were married or became civil union partners on   . The maiden/previous name of   was   .
   ☐ This Property has never been occupied as the principal matrimonial/civil union residence of any of us. (If it has, or if it was acquired before May 28, 1980, each spouse/partner must sign the Deed and Affidavit N.J.S.A. 3B:28-2,3.)
   ☐ Our complete marital or civil union history is listed above except as listed below under paragraph 7. This includes all marriages or civil unions not listed above, and any pending matrimonial or civil union actions. We include how each marriage or civil union ended. We have attached copies of any death certificates, judgments for divorce or annulment or dissolution of a civil union including any provisions in these judgments which relate to this Property.

7. **Exceptions and Additions**.   The following is a complete list of exceptions and additions to the above statements. This includes all liens or mortgages which are not being paid off as a result of this sale, as well as marital or civil union information not particularly set forth in paragraph 6 above.

We have been advised that recognizance and/or abstracts or recognizance of bail are not being indexed among the records of the   County Clerk/Register's office and that the Title Company, Buyer(s) and/or Mortgagee will rely on the truthfulness of this statement. The undersigned hereby certify that there are no recognizance filed against the undersigned as either principal or surety on the property which is the subject of this transaction. There are no unpaid fines or surcharges levied against us by the New Jersey Motor Vehicle Commission.

8. **Child Support.**
   ☐ There are no outstanding child support orders or judgments against this deponent.
   ☐ There is a child support order outstanding, Docket no.   against this deponent. All payments, however, are current as of this date.

9. **Reliance.**   We make this Affidavit in order to induce the Buyer(s) to accept our Deed. We are aware that the Buyer(s) and their Mortgage lender rely on our truthfulness and the statements made in this Affidavit.

Signed and sworn to before me on (date)

FIGURE 5–6

Affidavit of Title

STATE OF NEW JERSEY COUNTY OF   SS:

say(s) under oath:

1. Representations.   If only one person signs this Affidavit the words "we," "us" and "our" shall mean "I," "me" and "my." The statements in this Affidavit are true to the best of our knowledge, information and belief.

2. Name, Age and Residence.   We have never changed our names or used any other names. We are citizens of the United States and at least 18 years old. After today, we will live at

3. Ownership and Possession.   We are the only owners of Property located at
                                                                            called "this Property."

We now Mortgage this Property to

The date of the Mortgage is the same as this Affidavit. This Mortgage is given to secure a loan of $. We are in sole possession of this Property. There are no tenants or other occupants of this Property. We have owned this Property since . Since then no one has questioned our ownership or right to possession. We have never owned any Property which is next to this Property.

4. Improvements.   No additions, alterations or improvements are now being made or have been made to this Property since . We have always obtained all necessary permits, Certificates of Occupancy and other necessary approvals. All charges for municipal improvements such as sewers, sidewalks, curbs or similar improvements benefiting this Property have been paid in full. No building, addition, extension or alteration on this Property has been made or worked on within the past 90 days. We are not aware that anyone has filed or intends to file a mechanic's lien, Notice of Unpaid Balance and Right to File Lien Claim, Construction Lien Claim or building contract relating to this Property. No one has notified us that money is due and owing for construction, alteration or repair work on this Property.

5. Liens or Encumbrances.   We have not allowed any interests (legal rights) to be created which affects our ownership or use of this Property. No other persons have legal rights in this Property, except the rights of utility companies to use this Property along the road or for the purpose of serving this Property. There are no pending lawsuits or judgments against us or other legal obligations which may be enforced against this Property. No bankruptcy or insolvency proceedings have been started by or against us. We have never been declared bankrupt. No one has any security interest in any personal Property or fixtures on this Property. All liens (legal claims, such as judgments) listed on the attached judgment or lien search are not against us, but against others with similar names. There are no unpaid fines or surcharges levied against me by the New Jersey Motor Vehicle Commission.

6. Marital/Civil Union History   (Check where appropriate)
- ☐ We are not married or civil union partners.
- ☐ We are married to each other or are civil union partners. We were married or became civil union partners on . The maiden/previous name of   was   .
- ☐ This Property has never been occupied as the principal matrimonial/civil union residence of any of us. (If it has, or if it was acquired before May 28, 1980, each spouse/partner must sign the Mortgage and Affidavit N.J.S.A. 3B:28-2,3.)
- ☐ Our complete marital or civil union history is listed above except as listed below under paragraph 7. This includes all marriages or civil unions not listed above, and any pending matrimonial or civil union actions. We include how each marriage or civil union ended. We have attached copies of any death certificates, judgments for divorce or annulment or dissolution of a civil union including any provisions in these judgments which relate to this Property.

7. Exceptions and Additions.   The following is a complete list of exceptions and additions to the above statements. This includes all liens or Mortgages which are not being paid off as a result of this Mortgage, as well as marital information not particularly set forth in paragraph 6 above.

We have been advised that recognizance and/or abstracts or recognizance of bail are not being indexed among the records of the   County Clerk/Register's office and that the Title Company, Buyer(s) and/or Mortgagee will rely on the truthfulness of this statement. The undersigned hereby certify that there are no recognizance filed against the undersigned as either principal or surety on the property which is the subject of this transaction.

8. Child Support.
- ☐ There are no outstanding child support orders or judgments against this deponent.
- ☐ There is a child support order outstanding, Docket no.   against this deponent. All payments however, are current as of this date.

9. Reliance.   We make this Affidavit in order to obtain the Mortgage Loan. We are aware that our Lender will rely on our truthfulness and the statements made in this Affidavit.

Signed and sworn to before me on

_____ , 20_____

_____   _____

Notary Public _____   _____

1635 - Affidavit of Title - For Mortgage of Property by
Individual - Plain Language
Rev. 2/07 P12/08

©2007 by ALL-STATE LEGAL®
A Division of ALL-STATE International, Inc.
www.aslegal.com 800.222.0510

FIGURE 5–7

ATTORNEY'S REPORT OF TITLE

I have examined the record title to the real estate described in Schedule "A" to the date hereof for the protection of: OWNER or LEASEHOLDER to be insured:

LENDER to be insured:

Type of Mortgage/Deed of Trust Conv: VA   FHA   VRM   Conmt,   Other   (Specify)

Title vested in:

Estate or Interest: T ype of Tenancy:

Being (the same) (part of the same) premises acquired by Deed from
dated _____ and recorded _____ in Deed   Book page   Note: if acquired by more than one deed or through an estate set forth the additional information and attach hereto.

Schedule A
Attach complete description of Real Estate (including heading) to be insured.

Schedule B
ATTORNEY'S OBJECTIONS
NOTE: Please fill all spaces: "None" where applicable.

Property is occupied by:
If tenant, give particulars of lease:
1. Does tenant have renewal and/or purchase option?
2. Taxes are paid to and including the year   Parcel No.
3. Water Rent accruing from
4. Sewer Rent accruing from
   Note: if 3 and 4 are private sources, so state.
5. Any unpaid water and sewer connections, paving charges or other assessments
6. .... (define)
   Easements, servitudes, variation in dimensions or area content improper location of buildings and improvements, conflict with tines of adjoining property, encroachments, projections or other matters which might be disclosed by an accurate survey of the premises
7. Liability for claims for work done or materials furnished for which a lien might be filed.
   Construction (if applicable) is. (   ) contemplated (   ) in progress (   ) completed
   And statutory lien period has (   ) expired - (   ) has not expired.   (date)
8. Is property located in a coed area? Yes   No   . If as, Bituminoult; Anthracite   .
List all liens and other exceptions and conditions disclosed by the examinaticm. (Furnish verbatim copies of easements, rights of way and restrictions INCLUDING REVERTER CLAUSE, IF ANY).

Certified at   this   day of   19
                        (AM/PM)

(Signature} Attorney at Law

(Note -Please type name under signature.)

No liability is assumed by Meridian Title Insurance Company under this Attorney's Report of Title until a commitment, title binder or title policy is issued pursuant to this report.

TF5 (Rev. 11/84)

FIGURE 5–8

3. Remove exceptions and objections raised by buyer's attorney.

4. Obtain receipted proof from collectors to remove any governmental lien charges.

5. Obtain payoff statements or releases pertaining to previous mortgages and judgments.

6. If required, obtain releases of leases, easements, and other restrictions.

7. Prepare indemnities or letters to title company to remove exceptions to title report.

8. Prepare any other documents required by the title company.

9. Consult title officer in case of any doubts or need of special treatment.

Attached to the final certification are copies of:

- Restrictions
- Rights-of-way
- Subdivision plan
- Plotting of deed description
- Applicable portion of appropriate tax map
- Photocopies of any agreements, and so forth revealed by the title search, which should be brought to the attention of the buyer[24]

G. Title Policy

Once the title company is satisfied with the removal or remedy of objections, it will issue a title policy. The policy is supported by various schedules like coverage terms and exclusions. Typical title policies then proceed in a series of endorsements, another means of timing or altering the scope of coverage. In any standard policy, the endorsements may include:

- Variable rate mortgage losses due to miscalculation and other reasons
- Restriction as to residential use only
- Survey inconsistencies
- Limitation on liability
- Terms and conditions of liability

The standard endorsements, as published by the professional group C of the ALTA, are frequently reproduced. Endorsement 100 insures against a reversion of title by enforcing any existing, but unviolated, restrictions. Endorsement 101 insures against any loss by the enforcement or attempted enforcement of violated restrictions. This requires an additional premium payable to the title insurance company after additional consideration by them. Regarding the survey, Endorsement 300 insures the mortgage at a reasonable cost, while Endorsement 301 insures the buyer for an additional premium.

At times, the title company sees the risks of insuring as too prohibitive. Certainly, some encumbrances or conveyancing defects have considerable liability or may take too long or be too costly to remedy. An inability to formalize discharge on an underlying mortgage surely qualifies. See a frustrated attempt to gain a discharge in the letter in Figure 5–9.

If the buyer still desires the property, despite its potential or actual defects, and the lender mandates title insurance, a buyer can negotiate a title policy, not only excepting the impediments, but agreeing to indemnify the title company, holding it harmless in the event of an actual dispute. A sum of money is usually put in escrow with a corresponding promise to indemnify.

Anyone threatening litigation **clouds** a title. A title insurance company can be satisfied that it will be protected in the event of a full-fledged lawsuit by an indemnification agreement. In essence, title is made good and marketable, according to the title insurance standards by the indemnification agreement.

Date

Attn: Payoff Department
Lender
Address

Re: Borrower:

Property Location:

Date of Mortgage:

Recorded in Book Page:

Original Amount of Mortgage:

Loan No:

Dear Sir/Madam:

On [date], this office forwarded to your company by overnight delivery funds sufficient to pay in full the above-reference mortgage obligation. (See copy of letter and cancelled check which is enclosed.) Since that time, in excess of five (5) telephone calls have been made to your company to determine the whereabouts of the mortgage discharge. At first, the response to the calls was that the discharge would be prepared shortly. More recently upon receiving our telephone calls, the customer service department has requested a fax be forwarded to the Mortgage Release Department. Three requests have been faxed. A reasonable time in which to issue a discharge on a mortgage in Rhode Island is approximately thirty (30) days.

To date, I have incurred more than two (2) hours of my time in pursuing this discharge. My rate on matters such as this is $150.00 per hour. I have enclosed copies of R.I.G.L. 34–26–5, as well as a letter from the Department of Business Regulations pertaining to, among other things, this very issue. It would be very profitable for this office to take legal action against you, but I prefer not to practice law that way.

If I do not hear from you within ten (10) days of your receipt of this letter, I will initiate suit against you in the District Court for attorney's fees, triple costs, as well as an order from the Court discharging your mortgage. Furthermore, I will notify the Department of Business Regulations of your breach of the Rhode Island statutory provisions so that the same may be considered at the time you or anyone selling mortgages to you requests a license renewal from the Department.

Very truly yours,

Enclosures

FIGURE 5–9
Communication regarding mortgage discharge.

H. Closing Instructions

At the settlement, the title agent or other person must be certain that all documents are executed without error. The variety of title documents recorded makes attention to detail a necessity. At this stage, the buyer is often delivered the actual title insurance policy. Adhere to the title company's instructions that accompany title documentation. Some practitioners rely on a closing letter to lay out the parameters. See Figure 5–10.

CLOSING PROTECTION LETTER

_____ **TITLE INSURANCE COMPANY**

Lender (or Buyer) Name
Lender (or Buyer) Address
Lender (or Buyer) Address

Date

Agent ID
"Issuing Agent"
Agent Name
Agent Address
Agent Address

Transaction (hereafter, "the Real Estate Transaction"):

Re: Closing Protection Letter

Dear Madam or Sir:

_____Title Insurance Company (the "Company") agrees, subject to the Conditions and Exclusions set forth below, to reimburse you for actual loss incurred by you, in connection with the closing of the Real Estate Transaction conducted by the Issuing Agent, provided:

      (A) Title insurance of the Company is specified for your protection in connection with the closing; and,

      (B) You are to be the (i) lender secured by a mortgage (including any other security instrument) of an interest in land, its assignees or a warehouse lender, (ii) purchaser of an interest in land, or (iii) lessee of an interest in land;

and provided the loss arises out of:

1. Failure of the Issuing Agent to comply with your written closing instructions to the extent that they relate to (a) the status of the title to that interest in land or the validity, enforceability and priority of the lien of the mortgage on that interest in land, including the obtaining of documents and the disbursement of funds necessary to establish the status of title or lien, or (b) the obtaining of any other document, specifically required by you, but only to the extent the failure to obtain the other document affects the status of the title to that interest in land or the validity, enforceability and priority of the lien of the mortgage on that interest in land, and not to the extent that your instructions require a determination of the validity, enforceability or the effectiveness of the other document; or

2. Acts of theft of settlement funds or fraud with regard to settlement funds by the Issuing Agent in connection with such closings to the extent such theft or fraud affects the status of the title to said interest in land or the validity, enforceability or priority of the lien of said mortgage or deed of trust on said interest in land; or

3. Acts of theft of or fraud with regard to the purchaser's earnest money or settlement funds deposited with Issuing Agent.

FIGURE 5–10
(continues)

If you are a lender protected under the foregoing paragraph, your borrower, your assignee and your warehouse lender in connection with a loan secured by a mortgage shall be protected as if this letter were addressed to them.

Conditions and Exclusions

1. The Company will not be liable to you for loss arising out of:

   A. Failure of the Issuing Agent to comply with your closing instructions which require title insurance protection inconsistent with that set fort in the title insurance binder or commitment issued by the Company. Instructions which require the removal of specific exceptions to title or compliance with the requirements contained in the binder or commitment shall not be deemed to be inconsistent.

   B. Loss or impairment of your funds in the course of collection or while on deposit with a bank due to bank failure, insolvency or suspension, except as shall result from failure of the Issuing Agent to comply with your written closing instructions to deposit the funds in a bank which you designated by name.

   C. Defects, liens, encumbrances or other matters in connection with your purchase, lease or loan transactions except to the extent that protection against those defects, liens, encumbrances or other matters is afforded by a policy of title insurance not inconsistent with your closing instructions.

   D. Fraud, dishonesty or negligence of your employee, agent, attorney or broker.

   E. Your settlement or release of any claim without the written consent of the Company.

   F. Any matters created, suffered, assumed or agreed to by you or known to you.

2. The protection herein offered shall not exceed the amount of settlement funds you transmit to the Issuing Agent.

3. When the Company shall have reimbursed you pursuant to this letter, it shall be subrogated to all rights and remedies which you would have had against any person or property had you not been so reimbursed. Liability of the Company for reimbursement shall be reduced to the extent that you have knowingly and voluntarily impaired the value of this right of subrogation.

4. The Issuing Agent is the Company's agent only for the limited purpose of issuing title insurance policies, and is not the Company's agent for the purpose of providing other closing or settlement services. The Company's liability for your losses arising from those other closing or settlement services is strictly limited to the protection expressly provided in this letter. Any liability of the Company for loss does not include liability for loss resulting from the negligence, fraud or bad faith of any party to a real estate transaction other than an Issuing Agent, the lack of creditworthiness of any borrower connected with a real estate transaction, or the failure of any collateral to adequately secure a loan connected with a real estate transaction. However, this letter does not affect the Company's liability with respect to its title insurance binders, commitments or policies.

5. You must promptly send written notice of a claim under this letter to the Company at its principal office at _____. The Company is not liable for a loss if the written notice is not received within one year from the date of the closing.

6. The protection herein offered extends only to real property transactions in Missouri.

Any previous closing protection letter provided to you is hereby cancelled only with respect to the Real Estate Transaction.

_____ **TITLE INSURANCE COMPANY**

By: _____

FIGURE 5–10
(continued)

CHAPTER FIVE **SUMMARY**

Chapter Five discussed the following topics:

- The definition and requirements of a good title
- The purpose of a title company
- Defects and impediments to title
- Process of searching a title—conveyance search
- Encumbrance searches—definition and how to conduct
- Purpose of title insurance
- Process of acquiring title insurance

REVIEW **QUESTIONS**

1. Prove this statement true or false: Title insurance runs with the land upon conveyance.
2. Give three examples of impediments to title.
3. How could the three examples of impediments to title from question number 2 be rectified?
4. How does title insurance assure the buyer of a clear and protected exchange?
5. What are some of the expenses related to assuring good title?
6. When abstracting title, the paralegal can begin with varied information. Beside the name of the grantor or grantee, how can the chain of title be identified?
7. What are five records searched in the abstraction of title?
8. Explain the difference between a conveyance search and an encumbrance search.
9. Outline the process for obtaining title insurance.
10. What system of recording is used in your area? Briefly explain how mortgage, judgment, and deed books are organized.

DISCUSSION **QUESTION**

When performing a title search, impediments and encumbrances must be identified and subsequently removed. For what kind of problems should the paralegal look?

EXERCISE 1

Prepare an Owner's Affidavit of Title, Purchaser's Affidavit of Title, and Attorney's Report of Title using the following fact patterns:

Name of Buyers—John and Mary Smith

Address—394 Willow Drive, Mytown, US

Consideration—$75,000

File No. 987654

Address of Property—399 Bend Drive, Mytown, US

Description of Property—All the certain lot or piece of ground with buildings and improvements thereon erected, situated in the township of William, county of Brown, State of U.S., and described as follows:

Beginning at a point at the intersection of the southerly side of Bend Drive and the northwesterly side of Marveen Avenue. Containing in front or breadth on the said side of Bend

Drive 100 feet and extending of that width in length or depth, 100 feet, the southeasterly line thereof being the long, the northwesterly side of Marveen Avenue.

Name of Sellers—Joe and Jennifer Meyers

Amount of mortgage to be insured—$65,000

Type of Mortgage—Conventional

Mortgagors—Sunny Day Bank

Title by—Tenancy by the entireties

Deed Book—75 at page 120

Will Book—901 at page 6

Intestacy—Not applicable

Use of Property—Residential

Interim binder—Desired

Deliver binder to—Mark Matthews, Attorney at Law, 2nd Floor, National Bank Building, Mytown, US

Settlement to be held at—Sellers' home

Assessments paid until—July 31, 2010; all current

Taxes paid until—July 31, 2010; all current

Notary Public—Joan Williams, Brown County, US

Notary Commission Expires—February 8, 2010

All rent accrue—July 31 annually

Title Commitment No. 983B982

Tax Parcel No. 201

Conflicts with adjoining properties, easements, or variations—No

Liens—None

Mineral Region—No

Date of Deed Book—Deed from Mary Richey to seller dated June 1, 1975; recorded in Deed Book 75, page 120.

EXERCISE 2

Obtain a copy of a deed from a friend, family member, or a random deed in the office responsible for recording deeds. Using Figures 5–2 and 5–3, trace the deed back two transactions.

Assignment for the Case of John and Martha

Prepare an Owner's Affidavit of Title, Purchaser's Affidavit of Title, and Attorney's Report of Title using the following additional information. Please create any missing information.

File No. 635–BA–2005
Amount of mortgage to be insured—$65,000
Type of Mortgage—Conventional
Deed Book—101 at page 7
Use of Property—Residential
Interim binder—Desired
Settlement to be held at—Settlement agency's office
Assessments paid until—all current
Taxes paid until—July 1, 2010; April 1, 2010; all current

Notary Public—Renee Smith
Notary Commission Expires—December 5, 2010
Title Commitment No. 6725934
Tax Parcel No. 901
Conflicts with adjoining properties, easements, or variations—No
Liens—None
Mineral Region—No
Date of Deed Book—Deed from Ronald Amend to seller dated May 22, 1994; recorded in
  Deed Book 101, page 7.

REFERENCES

1. James J. Kelly, *Bringing Clarity to Title Clearing: Tax Foreclosure and Due Process in the Internet Age*, 77 U. CIN. L. REV. 63 (2008).

2. ROBERT BERNHARDT, REAL PROPERTY, 256 (1975).

3. *Id*. at 347.

4. TIMOTHY G. O'NEILL, LADNER ON CONVEYANCING IN PENNSYLVANIA, §20.01 (1988).

5. *Id*. at §20.01.

6. Charles B. Dewitt, III, *Title Insurance: A Primer*, 3 TENN. J. PRAC. & PROC. 15 (2000); *see also* Robert L. Tucker, *Disappearing Ink: The Emerging Duty to Remove Invalid Policy Provisions*, 42 AKRON L. REV. 519 (2009).

7. O'NEILL, *supra note* 4, at 523.

8. Rhode Island Bar Association, *Proposed Form, Letter, and Practice Standard Changes*, 51 RI BAR J. 37 (2002).

9. SUMMA PA. JUR. 2d, §8:72.

10. CHARLES P. NEMETH, THE PARALEGAL RESOURCE MANUAL, 2nd ed. (1995), 523–4.

11. O'Neill, *supra note* 4, at §19.02.

12. *Id*. at 569.

13. BURTON R. LAUB & W. EDWARD SELL, PENNSYLVANIA KEYSTONE, REAL ESTATE CLOSING at 9–10 (1993).

14. *Id*. at 11–12.

15. SUMMA, *supra note* 8, at §8:77.

16. *See Mechanic's Liens: Definition of Subcontractor Critical to Validity of Materialman's Lien*, 20 REAL EST. L. REP. (May 1991).

17. Dewitt, *supra note* 6, at 15.

18. LAUB & SELL, *supra note* 13, at 14.

19. DataSearch, 797 Cromwell Park Drive Suite A-F, Glen Burnie, Maryland 21061 www.data-search.com/html/partners/files/v33_Worksheet.pdf

20. Dewitt, *supra note* 15.

21. MARK WARDA, THE COMPLETE BOOK OF REAL ESTATE CONTRACTS 36 (2005).

22. All-State Legal, One Commerce Drive, Cranford, NJ, 05631, Form 1630.

23. All-State Legal, One Commerce Drive, Cranford, NJ 05631, Form, 1635.

24. WILLIAM F. HOFFMEYER, THE PENNSYLVANIA REAL ESTATE SETTLEMENT PROCEDURES MANUAL, 35 (1990).

Nature of a Deed

LEARNING OBJECTIVES

- To summarize the nature of a deed and its purpose.
- To identify the various elements for a formal and legally enforceable deed.
- To distinguish and differentiate a grant of right from other types of transfer.
- To recognize specialized deed clauses, such as mining and water rights.

JOB COMPETENCIES

- To prepare a deed in conjunction with an attorney.
- To interpret the restrictions and encumbrances placed within a deed.
- To identify the form of deed being granted and its resulting rights and obligations or limitations.
- To assemble a deed and record it.

ETHICAL CONSIDERATIONS

The paralegal must be aware of the following ethical dilemmas during this phase of a real estate transaction:

- Unauthorized practice of law
- Lawyer supervision of nonlawyers
- Confidentiality issues
- Communications with persons outside of law firm

I. INTRODUCTION

KEY WORDS

deed	indenture
grantee	Statute of Frauds
grantor	

A **deed**, which a paralegal routinely drafts, evidences the transfer and subsequent ownership of real property. The deed document has a long and illustrious history, and largely came about due to a need for a formal record of ownership in land. For many generations, even in the American experience, a deed was not required and property was even passed by oral promise over the generations. Over time, the sheer number of transactions, as the move from a feudal society become more evident, called for a recordation system of ownership. Deeds or other conveyancing documents were authored, collected, signed and recorded in some of office of governmental oversight. In a nutshell, deeds formalize the transaction and give permanency to it.

Web Exercise

For an interesting look at how deeds became part of the Anglo-Saxon, Western tradition, see the analysis of the Harvard Law Library at www.law.harvard.edu/library/special/exhibits/exhibitions/history-in-deed.html.

Deeds are simple documents in some ways. First, there are generally only two parties to the document. The seller on the deed, known as the **grantor**, agrees for a sum of consideration to transfer or alienate certain rights, covenants, restrictions, or other obligations to a buyer, known as the **grantee**. Deeds that contain mutual covenants between the parties are sometimes called **indentures** after the ancient practice of cutting an instrument in half in a jagged manner and supplying each party with a piece for later comparison if necessary.[1]

In most U.S. jurisdictions, under the **Statute of Frauds**, a deed must be in writing to be enforceable. This rule originates from the common law principle. While the statute does not prevent an oral contract for the sale of realty from coming into existence, it does prevent the specific enforcement of the agreement.

II. DEED COVENANTS

KEY WORDS		
covenant	Covenant of Warranty	perfecting the title
covenant of further assurances	express covenant	present covenant
	future covenant	Quiet Enjoyment
covenant of Seisin	implied covenant	Right to Convey
Covenant of Title		

Deeds transfer and alienate some level of ownership to the buying party. The seller signatory to the deed conveys in particular ways and gives varying levels of assurances on the quality of a property. In this sense, every deed includes provisions called covenants. A **covenant**, in loose terms, is a promise, an assurance, a representation about the property to be conveyed. Covenants may lay out the full rights of ownership and usage that bind the present buyers or successors, or set form in some restrictive language on how property can be used. Covenants are further classified into present and future categories. In the **present covenant**, the grantor conveys present rights; and in the **future covenant**, the grantor anticipates future usage with restriction. Covenants may also be expressly inserted into the language of the deed or implied by common law, rule, or regulation. An **express covenant** can be directly discovered in the content of the deed. An **implied covenant** is one intended or implied in other laws and public policy, such as deeds cannot discriminate based on race or gender. A quick look at the more common covenants follows.

A. Covenant of Seisin

The broadest and most extensive of the covenant class, Seisin, expressly indicates that the Seller of the property in question conveys a property that is fully owned by the grantor and not subject to the rights and obligations of other parties. The **covenant of seisin** warrants that the grantor is the owner of the estate described in the deed.[2]

The term Seisin imputes that the grantor is seized of a distinct interest property which he or she has every right to sell since they are the possesors with a legal interest. Hence, the grantor who owns a fee simple estate freehold, without restriction, may be said to warrant or covenant the extent of said possession. On the other hand, a grantor who sells more than possessed would be held to have breached the covenant.

B. Covenant of Right to Convey/Covenant of Title

Closely aligned to Seisin is the Covenant of **Right to Convey**. Sometimes referred to as the **Covenant of Title**, the grantor, by execution of the deed, indicates that he or she has the power and right to covey the title of said property. In other words, the grantor affirms not the extent of the owned interest but instead the legal power and right to convey whatever that title might be. Various American jurisdictions have codified this and other covenants. By way of example, review the West Virginia Code provison on the Right to Convey:

36-4-4. Right to convey.

A covenant by a grantor in a deed for land, "that he has the right to convey the said land to the grantee," or a covenant of like import, shall have the same effect as if the grantor had covenanted that he has good right, full power, and absolute authority to convey the said land, with all the buildings thereon, and the privileges and appurtenances thereto belonging, unto the grantee, in the manner in which the same is conveyed, or intended so to be by the deed, and according to its true intent.[3]

C. Covenant Against Encumbrances

Also spelled as an "Incumbrance", the Covenant gives assurances that the land is conveyed free and clear of the typical encumbrances. Buyers of the property are promised that any existing encumbrances have been dealt with or will be remedies in future circumstance. The covenant gives assurances regarding:

- Liens
- Judgments
- Attachments
- Levy
- Taxes
- Mortgages
- Local Assessments

It is possible that a grantee will assume, by consent, certain encumbrances, such as a mortgage, due to favorable rates.

Web Exercise

See how the Statute of Limitations impacts a claim for breach of the Covenant Against Encumbrances at www.websupp.org/data/WDMO/2:06-cv-04046-36-WDMO.pdf.

CASE DECISION

See how the Covenant Against Encumbrances was interpreted by a Texas Court.

TEXAS COURT OF APPEALS, THIRD DISTRICT, AT AUSTIN

NO. 03-97-00501-CV

Hugh Bob Spiller, Appellant

v.

Fidelity National Title Insurance Company, Appellee

FROM THE DISTRICT COURT OF CONCHO COUNTY, 119TH JUDICIAL DISTRICT

NO. 3207-B, HONORABLE JOHN E. SUTTON, JUDGE PRESIDING

We consider in this appeal the effect of a warrantee's settling an adverse claim to land covered by warranties of title given in a deed of real property. The trial court rendered a summary judgment against the warrantor, appellant Hugh Bob Spiller, ruling that his refusal to defend the warrantee estopped him from contesting the reasonableness of the settlement negotiated by the warrantee's title insurer, appellee Fidelity National Title Insurance Company. We will reverse the judgment of the trial court and remand the cause for further proceedings.

THE CONTROVERSY

In 1987, Thomas Rezzlle conveyed to his son Richard Rezzlle the land in question. To finance the purchase, Richard Rezzlle borrowed $50,000 from Junction National Bank, secured by a first lien given in a deed of trust, and $24,580 from Thomas secured by a second lien. The bank sold its note to Spiller. On May 1, 1990, Spiller foreclosed his lien on the property. Spiller and Thomas Rezzlle purchased the property from a substitute trustee. Spiller and Thomas Rezzlle conveyed the land on June 4 to Lee Bell by deed of general warranty, after which Bell subdivided the land and sold some of the lots. Bell obtained title insurance from Fidelity, and some of the remaining lot owners obtained insurance from Alamo Title Company.

In 1994, Richard Rezzlle and Sue McShan sued Spiller, Thomas Rezzlle, Lee Bell, thirteen lot owners, and the substitute trustee under the deeds of trust. Richard Rezzlle alleged that defects in the foreclosure proceedings rendered the foreclosure sale void. McShan claimed that, as Spiller's wife when he acquired it, she owned a community interest in the note. McShan further asserted that in 1988 the court hearing the divorce proceedings between her and Spiller temporarily enjoined disposition of the note, and that the court later awarded the entire note to her. McShan and Richard Rezzlle prayed that the deed to Bell be canceled and title to the land awarded to them.

Spiller initially appeared in the lawsuit pro se, but later was represented by counsel. Alleging breach of the warranties made in the deed to him, Bell cross-claimed against Spiller and Thomas Rezzlle. Fidelity intervened, as subrogee of Bell's rights, to sue Spiller for breaching his covenant of warranty of title and covenant against encumbrances. Fidelity also claimed to be the assignee of the claims of seven of the lot owners as well as all claims Alamo held by subrogation. Fidelity alleged that it paid to defend and settle the lawsuit against Bell and that it was entitled to recover the $60,000 paid to release claims against the land plus $13,222.40 in attorney's fees to defend the title. At the request of McShan and Richard Rezzlle, the trial court dismissed with prejudice their claims against all defendants, leaving only the cross-claims pending.

The trial court granted Fidelity's motion for summary judgment, rendering a final judgment that Fidelity recover $73,222.40 from Spiller.

DISCUSSION AND HOLDINGS

(continued)

In his first point of error, Spiller asserts that Fidelity's theory of estoppel cannot support the judgment. Fidelity moved for summary judgment on the ground that Spiller's refusal to defend Bell against McShan and Richard Rezzlle's claims estopped him from asserting that they were without merit and that the amount Fidelity and Alamo paid to settle them was unreasonable. Because the question in this case is one of law, we review the summary-judgment record to determine whether it establishes conclusively Fidelity's right to judgment. *Gibbs v. General Motors Corp.*, 450 S.W.2d 827, 828 (Tex. 1970).

In the deed conveying the land to Bell, Spiller and Thomas Rezzlle bound themselves "to warrant and forever defend the premises unto the grantees against every person whomsoever lawfully claiming or to claim the same or any part thereof." By this covenant, Spiller warranted that he had not conveyed the same estate to any person other than Bell, and that the property was free from encumbrances. *Compton v. Trico Oil Co.*, 120 S.W.2d 534, 537 (Tex. Civ. App.–Dallas 1938, writ ref'd). The covenant of general warranty is termed a contract of indemnity, its purpose being to indemnify the warrantee against loss he may sustain by a failure in the warrantor's title. *City of Beaumont v. Moore*, 202 S.W.2d 448, 453 (Tex. 1947).

By using the words "grant" and "convey" in the deed to Bell, Spiller additionally warranted that the land he sold was not encumbered. Tex. Prop. Code Ann. § 5.023(a) (West 1984). The covenant against encumbrances is distinct from the warranty of title and is intended to protect the grantee against rights or interests in third persons that, while consistent with the fee being in the grantor, diminish the value of the estate conveyed. *Moore*, 202 S.W.2d at 453. Like the covenant of warranty of title, however, the covenant against encumbrances is one of indemnity, promising compensation for damages that arise from an outstanding right or interest in a third person. *Id.*

To prevail on a claim for breach of warranty of title, the warrantee must show that his title has failed and that he has been evicted from the land. *Schneider v. Lipscomb County Nat'l Farm Loan Ass'n*, 202 S.W.2d 832, 834 (Tex. 1947); *Freeman v. Anderson*, 119 S.W.2d 1081, 1083 (Tex. Civ. App.–Waco 1938, no writ). An eviction may be either actual or constructive; if the latter, the warrantee must prove that paramount title has been positively asserted against him and that the asserted title is in fact paramount. *Schneider*, 202 S.W.2d at 834; *Whitaker v. Felts*, 155 S.W.2d 604, 606 (Tex. 1941). A warrantee cannot base a constructive eviction merely on his voluntary act; if he cedes to an opposing claim of title that is inferior to his own, he cannot hold the warrantor liable in damages. *Whitaker*, 155 S.W.2d at 606; *Rancho Bonito Land & Live-Stock Co. v. North*, 45 S.W. 994, 996 (Tex. 1898). Having ceded to McShan and Richard Rezzlle's claims to paramount title by settling, Bell must rely on a constructive eviction. Thus before Spiller could be held liable for a breach of warranty, he would ordinarily be entitled to an adjudication that McShan and Richard Rezzlle held superior title to the land. *Johns v. Hardin*, 16 S.W. 623, 623 (Tex. 1891). *E.g., Sherman v. Piner*, 91 S.W.2d 1185, 1185 (Tex. Civ. App.–Eastland 1936, no writ).

A claim for breach of the covenant against encumbrances arises when the covenantee is either dispossessed by foreclosure or compelled to discharge the encumbrance. *Seibert v. Bergman*, 44 S.W. 63, 63-64 (Tex. 1898); *Wolff v. Commercial Standard Ins. Co.*, 345 S.W.2d 565, (Tex. Civ. App.–Houston [1st Dist.] 1961, writ ref'd n.r.e.); *Hill v. Provine*, 260 S.W. 682, 683 (Tex. Civ. App.–El Paso 1924, writ dism'd). Spiller's liability for breach of the covenant against encumbrances depended on a showing that Bell was legally obligated to discharge the encumbrance. *See Johns*, 16 S.W. at 623.

Fidelity contends that Spiller is estopped from litigating the merits of the title claims and the reasonableness of the settlement because he refused to defend Bell against the adverse claims. Fidelity supports its contention with the affidavit of the attorney then representing Bell. The attorney states in his affidavit that when he asked Spiller to defend Bell's title, Spiller demanded that Bell in return agree to hold him harmless from any claim for breach of warranty. Bell rejected this demand, according to the attorney, and Spiller refused to defend Bell. Fidelity then negotiated a settlement by which McShan and Rezzlle released their claims to title and nonsuited Bell in return for $50,000 from Fidelity and $5,000 from Alamo. We will assume that Spiller refused to defend Bell's title to the land.

The consequences of Spiller's refusing to defend Bell and Bell's settling the adverse claims are governed by principles of indemnity. When an indemnitor such as Spiller denies that he owes any obligation under an indemnity contract, he waives the right to a judicial determination of the indemnitee's liability to an adverse claimant. *Gulf, Colo. & S. F. Ry. v. McBride*, 322 S.W.2d 492, 495 (Tex. 1958); *Mitchell's Inc. v. Friedman*, 303 S.W.2d 775, 779 (Tex. 1957), *overruled on other grounds*, *Ethyl Corp. v. Daniel Constr. Co.*, 725 S.W.2d 705, 708 (Tex. 1987). An indemnitee such as Bell, who cannot secure a defense by his indemnitor and who then settles the claim without an adjudication of liability, assumes the burden to prove facts that might have rendered him liable to the claimant as well as the reasonableness of the amount he paid. *Firemen's Fund Ins. Co. v. Commercial Standard Ins. Co.*, 490 S.W.2d 818, 824 (Tex. 1972), *overruled on other grounds*, *Ethyl Corp. v. Daniel Constr. Co.*, 725 S.W.2d 705, 708 (Tex. 1987); *Mitchell's Inc.*, 303 S.W.2d at 779; *H.S.M. Acquisitions Inc. v. West*, 917 S.W.2d 872, 879 (Tex. App.–Corpus Christi 1996, no writ). The indemnitee must prove that, from his standpoint, the settlement was made in good faith and was reasonable and prudent under the circumstances. *Firemen's Fund Ins. Co.*, 490 S.W.2d at 824; *Mitchell's Inc.*, 303 S.W.2d at 779; *Wolff*, 345 S.W.2d at 568. Thus, while Spiller's refusal to defend Bell constituted a waiver of Spiller's right to have Bell's liability adjudicated, it did not estop Spiller from requiring Bell, or Bell's subrogee Fidelity, to prove Bell's potential liability and the reasonableness of the settlement with McShan and Richard Rezzlle.

CONCLUSION

We conclude that Bell's settlement imposed on him the burden to prove its reasonableness. Fidelity's assertion that Spiller is estopped to contend that the settlement was unreasonable misconstrues this burden. We, therefore, sustain point of error one. In light of our disposition of this point, we need not address points two and three. Because Fidelity was not entitled to summary judgment on the ground of estoppel, we reverse the trial court's judgment and remand the cause for further proceedings.

John Powers, Justice

Before Justices Powers, Aboussie and B. A. Smith

Reversed and Remanded

Filed: October 15, 1998

1. Fidelity moves this Court to disregard the transcription of the hearing on the summary-judgment motion as well as two affidavits filed in opposition to the motion after the judgment was signed. We sustain the motion. Tex. R. Civ. P. 166a(c).

2. We decline to address Spiller's contention that his defense against the adverse-title claims, initially pro se and later through an attorney, fulfilled his duty to defend Bell's title. 1891). *E.g., Sherman v. Piner*, 91 S.W.2d 1185, 1185 (Tex. Civ. App.–Eastland 1936, no writ).

A claim for breach of the covenant against encumbrances arises when the covenantee is either dispossessed by foreclosure or compelled to discharge the encumbrance. *Seibert v. Bergman*, 44 S.W. 63, 63-64 (Tex. 1898); *Wolff v. Commercial Standard Ins. Co.*, 345 S.W.2d 565, (Tex. Civ. App.–Houston [1st Dist.] 1961, writ ref'd n.r.e.); *Hill v. Provine*, 260 S.W. 682, 683 (Tex. Civ. App.–El Paso 1924, writ dism'd). Spiller's liability for breach of the covenant against encumbrances depended on a showing that Bell was legally obligated to discharge the encumbrance. *See Johns*, 16 S.W. at 623.

Fidelity contends that Spiller is estopped from litigating the merits of the title claims and the reasonableness of the settlement because he refused to defend Bell against the adverse claims. Fidelity supports its contention with the affidavit of the attorney then representing Bell. The attorney states in his affidavit that when he asked Spiller to defend Bell's title, Spiller demanded that Bell in return agree to hold him harmless from any claim for breach of warranty. Bell rejected this demand, according to the attorney, and Spiller refused to defend Bell. Fidelity then negotiated a settlement by which McShan and Rezzlle released their claims to title and nonsuited Bell in return for $50,000 from Fidelity and $5,000 from Alamo. We will assume that Spiller refused to defend Bell's title to the land.

(*continued*)

The consequences of Spiller's refusing to defend Bell and Bell's settling the adverse claims are governed by principles of indemnity. When an indemnitor such as Spiller denies that he owes any obligation under an indemnity contract, he waives the right to a judicial determination of the indemnitee's liability to an adverse claimant.

D. Covenant of Warranty/Quiet Enjoyment

In the **covenant of warranty**, the grantor promises to defend the premises from lawful claims, from third parties who allege to have an ownership interest in said property. This is a covenant that runs with the land and must be expressly designated in the deed format. This covenant is merely a guarantee that there are no valid claims outstanding against the property conveyed. If an invalid or inferior claim is asserted, the covenantor has no liability.

The **Covenant of Quiet Enjoyment** applies to leasehold estates. Here the lessor warrants that the lessee will have free and unfettered enjoyment to his leased premises during the duration of the lease.

E. Covenant of Further Assurances

The **covenant of further assurances** is a promise that the grantor will effect any changes in deed construction or language to effect what the grantor and grantee intended. For example, a deed that was agreed to be fee simple without conditions or restriction may subsequently be discovered to suffer from some restriction by interpretation of the deed language. The Covenant of Further Assurances tells the grantee that grantor will take all reasonable steps to cure the defect in deed language, or to undergo any reasonable action that would remedy the ambiguity or defect in title. This is sometimes described as **perfecting the title**.[4]

Just what the deed contains is basically a reflection of the rights conveyed by the grantor to the grantee. The deed may expand or restrict certain rights regarding the use of land or impose obligations upon that grantee. Deeds, in the most generic sense, convey a right, a title to a specific estate. The parties to it, for example, a guardian who grants or buys on behalf of another, a corporate deed when property conveyed is owned by a corporate entity, or a sheriff's deed, will often dictate the type of deed when a forced public sale of a distressed property occurs. Conditional financing may also influence its type and content, usually a mortgage note that gives a bank enhanced rights. In this case, a deed of trust is authored. The deed may also set out specific rights to use easements—that form of real property interest regarding utility, electric and gas lines, or other minimal intrusions granted to governmental authority. In addition, the deed may, by specific and explicit mention, permit the grantee access through an adjoining property to another location.

Other items referenced in deeds might involve riparian or water rights, air space, mineral rights, and party walls or fences. Simply, deeds manifest what is conveyed.

III. ELEMENTS OF A DEED

KEY WORDS

acknowledgment

encumbrance clause

habendum clause

metes and bounds

nominal consideration

recital

recording

testimonium clause

All deeds contain the following provisions:

- Names of the parties
- Consideration, whether nominal or actual
- Specific words of conveyance, such grant or convey, bargain or sell
- Description of the property, another place where the legal description will be provided
- Habendum clause, that is, that the property is taken freely and clearly or with certain reservations or restrictions. Habendum is often known as the "to have and to hold" clause
- Execution and acknowledgment clause.[5]

Deeds are typically two to four pages long depending upon the length of the property description and an enumeration of the parties and their respective rights and obligations. Reproduced to Figure 6–1[6] is a standard deed produced by Easy Soft Inc. Another version of a deed form is re-produced (**general warranty deed)** in Figure 6–2. A closer inspection of the various deed components follows.

A. Deed Components

In most deed constructions, the date follows the introductory phrase "This deed" or "This indenture." See Figure 6–3.

1. Parties

Just who the grantor and the grantee are rests within the confines of the next deed clause (see Figure 6–4). Whether the grantor is a person, a corporation or partnership, or other legal entity, need be explicitly stated. The parties may be individuals, partnership or corporate entities or other legal entity.

2. Consideration

What sum is being paid by grantee to grantor for the property is cited in the consideration clause of the deed. A small amount of sum must be set even if that sum does not represent the actual value of the exchange. Even the practice of citing a "one dollar consideration" sum meets the criterion of a legal consideration. This practice is known as **nominal consideration**. If the actual price is not stated, calculate by computing the documentary and tax stamps affixed to a final, recorded deed. See Figure 6–5.

3. Habendum Clause

The **habendum clause** represents the action of exchange that the deed triggers. (See Figure 6–6).
Under the deed's habendum clause, that is the provision that indicates the extent and nature of title held, the grantor states that certain covenants will run with the land, covenants being certain rights and duties that are passed to grantees. Covenants like the covenant of quiet enjoyment pass with the land except in the case of a quit-claim or sheriff's deed. Other specific covenants or rights with the land require explicit express language within the deed. The granting clause generally employs words such as *to grant, to sell, to release, to convey,* or *to pass on.* The words employed in a habendum clause are often referred to as "operative words."

4. Property Description

The deed should describe with particularity the property to be conveyed. The legal description of the property should be identical to any survey conducted, or governmental or plat

DEED

Prepared by:

_____

This Deed is made on,

BETWEEN

whose address is   ,   ,   referred to as the Grantor,

AND

whose post office address is   ,   ,   referred to as the Grantee.

The words "Grantor" and "Grantee" shall mean all Grantors and all Grantees listed above.

1. Grantor. The Grantor makes this Deed as the Personal Representative of the Estate of who died on   late of the   of County of   and State of   . Letters were issued to the grantor herein by the surrogate of   County on   .

2. Transfer of Ownership. The Grantor grants and conveys (transfers ownership of) the property described below to the Grantee. This transfer is made for the sum of   (dollars). The Grantor acknowledges receipt of this money.

3. Tax Map Reference. (N.J.S.A. 46:15-2.1) Municipality of   Block No.   Lot No. Account No.   .

No property tax identification number is available on the date of this deed. (Check box if applicable)

4. Property. The property consists of the land and all the buildings and structures on the land in the of   County of   and the State of   .

Please see attached Legal Description annexed hereto and made a part hereof. (Check box if applicable)

The street address of the property is:

5. Promises by Grantor. The Grantor promises that the Grantor has done no act to encumber the property. This promise is called a "covenant as to grantor's acts" (N.J.S.A. 46:4-6). This promise means that the Grantor has not allowed anyone else to obtain any legal rights which affect the Property (such as by making a mortgage or allowing a judgment to be entered against the Grantor).

6. Signatures. The Grantor signs this Deed as of the date at the top of the first page. If the Grantor is a corporation, this Deed is signed and attested to by itd proper corporate officers and its corporate seal is affixed.

Witnessed or Attested by:

_____(Seal)

_____   _____(Seal)

_____   _____(Seal)

FIGURE 6–1
(continues)

STATE OF New Jersey, COUNTY OF Middlesex   SS.:

I CERTIFY that on

, personally came before me and stated to my satisfaction that this person (or if more than one, each person):

(a) was the maker of this Deed;
(b) executed this Deed as his or her capacity as personal representative of the deceased owner; and
(c) made this Deed for: as the full and actual consideration paid or to be paid for the transfer of title.

(Such consideration is defined in N.J.S.A. 46:15-5.)

STATE OF New Jersey, COUNTY OF Middlesex   SS.:

I CERTIFY that on

, personally came before me and stated to my satisfaction that this person (or if more than one, each person):

(a) was the maker of the attached Deed;
(b) was authorized to and did execute this Deed as   of   the entity named in this Deed; and
(c) made this Deed for: as the full and actual consideration paid or to be paid for the transfer of title.
(Such consideration is defined in N.J.S.A. 46:15-5.)
(d) executed this Deed as the act of the entity, in his or her capacity as personal representative of the deceased owner.

RECORD AND RETURN TO:

John Public Esq.
123 Pin Oak Drive
New Brunswick, New Jersey 09989

_____

FIGURE 6–1
(continued)

THIS INDENTURE, made the   day of   ,

BETWEEN

party of the first part, and

party of the second part,

WITNESSETH, that the party of the first part, in consideration of ten dollars and other valuable consideration paid by the party of the second part, does hereby grant and release unto the party of the second part, the heirs or successors and assigns of the party of the second part forever,

ALL that certain plot, piece or parcel of land, with the buildings and improvements thereon erected, situate, lying and being in the

TOGETHER with all right, title and interest, if any, of the party of the first part in and to any streets and roads abutting the above described premises to the center lines thereof; TOGETHER with the appurtenances and all the estate and rights of the party of the first part in and to said premises; TO HAVE AND TO HOLD the premises herein granted unto the party of the second part, the heirs or successors and assigns of the party of the second part forever.

AND the party of the first part covenants that the party of the first part will receive the consideration for this conveyance and will hold the right to receive such consideration as a trust fund to be applied first for the purpose of paying the cost of the improvement and will apply the same first to the payment of the cost of the improvement before using any part of the total of the same for any other purpose.

FIGURE 6–2
(continues)

AND the party of the first part covenants as follows: that said party of the first part is seized of the said premises in fee simple, and has good right to convey the same; that the party of the second part shall quietly enjoy the said premises; that the said premises are free from encumbrances, except as aforesaid; that the party of the first part will execute or procure any further necessary assurance of the title to said premises; and that said party of the first part will forever warrant the title to said premises.

The word "party" shall be construed as if it read "parties" whenever the sense of this indenture so requires.

IN WITNESS WHEREOF. the party of the first part has duly executed this deed the day and year first above written.

IN PRESENCE OF:

_____

_____

_____

FIGURE 6–2
(continued)

THIS INDENTURE, Made the _____ day of_____in the year of our Lord

two thousand _____

FIGURE 6–3
Introductory Phrase with Date Designation.

BETWEEN _____ (hereinafter called the grantor), of the first part, and

_____ (hereinafter called the grantee), of the second part.

FIGURE 6–4
Identification of Parties.

WITNESSETH that the said party of the first part, for and in consideration of the sum of
_____, lawful money of the United States of America, well and truly
paid by the said party of the second part to the said party of the first part, at and before the
unsealing and delivery of these presents.

FIGURE 6–5
Consideration Clause.

> . . . the receipt whereof is hereby acknowledged, hath granted, bargained, sold, aligned, enfeoffed, released, conveyed and confirmed, and by these presents doth grant, bargain, sell, alien, enfeoff, release, convey and confirm unto the said party of the second party, _____ heirs, successors and assigns.

FIGURE 6–6
Habendum Clause.

descriptions previously confirmed. There are four types of legal descriptions used in real estate in the USA.

- Metes and bounds
- Government land survey
- Lot and block numbers
- Monuments

Metes refer to distance and bounds to direction with a beginning point being the point to commence calculation. This is known as Point of Beginning (POB). Deeds will frequently see these types of land descriptions such as

> Beginning at a point (POB) on the North side of Mark Street 50 feet East from the corner formed by the intersection of the East boundary of Peter Road and the North boundary of Marks Street; thence East 90 degrees 200 feet; thence North 300 feet; thence West 200 feet; thence direct to the POB.

The description can be based on rectangular land survey system that has long been utilized. There are geographical locations all over the US that serve as a base reference. The principal meridians running North-South and East-West intersect at these locations.

Beginning at these points, the surveyors established lines every 6 miles North, South, East and West at a designated point. Each of these squares is called townships. These are 6 miles by 6 miles, having an area of 36 square miles. Lines running East-West are called township lines. Lines running North-South are called range lines. They are further divided up into areas of 1 square mile called sections. Thus there are 36 sections in a township. Each section contains 640 acres. See Figure 6–7.

Other methods utilized lots and blocks or some fixed position or monument to commence the measure. Whatever method is employed, "it is essential, in order that a deed may be operative as a legal conveyance, that the land granted and intended to be conveyed be described with sufficient definiteness and certainty to locate and distinguish it from other lands of the same kind."[7] (See Figure 6–8).

Web Exercise

Review the information on how to compute Metes and Bounds Deed Land descriptions at agecon2.tamu.edu/people/faculty/lard-curtis/432/PDFs/MetesAndBounds.pdf.

5. The Recital

While not a necessary component of the deed, the **recital** sets out the change of title as it relates to the previous grantor and grantee. The recital generally commences with the term "BEING," indented and capitalized. (See Figure 6–9.)

EXAMPLE 2

TOWNSHIP DIVIDED INTO SECTIONS

◄ONE MILE►					
6	5	4	3	2	1
7	8	9	10	11	12
18	17	16	15	14	13
19	20	21	22	23	24
30	29	28	27	26	25
31	32	33	34	35	36

◄ONE MILE►

SIX MILES

◄———————— SIX MILES ————————►

FIGURE 6–7

6. Encumbrance Clause

Deed language may also include references to encumbrances based on mortgages or other restrictive conditions in the conveyance. (See Figure 6–10.)

The deed may also set out explicit restrictions on the use of property such as a limitation on its use for manufacturing or machinery. Other typical restrictive encumbrances may limit the subdivision of lots, restrict the type and style of buildings, restrict uses for other than a private dwelling, or forbid the consumption or manufacture of intoxicating liquors. Easement, exceptions, and other reservations are proper subject matter for encumbrance clauses.

ALL that certain lot or piece of ground situated in the_____, County of _____ and State of _____ being Lot No._____, in the_____, as recorded in the Recorder's Office of _____County, _____, in Plan Book Volume _____, Pages _____, _____ and _____.

BEING DESIGNATED as Block and Lot No. _____, known and numbered as _____, _____, _____.

UNDER AND SUBJECT to covenants, conditions, restrictions, easements, coal and mining rights and right of way as contained in prior instruments of record.

FIGURE 6–8
Legal Description.

BEING the same premises which _____ and _____ his wife, by deed dated _____, _____, and recorded in _____ for the County of _____ in deed Book _____ No. ____ page ____, granted and conveyed unto the said _____ and his wife in _____, as _____

FIGURE 6–9
Recital.

ALSO UNDER AND SUBJECT to the payment of a certain mortgage debt or principal sum of thirty-five hundred dollars ($3,500) (reduced to two thousand dollars ($2,000) by payments on account), with interest thereon as the same may become due and payable.

FIGURE 6–10
Encumbrance Clause.

7. Testimonium Clause

The **testimonium clause**, where grantor executes the deed to grantee, is an administrative necessity for deed formality. Title does not pass to a grantee unless the grantor signs the deed document. Under the Statute of Frauds, the grantor alone must sign and execute. See Figure 6–11.

WITNESS WHEREOF, the said party of the first part has hereunto set their hands and seals the day, month and year first written above.

Signed, sealed and delivered in the presence of

_____

_____

FIGURE 6–11
Testimonium Clause.

8. *Acknowledgment*

Witnesses and notarial matters encompass the **acknowledgment** clause. See Figure 6–12.

IN WITNESS WHEREOF the said party of the first part to these presents hath hereunto set
_____ hand and seal.

Dated the day, month and year first above written.

SIGNED, SEALED and DELIVERED In the Presence of

_____; (SEAL)

_____; (SEAL)

On this _____ day of_____, _____, before me, the Subscriber, a
Notary Public for the State of _____, residing in _____ and
_____, came the above-named _____ and _____,
Husband and Wife, and acknowledged the foregoing to be their act and deed, and desired the
same to be recorded as such.

WITNESS my hand and notarial seal, the day, month and year aforesaid.

_____
Notary Public

(Seal)

My commission expires _____, _____

FIGURE 6–12
Acknowledgment.

9. *Certificate of Residence*

Some jurisdictions require that the grantee indicate whether or not the property transferred by this deed is the residence of the grantee. The purpose of this legal requirement is to aid the Recorder of Deeds which furnishes the names and address of county property owners to the tax authorities. (Figure 6–13.)

CERTIFICATE OF RESIDENCE

I, _____ do hereby certify that grantees' precise residence is

_____ _____, _____, _____,

_____.

Witness my hand this _____ day of _____, _____.

FIGURE 6–13

10. *Recording Information*

The final component relates to when a deed was recorded, as well as in what book and on what page the deed is referenced. This area of the deed is inscribed by an official agent in the governmental office entrusted with deed recordation. The formalization of deed **recording** is not merely a paper transaction since priority of recordation is partially proven by the inscription and in a case of competing title claims or challenges, the party with a prior recordation may have the superior right to the property.

Web Exercise

Learn how to request a copy of a deed from a large city registry at stlouis.missouri.org/citygov/recorder/forms/DeedCopyForm.pdf.

IV. TYPES OF DEEDS

KEY WORDS		
administrator	guardian deed	special warranty deed
bargain & sale deed	limited warranty deed	
corporate deed		trustee's deed
executor	quitclaim deed	
general warranty deed	sheriff's deed	

The purposes of and parties to the conveyance determine the type of deed needed, and this needs to be confirmed by the paralegal and supervising attorney. All deeds minimally contain the following provisions:

- Names of the parties
- Consideration, whether nominal or actual
- Specific words of conveyance, such as grant or convey, grant, bargain or sell, or the like
- Description of the property, another place where the legal description will be provided
- Habendum clause, which implies, that the property is taken freely and clearly or with certain reservations or restrictions. Habendum is often known as the "to have and to hold" clause
- Execution and acknowledgement clause

The grantor must be competent to convey, and the grantee must be capable of receiving the grant of the property. Any person who is competent to make a valid contract is competent to be a grantor. Minors or insane persons may avoid their contracts, and no one should propose a real estate transaction with such persons or take a deed from any grantor who is under age or non compos mentis.[8]

Deeds vary in terms of their covenants and warranties. A grantor who wishes to promise the minimum bundle of rights would utilize the **quitclaim deed**. The grantor in a quitclaim situation makes no promises and no warranties regarding the quality of its title. On the other hand, a buyer of property may wish numerous assurances, insisting upon a quality title with no encumbrances or restrictive covenants. In this case, another type of deed is employed, namely a general or **special warranty deed**. The **general warranty deed** can only be described as generous in its protections. "Unlike a quitclaim deed, which purports to convey no greater interest in property than that which the grantor actually owns, a general warranty deed incorporates certain promises of the grantor respecting the quality of title conveyed. Chief among these promises is the 'covenant of quiet enjoyment' by which the grantor warrants that the grantee's peaceable possession and use of the subject property shall be undisturbed by the grantor or by any third party lawfully claiming an interest in the property in opposition to the interest conveyed to the grantee. If 'undisturbed' is to be read literally, once the conveyance is made, the grantor is obliged to refrain forever from raising any issue as to the extent of the interest conveyed."[9] A summary review of all deed formats follows.

A. General Warranty Deed

The **general warranty deed** conveys the highest level of assurance to a buyer. "Under the 'general warranty deed' grantor warrants that the property is being alienated, transferred and conveyed without any reservation and is free and clear of any encumbrances or defects." For an example of a **warranty deed** see Figure 6–14.[10]

In a general warranty deed, "the grantor warrants that the grantee's peaceable possession and use of the subject property shall be undisturbed by the grantor or by any third party lawfully claiming an interest in the property in opposition to the interest conveyed to the grantee."[11]

In effect, the grantor gives a warranty relative to the whole world, comforting the buyer that any and all claims will be defended. Other warranty deeds provide less assurance.

B. Limited Warranty Deed

The **limited warranty deed** form more narrowly warrants some aspect of the grantor's interests. Usually, the grantor assures the grantee that the grantor's interest in the property is fully warranted, though the grantor gives no assurances of previous owners in the chain of title regarding the property. Some states, like Ohio, codify the limited warranty deed and provide suggested formats.

5302.07 Limited warranty deed form.

A deed in substance following the form set forth in this section, when duly executed in accordance with Chapter 5301. of the Revised Code, has the force and effect of a deed in fee simple to the grantee, the grantee's heirs, assigns, and successors, to the grantee's and the grantee's heirs', assigns', and successors' own use, with covenants on the part of the grantor with the grantee, the grantee's heirs, assigns, and successors, that, at the time of the delivery of that deed the premises were free from all encumbrances made by the grantor, and that the grantor does warrant and will defend the same to the grantee and the grantee's heirs, assigns, and successors, forever, against the lawful claims and demands of all persons claiming by, through, or under the grantor, but against none other.

"LIMITED WARRANTY DEED

.... (marital status), of.......... County, ... for valuable consideration paid, grant(s), with limited warranty covenants, to.........., whose tax-mailing address is.........., the following real property:

(description of land or interest therein and encumbrances, reservations, and exceptions, if any)

Prior Instrument Reference: Volume.........., Page..........

.........., wife (husband) of said grantor, releases to said grantee all rights of dower therein.

Executed this..........day of..........

....

(Signature of Grantor)

(Execution in accordance with Chapter 5301. of the Revised Code)"

Effective Date: 02-01-2002[12]

M 918—Bargain and sale deed, without covenant,
statutory deed language, ind. or corp., 11-83

© 1981 Julius Blumberg, Inc., Publisher, NYC 10013

Consult your Lawyer before signing this deed — it has important legal consequences.

Deed

This Deed is made on   19   between

Date

Parties   **Grantor**
            *Full name(s)
            and post
            office address*
                                                                      Grantor, and

            Grantee
            *Full name(s)
            and post
            office address*
                                                                      Grantee.

            (The words "Grantor" and "Grantee" include all Grantors and all
            Grantees under this Deed.)

Consideration   In return for the payment to them of
                                                      Dollars ($),
Conveyance   the Grantor grants and conveys to the Grantee all of the land located in the
                              of   County of
            and State of New Jersey, specifically described as follows:

**Description
of Land**

This Deed was prepared by   ....
                                        Print or type name.   *Signature*

FIGURE 6–14
(continues)

Municipal Lot and Block or Account Number

The land is now designated as Lot   in Block on the municipal tax map (or as Account No.   ).

Check box if applicable ☐ No property tax identification number for the land is available at the time of this conveyance.

Receipt of Consideration

The Grantor has received the full payment from the Grantee.

Signature of Grantor

The Grantor signs this Deed on the first date above. If the Grantor is a corporation this Deed is signed by its corporate officers and its corporate seal is affixed.

Signed, sealed and delivered in the presence of or attested by:

.... (SEAL)

.... (SEAL)

.... (SEAL)

.... (SEAL)

CERTIFICATE OF ACKNOWLEDGMENT BY INDIVIDUAL

State of New Jersey, County of

I am a
an officer authorized to take acknowledgments and proofs in this State. I sign this acknowledgment below to certify that it was made before me.

On.., 19............, ...

....
appeared before me in person. *(If more than one person appears, the words "this person" shall include all persons named who appeared before the officer and made this acknowledgment).* I am satisfied that this person is the person named in and who signed this Deed. This person acknowledged signing, sealing and delivering this Deed as this person's act and deed for the uses and purposes expressed in this Deed.

This person also acknowledged that the full and actual consideration paid or to be paid for the transfer of title to realty evidenced by this Deed, as such consideration is defined in P.L. 1968, c. 49, §1(c), is $...

....
Officers signature. Print, stamp or type name and title directly beneath.

FIGURE 6–14

(continued)

CORPORATE PROOF BY THE SUBSCRIBING WITNESS

State of New Jersey, County of

I am a
an officer authorized to take acknowledgments and proofs in this State.

On.., 19........., ...
(from now on called the "Witness") appeared before me in person. The Witness was duly sworn by me according to law under oath and
stated and proved to my satisfaction that:

    1. The Witness is the...Secretary of the Corporation which is the Grantor in this Deed.
    2. ....the officer who signed this Deed, is the..........................President
of the Corporation (from now on called the "Corporate Officer").
    3. The making, signing, sealing, and delivery of this Deed have been duly authorized by a proper resolution of the Board of
Directors of the Corporation.
    4. The Witness knows the corporate seal of the Corporation. The seal affixed to this Deed is the corporate seal of the Corpora-
tion. The seal was affixed to this Deed by the Corporate Officer. The Corporate Officer signed and delivered this Deed as and for the
voluntary act and deed of the Corporation. All this was done in the presence of the Witness who signed this Deed as attesting witness.
The Witness signs this proof to attest to the truth of these facts.

    The Witness also acknowledged that the full and actual consideration paid or to be paid for the transfer of title to realty
evidenced by this Deed, as such consideration is defined in P.L. 1968, c. 49, §1(c), is $...

Sworn to and signed before me on the date written above.

                                     ....
                                         Witness: sign above and print or type name below.

....
Officers signature. Print, stamp or type name and title directly beneath.

Deed *to*	*Record and return to:*

FIGURE 6–14
(continued)

Web Exercise

See John Murray's exceptional analysis on the nature of a special or limited warranty deed at www.abanet.org/rppt/publications/edirt/2001/2001winter/article1.pdf.

Limited warranty deeds do provide protections although the influence of these protections only relates to the grantor him or herself. All the grantor affirms is that they have not harmed or misrepresented as to the property. Minnesota publishes perfect limited language in the published library of deed documents at Figure 6–15.[13]

For an example of a limited warranty deed see Figure 6–16.

C. Quitclaim Deed

At the other end of the protection spectrum, as compared to the general warranty deed, is the **quitclaim deed**. The Quitclaim is often referred to as the **Bargain and Sale** deed. Within it, the grantor makes no assurances concerning the quality and content of title. Thus, the grantor relays no assurance regarding liens, remaining tax obligations, judgments attached to the interest, or hold-over lessees. Quitclaim deeds are frequently found in foreclosure proceedings, and certain executor and administrator settings in regard to estates and trusts. The paucity of language inserted within the deed instrument tells much of its minimal protection for buyers. See Figure 6–17.

For another example of a quitclaim deed see Figure 6–18.

(Top 3 inches reserved for recording data)

LIMITED WARRANTY DEED	Minnesota Uniform Conveyancing Blanks
Individual(s) to Individual(s)	Form 10.2.1 (2006)

DEED TAX DUE: $ _____   DATE: _____
(month/day/year)

FOR VALUABLE CONSIDERATION, _____
(insert name and marital status of each Grantor)

_____, ("**Grantor**"),

hereby conveys and quitclaims to _____
(insert name of each Grantee)

_____, ("**Grantee**"), real property

in _____ County, Minnesota, legally described as follows:

Check here if all or part of the described real property is Registered (Torrens) ☐

together with all hereditaments and appurtenances.

This Deed conveys after-acquired title. Grantor warrants that Grantor has not done or suffered anything to encumber the property, EXCEPT:

Check applicable box:
☐ The Seller certifies that the Seller does not know of
any wells on the described real property.
☐ A well disclosure certificate accompanies this
document.
☐ I am familiar with the property described in this
instrument and I certify that the status and number
of wells on the described real property have not changed
since the last previously filed well disclosure certificate.

Grantor

_____
(signature)

_____
(signature)

Page 1 of 2

FIGURE 6–15.
(continues)

Page 2 of 2 Minnesota Uniform Conveyancing Blanks **Form 10.2.1**

State of Minnesota, County of ______________________

This instrument was acknowledged before me on ______________________, by ______________________
(month/day/year)

____
(insert name and marital status of each Grantor)

______________________.

(Seal, if any)

____
(signature of notarial officer)

Title (and Rank): ______________________

My commission expires: ______________________
(month/day/year)

THIS INSTRUMENT WAS DRAFTED BY:
(insert name and address)

TAX STATEMENTS FOR THE REAL PROPERTY DESCRIBED IN THIS INSTRUMENT SHOULD BE SENT TO:
(insert name and address of Grantee to whom tax statements should be sent)

FIGURE 6–15
(continued)

LIMITED WARRANTY DEED

Date:

______________________, Grantor, hereby conveys and quitclaims to ______________________, as Grantees, for and in consideration of the sum of ______________________ ($__________) real property in ______________________ County, State of ______________, described as follows:

together with all hereditaments and appurtenances.

Grantor warrants that Grantor has not done or suffered anything to encumber the property, EXCEPT:

____
Grantor
By: ______________________

STATE OF)
) ss.
COUNTY OF)

The foregoing was acknowledged before me this _____ day of ______________,
20___, by ______________________, the ______________________
of ______________________, a ______________________, under the laws
of ______________________, on behalf of the ______________.

____
Notary

FIGURE 6–16

(Top 3 inches reserved for recording data)

QUIT CLAIM DEED Individual(s) to Individual(s)	**Minnesota Uniform Conveyancing Blanks** Form 10.3.1 (2006)

DEED TAX DUE: $ _____

DATE: _____
(month/day/year)

FOR VALUABLE CONSIDERATION, _____
(insert name and marital status of each Grantor)

_____, ("**Grantor**"),

hereby conveys and quitclaims to _____
(insert name of each Grantee)

_____, ("**Grantee**"), real property

in _____ County, Minnesota, legally described as follows:

Check here if all or part of the described real property is Registered (Torrens) ☐

together with all hereditaments and appurtenances.

Check applicable box:
☐ The Seller certifies that the Seller does not know of
   any wells on the described real property.
☐ A well disclosure certificate accompanies this
   document.
☐ I am familiar with the property described in this
   instrument and I certify that the status and number
   of wells on the described real property have not changed
   since the last previously filed well disclosure certificate.

Grantor

_____
(signature)

_____
(signature)

FIGURE 6–17
(continues)

Page 2 of 2 | Minnesota Uniform Conveyancing Blanks **Form 10.3.1**

State of Minnesota, County of ____________________

This instrument was acknowledged before me on ____________________, by ____________________
(month/day/year)

____
(insert name and marital status of each Grantor)

____.

(Seal, if any)

____
(signature of notarial officer)

Title (and Rank): ____________________

My commission expires: ____________________
(month/day/year)

THIS INSTRUMENT WAS DRAFTED BY:
(insert name and address)

TAX STATEMENTS FOR THE REAL PROPERTY DESCRIBED IN THIS INSTRUMENT SHOULD BE SENT TO:
(insert name and address of Grantee to whom tax statements should be sent)

FIGURE 6–17
(continued)

Deed

This Deed is made on
BETWEEN

whose post office address is

referred to as the Grantor,
AND

whose post office address is

referred to as the Grantee.
The words "Grantor" and "Grantee" shall mean all Grantors and all Grantees listed above.

1. Transfer of Ownership.   The Grantor grants and conveys (transfers ownership of) the property described below
to the Grantee. This transfer is made for the sum of

The Grantor acknowledges receipt of this money.

2. Tax Map Reference.   (N.J.S.A. 46:15-1.1) Municipality of
Block No.   Lot No.   Qualifier No.   Account No.
☐ No property tax identification number is available on the date of this Deed. (Check box if applicable.)

3. Property.   The Property consists of the land and all the buildings and structures on the land in the
of   County of   and State of New Jersey. The legal
description is:

☐ Please see attached Legal Description annexed hereto and made a part hereof. (Check box if applicable.)

Prepared by: *(print signer's name below signature)*   (For Recorder's Use Only)

_____

106 - Deed - Quitclaim - Ind. or Corp.
Plain Language
Rev. 7/01   P7/07

©2001 by ALL-STATE LEGAL®
A Division of ALL-STATE International, Inc.
www.aslegal.com   800.222.0510   Page 1

FIGURE 6–18
Reprinted courtesy of All-State Legal Supply Company.
(continues)

The street address of the Property is:

4. Type of Deed. This Deed is called a Quitclaim Deed. The Grantor makes no promises as to ownership or title, but simply transfers whatever interest the Grantor has to the Grantee.

5. Signatures. The Grantor signs this Deed as of the date at the top of the first page. If the Grantor is a corporation, this Deed is signed and attested to by its proper corporate officers and its corporate seal is affixed. (Print name below each signature).

Witnessed or Attested by:
_____ (Seal)

_____ (Seal)

STATE OF NEW JERSEY, COUNTY OF   SS:
I CERTIFY that on

personally came before me and stated to my satisfaction that this person (or if more than one, each person):
(a) was the maker of this Deed;
(b) executed this Deed as his or her own act; and
(c) made this Deed for $ as the full and actual consideration paid or to be paid for the transfer of title. (Such consideration is defined in N.J.S.A. 46:15-5.)

_____
Print name and title below signature

STATE OF NEW JERSEY, COUNTY OF   SS:
I CERTIFY that on

personally came before me and stated to my satisfaction that this person (or if more than one, each person):
(a) was the maker of the attached Deed;
(b) was authorized to and did execute this Deed as
of   the entity named in this Deed;
(c) made this Deed for $ as the full and actual consideration paid or to be paid for the transfer of title. (Such consideration is defined in N.J.S.A. 46:15-5.); and
(d) executed this Deed as the act of the entity.

```
RECORD AND RETURN TO:
```
_____
Print name and title below signature

106 - Deed - Quitclaim - Ind. or Corp.
Plain Language
Rev. 7/01   P7/07

FIGURE 6–18
(continued)

D. Executor or Administrator's Deed

After a person dies, a deed document's language will remain fixed, as if the owner of the realty, now deceased, was still capable of executing a transfer. If no spouse survives the deceased landowner, the formal estate exclusively retains the authority to sell. The **executor** or the **administrator** of the estate is generally empowered to prepare a deed, execute it, and transfer it to a grantee. The executor or administrator acts as a replacement for the testator or the decedent.

See Figure 6–19 for the Executor Deed format.

CASE DECISION

Read the Rhode Island Superior Court decision on the legality of an Executor's Deed.

STATE OF RHODE ISLAND AND PROVIDENCE PLANTATIONS

PROVIDENCE, SC	<u>Filed December 15, 2006</u>	SUPERIOR COURT
KEY FINANCIAL SERVICES	:	
	:	
vs.	:	C.A. No. PC 05-3234
	:	
ROBERT TESTA, as Administrator of	:	
the Estate of Jesse Oliver, Jr., C.T.A.	:	
and Robert Oliver, Sr., and his assignee,	:	
Dixon 5 Associates	:	

DECISION

GIBNEY, J. This matter is before the Court on plaintiff Key Financial Service's (Key Financial) Motion for Summary Judgment. The Defendants[1] object to this motion.

Facts and Travel

On August 19, 1988, Jesse Oliver, Jr. the owner of property located at 5 Dixon Avenue in Bristol, RI (the "Property"), died. Before his death, he had written a will (the "Will"), under which he bequeathed the Property to Robert Oliver, Sr. (Robert). Additionally, the Will named Robert as Executor of the estate. Shortly thereafter, Robert executed a promissory note and mortgage on the Property in the amount of $122,000. On April 6, 1989, the promissory note and mortgage were assigned to the plaintiff in this case, Key Financial Services (Key Financial). Approximately two weeks later, on April 21, 1989, Robert issued an executor's deed to himself and procured the remaining interests in the Property via a deed issued by Mary Carlone, who had been granted a life estate in the Property under the Will.

Subsequently, however, it was revealed that Robert had never posted the bond required by his appointment as Executor of Jesse Oliver's estate. Consequentially, Augustine Smith ("Mr. Smith") moved the Bristol County Probate Court (Probate Court) to remove Robert as Executor and appoint himself as administrator in his place. The Probate Court granted the petition on February 5, 1991, and thereafter Mr. Smith filed an affidavit in the Town of Bristol Land Records declaring that the executor's deed issued by Robert as null and void. On March 1, 2001, Mr. Smith died before any action regarding the executor's deed could be taken in the Probate Court. In his place, the Probate Court appointed Robert Testa (Mr. Testa) as administrator on June 16, 2005.

---

[1]The present Administrator of the estate, Robert Testa, is only a placeholder for the purposes of this civil action. The actual defendants in interest of this case, Robert Oliver Sr. and his assignees (collectively, "Defendants"), did not object to this appointment.

(continued)

Robert Oliver then defaulted on the promissory note assigned to Key Financial, and, as a result, Key Financial brought suit against him in this Court. The Court awarded partial summary judgment for Key Financial in the amount of $203,148.89. Execution was issued against Robert Oliver, and the Property was levied by Sheriff's action. Key Financial pursued the levy sale, and on November 27, 1996, it obtained all right and title held by Robert in the Property. The Sheriff's Deed of Execution Sale was issued on March 5, 1998.

On July 1, 2005, Key Financial filed this action against Robert Testa, as Administer of the Estate of Jesse Oliver, Jr., and Robert Oliver, Sr., seeking to quiet title as to any claims Robert Oliver Sr. may have to the Property. In response, Defendants argue that the title of the property never passed to Key Financial, and it still remains in the estate of Jesse Oliver, Jr.

Key Financial has now moved for summary judgment.

Standard of Review

The Court will grant a motion for summary judgment when, after "viewing the facts and all reasonable inferences therefrom in the light most favorable to the nonmoving party, the court determines that there are no issues of material fact in dispute[.]" Tavares v. Barbour, 790 A.2d 1110, 1112 (R.I. 2002) (citations omitted). The moving party bears the initial burden of establishing that no genuine issues of material fact exist; if it does so successfully, then the burden shifts to the nonmoving party. Heflin v. Koszela, 774 A.2d 25, 29 (R.I. 2001). If the nonmoving party can demonstrate that an issue of material fact exists, the motion will be denied. Palmisciano v. Burrillville Racing Ass'n., 603 A.2d 317, 320 (R.I. 1992) (citations omitted).

Analysis

The issue in this case is whether Robert's execution of the promissory note and mortgage were within his power as a devisee, thus making those encumbrances, and the ensuing levy sale, valid. Key Financial argues that Robert Oliver, as devisee, was entitled to mortgage his property. In contrast, Defendants argue that the Property is still owned by the estate of Jesse Oliver, and they rely on several arguments to support this assertion.

First, Defendants argue that the executor's deed Robert issued to himself should be declared null and void. First, they argue that because Robert was never qualified as Executor of the estate, he had no power to issue an executor's deed. Furthermore, they argue that under R.I.G.L. 1956 § 33-12-6[2], even if Robert had been qualified as Executor, he would not have been able to transfer the property from the estate without permission of the Court, which he never received. In addition, Defendants argue that the Probate Court's February 5, 1991 decree amounted to a finding that Robert's issuance of the executor's deed was illegal and therefore invalid. In this Decree, the Probate Court stated, in part, that as ". . . [Robert Oliver] has not filed a bond, has not filed an inventory, and has improperly conveyed real estate and has not qualified by law for appointment, he is forthwith removed." Decree of Probate Judge Raymond A. Thomas of the Town of Bristol, in the Estate of Jesse Oliver, Jr., No. 88-68. Defendants contend that the abovementioned "improperly conveyed real estate" refers to Robert's transfer of the Property to himself by executor's deed.

The Defendants' reliance on these arguments, however, is misplaced. In DiCristofaro v. Beaudry, 113 R.I. 313, 319; 320 A.2d 597, 601 (1974), the Rhode Island Supreme Court held that "[t]itle to real

---

[2]Section 33-12-6, in its entirety, provides:

"The executor or administrator may sell the real estate of a deceased person despite the sufficiency of the personal property to pay the debts, funeral expenses and the items above enumerated whenever in the discretion of the probate court this action seems desirable in effecting a prompt and efficient settlement of the estate; provided, however, that this authority shall not be given with reference to real estate specifically devised, unless the specific devisees consent in writing thereto. An executor with a valid power of sale under a will may convey specifically devised property with the written consent of the specific devisee."

property vests immediately upon a testator's death in the devisees." Thus, upon the death of Jesse Oliver, title to the Property immediately vested in Robert as the devisee, and did not need to be transferred to him by an executor's deed. Robert's failure to meet his required duties as Executor, therefore, did not affect this interest in the land as a devisee. Regardless of the validity of the executor's deed, Robert, as the devisee and owner of the Property, was free to execute a promissory note and mortgage on it.

In response, however, the Defendants argue that the instant case provides an exception to this general principle. They claim that the land did not vest at the moment of Jesse Oliver's death because it was still subject to being sold to pay the debts of the estate. This argument fails as well. The fact that a piece of property may be needed to pay the debts of the estate does not prevent the title from vesting immediately upon the death of the testator. See Votolato v. McCaull, 80 R.I. 301, 306 (R.I. 1953), Honeymail v. Kelliher, 20 R.I. 564, 40 A. 499 (1898). In Votolato, the Rhode Island Supreme Court found that "the legislature in enacting R.I. Gen. Laws § 33-12-6 has created in the devisee a fee simple subject to defeasance. Title to real property vests immediately upon a testator's death in the devisees. However, the title to such real estate is subject to defeasance, in that if an executor or administrator wishes to sell the property for the prompt and efficient settlement of the estate, he may do so with the probate court's permission." Id. Thus, the fact that the Property is still subject to the debts of the estate does not prevent it from vesting immediately to Robert upon the death of Jesse Oliver, Jr.

Secondly, Defendants argues that, even as a devisee, Robert could not have encumbered the Property under Section 33-13-3, which holds that

> "[n]o heir or devisee of a deceased person shall have power, within two (2) years and six (6) months after the first publication of the notice of the qualification of the first executor or administrator on the estate of the deceased person, to incumber or alien the real estate of the deceased so as to prevent or affect the sale of the real estate by the executor or administrator, if necessary, as prescribed by law . . ."

Defendants argue that under this statute, even if the Property had vested in Robert at the time of Jesse Oliver's death, he was statutorily barred from encumbering it for two and a half years after the Executor was qualified. When the mortgage and note were executed, argues Defendants, Robert had not been qualified as Executor, and thus the time period had not yet even begun to run.

However, Section 33-13-3 is inapplicable to the instant case. That statute bars encumbrances which are designed to "prevent or affect the sale of the real estate by the executor," and there is absolutely no evidence that the mortgage in this case was issued for this purpose. Thus, Robert was acting within his power as devisee when he encumbered the property with a mortgage.

Additionally, the Court's conclusion is further bolstered by this Court's award of $203,148.89 to Key Financial when Robert defaulted on his obligations. Had the Court not found that mortgage proper in that action, it would not have issued the judgment. Furthermore, in its Order Granting Key Financial Service Relief from the Automatic Stay To Continue with Eviction Action, the United States Bankruptcy Court allowed Key Financial to complete the eviction proceedings with respect to the Property, essentially finding that Key Financial had proper title to the Property. Had the mortgage and promissory notes been improperly issued, then these courts would not have confirmed Key Financial's right to the Property.

Conclusion

In conclusion, the Court finds that Robert's execution of the promissory note and mortgage on the Property were well within his power as devisee. His interest in the Property was never defeased by the estate of Jesse Oliver, and, as a result, Plaintiff lawfully obtained title to the Property at execution sale. Accordingly, summary judgment is granted to Key Financial on its claim to quiet title in the Property as it related to the Defendants, Robert Oliver, Sr. and 5 Dixon Ave. Associates.

CONSULT YOUR LAWYER BEFORE SIGNING THIS INSTRUMENT-THIS INSTRUMENT SHOULD BE USED BY LAWYERS ONLY

THIS INDENTURE, made the   day of

BETWEEN

as executor of   the last will and testament of
                                                                                        , late of
                                                                              , deceased,

party of the first part, and

party of the second part,

WITNESSETH, that the party of the first part, by virtue of the power and authority given in and by said last will and testament, and in consideration of

                                                                                                    dollars,
                                        paid by the party of the second part, does hereby grant and release unto the party of the second part, the heirs or successors and assigns of the party of the second part forever,

ALL that certain plot, piece or parcel of land, with the buildings and improvements thereon erected, situate, lying and being in the

TOGETHER with all right, title and interest, if any, of the party of the first part, in and to any streets and roads abutting the above described premises to the center lines thereof; TOGETHER with the appurtenances, and also all the estate which the said decedent had at the time of decedent's death in said premises, and also the estate therein, which the party of the first part has or has power to convey or dispose of, whether individually, or by virtue of said will or otherwise; TO HAVE AND TO HOLD the premises herein granted unto the party of the second part, the heirs or successors and assigns of the party of the second part forever.

AND the party of the first part covenants that the party of the first part has not done or suffered anything whereby the said premises have been encumbered in any way whatever, except as aforesaid.
AND the party of the first part, in compliance with Section 13 of the Lien Law, covenants that the party of the first part will receive the consideration for this conveyance and will hold the right to receive such consideration as a trust fund to be applied first for the purpose of paying the cost of the improvement and will apply the same first to the payment of the cost of the improvement before using any part of the total of the same for any other purpose. The word "party" shall be construed as if it read "parties" whenever the sense of this indenture so requires.

IN WITNESS WHEREOF, the party of the first part has duly executed this deed the day and year first above written.

IN PRESENCE OF:

_____

_____

Standard N.Y.B.T.U. Form 8005 – Executor's Deed – Uniform Acknowledgment
Form 3307

FIGURE 6–19
(continues)

TO BE USED ONLY WHEN THE ACKNOWLEDGMENT IS MADE IN NEW YORK STATE

State of New York, County of   ss:

On the   day of   in the year
before me, the undersigned, personally appeared

personally known to me or proved to me on the basis of satisfactory evidence to be the individual(s) whose name(s) is (are) subscribed to the within instrument and acknowledged to me that he/she/they executed the same in his/her/their capacity(ies), and that by his/her/their signature(s) on the instrument, the individual(s), or the person upon behalf of which the individual(s) acted, executed the instrument.

_____
(signature and office of individual taking acknowledgment)

State of New York, County of   ss:

On the   day of   in the year
before me, the undersigned, personally appeared

personally known to me or proved to me on the basis of satisfactory evidence to be the individual(s) whose name(s) is (are) subscribed to the within instrument and acknowledged to me that he/she/they executed the same in his/her/their capacity(ies), and that by his/her/their signature(s) on the instrument, the individual(s), or the person upon behalf of which the individual(s) acted, executed the instrument.

_____
(signature and office of individual taking acknowledgment)

TO BE USED ONLY WHEN THE ACKNOWLEDGMENT IS MADE OUTSIDE NEW YORK STATE

State (or District of Columbia, Territory, or Foreign Country) of   ss:

On the   day of   in the year   before me, the undersigned, personally appeared

personally known to me or proved to me on the basis of satisfactory evidence to be the individual(s) whose name(s) is (are) subscribed to the within instrument and acknowledged to me that he/she/they executed the same in his/her/their capacity(ies), and that by his/her/their signature(s) on the instrument, the individual(s), or the person upon behalf of which the individual(s) acted, executed the instrument, and that such individual made such appearance before the undersigned in the

_____ in _____
(insert the City or other political subdivision)   (and insert the State or Country or other place the acknowledgment was taken)

_____
(signature and office of individual taking acknowledgment)

EXECUTOR'S DEED

Title No. _____

TO

┌───┐
│ STANDARD FORM OF NEW YORK BOARD OF TITLE UNDERWRITERS │
│   │
│   │
└───┘

SECTION
BLOCK
LOT
COUNTY OR TOWN
STREET ADDRESS

Recorded at Request of

RETURN BY MAIL TO:

┌───┐
│   │
│   │
│   │
└───┘

RESERVE THIS SPACE FOR USE OF RECORDING OFFICE

Product of Imperial Web Designs

FIGURE 6–19
(continued)

E. Guardian Deed

Those appointed to handle the affairs of minors or the physically or mentally incompetent may be responsible for the maintenance, purchase, or sale of real property. In the event that a **guardian** has been appointed by the decedent's testator and the will's dispositive provisions indicate the guardian should sell off specific real property in the name of said minor and leave the proceeds to that same minor, a **guardian's deed** should be prepared.

F. Trustee's Deed

Trustee's have temporary authority over the disposition of property. In some cases, a bank or other financial institution may have the authority as trustee over designated property. Foreclosure actions often witness the **trustee's deed**. Not to be confused with a Deed of Trust, whereby a party holds legal right and claim to a property in the event of default, the trustee's deed is relational—a party that stands in stead of the actual owner.

Trustees are the subject of substantial codification and regulation though it is clear that their signatures have the power to alienate. See the Montana Code which lays out this reality.

> 71-1-318. Trustee's deed. (1) The trustee's deed to the purchaser at the trustee's sale may contain, in addition to a description of the property conveyed, recitals of compliance with the requirements of this part relating to the exercise of the power of sale and the sale, including recitals of the facts concerning the default, the notice given, the conduct of the sale, and the receipt of the purchase money from the purchaser.
>
> (2) When the trustee's deed is recorded in the deed records of the county or counties where the property described in the deed is situated, the recitals contained in the deed and in the affidavits required under 71-1-315(2) shall be prima facie evidence in any court of the truth of the matters set forth therein, except that the same shall be conclusive evidence in favor of subsequent bona fide purchasers and encumbrancers for value and without notice.
>
> (3) The trustee's deed shall operate to convey to the purchaser, without right of redemption, the trustee's title and all right, title, interest, and claim of the grantor and his successors in interest and of all persons claiming by, through, or under them in and to the property sold, including all such right, title, interest, and claim in and to such property acquired by the grantor or his successors in interest subsequent to the execution of the trust indenture.[14]

Frequently seen in wills, especially for wealthy clients, is the use of testamentary trusts for the remaining spouse and, upon, their demise, secondary trusts for any remaining children. Within the testamentary, usually located in the will's residuary clause, will be an appointed trustee who may have to dispense with realty. Trustees are given broad discretion in a trustee's deed for the care, maintenance, and alienation of trust property on behalf of its beneficiaries, including realty. A trustee's deed, made freely available by the Kansas Bar Association, is at Figure 6–20.[15]

G. Sheriff's Deed

By levy, order of execution, or any other extraordinary attachment, county sheriffs are empowered, upon order of court, to sell property. Without a **sheriff's deed**, sale and transfer would not be possible. With the rise of foreclosures across America, there has been a dramatic increase in this type of filing.[16] Sheriff's deeds are part of a larger foreclosure process or arising from attachment, levy or

TRUSTEE'S DEED

This indenture made this _____ day of _____, _____, by and between

_____ and

_____ as Trustee(s) of the _____

as set forth in the Trust Agreement dated _____, _____, as GRANTOR(S)

and _____ as GRANTEE(S).

The GRANTOR(S), by virtue of the terms and provisions of said trust instrument, in consideration of the sum of $_____, the receipt of which is hereby acknowledged, does hereby grant, sell and convey to GRANTEE(S) the following described real estate

in _____ County, Kansas:

Except and subject to:

GRANTOR(S) covenants that GRANTOR(S) has good right to convey GRANTOR's interest in the property conveyed by this Deed (the "Property") and warrants the quiet possession of the Property against the claims of those claiming any right, interest or title through GRANTOR(S), except as may be described above, and further covenants that the Property is free from all encumbrances created by GRANTOR(S), except as may be described above, and GRANTOR(S) will warrant and defend the Property against all lawful claims of those claiming any right, interest or title through GRANTOR(S), except as may be described above; but GRANTOR(S) does not warrant title against those claiming a right, interest or title that arose prior to, or separate from, GRANTOR's interest in the Property. GRANTOR(S) executes this Deed as trustee and not in an individual capacity. By the acceptance hereof, it is agreed that GRANTOR(S) is not and shall not be personally liable upon any covenant or warranty herein, whether express or implied, and that GRANTOR's liability as trustee shall be limited to the assets held by GRANTOR(S) as trustee at the time any such liability may be determined.

GRANTOR(S) certifies that GRANTOR(S) is duly appointed, qualified and acting Trustee(s) of the _____ Trust dated _____, _____ and has full power and authority to convey GRANTOR's interest in the Property, and has made this conveyance pursuant to the power and authority granted to GRANTOR(S) in Article or Section _____ of such Trust Agreement, which agreement is in full force and effect and has not been amended or revoked.

TO HAVE AND TO HOLD the Property, together with the apputrenances and hereditaments and every part thereof, unto the GRANTEE(S), _____ successors, heirs and assigns.

For Corporate Trustee	For individual Trustee(s)
_____ as Trustee	_____ as Trustee(s)
(name of corporation)	of the _____ as set forth in the
of the _____ as set forth in the	Trust Agreement dated _____, _____.
Trust Agreement dated _____, _____.	
By:_____	
Printed Name:_____	_____
Title:_____	Printed Name:_____
(SEAL)	
ATTEST:_____	_____
Printed Name:_____, Secretary	Printed Name:_____

STATE OF _____)	Reserved for Register of Deeds
) SS.	
COUNTY OF _____)	

This instrument was acknowledged before me on _____, _____ by

_____

as Trustee(s) under the Trust Agreement

dated_____, _____.

_____

(SEAL)   Printed Name:_____

Notary Public

My Appointment Expires:_____

Pursuant to K.S.A. 79-1437e, a real estate validation questionnaire is not required due to Exception No._____ (complete if applicable).

(see reverse side for corporate acknowledgement)

FIGURE 6–20

(*continues*)

STATE OF ⟩
⟩ SS.
COUNTY OF ⟩

This instrument was acknowledged before me on _____, _____

by _____,

as _____ of

_____

a _____ as Trustee under the Trust Agreement

dated_____, _____

(SEAL)

_____

Printed Name:_____

Notary Public

My Appointment Expires:_____

FIGURE 6–20
(continued)

garnishment processes. Consult local and state codifications to determine when this type of deed is appropriate. Washington State's oversight is fairly typical

> In all cases where real estate has been, or may hereafter be sold by virtue of an execution or other process, it shall be the duty of the sheriff or other officer making such sale to execute and deliver to the purchaser, or other person entitled to the same, a deed of conveyance of the real estate so sold. The deeds shall be issued upon request immediately after the confirmation of sale by the court in those instances where redemption rights have been precluded pursuant to RCW 61.12.093 et seq., or immediately after the time for redemption from such sale has expired in those instances in which there are redemption rights, as provided in RCW 6.23.060. In case the term of office of the sheriff or other officer making such sale shall have expired before a sufficient deed has been executed, then the successor in office of such sheriff shall, within the time specified in this section, execute and deliver to the purchaser or other person entitled to the same a deed of the premises so sold, and such deeds shall be as valid and effectual to convey to the grantee the lands or premises so sold, as if the deed had been made by the sheriff or other officer who made the sale.[17]

Figure 6–21[18] contains a simplified Sheriff's deed.

H. Corporate Deed

Corporations, like individuals, can own real estate. Therefore, the **corporate deed** document must be structured to reflect this entity. Increased attention to execution and signature requirements for corporations is mandatory. Usually the corporation's secretary executes the deed document. **Corporate deeds** usually include a section for a seal. Pay close attention to the names and officers' titles listed at the grantor's signature lines and conform strictly to them.

Web Exercise

The State of Connecticut promulgates introductory format for all types of deeds at law.justia.com/connecticut/codes/title47/sec47-36c.html.

SHERIFF'S DEED

Ohio Revised Code §2329.36

I, _____, Sheriff of _____ County, Ohio pursuant to the Judgment and Decree in Foreclosure entered on _____ in favor of _____

in the amount of _____, the Order of Sale entered on _____, the Confirmation of Sale entered on _____ and in consideration of the sum of _____ dollars the receipt whereof is hereby acknowledged, does hereby GRANT, SELL AND CONVEY unto

and his heirs and assigns forever, all the rights, title and interest of the parties in the Court of Common Pleas, _____ County, Ohio, Case number _____,

and all pleadings therein incorporated herein by reference in and to the following Lands and Tenements situated in the County of _____ and State of Ohio, known and described as follows, to-wit:

This deed does not reflect any restrictions, conditions or easements of record. Purchaser(s) / Grantee(s) take(s) subject to any such existing restrictions, conditions, easements and any and all real property taxes, assessments, interest and/or penalties from confirmation of sale, as provided by Ohio Revised Code 323.47.

Prior Owner:

Parcel Number(s):

Prior Instrument Reference:

Executed officially this _____ day of _____

_____, _____ County Sheriff

By:

_____, Chief Deputy Sheriff
Civil Division, _____ County Sheriff's Office

The State of Ohio
_____ COUNTY SS:

The foregoing was acknowledged before me this _____ day of _____ _____ by _____, Chief Deputy Sheriff, _____ County, Ohio

This Instrument was prepared by:

_____ Notary Public State of Ohio

My Commission Expires: _____

FIGURE 6–21

V. SPECIALIZED DEED CLAUSES

KEY WORDS

hereditaments	**riparian rights**
mining rights	**single family**
quiet enjoyment	**covenant**
restrictive covenant	

As discussed previously, the deed document fundamentally reflects the grantor's interests, obligations, and rights and what the extent or limitation is of the conveyance. The deed document also gives notice about **restrictive covenants clauses** in use for the grantee's benefit.

Geographical locations and the peculiarity of local custom and practice affect deed language. For example, it is rare to see a coal rights clause contained in topography without coal. The question of water rights of way is more likely to appear in a deed for property adjacent to a body of water than in a land-locked location. Insert or delete the clauses that follow, depending on custom and location.

A. Mining Rights

Mining rights including coal and other surface or underground minerals or materials can be included or excepted in the deed document. See Figure 6–22.

B. Riparian Rights

Most deeds will have some reference to bodies of water that boarder the property in question. Most deeds contain an **appurtenance** clause that usually looks like:

> Together with all and singular buildings, improvements, waters, woods, ways, rights, liberties, privileges, **hereditaments** and appurtenances to the same belonging, or in any

---

COAL CLAUSE

NOTICE—THIS DOCUMENT MAY NOT SELL, CONVEY, TRANSFER, INCLUDE OR INSURE THE TITLE TO THE COAL AND RIGHT TO SUPPORT UNDERNEATH THE SURFACE LAND DESCRIBED OR REFERRED TO HEREIN, AND THE OWNER OR OWNERS OF SUCH COAL MAY HAVE THE COMPLETE LEGAL RIGHT TO REMOVE ALL OF SUCH COAL AND IN THAT CONNECTION, DAMAGE MAY RESULT TO THE SURFACE OF THE LAND AND ANY HOUSE, BUILDING OR OTHER STRUCTURE ON OR IN SUCH LAND. THE INCLUSION OF THIS NOTICE DOES NOT ENLARGE, RESTRICT OR MODIFY AND LEGAL RIGHTS OR ESTATES OTHERWISE CREATED, TRANSFERRED, EXCEPTED OR RESERVED BY THIS INSTRUMENT.

(This notice is set forth in the manner provided in Section 1 of the Act of July 17, 1957, P.L. 984, as amended, and is not intended as notice of unrecorded instruments, if any). Unless this notice is stricken, the deed for the property will contain this notice and will also contain, and buyer will sign, the notice specified in the Bituminous Mine Subsidence and Land Conservation Act of 1966.

FIGURE 6–22

RIGHTS IN A RIVER

TOGETHER with all the grantor's easements and right of way necessary for grantee's easy access to the tract of land and adjoining river; and also the grantor's rights and privileges in and to the river, including the title to the river bed, the islands, banks, shores, lakes, ponds, tributary streams and springs, waterpower, flow of the stream; and also including the grantor's right of fishing, fishery and fishing ground; and also including all the grantor's rights to fords, ferries, landing places, and mill sites; and also including the grantor's rights to construct dams, embankments, levees, canals, etc.; and also including all other water rights of every kind and character whatsoever.

FIGURE 6–23

---

wise appertaining, and the reversions and remainders, rents, issues and profits thereof and of every part and parcel thereof.

For an example of **riparian rights** for a grantee's passage of rights in a river, see Figure 6–23.

C. Building-Zoning Restrictions

In an age of plat plans and uniform building and design codes, many deeds contain language that lists a series of building restrictions or reservations, whether style or design, architectural changes to an existing structure, permissibility of add-on structures, landscaping, outdoor improvements, or building encroachments. The deed's ability to control these activities largely depends upon its language. For a building restriction clause see Figure 6–24.

D. Covenant of Quiet Enjoyment

A covenant of **quiet enjoyment** is a standard deed provision, found in lease agreements as well, in which the grantor assures grantee that they may utilize the premises without intrusion or other harm. For an example, see Figure 6–25.

E. Covenant of Warranty

A more elaborate warranty given by grantor to grantee assures the buyer that any and all claims made regarding this property will be defended by grantor. See Figure 6–26.

BUILDING RESTRICTION

UNDER AND SUBJECT to the lot or building thereon erected shall be subject to the following conditions and restrictions:

That for the purpose of affording light and air and for the purpose of preserving uniformity of appearance of the entire tract of which the lot and building is a part, no building, porch or addition shall be erected within ____ feet of the present building line of Street and _____ _____ Street; nor shall any building, porch, or additions, other than bay windows and steps be erected nearer than _____ feet to the division line of the lot or the piece of ground immediately adjoining the hereby granted premises.

FIGURE 6–24

_____, for himself and his heirs, does covenant with _____, his heirs and assigns, that he, _____, his heirs and assigns, shall at all times hereafter, peaceably and quietly have, hold, and enjoy the premises hereby granted and released without hindrance or interruption of any person lawfully claiming any right, title, or interest at law or in equity, to the aforementioned property or any part thereof.

FIGURE 6–25
Covenant of Quiet Enjoyment.

_____, and his heirs, does hereby grant and agree, with _____ his heirs and assigns, that he, _____ and his heirs, the said above mentioned tract of land, hereditaments, and appurtenances, hereby granted unto _____ his heirs and assigns, against him, _____, and his heirs, and against all and every other person lawfully claiming any part thereof, shall and will warrant and forever defend by these presents.

FIGURE 6–26
Covenant of Warranty.

As a part of the consideration for this conveyance the grantee, for the benefit of the grantor, his successors and assigns, and every other person who becomes the owner of the aforementioned property, agree as follows:

The property shall be used for private, single-family residence purposes exclusively.

FIGURE 6–27
Single Faimly Restriction Clause.

F. Single Family Restriction

To assure stability in communities, many planned communities have initiated covenants to restrict the use of any residence to single families. For deed language that mandates the **single-family covenants** see Figure 6–27.

CHAPTER SIX **SUMMARY**

Chapter Six discussed the following topics:

■ The definition of a deed and its purpose
■ The deed and the Statute of Frauds
■ The elements of a deed
■ Types of deeds
■ Specialized deed clauses and when they are required

REVIEW **QUESTIONS**

1. Prove this statement true or false: The Statute of Frauds must be considered when drafting a deed.
2. Are deeds the only acceptable way to legally transfer a property? Why or why not?
3. Seller has no obligation to present clear and free title in a general warranty deed. Is this statement true? Explain.
4. What clauses must a deed minimally contain?
5. What is the purpose of a quitclaim deed?
6. Explain the difference between a general warranty deed and a limited warranty deed.
7. There are several special deed types. Name three and explain their purpose.
8. Define the term "hereditament."
9. What deed clause would be included to address natural resources that exist under the surface of the earth.
10. What is the purpose of the covenant of quiet enjoyment? Is it included in documents other than deeds?

DISCUSSION **QUESTION**

Your firm is being asked to prepare a deed which gives the most assurance and most freely and totally alienates the property. What type of deed works here? Explain why you decided on this type of deed in relation to other types of deeds.

EXERCISE 1

Using the facts below, draft a general warranty deed.

Date of Deed—October 21, 2009

Grantors—Joe and Jennifer Meyers

Grantees—John and Mary Smith

Consideration—$75,000

Property Description (metes and bounds)—All the certain lot or piece of ground with buildings and improvements thereon erected, situated in the township of William, county of Brown, State of U.S., recorded in the Recorder's Office of Brown County, in Deed Book Volume 75, page 120, and described as follows:

Beginning at a point at the intersection of the southerly side of Bend Drive and the northwesterly side of Marveen Avenue. Containing in front or breadth on the said side of Bend Drive 100 feet and extending of that width in length or depth, 100 feet, the southeasterly line thereof being the long, the northwesterly side of Marveen Avenue.

Having erected thereon a 1-½ story dwelling.

Notary Public—Joan Williams, Brown County, US

Location—County of Brown, State of US

EXERCISE 2

Using the facts in Exercise 1, complete a limited warranty deed.

EXERCISE 3

Using the facts in Exercise 1, complete a quitclaim deed.

ASSIGNMENT FOR THE CASE OF JOHN AND MARTHA

From the information previously given, prepare a deed for the property that John and Martha will be purchasing.

REFERENCES

1. Burton R. Laub, Pennsylvania Keystone Lawyer's Desk Library of Practice § 1.7 at 7 (1994); See the updated and 3rd edition of Charles P. Nemeth, The Paralegal Resource Manual, 3rd ed. (2008).
2. Herbert T. Tiffany, Tiffany Real Property 439 (1970).
3. W. Va. Code R. § 36-4-4 (2009).
4. Tiffany, supra note 2, at 445.
5. Charles P. Nemeth, Paralegal Resource Manual, 2nd ed., 529 (1995).
6. Easy Soft Inc., 212 North Center Drive, North Brunswick NJ 08902, www.easysoft-usa.com; See Charles P. Nemeth, Pennsylvania Real Estate Agreements Of Sale (1998).
7. New Jersey Forms, Real Property, Conveyances § 2:13.
8. James A. Webster Jr., Patrick K. Hetrick, & Larry A. Outlaw, North Carolina Real Estate For Brokers And Salesmen 83 (1986).
9. Deeds: Grantor under General Warranty Deed May Not Dispute Title Conveyed to Grantee, 20 Real Est. L. Rep. 7, 7 (1991).
10. Blumberg Excelsior, 62 White Street, New York, NY 10013, Form M 918.
11. Note, Deeds: Grantor under General Warranty Deed May Not Dispute Title Conveyed to Grantee, 20 Real Est. L. Rep. 7 (1991); see also Callon Institutional Royalty Investors I v. Cauphin Island Property Owners Ass'n, 569 So.2d 343 (Ala. 1990).
12. Ohio Rev. Code Ann. §5302.07 (2009).
13. Minnesota Department of Commerce Web site, Uniform Conveyancing Blanks Page, Limited Warranty Deed at www.commerce.state.mn.us/UCB/10.2.1.pdf.
14. Mont. Code Ann. §71-1-318 (2009).
15. Kansas Bar Association, 1200 SW Harrison, Topeka, KS 66612, www.ksbar.org/forms/TrusteesDeed012D.pdf.
16. Ralph R. Roberts et al., Foreclosure Self-Defense For Dummies (2008).
17. Wash. Rev. Code §6.21.120 (2009).
18. City of Indianapolis, IN Web site, Sheriff's Deed at www.indygov.org/eGov/County/MCSD/Documents/Sheriff20Deed.pdf.

Mortgages

LEARNING OBJECTIVES

- To discuss a mortgage, mortgage note, and mortgage commitment.
- To summarize the varied techniques of financing.
- To identify conditions and other requirements imposed by financial institutions before a mortgage will be granted.

JOB COMPETENCIES

- To compose a rough draft of the mortgage note and mortgage contract.
- To advise clients on the variety of financing techniques available, including adjustable rate mortgages, wraparounds, purchase money mortgages, FHA, VA, and other governmental mortgages, fixed rate mortgages, reverse annuity, and other creative financing techniques.
- To establish working relationships with banks and other financial institutions in the lending business.
- To prepare all documents necessary to secure mortgage funds at settlement.

ETHICAL CONSIDERATIONS

The paralegal must be aware of the following ethical dilemmas during this phase of a real estate transaction:

- Unauthorized practice of law
- Lawyer supervision of nonlawyers
- Confidentiality issues
- Conflicts of interest
- Partnerships between lawyers and nonlawyers
- Communications with persons outside of law firm

I. THE NATURE OF A MORTGAGE

Given the cost of real estate, and considering that the transaction is the most costly that people will normally make in a lifetime, there is generally a need for financing. Unfinanced transactions for the purchase of real property are seldom seen. As a result, real estate buyers usually rely on some type of financing to affect the purchase. The vehicle for addressing this need is the mortgage. Mortgages are the commercially acceptable means of pledging a house to insure the repayment of a debt. In essence, the mortgage holder, usually a bank, savings and loan, or other lending institution, is the first in line in the event of default. It is a holder of the supreme and superior lien in the event of sale when the mortgage obligations are not adhered to. Put another way, the mortgagee lends to a mortgagor; and as long as the debt remains, the mortgagor "owns" the home until satisfied. By "own," one means in a potential sense not an actual one though the implications of default blur the lines of actual ownership.

Mortgages come in all types and sizes, from fixed rates to variable; from government-backed to privately insured; and from loans with a plethora of charges such as points and closing costs to loans that are free of points. Paralegals will find many career opportunities in the financing end of the real estate transaction.

The United States Department of Labor's Bureau of Labor Statistics highlights the perfect suitability of the paralegal in the real estate transaction when describing the profession's common duties:

> One of a paralegal's most important tasks is helping lawyers prepare for closings, hearings, trials, and corporate meetings. Paralegals might investigate the facts of cases and ensure that all relevant information is considered. They also identify appropriate laws, judicial decisions, legal articles, and other materials that are relevant to assigned cases. After they analyze and organize the information, paralegals may prepare written reports that attorneys use in determining how cases should be handled. If attorneys decide to file lawsuits on behalf of clients, paralegals may help prepare the legal arguments, draft pleadings and motions to be filed with the court, obtain affidavits, and assist attorneys during trials. Paralegals also organize and track files of all important case documents and make them available and easily accessible to attorneys. In addition to this preparatory work, paralegals perform a number of other functions. For example, they help draft contracts, mortgages, and separation agreements. They also may assist in preparing tax returns, establishing trust funds, and planning estates. Some paralegals coordinate the activities of other law office employees and maintain financial office records. [1]

Amongst a host of other activities, paralegals earn their keep in the world of finance. Whether working for real estate agents or brokers, real estate attorneys, title or abstract companies, banks, lenders, or for governmental authorities possessing oversight over mortgage bond programs, the influence of the legal professional is felt in many quarters.

Borrowers should be creative in looking for lending sources. Banks, savings, and loans are not the only access to funds. Insurance companies, pension funds, and foreign capital investors are increasingly offering mortgage funding.[2] Additionally, a mortgage instrument can be negotiated with local entrepreneurs and individuals who have ties with the local community. Doctors, dentists, accountants, and lawyers are potential lenders because they usually have the money to invest and are known to prefer real estate as an investment vehicle.[3]

Given the competitive nature of the mortgage market, it is wise to comparison shop. Most media outlets now publish, on a daily basis, lender's rates. An example is at Figure 7–1.[4]

Web Exercise

Take the Freddie Mac Quiz on Mortgages. Measure your knowledge base at www.freddiemac.com/corporate/buyown/english/mortgages/mortgages_knowledge_check.html.

Summary of Survey Results

Fixed-Rate Mortgages					
	Average Conventional 30-Year Commitment Rate	Fees & Points	Average Conventional 15-Year Commitment Rate	Fees & Points
US	5.12	0.7	4.56	0.7
Northeast	5.12	0.8	4.56	0.7
Southeast	5.11	0.7	4.61	0.7
N. Central	5.19	0.7	4.58	0.7
Southwest	5.12	0.5	4.63	0.5
West	5.08	0.8	4.49	0.8

Five/One-Year Adjustable-Rate Mortgages			
	First Commitment Rate	Fees & Points	Margin
US	4.57	0.6	2.74
Northeast	4.59	0.5	2.73
Southeast	4.32	0.6	2.75
N. Central	4.82	0.8	2.74
Southwest	4.46	0.4	2.76
West	4.64	0.6	2.73

One-Year Adjustable-Rate Mortgages			
	First Commitment Rate	Fees & Points	Margin
US	4.69	0.5	2.75
Northeast	4.38	0.5	2.73
Southeast	4.98	0.4	2.75
N. Central	4.71	0.7	2.75
Southwest	5.03	0.5	2.78
West	4.58	0.6	2.75

FIGURE 7–1

II. MORTGAGE DOCUMENTS

KEY WORDS

deed of trust	**mortgagee**
mortgage	**mortgagor**
mortgage note	

Dealing with lenders and processing mortgages can only be described as a paper-driven exercise. There are many documents to be prepared, possibly by paralegals. Since the purchase of real estate is a conveyance subject to the Statute of Frauds, to be defensible, it should be in written form. While money can be lent without an underlying writing, the risk of unenforceability is simply too high. This is as true for the real estate agreement of sale as for the subsequent mortgage. A survey of the typical documents is now in order.

A. Mortgage

The content of a **mortgage**, being a security instrument that assures the collateral of the real property for the repayment of the debt, must precisely lay out the rights and obligations of the parties. In general, both borrower **(mortgagor)** and lender **(mortgagee)** agree to certain terms and conditions, including:

- Payment of principal and interest
- Prepayment and late charges
- Funds for taxes and insurance
- Application of mortgage payments
- Charges and liens
- Occupancy
- Preservation, maintenance, and protection of the property
- Leaseholds
- Lender's rights in the property
- Mortgage insurance
- Inspection rights
- Rights and obligations in event of condemnation
- Release and forbearance
- Successors and assigns
- Loan charges, including points
- Right of reinstatement
- Transfer of property
- Sale of Note
- Environmental consideration
- Acceleration clause

A comprehensive mortgage document from All-State Legal is provided in Figure 7–2.[5]

B. Mortgage Note

The second document seen in the mortgage finance transaction is the **mortgage note**. The mortgage note is the borrower's promise to pay a set sum of money, with a specific interest rate for a fixed duration. It includes various loan charges and failure terms or conditions that trigger default. A mortgage note, just as any other promissory note, sets out the terms and conditions of a promise made by the borrower. See Figure 7–3[6] for an example of a mortgage note from Easy Soft Inc.

C. Deed of Trust

In addition to the mortgage document, a **Deed of Trust** may evidence the relationship of a borrower to an underlying obligation. While the borrower, under traditional mortgage terms, promises the bank to repay, under a Deed of Trust includes a third party—a trustee, who curiously enough actually equitably holds title to the property until and when the proceeds of the mortgage are paid. Hence in a foreclosure, the power to sell belongs to the third party and not the bank, as under traditional mortgage/promissory note arrangements. Deeds of Trust are used in a minority of American jurisdictions. For a sample, see Figure 7–4.[7]

Mortgage

This mortgage is made on _____ .

BETWEEN the Borrower(s) _____

_____

whose address is _____

_____

referred to as "I,"
AND the Lender _____

_____

whose address is _____

_____

referred to as the "Lender."

If more than one Borrower signs this Mortgage, the word "I" shall mean each Borrower named above. The word "Lender" means the original Lender and anyone else who takes this Mortgage by transfer.

1. Mortgage Note. In return for a loan that I received, I promise to pay $_____ (called "Principal"), plus interest in accordance with the terms of a Mortgage Note (referred to as the "Note") dated _____ . The Note provides for monthly payments of $_____ and a yearly interest rate of _____%. All sums owed under the Note are due no later than _____ . All terms of the Note are made part of this Mortgage.

_____

_____

2. Property Mortgaged. The property mortgaged (called the "Property") to the Lender is located in the _____ of _____ , County of _____ and State of New Jersey. The Property includes: (a) the land; (b) all buildings that are now, or will be, located on the land; (c) all fixtures that are now, or will be, attached to the land or building(s) (for example, furnaces, bathroom fixtures and kitchen cabinets); (d) all condemnation awards and insurance proceeds relating to the land and building(s); and (e) all other rights that I have, or will have, as owner of the Property. The legal description is:

☐ Please see attached Legal Description annexed hereto and made a part hereof (check box if applicable).

_____

(For Recorder's Use Only)

204S - Note Mortgage
Ind. or Corp. - Plain Language
Rev. 3/06 P11/08

©2006 by ALL-STATE LEGAL
A Division of ALL-STATE International, Inc.
www.aslegal.com 800.222.0510 Page 1

FIGURE 7–2
(continues)

3. Rights Given to Lender. I mortgage the Property to the Lender. This means that I give the Lender those rights stated in this Mortgage and also those rights the law gives to lenders who hold mortgages on real property. When I pay all amounts due to the Lender under the Note and this Mortgage, the Lender's rights under this Mortgage will end. The Lender will then cancel this Mortgage at my expense.

4. Promises. I make the following promises to the Lender:

    a. Note and Mortgage. I will comply with all of the terms of the Note and this Mortgage.

    b. Payments. I will make all payments required by the Note and this Mortgage.

    c. Ownership. I warrant title to the premises (N.J.S.A. 46:9-2). This means I own the Property and will defend my ownership against all claims.

    d. Liens and Taxes. I will pay all liens, taxes, assessments and other government charges made against the Property when due. I will not claim any deduction from the taxable value of the Property because of this Mortgage. I will not claim any credit against the Principal and interest payable under the Note and this Mortgage for any taxes paid on the Property.

    e. Insurance. I must maintain extended coverage fire or property insurance on the Property. The Lender may also require that I maintain flood insurance or other types of insurance. The insurance companies, policies, amounts, and types of coverage must be acceptable to the Lender. I will notify the Lender in the event of any substantial loss or damage. The Lender may then settle the claim on my behalf if I fail to do so. All payments from the insurance company must be payable to the Lender under a "standard mortgage clause" in the insurance policy. The Lender may use any proceeds to repair and restore the Property or to reduce the amount due under the Note and this Mortgage. This will not delay the due date for any payment under the Note and this Mortgage.

    f. Repairs. I will keep the Property in good repair, neither damaging nor abandoning it. I will allow the Lender to inspect the Property upon reasonable notice to me.

    g. Statement of Amount Due. Upon request of the Lender, I will certify to the Lender in writing:

        (a) the amount due on the Note and this Mortgage, and

        (b) whether or not I have any defense to my obligations under the Note and this Mortgage.

204S - Note Mortgage
Ind. or Corp. - Plain Language
Rev. 3/06   P11/08

©2006 by ALL-STATE LEGAL
A Division of ALL-STATE International, Inc.
www.aslegal.com   800.222.0510   Page 2

FIGURE 7–2
(continued)

h. Rent. I will not accept rent from any tenant for more than one month in advance.

i. Lawful Use. I will use the Property in compliance with all laws, ordinances and other requirements of any governmental authority.

5. Eminent Domain. All or part of the Property may be taken by a government entity for public use. If this occurs, I agree that any compensation be given to the Lender. The Lender may use this to repair and restore the Property or to reduce the amount owed on the Note and this Mortgage. This will not delay the due date for any further payment under the Note and this Mortgage. Any remaining balance will be paid to me.

6. Tax and Insurance Escrow. If the Lender requests, I will make regular monthly payments to the Lender of: (a) 1/12 of the yearly real estate taxes and assessments on the Property; and (b) 1/12 of the yearly cost of insurance on the Property. These payments will be held by the Lender without interest to pay the taxes, assessments and insurance premiums as they become due.

7. Payments Made for Borrower(s). If I do not make all of the repairs or payments as agreed in this Mortgage, the Lender may do so for me. The cost of these repairs and payments will be added to the Principal, will bear interest at the same rate provided in the Note and will be repaid to the Lender upon demand.

8. Default. The Lender may declare that I am in default on the Note and this Mortgage if:
    a. I fail to make any payment required by the Note and this Mortgage within _____ days after its due date;
    b. I fail to keep any other promise I make in this Mortgage;
    c. the ownership of the Property is changed for any reason;
    d. the holder of any lien on the Property starts foreclosure proceedings; or
    e. bankruptcy, insolvency or receivership proceedings are started by or against any of the Borrowers.

9. Payments Due Upon Default. If the Lender declares that I am in default, I must immediately pay the full amount of all unpaid Principal, interest, other amounts due on the Note and this Mortgage and the Lender's costs of collection and reasonable attorney fees.

10. Lender's Rights Upon Default. If the Lender declares that the Note and this Mortgage are in default, the Lender will have all rights given by law or set forth in this Mortgage. This includes the right to do any one or more of the following:
    a. take possession of and manage the Property, including the collection of rents and profits;
    b. have a court appoint a receiver to accept rent for the Property (I consent to this);
    c. start a court action, known as foreclosure, which will result in a sale of the Property to reduce my obligations under the Note and this Mortgage; and
    d. sue me for any money that I owe the Lender.

11. Notices. All notices must be in writing and personally delivered or sent by certified mail, return receipt requested, to the address given in this Mortgage. Address changes may be made upon notice to the other party.

12. No Waiver by Lender. Lender may exercise any right under this Mortgage or under any law, even if Lender has delayed in exercising that right or has agreed in an earlier instance not to exercise that right. Lender does not waive its right to declare that I am in default by making payments or incurring expenses on my behalf.

13. Each Person Liable. This Mortgage is legally binding upon each Borrower and all who succeed to their responsibilities (such as heirs and executors). The Lender may enforce any of the provisions of the Note and this Mortgage against any one or more of the Borrowers who sign this Mortgage.

14. No Oral Changes. This Mortgage can only be changed by an agreement in writing signed by both the Borrower(s) and the Lender.

15. Signatures. I agree to the terms of this Mortgage and have set my hand and seal hereunto. If the Borrower is a corporation, its proper corporate officers sign and seal this mortgage.

Witnessed or Attested by:

_____ (Seal)

_____   _____ (Seal)

204S - Note Mortgage
Ind. or Corp. - Plain Language
Rev. 3/06 P11/08

©2006 by ALL-STATE LEGAL
A Division of ALL-STATE International, Inc.
www.aslegal.com 800.222.0510   Page 3

FIGURE 7–2
(continued)

STATE OF NEW JERSEY, COUNTY OF _____ SS:
I CERTIFY that on _____

_____

personally came before me and stated to my satisfaction that this person (or if more than one, each person):
(a) was the maker of the attached instrument; and,
(b) executed this instrument as his or her own act.

_____

Print name and title below signature

STATE OF NEW JERSEY, COUNTY OF _____ SS:
I CERTIFY that on _____

personally came before me and stated to my satisfaction that this person (or if more than one, each person):
(a) was the maker of the attached instrument;
(b) was authorized to and did execute this instrument as _____
of _____ the entity named in this instrument; and,
(c) executed this instrument as the act of the entity named in this instrument.

_____

Print name and title below signature

To the County Recording Officer of _____ County:

This Mortgage is fully paid. I authorize you to cancel it of record.

Dated _____   _____ (Seal)
                                                      , Lender

204S - Note Mortgage
Ind. or Corp. - Plain Language
Rev. 3/06   P11/08

FIGURE 7–2
(continued)

Mortgage

This mortgage is made on
BETWEEN the Borrower(s)

Whose address is

referred to as "I,"
AND the Lender

whose address is

referred to as the "Lender."

If more than one Borrower signs this Mortgage, the word "I" shall mean each Borrower named above. The word "Lender" means the original Lender and anyone else who takes this Mortgage by transfer.

1. Mortgage Note.   In return for a loan that I received, I promise to pay $ (called "Principal"), plus interest in accordance with the terms of a Mortgage Note (referred to as the "Note") dated   . The Note provides for monthly payments of $ and a yearly interest rate of   %. All sums owed under the Note are due no later than   . All terms of the Note are made part of this Mortgage.

2. Property Mortgaged.   The property mortgaged (called the "Property") to the Lender is located in the of   County of   and State of New Jersey. The Property includes: (a) the land; (b) all buildings that are now, or will be, located on the land; (c) all fixtures that are now, or will be, attached to the land or building(s) (for example, furnaces, bathroom fixtures and kitchen cabinets); (d) all condemnation awards and insurance proceeds relating to the land and building(s); and (e) all other rights that I have, or will have, as owner of the Property. The legal description is:

☐ Please see attached Legal Description annexed hereto and made a part hereof (check box if applicable).

(For Recorder's Use Only)

204S - Note Mortgage
Ind. or Corp. - Plain Language
Rev. 10/00   P 2/01

Powered by

©2000 by ALL-STATE LEGAL®
A Division of ALL-STATE International, Inc.
www.aslegal.com   800-222-0510   Page 1

FIGURE 7–3
(continues)

3. **Rights Given to Lender.** I mortgage the Property to the Lender. This means that I give the Lender those rights stated in this Mortgage and also those rights the law gives to lenders who hold mortgages on real property. When I pay all amounts due to the Lender under the Note and this Mortgage, the Lender's rights under this Mortgage will end. The Lender will then cancel this Mortgage at my expense.

4. **Promises.** I make the following promises to the Lender:

   a. **Note and Mortgage.** I will comply with all of the terms of the Note and this Mortgage.

   b. **Payments.** I will make all payments required by the Note and this Mortgage.

   c. **Ownership.** I warrant title to the premises (N.J.S.A. 46:9-2). This means I own the Property and will defend my ownership against all claims.

   d. **Liens and Taxes.** I will pay all liens, taxes, assessments and other government charges made against the Property when due. I will not claim any deduction from the taxable value of the Property because of this Mortgage. I will not claim any credit against the Principal and interest payable under the Note and this Mortgage for any taxes paid on the Property.

   e. **Insurance.** I must maintain extended coverage fire or property insurance on the Property. The Lender may also require that I maintain flood insurance or other types of insurance. The insurance companies, policies, amounts, and types of coverage must be acceptable to the Lender. I will notify the Lender in the event of any substantial loss or damage. The Lender may then settle the claim on my behalf if I fail to do so. All payments from the insurance company must be payable to the Lender under a "standard mortgage clause" in the insurance policy. The Lender may use any proceeds to repair and restore the Property or to reduce the amount due under the Note and this Mortgage. This will not delay the due date for any payment under the Note and this Mortgage.

   f. **Repairs.** I will keep the Property in good repair, neither damaging nor abandoning it. I will allow the Lender to inspect the Property upon reasonable notice to me.

2048 - Note Mortgage
Ind. or Corp. - Plain Language
Rev. 10/00   P 2/01

Powered by
HotDocs

FIGURE 7–3
(continued)

g. **Statement of Amount Due**.   Upon request of the Lender, I will certify to the Lender in writing:
(a) the amount due on the Note and this Mortgage, and
(b) whether or not I have any defense to my obligations under the Note and this Mortgage.

h. **Rent.**   I will not accept rent from any tenant for more than one month in advance.

i. **Lawful Use**.   I will use the Property in compliance with all laws, ordinances and other requirements of any governmental authority.

5. Eminent Domain.   All or part of the Property may be taken by a government entity for public use. If this occurs, I agree that any compensation be given to the Lender. The Lender may use this to repair and restore the Property or to reduce the amount owed on the Note and this Mortgage. This will not delay the due date for any further payment under the Note and this Mortgage. Any remaining balance will be paid to me.

6. Tax and Insurance Escrow.   If the Lender requests, I will make regular monthly payments to the Lender of: (a) 1/12 of the yearly real estate taxes and assessments on the Property; and (b) 1/12 of the yearly cost of insurance on the Property. These payments will be held by the Lender without interest to pay the taxes, assessments and insurance premiums as they become due.

7. Payments Made for Borrower(s).   If I do not make all of the repairs or payments as agreed in this Mortgage, the Lender may do so for me. The cost of these repairs and payments will be added to the Principal, will bear interest at the same rate provided in the Note and will be repaid to the Lender upon demand.

8. Default.   The Lender may declare that I am in default on the Note and this Mortgage if:
   a. I fail to make any payment required by the Note and this Mortgage within   days after its due date;
   b. I fail to keep any other promise I make in this Mortgage;
   c. the ownership of the Property is changed for any reason;
   d. the holder of any lien on the Property starts foreclosure proceedings; or
   e. bankruptcy, insolvency or receivership proceedings are started by or against any of the Borrowers.

9. Payments Due Upon Default.   If the Lender declares that I am in default, I must immediately pay the full amount of all unpaid Principal, interest, other amounts due on the Note and this Mortgage and the Lender's costs of collection and reasonable attorney fees.

10. Lender's Rights Upon Default.   If the Lender declares that the Note and this Mortgage are in default, the Lender will have all rights given by law or set forth in this Mortgage. This includes the right to do any one or more of the following:
   a. take possession of and manage the Property, including the collection of rents and profits;
   b. have a court appoint a receiver to accept rent for the Property (I consent to this);
   c. start a court action, known as foreclosure, which will result in a sale of the Property to reduce my obligations under the Note and this Mortgage; and
   d. sue me for any money that I owe the Lender.

11. Notices.   All notices must be in writing and personally delivered or sent by certified mail, return receipt requested, to the address given in this Mortgage. Address changes may be made upon notice to the other party.

12. No Waiver by Lender.   Lender may exercise any right under this Mortgage or under any law, even if Lender has delayed in exercising that right or has agreed in an earlier instance not to exercise that right. Lender does not waive its right to declare that I am in default by making payments or incurring expenses on my behalf.

13. Each Person Liable.   This Mortgage is legally binding upon each Borrower and all who succeed to their responsibilities (such as heirs and executors). The Lender may enforce any of the provisions of the Note and this Mortgage against any one or more of the Borrowers who sign this Mortgage.

14. No Oral Changes.   This Mortgage can only be changed by an agreement in writing signed by both the Borrower(s) and the Lender.

15. Signatures.   I agree to the terms of this Mortgage. If the Borrower is a corporation, its proper corporate officers sign.

Witnessed or Attested by:

_____   (Seal)

_____   _____   (Seal)

FIGURE 7–3
(continued)

STATE OF NEW JERSEY, COUNTY OF   SS:
I CERTIFY that on

personally came before me and stated to my satisfaction that this person (or if more than one, each person):
(a) was the maker of the attached instrument; and,
(b) executed this instrument as his or her own act.

_____

Print name and title below signature

STATE OF NEW JERSEY, COUNTY OF   SS:
I CERTIFY that on

personally came before me and stated to my satisfaction that this person (or if more than one, each person):
(a) was the maker of the attached instrument;
(b) was authorized to and did execute this instrument as

of   the entity named in this instrument; and,
(c) executed this instrument as the act of the entity named in this instrument.

STATE OF NEW JERSEY, COUNTY OF   SS:
I CERTIFY that on

personally came before me and stated to my satisfaction that this person (or if more than one, each person):
(a) was the maker of the attached instrument; and,
(b) executed this instrument as his or her own act.

_____

Print name and title below signature

NOTE MORTGAGE	*Dated:*
	Record & Return to:
Borrower(s),	
TO	
Lender(s).	

To the County Recording Officer of   County:

This Mortgage is fully paid. I authorize you to cancel it of record.

Dated   _____ (Seal)

                                                Lender

204S - Note Mortgage
Ind. or Corp. - Plain Language
Rev. 10/00   P 2/01

Powered by
Hot**D**ocs®

©2000 by ALL-STATE LEGAL®
A Division of ALL-STATE International, Inc.
www.aslegal.com   800-222-0510   Page 4

FIGURE 7–3
(continued)

The printed portions of this form, except differentiated additions, have been approved by the Colorado Real Estate Commission (TD72-9-08) (Mandatory 1-09)

IF THIS FORM IS USED IN A CONSUMER CREDIT TRANSACTION, CONSULT LEGAL COUNSEL.
THIS IS A LEGAL INSTRUMENT. IF NOT UNDERSTOOD, LEGAL, TAX OR OTHER COUNSEL SHOULD BE CONSULTED BEFORE SIGNING.

DEED OF TRUST
(Due on Transfer - Strict)

THIS DEED OF TRUST is made this _____ day of _____, 20 __, between _____
_____ (Borrower), whose address is _____ ;
and the Public Trustee of the County in which the Property (see paragraph 1) is situated (Trustee); for the benefit of
_____ (Lender), whose address is
_____ .

Borrower and Lender covenant and agree as follows:

1.   Property in Trust. Borrower, in consideration of the indebtedness herein recited and the trust herein created, hereby grants and conveys to Trustee in trust, with power of sale, the following legally described property located in the _____ County of _____, State of Colorado:

known as No. _____ (Property Address),
           Street Address   City   State   Zip
together with all its appurtenances (Property).

2.   Note: Other Obligations Secured. This Deed of Trust is given to secure to Lender:

A. the repayment of the indebtedness evidenced by Borrower's note (Note) dated _____ in the principal sum of _____ Dollars (U.S. $_____), with interest on the unpaid principal balance from _____ until paid, at the rate of _____ percent rate per annum, with principal and interest payable at _____ or such other place as Lender may designate, in _____ payments of _____ Dollars (U.S. $_____), due on the ____ day of each _____ beginning _____ ; such payments to continue until the entire indebtedness evidenced by said Note is fully paid; however, if not sooner paid, the entire principal amount outstanding and accrued interest thereon shall be due and payable on _____ ; and Borrower is to pay to Lender a late charge of _____ % of any payment not received by Lender within _____ days after payment is due; and Borrower has the right to prepay the principal amount outstanding under said Note, in whole or in part, at any time without penalty except _____ .

B. the payment of all other sums, with interest thereon at _____ % per annum, disbursed by Lender in accordance with this Deed of Trust to protect the security of this Deed of Trust; and

C. the performance of the covenants and agreements of Borrower herein contained.

3.   Title. Borrower covenants that Borrower owns and has the right to grant and convey the Property, and warrants title to the same, subject to general real estate taxes for the current year, easements of record or in existence, and recorded declarations, restrictions, reservations and covenants, if any, as of this date; and subject to _____ .

4.   Payment of Principal and Interest. Borrower shall promptly pay when due the principal of and interest on the indebtedness evidenced by the Note, and late charges as provided in the Note and shall perform all of Borrower's other covenants contained in the Note.

5.   Application of Payments. All payments received by Lender under the terms hereof shall be applied by Lender first in payment of amounts due pursuant to paragraph 23 (Escrow Funds for Taxes and Insurance), then to amounts disbursed by Lender pursuant to paragraph 9 (Protection of Lender's Security), and the balance in accordance with the terms and conditions of the Note.

6.   Prior Mortgages and Deeds of Trust; Charges; Liens. Borrower shall perform all of Borrower's obligations under any prior deed of trust and any other prior liens. Borrower shall pay all taxes, assessments and other charges, fines and impositions attributable to the Property which may have or attain a priority over this Deed of Trust, and leasehold payments or ground rents, if any, in the manner set out in paragraph 23 (Escrow Funds for Taxes and Insurance) or, if not required to be paid in such manner, by Borrower making payment when due, directly to the payee thereof. Despite the foregoing, Borrower shall not be required to make payments otherwise required by this paragraph if Borrower, after notice to Lender, shall in good faith contest such obligation by, or defend enforcement of such obligation in, legal proceedings which operate to prevent the enforcement of the obligation or forfeiture of the Property or any part thereof, only upon Borrower making all such contested payments and other payments as ordered by the court to the registry of the court in which such proceedings are filed.

7.   Property Insurance. Borrower shall keep the improvements now existing or hereafter erected on the Property insured against loss by fire or hazards included within the term "extended coverage" in an amount at least equal to the lesser of (a) the insurable value of the Property or (b) an amount sufficient to pay the sums secured by this Deed of Trust as well as any prior encumbrances on the Property. All of the foregoing shall be known as "Property Insurance."

The insurance carrier providing the insurance shall be qualified to write Property Insurance in Colorado and shall be chosen by Borrower subject to Lender's right to reject the chosen carrier for reasonable cause. All insurance policies and renewals thereof

TD72-9-08. **DEED OF TRUST (DUE ON TRANSFER - STRICT)**   Page 1 of 5

FIGURE 7–4
(continues)

shall include a standard mortgage clause in favor of Lender, and shall provide that the insurance carrier shall notify Lender at least ten (10) days before cancellation, termination or any material change of coverage. Insurance policies shall be furnished to Lender at or before closing. Lender shall have the right to hold the policies and renewals thereof.

In the event of loss, Borrower shall give prompt notice to the insurance carrier and Lender. Lender may make proof of loss if not made promptly by Borrower.

Insurance proceeds shall be applied to restoration or repair of the Property damaged, provided said restoration or repair is economically feasible and the security of this Deed of Trust is not thereby impaired. If such restoration or repair is not economically feasible or if the security of this Deed of Trust would be impaired, the insurance proceeds shall be applied to the sums secured by this Deed of Trust, with the excess, if any, paid to Borrower. If the Property is abandoned by Borrower, or if Borrower fails to respond to Lender within 30 days from the date notice is given in accordance with paragraph 16 (Notice) by Lender to Borrower that the insurance carrier offers to settle a claim for insurance benefits, Lender is authorized to collect and apply the insurance proceeds, at Lender's option, either to restoration or repair of the Property or to the sums secured by this Deed of Trust.

Any such application of proceeds to principal shall not extend or postpone the due date of the installments referred to in paragraphs 4 (Payment of Principal and Interest) and 23 (Escrow Funds for Taxes and Insurance) or change the amount of such installments. Notwithstanding anything herein to the contrary, if under paragraph 18 (Acceleration; Foreclosure; Other Remedies) the Property is acquired by Lender, all right, title and interest of Borrower in and to any insurance policies and in and to the proceeds thereof resulting from damage to the Property prior to the sale or acquisition shall pass to Lender to the extent of the sums secured by this Deed of Trust immediately prior to such sale or acquisition.

All of the rights of Borrower and Lender hereunder with respect to insurance carriers, insurance policies and insurance proceeds are subject to the rights of any holder of a prior deed of trust with respect to said insurance carriers, policies and proceeds.

8. **Preservation and Maintenance of Property.** Borrower shall keep the Property in good repair and shall not commit waste or permit impairment or deterioration of the Property and shall comply with the provisions of any lease if this Deed of Trust is on a leasehold. Borrower shall perform all of Borrower's obligations under any declarations, covenants, by-laws, rules, or other documents governing the use, ownership or occupancy of the Property.

9. **Protection of Lender's Security.** Except when Borrower has exercised Borrower's rights under paragraph 6 above, if Borrower fails to perform the covenants and agreements contained in this Deed of Trust, or if a default occurs in a prior lien, or if any action or proceeding is commenced which materially affects Lender's interest in the Property, then Lender, at Lender's option, with notice to Borrower if required by law, may make such appearances, disburse such sums and take such action as is necessary to protect Lender's interest, including, but not limited to:

    (a)   any general or special taxes or ditch or water assessments levied or accruing against the Property;

    (b)   the premiums on any insurance necessary to protect any improvements comprising a part of the Property;

    (c)   sums due on any prior lien or encumbrance on the Property;

    (d)   if the Property is a leasehold or is subject to a lease, all sums due under such lease;

    (e)   the reasonable costs and expenses of defending, protecting, and maintaining the Property and Lender's interest in the Property, including repair and maintenance costs and expenses, costs and expenses of protecting and securing the Property, receiver's fees and expenses, inspection fees, appraisal fees, court costs, attorney fees and costs, and fees and costs of an attorney in the employment of Lender or holder of the certificate of purchase;

    (f)   all other costs and expenses allowable by the evidence of debt or this Deed of Trust; and

    (g)   such other costs and expenses which may be authorized by a court of competent jurisdiction.

Borrower hereby assigns to Lender any right Borrower may have by reason of any prior encumbrance on the Property or by law or otherwise to cure any default under said prior encumbrance.

Any amounts disbursed by Lender pursuant to this paragraph 9, with interest thereon, shall become additional indebtedness of Borrower secured by this Deed of Trust. Such amounts shall be payable upon notice from Lender to Borrower requesting payment thereof, and Lender may bring suit to collect any amounts so disbursed plus interest specified in paragraph 2B (Note; Other Obligations Secured). Nothing contained in this paragraph 9 shall require Lender to incur any expense or take any action hereunder.

10. **Inspection.** Lender may make or cause to be made reasonable entries upon and inspection of the Property, provided that Lender shall give Borrower notice prior to any such inspection specifying reasonable cause therefore related to Lender's interest in the Property.

11. **Condemnation.** The proceeds of any award or claim for damages, direct or consequential, in connection with any condemnation or other taking of the Property, or part thereof, or for conveyance in lieu of condemnation, are hereby assigned and shall be paid to Lender as herein provided. However, all of the rights of Borrower and Lender hereunder with respect to such proceeds are subject to the rights of any holder of a prior deed of trust.

In the event of a total taking of the Property, the proceeds shall be applied to the sums secured by this Deed of Trust, with the excess, if any, paid to Borrower. In the event of a partial taking of the Property, the proceeds remaining after taking out any part of the award due any prior lien holder (net award) shall be divided between Lender and Borrower, in the same ratio as the amount of the sums secured by this Deed of Trust immediately prior to the date of taking bears to Borrower's equity in the Property immediately prior to the date of taking. Borrower's equity in the Property means the fair market value of the Property less the amount of sums secured by both this Deed of Trust and all prior liens (except taxes) that are to receive any of the award, all at the value immediately prior to the date of taking.

If the Property is abandoned by Borrower or if, after notice by Lender to Borrower that the condemnor offers to make an award or settle a claim for damages, Borrower fails to respond to Lender within 30 days after the date such notice is given, Lender is

TD72-9-08. **DEED OF TRUST (DUE ON TRANSFER - STRICT)** Page 2 of 5

FIGURE 7–4

(continued)

authorized to collect and apply the proceeds, at Lender's option, either to restoration or repair of the Property or to the sums secured by this Deed of Trust.

Any such application of proceeds to principal shall not extend or postpone the due date of the installments referred to in paragraphs 4 (Payment of Principal and Interest) and 23 (Escrow Funds for Taxes and Insurance) nor change the amount of such installments.

12.   Borrower not Released. Extension of the time for payment or modification of amortization of the sums secured by this Deed of Trust granted by Lender to any successor in interest of Borrower shall not operate to release, in any manner, the liability of the original Borrower, nor Borrower's successors in interest, from the original terms of this Deed of Trust. Lender shall not be required to commence proceedings against such successor or refuse to extend time for payment or otherwise modify amortization of the sums secured by this Deed of Trust by reason of any demand made by the original Borrower nor Borrower's successors in interest.

13.   Forbearance by Lender Not a Waiver. Any forbearance by Lender in exercising any right or remedy hereunder, or otherwise afforded by law, shall not be a waiver or preclude the exercise of any such right or remedy.

14.   Remedies Cumulative. Each remedy provided in the Note and this Deed of Trust is distinct from and cumulative to all other rights or remedies under the Note and this Deed of Trust or afforded by law or equity, and may be exercised concurrently, independently or successively.

15.   Successors and Assigns Bound; Joint and Several Liability; Captions. The covenants and agreements herein contained shall bind, and the rights hereunder shall inure to, the respective successors and assigns of Lender and Borrower, subject to the provisions of paragraph 24 (Transfer of the Property; Assumption). All covenants and agreements of Borrower shall be joint and several. The captions and headings of the paragraphs in this Deed of Trust are for convenience only and are not to be used to interpret or define the provisions hereof.

16.   Notice. Except for any notice required by law to be given in another manner, (a) any notice to Borrower provided for in this Deed of Trust shall be in writing and shall be given and be effective upon (1) delivery to Borrower or (2) mailing such notice by first class U.S. mail, addressed to Borrower at Borrower's address stated herein or at such other address as Borrower may designate by notice to Lender as provided herein, and (b) any notice to Lender shall be in writing and shall be given and be effective upon (1) delivery to Lender or (2) mailing such notice by first class U.S. mail, to Lender's address stated herein or to such other address as Lender may designate by notice to Borrower as provided herein. Any notice provided for in this Deed of Trust shall be deemed to have been given to Borrower or Lender when given in any manner designated herein.

17.   Governing Law; Severability. The Note and this Deed of Trust shall be governed by the law of Colorado. In the event that any provision or clause of this Deed of Trust or the Note conflicts with the law, such conflict shall not affect other provisions of this Deed of Trust or the Note which can be given effect without the conflicting provision, and to this end the provisions of the Deed of Trust and Note are declared to be severable.

18.   Acceleration; Foreclosure; Other Remedies. Except as provided in paragraph 24 (Transfer of the Property; Assumption), upon Borrower's breach of any covenant or agreement of Borrower in this Deed of Trust, or upon any default in a prior lien upon the Property, (unless Borrower has exercised Borrower's rights under paragraph 6 above), at Lender's option, all of the sums secured by this Deed of Trust shall be immediately due and payable (Acceleration). To exercise this option, Lender may invoke the power of sale and any other remedies permitted by law. Lender shall be entitled to collect all reasonable costs and expenses incurred in pursuing the remedies provided in this Deed of Trust, including, but not limited to, reasonable attorney's fees.

If Lender invokes the power of sale, Lender shall give written notice to Trustee of such election. Trustee shall give such notice to Borrower of Borrower's rights as is provided by law. Trustee shall record a copy of such notice as required by law. Trustee shall advertise the time and place of the sale of the Property, for not less than four weeks in a newspaper of general circulation in each county in which the Property is situated, and shall mail copies of such notice of sale to Borrower and other persons as prescribed by law. After the lapse of such time as may be required by law, Trustee, without demand on Borrower, shall sell the Property at public auction to the highest bidder for cash at the time and place (which may be on the Property or any part thereof as permitted by law) in one or more parcels as Trustee may think best and in such order as Trustee may determine. Lender or Lender's designee may purchase the Property at any sale. It shall not be obligatory upon the purchaser at any such sale to see to the application of the purchase money.

Trustee shall apply the proceeds of the sale in the following order: (a) to all reasonable costs and expenses of the sale, including, but not limited to, reasonable Trustee's and attorney's fees and costs of title evidence; (b) to all sums secured by this Deed of Trust; and (c) the excess, if any, to the person or persons legally entitled thereto.

19.   Borrower's Right to Cure Default. Whenever foreclosure is commenced for nonpayment of any sums due hereunder, the owners of the Property or parties liable hereon shall be entitled to cure said defaults by paying all delinquent principal and interest payments due as of the date of cure, costs, expenses, late charges, attorney's fees and other fees all in the manner provided by law. Upon such payment, this Deed of Trust and the obligations secured hereby shall remain in full force and effect as though no Acceleration had occurred, and the foreclosure proceedings shall be discontinued.

20.   Assignment of Rents; Appointment of Receiver; Lender in Possession. As additional security hereunder, Borrower hereby assigns to Lender the rents of the Property; however, Borrower shall, prior to Acceleration under paragraph 18 (Acceleration; Foreclosure; Other Remedies) or abandonment of the Property, have the right to collect and retain such rents as they become due and payable.

TD72-9-08. **DEED OF TRUST (DUE ON TRANSFER - STRICT)**   Page 3 of 5

FIGURE 7–4
(continued)

Lender or the holder of the Trustee's certificate of purchase shall be entitled to a receiver for the Property after Acceleration under paragraph 18 (Acceleration; Foreclosure; Other Remedies), and shall also be so entitled during the time covered by foreclosure proceedings and the period of redemption, if any; and shall be entitled thereto as a matter of right without regard to the solvency or insolvency of Borrower or of the then owner of the Property, and without regard to the value thereof. Such receiver may be appointed by any Court of competent jurisdiction upon ex parte application and without notice; notice being hereby expressly waived.

Upon Acceleration under paragraph 18 (Acceleration; Foreclosure; Other Remedies) or abandonment of the Property, Lender, in person, by agent or by judicially-appointed receiver, shall be entitled to enter upon, take possession of and manage the Property and to collect the rents of the Property including those past due. All rents collected by Lender or the receiver shall be applied, first to payment of the costs of preservation and management of the Property, second to payments due upon prior liens, and then to the sums secured by this Deed of Trust. Lender and the receiver shall be liable to account only for those rents actually received.

21.   Release. Upon payment of all sums secured by this Deed of Trust, Lender shall cause Trustee to release this Deed of Trust and shall produce for Trustee the Note. Borrower shall pay all costs of recordation and shall pay the statutory Trustee's fees. If Lender shall not produce the Note as aforesaid, then Lender, upon notice in accordance with paragraph 16 (Notice) from Borrower to Lender, shall obtain, at Lender's expense, and file any lost instrument bond required by Trustee or pay the cost thereof to effect the release of this Deed of Trust.

22.   Waiver of Exemptions. Borrower hereby waives all right of homestead and any other exemption in the Property under state or federal law presently existing or hereafter enacted.

23.   Escrow Funds for Taxes and Insurance. This paragraph 23 is not applicable if Funds, as defined below, are being paid pursuant to a prior encumbrance. Subject to applicable law, Borrower shall pay to Lender, on each day installments of principal and interest are payable under the Note, until the Note is paid in full, a sum (herein referred to as "Funds") equal to _____ of the yearly taxes and assessments which may attain priority over this Deed of Trust, plus _____ of yearly premium installments for Property Insurance, all as reasonably estimated initially and from time to time by Lender on the basis of assessments and bills and reasonable estimates thereof, taking into account any excess Funds not used or shortages.

The principal of the Funds shall be held in a separate account by Lender in trust for the benefit of Borrower and deposited in an institution, the deposits or accounts of which are insured or guaranteed by a federal or state agency. Lender shall apply the Funds to pay said taxes, assessments and insurance premiums. Lender may not charge for so holding and applying the Funds, analyzing said account or verifying and compiling said assessments and bills. Lender shall not be required to pay Borrower any interest or earnings on the Funds. Lender shall give to Borrower, without charge, an annual accounting of the Funds showing credits and debits to the Funds and the purpose for which each debit to the Funds was made. The Funds are pledged as additional security for the sums secured by this Deed of Trust.

If the amount of the Funds held by Lender shall not be sufficient to pay taxes, assessments and insurance premiums as they fall due, Borrower shall pay to Lender any amount necessary to make up the deficiency within 30 days from the date notice is given in accordance with paragraph 16 (Notice) by Lender to Borrower requesting payment thereof. Provided however, if the loan secured by this Deed of Trust is subject to RESPA or other laws regulating Escrow Accounts, such deficiency, surplus or any other required adjustment shall be paid, credited or adjusted in compliance with such applicable laws.

Upon payment in full of all sums secured by this Deed of Trust, Lender shall simultaneously refund to Borrower any Funds held by Lender. If under paragraph 18 (Acceleration; Foreclosure; Other Remedies) the Property is sold or the Property is otherwise acquired by Lender, Lender shall apply, no later than immediately prior to the sale of the Property or its acquisition by Lender, whichever occurs first, any Funds held by Lender at the time of application as a credit against the sums secured by this Deed of Trust.

24.   Transfer of the Property; Assumption. The following events shall be referred to herein as a "Transfer": (i) a transfer or conveyance of title (or any portion thereof, legal or equitable) of the Property (or any part thereof or interest therein), (ii) the execution of a contract or agreement creating a right to title (or any portion thereof, legal or equitable) in the Property (or any part thereof or interest therein), (iii) or an agreement granting a possessory right in the Property (or any portion thereof), in excess of 3 years, (iv) a sale or transfer of, or the execution of a contract or agreement creating a right to acquire or receive, more than fifty percent (50%) of the controlling interest or more than fifty percent (50%) of the beneficial interest in Borrower, (v) the reorganization, liquidation or dissolution of Borrower. Not to be included as a Transfer are (i) the creation of a lien or encumbrance subordinate to this Deed of Trust, (ii) the creation of a purchase money security interest for household appliances, or (iii) a transfer by devise, descent or by operation of the law upon the death of a joint tenant. At the election of Lender, in the event of each and every Transfer:

(a)   All sums secured by this Deed of Trust shall become immediately due and payable (Acceleration).

(b)   If a Transfer occurs and should Lender not exercise Lender's option pursuant to this paragraph 24 to Accelerate, Transferee shall be deemed to have assumed all of the obligations of Borrower under this Deed of Trust including all sums secured hereby whether or not the instrument evidencing such conveyance, contract or grant expressly so provides. This covenant shall run with the Property and remain in full force and effect until said sums are paid in full. Lender may without notice to Borrower deal with Transferee in the same manner as with Borrower with reference to said sums including the payment or credit to Transferee of undisbursed reserve Funds on payment in full of said sums, without in any way altering or discharging Borrower's liability hereunder for the obligations hereby secured.

(c)   Should Lender not elect to Accelerate upon the occurrence of such Transfer then, subject to (b) above, the mere fact of a lapse of time or the acceptance of payment subsequent to any of such events, whether or not Lender had actual or constructive notice of such Transfer, shall not be deemed a waiver of Lender's right to make such election nor shall Lender be estopped therefrom

TD72-9-08. **DEED OF TRUST (DUE ON TRANSFER - STRICT)**   Page 4 of 5

FIGURE 7–4
(continued)

by virtue thereof. The issuance on behalf of Lender of a routine statement showing the status of the loan, whether or not Lender had actual or constructive notice of such Transfer, shall not be a waiver or estoppel of Lender's said rights.

25. **Borrower's Copy.** Borrower acknowledges receipt of a copy of the Note and this Deed of Trust.

EXECUTED BY BORROWER.

IF BORROWER IS NATURAL PERSON(s):

_____

_____ doing business as _____

IF BORROWER IS CORPORATION:
ATTEST:

                                                _____
                                                Name of Corporation

_____ By _____
               Secretary   President

(SEAL)
IF BORROWER IS PARTNERSHIP:
                                                  _____
                                                Name of Partnership

                                          By _____
                                                A General Partner

IF BORROWER IS LIMITED LIABILITY COMPANY: _____
                                                Name of Limited Liability Company

                                          By _____
                                                Its authorized representative

                                                _____
                                                Title of authorized representative

STATE OF COLORADO   ⎫
                                 ⎬ ss.
_____ COUNTY OF _____ ⎭

The foregoing instrument was acknowledged before me this _____ day of _____, 20 ___, by*
_____.

Witness my hand and official seal.
My commission expires: _____.

                                                _____
                                                Notary Public

*If a natural person or persons, insert the name(s) of such person(s). If a corporation, insert, for example, "John Doe as President and Jane Doe as Secretary of Doe & Co., a Colorado corporation." If a partnership, insert, for example, "Sam Smith as general partner in and for Smith & Smith, a general partnership." A Statement of Authority may be required if borrower is a limited liability company or other entity (38-30-172, C.R.S.)

FIGURE 7–4
(continued)

III. BUYER'S PRELIMINARY QUALIFICATION

Financing for the real estate transaction has little possibility of award if the buyer is short on cash or lacks the qualifications for the mortgage. Most real estate brokers and agents and the paralegals they employ now screen potential buyers in the real estate transaction. The screening process attempts to weigh and evaluate the assets of the buyer. The vehicle most often used to accomplish this purpose is an income-to-debt ratio that paints an accurate income-liability picture. Therefore, it is a wise practice to screen any prospective buyer under a test of eligibility for a specific loan product. One way this can be accomplished is the Buyer's Financial Information sheet, reproduced in Figure 7–5.[8]

Information on assets, liabilities, annual income, and current real property owned is solicited and then calculated. Personal information that leads to an expansive credit history is also reported. In general, this type of prequalification and eligibility determination looks at the gross monthly income, which includes verifiable salaries, dividends, net rental income, child support, yearly verifiable bonuses, trust fund income, mortgage differential, commissions, verifiable overtime, disability payments, pension payments, part-time employment, annuities, and alimony. Figured against the total amount of income is the total amount of debt, including installment loans, credit cards, auto loans, other mortgages, and any other liabilities with generally more than ten or more payments remaining. As to the mortgage calculation, eligibility also depends on the amount of tax, insurance, and association dues. In general, the lender analyzes both the property and the buyer who seeks it. In the case of property, these questions are pertinent:

- Are sufficient casualty, liability, and title insurance in effect?
- Have tax, judgment, or mechanics' liens been placed on the property?
- Is there a recent appraisal and on-site inspection report?
- Are there potential environmental problems?[9]

In the case of a borrower, the central points are:

- Integrity
- Financial ability
- Expertise
- Motivation[10]

In the final analysis, the lender must be satisfied with not only the credit history of the applicant, but also the balance of assets when compared to liabilities.

For an investor, income analysis of the commercial property under consideration helps a prospective buyer, as well as a lender, determine whether or not a commercial loan is a wise business strategy.

Aside from income and asset eligibility determinations, the assessment of a prospective buyer's eligibility depends upon the type of mortgage loans available. Criteria for loans differ markedly, from a rigorous set of eligibility criteria for the straight conventional loan to an almost nonexistent set of variables for a no-documentation loan. With the tremendous variety of loan products available in the real estate marketplace, prospective buyers should be guided to loan products that are tailored to their particular situation.

BUYER'S FINANCIAL INFORMATION

BFI

This form recommended and approved for, but not restricted to use by, the members of the Pennsylvania Association of REALTORS® (PAR).

1 BUYER 1 _____
2 ADDRESS _____
3 _____
4 BUYER 2 _____
5 ADDRESS _____
6 _____
7
8
9 **The following information is requested to determine the buyer's financial ability to purchase the property.**
10
11 1. Will you occupy the premises? ☐ Yes ☐ No
12 2. Have you in the last 7 years declared bankruptcy, suffered foreclosure, had an account for collection action, had a history of late pay-
13 ments, or had any legal action affecting ability to finance? ☐ Yes ☐ No
14 If yes, explain. _____
15 3. Is any part of purchase price or settlement costs being obtained from a source other than shown below? ☐ Yes ☐ No
16 If yes, explain. _____
17 4. Have you at any time on or since January 1, 1998, been obligated to pay support under an order that is on record in any Pennsylvania
18 county? ☐ Yes ☐ No
19 If yes, list the county and the Domestic Relations File or Docket Number: _____
20 5. Are there any arrearages for alimony or child/spousal support due in this, or any other, jurisdiction? ☐ Yes ☐ No
21 If yes, explain: _____
22
23 **For a purchase involving mortgage financing, disclose at least a minimum net worth of liquid assets in the amount of the down**
24 **payment plus settlement costs. For cash sales, disclose at least a minimum amount equal to the purchase price plus settlement**
25 **costs.**
26
27 **ASSETS (Bank accounts, stocks, etc.)** **BUYER 1** **BUYER 2**
28
29 _____ $ _____ $ _____
30 _____ $ _____ $ _____
31 _____ $ _____ $ _____
32 _____ $ _____ $ _____
33 _____ $ _____ $ _____
34 TOTAL $ _____ $ _____
35
36 **The information in this section must be provided if Buyer(s) require a mortgage loan.**
37

38 **LIABILITIES (list all liabilities,** **BUYER 1** **BUYER 2**
39 **including alimony or child/spousal support, if any)** **Balance** **Per Month** **Balance** **Per Month**

40	$	$	$	$
41	$	$	$	$
42	$	$	$	$
43	$	$	$	$
44	$	$	$	$
45 TOTAL	$	$	$	$

46
47 **Real Estate Currently Owned** (First Property)   **Real Estate Currently Owned** (Second Property)
48
49 Address _____   Address _____
50
51 Value $ _____ Mo. Payment $ _____   Value $ _____ Mo. Payment $ _____
52 Mortgage/Equity Loan Balance $ _____   Mortgage/Equity Loan Balance $ _____
53
54 **Buyer Initials:** _____ / _____   BFI Page 1 of 2

Pennsylvania Association of REALTORS®

FIGURE 7–5
(continues)

55 **The information in this section must be provided if Buyer(s) require a mortgage loan, but only to the extent necessary to prove**
56 **the ability to qualify for the mortgage loan.**

57
58 **EMPLOYMENT INFORMATION -- BUYER 1**   **EMPLOYMENT INFORMATION -- BUYER 2**
59
60 Current Employer: _____   Current Employer: _____
61 Address: _____   Address: _____
62 _____   _____
63 Occupation: _____   Occupation: _____
64 Years at job: _____   Years at job: _____
65
66 Prior Employer: _____   Prior Employer: _____
67 Address: _____   Address: _____
68 _____   _____
69 Occupation: _____   Occupation: _____
70 Years at job: _____   Years at job: _____
71
72 **ANNUAL INCOME**   <u>**BUYER 1**</u>   **ANNUAL INCOME**   <u>**BUYER 2**</u>
73
74 Basic Salary $ _____   Basic Salary $ _____
75 Overtime $ _____   Overtime $ _____
76 Bonuses $ _____   Bonuses $ _____
77 Commissions $ _____   Commissions $ _____
78 Dividends $ _____   Dividends $ _____
79 Interest $ _____   Interest $ _____
80 _____ $ _____   _____ $ _____
81 _____ $ _____   _____ $ _____
82   TOTAL $ _____   TOTAL $ _____
83   **COMBINED TOTAL INCOMES** $ _____
84
85 ADDITIONAL INFORMATION: _____
86 _____
87 _____
88 _____
89 ══

90 Buyer(s) affirm that the above information is true and correct. Buyer(s) understand that the information may be used as a basis for
91 the acceptance or rejection of an offer by the seller. Buyer(s) further understand that the information may be provided to a lender in
92 conjunction with the placement of a mortgage loan. Buyer(s) acknowledge that failure to provide truthful and correct information
93 may result in the forfeiture of any deposits made by Buyer(s) and may subject Buyer(s) to other financial loss or penalties.

94 ┌─ □ If checked, Buyer(s) expressly authorize and direct _____
95 │   (Broker) acting as □ Broker for Seller □ Broker for Buyer □ Transaction Licensee, to obtain any information or
96 │   reports from a credit reporting agency including, but not limited to consumer reports, credit reports, criminal histo-
97 │   ry reports, judgments of record and verification of employment and salary history deemed necessary for furthering
98 │   the completion of this and any related transactions, and for the evaluation of the information provided by Buyer(s).
99 │   Upon signing this form, Buyer(s) agree to provide their social security number(s) to the broker identified above for the
100 │   purposes of obtaining such reports and information.
    └──

101 Buyer(s) expressly authorize Broker to provide the information contained in this form and any reports or information obtained by
102 Broker for the purposes stated above, to the seller(s), cooperating broker(s), mortgage broker(s) and lender(s) involved in this trans-
103 action or any related transaction. BUYER(S) UNDERSTAND THAT BROKER HAS NO CONTROL OVER THE USE OF ANY
104 INFORMATION AFTER IT IS DISCLOSED TO A THIRD PARTY; BUYER(S) AGREE TO RELEASE AND HOLD BROKER
105 HARMLESS FROM ANY AND ALL LIABILITY FOR ANY MISUSE OR SUBSEQUENT DISCLOSURE BY ANY THIRD PARTY
106 OF THE INFORMATION OR REPORTS DISCLOSED BY BROKER PURSUANT TO THE TERMS OF THIS AUTHORIZATION.
107
108 Buyers' signatures serve as an acknowledgement of receipt of a copy of this financial information sheet.
109
110 **BUYER**_____ **DATE** _____
111 **BUYER**_____ **DATE** _____
112 **BUYER**_____ **DATE** _____

FIGURE 7–5
(continued)

IV. TYPES OF MORTGAGE PRODUCTS

Familiarity with the diverse range of products and services in the mortgage sector is crucial to any real estate paralegal. Mortgages should be thought of as competitive products, with a whole host of private financiers, banks, savings and loans, lenders, insurance companies, and other investors vigorously competing for a share of the real estate mortgage marketplace listings. As a result, there are often stark differences in the terms and conditions of loan products. A summary review of the various types of mortgages follows. All are **conventional mortgages** with the exception of VA or FHA mortgages.

Web Exercise

The Federal Reserve Board publishes excellent guidance on the types and characteristics of the diverse product line in mortgages. Visit www.federalreserve.gov/pubs/mortgage/mortb_1.htm.

A. Fixed Rate Mortgage

Historically, **fixed rate mortgages** have been the preferred choice of prospective home buyers. A fixed rate mortgage generally ranges from 3% to 21%, depending on economic conditions and Federal Reserve policy. The loan is generally amortized over a period of ten through forty years. An **amortization** schedule can describe to a client what their payments of interest and principal will be over the life of a loan. See the amortization schedule in Figure 7–6.

Favorable features of a fixed rate note rest in its predictability and consistency over the life of the loan. Its main disadvantage rests in its inability to react to market conditions, a fact especially distressing to a mortgagee who has locked in a high interest rate in a declining interest climate.

B. Adjustable Rate Mortgage

The **adjustable rate mortgage** (ARM) completely contrasts the fixed rate format. ARMs usually start at a lower and more enticing rate than fixed rate mortgages. The interest rate will subsequently adjust to a higher or lower rate depending on interest rate fluctuations. Adjustment periods can be anywhere from thirty days to a span of years. Adjustable rate mortgages are amortized over a ten- to forty-year period but can change depending upon refinancing options or conversion rights exercisable over three- to five-year periods. Adjustable rate mortgages also have a **cap** feature; that is, the base mortgage can only rise one or two points in a given year and up to five to six points over the life of the loan. The same is true about how the rate might decline. An ARM is set at an initial rate, but it is indexed to some measure of the **prime rate of interest**. The borrower's

Principal borrowed: $100000.00
Annual Payments: 12   Total Payments: 360 (30.00 years)
Annual interest rate: 8.00%   Periodic interest rate: 0.6667%
Regular Payment amount: $733.76   Final Balloon Payment: $0.00
Annual Debt Service Constant: 8.8051%
Minimum amortizing payment for this Principal and Interest rate: $666.68

The following results are estimates which do not account for values being rounded to the nearest cent.
See the amortization schedule for more accurate values.

Total Repaid: $264153.60
Total Interest Paid: $164153.60
Interest as percentage of Principal: 164.154%

PMT	PRINCIPAL	INTEREST	PRIN BAL	PMT	PRINCIPAL	INTEREST	PRIN BAL
1	67.09	666.67	99932.91	38	85.79	647.97	97109.34
2	67.54	666.22	99865.37	39	86.36	647.40	97022.98
3	67.99	665.77	99797.38	40	86.94	646.82	96936.04
4	68.44	665.32	99728.94	41	87.52	646.24	96848.52
5	68.90	664.86	99660.04	42	88.10	645.66	96760.42
6	69.36	664.40	99590.68	43	88.69	645.07	96671.73
7	69.82	663.94	99520.86	44	89.28	644.48	96582.45
8	70.29	663.47	99450.57	45	89.88	643.88	96492.57
9	70.76	663.00	99379.81	46	90.48	643.28	96402.09
10	71.23	662.53	99308.58	47	91.08	642.68	96311.01
11	71.70	662.06	99236.88	48	91.69	642.07	96219.32
12	72.18	661.58	99164.70	49	92.30	641.46	96127.02
13	72.66	661.10	99092.04	50	92.91	640.85	96034.11
14	73.15	660.61	99018.89	51	93.53	640.23	95940.58
15	73.63	660.13	98945.26	52	94.16	639.60	95846.42
16	74.12	659.64	98871.14	53	94.78	638.98	95751.64
17	74.62	659.14	98796.52	54	95.42	638.34	95656.22
18	75.12	658.64	98721.40	55	96.05	637.71	95560.17
19	75.62	658.14	98645.78	56	96.69	637.07	95463.48
20	76.12	657.64	98569.66	57	97.34	636.42	95366.14
21	76.63	657.13	98493.03	58	97.99	635.77	95268.15
22	77.14	656.62	98415.89	59	98.64	635.12	95169.51
23	77.65	656.11	98338.24	60	99.30	634.46	95070.21
24	78.17	655.59	98260.07	61	99.96	633.80	94970.25
25	78.69	655.07	98181.38	62	100.62	633.14	94869.63
26	79.22	654.54	98102.16	63	101.30	632.46	94768.33
27	79.75	654.01	98022.41	64	101.97	631.79	94666.36
28	80.28	653.48	97942.13	65	102.65	631.11	94563.71
29	80.81	652.95	97861.32	66	103.34	630.42	94460.37
30	81.35	652.41	97779.97	67	104.02	629.74	94356.35
31	81.89	651.87	97698.08	68	104.72	629.04	94251.63
32	82.44	651.32	97615.64	69	105.42	628.34	94146.21
33	82.99	650.77	97532.65	70	106.12	627.64	94040.09
34	83.54	650.22	97449.11	71	106.83	626.93	93933.26
35	84.10	649.66	97365.01	72	107.54	626.22	93825.72
36	84.66	649.10	97280.35	73	108.26	625.50	93717.46
37	85.22	648.54	97195.13	74	108.98	624.78	93608.48

FIGURE 7–6
(continues)

PMT	PRINCIPAL	INTEREST	PRIN BAL	PMT	PRINCIPAL	INTEREST	PRIN BAL
75	109.70	624.06	93498.78	125	152.93	580.83	86970.91
76	110.43	623.33	93388.35	126	153.95	579.81	86816.96
77	111.17	622.59	93277.18	127	154.98	578.78	86661.98
78	111.91	621.85	93165.27	128	156.01	577.75	86505.97
79	112.66	621.10	93052.61	129	157.05	576.71	86348.92
80	113.41	620.35	92939.20	130	158.10	575.66	86190.82
81	114.17	619.59	92825.03	131	159.15	574.61	86031.67
82	114.93	618.83	92710.10	132	160.22	573.54	85871.45
83	115.69	618.07	92594.41	133	161.28	572.48	85710.17
84	116.46	617.30	92477.95	134	162.36	571.40	85547.81
85	117.24	616.52	92360.71	135	163.44	570.32	85384.37
86	118.02	615.74	92242.69	136	164.53	569.23	85219.84
87	118.81	614.95	92123.88	137	165.63	568.13	85054.21
88	119.60	614.16	92004.28	138	166.73	567.03	84887.48
89	120.40	613.36	91883.88	139	167.84	565.92	84719.64
90	121.20	612.56	91762.68	140	168.96	564.80	84550.68
91	122.01	611.75	91640.67	141	170.09	563.67	84380.59
92	122.82	610.94	91517.85	142	171.22	562.54	84209.37
93	123.64	610.12	91394.21	143	172.36	561.40	84037.01
94	124.47	609.29	91269.74	144	173.51	560.25	83863.50
95	125.30	608.46	91144.44	145	174.67	559.09	83688.83
96	126.13	607.63	91018.31	146	175.83	557.93	83513.00
97	126.97	606.79	90891.34	147	177.01	556.75	83335.99
98	127.82	605.94	90763.52	148	178.19	555.57	83157.80
99	128.67	605.09	90634.85	149	179.37	554.39	82978.43
100	129.53	604.23	90505.32	150	180.57	553.19	82797.86
101	130.39	603.37	90374.93	151	181.77	551.99	82616.09
102	131.26	602.50	90243.67	152	182.99	550.77	82433.10
103	132.14	601.62	90111.53	153	184.21	549.55	82248.89
104	133.02	600.74	89978.51	154	185.43	548.33	82063.46
105	133.90	599.86	89844.61	155	186.67	547.09	81876.79
106	134.80	598.96	89709.81	156	187.91	545.85	81688.88
107	135.69	598.07	89574.12	157	189.17	544.59	81499.71
108	136.60	597.16	89437.52	158	190.43	543.33	81309.28
109	137.51	596.25	89300.01	159	191.70	542.06	81117.58
110	138.43	595.33	89161.58	160	192.98	540.78	80924.60
111	139.35	594.41	89022.23	161	194.26	539.50	80730.34
112	140.28	593.48	88881.95	162	195.56	538.20	80534.78
113	141.21	592.55	88740.74	163	196.86	536.90	80337.92
114	142.16	591.60	88598.58	164	198.17	535.59	80139.75
115	143.10	590.66	88455.48	165	199.49	534.27	79940.26
116	144.06	589.70	88311.42	166	200.82	532.94	79739.44
117	145.02	588.74	88166.40	167	202.16	531.60	79537.28
118	145.98	587.78	88020.42	168	203.51	530.25	79333.77
119	146.96	586.80	87873.46	169	204.87	528.89	79128.90
120	147.94	585.82	87725.52	170	206.23	527.53	78922.67
121	148.92	584.84	87576.60	171	207.61	526.15	78715.06
122	149.92	583.84	87426.68	172	208.99	524.77	78506.07
123	150.92	582.84	87275.76	173	210.39	523.37	78295.68
124	151.92	581.84	87123.84	174	211.79	521.97	78083.89

FIGURE 7–6
((continued))

PMT	PRINCIPAL	INTEREST	PRIN BAL	PMT	PRINCIPAL	INTEREST	PRIN BAL
175	213.20	520.56	77870.69	225	297.22	436.54	65184.26
176	214.62	519.14	77656.07	226	299.20	434.56	64885.06
177	216.05	517.71	77440.02	227	301.19	432.57	64583.87
178	217.49	516.27	77222.53	228	303.20	430.56	64280.67
179	218.94	514.82	77003.59	229	305.22	428.54	63975.45
180	220.40	513.36	76783.19	230	307.26	426.50	63668.19
181	221.87	511.89	76561.32	231	309.31	424.45	63358.88
182	223.35	510.41	76337.97	232	311.37	422.39	63047.51
183	224.84	508.92	76113.13	233	313.44	420.32	62734.07
184	226.34	507.42	75886.79	234	315.53	418.23	62418.54
185	227.85	505.91	75658.94	235	317.64	416.12	62100.90
186	229.37	504.39	75429.57	236	319.75	414.01	61781.15
187	230.90	502.86	75198.67	237	321.89	411.87	61459.26
188	232.44	501.32	74966.23	238	324.03	409.73	61135.23
189	233.99	499.77	74732.24	239	326.19	407.57	60809.04
190	235.55	498.21	74496.69	240	328.37	405.39	60480.67
191	237.12	496.64	74259.57	241	330.56	403.20	60150.11
192	238.70	495.06	74020.87	242	332.76	401.00	59817.35
193	240.29	493.47	73780.58	243	334.98	398.78	59482.37
194	241.89	491.87	73538.69	244	337.21	396.55	59145.16
195	243.50	490.26	73295.19	245	339.46	394.30	58805.70
196	245.13	488.63	73050.06	246	341.72	392.04	58463.98
197	246.76	487.00	72803.30	247	344.00	389.76	58119.98
198	248.40	485.36	72554.90	248	346.29	387.47	57773.69
199	250.06	483.70	72304.84	249	348.60	385.16	57425.09
200	251.73	482.03	72053.11	250	350.93	382.83	57074.16
201	253.41	480.35	71799.70	251	353.27	380.49	56720.89
202	255.10	478.66	71544.60	252	355.62	378.14	56365.27
203	256.80	476.96	71287.80	253	357.99	375.77	56007.28
204	258.51	475.25	71029.29	254	360.38	373.38	55646.90
205	260.23	473.53	70769.06	255	362.78	370.98	55284.12
206	261.97	471.79	70507.09	256	365.20	368.56	54918.92
207	263.71	470.05	70243.38	257	367.63	366.13	54551.29
208	265.47	468.29	69977.91	258	370.08	363.68	54181.21
209	267.24	466.52	69710.67	259	372.55	361.21	53808.66
210	269.02	464.74	69441.65	260	375.04	358.72	53433.62
211	270.82	462.94	69170.83	261	377.54	356.22	53056.08
212	272.62	461.14	68898.21	262	380.05	353.71	52676.03
213	274.44	459.32	68623.77	263	382.59	351.17	52293.44
214	276.27	457.49	68347.50	264	385.14	348.62	51908.30
215	278.11	455.65	68069.39	265	387.70	346.06	51520.60
216	279.96	453.80	67789.43	266	390.29	343.47	51130.31
217	281.83	451.93	67507.60	267	392.89	340.87	50737.42
218	283.71	450.05	67223.89	268	395.51	338.25	50341.91
219	285.60	448.16	66938.29	269	398.15	335.61	49943.76
220	287.50	446.26	66650.79	270	400.80	332.96	49542.96
221	289.42	444.34	66361.37	271	403.47	330.29	49139.49
222	291.35	442.41	66070.02	272	406.16	327.60	48733.33
223	293.29	440.47	65776.73	273	408.87	324.89	48324.46
224	295.25	438.51	65481.48	274	411.60	322.16	47912.86

FIGURE 7–6
(continued)

PMT	PRINCIPAL	INTEREST	PRIN BAL	PMT	PRINCIPAL	INTEREST	PRIN BAL
275	414.34	319.42	47498.52	320	558.75	175.01	25693.47
276	417.10	316.66	47081.42	321	562.47	171.29	25131.00
277	419.88	313.88	46661.54	322	566.22	167.54	24564.78
278	422.68	311.08	46238.86	323	569.99	163.77	23994.79
279	425.50	308.26	45813.36	324	573.79	159.97	23421.00
280	428.34	305.42	45385.02	325	577.62	156.14	22843.38
281	431.19	302.57	44953.83	326	581.47	152.29	22261.91
282	434.07	299.69	44519.76	327	585.35	148.41	21676.56
283	436.96	296.80	44082.80	328	589.25	144.51	21087.31
284	439.87	293.89	43642.93	329	593.18	140.58	20494.13
285	442.81	290.95	43200.12	330	597.13	136.63	19897.00
286	445.76	288.00	42754.36	331	601.11	132.65	19295.89
287	448.73	285.03	42305.63	332	605.12	128.64	18690.77
288	451.72	282.04	41853.91	333	609.15	124.61	18081.62
289	454.73	279.03	41399.18	334	613.22	120.54	17468.40
290	457.77	275.99	40941.41	335	617.30	116.46	16851.10
291	460.82	272.94	40480.59	336	621.42	112.34	16229.68
292	463.89	269.87	40016.70	337	625.56	108.20	15604.12
293	466.98	266.78	39549.72	338	629.73	104.03	14974.39
294	470.10	263.66	39079.62	339	633.93	99.83	14340.46
295	473.23	260.53	38606.39	340	638.16	95.60	13702.30
296	476.38	257.38	38130.01	341	642.41	91.35	13059.89
297	479.56	254.20	37650.45	342	646.69	87.07	12413.20
298	482.76	251.00	37167.69	343	651.01	82.75	11762.19
299	485.98	247.78	36681.71	344	655.35	78.41	11106.84
300	489.22	244.54	36192.49	345	659.71	74.05	10447.13
301	492.48	241.28	35700.01	346	664.11	69.65	9783.02
302	495.76	238.00	35204.25	347	668.54	65.22	9114.48
303	499.07	234.69	34705.18	348	673.00	60.76	8441.48
304	502.39	231.37	34202.79	349	677.48	56.28	7764.00
305	505.74	228.02	33697.05	350	682.00	51.76	7082.00
306	509.11	224.65	33187.94	351	686.55	47.21	6395.45
307	512.51	221.25	32675.43	352	691.12	42.64	5704.33
308	515.92	217.84	32159.51	353	695.73	38.03	5008.60
309	519.36	214.40	31640.15	354	700.37	33.39	4308.23
310	522.83	210.93	31117.32	355	705.04	28.72	3603.19
311	526.31	207.45	30591.01	356	709.74	24.02	2893.45
312	529.82	203.94	30061.19	357	714.47	19.29	2178.98
313	533.35	200.41	29527.84	358	719.23	14.53	1459.75
314	536.91	196.85	28990.93	359	724.03	9.73	735.72
315	540.49	193.27	28450.44	360	*735.72	4.90	0.00
316	544.09	189.67	27906.35				
317	547.72	186.04	27358.63				
318	551.37	182.39	26807.26				
319	555.04	178.72	26252.22				

*The final payment has been adjusted to account for payments having been rounded to the nearest cent.

FIGURE 7–6
(continued)

payments are periodically adjusted. The variability of any rate depends upon some other indicator, whether it is treasury bonds, the eleventh district cost of Treasury funds, the prime rate of interest, or any other acceptable measure laid out in the mortgage and note.[11]

In the event a buyer selects the adjustable rate option, a rider should be prepared and attached to the agreement of sale. The rider relays the interest rate—monthly, annual, or lifetime caps—and other duties relative to the buyer's commitment and contingencies to obtain the mortgage and the seller's options in the event of a failure to acquire mortgage funding.

C. Balloon Mortgage

A **balloon mortgage** has both short-term and long-term features. On one hand, the interest rate is amortized over a period of twenty or thirty years, while the pay-off day is in an extremely short span of time, usually between three and seven years. In this sense, a balloon goes up, signaling a demand of complete payment of the principal on the third- through seventh-year anniversaries. Thus, the borrower has a principal and interest rate favorable on a thirty-year calculation but must be aware that the entire principal will be due and payable in a very brief period of time.

An often seen balloon product is the 7/23-year balloon. While the principal and interest are amortized over a twenty-three years period, the remaining principal will be due and payable at the end of the seventh year.

D. Graduated Payment Mortgage

A **Graduated Payment Mortgage (GPM)** has an initial low rate affording first-time home buyers a lower payment option and gradually increasing payments. In the future, monthly payments increase to level out the amortization deficit that resulted from deferred principal in the earlier loan payment period.

E. Governmental Mortgages

While federal, state, and local governments are not in the practice of directly lending funds to borrowers, these entities have not been shy about insuring the interests of banks making such loans. If a hometown bank wishes an assurance that its loan will be repaid in case of default by the borrower, the government provides an assurance to the lenders guaranteeing the repayment of the loan.

The three federal agencies most often involved in the lending insurance area are: the **Veterans' Administration (VA)**, the **Federal Housing Administration (FHA)**, and the **Farmer's Home Administration (FMHA)**. All three of these guarantee types require much more documentation, are subject to more rules and regulations during the financing application and processing period, and other bureaucratic requirements exist that need to be fulfilled. Some of the burdens imposed by these federal programs are so onerous that a seller may expressly reject any offer that is based on FHA, VA, or FMHA programs. One can appreciate the rigidity of the VA, FHA, and other governmental mortgage programs after reviewing the following FHA/VA appraisal requirements:

1. Properties are not acceptable in industrial, commercial, or main highway areas.
2. Exterior paint must be in good condition.
3. Porches must be in good repair.
4. Stairs must have handrails on one side.
5. All windows must be operable with no broken or cracked glass.
6. No captive bathrooms or baths allowed off the kitchen.
7. Furnaces must be in good repair; gas conversion furnaces must be inspected and proved energy efficient.
8. The roof must prevent entrance of moisture.
9. Repair of a broken sidewalk will be required.

10. The plumbing should be copper; steel is acceptable if in good condition.

11. Gas water heaters must have relief valves and drains and be of such a size as to provide an adequate supply of hot water.

12. Downspouts must be in good repair with property drainage or splash blocks.

13. Homes with integral garages must have a firewall with fire-resistant door.

14. Home must have a proper sewage disposal system.

15. The attic window must allow proper ventilation.

16. Home should be free of flood, subsidence, or badly eroded areas.

17. No water seepage is allowed in basement.

18. Knob and tube wiring is not acceptable unless in very good condition.

19. Townhouses should be separated by an adequate firewall to the roof.

1. *Veterans' Administration*

The VA loan program dates back to the *Serviceman's Readjustment Act of 1944*, amended by the *Korean Conflict GI Bill (July 1952)*, and followed by the *Veteran's Housing Acts of 1970 and 1974*.

Under these laws, eligible veterans having served at least 180 days active military service as of September 16, 1940, and having been honorably discharged may obtain partially guaranteed loans for the purchase or construction of a home. Additionally, widows or widowers of veterans who died in the service or from service-related causes, who have not remarried, may make use of this privilege.

This VA loan program has served hundreds of thousands of soldiers since the World War II era. Although the veteran usually receives the mortgage money from a local lender, the VA may lend money directly if no VA-approved lender is available.

Some of the characteristics of the VA guarantee mortgages are:

1. **Guarantee:** The VA guarantees a part of the loan to the lender in case the buyer defaults. The VA only guarantees the loan, not the condition of the property. The VA guarantees first mortgages, new construction, additions to existing homes, and ability to refinance an existing home loan or VA loan.

2. **Cost:** The cost of the VA guarantee to the buyer may be quite substantial, as indicated in the Loan Guaranty Circular No. 93-23, distributed on August 20, 1993, to all program participants. See Figure 7–7[12] for the VA's Funding Fee Table.

3. **Maximum Mortgage:** The VA sets no maximum mortgage amount, but the basic entitlement is $36,000. For loans in excess of $144,000 to purchase or construct a home, additional entitlement up to an amount equal to 25% of the VA county loan limit for a single family home may be available. This loan limit can change yearly. The maximum guarantee amount for most U.S. counties is $417,000. After inspecting the property, the VA will state their maximum mortgage amount on a specific property on the VA "Certificate of Reasonable Value."

4. **Down Payment:** The VA requires no down payment from the veteran, but the lender may require one. The VA allows secondary financing.

5. **Interest Rate:** The interest rate is negotiated between the lender and the borrower based on the current rate of the mortgage market.

6. **Mortgage Term:** The maximum mortgage term is thirty years.

7. **Repairs:** Repairs may be required for property not meeting minimum standards, but the VA at a written request of the veteran may waive repairs. Structural items may not be waived.

8. **Occupancy:** The VA requires the buyer to occupy the structure on which the VA mortgage is placed within a reasonable time after settlement. The structure may have up to four (4) units.

Funding Fee Tables Purchase And Construction Loans

Note: The funding fee for regular military first time use from 1/1/04 to 9/30/04 is 2.2 percent. This figure drops to 2.15 percent on 10/1/04.

Type of Veteran	Down Payment	First Time Use	Subsequent Use for loans from 1/1/04 to 9/30/2011
Regular Military	None 5% or more (up to 10%) 10% or more	2.15% 1.50% 1.25%	3.3%* 1.50% 1.25%
Reserves/ National Guard	None 5% or more (up to 10%) 10% or more	2.4% 1.75% 1.5%	3.3%* 1.75% 1.5%

Cash-Out Refinancing Loans

Type of Veteran	Percentage for First Time Use	Percentage for Subsequent Use
Regular Military	2.15%	3.3%*
Reserves/National Guard	2.4%	3.3%*

*The higher subsequent use fee does not apply to these types of loans if the veteran's only prior use of entitlement was for a manufactured home loan.

Other Types Of Loans

Type of Loan	Percentage for Either Type of Veteran Whether First Time or Subsequent Use
Interest Rate Reduction Refinancing Loans	.50%
Manufactured Home Loans	1.00%
Loan Assumptions	.50%

FIGURE 7–7

9. **Settlement Costs:** The seller may pay on behalf of the veteran buyer, both the closing costs and prepaid items. The VA allows the lender to charge an origination fee.

10. **Assumption:** VA loans are assumable to both a veteran and nonveteran, but a funding fee of 0.5% must be paid on all loan amounts. However, the original mortgagor usually retains liability, and the new purchaser will be asked to sign a collateral bond. This is a very complicated matter and requires a lot of experience and expertise to handle it properly.

11. **Presettlement Inspection:**   The veteran buyer must be escorted through the property within three days prior to settlement.

12. **Eligibility:**   When a veteran disposes of the property, and has satisfied the mortgage, or is released from the liability of the mortgage, the veteran may have eligibility fully restored. Veterans using the program more than once, except for refinancing at a lower interest rate, will be required to pay a 3.3% funding fee with no down payment, or a 1.5% funding fee with a minimum of 5% down payment, or a 1.25% funding fee with a minimum of 10% down payment.

13. **Vendee Loans:**   Vendee loans and loans for manufactured homes under Title 38, U.S.C. Section 3712 (formerly 1812) will be 1% of the loan amount.

14. **Current Base Eligibility:** $36,000.

2. Federal Housing Administration

The *National Housing Act of 1934* created the Federal Housing Administration for the purposes of assisting first-time homebuyers and stimulating the housing market. The FHA does not lend money directly to the purchaser, but instead serves as a guarantor to the bank for any money lent. Some of the features of FHA-insured mortgages are:

1. **Insurance:**   The FHA insures the mortgagee against loss in the event of foreclosure. The FHA insures first mortgages and home improvements.

2. **Cost:**   The FHA charges the purchaser a mortgage insurance premium (MIP) for this insurance. This premium amounts to 0.5% of the unpaid principal balance in addition to a 1.5% up-front fee.

3. **Maximum Mortgage:**   The maximum mortgage amount is established by the FHA and will vary between $271,050 and $417,000, depending upon the prevailing housing costs in the area. After inspecting a property, the FHA will state their maximum mortgage amount for a specific property on their "FHA Conditional Commitment."

4. **Down Payment:**   The FHA established a formula to arrive at the minimum down payment (loan to value ratio). This formula depends on the FHA program being used. Secondary financing is not allowed on unsecured notes.

5. **Interest Rate:**   The interest rate is negotiated between the lender and the borrower based on the current rate of the mortgage market.

6. **Mortgage Term:**   An FHA loan may be amortized for up to thirty years.

7. **Repairs:**   The FHA may require repairs to be completed on a property that does not meet minimum standards.

8. **Occupancy:**   The FHA has only one program that will insure financing for a nonoccupant owner. All other programs require owner occupancy within a reasonable time after settlement.

9. **Closing Costs:**   The seller may pay closing costs on behalf of the purchaser, but the seller may not pay for the purchaser's prepaid items. The FHA allows the lender to charge an origination fee.

10. **Assumption:**   FHA mortgages may be assumable. However, the original mortgagor usually retains liability unless released by the mortgagee.

F. Reverse Mortgages

Reverse mortgages are a new type of mortgage designed specifically to be appealing to older homeowners. In regular mortgages, the homeowner pays the lender. In reverse mortgages, the opposite is true—homeowners receive money that does not need to be repaid until the home is sold, the homeowner dies, or does not use the home as the primary residence.

There are advantages to reverse mortgages, including:

■ There are tax advantages.

■ Reverse mortgages can supplement retirement income.

They may be a good idea for a homeowner who has a great deal of equity in his/her home but not other assets or sufficient retirement savings, and wishes to stay in his/her home rather than downsize.

There are other factors to consider. If you dream of giving your home to your children after you die, a reverse mortgage may make that difficult since the equity in the home will have been depleted. Reverse mortgages require research to make sure it is right for each homeowner, and there are usually requirements, such as:

■ The homeowners must be at least sixty-two years of age.

■ The home must be the primary residence.

Web Exercise

To find out the potential for fraud in the Reverse Mortgage, visit the Federal Trade Commission (FTC)'s Advisory at www.ftc.gov/bcp/edu/pubs/consumer/homes/rea13.shtm.

G. Assumed Mortgage

Many mortgage instruments and notes provide for the option of assumption by a third party. **Assumption** is an attractive feature when a seller has locked in an enticing interest rate. This is possible only if the lender/mortgagee did not prohibit assumption in the mortgage document. The applicant wishing to avail himself or herself of the assumption will be subject to all the traditional processes: application review, credit suitability, appraisal, and other processing requirements.

If a paralegal reviews the mortgage documentation, they make sure that the lenders have explicitly stated whether or not assumption is permitted. If assumption is prohibited, an attempt to transfer is impossible. Generally speaking, the impact of an unauthorized assumption is outlined in a **due-on-transfer rider**. This document usually indicates that any attempt to sell or alienate the property during the life of the mortgage will obligate the homeowner to pay full balance, thereby accelerating the mortgage obligation. See the Due-on-Transfer Rider in Figure 7–8.

This rider adds a provision to the security instrument allowing the lender to require repayment of the note in full upon transfer of the property. Of course, the interest rate and balance remaining on the amount of the assumed mortgage will influence any decision to exercise this tactic.

The real estate agreement of sale should reflect the parties' intentions to allow assumption. An acceptable Mortgage Assumption Clause is reproduced in Figure 7–9.

H. Purchase Money Mortgage

There are occasions when a seller finances the transaction. This will occur if the buyer lacks the capacity to get financing, or the seller wishes to maintain a longer-term interest in the property, or the terms and conditions of the financing offered by the seller bests the bank. This type of mortgage is referred to as a **Purchase Money Mortgage (PMM)**.

There are many advantages to this mortgage. First and foremost, there are less parties involved starting with the banks and financial institutions. Second, given the lack of these types of parties, there is less documentary preparation and fewer regulatory requirements. For example, the PMM purchaser is not even entitled to the traditional *Real Estate Settlement and Procedures Act* (RESPA) Closing or Settlement Sheet. Third, the speed of this informal underwriting can only be described as impressive. Fourth, there are far fewer costs, from survey if agreed, to a host of transactional fees that pile up on the ordinary mortgage. Fifth, the parties may agree to less stringent down payment terms.

DUE-ON-TRANSFER RIDER

THIS DUE-ON-TRANSFER RIDER, is made this _____ day of _____, _____, and is incorporated into and shall be deemed to amend and supplement the Mortgage, Deed of Trust, or Security Deed (the Security Instrument) of the same date given by the undersigned (the "Borrower") to secure Borrower's note to _____ (the "Lender") of the same date (the "Note") and covering the property described in the Security Instrument and located at:

_____

(Property Address)

AMENDED COVENANT, In addition to the covenants and agreements made in the Security Instrument, Borrower and Lender further covenant and agree as follows:

TRANSFER OF THE PROPERTY OR A BENEFICIAL INTEREST IN BORROWER

Uniform Covenant 17 of the Security Instrument is amended to read as follows:

Transfer of the Property or a Beneficial Interest in Borrower. If all or any part of the Property or any interest in it is sold or transferred (or if a beneficial interest in Borrower is sold or transferred and Borrower is not a natural person) without Lender's prior written consent, Lender may, at its option, require immediate payment in full of all sums secured by this Security Instrument. However, this option shall not be exercised by Lender if exercise is prohibited by federal law as of the date of this Security Instrument. Lender also shall not exercise this option if: (a) borrower causes to be submitted to Lender information required by Lender to evaluate the intended transferee as if a new loan were being made to the transferee; and (b) Lender reasonably determines that Lender's security will not be impaired by the loan assumption and the risk of a breach of any covenant or agreement in this Security Instrument is acceptable to Lender.

To the extent permitted by applicable law, Lender may charge a reasonable fee as a condition to Lender's consent to the loan assumption. Lender may also require the transferee to sign an assumption agreement that is acceptable to Lender and agreements made in the Note and in this Security Instrument. Borrower will continue to be obligated under the Note and this Security Instrument unless Lender releases Borrower in writing.

If Lender exercises the option to require payment in full, Lender shall give Borrower notice of acceleration. The notice shall provide a period of not less than 30 days for the date the notice is delivered or mailed within which Borrower must pay all sums secured by this Security Instrument. If Borrower fails to pay these sums prior to the expiration of this period, Lender may invoke any remedies permitted by this Security Instrument without further notice or demand on Borrower.

BY SIGNING BELOW, Borrower accepts and agrees to the terms and covenants contained in this Due-On-Transfer Rider.

_____ (Seal)

_____ (Seal)

FIGURE 7–8

Even with the PMM, legal counsel and the paralegal will likely be involved in closing the transaction. A sample PMM is at Figure 7–10.[13]

Web Exercise

The United States Department of Housing and Urban Development (HUD) publishes a PMM Worksheet for prospective sellers at www.hudclips.org/download/HUD-92900-PUR.

MORTGAGE ASSUMPTION CLAUSE

Seller and Buyer acknowledge and agree that the consummation of this transaction is specifically contingent upon buyer's assumption, without change as to terms and conditions, of seller's existing mortgage to _____. Said mortgage has an outstanding balance of approximately $_____, bears interest at the rate of _____% per annum, with monthly payments of principal and interest in the amount of $_____ (together with 1/12th of the annual real estate taxes and hazard insurance premiums) for a remaining term of _____ years. Seller shall take any steps which must be completed to enable buyer to assume said mortgage. Upon settlement of this transaction, buyer personally assumes and agrees to pay said mortgage in accordance with the terms and conditions thereof, as a part of the consideration for the conveyance. Buyer shall pay any required assumption fees, with seller to incur no costs by reason of said assumption.

FIGURE 7–9

Document Number	State Bar of Wisconsin Form 21-2003 **MORTGAGE** Document Name	

_____
_____

("Mortgagor," whether one or more) mortgages to _____

_____
its successors or assigns ("Mortgagee," whether one or more), to secure payment of $ _____ evidenced by a note or notes, or other obligation ("Obligation") dated _____ executed by _____

_____
to Mortgagee, and any extensions, renewals and modifications of the Obligation and refinancings of any such indebtedness on any terms whatsoever (including increases in interest) and the payment of all other sums, with interest, advanced to protect the Property and the security of this Mortgage, and all other amounts paid by Mortgagee hereunder, the following property, together with all rights and interests appurtenant thereto in law or equity, all rents, issue and profits arising therefrom, including insurance proceeds and condemnation awards, all structures, improvements and fixtures located thereon, in _____ County, State of Wisconsin ("Property"):

Recording Area
Name and Return Address

Parcel Identification Number (PIN)
This _____ homestead property.
(is) (is not)
This _____ a purchase money mortgage.
(is) (is not)

FIGURE 7–10
(continues)

1. **MORTGAGOR'S COVENANTS.**

   a. **COVENANT OF TITLE.** Mortgagor warrants title to the Property, except restrictions and easements of record, if any, and further excepting:

   b. **FIXTURES.** Any property which has been affixed to the Property and is used in connection with it is intended to become a fixture. Mortgagor waives any right to remove such fixture from the Property which is subject to this Mortgage.

   c. **TAXES**. Mortgagor promises to pay when due all taxes and assessments levied on the Property or upon Mortgagee's interest in it and to deliver to Mortgagee on demand receipts showing such payment.

   d. **INSURANCE**. Mortgagor shall keep the improvements on the Property insured against loss or damage occasioned by fire, extended coverage perils and such other hazards as Mortgagee may require, without co-insurance, through insurers approved by Mortgagee, in the amount of the full replacement value of the improvements on the Property. Mortgagor shall pay the insurance premiums when due. The policies shall contain the standard mortgage clause in favor of Mortgagee, and evidence of all policies covering the Property shall be provided to Mortgagee. Mortgagor shall promptly give notice of loss to insurance companies and Mortgagee. Unless Mortgagor and Mortgagee otherwise agree in writing, insurance proceeds shall be applied to restoration or repair of the Property damaged, provided Mortgagee deems the restoration or repair to be economically feasible.

   e. **OTHER COVENANTS**. Mortgagor covenants not to commit waste nor suffer waste to be committed on the Property, to keep the Property in good condition and repair, to keep the Property free from future liens superior to the lien of this Mortgage and to comply with all laws, ordinances and regulations affecting the Property. Mortgagor shall pay when due all indebtedness which may be or become secured at any time by a mortgage or other lien on the Property superior to this Mortgage and any failure to do so shall constitute a default under this Mortgage.

2. **DEFAULT AND REMEDIES**. Mortgagor agrees that time is of the essence with respect to payment of principal and interest when due, and in the performance of the terms, conditions and covenants contained herein or in the Obligation secured hereby. In the event of default, Mortgagee may, at its option, declare the whole amount of the unpaid principal and accrued interest due and payable, and collect it in a suit at law or by foreclosure of this Mortgage or by the exercise of any other remedy available at law or equity. If this Mortgage is subordinate to a superior mortgage lien, a default under the superior mortgage lien constitutes a default under this Mortgage.

3. **NOTICE**. Unless otherwise provided in the Obligation secured by this Mortgage, prior to any acceleration (other than under paragraph 9, below) Mortgagee shall mail notice to Mortgagor specifying: (a) the default; (b) the action required to cure the default; (c) a date, not less than 15 days from the date the notice is mailed to Mortgagor by which date the default must be cured; and (d) that failure to cure the default on or before the date specified in the notice may result in acceleration.

4. **EXPENSES AND ATTORNEY FEES**. In case of default, whether abated or not, all costs and expenses, including, but not limited to, reasonable attorney fees, to the extent not prohibited by law shall be added to the principal, become due as incurred, and in the event of foreclosure be included in the judgment.

5. **FORECLOSURE WITHOUT DEFICIENCY**. Mortgagor agrees to the provisions of Sections 846.101 and 846.103, Wis. Stats., as may apply to the Property and as may be amended, permitting Mortgagee in the event of foreclosure to waive the right to judgment for deficiency and hold the foreclosure sale within the time provided in such applicable Section.

6. **RECEIVER**. Upon default or during the pendency of any action to foreclose this Mortgage, Mortgagor consents to the appointment of a receiver of the Property, including homestead interest, to

FIGURE 7–10
(continued)

collect the rents, issues and profits of the Property during the pendency of such an action, and such rents, issues and profits when so collected shall be held and applied as the court shall direct.

7. **WAIVER**. Mortgagee may waive any default without waiving any other subsequent or prior default by Mortgagor.

8. **MORTGAGEE MAY CURE DEFAULTS**. In the event of any default by Mortgagor of any kind under this Mortgage or any Obligation secured by this Mortgage, Mortgagee may cure the default and all sums paid by Mortgagee for such purpose shall immediately be repaid by Mortgagor with interest at the rate then in effect under the Obligation secured by this Mortgage and shall constitute a lien upon the Property.

9. **CONSENT REQUIRED FOR TRANSFER**. Mortgagor shall not transfer, sell or convey any legal or equitable interest in the Property (by deed, land contract, option, long-term lease or in any other way) without the prior written consent of Mortgagee, unless either the indebtedness secured by this Mortgage is first paid in full or the interest conveyed is a mortgage or other security interest in the Property, subordinate to the lien of this Mortgage. The entire indebtedness under the Obligation secured by this Mortgage shall become due and payable in full at the option of Mortgagee without notice, which notice is hereby waived, upon any transfer, sale or conveyance made in violation of this paragraph. A violation of the provisions of this paragraph will be considered a default under the terms of this Mortgage and the Obligation it secures.

10. **ASSIGNMENT OF RENTS**. Mortgagor hereby transfers and assigns absolutely to Mortgagee, as additional security, all rents, issues and profits which become or remain due (under any form of agreement for use or occupancy of the Property or any portion thereof), or which were previously collected and remain subject to Mortgagor's control following any default under this Mortgage or the Obligation secured hereby and delivery of notice of exercise of this assignment by Mortgagee to the tenant or other user(s) of the Property in accordance with the provisions of Section 708.11, Wis. Stats., as may be amended. This assignment shall be enforceable with or without appointment of a receiver and regardless of Mortgagee's lack of possession of the Property.

11. **ENVIRONMENTAL PROVISION**. Mortgagor represents, warrants and covenants to Mortgagee that (a) during the period of Mortgagor's ownership or use of the Property no substance has been, is or will be present, used, stored, deposited, treated, recycled or disposed of on, under, in or about the Property in a form, quantity or manner which if known to be present on, under, in or about the Property would require clean-up, removal or other remedial action ("Hazardous Substance") under any federal, state or local laws, regulations, ordinances, codes or rules ("Environmental Laws"); (b) Mortgagor has no knowledge, after due inquiry, of any prior use or existence of any Hazardous Substance on the Property by any prior owner of or person using the Property; (c) without limiting the generality of the foregoing, Mortgagor has no knowledge, after due inquiry, that the Property contains asbestos, polychlorinated biphenyl components ("PCBs") or underground storage tanks; (d) there are no conditions existing currently or likely to exist during the term of this Mortgage which would subject Mortgagor to any damages, penalties, injunctive relief or clean-up costs in any governmental or regulatory action or third-party claims relating to any Hazardous Substance; (e) Mortgagor is not subject to any court or administrative proceeding, judgment, decree, order or citation relating to any Hazardous Substance; and (f) Mortgagor in the past has been, at the present is and in the future will remain in compliance with all Environmental Laws. Mortgagor shall indemnify and hold harmless Mortgagee from all loss, cost (including reasonable attorney fees and legal expenses), liability and damage whatsoever directly or indirectly resulting from, arising out of or based upon (i) the presence, use, storage, deposit, treatment, recycling or disposal, at any time, of any Hazardous Substance on, under, in or about the Property, or the transportation of any Hazardous Substance to or from the Property, (ii) the violation or alleged violation of any Environmental Law, permit, judgment or license relating to the presence, use, storage, deposit, treatment, recycling or disposal of any Hazardous Substance on, under, in or about the Property, or the trans-

FIGURE 7–10
(continued)

portation of any Hazardous Substance to or from the Property, or (iii) the imposition of any governmental lien for the recovery of environmental clean-up costs expended under any Environmental Law. Mortgagor shall immediately notify Mortgagee in writing of any governmental or regulatory action or third-party claim instituted or threatened in connection with any Hazardous Substance on, in, under or about the Property.

12. **SECURITY INTEREST ON FIXTURES**. To further secure the payment and performance of the Obligation, Mortgagor hereby grants to Mortgagee a security interest in:

CHOOSE ONE OF THE FOLLOWING OPTIONS; IF NEITHER IS CHOSEN, OPTION A SHALL APPLY:

☐ A. All fixtures and personal property located on or related to the operations of the Property whether now owned or hereafter acquired.

☐ B. All property listed on the attached schedule.

This Mortgage shall constitute a security agreement within the meaning of the Uniform Commercial Code with respect to those parts of the Property indicated above. This Mortgage constitutes a fixture filing and financing statement as those terms are used in the Uniform Commercial Code. This Mortgage is to be filed and recorded in the real estate records of the county in which the Property is located, and the following information is included: (1) Mortgagor shall be deemed the "debtor"; (2) Mortgagee shall be deemed to be the "secured party" and shall have all of the rights of a secured party under the Uniform Commercial Code; (3) this Mortgage covers goods which are or are to become fixtures; (4) the name of the record owner of the land is the debtor; (5) the legal name and address of the debtor are _____

_____

(6) the state of organization and the organizational identification number of the debtor (if applicable) are
_____;

(7) the address of the secured party is _____; and

_____

13. **SINGULAR; PLURAL**. As used herein, the singular shall include the plural and any gender shall include all genders.

14. **JOINT AND SEVERAL/LIMITATION ON PERSONAL LIABILITY**. The covenants of this Mortgage set forth herein shall be deemed joint and several among Mortgagors, if more than one. Unless a Mortgagor is obligated on the Obligation secured by this Mortgage, Mortgagor shall not be liable for any breach of covenants contained in this Mortgage.

15. **INVALIDITY.** In the event any provision or portion of this instrument is held to be invalid or unenforceable, this shall not impair or preclude the enforcement of the remainder of the instrument.

16. **MARITAL PROPERTY STATEMENT**. Any individual Mortgagor who is married represents that the obligation evidenced by this instrument was incurred in the interest of Mortgagor's marriage or family.

Dated _____

_____.(SEAL) _____ (SEAL)

*_____ *_____

_____.(SEAL) _____ (SEAL)

*_____ *_____

FIGURE 7–10
(continued)

AUTHENTICATION	ACKNOWLEDGMENT

Signature(s) _____
 	
 _____
 authenticated on _____
 	
 _____
 *_____
 	
 TITLE: MEMBER STATE BAR OF WISCONSIN)
   (If not, _____
   authorized by Wis. Stat. § 706.06)
 	
 THIS INSTRUMENT DRAFTED BY:
 	
 _____
 	
 _____
	STATE BAR OF WISCONSIN)
	                     ) ss.
	 _____COUNTY)
	 Personally came before me on _____
	 the above-named _____
	
	 _____
	 to me known to be the person(s) who executed the foregoing instrument and acknowledged the same.
	
	 _____
	 *_____
	 Notary Public, State of Wisconsin
	 My Commission (is permanent) (expires: _____)

(Signatures may be authenticated or acknowledged. Both are not necessary.)

NOTE: THIS IS A STANDARD FORM. ANY MODIFICATIONS TO THIS FORM SHOULD BE CLEARLY IDENTIFIED.

MORTGAGE	STATE BAR OF WISCONSIN	FORM NO. 21-2003

*Type name below signatures.

© 2003 STATE BAR OF WISCONSIN

FIGURE 7–10
(continued)

V. MORTGAGE APPLICATION

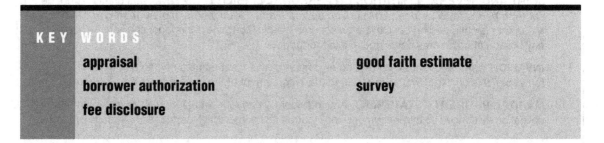

KEY WORDS

appraisal   good faith estimate

borrower authorization   survey

fee disclosure

An application should be made once the real estate buyer has reviewed all available mortgage products, their advantages and disadvantages, their costs and savings, and as soon as an eligibility determination has been positively made and the buyer can qualify for one of these programs. Unfortunately, the present economic decline directly results from careless, and even negligent underwriting practices fostered by both government and lending entities. Known as the "sub-prime" crisis, loans were disbursed to parties lacking creditworthiness and even regularly to those who paid nothing down. Prompted by regulatory rules that sought to expand home ownership, the net effect was to set up a fall of dominoes—namely millions of loans that could not be supported in the marketplace.[14]

    With the effects of the mortgage crisis still being felt, state legislators hold accountable both the lenders and the borrowers for misrepresentation during the application process. In Florida, an applicant who intentionally misrepresents may be guilty of fraud.

817.545 Mortgage fraud:

(1) For the purposes of the section, the term "mortgage lending process" means the process through which a person seeks or obtains a residential mortgage loan, including, but not limited to, the solicitation, application or origination, negotiation of terms, third-party provider services, underwriting, signing and closing, and funding of the loan. Documents involved in the mortgage lending process include, but are not limited to, mortgages, deeds, surveys, inspection reports, uniform residential loan applications, or other loan applications; appraisal reports; HUD-1 settlement statements; supporting personal documentation for loan applications such as W-2 forms, verifications of income and employment, credit reports, bank statements, tax returns, and payroll stubs; and any required disclosures.

(2) A person commits the offense of mortgage fraud if, with the intent to defraud, the person knowingly:

(a) Makes any material misstatement, misrepresentation, or omission during the mortgage lending process with the intention that the misstatement, misrepresentation, or omission will be relied on by a mortgage lender, borrower, or any other person or entity involved in the mortgage lending process; however, omissions on a loan application regarding employment, income, or assets for a loan which does not require this information are not considered a material omission for purposes of this subsection.

(b) Uses or facilitates the use of any material misstatement, misrepresentation, or omission during the mortgage lending process with the intention that the material misstatement, misrepresentation, or omission will be relied on by a mortgage lender, borrower, or any other person or entity involved in the mortgage lending process; however, omissions on a loan application regarding employment, income, or assets for a loan which does not require this information are not considered a material omission for purposes of this subsection.

(c) Receives any proceeds or any other funds in connection with the mortgage lending process that the person knew resulted from a violation of paragraph (a) or paragraph (b).

(d) Files or causes to be filed with the clerk of the circuit court for any county of this state a document involved in the mortgage lending process which contains a material misstatement, misrepresentation, or omission.

(3) An offense of mortgage fraud may not be predicated solely upon information lawfully disclosed under federal disclosure laws, regulations, or interpretations related to the mortgage lending process.

(4) For the purpose of venue under this section, any violation of this section is considered to have been committed:

(a) In the county in which the real property is located or

(b) In any county in which a material act was performed in furtherance of the violation.[15]

The application process is intensive in terms of documentation, from the initial application to verification of deposits and assets, to the issuance of a mortgage commitment. In sum, the mortgage application is "broken down into five parts:

- Originating a loan
- Structuring and documenting the loan
- Providing credit enhancement in the form of guarantees or additional collateral
- Placing and trading of the loan with investors, and
- Servicing the loan."[16]

A. The Mortgage Questionnaire

No mortgage application process can commence without a completed questionnaire. Figure 7–11 contains a typical mortgage questionnaire that garners the following information:

- Institutional information
- Property information

Uniform Residential Loan Application

This application is designed to be completed by the applicant(s) with the Lender's assistance. Applicants should complete this form as "Borrower" or "Co-Borrower," as applicable. Co-Borrower information must also be provided (and the appropriate box checked) when ☐ the income or assets of a person other than the Borrower (including the Borrower's spouse) will be used as a basis for loan qualification or ☐ the income or assets of the Borrower's spouse or other person who has community property rights pursuant to state law will not be used as a basis for loan qualification, but his or her liabilities must be considered because the spouse or other person has community property rights pursuant to applicable law and Borrower resides in a community property state, the security property is located in a community property state, or the Borrower is relying on other property located in a community property state as a basis for repayment of the loan.

If this is an application for joint credit, Borrower and Co-Borrower each agree that we intend to apply for joint credit (sign below):

Borrower	Co-Borrower

I. TYPE OF MORTGAGE AND TERMS OF LOAN

Mortgage Applied for:	☐ VA ☐ FHA	☐ Conventional ☐ USDA/Rural Housing Service	☐ Other (explain):	Agency Case Number	Lender Case Number
Amount $	Interest Rate %	No. of Months	**Amortization Type:**	☐ Fixed Rate ☐ GPM	☐ Other (explain): ☐ ARM (type):

II. PROPERTY INFORMATION AND PURPOSE OF LOAN

Subject Property Address (street, city, state & ZIP)		No. of Units
Legal Description of Subject Property (attach description if necessary)		Year Built

Purpose of Loan	☐ Purchase ☐ Construction ☐ Refinance ☐ Construction-Permanent	☐ Other (explain):	Property will be: ☐ Primary Residence ☐ Secondary Residence ☐ Investment

Complete this line if construction or construction-permanent loan.

Year Lot Acquired	Original Cost $	Amount Existing Liens $	(a) Present Value of Lot $	(b) Cost of Improvements $	Total (a + b) $

Complete this line if this is a refinance loan.

Year Acquired	Original Cost $	Amount Existing Liens $	Purpose of Refinance	Describe Improvements ☐ made ☐ to be made Cost: $

Title will be held in what Name(s)	Manner in which Title will be held	Estate will be held in: ☐ Fee Simple ☐ Leasehold (show expiration date)

Source of Down Payment, Settlement Charges, and/or Subordinate Financing (explain)

III. BORROWER INFORMATION

Borrower	Co-Borrower
Borrower's Name (include Jr. or Sr. if applicable)	Co-Borrower's Name (include Jr. or Sr. if applicable)

Social Security Number	Home Phone (incl. area code)	DOB (mm/dd/yyyy)	Yrs. School	Social Security Number	Home Phone (incl. area code)	DOB (mm/dd/yyyy)	Yrs. School

☐ Married ☐ Unmarried (include ☐ Separated single, divorced, widowed)	Dependents (not listed by Co-Borrower) no. ages	☐ Married ☐ Unmarried (include ☐ Separated single, divorced, widowed)	Dependents (not listed by Borrower) no. ages
Present Address (street, city, state, ZIP) ☐ Own ☐ Rent ___ No. Yrs.		Present Address (street, city, state, ZIP) ☐ Own ☐ Rent ___ No. Yrs.	
Mailing Address, if different from Present Address		Mailing Address, if different from Present Address	

If residing at present address for less than two years, complete the following:

Former Address (street, city, state, ZIP) ☐ Own ☐ Rent ___ No. Yrs.	Former Address (street, city, state, ZIP) ☐ Own ☐ Rent ___ No. Yrs.

IV. EMPLOYMENT INFORMATION

Borrower	Co-Borrower
Name & Address of Employer ☐ Self Employed	Yrs. on this job	Name & Address of Employer ☐ Self Employed	Yrs. on this job
	Yrs. employed in this line of work/profession		Yrs. employed in this line of work/profession
Position/Title/Type of Business	Business Phone (incl. area code)	Position/Title/Type of Business	Business Phone (incl. area code)

If employed in current position for less than two years or if currently employed in more than one position, complete the following:

FIGURE 7–11
(continues)

Borrower		IV. EMPLOYMENT INFORMATION (cont'd)		Co-Borrower	
Name & Address of Employer	☐ Self Employed	Dates (from – to)	Name & Address of Employer	☐ Self Employed	Dates (from – to)
		Monthly Income $			Monthly Income $
Position/Title/Type of Business		Business Phone (incl. area code)	Position/Title/Type of Business		Business Phone (incl. area code)
Name & Address of Employer	☐ Self Employed	Dates (from – to)	Name & Address of Employer	☐ Self Employed	Dates (from – to)
		Monthly Income $			Monthly Income $
Position/Title/Type of Business		Business Phone (incl. area code)	Position/Title/Type of Business		Business Phone (incl. area code)

V. MONTHLY INCOME AND COMBINED HOUSING EXPENSE INFORMATION

Gross Monthly Income	Borrower	Co-Borrower	Total	Combined Monthly Housing Expense	Present	Proposed
Base Empl. Income*	$	$	$	Rent	$	
Overtime				First Mortgage (P&I)		$
Bonuses				Other Financing (P&I)		
Commissions				Hazard Insurance		
Dividends/Interest				Real Estate Taxes		
Net Rental Income				Mortgage Insurance		
Other (before completing, see the notice in "describe other income," below)				Homeowner Assn. Dues		
				Other:		
Total	$	$	$	Total	$	$

* Self Employed Borrower(s) may be required to provide additional documentation such as tax returns and financial statements.

Describe Other Income   *Notice:* Alimony, child support, or separate maintenance income need not be revealed if the Borrower (B) or Co-Borrower (C) does not choose to have it considered for repaying this loan.

B/C		Monthly Amount
		$

VI. ASSETS AND LIABILITIES

This Statement and any applicable supporting schedules may be completed jointly by both married and unmarried Co-Borrowers if their assets and liabilities are sufficiently joined so that the Statement can be meaningfully and fairly presented on a combined basis; otherwise, separate Statements and Schedules are required. If the Co-Borrower section was completed about a non-applicant spouse or other person, this Statement and supporting schedules must be completed about that spouse or other person also.

Completed ☐ Jointly ☐ Not Jointly

ASSETS Description	Cash or Market Value	Liabilities and Pledged Assets. List the creditor's name, address, and account number for all outstanding debts, including automobile loans, revolving charge accounts, real estate loans, alimony, child support, stock pledges, etc. Use continuation sheet, if necessary. Indicate by (*) those liabilities, which will be satisfied upon sale of real estate owned or upon refinancing of the subject property.		
Cash deposit toward purchase held by:	$			
List checking and savings accounts below		**LIABILITIES**	**Monthly Payment & Months Left to Pay**	**Unpaid Balance**
Name and address of Bank, S&L, or Credit Union		Name and address of Company	$ Payment/Months	$
Acct. no.	$	Acct. no.		
Name and address of Bank, S&L, or Credit Union		Name and address of Company	$ Payment/Months	$
Acct. no.	$	Acct. no.		
Name and address of Bank, S&L, or Credit Union		Name and address of Company	$ Payment/Months	$
Acct. no.	$	Acct. no.		

Freddie Mac Form 65 6/09   Page 2 of 5   Fannie Mae Form 1003 6/09

FIGURE 7–11
(continued)

VI. ASSETS AND LIABILITIES (cont'd)

Name and address of Bank, S&L., or Credit Union		Name and address of Company	$ Payment/Months	$
Acct. no.	$	Acct. no.		
Stocks & Bonds (Company name/ number & description)	$	Name and address of Company	$ Payment/Months	$
		Acct. no.		
Life insurance net cash value Face amount: $	$	Name and address of Company	$ Payment/Months	$
Subtotal Liquid Assets	$			
Real estate owned (enter market value from schedule of real estate owned)	$			
Vested interest in retirement fund	$			
Net worth of business(es) owned (attach financial statement)	$	Acct. no.		
Automobiles owned (make and year)	$	Alimony/Child Support/Separate Maintenance Payments Owed to:	$	
Other Assets (itemize)	$	Job-Related Expense (child care, union dues, etc.)	$	
		Total Monthly Payments	$	
Total Assets a.	$	Net Worth (a minus b) ▶	$	**Total Liabilities b.** $

Schedule of Real Estate Owned (If additional properties are owned, use continuation sheet.)

Property Address (enter S if sold, PS if pending sale or R if rental being held for income) ▼	Type of Property	Present Market Value	Amount of Mortgages & Liens	Gross Rental Income	Mortgage Payments	Insurance, Maintenance, Taxes & Misc.	Net Rental Income
		$	$	$	$	$	$
Totals		$	$	$	$	$	$

List any additional names under which credit has previously been received and indicate appropriate creditor name(s) and account number(s):

Alternate Name	Creditor Name	Account Number

VII. DETAILS OF TRANSACTION

a.	Purchase price	$
b.	Alterations, improvements, repairs	
c.	Land (if acquired separately)	
d.	Refinance (incl. debts to be paid off)	
e.	Estimated prepaid items	
f.	Estimated closing costs	
g.	PMI, MIP, Funding Fee	
h.	Discount (if Borrower will pay)	
i.	Total costs (add items a through h)	

VIII. DECLARATIONS

If you answer "Yes" to any questions a through i, please use continuation sheet for explanation.

	Borrower Yes No	Co-Borrower Yes No
a. Are there any outstanding judgments against you?	☐ ☐	☐ ☐
b. Have you been declared bankrupt within the past 7 years?	☐ ☐	☐ ☐
c. Have you had property foreclosed upon or given title or deed in lieu thereof in the last 7 years?	☐ ☐	☐ ☐
d. Are you a party to a lawsuit?	☐ ☐	☐ ☐
e. Have you directly or indirectly been obligated on any loan which resulted in foreclosure, transfer of title in lieu of foreclosure, or judgment?	☐ ☐	☐ ☐

(This would include such loans as home mortgage loans, SBA loans, home improvement loans, educational loans, manufactured (mobile) home loans, any mortgage, financial obligation, bond, or loan guarantee. If "Yes," provide details, including date, name, and address of Lender, FHA or VA case number, if any, and reasons for the action.)

FIGURE 7–11
(continued)

VII. DETAILS OF TRANSACTION		VIII. DECLARATIONS					
		If you answer "Yes" to any question a through I, please use continuation sheet for explanation.		Borrower		Co-Borrower	
				Yes	No	Yes	No
j.	Subordinate financing						
		f. Are you presently delinquent or in default on any Federal debt or any other loan, mortgage, financial obligation, bond, or loan guarantee?		☐	☐	☐	☐
k.	Borrower's closing costs paid by Seller	g. Are you obligated to pay alimony, child support, or separate maintenance?		☐	☐	☐	☐
		h. Is any part of the down payment borrowed?		☐	☐	☐	☐
l.	Other Credits (explain)	i. Are you a co-maker or endorser on a note?		☐	☐	☐	☐
m.	Loan amount (exclude PMI, MIP, Funding Fee financed)	-- j. Are you a U.S. citizen?		☐	☐	☐	☐
n.	PMI, MIP, Funding Fee financed	k. Are you a permanent resident alien?		☐	☐	☐	☐
o.	Loan amount (add m & n)	**l. Do you intend to occupy the property as your primary residence?**		☐	☐	☐	☐
		If "Yes," complete question m below.					
p.	Cash from/to Borrower (subtract j, k, l & o from i)	m. Have you had an ownership interest in a property in the last three years?		☐	☐	☐	☐
		(1) What type of property did you own—principal residence (PR), second home (SH), or investment property (IP)?		____		____	
		(2) How did you hold title to the home— by yourself (S), jointly with your spouse or jointly with another person (O)?		____		____	

IX. ACKNOWLEDGEMENT AND AGREEMENT

Each of the undersigned specifically represents to Lender and to Lender's actual or potential agents, brokers, processors, attorneys, insurers, servicers, successors and assigns and agrees and acknowledges that: (1) the information provided in this application is true and correct as of the date set forth opposite my signature and that any intentional or negligent misrepresentation of this information contained in this application may result in civil liability, including monetary damages, to any person who may suffer any loss due to reliance upon any misrepresentation that I have made on this application, and/or in criminal penalties including, but not limited to, fine or imprisonment or both under the provisions of Title 18, United States Code, Sec. 1001, et seq.; (2) the loan requested pursuant to this application (the "Loan") will be secured by a mortgage or deed of trust on the property described in this application; (3) the property will not be used for any illegal or prohibited purpose or use; (4) all statements made in this application are made for the purpose of obtaining a residential mortgage loan; (5) the property will be occupied as indicated in this application; (6) the Lender, its servicers, successors or assigns may retain the original and/or an electronic record of this application, whether or not the Loan is approved; (7) the Lender and its agents, brokers, insurers, servicers, successors, and assigns may continuously rely on the information contained in the application, and I am obligated to amend and/or supplement the information provided in this application if any of the material facts that I have represented herein should change prior to closing of the Loan; (8) in the event that my payments on the Loan become delinquent, the Lender, its servicers, successors or assigns may, in addition to any other rights and remedies that it may have relating to such delinquency, report my name and account information to one or more consumer reporting agencies; (9) ownership of the Loan and/or administration of the Loan account may be transferred with such notice as may be required by law; (10) neither Lender nor its agents, brokers, insurers, servicers, successors or assigns has made any representation or warranty, express or implied, to me regarding the property or the condition or value of the property; and (11) my transmission of this application as an "electronic record" containing my "electronic signature," as those terms are defined in applicable federal and/or state laws (excluding audio and video recordings), or my facsimile transmission of this application containing a facsimile of my signature, shall be as effective, enforceable and valid as if a paper version of this application were delivered containing my original written signature.

Acknowledgement. Each of the undersigned hereby acknowledges that any owner of the Loan, its servicers, successors and assigns, may verify or reverify any information contained in this application or obtain any information or data relating to the Loan, for any legitimate business purpose through any source, including a source named in this application or a consumer reporting agency.

Borrower's Signature X	Date	Co-Borrower's Signature X	Date

X. INFORMATION FOR GOVERNMENT MONITORING PURPOSES

The following information is requested by the Federal Government for certain types of loans related to a dwelling in order to monitor the lender's compliance with equal credit opportunity, fair housing and home mortgage disclosure laws. You are not required to furnish this information, but are encouraged to do so. The law provides that a lender may not discriminate either on the basis of this information, or on whether you choose to furnish it. If you furnish the information, please provide both ethnicity and race. For race, you may check more than one designation. If you do not furnish ethnicity, race, or sex, under Federal regulations, this lender is required to note the information on the basis of visual observation and surname if you have made this application in person. If you do not wish to furnish the information, please check the box below. (Lender must review the above material to assure that the disclosures satisfy all requirements to which the lender is subject under applicable state law for the particular type of loan applied for.)

BORROWER ☐ I do not wish to furnish this information	**CO-BORROWER** ☐ I do not wish to furnish this information
Ethnicity: ☐ Hispanic or Latino ☐ Not Hispanic or Latino	**Ethnicity:** ☐ Hispanic or Latino ☐ Not Hispanic or Latino
Race: ☐ American Indian or Alaska Native ☐ Asian ☐ Black or African American ☐ Native Hawaiian or Other Pacific Islander ☐ White	**Race:** ☐ American Indian or Alaska Native ☐ Asian ☐ Black or African American ☐ Native Hawaiian or Other Pacific Islander ☐ White
Sex: ☐ Female ☐ Male	**Sex:** ☐ Female ☐ Male

To be Completed by Loan Originator:
This information was provided:
☐ In a face-to-face interview
☐ In a telephone interview
☐ By the applicant and submitted by fax or mail
☐ By the applicant and submitted via e-mail or the Internet

Loan Originator's Signature X	Date
Loan Originator's Name (print or type)	Loan Originator Identifier	Loan Originator's Phone Number (including area code)
Loan Origination Company's Name	Loan Origination Company Identifier	Loan Origination Company's Address

FIGURE 7–11
(continued)

CONTINUATION SHEET/RESIDENTIAL LOAN APPLICATION		
Use this continuation sheet if you need more space to complete the Residential Loan Application. Mark **B** f or Borrower or **C** for Co-Borrower.	Borrower:	Agency Case Number:
	Co-Borrower:	Lender Case Number:

I/We fully understand that it is a Federal crime punishable by fine or imprisonment, or both, to knowingly make any false statements concerning any of the above facts as applicable under the provisions of Title 18, United States Code, Section 1001, et seq.

Borrower's Signature	Date	Co-Borrower's Signature	Date
X		X	

FIGURE 7–11
(continued)

- Applicant information
- Applicant's employment
- Applicant's housing
- Applicant's residency
- Applicant's bank accounts
- Applicant's assets
- Applicant's debts
- Applicant's real estate loans and real estate owned

The application's contents are verified and confirmed through a host of other practices. Given this, a variety of exhibits should be attached to the loan questionnaire, including:

1. Names, addresses, telephone numbers, and dates worked for each employer for the past two years.

2. Names, addresses, and account numbers of all charge accounts or installment loans that applicant pays now.

3. Names, addresses, and account numbers of all bank accounts (checking, savings, or deposit) that are now open.

4. Names, addresses, and account numbers of all charge accounts that were recently closed.

5. The applicants' Social Security numbers.

6. If applicant receives Social Security payments, public assistance, or a pension of any kind, a copy of the letter showing the amount you receive or a copy of the most recent check.

7. If applicants are applying for a VA mortgage, obtain a copy of the DD-214 form or discharge papers or a current Certificate of Eligibility.

8. If applicant has a mortgage on any type of property, obtain name, address, and account number of the mortgage company to which payments are made.

9. If applicant is self-employed, obtain a copy of the profit and loss statement and balance sheets for the past two years and copies of federal tax returns for the past two years.

10. If there is difficulty in locating previous employers, obtain copies of W-2 forms for the past two years.

11. If income is on a commission basis, obtain W-2 forms for the past two years.

12. Obtain a check to cover cost of appraisal and credit report under the VA program or the FHA program.

13. Obtain from the selling agent a signed copy of sales agreement, a copy of the deed (legal description), and a copy of the listing sheet.

CASE DECISION

There are has been ample litigation on the good faith effort's applicants during the application process. When is the application complete? Consider this Circuit Court of Appeals case.

United States Court of Appeals for the Federal Circuit

01-3280

WILLIAM A. O'KEEFE,

Petitioner,

v.

UNITED STATES POSTAL SERVICE,

Respondent.

01-3280

WILLIAM A. O'KEEFE,

Petitioner,

v.

UNITED STATES POSTAL SERVICE,

Respondent.

DECIDED: November 6, 2002

Before CLEVENGER, BRYSON, and PROST, <u>Circuit Judges</u>.

PROST, *Circuit Judge*.

William A. O'Keefe ("O'Keefe") petitions for review of the decision of the Merit Systems Protection Board ("Board"), No. PH-0752–00-0022-I-1, affirming the decision by the administrative judge that O'Keefe engaged in improper conduct, but reversing the judge's mitigation of the agency's penalty from removal to a sixty-day suspension. We have jurisdiction under 5 U.S.C. § 7703(b)(1). We vacate the Board's decision and remand this case for further proceedings consistent with this opinion.

BACKGROUND

On September 2, 1999, the United States Postal Service ("Postal Service") issued O'Keefe a letter of proposed removal, claiming that he engaged in "improper conduct/fraudulent use of personal identifiers." The Notice accuses O'Keefe of improperly using the personal information of a co-worker, Joseph Cummins ("Cummins"), to help another coworker, Valerie Davis Taylor ("Taylor"), obtain a mortgage.

The alleged plan to help Taylor obtain a mortgage developed from Taylor's having made an $18,000 deposit towards the purchase of a new home, without first securing approval for a mortgage. In late 1996, Taylor applied for a mortgage with American Financial Mortgage Corporation, but was told that she was unable, on her own, to qualify for the loan. To avoid losing her deposit, Taylor and O'Keefe approached Cummins and asked if he would assist Taylor in obtaining the mortgage. Cummins agreed, at least initially. On October 27, 1996, someone completed a loan application, employment verification request, and credit verification request in the name of Joseph Cummins. These forms contained Cummins' personal information, including his address, social security number, and description of assets and liabilities. Someone signed Cummins' name on the forms. The employment verification form was sent to Cummins' employer, Mr. Henzy at the Havertown Branch Post Office. Mr. Henzy completed the form, returned it to the mortgage company, and gave a copy to Cummins, who expressed confusion about the form because he claimed to have no knowledge of applying for a mortgage. Cummins stated that the signature on the form was not his own and that he did not give anyone permission to use or sign his name. Mr. Henzy then initiated an investigation that eventually led to the removal and arrest of O'Keefe and Taylor.

O'Keefe denies that he completed the mortgage application and related forms using Cummins' name and information. However, he does admit that he accompanied Taylor to the build site of the home she wished to purchase and identified himself to the builder as Cummins. O'Keefe also admits calling the mortgage company on at least one occasion, purporting to be Cummins. According to O'Keefe, Cummins consented to these actions when he agreed to help Taylor obtain a mortgage. Cummins, on the other hand, contends that he withdrew his consent shortly after agreeing to help Taylor.

In November 1998, O'Keefe and Taylor were arrested for theft and forgery based on their attempt to help Taylor obtain the mortgage. The charges against O'Keefe were dismissed when he completed the Accelerated Rehabilitative Disposition Program. On September 2, 1999, the Postal Service issued its notice of proposed removal. O'Keefe failed to respond to the notice and on October 4, 1999, the Postal Service terminated O'Keefe's employment. O'Keefe then filed an appeal with the Board. After a hearing, the administrative judge found that O'Keefe engaged in improper conduct by using Cummins' personal information without his consent, but that the penalty of removal should be mitigated to a sixty-day suspension because removal exceeded the bounds of reasonableness. *O'Keefe v. United States Postal Serv.*, No. PH-0752-00-0022-I-1, slip op. at 12, 16 (M.S.P.B. Mar. 28, 2000) ("Initial Decision"). The Postal Service then filed a petition for review with the Board, which reinstated the agency's penalty of removal because it found O'Keefe's conduct to be egregious and removal a reasonable penalty. *O'Keefe v. United States Postal Serv.*, No. PH-0752-00-0022-I-1, slip op. at 4-8 (M.S.P.B. Apr. 26, 2001) ("Final Decision").

O'Keefe now petitions for review of the Final Decision, arguing that his conduct was not so egregious as to warrant removal and, moreover, that removal is an unreasonably harsh penalty when all of the relevant factors are considered under *Douglas v. Veterans Administration*, 5 M.S.P.R. 280, 305-06 (1981). O'Keefe also argues that the administrative judge erred by not informing him that he needed to present sworn testimony in support of his version of what happened, thus leading the judge to erroneously conclude that O'Keefe engaged in improper conduct. According to O'Keefe, who appeared pro se, the judge should have told him that his unsworn statements were not evidence.

I

In reviewing a final decision of the Merit Systems Protection Board, this court shall review the record and hold unlawful and set aside any agency action, findings, or conclusions found to be—(1) arbitrary, capricious, an abuse of discretion, or otherwise not in accordance with law; (2) obtained without procedures required by law, rule, or regulation having been followed; or (3) unsupported by substantial evidence;. . . .

5 U.S.C. § 7703(c) (2000). "When, as here, the decision of the full board differs from that of its presiding official [the administrative judge], this court will engage in a more searching scrutiny of the record." *Connolly v. United States Dep't of Justice*, 766 F.2d 507, 512 (Fed. Cir. 1985).

An agency's decision "to dismiss a federal employee must have a 'rational basis supported by substantial evidence from the record taken as a whole.'" *Mitchum v. Tenn. Valley Auth.*, 756 F.2d 82, 85 (Fed. Cir. 1985) (quoting *VanFossen v. Dep't of Hous. & Urban Dev.*, 748 F.2d 1579, 1580 (Fed. Cir. 1984)). When all of the agency's charges are sustained, the agency's original penalty may nevertheless be mitigated to a maximum reasonable penalty when the agency's penalty is too severe. *LaChance v. Devall*, 178 F.3d 1246, 1260 (Fed. Cir. 1999).

The administrative judge found that the Postal Service's removal of O'Keefe was too severe a penalty because several factors weighed in favor of mitigation, including:

First, while the charged act of misconduct is serious, it is not egregious. Second, the appellant's more than 28 years of service of consistently satisfactory service is a significant factor to be considered. Third, the record does not show that the appellant gained financially from his misconduct. Fourth, the appellant's potential for rehabilitation.

Initial Decision at 15. The Board disagreed with the administrative judge, finding that O'Keefe's conduct was egregious. Final Decision at 5-6. The Board's opinion, however, is based on an erroneous version of the facts that is not supported by the record or the original charge against O'Keefe.

First, the Final Decision states that O'Keefe filed the mortgage application using Cummins' personal information. *Id.* at 2, 6. The Notice of Proposed Removal, however, does not specifically charge O'Keefe with filing the mortgage application. Rather, to support the general charge of "improper

(continued)

conduct/fraudulent use of personal identifiers," the Notice specifies that Engaging in Criminal Activity is a violation of Postal Service regulations contained in the Postal Service Code of Ethical Conduct. By your actions you are in violations of but not limited to the following sections of the Employee and Labor Relations Manual part 666.2 Behavior and Personal Habits and 661.53, Unacceptable Conduct, which states:

"No employee will engage in criminal, dishonest, notoriously disgraceful or immoral conduct. Conviction of any criminal statute may be grounds for disciplinary action by the Postal Service."

By your actions you have violated the provisions of the Employee and Labor Relations Manual, [including] but not limited to, the Code of Conduct, and the Administrative Support Manual. Your behavior can not and will not be tolerated by the United States Postal Service.

While the Notice details various suspected aspects of Taylor's attempt to secure a mortgage, the only conduct specifically attributed to O'Keefe is his arrest, his admission that he accompanied Taylor to the home site while purporting to be Cummins, and his admission that he called American Financial Mortgage Company purporting to be Cummins. The Notice does not accuse O'Keefe of forging and filing the mortgage application. The agency's counsel also stated at the hearing before the administrative judge that "we never charged him with signing the forms."

Similarly, the Final Decision states that the "investigative memorandum indicates that the appellant and Taylor even went so far as to falsify Cummins' address on W-2 forms so that it would appear that Cummins lived with Taylor." *Id.* at 5. In fact, the two Investigative Memoranda in the record implicate Taylor for falsifying Cummins' W-2 forms, which Taylor admitted faxing to American Financial Mortgage Company. The Notice of Proposed Removal also did not specifically charge O'Keefe with falsifying Cummins' address on the W-2 forms. Rather, the Notice merely reported that O'Keefe told the investigator that he "never saw Mr. Cummins' W-2 or pay stubs" and that he "did not know why Mr. Cummings' [sic] address would be changed on his W-2 unless it was to look like Mr. Cummins lived with Ms. Taylor." The administrative judge's opinion does not refer to these W-2 forms as a basis for sustaining the agency's charge against O'Keefe. To the contrary, the Initial Decision notes that the evidence "fails to establish any participation on the part of the appellant, other than by suggestion and innuendo." Initial Decision at 8 n.4.

Finally, the Board's assessment of the egregiousness of O'Keefe's conduct rests in part on its belief that O'Keefe "obtained Cummins' mother's maiden name without revealing his purpose to use the name in the mortgage application process." Final Decision at 6. In fact, Cummins' mother's maiden name appears nowhere on the mortgage application papers in the record. And, as with the other items of misinformation relied on by the Board, the Notice of Proposed Removal makes no charge against O'Keefe for misusing Cummins' mother's maiden name. The Notice merely states that "Mr. Cummins advised that you had a relationship with Ms. Taylor and that you had previously inquired to Mr. Cummins mothers maiden name." Neither of these facts, even if true, constitutes wrongdoing or is sufficient to support the Board's conclusion that O'Keefe did in fact misuse Cummins' mother's maiden name on the mortgage application.

The Board's reliance on erroneous facts to determine that O'Keefe's conduct was egregious and, therefore, that the agency's penalty should not be mitigated, is an abuse of discretion for two reasons. "The Board necessarily abuses its discretion when it rests its decision on factual findings unsupported by substantial evidence." *Pyles v. Merit Sys. Prot. Bd.*, 45 F.3d 411, 414 (Fed. Cir. 1995). As detailed above, many of the facts relied on by the Board are not supported by the record. The Board's determination that O'Keefe's conduct was egregious based on these unsupported facts cannot stand.

The Board also abused its discretion by exceeding the scope of the Notice of Proposed Removal. Only the charge and specifications set out in the Notice may be used to justify punishment because due process requires that an employee be given notice of the charges against him in sufficient detail to allow the employee to make an informed reply. *See Brook v. Corrado*, 999 F.2d 523, 526-27 (Fed. Cir. 1993); *LaChance v. Merit Sys. Prot. Bd.*, 147 F.3d 1367, 1371 (Fed. Cir. 1998). The Board's review of the agency's decision is likewise limited solely to the grounds invoked by the agency. *McIntire v. Fed. Emergency Mgmt. Agency*, 55 M.S.P.R. 578, 583 n.4 (1992) (stating that the Board will not consider allegations of misconduct related to the charges "because they were not specified in the agency's proposal notice"); *Riley v. Dep't of the Army*, 53 M.S.P.R. 683, 688 (1992) (finding that the administrative judge erred by sustaining a charge that was not specified by the agency). Nor may the Board substitute what it considers to be a better basis for removal than what was identified by the agency. *Shaw v. Dep't of the Air Force*, 80 M.S.P.R. 98, 106-07 (1998) ("The Board cannot adjudicate an adverse action on the basis of a charge that could have been brought but was not. Rather, the Board is required to adjudicate an appeal solely on the grounds invoked by the agency, and it may not substitute what it considers to be a more appropriate charge." (citations omitted)); *Riley*, 53 M.S.P.R. at 688; *Gottlieb v. Veterans Admin.*, 39 M.S.P.R. 606, 609-10 (1989) (reversing a judge's adjudication that the agency proved a charge on different grounds than those stated in the charge itself). By accusing O'Keefe of specific misdeeds that were not within the scope of the Notice of Proposed Removal, the Board has exceeded the scope of its review of the agency's decision. As such, the Board has abused its discretion in finding that O'Keefe's conduct was so egregious as to require removal.

Because the Board's conclusion that O'Keefe's conduct was egregious relies on facts that are neither supported by substantial evidence nor contained within the charge against O'Keefe, we vacate the Board's reversal of the administrative judge's mitigation of the agency's penalty and remand for further proceedings consistent with this opinion.

II

O'Keefe argues that his Fifth Amendment due process rights were violated in this case because the administrative judge failed to advise O'Keefe, a pro se appellant, that he needed to present sworn testimony in support of his case. O'Keefe did not testify under oath at the hearing before the administrative judge. Instead, he presented his case through cross-examination of the agency's witnesses, direct examination of other witnesses, and closing argument. According to O'Keefe, he thought that he sufficiently presented evidence in support of his version of what happened and that at all times he was subject to the penalties of perjury. O'Keefe believes that his Fifth Amendment rights to due process were violated because the ultimate issue of whether the agency proved the charge came down to a credibility determination by the administrative judge as to whether to believe O'Keefe or Cummins. As a pro se appellant, O'Keefe claims that he should have been advised that his version could not be credited without supporting sworn testimony and that he was thus deprived of a fair and impartial opportunity to defend himself.

O'Keefe is correct that the administrative judge's decision depended in large part on whether to believe Cummins or O'Keefe. In particular, the judge "credit[ed] Mr. Cummins' testimony that while he agreed to help Ms. Taylor, he did not give her or the appellant permission to use his personal information to apply for a mortgage." Initial Decision at 9. The judge also noted that the "only evidence in the record that refutes Mr. Cummins' sworn testimony regarding his lack of consent are the unsworn statements of the appellant and Ms. Taylor given to Insp. Cunicelli during his investigation and the detailed nature of the mortgage application." *Id.* at 10. The administrative judge then concluded that these unsworn statements were unreliable hearsay. *Id.* at 11.

One of the pivotal disputed facts in this case—when Cummins withdrew his consent to help Taylor— was resolved by the administrative judge based on O'Keefe's failure to provide sworn testimony to contradict Cummins' sworn testimony. *Id.* at 10-11. Cummins testified that he withdrew his consent to help Taylor obtain a mortgage three weeks after agreeing to help, before the mortgage application forms were filled out and signed with his name. O'Keefe claims that Cummins withdrew his consent much later and that he and Taylor dropped the attempt to obtain a mortgage after Cummins changed his mind. One postal employee corroborated O'Keefe's version by testifying that Cummins told him as late as January 1997 that he was helping Taylor obtain a mortgage. Nevertheless, the judge concluded that she "[could] not find that the unsworn statements made by the appellant and Ms. Taylor, who are obviously interested parties, outweigh[ed] the sworn testimony of Mr. Cummins" and that O'Keefe "advanced no evidence to corroborate his version that Mr. Cummins authorized his actions." *Id.* at 11.

While we are not prepared to say that O'Keefe's Fifth Amendment rights have been violated by the judge's failure to instruct him about the need for sworn testimony, we do note that the Board appears to have imposed a special duty on administrative judges to assist pro se appellants. The Board's regulations require judges to "conduct fair and impartial hearings," granting judges "all powers neces-sary" to meet this requirement. 5 C.F.R. § 1201.41(b) (2002). To that end, "[t]he Board has held that administrative judges should provide more guidance to pro se appellants and interpret their arguments in the most favorable light." *Miles v. Dep't of Veterans Affairs*, 84 M.S.P.R. 418, 421 (1999); *see also Patterson v. United States Postal Serv.*, 71 M.S.P.R. 332, 335 (1996), *aff'd*, 106 F.3d 425 (Fed. Cir. 1997) (Table). Moreover, "the Board and its administrative judges have an obligation to inform the parties what is required to establish their cases. This obligation is particularly significant where, as here, the appellant is appearing pro se." *Harless v. Office of Pers. Mgmt.*, 71 M.S.P.R. 110, 113 (1996) (remanding because the administrative judge failed to instruct the appellant that he must support his claim of financial hard-ship with appropriate evidence); *see also Goodnight v. Office of Pers. Mgmt.*, 49 M.S.P.R. 184, 187-89 (1991) (stating that "to ensure fairness, the administrative judge should have advised the appellant prior to the close of the record that she had not provided the evidence to prove her claim"); *cf. Wilson v. Dep't of Health & Human Servs.*, 834 F.2d 1011, 1012 (Fed. Cir. 1987) (finding that an administrative judge should have informed appellant of deficiencies in her proof of entitlement to attorney's fees).

Had O'Keefe's arguments been presented in the form of sworn testimony, we cannot say whether the administrative judge could have properly found that the agency proved the charges against O'Keefe. In addition, the Board has not had an opportunity to consider whether the administrative judge should have instructed O'Keefe about the need for sworn testimony because this issue was first raised in O'Keefe's petition to this court. (We note that O'Keefe, having apparently been satisfied with the administrative judge's mitigation of the penalty, had no reason to raise this issue until after the Board reversed the ad-ministrative judge). We believe the Board should consider this issue in the first instance on remand.

CONCLUSION

For the foregoing reasons, we vacate the decision of the Board and remand this case for further pro-ceedings consistent with the opinion.

VACATE AND REMAND

B. Release and Authorization

All lenders will ask for a **borrower authorization** or release that will permit their agents to check credit background and any other information that will bear on the business sensibility of the loan. Authorization to release information may be utilized as well.

C. Fee Disclosure

Most lenders provide an application **fee disclosure** form that outlines the application fee, points, or other costs associated with funds for this loan, including mortgage broker compensation. See Figure 7–12.

D. Notice of Federal Rights during the Application Process

At the same time all disclosures and waivers are requested, notice is required under the *Fair Credit Reporting Act, Equal Credit Opportunity Act*, and *Right to Financial Privacy Act*. Figure 7–13 addresses the *Right to Financial Privacy Act*. Under the *Federal Truth in Lending Act*, a notice of the applicant's right to cancel the agreement may be needed. See Figure 7–14.

E. Fair Credit Reporting Act

The federal *Fair Credit Reporting Act* (FCRA)[17] promotes the accuracy, fairness, and privacy of in-formation in the files of consumer reporting agencies. In the world of real estate, the question of credit is crucial to a successful application or a denied one. Credit reporting agencies are subject to these rules and consumers are granted explicit rights under the act. The Federal Trade Commission oversees the implementation of the act.

LOAN APPLICATION DISCLOSURE

DISCLAIMER OF COMMITMENT: The signing of an application form and/or any related documents in connection with our application for a home loan with _____ does not mean or imply that there is a commitment on the part of _____ to grant us any loan. Any expression to us of confidence that we might obtain a loan, at a particular rate or amount, is an expression of belief and opinion only by the one making it, and not to relied upon by us as a representation by an authorized agent of _____. I/We further understand that if I/we should cause escrow to cancel after the loan application has been accepted and approved, I/we may be liable for, and agree to pay a cancellation fee, not to exceed 1% of the loan amount.

RIGHT OF PRIVACY ACT: This is notice to you, as required by the Right to Financial Privacy Act of 1978, that the Department of Housing and Urban Development has a right of access to financial records held by a financial institution in connection with the consideration or administration of assistance to you. Financial records involving your transaction will be available to the Department of Housing and Urban Development without further notice or authorization but will not be disclosed or released to another Government agency or Department without your consent except as required or permitted by law.

FAIR CREDIT REPORTING ACT: _____ as part of processing your application for a Real Estate loan, may request a consumer report bearing on your credit worthiness, credit standing and credit capacity. This notice is given pursuant to the Fair Credit reporting Act of 1970, Section 601 to Section 622, inclusive. You are entitled to such information within 60 days of written demand therefore made to the credit reporting agency pursuant to Section 606(b) of the Fair Credit Reporting Act.

EQUAL CREDIT REPORTING ACT: The Federal Equal Credit Opportunity Act, 15 U.S.C. 1961 set.seq., prohibits discrimination against credit applicants on the basis of sex and marital status. Beginning March 23, 1977, the Act extends this protection to race, color, religion, national origin, age (provided the applicant has the capacity to contract), whether all or part of the applicant's income is derived from any public assistance program, or if the applicant has in good faith exercised any right under the Consumer Credit Protection Act. The Federal Agency which administers compliance with this law concerning the Lender is the Federal Trade Commission, 450 Golden Gate Avenue, San Francisco, CA 94102.

Initials _____ Initials _____

STATE OF CALIFORNIA FAIR LENDING NOTICE: Under the Housing Financial Discrimination Act of 1977, it is unlawful for a financial institution to refuse to make a

---

FIGURE 7–12
(continues)

loan or to offer less favorable terms than normal (such as higher interest rate, larger down payment or shorter maturity) based on any of the following considerations:

1. Neighborhood characteristics (such as the average age of the homes or the income level in the neighborhood) except to a limited extent necessary to avoid unsafe and unsound business practice.
2. Race, sex, color, religion, marital status, national origin or ancestry.
3. It is also unlawful to consider, in appraising a residence, the racial, ethnic, or religious composition of a particular neighborhood, whether or not such composition is under going change or is expected to undergo change.

RIGHT TO COPY OF APPRAISAL: I/We have been informed of our right to receive a copy of our residential mortgage appraisal. **MORTGAGE RESOURCES** will supply a copy of this appraisal, upon demand, to the client. (The appraisal company may have an additional charge for this service.)

BROKER DISCLOSURE: A Good Faith Estimate will be provided by _____, a Mortgage Broker, within three days of application and ( ) a lender has been obtained; ( ) no lender has yet been obtained. A lender will provide you with an additional Good Faith Estimate within three business days of receipt of your loan application.

If you wish to file a complaint, or if you have any questions about your rights, contact: Department of Real Estate, 1515 Clay Street, Suite 702, Oakland, CA 94612-1402, (510) 622-2552 or 320 West 4th Street, Suite 350, Los Angeles, CA 90013-1105, (213) 620-2072. If you file a complaint, the law requires that you receive a decision within thirty (30) days. I/We have received a copy of this notice.

Borrower: _____ **Date:** _____

Borrower: _____ **Date:** _____

FIGURE 7–12
(continued)

Web Exercise

Visit www.ftc.gov/credit.

FCRA grants specific rights. First, if a negative determination has come forward, you have the right to know the specific content of that information. Second, you have the right to know what is in your file. You may request and obtain all the information about yourself in the files of a consumer reporting agency. Third, you have the right to ask for a credit score. Credit scores are calculated computations of your creditworthiness based on information from credit bureaus. You may request a credit score from consumer reporting agencies that create scores or distribute scores used in residential real property loans. Fourth, you have the right to dispute incomplete or inaccurate information. Fifth,

NOTICE REQUIRED UNDER THE FAIR CREDIT REPORTING ACT

In compliance with the Fair Credit Reporting Act, we are informing you that an investigative report will be made. We are also informing you that you have the right to make a written request, within a reasonable period of time after you receive this notice, for an additional disclosure of the nature and scope of the investigation requested. To save you the trouble of writing, we are furnishing this additional information as follows:

> The nature and scope of the investigation requested may include information obtained through personal interviews concerning residence verification, number of dependents, employment, occupation, general health, habits, reputation, and mode of living.

INTENT TO OCCUPY STATEMENT AND ECOA

FEDERAL EQUAL CREDIT OPPORTUNITY ACT -- NOTICE TO APPLICANT

The Federal Equal Credit Opportunity Act prohibits creditors from discriminating against applicants on the basis of race, color, religion, national origin, sex, marital status, age, (provided that the applicant has the capacity to enter into a binding contract); because all or part of the applicant's income is derived from a public assistance program; or because the applicant has in good faith exercised any right under the Consumer Credit Protection Act. The Federal Agency that administers compliance with this law concerning this creditor is the Federal Trade Commission, Washington, D. C. 20580, Telephone (202) 724-1140.

RIGHT TO FINANCIAL PRIVACY ACT -- NOTICE TO APPLICANT

This is notice to you as required by the Right to Financial Privacy Act of 1978 that the Department of Housing and Urban Development has a right to access financial records held in a financial institution in connection with the consideration or administration of assistance to you. Financial records involving your transaction will be available to the Department of Housing and Urban Development without further notice or authorization but will not be disclosed or released to another Government Agency or department without your consent except as required or permitted.

I / We the undersigned DO Intend _____ or DO NOT Intend _____ to occupy the below stated property as our primary residence.

Property Address: _____

_____

_____

_____   _____
Signature of Borrower   Date

_____   _____
Signature of Borrower   Date

FIGURE 7–13

NOTICE OF RIGHT TO CANCEL

Loan Number: Date:
Borrowers:

Property Address:

YOUR RIGHT TO CANCEL:

You are entering into a transaction that will result in a mortgage, lien, or security interest on/in your home. You have a legal right under federal law to cancel this transaction, without cost, within THREE BUSINESS DAYS from whichever of the following events occurs last:

1. the date of the transaction, which is   ; or
2. the date you receive your Truth in Lending disclosures; or
3. the date you receive this notice of your right to cancel.

If you cancel the transaction, the mortgage, lien, or security interest is also cancelled. Within 20 CALENDAR DAYS after we receive your notice, we must take the steps necessary to reflect the fact that the mortgage, lien, or security interest on/in your home has been cancelled, and we must return to you any money or property you have given to us or to anyone else in connection with this transaction.

You may keep any money or property we have given you until we have done the things mentioned above, but you must then offer to return the money or property. If it is impractical or unfair for you to return the property, you must offer its reasonable value. You may offer to return the property at your home or at the location of the property. Money must be returned to the address below. If we do not take possession of the money or property within 20 CALENDAR DAYS of your offer, you may keep it without further obligation.

HOW TO CANCEL:

If you decide to cancel this transaction, you may do so by notifying us in writing,

Name of Creditor:
at

You may use any written statement that is signed and dated by you and states your intention to cancel, or you may use this notice by dating and signing below. Keep one copy of this notice because it contains important information about your rights.

If you cancel by mail or telegram, you must send a notice no later than midnight of   (or midnight of the THIRD BUSINESS DAY following the latest of the three events listed above.) If you send or deliver your written notice to cancel some other way, it must be delivered to the above address no later than that time.

I WISH TO CANCEL

_____   _____
Date   Signature

I/WE ACKNOWLEDGE RECEIPT OF TWO COPIES OF NOTICE OF RIGHT TO CANCEL AND ONE COPY OF THE FEDERAL TRUTH-IN-LENDING DISCLOSURE STATEMENT, ALL GIVEN BY LENDER IN COMPLIANCE WITH TRUTH-IN-LENDING SIMPLIFICATION AND REFORM ACT OF 1980 (PUBLIC LAW 96-221).

Each borrower in this transaction has the right to cancel. The excercise of this right by one borrower shall be effective as to all borrowers.

_____   _____   _____   _____
Borrower's Signature   Date   Borrower's Signature   Date

_____   _____   _____   _____
Borrower's Signature   Date   Borrower's Signature   Date

Ellie Mae, Inc.   Form **NRTC** (03/95)

FIGURE 7–14

credit reporting agencies must correct or delete inaccurate, incomplete, or unverifiable information upon request and proof. The three most often seen credit reporting agencies are:

Equifax: 1-800-685-1111; equifax.com

Experian: 1-888-397-3742; experian.com

TransUnion: 1-800-916-8800; transunion.com

Sixth, consumer reporting agencies may not report outdated negative information. Seventh, you may seek damages from any violators of the act.

Web Exercise

Check out the Complaint Process that is available online with the FTC at www.ftccomplaintassistant.gov/FTC_Wizard.aspx?Lang=en.

F. Equal Credit Opportunity Act

The Equal Credit Opportunity Act (ECOA)[18] prohibits credit discrimination on the basis of race, color, religion, national origin, sex, marital status, age, or because one receives public assistance. Creditors may appropriately ask most questions involving income, expenses, debts, and credit history. Lenders may not engage in the following practices:

- Discourage or reject applications because of race, color, religion, national origin, sex, marital status, age, or receipt of public assistance.

- Consider race, sex, or national origin, although this information may be voluntarily given for affirmative action assessment.

- Impose different terms or conditions, like a higher interest rate or higher fees, on a loan based on your race, color, religion, national origin, sex, marital status, age, or because of public assistance.

- Ask the applicant works or he/she is divorced. A creditor may use only the terms: married, unmarried, or separated.

- Ask about marital status if you're applying for a separate, unsecured account. A creditor may ask for this information if living in "community property" states: Arizona, California, Idaho, Louisiana, Nevada, New Mexico, Texas, Washington, and Wisconsin. A creditor in any state may ask for this information if you apply for a joint account or one secured by property.

- Ask about plans for having or raising children, but they can ask questions about expenses related to dependents.

- Ask about alimony, child support, or separate maintenance payments, unless told first that you don't have to provide this information if you are not relying on these payments to get credit.

The grant or denial of credit should not be based upon race, color, religion, national origin, sex, marital status, or whether on public assistance, nor consider the racial composition of the neighborhood where the property is located.

Web Exercise

The United States Department of Justice (DOJ) enforces the provisions of the Equal Credit Opportunity Act. Visit their list of current cases on the docket with corresponding briefs at www.usdoj.gov/crt/app/briefs_hous.php.

The Equal Credit Opportunity Act, joining with the DOJ, looks for patterns of discriminatory lending. The courts have found a "pattern or practice" when the evidence establishes that the discriminatory actions were the defendant's regular practice, rather than an isolated instance. A "pattern or practice" means that the defendant has a policy of discriminating, even if the policy is not always followed. See Figure 7–15.

G. Right to Financial Privacy Act

Other consumer protections are afforded homebuyers by the Federal Deposit Insurance Corporation, commonly known as the FDIC. Its enforcement power oversees the *Right to Financial Privacy Act*.[19]

Given the extraordinary amount of paperwork and documents that flow throughout the real estate transaction, and understanding the private sensitivity much of this financial information by nature contains, Congress legislates a series of protections of these records and corresponding content. The act deals with the power of government to gain access; the power of financial institutions and the right of the financial consumer, or customer as the act describes, to protect the records in question. Without a release or authorization, the privacy of the record remains intact. As to the power of government to gain access, the act lays out express access approaches, which are:

- There is an appropriate administrative subpoena or summons.
- There is a qualified search warrant.
- There is an appropriate judicial subpoena.
- There is an appropriate written request from an authorized government authority.

The part of the legislation dealing with consumers notes:

a. A customer may authorize disclosure under Section 3402(1) of this title if he furnishes to the financial institution and to the government authority seeking to obtain such disclosure signed and dated statement which:

1. authorizes such disclosure for a period not in excess of three months;
2. states that the customer may revoke such authorization at any time before the financial records are disclosed;
3. identifies the financial records which are authorized to be disclosed;
4. specifies the purposes for which, and the government authority to which, such records may be disclosed; and
5. states the customer's rights under this title.

b. No such authorization shall be required as a condition of doing business with any financial institution.

c. The customer has the right, unless the government authority obtains a court order as provided in Section 3409 of this title, to obtain a copy of the record which the financial institution shall keep of all instances in which the customer's record is disclosed to a government authority pursuant to this section, including the identity of the government authority to which such disclosure is made.[20]

Other acts such as the Federal Truth in Lending Act and various consumer protections statutes are tangentially dealing disclosure of loan rates, term and remedies in the event of default.[21]

H. Estimate of Buyer's Settlement Cost

A **good faith estimate** of buyer's settlement cost consists of an itemization of possible loan origination fees, abstract and title search fees, title insurance, prepaid items, and escrow reserves such as taxes. See Figure 7–16.

Many documents in the mortgage transaction have this disclosure quality since the costs of financing and the fees associated with the processing are increasingly prohibitive.

U. S. Department of Housing and Urban Development

EQUAL HOUSING OPPORTUNITY

We Do Business in Accordance With the Federal Fair Housing Law

(The Fair Housing Amendments Act of 1988)

It is illegal to Discriminate Against Any Person Because of Race, Color, Religion, Sex, Handicap, Familial Status, or National Origin

---

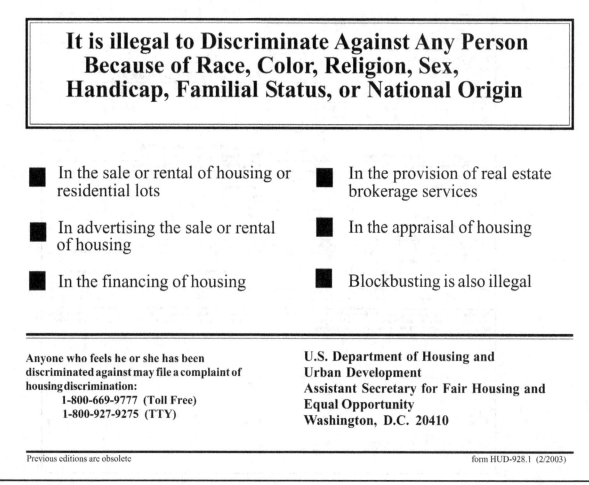

■ In the sale or rental of housing or residential lots

■ In advertising the sale or rental of housing

■ In the financing of housing

■ In the provision of real estate brokerage services

■ In the appraisal of housing

■ Blockbusting is also illegal

Anyone who feels he or she has been discriminated against may file a complaint of housing discrimination:
    1-800-669-9777 (Toll Free)
    1-800-927-9275 (TTY)

U.S. Department of Housing and Urban Development
Assistant Secretary for Fair Housing and Equal Opportunity
Washington, D.C. 20410

Previous editions are obsolete   form HUD-928.1 (2/2003)

FIGURE 7–15

GOOD FAITH ESTIMATE

Lender:	Sales Price:
Address:	Base Loan Amount:
	Total Loan Amount:
Applicant(s):	Interest Rate:
	Type of Loan:
Property Address:	Preparation Date:
	Loan Number:

The information provided below reflects estimates of the charges which you are likely to incur at the settlement of your loan. The fees listed are estimates - actual charges may be more or less. Your transaction may not involve a fee for every item listed.
The numbers listed beside the estimates generally correspond to the numbered lines contained in the HUD-1 or HUD-1A settlement statement which you will be receiving at settlement. The HUD-1 or HUD-1A settlement statement will show you the actual cost for items paid at settlement.

800	ITEMS PAYABLE IN CONNECTION WITH LOAN:		1100	TITLE CHARGES:	
801	Origination Fee @ % + $	$ _____	1101	Closing or Escrow Fee	$ _____
802	Discount Fee @ % + $	$ _____	1102	Abstract or Title Search	$ _____
803	Appraisal Fee	$ _____	1103	Title Examination	$ _____
804	Credit Report	$ _____	1105	Document Preparation Fee	$ _____
805	Lender's Inspection Fee	$ _____	1106	Notary Fee	$ _____
806	Mortgage Insurance Application Fee	$ _____	1107	Attorney's Fee	$ _____
807	Assumption Fee	$ _____	1108	Title Insurance	$ _____
808	Mortgage Broker Fee	$ _____			$ _____
810	Tax Related Service Fee	$ _____			$ _____
811	Application Fee	$ _____			$ _____
812	Commitment Fee	$ _____			$ _____
813	Lender's Rate Lock-In Fee	$ _____			$ _____
814	Processing Fee	$ _____			$ _____
815	Underwriting Fee	$ _____	1200	GOVERNMENT RECORDING AND TRANSFER CHARGES:	
816	Wire Transfer Fee	$ _____	1201	Recording Fee	$ _____
		$ _____	1202	City/County Tax/Stamps	$ _____
900	ITEMS REQUIRED BY LENDER TO BE PAID IN ADVANCE:		1203	State Tax/Stamps	$ _____
901	Interest for days @ $ /day	$ _____	1204	Intangible Tax	$ _____
902	Mortgage Insurance Premium	$ _____			$ _____
903	Hazard Insurance Premium	$ _____			$ _____
904	County Property Taxes	$ _____			$ _____
905	Flood Insurance	$ _____			$ _____
		$ _____	1300	ADDITIONAL SETTLEMENT CHARGES:	
		$ _____	1301	Survey	$ _____
1000	RESERVES DEPOSITED WITH LENDER:		1302	Pest Inspection	$ _____
1001	Hazard Ins. Mo. @ $ Per Mo.	$ _____			$ _____
1002	Mortgage Ins. Mo. @ $ Per Mo.	$ _____			$ _____
1004	Tax & Assmt. Mo. @ $ Per Mo.	$ _____			$ _____
1006	Flood Insurance	$ _____			$ _____
		$ _____		TOTAL ESTIMATED SETTLEMENT CHARGES:	$ _____
"S"/"B" designates those costs to be paid by Seller/Broker.			"A" designates those costs affecting APR.		

TOTAL ESTIMATED MONTHLY PAYMENT:		TOTAL ESTIMATED FUNDS NEEDED TO CLOSE:	
Principal & Interest	$ _____	Down Payment	$ _____
Real Estate Taxes	$ _____	Estimated Closing Costs	$ _____
Hazard Insurance	$ _____	Estimated Prepaid Items / Reserves	$ _____
Flood Insurance	$ _____	Total Paid Items (Subtract)	$ _____
Mortgage Insurance	$ _____	Other	$ _____
Other	$ _____	CASH FROM BORROWER	$ _____
TOTAL MONTHLY PAYMENT	$ _____		

THIS SECTION IS COMPLETED ONLY IF A PARTICULAR PROVIDER OF SERVICE IS REQUIRED. Listed below are providers of service which we required you to use. The charges indicated in the Good Faith Estimate above are based upon the corresponding charge of the below designated providers.

ITEM NO.	NAME & ADDRESS OF PROVIDER	TELEPHONE NO.	NATURE OF RELATIONSHIP

These estimates are provided pursuant to the Real Estate Settlement Procedures Act of 1974, as amended (RESPA). Additional information can be found in the HUD Special Information Booklet, which is to be provided to you by your mortgage broker or lender, if your application is to purchase residential property and the Lender will take a first lien on the property.

Applicant	Date	Applicant	Date
Applicant	Date	Applicant	Date

☐ This Good Faith Estimate is being provided by a mortgage broker, and no lender has yet been obtained.

Page 1 of 1

FIGURE 7–16

The RESPA is a federal law guiding credit and financial transactions. RESPA instructs lenders to disclose the particular or unique features of their loan products and the techniques and methods of loan servicing. For example, some banks may be required to announce restrictions on transfer, the impact of contractual contingencies, late payment or prepayment penalties, and escrow requirements.

If the loan product allows an interest rate lock during the application period, an agreement is usually delivered to the buyer for signature. Interest rate lock periods usually run between thirty, sixty, and ninety days. Some lenders may charge a point or a percentage thereof or some other type of fee associated with locking a rate, particularly in volatile interest rate periods. The application process also includes the types of services available by lender or through subsidiaries or related companies. Many lenders provide title services, closing and settlement agents, and have access to homeowners or private mortgage insurance. Under federal and state law, applicants should be put on notice as to their right to refuse such services and to select their own agents.

Federal law mandates that lenders provide borrowers with a brochure published by the secretary of HUD entitled RESPA. The RESPA booklet outlines all the nuances of a typical real estate transaction and attempts to explain, in plain English, what buyers and sellers can expect during the transaction. In particular, RESPA covers the buyer's and seller's costs and the kinds of expenses that are likely to be seen in a transaction. It is not a document of legal authority, but only a booklet of guidance for both the uninitiated and the experienced.

I. Purchaser's Certification or Affidavit

The lender will also provide applicants with an affidavit that memorializes the purchaser's intention to occupy the property as a primary residence for a designated period beyond the closing date. This type of borrower's affidavit addresses the secondary mortgage market's underwriting guidelines.

J. Tax Forms

During the application process, a variety of tax returns are generally submitted for full documentation loans. If a taxpayer has difficulty in locating the returns, the lender will make formal communication with the Internal Revenue Service (IRS) for copies of them. A third-party request for a tax return can be accomplished by completing IRS Form 4506.

K. Verifications

1. Loan Verification

Lenders, banks, and private investors must conduct due diligence on the affirmation of the facts listed on the questionnaire or application. A variety of verifications requested will be prepared by paralegals working in a lender's environment.

2. Rent or Mortgage Verification

Verification of rent or mortgage account, which is a sign of creditworthiness, is routinely undertaken.

3. Funds Verification

Verification of the amount of deposits in savings or checking accounts must also be done. In full or limited documentation loans, borrowers are required to certify the amount and location of funds that will be utilized to close.

4. Employment Verification

Finally, verification as to present employment as well as pay and other benefits must be accomplished.

L. Appraisal

No mortgage application can be successful without an **appraisal** of the property's value. The appraiser, who is certified or licensed by governmental authority, arrives at appraised value by either the cost of actual construction or by a comparative marketplace analysis by looking at other properties in similar locales that have recently sold. There are numerous other factors that can be considered in arriving at appraised value such as:

- The issue of cost
- Intrinsic value
- Economic value
- Liquidation value
- "As is" value
- Stabilized value[22]

Appraisal values are highly relative in the real estate marketplace. In boom times, properties tend to be appraised at higher values, while the reverse is true in times of depression.[23] A home once worth a fortune can easily deflate, depending on market conditions, neighborhood changes, or environmental hazards.

The content of this appraisal is broken down into these categories:

- Photographic portrayals
- Market value or cost value analysis
- Comparative transactions
- Location and survey
- Disclaimers and other caveats

The appraiser performs a key role in the mortgage process. If the analysis of the mortgage exceeds the appraised value of the property, lenders are rightfully wary. The appraised value should, at least, be the same as or exceed the value of any underlying mortgage. If the appraisal comes in lower than expected, borrowers or sellers are permitted to lower the price of the real estate transaction to meet the appraisal figure.

Appraisers and the appraisal process have also been severely critiqued during the mortgage crisis. In some ways, there was too much closeness to appraiser and lender; there was an incentive-based system that fostered appraisals that were exaggerated and there was a loose attitude about professional standards in the appraisal business. Much has been done to tighten up these processes since the debacle of loans to value. Even Congress has authorized the formation and oversight of appraisers by its erection of the Appraisal Foundation. Publishing a Uniform Standards of Professional Appraisal Practice (USAP), the foundation promulgates uniform expectations for professional behavior. The standards fall into these categories:

Standard 1: Real Property Appraisal, Development: In developing a real property appraisal, an appraiser must identify the problem to be solved, determine the scope of work necessary to solve the problem, and correctly complete research and analyses necessary to produce a credible appraisal.

Standard 2: Real Property Appraisal, Reporting: In reporting the results of a real property appraisal, an appraiser must communicate each analysis, opinion, and conclusion in a manner that is not misleading.

Standard 3: Appraisal Review, Development, and Reporting: In performing an appraisal review assignment, an appraiser acting as a reviewer must develop and report a credible opinion as to the quality of another appraiser's work and must clearly disclose the scope of work performed.

Standard 4: Real Property Appraisal Consulting, Development: In developing a real property appraisal consulting assignment, an appraiser must identify the problem to be solved, determine the scope of work necessary to solve the problem, and correctly complete the research and analyses necessary to produce credible results.

Standard 5: Real Property Appraisal Consulting, Reporting: In reporting the results of a real property appraisal consulting assignment, an appraiser must communicate each analysis, opinion, and conclusion in a manner that is not misleading.

Standard 6: Mass Appraisal, Development, and Reporting: In developing a mass appraisal, an appraiser must be aware of, understand, and correctly employ those recognized methods and techniques necessary to produce and communicate credible mass appraisals.

Standard 7: Personal Property Appraisal, Development: In developing a personal property appraisal, an appraiser must identify the problem to be solved, determine the scope of work necessary to solve the problem, and correctly complete research and analyses necessary to produce a credible appraisal.

Standard 8: Personal Property Appraisal, Reporting: In reporting the results of a personal property appraisal, an appraiser must communicate each analysis, opinion, and conclusion in a manner that is not misleading.

Standard 9: Business Appraisal, Development: In developing and appraisal of an interest in a business enterprise or intangible asset, an appraiser must identify the problem to be solved, determine the scope of work necessary to solve the problem, and correctly complete the research and analyses necessary to produce a credible appraisal.

Standard 10: Business Appraisal, Reporting: In reporting the results of an appraisal of an interest in a business enterprise or intangible asset, an appraiser must communicate each analysis, opinion, and conclusion in a manner that is not misleading.[24]

Web Exercise

Most states now heavily regulate the actions of appraisers by license and corresponding oversight. See North Dakota's Board standards on appraisers at www.legis.nd.gov/cencode/T43C233.pdf.

M. Survey

Usually coupled with an appraisal request is the lender's desire for a **survey**. The survey graphically portrays the boundary lines of the property purchased. If there are encroachments, easements, violations of rights-of-way, setback violations, or other zoning errors, the survey will identify them. A completed survey may appear as portrayed in Figure 7–17.

For a survey review checklist, see Figure 7–18.[25]

VI. MORTGAGE COMMITMENT

Once the application and the underwriting process are complete and the applicant has met all of the documentary demands placed upon him or her during an increasingly rigorous process, the lender is ready to either grant or deny the loan request. When the loan is denied, a notice and explanation of why the loan was not approved is forwarded to the applicant. When a loan has been approved, the lender is then prepared to "commit." Commitments come in many shapes and sizes. Some are "full," that is without restriction or condition. Others are "conditional," which means that some issue remains before the commitment is unconditional and full. One usually witnesses conditions related to finance or appraisal. To commit means to agree, to approve, and to let the borrower know that the terms and conditions of a loan applied for are now available. It is rare for a lender to commit without conditions or other contingent language.

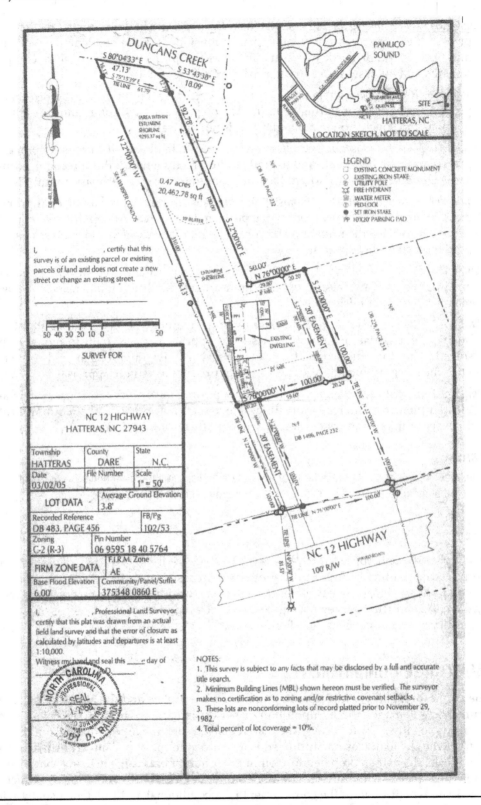

FIGURE 7–17

SURVEY REVIEW CHECKLIST

Date: _____

File name: _____

Reviewed by: _____

Survey date: _____

Last Revision: _____

Surveyor: _____

Phone: _____

Prepared for: _____

Type of Survey: _____

Title Report Reference: _____

SURVEY REQUIREMENTS

1. _____ Scale
2. _____ Basis of bearing
3. _____ North arrow
4. _____ Legend
5. _____ Signed, sealed, and dated
6. _____ Property description and location

    A. _____ Legal Description (on survey; match title commitment): _____
    Description closes: _____

    B. _____ Boundaries: _____

        _____ point of commencement/point of beginning shown (and description returns to POB)

        _____ corners set

        _____ iron pins placed at deflection points

        _____ curves (length and arc or radius, tangent)

        _____ monuments found

        _____ azimuth baseline shown

        _____ platted property: lots, blocks, section and recording numbers of plat

        _____ platted property: metes and bounds match plat

    C. _____ Adjoining properties (noted with any overlaps or gaps shown): _____

    D. _____ Multiple parcels contiguous: _____

7. _____ Easements and other physical encumbrances shown on title (locate all with corresponding number of title commitment; include appurtenant easements): _____

8. _____ Improvements:

    A. _____ Building and structures (height, area, perimeter dimensions; frame, roof and exterior finish): _____

    B. _____ Other improvements or physical objects (fences rockeries, landscaping, planter boxes, out-buildings—determine ownership and issues): _____

FIGURE 7–18

(continues)

9. _____ Encroachments (improvements over easements/boundaries; subject property onto adjoiner, adjoiner onto subject property):_____

10. _____ Access:

    A. _____ Roads (adjoining streets, highways, alleys _____ public v. private), right of ways; labeled, distance to property and restrictions shown): _____

    B. _____ Ingress and egress (curb cuts and driveways): _____

11. _____ Utilities (locate electricity), sewer (storm and sanitary), telephone, water, gas; all connected to public utility lines either through public street or easement over private adjoiner): _____

12. _____ Storm drainage ponds and systems (if any; easement for run off): _____

13. _____ Parking (number and size of spaces): _____

14. _____ Building set-back lines: _____

15. _____ Street address (of each building): _____

16. _____ Area of land and area of buildings: _____

17. _____ Water (locate including flow direction all creeks, rivers, ponds, bays, lakes adjacent to or on property, or within flood plains or flood prone area): _____

18. _____ Cemeteries (if any): _____

19. _____ Vicinity sketch (show closest thoroughfare intersection): _____

20. _____ Field notes on survey: _____

21. _____ Flood Hazard Area Certification (map number, zone): _____

22. _____ Certification (compare to requirement; client named): _____

23. _____ Other: _____

FIGURE 7–18
(continued)

CASE DECISION

Read and interpret a Tennessee decision that evaluates conditional language.

IN THE COURT OF APPEALS OF TENNESSEE
AT NASHVILLE
July 11, 2001 Session

MARTIN HERRICK, ET UX. v. MIKE FORD CUSTOM BUILDERS, LLC

Direct Appeal from the Chancery Court for Williamson County
No. 26004   Russ Heldman, Judge

No. M2000–02569-COA-R3-CV – Filed August 13, 2001

The Herricks entered into a sales agreement with Mike Ford for the construction of a home. The sales agreement provided that the deposit paid by the Herricks became non-refundable upon the presentation of a loan commitment letter. The Herricks presented Mike Ford with a loan commitment letter from Southeastern Mortgage Company which was conditioned upon proof of employment. Mr. Herrick was terminated from his employment, and, as a result, Southeastern denied the Herricks' loan application.

The Herricks demanded Mike Ford return their deposit. Mike Ford refused, contending that the deposit became non-refundable at the time the Southeastern loan commitment letter was presented. Both parties filed motions for summary judgment. The trial court granted summary judgment in favor of the Herricks. We reverse and remand.

Tenn. R. App. P. 3 Appeal as of Right; Judgment of the Chancery Court Reversed; and Remanded

DAVID R. FARMER, J., delivered the opinion of the court, in which W. FRANK CRAWFORD, P.J., W.S. and ALAN E. HIGHERS, J., joined.

R. Francene Kavin, Brentwood, Tennessee, for the appellant, Mike Ford Custom Builders, LLC.

P. Edward Schell, Franklin, Tennessee, for the appellees, Martin Herrick and Lydia Herrick.

OPINION

Martin Herrick (Mr. Herrick) and Lydia Herrick (Mrs. Herrick, or collectively, the Herricks) entered into a sales agreement (the agreement) with Mike Ford Custom Builders (Mike Ford) for the construction of a home in Williamson County, Tennessee. The agreement provided that the Herricks would pay a deposit of $22,495 upon the signing of the agreement which would be credited against the purchase price of $449,900 at closing. The deposit became non-refundable upon presentation of a loan commitment letter or other evidence of financial ability. Regarding the loan commitment, the agreement provided as follows:

> LOAN COMMITMENT: Buyer will apply for mortgage loan within (3) working days of the acceptance of this offer and shall present loan commitment or other evidence of financial ability to Seller within fourteen (14) days from said acceptance. This agreement [is] contingent upon Buyers ability to obtain loan commitment letter. All of buyer's deposit(s) shall be non-refundable upon Buyer['s] presentation of loan commitment or evidence of financial ability to Seller.

Mr. Herrick applied with Southeastern Mortgage Company (Southeastern) and received a conditional loan approval which read as follows:

> Southeastern Mortgage of Tennessee, Inc. is pleased to issue this conditional loan approval to you on the house located at 9462 Waterfall Road, Brentwood, Tennessee 37027. Your loan application and supporting documentation has been reviewed and conditionally approved subject to meeting the following: . . . . No adverse changes in employment/income/assets/liabilities or credit.

Mr. Herrick accepted the loan commitment and presented the Southeastern letter to Mike Ford. Mike Ford contacted Southeastern and was assured by Southeastern that the letter received from Mr. Herrick containing the language, "conditional loan approval," was a standard commitment letter and that the approval was given conditionally upon certain criteria being met by the Herricks at the time of closing.

Construction of the home began during late summer, 1998. In November of 1998, Mr. Herrick notified Southeastern that his employment had been terminated. He then made a demand on Mike Ford for the return of the deposit. Mike Ford refused, saying that the deposit became nonrefundable at the presentation of the Southeastern loan commitment letter. The Herricks then filed suit against Mike Ford, alleging that their ability to obtain financing was a condition precedent to their obligation to perform under the agreement. Both parties filed a motion for summary judgment. The trial court determined that the financing contingency was a condition precedent to the parties' performanceunder the agreement; the Herricks were unable to obtain financing and thus were unable to perform their obligations under the agreement; and, as such, the Herricks were entitled to the return of their deposit. This appeal ensued.

(continued)

Mike Ford raises the following issues, as we perceive them, for this court's review:

1. Whether the trial court erred in granting summary judgment in favor of the Herricks.

2. Whether the trial court erred in finding that the agreement contained a condition precedent which served to excuse the Herricks from performance under the agreement.

3. Whether the trial court erred by finding the requirement of providing a loan commitment letter and the Herricks' inability to obtain a loan not to be severable and independent of each other.

4. Whether the trial court erred in its contract interpretation.

This appeal is from a grant of summary judgment. In their respective briefs, both parties concede that there are no genuine issues of material fact as is evidenced by the filing of cross motions for summary judgment. Summary judgment is appropriate if no genuine issues of material fact exist and the movant proves it is entitled to a judgment as a matter of law. *See* Tenn. R. Civ. P. 56.03. On appeal, we must take the strongest view of the evidence in favor of the nonmoving party, allowing all reasonable inferences in its favor and discarding all countervailing evidence. *See Shadrick v. Coker*, 963 S.W.2d 726, 731 (Tenn. 1998) (citing *Byrd v. Hall*, 847 S.W.2d 208, 210–11 (Tenn. 1993)). Since our review only concerns questions of law, we review the record *de novo* with no presumption of correctness of the judgment below. *See* Tenn. R. App. P. 13(d); *Bain v. Wells*, 936 S.W.2d 618, 622 (Tenn. 1997).

The main issue before this court is the interpretation of the following agreement provision, "All of buyer's deposit(s) shall be non-refundable upon Buyer['s] presentation of loan commitment or evidence of financial ability to Seller." It is settled law in Tennessee that the meaning of a contract provision is a question of law. *See Bradson Mercantile, Inc. v. Crabtree*, 1 S.W.3d 648 (Tenn. Ct. App. 1999). If the contract language is plain and unambiguous, it is the court's duty to interpret the contract as it is written, applying to the words of the contract their usual, natural, and ordinary meaning. *See Johnson v. Johnson*, 37 S.W.3d 892, 896 (Tenn. 2001); *Hardeman County Bank v. Stallings*, 917 S.W.2d 695 (Tenn. Ct. App. 1995) *perm. app. denied*. A contract is ambiguous when its meaning is uncertain and can fairly be understood in more ways than one. *See Johnson*, 37 S.W.3d at 896 (citing *Farmers-Peoples Bank v. Clemmer*, 519 S.W.2d 801, 805 (Tenn. 1975)). We believe the language in the agreement before this court is clear: the Herricks' deposit becomes non-refundable upon the presentation of a loan commitment letter. The agreement does not state that the loan commitment letter had to be free of conditions; rather, it simply says that upon presentment of loan commitment, the deposit becomes non-refundable. It is uncontested that the conditions listed in the Southeastern loan commitment letter were for the benefit of the mortgage company. Further, Southeastern stated in its affidavit that the loan commitment letter containing the language, "conditional loan approval," was a standard commitment letter and that the criteria contained in the loan commitment letter had to be met by the Herricks *at the time of closing*. We conclude that the presentation of the Southeastern loan commitment letter to Mike Ford made the Herricks' deposit non-refundable. Due to our finding, all remaining issues are pretermitted.

Based upon the foregoing, we reverse the judgment of the trial court, and remand this case for entry of summary judgment in favor of the appellants, Mike Ford Custom Builders, LLC. The costs of this appeal are taxed to the appellees, Martin Herrick and Lydia Herrick, and their surety, for which execution may issue if necessary.

DAVID R. FARMER, JUDGE

A sample commitment letter is at Figure 7–19.

Congratulations! Your loan application has been approved subject to the terms and conditions included in this commitment letter. You may be required to provide documentation that is acceptable to the Lender. If the documentation you provide does not satisfy the terms and conditions, your final approval is not guaranteed and the Lender may require additional information and review. This commitment is also subject to reconsideration if there is any material change in your financial status, in the information provided in your application or on the condition of the property.

Loan Type _____ Loan amount $_____ Loan term (months) _____

Simple Interest rate_____%.

Unless the section titled "Locked-In" below is checked, you have elected to FLOAT and the interest rate designated above reflects the interest rate used for qualifying. The interest rate and discount points for your loan application will go up and down depending on market conditions until you loan is price protected.

Your monthly payments will consist of principal and interest in the approximate amount of $_____ and escrow payments. Your payment is due on the first day of each month without exception. A late payment service charge of _____ % will be charged on payments received after the end of 15 calendar days after the payment is due. Your loan must close and fund prior to the interest rate lock-in expiration date and prior to the commitment expiration date. Your interest rate lock-in expiration date is _____. If you cannot close and fund prior to this date for any reason, you will be required to re-price your loan. Your commitment expiration date is _____. If you cannot close and fund prior to this date, you may be required to provide additional documentation and your loan will be resubmitted for credit approval.

Interest Rate Adjustment - ARM Option

_____ If this line is checked, you have been approved for an Adjustable Rate Mortgage (ARM). You will be notified of your First Interest Rate Change Data and your interest rate will be adjusted every twelve months thereafter. Your adjusted interest rate will be based on an Index plus a Margin, subject to the interest rate caps explained in the ARM Disclosure and Description of Program provided to your earlier.

FHA/VA

All conditions set forth on the FHA Conditional Commitment or the VA Certificate of Reasonable Value (CRV) must be satisfied.

Lock-in

_____ If this line is checked, you have elected to lock in the interest rate and discount points for your application, which means that if your loan is closed and funded within the Price Protection Period, we will make the loan at the interest rate and discount points specified in this letter.

Assumability

_____ If this line is checked, your loan may be assumed by a qualified borrower who meets investor guidelines at time of assumption.

Escrow

Your monthly payment will include an amount for taxes, hazard insurance premiums, premiums for other insurance you may have (such as flood insurance or FHA mortgage insurance), and other items that may be required to be escrowed under the terms of the Loan agreement.

FIGURE 7–19

Mortgage Commitment Letter.

(continues)

Flood Insurance

_____ If this line is checked, we must be furnished at closing with an original policy of flood insurance (or application for insurance) under the National Flood Insurance Act of 1968, along with a paid receipt for the first year's premium. This insurance policy must be obtained from an acceptable company, must be in a form acceptable to us, and must have a loss payable provision as described under the Hazard Insurance requirements below.

Origination Fee and Loan Discount

Buyer/Seller must pay, at closing, a total Loan Origination Fee of _____% of the principal amount of the loan (not including the MIP if financed) and a total loan discount of _____ % of the principal amount of the loan to be paid on the total loan amount (including the MIP if financed). If you've elected to float your rate and points, refer to the Election Form given to you at the time of application. For an FHA loan, Buyer must either pay or finance the up-front Mortgage Insurance Premium of $_____ and must pay a monthly MIP charge to start at $_____ per month. For a VA loan Buyer must also pay and/or finance the VA Funding Fee of $_____.

New Construction

New construction is subject to the proposed home being 100 percent completed prior to loan closing in accordance with the approved plans and specifications. We must receive evidence that all contractors and materialmen have waived their rights to a mechanic's lien. An approved final inspection will be required prior to closing along with photos of the completed property.

Credit Documents

All credit documents over 120 days old as of the date of the closing will need to be updated prior to loan closing to ascertain that your ability to repay has not changed adversely. (New construction credit documents over 180 days old at time of closing must be updated.)

Program Availability

We reserve the right to modify or eliminate this loan program at any time without notice to you. If the program is eliminated or you no longer qualify because of program modifications, this Approval will be void and you will be required to submit a new application for a different loan program.

Title Insurance or Attorney's Certificate

We must be furnished with an acceptable title insurance policy (or title guarantee policy) issued by a company or attorney satisfactory to us. The policy must name us as an insured in the amount of the loan and must insure the Security Instrument to be valid first lien on the property, free from all exceptions except those approved by us. If questions of survey are raised in connection with the title policy, we may/will require you to furnish us with a survey of the subject property.

Hazard Insurance

We must be furnished at closing with a copy of an original policy of hazard insurance or an original 90-day binder with a paid receipt for the first year's insurance premium insuring the subject property against loss by fire and hazards included in the term "extended coverage", and such other hazards as is customary to insure against in the area where the property is located. Coverage should be for at least the amount of the loan or the replacement cost of the property, whichever is less. If replacement cost is less than the loan amount, your appraisal must include a breakdown of land value and replacement cost. This insurance policy must be obtained from an acceptable company (Best general rating of at least B and a financial size rating of at least III),

FIGURE 7–19
(continued)

must be in a form acceptable to us, and must have a loss payable provision designating the mort-gagee as follows:

[Name of Bank], its successors and/or assigns,

Address _____

Loan # _____

Assessments

Special assessments may be assumed provided that the assessment is recognized on the Appraisal or CRV or an amendment to the Appraisal or CRV. The appraised value must be reduced by the un-paid amount of the special assessment which will reduce your maximum mortgage amount.

Legal Documents

The Note and Security Instrument evidencing and securing the loan must be executed and delivered to us at the loan closing and must be acceptable to us in the form and substance.

Payment of Fees

By accepting this commitment, Buyer/Seller agrees to pay all closing costs, including recording fees, mortgage registration tax, tax service fees, fees or premiums for title examination, abstract of title, title insurance, survey expenses, appraisal fees, private mortgage insurance (if applicable), cost of credit report, document preparation fees, and attorney's fees (if outside counsel is engaged by us).

Legal Compliance

The Property must comply with applicable zoning, building, and other laws and regulations.

Modification

We reserve the right to withdraw this approval, or to modify the terms as required, if any material facts appear which have not been previously revealed to us by you.

FIGURE 7–19
(continued)

Web Exercise

Commitments can be subject to regulatory oversight. See the State of Vermont's policy and corresponding regulation at www.bishca.state.vt.us/BankingDiv/regsbulletins/bnkregs/REG_B-98–1.htm.

Commitments may also pose other request such as asking the borrower to submit evidence of a satisfactory credit report, appraisal, receipt of mortgage insurance, verification of information and application documents, and satisfaction of all other terms and conditions that involves dis-count points. Some standard qualifications involved in commitments are:

- Approved plans and specifications
- Architect's/engineer's report
- Certificate of Completion
- Certificate of Occupancy
- Permits, licenses, and approvals
- Surveys

- Compliance with environmental regulations
- Hazardous materials report
- Casualty
- Flood insurance
- Appraisal
- Legal counsel's report
- Organizational compliance
- Financial certification
- Choice of law
- Title insurance policy
- Encumbrance of chattels
- Lease approval
- Leasing status
- Subordination of leases
- Tenant estoppel certificates
- Assignment of rents and leases
- Proof of insurance
- Tax information/deposits
- Restrictions
- Acceleration prepayment charge
- Submission of documents
- Closing costs
- Nonassignment of commitment
- Expiration of commitment
- Commitment fee
- Payment of processing fee
- Payment of nonrefundable fee
- Loan discount fees
- Payoff of current loan
- Ground lease approval
- Subordination of ground lease
- Personal liability
- Guaranty agreement
- Master lease
- Letter of credit
- Escrow funds
- Certificate of deposit
- Tenant improvements
- Declaration of easements and restrictions
- Partial release or subordination of lien
- Buy and sell agreement
- Interest rate subject to adjustment[26]

Failure to meet one or any of these conditional requirements makes the commitment either a nullity or voidable. As an example, unsatisfactory environmental findings or well water pump rate may negate the commitment. Paul Katcher writes:

> The commitment letter generally conditions the lender's obligation to close the loan on the collateral being free from environmental contamination. This gives the lender the option of terminating the commitment if an environmental problem is discovered during the commitment stage. Generally, the lender agrees to return the borrower's commitment fees less the lender's out-of-pocket legal and environmental survey expenses if the commitment is terminated for this reason.[27]

With this style of conditional language, lenders can protect their financial integrity by verifying the information contained in the application. Let us face it; lenders cannot be naive about all material facts posed in the application documents. Simply put, borrowers can and do lie. On the other hand, lenders can be just as underhanded and fraudulent. At times, lenders have been known to exercise business in an arbitrary way. The courts are seeing increasing litigation on the matter of lender negligence. Robert Shadur, in *Avoiding Lender Liability in the Loan Commitment Stage*, points this out:

> As a corollary to the contract obligation of good faith, borrowers may allege that lender was negligent in exercising its duty to process or administer loan applications and commitments. Some courts have found that lenders owe borrowers a duty to process a loan application with reasonable care. However, lenders do not incur a duty to exercise reasonable care when they demand documents under a loan commitment to assure the adequacy of loan collateral.[28]

To be sure, nervousness in the mortgage market reaches its apex at the commitment stage. Loan commitments should be defensively drafted. Shadur continued, "When preparing a loan commitment, be sure to include all material terms; a commitment cannot be too complete. Consider the following items:

- Detailed statement of purpose of loan and use of funds
- Expiration date
- Type of loan
- Nature of financing (accounts, inventory, equipment, and similar items)
- List of collateral
- Terms of the note (i.e., interest rate, prepayment penalty, period of payment, and repayment terms)
- Cross-default provisions, if any
- Cross-collateralization provisions, if any
- Restrictions on sale or transfer
- Nature and scope of required guarantees
- Specific default provisions
- Waiver of borrower's right of redemption
- The nature of any escrows to be established
- Special title insurance endorsement
- Documents to be required from or by third parties."[29]

Proponents of easier mortgage application processes and greater credit fluidity have criticized this type of defensive posturing.

Conditional commitments travel all the way to the closing table. Banks will reiterate these closing conditions in loan transmittal packages, closing instructions, and other documentation relative to the settlement process. See the example entitled Notification of Underwriting Approval and Closing Conditions in Figure 7–20.

DATE:
BORROWER:
CASE #:
LOAN #:
PROPERTY ADDRESS:

NOTIFICATION OF UNDERWRITING APPROVAL AND CLOSING CONDITIONS

We are pleased to inform you that your application has been underwritten, and you qualify for a loan with the following terms:

Loan Type: _____
Loan Amount: $_____
Interest Rate: _____ %
Term: _____ years

This approval is subject to the following conditions:
   If a condition is changed, it must be certified prior to the issuance of loan documents.

1. Hazard Insurance in the amount of $_____ (required prior to closing)
2. The loan must contain in all respects with the requirements of FHA, VA, FHMA, FHLMC, or the applicable investor.

( ) 3. _____
( ) 4. _____
( ) 5. _____
( ) 6 _____
( ) 7. _____

Underwriting approval is valid for 30 days from the date of this notification. If the documentation used to underwrite your loans expires during this 30-day period, the information must be cancelled and updated. If there is any material change to your income or credit standing prior to loan closing, this approval is void.

NOTIFICATION OF UNDERWRITING APPROVAL IS **(name of company)** DETERMINATION OF YOUR ABILITY TO MEET THE FINANCIAL OBLIGATIONS OF THE LOAN. IT IS NOT A COMMITMENT TO MAKE A LOAN AT ANY PARTICULAR RATE OR TERMS OR FOR ANY PARTICULAR PERIOD OF TIME, NOR DOES IT GUARANTEE THE AVAILIABILITY OF THE TYPE OF LOAN FOR WHICH UNDERWRITING APPROVAL IS GIVEN. SUCH A COMMITMENT CAN BE OBTAINED ONLY THROUGH EXECUTION OF **(name of company)** DISCOUNT POINT COMMITMENT.

( ) A Discount Point Commitment has been issued for this loan and expires on _____

( ) No Discount Point Commitment has been issued for this loan. Interest rate and discount points must be negotiated prior to loan closing.

Sincerely,

(name of company)
By: _____ Date: _____

We, the undersigned, understand and accept the terms and conditions set forth above

_____   _____   _____   _____
Borrower   Date   Borrower   Date

_____   _____   _____   _____
Borrower   Date   Borrower   Date

FIGURE 7–20

CHAPTER SEVEN **SUMMARY**

Chapter Seven discussed the following topics:

- The nature of a mortgage or deed of trust
- The contents and purpose of a mortgage document
- The contents and purpose of a mortgage note
- Information collected prior to the application phase
- Different types of mortgage products and their advantages and disadvantages
- The process of mortgage application and the various corresponding documentation
- Notification documents required by law
- Real Estate Settlement and Procedures Act requirements and the good faith estimate
- Appraisal and survey requirements
- The purpose and necessity of a mortgage commitment

REVIEW **QUESTIONS**

1. Explain the basic features of a balloon mortgage.
2. What government document estimates the costs of a loan?
3. What is the purpose of an acceleration clause?
4. Explain the difference between a mortgage and a note.
5. In addition to credit rating, what other factors are considered by a lender when deciding to approve or disapprove a loan?
6. What various types of governmental mortgage programs exist?
7. What type of mortgage uses a due-on-transfer rider?
8. Name three government notification documents that are used during the application process.
9. What is the purpose of a mortgage commitment?
10. What is mortgage insurance?

DISCUSSION **QUESTION**

Your client discusses financial capacity in light of mortgage selection. The client is young, shows promise for the future, but is presently cash short. What mortgage products should be recommended? Name four and discuss why you would recommend them.

EXERCISE 1

Using the following fact pattern, complete a Uniform Residential Loan Application:

Borrower—Joy Johnson
Mortgage Type—Conventional
Mortgage Amount—$100,000
Interest Rate—7.5%
Number of Months—360

Insurance and Taxes in Escrow—Yes

Prepayment Option—Yes

Property Street Address—303 Wayside Lane

City—Mytown

County—Brown

State and Zip Code—US, 00000

Purpose of Loan—Purchase

Address—Apt. 6, Firefly Road, Mytown, US 00001

Length of Residency—7 years

Annual Income—$75,000

Dividends and Interest—$1,200 per year

Current Rent Payment—$600 per month

Purchase Price—$110,000

Closing Costs—$10,000

Prepaid Escrow—$2,000

Other Financing—No

Cash Deposit—$10,000

Marital Status—Single

Dependents—No

Employer—Widget Corp., 2 West End Drive, Mytown, US

Years Employed—10

Position Title—Division Manager

Type of Business—Manufacturing

Social Security Number—000-00-0000

Phone—555-111-2222

Business Phone—555-222-1111

Reference—Platinum Card, Plaza Eight, Mytown, US; Acct. # 098765; revolving credit line, highest balance—$7,000

Reference—National Bank, Plaza Two, Mytown, US, Acct. # 123456; auto loan, $17,500

Checking and Saving Account—$12,000

Stocks and Bonds—$25,000

Life Insurance Value—$50,000

Retirement Fund—$12,000

Automobiles—2001 Saturn; $12,000

Personal Property—$50,000

Debt—National Bank, $422 per month; $6,250 unpaid balance

Debt—The Platinum Card; $140 per month; $4,200 unpaid balance

Year Property Built—1984

EXERCISE 2

Locate an online Amortization Table generator. Using the facts from Exercise 1 and from the Case of John and Martha, generate two amortization tables.

Assignment for the Case of John and Martha

Complete a mortgage application using the following additional information:

Mortgage Type—Conventional
Interest Rate—6.5%
Number of Months—120
Insurance and Taxes in Escrow—Yes
Prepayment Option—Yes
Purpose of Loan—Purchase
Dividends and Interest—$1,200 per year
Closing Costs—$10,000
Prepaid Escrow—$2,000
Reference for John—the Platinum Card, Plaza Eight, Mytown, US; Acct. # 098765; revolving credit line, highest balance—$7,000
Reference for Martha—National Bank, Plaza Two, Mytown, US, Acct. # 123456; auto loan, $17,500
Checking and Saving Account—John—$12,000
Checking and Saving Account—Martha—$8,000
Stocks and Bonds—John—$25,000
Stocks and Bonds—Martha—$2,000
Life Insurance Value—Martha—$50,000
Life Insurance Value—John—$500,000
Retirement Fund—John—$12,000
Automobiles—Martha—2001 Saturn; $12,000
Automobiles—John—2005 Chrysler 300M; $25,000
Personal Property—John—$50,000
Personal Property—Martha—$30,000
Debt—Martha—National Bank, $422 per month; $6,250 unpaid balance
Debt—John—The Platinum Card; $140 per month; $4,200 unpaid balance
Year Property Built—1984

REFERENCES

1. U.S. Dept. Of Labor, Bureau Of Labor Statistics: Occupational Handbook: 2008–2009.

2. Daniel R. Levitan, *Alternative Financing Sources for the 1990s*, 6 Real Est. Fin. J. 42, 25 (1990); *see also* Fred Wright, *Commentary: The Effect of New Deal Real Estate Residential Finance and Foreclosure Policies in Response to the Real Estate Conditions of the Great Depression*, 57 Ala. L. Rev. 321 (2005); Robert M. Zimman and Novica Petrosvski, *The Home Mortgage and Chapter 13: An Essay in Unintended Consequences*, 17 Am. Bankr. Inst. L. Rev. 133 (2009); Jack Cummings, The Real Estate Finance And Investment Manual (1997); William Miles, *Irreversibility, Uncertainty and Housing Investment*, 38 J. Real Est. (2007).

3. *Id.* at 25.

4. Freddie Mac, *Primary Mortgage Market Survey*, at www.freddiemac.com/pmms/release.html.

5. All-State Legal, One Commerce Drive, Cranford, NJ, Form 204S.

6. Easy Soft Inc., 212 North Center Drive, North Brunswick NJ 08902, www.easysoft-usa.com, Mortgage Note.

7. Colorado Department of Regulatory Agencies, Division of Real Estate, *Deed of Trust* at www.dora.state.co.us/real-estate/contracts/2008Contracts/TD72%20_Strict_91708.pdf.

8. Pennsylvania Association of REALTORS®, 4501 Chambers Hill Road, Harrisburg, PA 17111–2406.

9. Joseph L. Fishman & Richard E. Strauss, *What to Do Upon Discovery of a Problem Real Estate Loan,* 37 Prac. Law. Jan. 1991, at 89, 90–91.

10. *Id.* at 91.

11. David Crump & Jerome Curtis Jr., The Anatomy of a Real Property Transaction 19 (1984).

12. Veteran's Administration, *Funding Fee Table* at www.homeloans.va.gov/docs/funding_fee_tables.doc.

13. Reprinted courtesy of The State Bar of Wisconsin. Available at http://www.wi.ctic.com/documents/mortgage.doc

14. Federal Reserve Bank of Boston, Public Policy Discussion Papers, *Making Sense of the Subprime Crisis* (2008) at www.bos.frb.org/economic/ppdp/2009/ppdp0901.pdf.

15. Fla. Stat. §817.545 (2008).

16. Shaun M. Brady, *Greater Efficiencies Needed in Bank Loan Process,* 7 Real Est. Fin. J. 49, 54 (1992); *see also* Anthony Faranda-Diedrich, *Recent Case: Pennsylvania Commonwealth Courts Holds That a Lawyer May Be Liable for Malpractice for Failure to Ensure That a Mortgage Is Properly Filed and Indexed,* 49 Vill. L. Rev. 233 (2004).

17. 15 U.S.C. §1681 et seq. (2009).

18. 15 U.S.C. §1691 (2009).

19. 12 U.S.C. §3401 et seq. (2009).

20. 12 U.S.C. §3404 (2009).

21. *See* Office of the Comptroller of the United States, Truth in Lending: Compliance Handbook (2008) www.occ.treas.gov/handbook/til.pdf.

22. Webster A. Collins, *There Is No Such Thing as a Final Estimate of Value,* 8 Real Est. Fin. J. 85 (1993).

23. Fishman & Strauss, *supra* note 9, *at* 89.

24. Uniform Standards of Professional Appraisal Practice, 2008–2009 edition, 209.190.242.26/html/USPAP2008/index.htm.

25. Shannon J. Skinner, *A Practical Guide to Survey Review* (with Checklist), 9 Prac. Real Est. Law, 45, 54–5 (1993).

26. *See* Sidney A. Keyles, *How to Draft Mortgage Loan Commitments from the Lender's Perspective,* 8 Prac. Real Est. Law., Jan. 1992, at 41, 45 et seq.; *see also* Tracie R. Porter, *The Anatomy of Real Estate Contract Forms for New Real Estate Attorneys,* 17 CBA Record 34 (2009).

27. Paul Katcher, *Lending Practices That Guard Against Environmental Liability,* 7 Real Est. Fin. J., Fall 1991, at 14, 15.

28. Robert Shadur, *Avoiding Lender Liability at the Loan Commitment Stage,* 6 Prac. Real Est. Law, 47, 50 (1990).

29. *Id.* at 53.

Closing and Settlement

LEARNING OBJECTIVES

- To prepare and compute closing documents.
- To schedule the closing process.
- To describe the nature of RESPA and client education.
- To explain prorations and their computation.
- To compute a settlement sheet and have all necessary documents recorded by the appropriate government authority.

JOB COMPETENCIES

- To educate the client regarding RESPA.
- To conduct a closing.
- To compute a settlement sheet.
- To make settlement distributions.
- To resolve settlement disputes.
- To create a closing tickler or checklist system.
- To record documents in one's particular jurisdiction.
- To verify and distribute all remaining escrow funds.

ETHICAL CONSIDERATIONS

The paralegal must be aware of the following ethical dilemmas during this phase of a real estate transaction:

- Unauthorized practice of law
- Lawyer supervision of nonlawyers
- Confidentiality issues
- Conflicts of interest
- Partnerships between lawyers and nonlawyers
- Communications with persons outside of law firm

I. INTRODUCTION

Once a title search is complete, a mortgage or other financing is arranged, and all conditions and contingencies set out in the agreement of sale are met or satisfied, the parties will commence the closing on the property. To close is synonymous with the term "settle," the agreement reaching its fruition, the transfer of property taking place. The party entrusted with closing varies according to jurisdiction but can and does include lawyers, title clerks, paralegals, and other closers. Some states have historically designated only attorneys, though these limitations are under severe pressure. New Jersey's exclusive lawyer closing system has just been overturned by the state's highest court, allowing for abstract and title companies to enter the marketplace. It would appear that the exclusivity club for lawyers and lawyers alone is on the wane. While paralegals must ever be mindful of their proper role, it is clear that the tasks of closing and settlement are highly administrative rather than legalistic. A recent joint opinion by the United States Department of Justice and the Federal Trade Commission broke down historic barriers to all but lawyers. See Figure 8–1.

This opinion reflects the historic protectionism to the advantage of the paralegal and legal assistant, and given the tasks of closing, a better fit is unlikely.

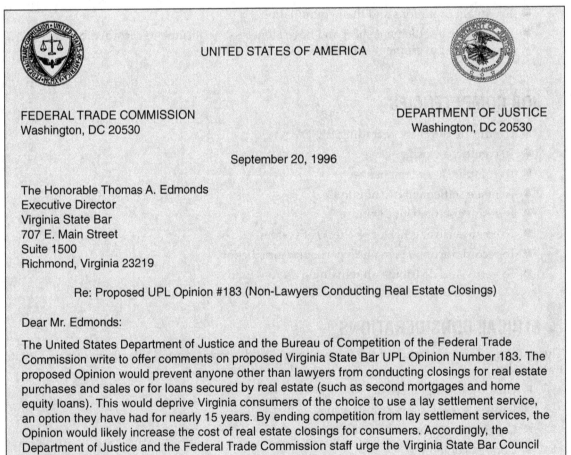

UNITED STATES OF AMERICA

FEDERAL TRADE COMMISSION
Washington, DC 20530

DEPARTMENT OF JUSTICE
Washington, DC 20530

September 20, 1996

The Honorable Thomas A. Edmonds
Executive Director
Virginia State Bar
707 E. Main Street
Suite 1500
Richmond, Virginia 23219

Re: Proposed UPL Opinion #183 (Non-Lawyers Conducting Real Estate Closings)

Dear Mr. Edmonds:

The United States Department of Justice and the Bureau of Competition of the Federal Trade Commission write to offer comments on proposed Virginia State Bar UPL Opinion Number 183. The proposed Opinion would prevent anyone other than lawyers from conducting closings for real estate purchases and sales or for loans secured by real estate (such as second mortgages and home equity loans). This would deprive Virginia consumers of the choice to use a lay settlement service, an option they have had for nearly 15 years. By ending competition from lay settlement services, the Opinion would likely increase the cost of real estate closings for consumers. Accordingly, the Department of Justice and the Federal Trade Commission staff urge the Virginia State Bar Council to reject this Opinion.

FIGURE 8–1
(continues)

The Interest And Experience Of The U.S. Department of Justice And The Federal Trade Commission

The United States Department of Justice and the Federal Trade Commission are entrusted with enforcing this nation's antitrust laws.

For more than 100 years, since the passage of the Sherman Antitrust Act, the United States Department of Justice has worked to promote free and unfettered competition in all sectors of the American economy. Restraints on competition can force consumers to pay higher prices or accept goods and services of lower quality. Accordingly, such restraints are of significant concern, whether they are imposed by a "smokestack" industry or by a profession. Restraints on competition in any market have the potential to harm consumers. The Justice Department's civil and criminal enforcement programs are directed at eliminating such restraints. The Justice Department also encourages competition through advocacy letters such as this.

Congress has directed the Federal Trade Commission to prevent unfair methods of competition and unfair or deceptive acts or practices in or affecting commerce. The Federal Trade Commission has particular concern about restrictions that may adversely affect the competitive process and raise prices (or decrease quality or services) to consumers. Because the Commission has broad responsibility for consumer protection, it is also concerned about acts or practices in the marketplace that injure consumers through unfairness or deception. Pursuant to this statutory mandate, the Federal Trade Commission encourages competition in the licensed professions, including the legal profession, to the maximum extent compatible with other state and federal goals. The Commission has challenged anticompetitive restrictions on the business practices of state-licensed professionals, including lawyers. In addition, the staff has conducted studies of the effects of occupational regulation and submitted comments about these issues to state legislatures, administrative agencies, and others. The Commission also has had significant experience in analyzing and challenging restrictions on competition in the real estate industry.

UPL Opinion No. 183

UPL Opinion Number 183 would declare the conduct of real estate closings by anyone other than an attorney to be the unauthorized practice of law. The proposed Opinion would prohibit lay settlement services from conducting closings for real estate sales and for any loans secured by real estate, such as home equity loans and refinancings. Although the proposed Opinion permits the closing attorney to delegate certain tasks to lay people, it requires that the attorney "actively oversee all aspects of the closing." Moreover, the proposed Opinion would bar a Virginia attorney who is employed by a title agency from performing real estate closings. Consequently, the proposed Opinion would require a consumer who otherwise might retain a real estate agent, title company, bank or other lay settlement service for a closing instead to hire his or her own lawyer.

UPL Opinion No. 183 was issued by The Standing Committee on the Unauthorized Practice of Law at the request of a member of the Virginia State Bar. The Virginia State Bar Council and the Supreme Court of Virginia must approve the Opinion to make it binding authority.

The Proposed Opinion Will Likely Adversely Affect Consumers

Free and unfettered competition is at the heart of the American economy. As the United States Supreme Court has observed, "ultimately competition will produce not only lower prices but also better goods and services. The heart of our national economic policy long has been faith in the value of competition.'" National Society of Professional Engineers v. United States, 435 U.S. 679, 695 (1978); accord Superior Court Trial Lawyers' Association, 493 U.S. 411, 423 (1990). Competition benefits consumers of both traditional manufacturing industries and the learned professions. Goldfarb v. Virginia State Bar, 421 U.S. 773, 787 (1975); National Society of Professional Engineers, 435 U.S. at 689.

FIGURE 8–1
(continued)

The proposed Opinion would restrain competition by erecting an artificial barrier to competition from lay settlement services and would deprive Virginia consumers of the option of closing real estate transactions without the services of an attorney. The proposed Opinion has the potential to increase costs for consumers in two ways. First, it would force consumers who would not otherwise hire an attorney for a real estate closing to do so. The restriction would adversely affect all consumers who might prefer the combination of price, quality, and service that a lay settlement service offers. It would particularly affect consumers who are obtaining home equity loans or refinancing existing real estate loans. A number of banks currently handle such closings without charge. Second, the proposed Opinion, by eliminating competition from lay settlement services, would likely cause the price of lawyers' settlement services to increase. Even consumers who choose a lawyer over a settlement company would likely pay higher prices.

This has been the experience elsewhere. The New Jersey Supreme Court, in holding last year that non-lawyers may conduct closings and settlements, found that real estate closing fees were lower in southern New Jersey, where lay settlements were commonplace, than in the northern part of the State, where lawyers conducted almost all settlements. Southern New Jersey buyers who were represented by counsel throughout the entire transaction, including closing, paid, on average, $650, while sellers there paid $350. Northern New Jersey sellers paid $750 in lawyers' fees on average and buyers, $1,000. In re Opinion No. 26 of the Committee On The Unauthorized Practice of Law, 654 A.2d 1344, 1348–49 (N.J. 1995).

There is no reason to expect Virginia's experience to be different. In 1981, the Attorney General of Virginia issued an Economic Impact Statement analyzing proposed UPL rules that would have permitted only lawyers to conduct real estate closings and would have required title insurance companies to issue policies only through attorneys. The Attorney General found that there was "significant evidence that costs to the consumer will remain higher in Virginia than they otherwise might be." He based his conclusion, in part, on data from 1979–80 HUD studies that appeared to show that consumers pay more when lawyers are involved in all residential real estate closings. Attorney General of Virginia, Economic Impact Statement, 1980–81 Op. Atty. Gen. Va. 427 (March 12, 1981). Moreover, according to information the staff has gathered from industry representatives, costs for settlement in Virginia have fallen since lay settlement services began operating about 15 years ago.

During the past 15 years, the use of lay closing services has grown steadily in Virginia. In northern Virginia, lay settlement services now perform a large number of closings. In the Richmond area, they perform a substantial number, and in the Norfolk-Virginia Beach area, the number is growing. In many other States as well, lay settlement services and attorneys compete in the provision of real estate closings.

Notwithstanding the popularity of lay settlement services, in many situations, the assistance of a licensed lawyer is necessary. A consumer might choose an attorney to answer legal questions, negotiate disputes, or offer various protections. Consumers who hire attorneys may get better service and representation at the closing than those who do not. But, as the New Jersey Supreme Court has concluded, this is not a reason to eliminate lay closing services as an alternative for consumers who wish to utilize them. In re Opinion No. 26, 654 A.2d at 1360. Rather, the choice of using a lawyer or a non-lawyer should rest with the consumer. Id. As the United States Supreme Court noted,

> The assumption that competition is the best method of allocating resources in a free market recognizes that all elements of a bargain—quality, service, safety, and durability—and not just the immediate cost, are favorably affected by the free opportunity to select among alternative offers.

National Society of Professional Engineers, 435 U.S. at 695 (emphasis added); accord Superior Court Trial Lawyers' Association, 493 U.S. at 423. Permitting competition by lay services allows consumers to consider more relevant factors in selecting a provider of settlement services, such as cost, convenience, and the degree of assurance that the necessary documents and commitments are sufficient.

FIGURE 8–1
(continued)

Restraints similar to the one proposed here have been adopted in the past, with similar anticompetitive effects. For example, the Justice Department obtained a judgment against a county bar association that restrained title insurance companies from competing in the business of certifying title. The bar association had adopted a resolution requiring lawyers' examinations of title abstracts and had induced banks and others to require the lawyers' examinations in real estate transactions. United States v. Allen County Indiana Bar Association, Civ. No. F-79-0042 (N.D. Ind. 1980). Likewise, the Justice Department obtained a court order prohibiting another county bar association from restricting the trust and estate services that corporate fiduciaries could provide in competition with attorneys. United States v. New York County Lawyers' Association, No. 80 Civ. 6129 (S.D.N.Y. 1981).

The basis for the proposed Opinion—and for all regulation of the unauthorized practice of law—is the risk that a lay person will make a mistake that a lawyer would not and thereby harm a consumer. Significantly, the proposed Opinion cites no actual instances of consumer injury. Instead, it relies upon hypotheticals. Hypotheses alone are an insufficient basis for restricting competition in a way that is likely to harm consumers, especially in the face of 15 years of favorable experience with lay services in Virginia. One reason for the absence of problems may be the increasing use of standardized loan forms, now necessary for reselling a mortgage in the secondary market. These reduce the likelihood of error and the need for independent legal judgment. In addition, a substantial number of closings now involve home equity loans or refinancings of existing loans. Because a related transaction has already gone through the closing process once, legal questions are less likely to arise.

Moreover, uninformed consumers could be protected by measures far less anticompetitive than an outright ban on non-lawyer closings. For example, the New Jersey Supreme Court required written notice of the risk involved in proceeding with a real estate transaction without an attorney. In re Opinion No. 26, 654 A.2d at 1363. Disclosure, and an appropriate opportunity for consumer waiver, would appear to address the possibility of a conflict of interest on the part of the settlement company (see page 4 of the proposed Opinion). Alternatively, the State may wish to regulate lay settlement services more closely. We urge the Council to consider these alternatives if it deems additional consumer protections warranted.

Conclusion

In sum, proposed UPL Opinion Number 183, which would prevent non-lawyers from conducting settlements, is likely to have significant anticompetitive consequences. Consumers are likely to pay higher prices and face restricted choice without obtaining significant countervailing benefits. Accordingly, we urge the Council to reject the proposed Opinion.

We appreciate the opportunity to present our views. Please contact us if you have any questions or if we can help in any way.

Sincerely yours,

Anne K. Bingaman
Assistant Attorney General
Jessica N. Cohen, Trial Attorney
United States Department of Justice
Antitrust Division

William J. Baer
Director
Randall Marks, Attorney
Federal Trade Commission
Bureau of Competition

FIGURE 8–1
(continued)

To close is to make permanent the buyer's and seller's intentions. If one agrees that a residential home purchase is the most serious investment the average person makes, it is easy to appreciate how buyers and sellers view the closing transaction. Most parties are nervous and somewhat intimidated by the process. Anticipation, coupled with natural suspicions about legal and banking requirements, make the settlement environment a testy place at times. This is the place where paralegals endure and flourish. Settlement tables can be emotional settings. Paralegals can alleviate the tension by having control of the documents, a cool demeanor, and a professional preparedness. Too frequently the players in a real estate transaction act as adversaries. Small inconveniences and trifles become major catastrophes and landslides. Attorney John H. Kupillas Jr. recognizes this tendency:

> Little things get blown out of proportion. Of course, clients can often get extremely upset over "little" things. Missing light fixtures, tables and chairs as well as other items of personal property can be the source of much conflict. Why? Surely the purchase and sale of residential real estate is, to a very large degree, an emotional event. Therefore, seemingly insignificant things can set off these emotions. It is our job as attorneys to diffuse this over-reaction by putting things in perspective. An effective attorney in this area (as in most areas) must be a good psychologist. The ability to deal with people in this area is a far greater asset than legal knowledge.[1]

The climate is essentially developed by those who orchestrate the closing. This being so, confrontations can be avoided if the paralegal ensures that all is in order before the assigned date and time. Communicate the content and calculations of closing before the parties ever reach the table. No surprises mean no chance for argument.

The sheer number of players involved in the typical real estate closing causes some problems. To illustrate the following parties are likely participants:

- Seller
- Attorney for seller
- Buyer
- Attorney for buyer
- Banker
- Title insurance company
- Hazard policy insurance company
- Practitioners and paralegals from other offices
- Government agencies
- Mortgage authorities
- Tax officials
- Zoning authorities
- Parties who must attend the closing
- Real estate agents
- Brokers

Communication to, by, and between these parties is essential to effective closing and settlement.

II. SOFTWARE PROGRAMS FOR CLOSING AND SETTLEMENT

Rarely will a Closing and Settlement take place by pen and pencil. Today's software packages, that assist the closer, are simply amazing. Aside from computation, modern software programs organize the entire process; track and trace the parties and necessary documentation and deliver key reminders and suggestions throughout the entire process. It is almost impossible to live without the software. Sprinkled throughout this text are samples from various delivery systems, including

FIGURE 8-2
Courtesy of Easy Soft Inc., 212 North Center Drive, North Brunswick NJ 08902, www.easysoft-usa.com.

Easy Soft—whose Easy HUD program is a dream product for the closer. Easy HUD cuts the demands of closing time and incorporates all new HUD Closing forms. See Figure 8–2.

The Nation's Top Real Estate Closing Software with Automated HUD Settlement Statements—Easy HUD simplifies the entire real estate closing process with automated HUD settlement statement preparation (HUD-1 & HUD-1A), disbursement check preparation/printing and 1099-S electronic filing. Real estate closings are always balanced. Plus, with Easy HUD you can automatically export real estate closing transactions to Easy Trust or QuickBooks for trust account bookkeeping.

Web Exercise

Download Easy HUD's free Demo at *www.easysoft-usa.com/download_demo.html?_pN_=EasyHUD&type= dHIwZV8x.*

Another reputable program is Argosy Power Closer. See Figure 8–3.

FIGURE 8-3
Courtesy Argosy Legal Systems.

Just as Easy Soft accomplishes, Power Closer does the standard documentation for the real estate transaction. In addition:

- Power Closer real estate closing software calculates and prints HUD-1 and HUD-1A settlement statements, buyer/borrower statements, seller statements, balance sheet and disbursement summary and 1099-S forms.
- Power Closer works with QuickBooks, Quicken 98 through 2004, and similar systems to print disbursement checks and balance and audit your trust accounts
- Create custom closing documents with WordPerfect or Microsoft Word by merging over 800 items from Power Closer.
- Add-on modules include end-of-year 1099 reporting and multiuser network support.
- Power Closer runs with Windows 95, 98, Me, NT, 2000, XP, or Vista.

Power Closer not only prepares the standard closing documentation, but also computes and keeps running tabs on money and disbursements. The program is capable of generating the following reports:

- Net Lender check, include or exclude any disbursement
- Broker commissions by points or percent
- Split sales commissions by points or percent
- Prorations: annual, semiannual, quarterly, monthly
- New loan principal and interest payment
- New loan prepaid (interim) interest payment
- New loan origination fee, loan discount
- Loan payoffs by seller
- Seller-financed real estate transactions
- Construction loan closings
- Refinance transactions
- Loan payoffs for refinance transactions
- Recording fees, look up city/county/state calculations
- Recording fees, payee is recalled by city/county/state
- Transfer fees, look up city/county/state calculations
- Transfer fees, payee is recalled by city/county/state
- Refund check(s) for excess payment by buyer or seller
- Monetary balances are continuously updated in real time

Web Exercise

Download and try Power Closer at *www.argosylegal.com/powerdn.htm*.

A third and final example of technology aiding the paralegal and the real estate team is a software product names ALTASTAR. As its competitors do, ALTASTAR generates basic documentation, computes and calculates costs and proceeds and delivers effective tracking tools to orchestrate the closing and settlement. Other features of the software include:

- Prepare and print HUD-1 Settlement Statement for Purchases, New Loans, and Refinances
- Automated Good Faith Estimate (GFE) entries' view

- Balance receipts, disbursements and net loan proceeds (cash from lender)
- Automatically create balanced list of deposits and checks
- Include form HUD-1A for refinances
- HUD-1 Addendum adds additional lines
- Change descriptions that print for most lines
- Convert to PDF to e-mail completed settlement statement
- Easily balance commissions retained by broker and excess deposits
- Check for program updates on Internet
- Automatic prorations
- Calculate loan payoff
- Computes advance interest to lender
- Calculates loan origination fee and loan discount
- A change of proration date or disbursement date automatically recalculates prorations, loan payoff and advance interest to lender
- Broker commissions may be entered by percent or amount
- Calculates recording fees
- Calculates stamps/taxes automatically
- Repeat payees without reentering
- Print 1099-S on blank Internal Revenue Service (IRS) forms
- Calculate transfer, stamp, intangible and mortgage taxes (Lines 1201–1205)
- Store transfer, stamp, intangible and mortgage tax rates for multiple jurisdictions to use for Lines 1201–1205 as needed
- Cash to/from buyer/seller updated instantly as amounts change
- Option to print "Draft" until HUD-1 Statement is finalized
- Access Windows calculator from program
- Pop-up Calendar for date entry
- 90 Days toll-free product

III. CLOSING DOCUMENTATION

KEY WORDS

Real Estate Settlement and
    Procedures Act (RESPA)

settlement statement

truth in lending
    disclosure

Paperwork drives closings. Preparation of the deed, mortgage, note and riders, and other documentation in the real estate transaction, as discussed in chapters 6 and 7, constitute the closing file. That file contains:

1. Survey
2. Loan payoff documents
3. Judgment certificates
4. Assumption statements and other documentation
5. Notice requirements under government loan programs
6. Leases, if applicable
7. Receipts for payment of all taxes, whether state, local, or special assessments
8. Certificates for septic, soil, percolation, and zoning rights
9. Insurance policies that cover hazard and occupational activities
10. Rough draft of a settlement sheet to be submitted to all the parties for their inspection before a settlement; a general form is provided by most title insurance companies who assist in the settlement process
11. Certificate of attorney as required
12. Termite inspection report: contracts are usually conditional upon satisfactory termite reports
13. Satisfaction pieces for mortgages
14. Evidence of satisfied judgments
15. Evidence of satisfied liens
16. Releases as needed
17. Septic tank inspection reports
18. Premise inspection documents
19. Certificate of occupancy
20. Final accounting
21. Checks from escrow account, whether real estate or attorney's office
22. Zoning certificates and waivers
23. Utility bills
24. Calculation on earnest money deposit interest.

These staggering paper requirements and the general lack of consumer sophistication have caused the U.S. Congress to enact laws that govern the real estate settlement. "Enacted by Congress in 1974, the **Real Estate Settlement and Procedures Act** (RESPA) (12 U.S.C. 2601, et seq.) was intended to regulate and reform various lending practices and closing and settlement procedures 'to insure that consumers throughout the Nation are provided with greater and more timely information on the nature and costs of the settlement process and are protected from unnecessarily high settlement charges caused by certain abusive practices.'"[2,3] RESPA attempts to give regularity to the settlement process and to thwart unfair and fraudulent practices. Any loan that has a federal connection, FHA, VA, underwritten by Fannie Mae, and so forth, is subject to the act. Cash deals and private owner mortgages (sometimes called purchase money mortgages) are beyond RESPA scrutiny.

CASE DECISION

The intricacies of closing and settlements often give rise to ethical complaints against the conduct of those conducting same. In 2006, Delaware disciplined an attorney.

IN THE SUPREME COURT OF THE STATE OF DELAWARE

IN THE MATTER OF A MEMBER	§	No. 313, 2006
OF THE BAR OF THE SUPREME	§	
COURT OF THE STATE OF	§	
DELAWARE	§	

Submitted: August 15, 2006
Decided: September 22, 2006

Before **STEELE,** Chief Justice, **HOLLAND,** and **RIDGELY,** Justices.

ORDER

This 22nd day of September 2006, it appears to the Court that the Board on Professional Responsibility filed its Report in this disciplinary matter recommending that the respondent-lawyer receive a private admonition for violating several of the Delaware Lawyers' Rules of Professional Conduct. Despite its recommendation of a private sanction in this case, the Board also recommended that its decision be made public in order to clarify for other members of the Delaware Bar a lawyer's responsibility to directly supervise the disbursement of funds from real estate transactions. Neither the ODC nor the respondent had any objections to the Board's Report and Recommendations. Accordingly, the Court directed the Board to file a public version of its Report redacting the name of the respondent. The Court has reviewed the matter pursuant to Rule 9(e) and concludes that the Board's Report and Recommendations should be approved.

NOW, THEREFORE, IT IS ORDERED that the redacted Report of the Board on Professional Responsibility filed on August 15, 2006 (copy attached) is hereby APPROVED. The matter is hereby CLOSED.

BY THE COURT:

_____
Chief Justice

(*continues*)

THE BOARD ON PROFESSIONAL RESPONSIBILITY
OF THE
SUPREME COURT OF THE STATE OF DELAWARE

In the Matter of a Member of	)	CONFIDENTIAL
the Bar of the Supreme Court	)	
of Delaware	)	Board Case No. 33, 2005

REPORT OF THE BOARD ON PROFESSIONAL RESPONSIBILITY

The Panel of the Board on Professional Responsibility appointed to hear this matter consisted of David J. Ferry, Jr., Esquire (Chair), Donald A. Blakey, Ph.D. and R. Brandon Jones, Esquire. A hearing was held in the Supreme Court Courtroom in Wilmington, Delaware on February 21, 2006. The Office of Disciplinary Counsel ("ODC") was represented by Mary S. Much, Esquire, who has subsequently been replaced by Andrea L. Rocanelll, Esquire and Respondent, ("respondent") was represented by Ian Connor Bifferato, Esquire, and Joseph R. Biden, III, Esquire. After the hearing, the Panel received submissions from both parties and an *amicus* memorandum of law from the Real and Personal Property Section of the Delaware State Bar Association.

BACKGROUND

A Petition for Discipline was filed against the respondent by the ODC on October 5, 2005. The Petition for Discipline alleged four counts charging the respondent with violations of Rule 1.4(b), Rule 1.16 Interpretive Guideline Re: Residential real estate transactions, Rule 5.3, and Rule 5.5(a), as follows:

COUNT ONE: Failure to Explain a Matter to the Extent Reasonably Necessary to Make an Informed Decision in violation of Rule 1.4(b).

COUNT TWO: Failure to Provide a Written Statement in violation of Rule 1.16 Interpretive Guideline Re: Residential real Estate transactions.

COUNT THREE: Responsibilities Regarding Non-Lawyer Assistants in violation of Rule 5.3.

COUNT FOUR: Assisting in the Unauthorized Practice of Law in violation of Rule 5.5(a).

Respondent filed an answer to the petition and denied all four counts of the petition and requested that the petition be dismissed.

FACTS AND EVIDENCE PRESENTED AT THE HEARING

The ODC's opening statement to the Board indicated that the issue in this matter was whether a lawyer can permit disbursement of real estate proceeds through a third party, that is, a title company. The ODC submitted that when Delaware attorneys delegate this function to an outside party, there is no way for the attorney to supervise the matter and they can, therefore, not protect the public. The ODC indicated its intention to call Edward Tarlov, Esquire and Michelle Nadeau to testify.

Respondent's counsel acknowledged that the ODC has the ability to protect the public by seeking redress against members of the bar, but in this case argued that the respondent complied with all but one issue which was that the attorney must have in writing a document that confirms the client's right to choose their counsel. In their opening comments to the Board, respondent's counsel indicated that an attorney must have in writing a document that expressly presents to his client that client's right to have separate counsel and that respondent would testify that he believes he, in fact, did present his client with the right to separate counsel and explained that right, but admitted that he did not have a written document to present at the hearing. Respondent's counsel, therefore, indicated that was one area in which respondent does not contest the ODC's complaint.

The ODC clarified that it was asking the Board to make findings of fact that the respondent's failure to provide his client with a writing outlining her absolute right to retain an attorney of her choice to

(*continued*)

represent her in the real estate transaction and then charging a fee for his services was in violation of Rule 1.16, Interpretative Guideline Re: Residential real estate transactions. The ODC further confirmed that this matter has been brought to clarify an existing ruling of court in the matter of Mid-Atlantic Settlement Services, Inc., et al.—Board of the Unauthorized Practice of Law case (2000 WL 97-5062 Del.Supr.) ("Mid-Atlantic"). A copy of the Mid-Atlantic decision was attached to the Petition for Discipline.

The ODC's first witness, Edward Tarlov, testified that he has been a practicing Delaware attorney for twenty years and is the chair of the Real and Personal Property Section of the Delaware State Bar Association. His business consists strictly of real estate transactions with the majority of his practice handling residential real estate transactions.

Mr. Tarlov indicated that when he receives a referral to represent a buyer, he sends a Rule 1.16 conflict letter out to the buyer. The conflict letter insures that the buyer is aware that they have an absolute right to choose any attorney. Mr. Tarlov explained the process of representing a client in a real estate transaction. He confirmed that to ensure that the funds are in his account, someone in his office pulls up the account using a computer program and ensures that the funds were issued on a certified check. Mr. Tarlov and his CPA review accounts to ensure that they are reconciled. He indicated that he uses settlement software to write the checks for settlements and an attorney in his office is required to sign the checks. Mr. Tarlov does not believe that funds in the case involving the respondent would have "bounced" if they came from the attorney escrow account.

Mr. Tarlov's belief is that the Mid-Atlantic case requires that a Delaware lawyer perform real estate transactions for the transfer of property and refinancing. One of the protections to the client having a lawyer perform the settlement includes a required compliance whereby the bank that has the escrow account must notify the Supreme Court if there are insufficient funds in the account. He believes the Mid-Atlantic decision requires that all funds flow through the real estate firm's escrow account if the attorney is the settlement agent.

Respondent's client, Michelle Nadeau (formerly Michelle Flanders), also testified in this matter. She indicated that she decided to refinance her home in January of 2003 and contacted First Central Mortgage after receiving a mailing from them. Ms. Nadeau first learned of the respondent's involvement with the refinance after the mortgage broker at First Central Mortgage informed her that he would be the attorney who would be conducting the real estate refinancing settlement. Respondent's office contacted Ms. Nadeau about a week prior to the September 22, 2003 settlement. Ms. Nadeau testified she did not receive anything from respondent's office regarding her absolute right to retain any attorney. She also testified that she was unaware that the funds from the settlement would be coming to her from Advance Settlement Services ("Advance"). She believed that she would receive funds from respondent's office. She did not discuss who would be disbursing the funds with respondent or First Central Mortgage. She knew the funds would not be disbursed until after the three day recision period required under refinancing transactions. She did not believe the respondent thoroughly reviewed all of the mortgage documents with her although she agreed that she signed all of the documents. She did not recall asking respondent to change the credit cards that were to be paid from the refinance.

Ms. Nadeau received three disbursement checks in the mail. The checks were issued on September 26, 2003 by Advance Settlement Agency. She received a check for $9,114.00 payable to MBNA, a check for $8,732.00 payable to CitiBank, and a check for $1,994.06 payable to herself. She understood that the $1,194.06 check was to go into an escrow account for her taxes and insurance after she made her first payment. She testified the CitiBank check was immediately mailed to CitiBank and cashed. She testified the other checks were not cashed because she was out of town immediately following the arrival of the checks. When she returned, she mailed the MBNA check, but it did not clear because the account on which the check was written had been closed.

Ms. Nadeau tried to contact respondent and First Central Mortgage, but received little to no assistance. She eventually contacted the Delaware State Police. Based on their efforts, Dwayne Pope of Advance Settlement Agency is currently incarcerated in Pennsylvania. Ms. Nadeau and respondent have been in contact with the title insurance company. Respondent told Ms. Nadeau that he would not

(*continued*)

be able to recover her funds because it is an unsecured debt. Respondent assisted Ms. Nadeau in filing a complaint with the Pennsylvania Board for Client Protection. That board informed her that Mr. Pope had never been a licensed attorney in Pennsylvania and, therefore, they could not give her any relief. She has not filed a claim with the Delaware Lawyers Fund for Protection because the Attorney General's Office advised her that she should contact the police. Ms. Nadeau paid off her MBNA account in September of 2005 with money from her late father's estate. She subsequently sold the house that she refinanced because of her debt and her inability to obtain any more equity from the home.

A law clerk in respondent's office testified on behalf of respondent. The law clerk is a member of the Delaware, New Jersey and New York Bars. Since September of 2005, he has handled residential real estate settlements in Delaware. He was present at the refinancing settlement of Ms. Nadeau to fulfill his Delaware clerkship requirements. He arrived to the settlement late and noticed about half of the documents had already been signed. Upon his arrival, respondent stopped the proceedings and explained the documents to him that had already been discussed and signed by Ms. Nadeau. The respondent also went over the general procedures of a refinancing settlement.

The law clerk stated that he believed that Ms. Nadeau was rushing through the settlement and signing the documents in a hurried manner. He testified that respondent was trying to explain the documents to Ms. Nadeau, but she seemed to have little interest in what he was saying to her. The entire process took fifteen to twenty minutes from the time the law clerk entered the room to the end of the settlement conference. He believes that he entered the room approximately half-way through the completion of the settlement and that it normally takes thirty to forty minutes to complete a settlement.

Respondent testified that he was admitted to practice in Delaware in 1994. He presently works as a solo practitioner primarily in the area of real estate law. He is a member of the Real and Personal Property Section of the Delaware State Bar Association, has been performing real estate closings on his own for the past ten years, and in his cases he has disbursed funds from his attorney escrow account as well as through third party accounts.

Respondent was first contacted about Ms. Nadeau's settlement in the summer of 2003. He was asked to prepare a new deed for the property that would remove Ms. Nadeau's ex-husband from the title. He receives referral cases much the same way as other members of the Bar. He testified that Advance is the title company that contacted him and First Central Mortgage was the mortgage broker.

Respondent indicated that he received referrals from Advance on a regular basis. He never disbursed funds from his escrow account when he worked with Advance. His relationship with Advance occurred in 2002 and 2003. He has not had any other cases that involved a theft by a third party. He testified that Advance Title Company and Advance Settlement Agency were both title companies. Advance performed closings in Pennsylvania, but does not perform closings in Delaware. In this case, Advance Title Company through their title company, Stewart Title, submitted a closing protection letter ("CPL") to the lender. The purpose of the CPL is to protect the bank in the case of misuse or fraud of the funds from Advance Title. Respondent believed that the CPL protected the borrower as well as the lender because the lender issued a commitment letter to the borrower. The bank is protected by the CPL from the title company and, in turn, the borrower is protected by the commitment letter from the bank. The complication arose in this case because the CPL was issued by Stewart Title Company and the title binder was issued by Security Title. Respondent does not know why two title companies were used in this case, but the result was that the two title companies lay blame on each other. Respondent is under the assumption that the title company is required to make the borrower whole in a case of misappropriation of funds by their closing agent pursuant to the terms of the CPL.

Respondent testified as to the process in handling the settlement. He testified that he asked Ms. Nadeau if it was acceptable for the law clerk to sit in on the closing. The respondent stated that he included as part of his regular practice a Supreme Court conflict notice that puts the borrower on notice of their absolute ability to retain counsel of their choosing at the time of closing; however, he cannot produce the conflict letter that he states Ms. Nadeau signed. He indicated his practice at the time was to have borrowers sign the Supreme Court letter at the time of closing.

(continued)

Respondent spoke with Ms. Nadeau about Advance's role in the refinance. Their discussion arose regarding Ms. Nadeau's request to change some of the refinance disbursements. Respondent said he made it clear Ms. Nadeau's disbursements would come from Advance. The disbursement sheet from the settlement indicates that respondent was in contact with Advance regarding changes to Ms. Nadeau's disbursements. He never mentioned that the payments would be coming from his escrow account.

Respondent became aware of the problems with the checks when a check written to him for his work on Ms. Nadeau's case bounced. He spoke with Ms. Nadeau in October regarding her MBNA check. That check had bounced because Stewart Title obtained an injunction against Dwayne Pope's real estate escrow account due to his fraud. Respondent was not able to collect his fee in this case. He spoke to Ms. Nadeau about remedying the problem. He contacted the title company and recommended that she file a claim with the Lawyer's Fund for Client Protection in Pennsylvania. Respondent was under the impression that Mr. Pope was a Pennsylvania attorney, but he was not.

Respondent testified that he stays current in real estate law through his membership in the Real and Personal Property Section of the Bar and discussions with other attorneys. He became aware of the Mid-Atlantic decision around a year after it was issued. He did not receive any indication that real estate rules had changed as a result of the Mid-Atlantic decision. He testified no one contacted him about ceasing to do third party closings. He testified there are a number of other attorneys that allow third parties to disburse funds. Respondent believes he is able to oversee the disbursement of funds because a third party cannot disburse funds without his approval. When a settlement occurs, respondent gives the title company a signed settlement sheet with notes on post-closing disbursement issues. Respondent only inquires about the disbursement if there is a delay or if the borrower inquires as to why funds have not been disbursed. Respondent did not receive a call that Ms. Nadeau's funds had been disbursed nor did he contact Advance to be sure that the lender had sent the funds to Advance. Respondent does not receive copies of checks that are sent to the borrower.

Respondent testified that he is protected from a stop payment on a check written from his escrow account because of the commitment letter from the bank. A borrower in a third party case is protected because of the CPL. A lender will not release funds until they receive the CPL. A title company has the right to audit an attorney's books to see if they have any stale checks in violation of the Delaware rules.

Respondent testified he has not personally reviewed any of Advance's records, but LandAmerica, a title agency, reviewed their agent's reconciliations and bank accounts to insure that there were no stale checks. Respondent believes Mr. Pope's business was shut down because Stewart Title discovered that there were problems with the accounts. Respondent is not aware of the details of Mr. Pope's criminal case. He was not aware that Mr. Pope had pled guilty to charges of conspiracy.

Respondent testified he is ultimately responsible for reviewing all paperwork that is completed in his office. He engages in monthly reconciliations of his account required by Rule 1.15. He realizes that if a check bounced in his account, a notice would be sent to the ODC. Respondent believes the title insurance company that issued the CPL is responsible to make sure that the funds are good funds and, therefore, would be responsible for paying Ms. Nadeau's claim. He believes Ms. Nadeau is protected by the CPL because of the lender's commitment letter. Respondent believes that the Real and Personal Property Section of the Bar Association should provide a bright line rule for the Mid-Atlantic case and how that case affects real estate closings.

The ODC submitted one exhibit which spelled out the traditional role of Delaware attorneys in transactions involving Delaware real property. Respondent submitted ten exhibits as follows:

Respondent's Exhibit 1 was a letter from Advance Settlement Agency to the attorney's office dated 8/22/03 directing that a new deed be prepared removing Dean Flanders from the title;

Respondent's Exhibit 2 was not admitted;

Respondent's Exhibit 3 was an addendum to note signed by Ms. Nadeau on 9/22/03;

(*continued*)

Respondent's Exhibit 4 was a copy of the HUD-1 Settlement Statement dated 9/22/03;

Respondent's Exhibit 5 was a signed copy of the HUD-1 Settlement Sheet dated 9/22/03;

Respondent's Exhibit 6 was a document copy policy/receipt acknowledgment signed by Ms. Nadeau on 9/22/03;

Respondent's Exhibit 7 was a note from respondent to Dennis regarding Ms. Nadeau's questions about pay-offs and escrows in her monthly payment;

Respondent's Exhibit 8 was a closing service letter dated 9/5/03;

Respondent's Exhibit 9 was a fax confirmation dated 9/5/03 for the closing service letter dated 9/5/03;

Respondent's Exhibit 10 was an unsigned document titled "In anticipation of your upcoming purchase or refinance, the following is the required Delaware Supreme Court conflict notice".

ANALYSIS, FINDINGS AND DECISION

As framed by the ODC in its opening statement to the Board, the question presented is whether it is a breach of professional responsibility for a Delaware attorney performing a real estate settlement to permit a non-licensed party to be responsible for the disbursement of settlement funds in connection with the real estate settlement.

It is clear that respondent has failed to provide a written statement in violation of Rule 1.16 Interpretive Guideline Re: Residential real estate transactions as the respondent was unable to produce a signed copy of the document at the hearing. In addition, respondent testified that it was his practice in 2003 to have a borrower sign such a document at the settlement table. This practice violated Rule 1.16 Interpretive Guideline as the written disclosure, even if it was provided, was not provided in writing at the earliest practicable time as required by Rule 1.16(a).

The more difficult question is whether respondent committed other ethical violations in allowing Advance to act as the disbursing agent for the refinancing proceeds. The Board has concluded that the respondent has committed a violation of Rule 5.3—Responsibilities Regarding Non-Lawyer Assistants—because by allowing Advance to disburse the settlement funds, the respondent could not properly supervise the disbursement of funds and comply with the requirements, accountability, and oversight embodied in Rule 1.15 and Rule 1.15(A) of the Delaware Lawyers Rules of Professional Conduct.

It would also appear to be a violation of Rule 5.5(a)—Assisting in the Unauthorized Practice of Law—to permit a non-licensed party (the title company) to receive and be responsible for the disbursement of loan proceeds in a real estate settlement.

The latest expression of what constitutes the practice of law in connection with real estate settlements is found in the Mid-Atlantic decision. In Mid-Atlantic, the Board held that real estate settlements constitute the practice of law and, therefore, it was necessary for settlements to be held by a Delaware attorney. The Board set forth aspects of a real estate settlement that constituted the practice of law which, among other things, included "supervising the disbursement of funds" . . .

Although the Board's decision in Mid-Atlantic did not specifically address what supervising the disbursement of funds entailed, it is clear from the decision that the Board wished to provide clients with the benefit and protection of the control and oversight of the Delaware Supreme Court. The accountability and oversight was later embodied in Rule 1.15 and Rule 1.15(A) of the Delaware Lawyers Rules of Professional Conduct. These procedures, among other things, require an attorney to keep funds separate from his own property, to maintain funds in a separate trust or escrow account, to reconcile the account monthly, and to allow those accounts to be subject to examination by the auditor for the Lawyers Fund for Client Protection. The rules also govern trust account overdraft notification. With respect to trust or escrow accounts maintained pursuant to the rules, the ODC is provided notice if a trust or escrow account has insufficient funds. This allows for immediate response by the ODC if a situation such as the one that occurred here had arisen.

(continued)

The protections afforded under Rules 1.15 and 1.15(A) will be rendered meaningless if a Delaware attorney could obviate responsibility under the rules by permitting non-licensed persons or entities to control the disbursement of funds in a real estate settlement. The Board concludes that a Delaware attorney who permits a non-licensed party to receive and control the disbursement of loan proceeds on behalf of a real estate client has violated the responsibilities regarding non-lawyer assistants pursuant to Rule 5.3 and has assisted in the unauthorized practice of law in violation of Rule 5.5(a).

RECOMMENDATIONS

In light of the fact that respondent's case appears basically to be a test case to obtain clarification of the <u>Mid-Atlantic</u> decision and the respondent appears to have no improper motive in his handling of this matter, it is the recommendation of the Board that respondent receive a private reprimand for his violation of Rule 1.16 Interpretive Guideline Re: residential real estate transactions, Rule 5.3 and Rule 5.5(a), and that the Court make public its determination and ruling that attorneys must directly supervise the disbursement of funds from real estate transactions and do so only through Rule 1.15(A) trust accounts in the future.

DONALD A. BLAKEY, Ph.D.

R. BRANDON JONES

DAVID J. FERRY, JR.

A. Compliance Documentation

Since most residential settlements have significant document volume, errors can sometimes occur in document preparation. Lenders ask for authorization to correct errors. See Figure 8–4.

B. Inspection Contract

For the most part, agreements of sale describe a buyer's right to inspect the subject property before final closing. This inspection right is exercisable usually between 24 to 48 hours before settlement. In the absence of a major system's malfunction or the agreement specifying other rights, the closing process will continue. The other major force in the closing process, aside from governmental demands, is the banking industry, which finances the transaction; the bulk of documentation and agreements at closing is generated at their insistence. A review of the more frequently witnessed closing documents and correspondence steps follow.

Web Exercise

There have been a host of abuses in the world of home inspections. Professional standards are urgently needed. Visit National Association of Certified Home Inspectors—*www.nachi.org*.

C. Mortgages, Notes, and Related Documents

Mortgages and notes are discussed in Chapter 7. Any mortgage applicant will soon experience the incredible array of related documents, at both the time of application and as a requirement for closing. The amount and style of such documentation differs widely and depends upon the type of mortgage product.

Most lenders will demand a series of executed addenda that will deal with the terms of the loan, governmental conditions, escrow, insurance, floor plan, and zoning. Basically, the lender, secondary mortgage markets like Fannie Mae and Freddie Mac insurance, and governmental

---

ERRORS AND OMISSIONS/COMPLIANCE AGREEMENT

LENDER: _____

BORROWERS:_____

PROPERTY ADDRESS:_____

LOAN NO.:_____

In consideration of the Lender's funding and closing of this loan, the borrower(s) agree(s), if requested by Lender or Closing Agent for Lender, to fully cooperate and adjust for clerical error, any or all loan closing documentation if deemed necessary or desirable in the reasonable discretion of Lender to enable Lender to sell, convey, seek guaranty or market the loan to any entity, including but not limited to an investor, Federal national Mortgage Association, Federal Home Loan Mortgage Corporation, Government National Mortgage Association, Federal Housing Authority or the Department of Veterans Affairs, or any Municipal Bonding Authority.

The borrower(s) agree(s) to comply with all above noted requests by the Lender within 30 days from date of mailing of the requests. Borrower(s) agree(s) to assume all costs including, by way of illustration and not limitation, actual expenses, legal fees and marketing losses for failing to comply with correction requests in the above noted time period.

The borrower(s) do hereby so agree in order to assure that this loan documentation executed will conform and be acceptable in the marketplace in the instance of transfer, sale or conveyance by Lender of its interest in and to the loan documentation, and to assure marketable title in the borrower(s).

Dated this _____ day of _____, 20___.

_____   _____

(Borrower)   (Borrower)

FIGURE 8–4

authorities mandate the extent of documentation. At the federal level under the RESPA, lenders have many performance requirements, such as differentiating between total loan payments and the amount of interest over a designated term. See the **Truth in Lending Disclosure** Statement, commonly known as the Regulation Z document, in Figure 8–5.

A Good Faith Estimate of all relevant costs in the Closing and Settlement should also be finalized. HUD has just published a new format for the Good Faith Estimate. See Figure 8–6.

If the total loan sum includes closing costs added to principal, a declared itemization is necessary. See Figure 8–7.

Escrow agreements, whereby a borrower is required to deposit reserves covering taxes, insurance, and mortgage payments are a typical banking disclosure. See Figure 8–8.

D. Leases

The closing officer must recognize any remaining leasehold right or obligation. If an existing lease on a property to be conveyed is still in force, the tenant has a superior right of possession despite the conveyance. Leases that extend beyond the closing date must be renegotiated and drafted.

E. Title Documentation

Chapter 5 addressed the subject of title and its related documentation. From the attorney's abstract to a final certificate of title, this type of documentation is generally conveyed to the lender or title company. Title policies, affidavits, and related applications are usually produced at settlement. Correspondence to both the buyer and lender on the importance of the title policy should be provided.

TRUTH IN LENDING DISCLOSURE STATEMENT

Creditor	Applicant(s)
Mailing Address	Property Address
Loan Number	Preparation Date

ANNUAL PERCENTAGE RATE The cost of your credit as a yearly rate.	FINANCE CHARGE The dollar amount the credit will cost you.	Amount Financed The amount of credit provided to you or on your behalf.	Total of Payments The amount you will have paid after you have made all payments as scheduled.
E %	ES	ES	ES

PAYMENT SCHEDULE:

NUMBER OF PAYMENTS	* AMOUNT OF PAYMENTS	MONTHLY PAYMENTS ARE DUE BEGINNING	NUMBER OF PAYMENTS	* AMOUNT OF PAYMENTS	MONTHLY PAYMENTS ARE DUE BEGINNING

* Includes mortgage insurance premiums, excludes taxes, hazard insurance or flood insurance.

DEMAND FEATURE: ☐ This loan does not have a Demand Feature   ☐ This loan has a Demand Feature.

ITEMIZATION: You have a right at this time to an ITEMIZATION OF AMOUNT FINANCED.
I/We ☐ do ☐ do not want an itemization.

REQUIRED DEPOSIT:
☐ The annual percentage rate does not take into account your required deposit.

VARIABLE RATE FEATURE:
☐ This Loan has a Variable Rate Feature. Variable Rate Disclosures have been provided to you earlier.

SECURITY: You are giving a security interest in:

ASSUMPTION: Someone buying this property
☐ cannot assume the remaining balance due under original mortgage terms.
☐ may assume, subject to lender's conditions, the remaining balance due under original mortgage terms.

FILING / RECORDING FEES: $

PROPERTY INSURANCE:
☐ Property / hazard insurance is a required condition of this loan. Borrower may purchase this insurance from any insurance company acceptable to the lender.
Hazard insurance ☐ is ☐ is not available through the lender at an estimated cost of   for a   month term.

LATE CHARGES: If your payment is more than   days late, you will be charged a late charge of   % of the overdue payment.

PREPAYMENT: If you prepay this loan in full or in part, you
☐ may ☐ will not have to pay a penalty.
☐ may ☐ will not be entitled to a refund of part of the finance charge.

See your contract documents for any additional information regarding non-payment, default, required repayment in full before scheduled date, and payment refunds and penalties.
E means estimate.

I/We hereby acknowledge reading and receiving a complete copy of this disclosure. I/We understand there is no commitment for the creditor to make this loan and there is no obligation for me/us to accept this loan upon delivery or signing of this disclosure.

_____	_____	_____	_____
	Date		Date
_____	_____	_____	_____
	Date		Date

GENESIS 2000, INC. * W15.0 * (800) 882-0504   Form RegZD (03/95)

FIGURE 8–5

OMB Approval No. 2502-0265

Good Faith Estimate (GFE)

Name of Originator	Borrower
Originator Address	Property Address
Originator Phone Number	
Originator Email	Date of GFE

Purpose

This GFE gives you an estimate of your settlement charges and loan terms if you are approved for this loan. For more information, see HUD's *Special Information Booklet* on settlement charges, your *Truth-in-Lending Disclosures,* and other consumer information at www.hud.gov/respa. If you decide you would like to proceed with this loan, contact us.

Shopping for your loan

Only you can shop for the best loan for you. Compare this GFE with other loan offers, so you can find the best loan. Use the shopping chart on page 3 to compare all the offers you receive.

Important dates

1. The interest rate for this GFE is available through [   ]. After this time, the interest rate, some of your loan Origination Charges, and the monthly payment shown below can change until you lock your interest rate.

2. This estimate for all other settlement charges is available through [   ].

3. After you lock your interest rate, you must go to settlement within [ ] days (your rate lock period) to receive the locked interest rate.

4. You must lock the interest rate at least [ ] days before settlement.

Summary of your loan

Your initial loan amount is	$
Your loan term is	years
Your initial interest rate is	%
Your initial monthly amount owed for principal, interest, and any mortgage insurance is	$ per month
Can your interest rate rise?	☐ No ☐ Yes, it can rise to a maximum of %. The first change will be in
Even if you make payments on time, can your loan balance rise?	☐ No ☐ Yes, it can rise to a maximum of $
Even if you make payments on time, can your monthly amount owed for principal, interest, and any mortgage insurance rise?	☐ No ☐ Yes, the first increase can be in and the monthly amount owed can rise to $. The maximum it can ever rise to is $
Does your loan have a prepayment penalty?	☐ No ☐ Yes, your maximum prepayment penalty is $
Does your loan have a balloon payment?	☐ No ☐ Yes, you have a balloon payment of $ due in years.

Escrow account information

Some lenders require an escrow account to hold funds for paying property taxes or other property-related charges in addition to your monthly amount owed of $ [   ].

Do we require you to have an escrow account for your loan?

☐ No, you do not have an escrow account. You must pay these charges directly when due.

☐ Yes, you have an escrow account. It may or may not cover all of these charges. Ask us.

Summary of your settlement charges

A	Your Adjusted Origination Charges *(See page 2)*	$
B	Your Charges for All Other Settlement Services *(See page 2)*	$
A + **B**	Total Estimated Settlement Charges	$

FIGURE 8–6
(continues)

Understanding
your estimated
settlement charges

Your Adjusted Origination Charges	
1. Our origination charge This charge is for getting this loan for you.	
2. Your credit or charge (points) for the specific interest rate chosen ☐ The credit or charge for the interest rate of [____] % is included in "Our origination charge." (See item 1 above.) ☐ You receive a credit of $[_____] for this interest rate of [____] %. This credit **reduces** your settlement charges. ☐ You pay a charge of $[_____] for this interest rate of [____] %. This charge (points) **increases** your total settlement charges. The tradeoff table on page 3 shows that you can change your total settlement charges by choosing a different interest rate for this loan.	
A Your Adjusted Origination Charges	$

Some of these charges can change at settlement. See the top of page 3 for more information.

Your Charges for All Other Settlement Services	
3. Required services that we select These charges are for services we require to complete your settlement. We will choose the providers of these services. *Service* *Charge*	
4. Title services and lender's title insurance This charge includes the services of a title or settlement agent, for example, and title insurance to protect the lender, if required.	
5. Owner's title insurance You may purchase an owner's title insurance policy to protect your interest in the property.	
6. Required services that you can shop for These charges are for other services that are required to complete your settlement. We can identify providers of these services or you can shop for them yourself. Our estimates for providing these services are below. *Service* *Charge*	
7. Government recording charges These charges are for state and local fees to record your loan and title documents.	
8. Transfer taxes These charges are for state and local fees on mortgages and home sales.	
9. Initial deposit for your escrow account This charge is held in an escrow account to pay future recurring charges on your property and includes ☐ all property taxes, ☐ all insurance, and ☐ other [_____].	
10. Daily interest charges This charge is for the daily interest on your loan from the day of your settlement until the first day of the next month or the first day of your normal mortgage payment cycle. This amount is $[_____] per day for [____] days (if your settlement is [_____]).	
11. Homeowner's insurance This charge is for the insurance you must buy for the property to protect from a loss, such as fire. *Policy* *Charge*	
B Your Charges for All Other Settlement Services	$
A + **B** Total Estimated Settlement Charges	$

Good Faith Estimate (HUD-GFE)   2

FIGURE 8–6
(*continued*)

Instructions

Understanding which charges can change at settlement

This GFE estimates your settlement charges. At your settlement, you will receive a HUD-1, a form that lists your actual costs. Compare the charges on the HUD-1 with the charges on this GFE. Charges can change if you select your own provider and do not use the companies we identify. (See below for details.)

These charges **cannot increase** at settlement:	The total of these charges **can increase up to 10%** at settlement:	These charges **can change** at settlement:
■ Our origination charge ■ Your credit or charge (points) for the specific interest rate chosen *(after you lock in your interest rate)* ■ Your adjusted origination charges *(after you lock in your interest rate)* ■ Transfer taxes	■ Required services that we select ■ Title services and lender's title insurance *(if we select them or you use companies we identify)* ■ Owner's title insurance *(if you use companies we identify)* ■ Required services that you can shop for *(if you use companies we identify)* ■ Government recording charges	■ Required services that you can shop for *(if you do not use companies we identify)* ■ Title services and lender's title insurance *(if you do not use companies we identify)* ■ Owner's title insurance *(if you do not use companies we identify)* ■ Initial deposit for your escrow account ■ Daily interest charges ■ Homeowner's insurance

Using the tradeoff table

In this GFE, we offered you this loan with a particular interest rate and estimated settlement charges. However:

■ If you want to choose this same loan with **lower settlement charges,** then you will have a **higher interest rate.**
■ If you want to choose this same loan with a **lower interest rate,** then you will have **higher settlement charges.**

If you would like to choose an available option, you must ask us for a new GFE.

Loan originators have the option to complete this table. Please ask for additional information if the table is not completed.

	The loan in this GFE	The same loan with lower settlement charges	The same loan with a lower interest rate
Your initial loan amount	$	$	$
Your initial interest rate[1]	%	%	%
Your initial monthly amount owed	$	$	$
Change in the monthly amount owed from this GFE	No change	You will pay $ **more** every month	You will pay $ **less** every month
Change in the amount you will pay at settlement with this interest rate	No change	Your settlement charges will be **reduced** by $	Your settlement charges will **increase** by $
How much your total estimated settlement charges will be	$	$	$

[1] *For an adjustable rate loan, the comparisons above are for the initial interest rate before adjustments are made.*

Using the shopping chart

Use this chart to compare GFEs from different loan originators. Fill in the information by using a different column for each GFE you receive. By comparing loan offers, you can shop for the best loan.

	This loan	Loan 2	Loan 3	Loan 4
Loan originator name				
Initial loan amount				
Loan term				
Initial interest rate				
Initial monthly amount owed				
Rate lock period				
Can interest rate rise?				
Can loan balance rise?				
Can monthly amount owed rise?				
Prepayment penalty?				
Balloon payment?				
Total Estimated Settlement Charges				

If your loan is sold in the future

Some lenders may sell your loan after settlement. Any fees lenders receive in the future cannot change the loan you receive or the charges you paid at settlement.

 Good Faith Estimate (HUD-GFE) 3

FIGURE 8–6
(*continued*)

ITEMIZATION OF AMOUNT FINANCED

Creditor:	Applicant(s):
Mailing Address:	Property Address:
Loan Number: Loan Type:	Preparation Date: Estimated Interest Rate:

Loan Amount
Prepaid Finance Charge   – _____

Amount Financed   =

I/We hereby acknowledge reading and receiving a complete copy of this disclosure. I/We understand there is no commitment for the creditor to make this loan and there is no obligation for me/us to accept this loan upon delivery or signing of this disclosure.

_____ Date   _____ Date

_____ Date   _____ Date

Ellie Mae, Inc.   Form ItemDisc (03/95)

FIGURE 8–7

ESCROW AGREEMENT

AGREEMENT this _____ day of _____ _____ between

(hereinafter "Seller"),

(hereinafter "Borrower"),

ABC MORTGAGE CORPORATION (hereinafter "Lender")

In consideration of the mutual covenants contained herein and of completion of settlement for premises at:

subject to certain conditions on BORROWER'S Commitment not yet fulfilled, the undersigned covenant and agree that the sum of $ _____ is hereby deposited with LENDER as ESCROWEE PENDING completion of the following items:

and that SELLER shall complete this work on or before _____ in a manner acceptable to LENDER, its successors or assigns, and or the Veterans Administration, and the Federal Housing Administration, as the case may be.

IT IS UNDERSTOOD AND AGREED THAT LENDER SHALL MAKE ONLY SUCH INSPECTIONS OF THE PREMISES AS IT DEEMS NECESSARY AND THAT ANY SUCH INSPECTIONS AND ANY DISBURSEMENTS MADE HEREUNDER SHALL BE SOLELY WITHIN LENDER'S JUDGMENT AND ONLY FOR THE PROTECTION OF LENDER'S COLLATERAL INTEREST AND NOT AS THE AGENT FOR EITHER PARTY HERETO. LENDER ASSUMES NO RESPONSIBILITY TO INSPECT THE QUALITY OF WORKMANSHIP AND ASSUMES NO RESPONSIBILITY FOR THE COMPLETION OF THE AFORESAID ITEMS, EITHER IN ACCORDANCE WITH THE PLANS AND SPECIFICATIONS OR FOR THE PRICE CONTRACTED FOR, WHICH RESPONSIBILITIES REMAIN SOLELY WITH BORROWER.

If the said work is not completed and approved within time specified, this is to authorize, empower and direct LENDER or its nominees, as its or their option, to enter into and upon the premises and to finish the work to its satisfaction without liability for any entry, trespass, damages, or any other act committed.

It is further agreed that in the event of failure to comply with the terms of this covenant and agreement, the above funds may be used and expended without notice to complete the work in whatever manner LENDER may deem fit and for any costs, expenses or any loss incurred by LENDER in connection with obtaining insurance of the mortgage loan by the Federal Housing Administration (or guarantee of the loan by the Veterans Administration), without liability to see to the proper application or distribution thereof or accounting thereof; and that the SELLER AND BORROWER shall be jointly and severally liable for the payment of any costs or expenses incident to completion, or for any action necessary to defray expenses caused by failure to comply with the foregoing which shall not be covered by said escrow deposit.

If the work is completed by the Seller and approved by LENDER, its successors, assigns, and / or the aforesaid Governmental Agencies, if required, within the time specified the above funds shall be PAID TO SELLER upon production of receipts from parties furnishing labor and material for the completion of said work, in the event such proof is deemed necessary, unless there is an unpaid obligation of the SELLER due and owing to LENDER at the time the funds are to be released; in which event the SELLER hereby authorizes LENDER to apply all or part of the funds held under this agreement in full payments or as a partial payment of any indebtedness which may then be due. An inspection fee will be charged for any inspection made prior to the release of all escrow monies.

It is specifically agreed that NEITHER SELLER NOR BORROWER will assign the aforementioned funds, and that LENDER, its successors or assigns, shall not be bound to honor any assignment made in violation of this agreement and the SELLER AND BORROWER hereby agree to hold harmless, DEFEND and indemnify LENDER, its successors and assigns, against any loss or damage including court costs and attorney's fees which may result in the event the funds deposited herewith are assigned in contravention of this agreement.

This covenant and agreement shall be binding upon the HEIRS successors or assigns of the PARTIES.

THIS WRITTEN AGREEMENT CONTAINS THE ENTIRE AGREEMENT BETWEEN THE PARTIES RELATING TO THIS ESCROW DEPOSIT AND THERE ARE NO OTHER TERMS OR CONDITIONS, ORAL

FIGURE 8–8
(continues)

OR WRITTEN, CONCERNING THIS ESCROW DEPOSIT. THE PARTIES AGREE THAT THIS AGREEMENT SHALL NOT BE ALTERED, AMENDED, CHANGED OR MODIFIED, EXCEPT IN WRITING EXECUTED BY THE PARTIES HERETO AND THAT NEITHER LENDER, NOR ITS AGENTS, SUCCESSORS OR ASSIGNS, HAVE AUTHORITY TO MAKE ANY ORAL MODIFICATIONS OF THIS AGREEMENT. THEREFORE, THE PARTIES FURTHER AGREE THAT NO ORAL REPRESENTATION MADE BY ANY PARTY OR ITS AGENT AFTER THE EXECUTION OF THIS AGREEMENT SHALL BE BINDING OR HAVE ANY LEGAL FORCE OR EFFECT.

BY SIGNING THIS AGREEMENT, THE PARTIES AGREE THAT THEY HAVE READ, UNDERSTOOD AND INTENT TO BE BOUND BY THIS AGREEMENT.

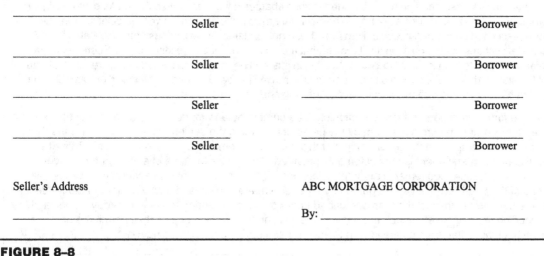

_____ Seller	_____ Borrower
_____ Seller	_____ Borrower
_____ Seller	_____ Borrower
_____ Seller	_____ Borrower

Seller's Address

ABC MORTGAGE CORPORATION

_____

By: _____

FIGURE 8–8
(*continued*)

F. Deed

It is customary for the seller to prepare, execute, and submit a deed to the presettlement agent. Types of deeds and their various components and provisions are discussed in Chapter 6.

G. The Settlement Sheet or Statement

Whether the property purchased is subject to mortgage financing is an integral factor in settlement. If nonowner/seller financing is involved, the RESPA basically dictates the method of reporting and calculation.

Web Exercise

Visit the United States Department of Housing and Urban Development's web location for information on the settlement process at *www.hud.gov/offices/hsg/ramh/res/respa_hm.cfm*.

Housing and Urban Development has promulgated a new format for the **Settlement Statement**. For the first time in more than thirty years, the U.S. Department of Housing and Urban Development (HUD) has issued long-anticipated mortgage reforms that will help consumers to shop for the lowest cost mortgage and avoid costly and potentially harmful loan offers. HUD will require, for the first time ever, that lenders and mortgage brokers provide consumers with a standard Good Faith Estimate (GFE) that clearly discloses key loan terms and closing costs. HUD estimates its new regulation will save consumers nearly $700 at the closing table. The entire RESPA process is guided by new statutory provisions, administrative regulations and the promulgation of new standards for the Closing process.

Sec. 2603. Uniform settlement statement

(a) The Secretary, in consultation with the Administrator of Veteran's Affairs, the Federal Deposit Insurance Corporation, and the Director of the Office of Thrift Supervision, shall develop and prescribe a standard form for the statement of settlement costs which shall be used (with such variations as may be necessary to reflect differences in legal and administrative requirements or practices in different areas of the country) as the standard real estate settlement form in all transactions in the United States which involve federally related mortgage loans. Such form shall conspicuously and clearly itemize all charges imposed upon the borrower and all charges imposed upon the seller in connection with the settlement and shall indicate whether any title insurance premium included in such charges covers or insures the lender's interest in the property, the borrower's interest, or both. The Secretary may, by regulation, permit the deletion from the form prescribed under this section of items which are not, under local laws or customs, applicable in any locality, except that such regulation shall require that the numerical code prescribed by the Secretary be retained in forms to be used in all localities. Nothing in this section may be construed to require that that part of the standard form which relates to the borrower's transaction be furnished to the seller, or to require that that part of the standard form which relates to the seller be furnished to the borrower.

(b) The form prescribed under this section shall be completed and made available for inspection by the borrower at or before settlement by the person conducting the settlement, except that (1) the Secretary may exempt from the requirements of this section settlements occurring in localities here the final settlement statement is not customarily provided at or before the date of settlement, or settlements where such requirements are impractical and (2) the borrower may, in accordance with regulations of the Secretary, waive his right to have the form made available at such time. Upon the request of the borrower to inspect the form prescribed under this section during the business day immediately preceding the day of settlement, the person who will conduct the settlement shall permit the borrower to inspect those items which are known to such person during such preceding day.[4]

1. Non-RESPA Settlement

In a cash deal, payment of the home purchase price and all related terms are within the standard agreement of sale. Instead of a full-blown settlement sheet, the parties conclude their transaction in memorandum form. Compared to the RESPA statement, there are far fewer calculations and reporting items. See Figure 8–9.

2. RESPA Settlement

The anchor document in a RESPA closing is the HUD-1 Settlement Statement, fully reproduced in Figure 8–10.

Inside the top border, items 1 through 8 and A–I, is information designating parties, agents, and the type of loan. Items J and K, Lines 100–603 cannot be completed until page 2 of the same form is completed. A summary review of the crucial lines on the sheet follows.

Lines 700–704: Total Sales/Broker's Commission If there is only one broker involved in the sale of the property, the broker's commission is normally paid in one lump sum. The commission can also be divided into installments if previously agreed upon. This calculation is made based on a percentage of the purchase price, usually 6 or 7 percent. Land or certain commercial transactions usually carry a higher rate of commission.

Lines 800–808: Items Payable in Connection with Loan Charges also relating to financing of the purchase price are listed as follows:

801–803: Points and up-front charges (loan origination and loan discount fees) are calculated. The borrower is always responsible for points under a real estate contract, unless another arrangement has previously been agreed upon. Certain governmental programs, such as FHA, defer the point expense to the seller.

MEMORANDUM OF SETTLEMENT

No. ....

Settlement made by

with

for purchase of Premises No.

Settled 20

Dr.

Consideration,

Taxes of Current year, $ from   20   to   20

House Rent

Cr.

Paid on account,

Water Rent, $ from   20   to   20

Interest on Mortgage,

House Rent,

Balance due Grantor

SETTLEMENT WITH GRANTOR	SETTLEMENT WITH GRANTEE
Fund Due Grantor in settlement .... $...........	Fund Due Grantor .... $.........
Mortgage .... $............	Title Charges .... $ ....
Mortgage .... $............	Title Charges ....$...........
Taxes and Water Rents .... $............	Taxes and Water Rents .... $............
Taxes and Water Rents ... . $............	Taxes and Water Rents .... $............
.... $...........	.... $...........
.... $...........	.... $...........
.... $...........	.... $...........
.... $........... $..........	.... $........... $........
	Credit deposited by ....
	.... $.........
Balance of settlement payable to Grantor $..........	Fund necessary to complete settlement $.........

The above settlement examined and approved, in consideration of which ....
is directed and authorized to make distribution and payments in accordance herewith.

Approved, and receipt of balance acknowledged   Approved,

....

            Grantor   Grantee

FIGURE 8–9

OMB Approval No. 2502-0265

A. Settlement Statement (HUD-1)

B. Type of Loan

1. ☐ FHA	2. ☐ RHS	3. ☐ Conv. Unins.	6. File Number:	7. Loan Number:	8. Mortgage Insurance Case Number:
4. ☐ VA	5. ☐ Conv. Ins.				

C. Note: This form is furnished to give you a statement of actual settlement costs. Amounts paid to and by the settlement agent are shown. Items marked "(p.o.c.)" were paid outside the closing; they are shown here for informational purposes and are not included in the totals.

D. Name & Address of Borrower:	E. Name & Address of Seller:	F. Name & Address of Lender:
G. Property Location:	H. Settlement Agent:	I. Settlement Date:
	Place of Settlement:	

J. Summary of Borrower's Transaction		K. Summary of Seller's Transaction	
100. Gross Amount Due from Borrower		**400. Gross Amount Due to Seller**	
101. Contract sales price		401. Contract sales price	
102. Personal property		402. Personal property	
103. Settlement charges to borrower (line 1400)		403.	
104.		404.	
105.		405.	
Adjustment for items paid by seller in advance		**Adjustments for items paid by seller in advance**	
106. City/town taxes to		406. City/town taxes to	
107. County taxes to		407. County taxes to	
108. Assessments to		408. Assessments to	
109.		409.	
110.		410.	
111.		411.	
112.		412.	
120. Gross Amount Due from Borrower		**420. Gross Amount Due to Seller**	
200. Amounts Paid by or in Behalf of Borrower		**500. Reductions In Amount Due to Seller**	
201. Deposit or earnest money		501. Excess deposit (see instructions)	
202. Principal amount of new loan(s)		502. Settlement charges to seller (line 1400)	
203. Existing loan(s) taken subject to		503. Existing loan(s) taken subject to	
204.		504. Payoff of first mortgage loan	
205.		505. Payoff of second mortgage loan	
206.		506.	
207.		507.	
208.		508.	
209.		509.	
Adjustments for items unpaid by seller		**Adjustments for items unpaid by seller**	
210. City/town taxes to		510. City/town taxes to	
211. County taxes to		511. County taxes to	
212. Assessments to		512. Assessments to	
213.		513.	
214.		514.	
215.		515.	
216.		516.	
217.		517.	
218.		518.	
219.		519.	
220. Total Paid by/for Borrower		**520. Total Reduction Amount Due Seller**	
300. Cash at Settlement from/to Borrower		**600. Cash at Settlement to/from Seller**	
301. Gross amount due from borrower (line 120)		601. Gross amount due to seller (line 420)	
302. Less amounts paid by/for borrower (line 220)	( )	602. Less reductions in amount due seller (line 520)	( )
303. Cash ☐ From ☐ To Borrower		**603. Cash** ☐ To ☐ From Seller	

The Public Reporting Burden for this collection of information is estimated at 35 minutes per response for collecting, reviewing, and reporting the data. This agency may not collect this information, and you are not required to complete this form, unless it displays a currently valid OMB control number. No confidentiality is assured; this disclosure is mandatory. This is designed to provide the parties to a RESPA covered transaction with information during the settlement process.

FIGURE 8–10
(continues)

L. Settlement Charges

700. Total Real Estate Broker Fees		Paid From Borrower's Funds at Settlement	Paid From Seller's Funds at Settlement
Division of commission (line 700) as follows:			
701. $ to			
702. $ to			
703. Commission paid at settlement			
704.			

800. Items Payable in Connection with Loan			
801. Our origination charge $	(from GFE #1)		
802. Your credit or charge (points) for the specific interest rate chosen $	(from GFE #2)		
803. Your adjusted origination charges	(from GFE A)		
804. Appraisal fee to	(from GFE #3)		
805. Credit report to	(from GFE #3)		
806. Tax service to	(from GFE #3)		
807. Flood certification	(from GFE #3)		
808.			

900. Items Required by Lender to Be Paid in Advance			
901. Daily interest charges from to @ $ /day	(from GFE #10)		
902. Mortgage insurance premium for months to	(from GFE #3)		
903. Homeowner's insurance for years to	(from GFE #11)		
904.			

1000. Reserves Deposited with Lender			
1001. Initial deposit for your escrow account	(from GFE #9)		
1002. Homeowner's insurance months @ $ per month $			
1003. Mortgage insurance months @ $ per month $			
1004. Property taxes months @ $ per month $			
1005. months @ $ per month $			
1006. months @ $ per month $			
1007. Aggregate Adjustment –$			

1100. Title Charges			
1101. Title services and lender's title insurance	(from GFE #4)		
1102. Settlement or closing fee $			
1103. Owner's title insurance	(from GFE #5)		
1104. Lender's title insurance $			
1105. Lender's title policy limit $			
1106. Owner's title policy limit $			
1107. Agent's portion of the total title insurance premium $			
1108. Underwriter's portion of the total title insurance premium $			

1200. Government Recording and Transfer Charges			
1201. Government recording charges	(from GFE #7)		
1202. Deed $ Mortgage $ Releases $			
1203. Transfer taxes	(from GFE #8)		
1204. City/County tax/stamps Deed $ Mortgage $			
1205. State tax/stamps Deed $ Mortgage $			
1206.			

1300. Additional Settlement Charges			
1301. Required services that you can shop for	(from GFE #6)		
1302. $			
1303. $			
1304.			
1305.			

1400. Total Settlement Charges (enter on lines 103, Section J and 502, Section K)		

FIGURE 8–10
(*continued*)

Comparison of Good Faith Estimate (GFE) and HUD-1 Charges		Good Faith Estimate	HUD-1
Charges That Cannot Increase	**HUD-1 Line Number**		
Our origination charge	# 801		
Your credit or charge (points) for the specific interest rate chosen	# 802		
Your adjusted origination charges	# 803		
Transfer taxes	#1203		

Charges That in Total Cannot Increase More Than 10%		Good Faith Estimate	HUD-1
Government recording charges	# 1201		
	# 1201		
	# 1201		
	# 1201		
	# 1201		
	#1201		
	#1201		
	#		
Total			
Increase between GFE and HUD-1 Charges		$	or %

Charges That Can Change		Good Faith Estimate	HUD-1
Initial deposit for your escrow account	#1001		
Daily interest charges	# 901 $ /day		
Homeowner's insurance	# 903		
	#		
	#		
	#		

Loan Terms

Your initial loan amount is	$
Your loan term is	years
Your initial interest rate is	%
Your initial monthly amount owed for principal, interest, and and any mortgage insurance is	$ includes ☐ Principal ☐ Interest ☐ Mortgage Insurance
Can your interest rate rise?	☐ No. ☐ Yes, it can rise to a maximum of %. The first change will be on and can change again every after . Every change date, your interest rate can increase or decrease by %. Over the life of the loan, your interest rate is guaranteed to never be **lower** than % or **higher** than %.
Even if you make payments on time, can your loan balance rise?	☐ No. ☐ Yes, it can rise to a maximum of $.
Even if you make payments on time, can your monthly amount owed for principal, interest, and mortgage insurance rise?	☐ No. ☐ Yes, the first increase can be on and the monthly amount owed can rise to $. The maximum it can ever rise to is $.
Does your loan have a prepayment penalty?	☐ No. ☐ Yes, your maximum prepayment penalty is $.
Does your loan have a balloon payment?	☐ No. ☐ Yes, you have a balloon payment of $ due in years on .
Total monthly amount owed including escrow account payments	☐ You do not have a monthly escrow payment for items, such as property taxes and homeowner's insurance. You must pay these items directly yourself. ☐ You have an additional monthly escrow payment of $ that results in a total initial monthly amount owed of $. This includes principal, interest, any mortgage insurance and any items checked below: ☐ Property taxes ☐ Homeowner's insurance ☐ Flood insurance ☐ ☐ ☐

Note: If you have any questions about the Settlement Charges and Loan Terms listed on this form, please contact your lender.

FIGURE 8–10
(*continued*)

804: The borrower usually pays an appraisal fee. This expense can range from $150 to $400 for a typical residential appraisal.

805: The borrower also pays for a credit report, required for all mortgage applications, ranging from $25 to $100.

806–807: Listed here are any tax service fees or flood certifications necessary to obtain the loan. Usually, these amounts are payable by the borrower.

Lines 900–904: Items Required by Lender to be Paid in Advance All lenders require certain items to be prepaid to ensure the economic viability of the loan. Interest is required to be paid in advance of the settlement as the borrower's expense.

Lines 1000–1007: Reserves Deposited with Lender A lender will require certain reserves such as hazard insurance, mortgage insurance, city and county taxes, and assessments to be deposited. Normally, lenders require between three and five months of reserves deposited with them.

Lines 1100–1108: Title Charges In this section, settlement closing fees, abstract searches, title searches, title binders, document preparation, notary fees, and title insurance acquisition are all calculated. These are buyer's expenses.

Lines 1200–1206: Government Recording and Transfer Charges This section includes recordation expenses for deeds, equally borne by the buyer and seller; mortgages and releases, which are usually the seller's responsibility; and the joint, equally divided, payment of transfer taxes, and apportioned city and county taxes.

Lines 1300–1305: Additional Settlement Charges Additional settlement charges may be either the buyer or seller's responsibility. Survey costs, pest inspection, water and sewer assessments, and other extraordinary charges are listed in the section. Once all of the charges are calculated, the total settlement charges for both the buyer and seller are entered in lines 103 and 502, respectively, on the front of the settlement sheet.

Personalty and settlement charges are added to the sales price at lines 102 and 402. City, town, and county taxes and other assessments are always prorated across the board. Stevens A. Carey writes: "A contractual obligation to prorate is therefore essential. It is not sufficient, however, to require only that prorations be made. The purchase contract should identify the method of proration with clear and precise language. Moreover, local counsel should be consulted regarding any local statutes or case law that might affect the interpretation of the language used."[5]

On lines 201–209, deposit or earnest money, new loans or existing loans, and so forth are listed. At line 220 the total paid by or for the borrower is subtracted from the total due, resulting in an outstanding balance or refund for the borrower at line 303.

The sales price, plus any personalty charges due to the seller, subtracted from any adjustments from line 420, is listed. At lines 501–509, the seller has to meet any existing cash obligations that are unpaid up to the settlement. A total reduction amount due the seller is at line 520. At line 600 the cash at settlement due to or from the seller is listed. The gross amount due to seller is listed at line 601. Line 603 lists the net cash due to or from the seller.

The newly revised HUD-1 includes a third page where a comparison is made between the settlement statement and the GFE. The first section includes a section on charges that cannot increase between the time the estimate was prepared and closing. Section 2 lists charges that cannot increase by more than 10%. Charges that can change are listed in section 3. There is also a section with loan specifics such as the loan amount, term, interest rate and type, pre-payment penalties, and balloon payment options.

Review the following facts. Tabulate them and insert in a blank settlement sheet. For the answer, see Appendix B.

Contract sales price—$260,000

Pro rata expenses:

City/town taxes—$445.95

County/state taxes—$1,980.90

School tax—$1,639.25

Borrower's Information

Deposit—$5,000

Principal amount of new loan—$175,000

Additional funds—$89,000

Loan expenses:

Document preparation—$100

Processing—$250

Tax service fee—$90

Interest paid in advance to lender—11/01/09 to 11/05/09; at $22.77/day

Settlement fee—$150

Title examination—$75

Title insurance binder—$25

Notary fees—$20

Title insurance—$487.50

Charge for endorsements 100 and 300—$80

Overnight delivery charge—$29

Recording fees:

Deed—$19.50

Mortgage—$23.50

Releases—$31

City/county tax/stamps for deed—$2,600

Seller's Information

Payoff of first mortgage loan—$66,680.77

Payoff of second mortgage loan—$119,060.70

Commission on contract sales price is 5.28%, divided equally between two brokers

Seller's distribution—$15

Overnight delivery—$30

State tax/stamps for deed—$2,600

Louise Friend is due $2,295 from seller

Borough certifications are due in the amount of $40

Final water bill—$44.98

Final sewage bill—$93.13

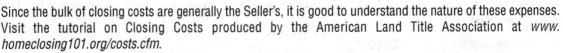

Web Exercise

Since the bulk of closing costs are generally the Seller's, it is good to understand the nature of these expenses. Visit the tutorial on Closing Costs produced by the American Land Title Association at *www.homeclosing101.org/costs.cfm*.

IV. CLOSING

Once all documentation is prepared and information is calculated, the parties are ready to close. Depending on local custom and practice principles, the party overseeing closing will vary. In some jurisdictions, the lawyer will be the preeminent figure. In others, the title company will tackle the task. In some circles, the paralegal will be entrusted with the responsibility. What is clear is that the allegation of "unauthorized practice of law" will have few supporters.

CASE DECISION

Virginia's recent claim, driven by the unauthorized practice claim, fell short in a 2007 ruling.

UNITED STATES OF AMERICA

January 3, 1997

David B. Beach, Clerk of Court

Supreme Court of Virginia

100 N. 9th Street, Fourth Floor

Richmond, Virginia 23219

Re: Proposed UPL Opinion #183

Dear Mr. Beach:

The United States Department of Justice and the Bureau of Competition of the Federal Trade Commission (1) submit these comments in opposition to proposed Virginia State Bar UPL Opinion Number 183. The Justice Department and the Federal Trade Commission do not generally comment on proposed unauthorized practice of law rule-makings, but offer these comments to prevent harm to competition and consumers. The proposed Opinion would generally prevent anyone other than lawyers from conducting closings for real estate purchases and sales or for loans secured by real estate. Adoption of the proposed Opinion will deprive Virginia consumers of the choice to use a lay settlement service, a choice they have had, and have increasingly exercised, for 15 years. Ending competition from lay settlement services will very likely increase real estate closing costs for consumers and has not been justified by a showing of increased consumer protection.

The Interest And Experience Of The Department of Justice And The Federal Trade Commission

The United States Department of Justice and the Federal Trade Commission are entrusted with enforcing this nation's antitrust laws.

For more than 100 years, since the passage of the Sherman Antitrust Act, the United States Department of Justice has worked to promote free and unfettered competition in all sectors of the American economy. Restraints on competition can force consumers to pay higher prices or accept goods and services of lower quality. Accordingly, such restraints are of significant concern, whether they are imposed by a "smokestack" industry or by a profession. Restraints on competition in any market have the potential to harm consumers. The Justice Department's civil and criminal enforcement programs are directed at eliminating such restraints. The Justice Department also encourages competition through advocacy letters such as this one. (2) Congress has directed the Federal Trade Commission to prevent unfair methods of competition and unfair or deceptive acts or practices in or affecting commerce. (3) The Federal Trade Commission has particular concern about restrictions that may adversely affect the competitive process and raise prices (or decrease quality or services) to consumers. Because the Commission has broad responsibility for consumer protec-

---

(continues)

tion, it is also concerned about acts or practices in the marketplace that injure consumers through unfairness or deception. Pursuant to this statutory mandate, the Federal Trade Commission encourages competition in the licensed professions, including the legal profession, to the maximum extent compatible with other state and federal goals. The Commission has challenged anticompetitive restrictions on the business practices of state-licensed professionals, including lawyers. (4) In addition, the staff has conducted studies of the effects of occupational regulation (5) and submitted comments about these issues to state legislatures, administrative agencies, and others. (6) The Commission also has had significant experience in analyzing and challenging restrictions on competition in the real estate industry. (7)

UPL Opinion #183

UPL Opinion #183 would declare real estate closings conducted by anyone other than an attorney to be the unauthorized practice of law. (8) The proposed Opinion would prohibit lay settlement services from conducting closings for real estate sales and for any loans secured by real estate. Although the proposed Opinion permits the closing attorney to delegate certain tasks to laypersons, it requires that the attorney "actively oversee all aspects of the closing." The closing attorney need not be present at the actual closing, however. The attorney's lay employees may conduct the closing. Moreover, the proposed Opinion would bar a Virginia attorney, who is employed by a title agency, from performing real estate closings. Consequently, the proposed Opinion would require a consumer who otherwise might retain a real estate agent, title company, bank, or other lay settlement service for a closing to retain a lawyer instead.

UPL Opinion #183 was issued by The Standing Committee on the Unauthorized Practice of Law at the request of a member of the Virginia State Bar. It was opposed by more than 500 of the 622 comments filed with the State Bar Council, as well as by the State Bar Counsel who stated that the proposed rule is not "appropriate or helpful to consumers."(9) Nonetheless, the State Bar Council approved the proposed Opinion on October 17.

The Public Interest Standard Should Guide

Pronouncements About the Practice of Law

In considering whether to declare that a service constitutes the practice of law in Virginia, the Court should consider the public interest. The rules against the unauthorized practice of law are themselves intended to protect the public interest and should not be construed in a manner inconsistent with that purpose. Indeed, the Court's own statement of these principles expressly provides that their ultimate aim is "the protection of the public." Va. S.Ct. R. Pt. 6, I (Introduction).

In determining how best to protect the public and where the public interest lies, the Court should consider both the harm that might be caused by permitting lay persons to provide closing services and the harm that would be caused by prohibiting them from doing so. These harms should be balanced against each other. As the Supreme Court of New Jersey wrote, when considering the same issue:

The question of what constitutes the unauthorized practice of law involves more than an academic analysis of the function of lawyers, more than a determination of what they are uniquely qualified to do. It also involves a determination of whether nonlawyers should be allowed, in the public interest, to engage in activities that may constitute the practice of law. . . .

We determine the ultimate touchstone—the public interest—through the balancing of the factors involved in the case, namely, the risks and benefits to the public of allowing or disallowing such activities.

In re Opinion No. 26, 654 A.2d at 1345–46.

As we explain below, an assessment of the relative costs of permitting and prohibiting lay closings in Virginia provides no basis to believe that the public interest would be served by prohibiting purchasers and sellers of real estate in Virginia from choosing whether they wish to be represented by an attorney.

(continued)

The Proposed Opinion Will Likely Adversely Affect The Public

Free and unfettered competition is at the heart of the American economy. As the United States Supreme Court has observed, "ultimately competition will produce not only lower prices but also better goods and services. 'The heart of our national economic policy long has been faith in the value of competition.'" *National Society of Professional Engineers v. United States*, 435 U.S. 679, 695 (1978); accord *Superior Court Trial Lawyers' Association*, 493 U.S. 411, 423 (1990). Competition benefits consumers of both traditional manufacturing industries and the learned professions. *Goldfarb v. Virginia State Bar*, 421 U.S. 773, 787 (1975); National Society of Professional Engineers, 435 U.S. at 689.

The proposed Opinion would restrain competition by erecting an insurmountable barrier against competition from lay settlement services, thereby depriving Virginia consumers of the choice of closing real estate transactions without the services of an attorney. The proposed Opinion could increase costs for consumers in two ways. First, by forcing consumers who would not otherwise hire an attorney for a real estate closing to do so, the restriction would adversely affect all consumers who prefer the combination of price, quality, and service that a lay settlement service offers.

A 1996 Media General study submitted by the Coalition for Choice in Real Estate found that lay closing services are significantly less costly than attorneys.

	Average Closing Costs	Median Closing Costs
Attorneys	$ 366	$ 350
Lay Services	$ 208	$ 200

Residential Real Estate Closing Cost Survey, September 1996 at 5. Media General surveyed 425 law firms and 64 lay firms in Virginia. The survey also reported that total closing costs, including the title examination, averaged $451 for lawyer closings and $272 for lay settlements. Title examination cost figures were submitted by 165 law firms and 41 lay providers. We are informed that nonlawyers closed about 75% of the approximately 20,000 home sales in Northern Virginia in 1995, and estimate that lay settlement firms handled about one-half of the 60,000 Virginia real estate closings. Admittedly, these figures are estimations, but they indicate that the elimination of lay settlements could cost Virginia consumers over $5 million annually, even assuming that lawyers do not raise their fees once lay settlement firms have been eliminated.

Second, by eliminating competition from less costly lay settlement services, the proposed Opinion would likely cause the price of lawyers' settlement services to increase, since the availability of alternative, lower-cost lay settlement services restrains the fees that lawyers can charge. Thus, even consumers who prefer to retain a lawyer for a real estate settlement are likely to pay higher prices, if the proposed Opinion is approved. This has been the experience elsewhere. The New Jersey Supreme Court, in holding that nonlawyers may conduct closings and settlements, found that real estate closing fees were lower in southern New Jersey (where lay settlements were commonplace), even for consumers who chose attorney closings, than in the northern part of the State, where lawyers conducted almost all settlements. Southern New Jersey buyers represented by counsel throughout the entire transaction, including closing, paid on average, $650, while sellers paid $350. Northern New Jersey buyers, represented by counsel, paid on average, $1,000 and sellers, $750. *In re Opinion No. 26 of the Committee On The Unauthorized Practice of Law, 654 A.2d 1344, 1348–49 (N.J. 1995).*

Consumers' settlement costs in Virginia have fallen since the Supreme Court's *Goldfarb* decision, *supra*, (10) and since lay settlement services began operating about 15 years ago. This was predicted in the Virginia Attorney General's 1981 Economic Impact Statement, analyzing a proposed UPL rule that would have permitted only lawyers to conduct real estate closings and would have required title insurance companies to issue policies only through attorneys. The Attorney General found that there was "significant evidence that costs to the consumer will remain higher in Virginia than they otherwise might be." He based his conclusion, in part, on data from 1979–80 HUD studies that appeared to show that consumers pay more when lawyers are involved in all residential real estate closings. Attorney General of Virginia, *Economic Impact Statement,* 1980–81 Op. Atty. Gen. Va. 427 (March 12, 1981).

(*continued*)

The use of lay closing services has grown steadily in Virginia during the past 15 years. We are informed that, in Northern Virginia, lay settlement services perform most residential closings, and in the Hampton Roads area, about half. In this respect, the Virginia experience is shared by nearly all the other States. Only in South Carolina are lawyer settlements required by a UPL rule.

Restraints similar to the one proposed here have been adopted in the past, with similar anticompetitive effects. For example, the Justice Department obtained a judgment against a county bar association that restrained title insurance companies from competing in the business of certifying title. The bar association had adopted a resolution requiring lawyers' examinations of title abstracts and had induced banks and others to require the lawyers' examinations in real estate transactions. *United States v. Allen County Indiana Bar Association*, Civ. No. F-79–0042 (N.D. Ind. 1980). Likewise, the Justice Department obtained a court order prohibiting another county bar association from restricting the trust and estate services that corporate fiduciaries could provide in competition with attorneys. *United States v. New York County Lawyers' Association,* No. 80 Civ. 6129 (S.D.N.Y. 1981). (11)

Notwithstanding the popularity of lay settlement services, the assistance of a licensed lawyer is necessary in many situations. A consumer might choose an attorney to answer legal questions, negotiate disputes, or offer various protections. Consumers who hire attorneys may get better service and representation at the closing than those who do not. But, as the New Jersey Supreme Court concluded, this is not a reason to eliminate lay closing services as an alternative for consumers who wish to utilize them. In re Opinion No. 26, 654 A.2d at 1360. Rather, the choice of using a lawyer or a nonlawyer should rest with the consumer. *Id.* As the United States Supreme Court noted:

The assumption that competition is the best method of allocating resources in a free market recognizes that all elements of a bargain—quality, service, safety, and durability, and not just the immediate cost—are favorably affected by the free opportunity to select among alternative offers.

National Society of Professional Engineers, 435 U.S. at 695 (emphasis added); accord *Superior Court Trial Lawyers' Association,* 493 U.S. at 423. Permitting competition by lay services allows consumers to consider more relevant factors in selecting a provider of settlement services, such as cost, convenience, and the degree of assurance that the necessary documents and commitments are sufficient.

The basis for the proposed Opinion—and for all regulation of the unauthorized practice of law—is the risk that a lay person will make a mistake that a lawyer would not and thereby harm a consumer. The UPL Opinion states that "both the potential and actual harm to consumers is very significant when lay settlement companies are permitted to close real estate transactions. . . . This Committee has received many reports of specific instances of harm . . . too numerous and detailed to set out in this opinion." UPL Opinion at 9–10 (October 17, 1996 draft) (*Opinion*). In a separate report, the Standing Committee provided 31 examples of harm that lay settlement services have allegedly caused to consumers. *Report of the Standing Committee on the Unauthorized Practice of Law Regarding Advisory UPL Opinion Number 183* (October 2, 1996). Exhibit 1, *Examples of Problems Which Occur When Lay Settlement Companies Conduct Closings and Why Attorneys Are Necessary in Real Estate Transactions.* The Committee's report, however, provides an inadequate factual basis for the adoption of the proposed UPL Opinion.

The Committee states that "there is no requirement that the harm . . . affect a significant segment of the population." *Committee Report* at 4. In general, however, the antitrust laws and competition policy require that a sweeping restriction on competition be justified by a credible showing of need for the restriction and that the restriction is narrowly drawn to minimize its anticompetitive impact. *See generally F.T.C. v. Indiana Federation of Dentists,* 476 U.S. 447, 459 (1986) ("Absent some countervailing procompetitive virtue... such an agreement limiting consumer choice . . . cannot be sustained under the Rule of Reason"). As explained on page 4, the average closing costs for lawyer settlements in Virginia are $451, while the average costs for lay settlements are only $272, a difference of $179. If consumers were required to pay that difference for each of the estimated 30,000 Virginia real estate closings currently handled by nonlawyers, the additional direct cost to consumers would be over $5 million each year. Moreover, the total cost each year of eliminating lay settlements in Virginia is likely to be even higher because the elimination of lay settlements would also likely cause a substantial increase in lawyer

(*continued*)

settlement charges. In New Jersey, the percentage difference between average lawyer settlement charges in areas where lay settlements were allowed and in areas where they were not was 75 percent. If the same difference applies in Virginia, and average lawyer settlement costs increased 75 percent with the adoption of UPL Opinion Number 183, then the proposed opinion would cost Virginia consumers more than $20 million in increased legal fees, and the total cost to Virginia consumers annually could exceed $25 million. (12) To justify UPL Opinion Number 183, the Virginia State Bar should demonstrate that any harm resulting from lay settlements exceeds the likely substantial cost of the proposed regulation.

A showing of harm is particularly important where, as here, the proposed Opinion radically changes the status quo by eliminating consumers' opportunity to use an entire class of providers. However, the Committee provided no studies or statistics showing the proportion of lay settlements that are problematic as opposed to the proportion of problematic attorney settlements. Instead, it relied entirely on anecdotal information, illustrated in the 31 examples of alleged harm from lay settlement services, all or nearly all of which were provided by members of the real estate bar seeking protection from competition from lay services.

Whether or not the 31 examples produced consumer injury (e.g., #31—the withholding of a broker's commission by a settlement agency pending a dispute between the broker and the home builder may have been prudent), or even whether the retention of a lawyer would have made a difference (e.g., #2—in which attorneys represented both buyer and seller) are unanswered questions. What is clear, however, is that 31 examples of alleged consumer harm is a minuscule fraction of the tens of thousands of lay settlements in Virginia during the past 15 years and suggests a safety record that other industries might envy.

We realize that conversions of settlement funds or misrecordations of title, however seldom, can be a terribly serious matter to consumers whose single most important investment is their home. Retaining a lawyer may be prudent, but it is no guarantee of safety. The greatest frauds involving Virginia real estate settlements in the 1990s were probably perpetrated by attorneys David Murray, Sr. in Tidewater (13) and Thomas Dameron in Northern Virginia. (14) If the Supreme Court is concerned that the 31 examples of alleged harm from lay settlements are an indication of more widespread problems with lay settlements, it may wish to develop a more complete record from interested parties. (15) Despite the Committee's list of 31 examples, one cannot conclude that consumer harm is a more prevalent result from lay settlements or lawyer settlements. (16) Approval of the proposed Opinion may impose substantial additional closing costs on Virginia consumers. These additional costs should not be imposed without a convincing showing that lay settlements have imposed injuries on consumers that cannot be cured by a less drastic measure.

In addition, even if substantial harm could be shown to result from lay settlements, the high cost of the proposed UPL Opinion would seem to require consideration of the possibility that such harm could be avoided by a remedy less restrictive of competition. Consumers can be protected by measures that restrain competition less than a complete ban on lay real estate settlements. For example, the New Jersey Supreme Court required written notice of the risks involved in proceeding with a real estate transaction without an attorney. *In re Opinion No. 26*, 654 A.2d at 1363. Alternatively, the Commonwealth may wish to regulate lay and lawyer settlement services more closely. The Supreme Court should consider the availability of these alternatives in passing on the proposed UPL Opinion.

When, in 1978, segments in the Virginia bar previously proposed to ban lay settlements through a UPL rule, the "Horsley Committee" was formed to study UPL regulations and review specifically the proposed UPL rule prohibiting lay real estate settlements. In its April 3, 1981 report, the Horsley Committee stated that:

The guiding principle for adopting UPL regulations in a free enterprise society should be whether limiting the activity of non-lawyers is needed to provide protection to a significant segment of the public. This Committee declines to characterize the "practice of law" aspects involved in a typical real estate closing as "the unauthorized practice of law" in the degree needed today to justify a broad prior restraint.

That "guiding principle" is an even more appropriate standard today, after tens of thousands of Virginia lay settlements, than it was 15 years ago. Adopting a draconian UPL rule that eliminates a service chosen by thousands of Virginia consumers and terminates the businesses of lay settlement firms should be undertaken only after a clear showing of consumer injury. The 31 examples of alleged injury

(*continued*)

appended to the October 17 Committee letter fall far short of the standard set by the Horsley Committee. (17) Some other factors should be considered with respect to the proposed Opinion. Even under the proposed UPL Opinion, lawyers need not be present at the actual closing. Rather, the closing can be handled by a paralegal or other lay person employed by the attorney. Hence, if, as the Committee believes, it is the "practiced legal eye" of the lawyer that protects consumers at closing, this eye does not witness the actual closing. No lawyer need be present to see that a consumer may be having legal problems that only the lawyer can identify and understand. Instead, the consumer receives protection similar to that from a lay settlement agent. In both situations, the lay person conducting the closing must determine whether to call a lawyer because a question is outside his or her expertise.

Conclusion

By prohibiting lay settlements, proposed UPL Opinion #183 will likely reduce competition and raise prices to consumers, without having demonstrated that lay settlements harm consumers in a way that would be prevented by restricting real estate closings to lawyers. Accordingly, we recommend that the Supreme Court of Virginia reject the proposed UPL Opinion.

We appreciate this opportunity to present our views and would be pleased to address any questions or comments regarding competition policies.

Sincerely yours,

Joel I. Klein

Acting Assistant Attorney General

Jessica N. Cohen, Attorney

United States Department of Justice

Antitrust Division

William J. Baer

Director

Randall Marks, Attorney

Federal Trade Commission

Bureau of Competition

cc: The Honorable Thomas A. Edmonds, Executive Director, Virginia State Bar

1. This letter presents the views of the staff of the Bureau of Competition of the Federal Trade Commission. They are not necessarily the views of the Commission or of any individual Commissioner.

2. *See, e.g., National Society of Professional Engineers v. United States,* 435 U.S. 679 (1978); *United States v. American Medical Association,* 130 F.2d 233 (D.C. Cir. 1939), *aff'd,* 317 U.S. 519 (1939); *United States v. American Bar Association,* Civ. No. 95-1211 (CRR) (D.D.C. 1996); *United States v. Brown University, et al.,* 1993-2 Trade Cas. (CCH) 70,391 (E.D. Pa. 1991); *United States v. A. Lanoy Alston,* D.M.D., P.C., Crim. No. 90-042-TUC (D. Ariz. 1990); *United States v. American Institute of Architects,* 1990-2 Trade Cases 69,256 (D.D.C., 1990); *United States v. Association of Engineering Geologists,* 1985-1 Trade Cas. (CCH) 66,349 (C.D. Cal. 1984); *United States v. New York County Lawyers' Association,* No. 80 Civ. 6129 (S.D.N.Y. 1981); *United States v. Geneva County Bar Association,* Civ. No. 80-113-S (M.D. Ala. 1980); *United States v. Allen County Indiana Bar Association Inc.,* Civ. No. F-79-0042 (N.D. Ind. 1979).

3. 15 U.S.C. 41 *et seq.*

4. *See, e.g., California Dental Association,* D-9259 (decision and order issued March 25, 1996); *Superior Court Trial Lawyers' Association,* 107 F.T.C. 562 (1986), *aff'd in part, rev'd in part sub nom. Superior Court Trial Lawyers' Association v. Federal Trade Commission,* 856 F.2d 226

(continued)

(D.C. Cir. 1988), *aff'd in part, rev'd in part*, 493 U.S. 411 (1990); *American Medical Association*, 94 F.T.C. 701 (1979), *aff'd sub nom. American Medical Association v. Federal Trade Commission*, 638 F.2d 443 (2d Cir. 1980), *aff'd by an equally divided court*, 455 U.S. 476 (1982).

5. Carolyn Cox, Susan Foster, "The Costs and Benefits of Occupational Regulation," Bureau of Economics, FTC, October 1990.

6. Recent recipients of Commission staff comments about lawyer advertising include the American Bar Commission on Advertising, June 24, 1994; Supreme Court of Mississippi, January 14, 1994; Supreme Court of New Mexico, July 29, 1991; State Bar of Arizona, April 17, 1990.

7. *Port Washington Real Estate Board*, C-3625 (November 6, 1995); *Industrial Multiple and American Industrial Real Estate Association*, C-3449 (consent order issued July 6, 1993, 58 Fed. Reg. 42,552 (Aug. 10, 1993)); *United Real Estate Brokers of Rockland Ltd.* (Rockland County Multiple Listing System), C-3461 (consent order issued Sept. 27, 1993, 58 Fed. Reg. 59,042 (Nov. 5, 1993)); *Bellingham-Whatcom County Multiple Listing Bureau*, 113 F.T.C. 724 (1990) (consent order); *Puget Sound Multiple Listing Association*, 113 F.T.C. 733 (1990) (consent order).

8. The Opinion indicates that the UPL prohibition applies only to third parties to a real estate closing. Consequently, a bank could use its employees to close a real estate loan to an unrepresented customer but could make no separate charge for the preparation of title documents. Opinion, p. 10.

9. Virginia's Attorney General has advised that less restrictive means than the proposed Opinion should be considered. In commenting on a similar proposed opinion 16 years ago, the Attorney General noted "the manifest anticompetitive effect of the proposal."

10. The fee schedules challenged in *Goldfarb* fixed lawyer's fees for residential real estate closings at 1% of the selling price. *See* 421 U.S. at 776.

11. If the Supreme Court of Virginia approves the proposed Opinion, the state action doctrine would likely exempt it from federal antitrust challenge. *Parker v. Brown*, 317 U.S. 341 (1943); *Bates v. State Bar of Arizona*, 433 U.S. 350 (1977). This doctrine immunizes some state government actions that, if taken by private parties, could violate the antitrust laws.

12. As noted above, the New Jersey Supreme Court found that the average cost for lawyer assisted closings in Northern New Jersey, where legal representation was required, was $1,750, while the average cost for lawyer assisted closings in Southern New Jersey, where legal representation was not required, was only $1,000, a 75 percent difference. If the average cost of a lawyer assisted closing in Virginia were to increase by 75 percent, it would rise from $451 to $789, for an increase of $338 per closing. If the average closing cost rises by that amount and lawyers handle all of the estimated 60,000 annual Virginia real estate closings, costs to Virginia consumers would increase by $20.28 million (60,000 x $338). Thus, the total cost to Virginia consumers, including the more than $5 million in direct costs of eliminating lay settlement providers, could exceed $25 million.

13. "See No Evil: How David Murray Got Away With It," *The Daily Press* (Newport News), November 15–19, 1992, p. A1, *et seq.*

14. "Realty Attorney Sentenced To Prison In Fraud Case: Scheme Cost Home Sellers, Lenders $5 Million," *The Washington Post*, October 12, 1996, 1996 WL 13425939.

15. Before rejecting a proposed UPL rule prohibiting lay settlements in 1995, the New Jersey Supreme Court retained a Special Master who conducted 16 days of hearings and submitted a report.

16. An attorney for an interested party in this proceeding forwarded to the Justice Department a December 12, 1996 letter from the Senior Vice President of Lawyers Title Insurance Corporation, which issues thousands of Virginia title insurance policies annually. The letter notes that Lawyers Title "has experienced no greater incidents of problems arising from the conduct of a settlement by a lay entity than we have from an attorney" (appended as Attachment A). Additionally, the Virginia State Bar

(*continued*)

Commission Department of Professional Regulation has reported that ". . . the major complaints against attorneys continue to be in the areas of neglect and communications, and these complaints typically come from the fields of real estate, family law and criminal law." *57th Annual Report of the Virginia State Bar*, p. 9. In each year from 1991 to 1995, between 10% and 14% of all complaints to the State Bar involved real estate—over 200 each year. *57th Annual Report*, pp. 8–13.

17. Its use also suggests due process concerns. We understand that the 31 examples were largely provided by lawyers with a real estate practice and that other commenters did not have the opportunity to respond to these 31 instances or to develop a record of settlement abuses by lawyers. When a proposed UPL rule prohibiting lay settlements was last before the Virginia Supreme Court, it required the Attorney General of Virginia to analyze the economic effect on competition of the proposed restraint supported by statistical data.

Whoever is given the obligation to close, must first and foremost educate the parties. The paralegal should inform all parties about the following:

1. Settlement sheet
2. Financing documents and other related matters
3. Document signing
4. Collection of monies
5. Collection of certified, accountable checks
6. Payment of debts and obligations
7. Liens, judgments, or other matters
8. Surrender of keys
9. Transfer of utilities
10. Tax bills
11. Mortgage satisfaction information
12. Hazard policy submission
13. Title binder
14. Other activities

Instructing on what is about to occur is time well spent. The best analogy one can give is that those entrusted with closing are "ringmasters," keeping the players and the papers in line and on schedule. This is no easy task! The needs and expectations of lenders, attorneys, buyers and sellers, brokers, and agents are important concerns for the paralegal. While the prime reason for closing is simple, namely that buyers buy and sellers sell, the road to settlement is laden with obstacles. Ponder these examples:

■ Broker and agent disagree on commission split.
■ Seller becomes suspicious of whether buyer has sufficient funds.
■ Buyer distrusts the representation of the house's quality by the seller.
■ Seller thinks buyer is making too many demands.
■ Lender wants more information than the buyer is willing to give.
■ Attorneys for buyer and seller become contentious.
■ Seller fails to prepare a deed or other documents.
■ Buyer forgets paperwork.

The possibility for these and other disputes is real. Can you see why so many settlements falter? As stated earlier, being prepared is the key. Having all the paperwork authored, instructing all parties aware of content, disseminating all information freely, and making plain to all parties the real purpose for settlement tends to make the settlement a breeze. Consider how the timing of settlement can cause disputes. Robert E. Schreiner sees the impact of unilateral closing date choice.

The right of the listing broker to set closing, however, should be exercised with diplomacy and discretion, since cooperation of all parties is vital. At the same time, the other parties need to appreciate that, with so many parties participating, a time and place fully acceptable to all is not likely and that some compromise and sacrifice may be necessary. Buyers and seller, particularly, must appreciate that closings should be held during regular business hours and that they may need to lose some time from their work. If needed, most items related to the settlement and other documents can be checked and verified only during regular business hours. The closing hour and place may need to be coordinated and confirmed with the co-op office, the loan company, the seller, the buyer, attorneys for buyer and seller, listing broker and salesman, and a private mortgagee who is being paid off.[6]

Settlement should be as informal and casual an atmosphere as feasible. Keep to schedule; be precise about starting time and the length of settlement. The paralegal should commence settlement proceedings by reviewing the Closing Checklist in Figure 8–11.

CLOSING CHECKLIST

1. What is the current real estate commission rate in your jurisdiction? _____%

2. Are the current agreement of sale and all attached extensions, addenda, and endorsements legally enforceable and timely? _____ Yes _____ No

3. State specifically (name, address, and telephone) to whom you make tax payments in your jurisdiction. Real Estate Tax Payments: _____

4. State specifically (name, address, and telephone) to whom you pay sewer assessments.

5. State specifically (name, address, and telephone) to whom you pay water rent, water bills, and other assessments relating to water. _____

6. What are the recording fees on a page-by-page basis in your jurisdiction? _____

7. How much of a transfer tax is required to be paid on a real estate transaction? _____%

8. Is the transfer tax divisible between the buyer and the seller? _____Yes _____ No If yes, by what formula? _____

9. What are the names, addresses, and telephone numbers of your local gas, electric, and telephone companies? Gas _____ Electric _____ Telephone _____

10. What are the names, addresses, and telephone numbers of three infestation carriers that might be required to perform an inspection on the property?

11. What is the name, address, and telephone number of a notary who will assist you in the preparation and completion of closing documentation?

12. What is the name, address, and telephone number of the bank official or officer who serves as a liaison between the closing and settlement parties for financing parties?

13. What are the names, addresses, and telephone numbers of the agents involved for seller and buyer, if applicable? Seller's Agent _____
Buyer's Agent _____

FIGURE 8–11
(continues)

14. What are the names, addresses, and telephone numbers of two or three hazard insurance agencies most likely to issue a policy in your jurisdiction?

15. What are the names, addresses, and telephone numbers of the most prominent and commonly employed title insurance companies in your region?

16. Do title agents perform the functions of closing in your region? _____ Yes _____ No

17. Have all the terms and conditions of the agreement of sale been met?
    financing conditions? _____ Yes _____ No
    zoning conditions? _____ Yes _____ No
    appraisal? _____ Yes_____ No
    engineering report? _____ Yes _____ No
    percolation test? _____ Yes _____ No
    repairs? _____ Yes _____ No

18. Have all mortgages been satisfied? _____ Yes _____ No

19. Will the mortgage subject to this property be assumed? _____ Yes _____ No

20. Have all assumption documents been prepared? _____ Yes _____ No

21. What are the names, addresses, and telephone numbers of the attorneys for buyers and sellers?
    Buyer's Attorney _____
    Seller's Attorney _____

22. What documents need to be prepared?
    _____ Indenture or deed
    _____ Deed of trust
    _____ Note
    _____ Bill of sale
    _____ Leases
    _____ Truth in lending disclosures
    _____ Release of trust
    _____ Right of rescission
    _____ Settlement abstract
    _____ Title abstraction
    _____ Escrow documentation
    _____ Insurance assignments
    _____ Commission agreements
    _____ Title insurance documentation
    _____ Mortgage assumption statements
    _____ Loan payoff statements
    _____ Attorney's opinion of title
    _____ Judgment certificate
    _____ Personal property tax statements
    _____ Releases
    _____ Lien documentation
    _____ Affidavits

23. Does your jurisdiction require that a survey be performed? _____ Yes _____ No

24. What are the names, addresses, and telephone numbers of three reliable surveyors in your area?

FIGURE 8–11
(continued)

OTHER CONSIDERATIONS

CHECKLIST OF QUESTIONS IN THE CLOSING AND SETTLEMENT PROCESS

1. Are documents properly notarized? _____ Yes _____ No

2. Are all lender's financing documents properly completed and filled out? _____Yes_____ No

3. Are all monies deposited in escrow accounts properly accounted for and ready to be distributed? _____ Yes _____ No

4. Have all bills been accounted for as to be noted on the settlement sheet?_____ Yes _____ No

5. Do you have the seller's new address?_____ Yes_____ No

6. What provisions have you taken for the surrender of keys? _____

7. Are all checks properly signed and endorsed?_____ Yes _____ No

8. Have buyer and seller adjusted their obligations and liabilities regarding gas, electric, water, and telephone services?_____ Yes _____ No

9. Are all insurance documents available? _____ Yes _____ No

10. Have insurance policies been acquired or canceled as needed? _____Yes _____ No

11. Have all settlement sheets been signed and executed?_____ Yes _____ No

12. Have buyer and seller exchanged telephone numbers?_____ Yes _____ No

---

FIGURE 8–11
(continued)

A. Seller at Closing

In terms of paperwork, the seller's responsibilities are relatively minor.

1. Deed

The deed, the centerpiece of transfer and one of the first documents to be prepared, lacks only formal execution. The closing agent will verify the accuracy of the deed and then advise on the location for endorsement. At the bottom of the deed, on the front cover, insert the buyer's address so the recorder knows where to forward the document after recordation.

2. Owner's Affidavit

Both title companies and counsel representing the seller or buyer may desire an affidavit by seller attesting to:

- Identity of the parties
- Heirship
- Marital status
- Capacity of the parties
- Rights of possession
- Possibility of mechanic's liens and municipal claims, and so forth

The policy behind the affidavit is to protect the title company against misrepresentations and to limit coverage in the event of falsehood.

3. Settlement Sheet

Seller's estimated disbursements will reflect expenses, existing liabilities, and other responsibilities. On the expense side (Figure 8–10), there is:

- Transfer tax: Line 1203
- Commissions: Line 703
- Mortgage balances: Lines 504 and 505
- Due taxes or assessments: Lines 510, 511, and 512
- Pest inspections
- Repairs

Proceeds are the difference between selling price and those obligations yet to be paid by the seller.

Fully explain how the gross sum owed to seller is computed. Expect queries on how taxes and other pro rata sums are calculated. There are numerous local and state differences in these practices.

The seller should receive an executed copy of the settlement sheet.

4. Leases

Naturally, any lease that allows a seller to stay over should be executed and delivered to the seller. Leases for buyers and sellers are fully discussed in Chapter 9.

5. Utilities

On the closing date, water, oil, gas, electric, and sewage accounts should be transferred. Any bills paid in advance or on a budget plan should be fully credited to the seller. Oil or propane gas left in the tank can be measured, priced at the current index, and credited in the settlement sheet, or depending on the description in the agreement of sale, it may be pumped out.

6. Insurance Refunds

The seller is entitled to an insurance premium refund as of the day of closing. Insurance return paperwork should be ordered in advance and be ready for execution at the closing table.

7. Releases or Satisfaction

The seller should provide the buyer an executed release or mortgage satisfaction document for any outstanding mortgages or other indebtedness.

B. Buyer at Closing

Buyers are besieged by documentary requirements. The paralegal should thoroughly review the closing checklist for buyer in Figure 8–12 which illustrates the dramatic amount of closing requirements. Buyers are mostly buffeted by financing demands, but the transfer from the old residence to the new triggers numerous tasks, from moving expenses to certified checks.

1. Financing Documents

At closing, buyers execute the mortgage, the corresponding note, and a host of other documents. Closing is a good time to disclose the consequences of late payment or default. The lender may

CLOSING CHECKLIST

BEFORE YOU GO TO THE CLOSING, YOU WILL WANT TO ANSWER THE FOLLOWING QUESTIONS:

	Yes	No
1. Are all necessary inspections done? (Bring inspection reports with you to the closing.)	☐	☐
2. Are all required repairs complete? (Bring certificate of completion to the closing.)	☐	☐
3. Do you have a paid insurance policy or binder in effect the day of the closing?	☐	☐
4. Did you give your old landlord notion?	☐	☐
5. Have you made a final inspection of the house?	☐	☐
6. Have you confirmed with the seller the move-out data?	☐	☐
7. Have you confirmed with your mover the move-in date?	☐	☐
8. Have you confirmed with your mover the time of pickup and delivery?	☐	☐
9. Have you confirmed with your mover the cost of the move?	☐	☐
10. Do you have enough money for moving?	☐	☐
11. Have you obtained from the lender or escrow agent the exact amount of money you will need for closing? (Ask about prepayable and other costs that did not appear on your RESPA statement.)	☐	☐
12. Do you have a certified check for that amount?	☐	☐
13. Do you have additional cash "just in case"?	☐	☐
14. Have you confirmed with your lawyer of escrow agent the TIME, DATE, PLACE of the closing?	☐	☐
15. Do you have receipts for those items you have already paid for on the house?	☐	☐

FIGURE 8–12

dictate completion of other documents that usually deal with matters of disclosure. Examples of these disclosures could involve:

- Price of the property
- Down payment
- The unpaid balance
- Finance charge
- The prepaid amount of the finance charge

- All other charges
- The total amount to be financed
- The deferred payment price
- The number, amount, and due dates of payments
- The amount of default, delinquency, or similar charges
- The type of any security interest held
- Any penalty charge
- Any unearned portion of the finance charge

2. Liens

Liens are existing obligations that make a completely free conveyance impossible until satisfied or removed. Taxes, mechanic's, or municipal liens are examples. The buyers may still proceed with a purchase even though the property has identifiable liens. This may occur when the seller credits the buyer for those costs, leaving the buyer responsible for its payment and removal, or it may occur when a buyer gets a bargain price that reflects the liens. In any case, the buyer may waive the title encumbrance created by the lien and accept the property as encumbered. See Figure 8–13.

Seller may also produce a release of liens document that satisfies any controversy.

3. Permits and Certifications

Any buyer should be apprised of permit or certification requirements and results. Most commonly seen will be the wood infestation certification. All other types of physical certifications or permits are fully covered in Chapter 4.

Home inspection reports should be discussed to determine whether any outstanding repairs still need attention.

4. Settlement Sheet

The buyer's involvement in the settlement sheet is far more intense. Charges, expenses, and costs of settlement, on even the average house, can be substantial. The closing agent should diligently explain all computational details relative to the buyer. Some of the most pertinent (Figure 8–10) are:

- Loan and financing expense: Line 202
- Advance payments: Line 201
- Escrow reserves: Lines 1001 through 1007
- Title expense: Lines 1101 through 1108
- Recording/transfer: Lines 1201 and 1202
- Miscellaneous settlement: Lines 1301 through 1305
- Pro rata taxes, assessments: Lines 210, 211, and 212
- Gross amount due agent: Line 703

After a complete explanation and execution, deliver a copy to the buyer.

5. Hazard Policy

A majority of lenders require delivery of the hazard or a flood policy, as well as advance escrow payment for one year, before closing. Documents are prepared, executed, and payments remitted at or before closing.

WAIVER OF LIEN

FINAL

State of _____, _____ County, ss:

WHEREAS, the undersigned _____ has been

heretofore employed by _____ to furnish certain material and

labor, to wit:_____

for the building owned by_____ and located on _____

_____

NOW THEREFORE, KNOW YE, That the undersigned, for a good and valuable consideration, the

receipt of which is hereby acknowledged, hereby and now waives and releases unto the said

_____ the owner of said premises, any and all lien, right of lien, or claim of

whatsoever kind of character on the above described building and real estate, on account of any and all labor

or material, or both, furnished for or incorporated into said building by the undersigned; and

_____ further certify that the consideration moving to the undersigned for

executing this Waiver of Lien has been mutually given and accepted as absolute cash payment and not as a

conditional or part payment or as security for payment.

Signed, sealed and delivered this _____ day of _____ , _____.

Signed _____

_____

Personally appeared before me this _____ day of _____ , _____.

_____ who, being duly sworn on oath, says: That he is

_____of the _____ and that he hereby acknowledges the

execution of the foregoing instrument for and on behalf of said_____

and at _____ special instance and request.

My Commission Expires: Notary Public

_____   _____

This instrument prepared by: _____

FIGURE 8–13

6. Title Insurance: Binder or Policy

If title insurance is part of the bargain, the buyer will minimally have to submit a binder at settlement. A binder is not a full-fledged policy but only a temporary commitment to issue one upon certain conditions once a closing occurs.

The settlement officer may be ready to issue a complete policy. In such case, before a policy can be issued, the title company will insist on purchase completeness in an affidavit.

7. Leases

The same rules applicable to seller for leases apply to the buyer. See Chapter 9.

8. Survey

If not already done, the settlement agent will transmit an official copy of the survey upon disbursement of the funds at settlement.

9. Escrow Agreement

Buyer and sellers, due to inadequacies discovered in inspection, may enter into a temporary escrow agreement whereby seller places sufficient funds to cover the cost of repairs.

C. Settlement

Once all the documents are authored and executed, they comprise the settlement package. In accordance with the lender's instructions, transmit the package. See Figure 8–14 for a settlement checklist.

D. Disbursement

The settlement sheet guides the disbursement of funds and proceeds, both as to amount and party. Disbursement ledgers or sheets organize the plan of disbursement. See Figure 8–15.[7]

The funds, as disbursed, should be fully reconciled with the data presented on the information sheet.

Generally speaking, fund distributions include these:

- Cash to seller
- Taxes to governments
- Commission to agents and brokers
- Lender's fees
- Points
- Appraisal
- Credit Report
- Tax service
- Processing
- Escrow/reserves
- Title company charges
- Attorneys
- Notary and express
- County governments
- Recorder of deeds
- Transfer tax
- Local governments

WORKSHEET FOR REAL ESTATE SETTLEMENT

SELLER _____ BUYER _____

PROPERTY ADDRESS _____

SETTLEMENT DATE _____ DATE OF PRORATION _____

LEGAL DESCRIPTION _____

	SELLER			BUYER			BROKER	
	Debit	Credit	Debit	Credit		Debit	Credit
1 Selling Price							
2 Deposit paid to							
3 Trust Deed, Payable to							
4 Trust Deed, Payable to							
5 Trust Deed, Payoff to							
6 Interest on Loan Assumed							
7 Title Ins. Premium							
8 Abstracting: Before Sale							
9 After Sale							
10 Title Exam by							
11 Recording: Warranty Deed							
12 Trust Deed							
13 Release							
14 Other							
15 Documentary Fee							
16 Certificate of Taxes Due							
17 Taxes for Preceding Year(s)							
18 Taxes for Current Year							
19 Tax Reserve							
20 Special Taxes							

WORKSHEET FOR REAL ESTATE SETTLEMENT   Page 1 of 2

FIGURE 8-14

(continues)

21 Personal Property Taxes				
22 Hazard Ins. Prem. Assumed				
23 Premium for New Insurance				
24 Hazard Ins. Reserve				
25 FHA Mortgage Ins. Assumed				
26 FHA Mortgage Ins. Reserve				
27 Loan Service Fee (Buyer)				
28 Loan Discount Fee (Seller)				
29 Interest on New Loan				
30 Survey, and/or Credit Report				
31 Appraisal Fee				
32 Water and/or Sewer				
33 Rents				
34 Security Deposits				
35 Loan Transfer Fee				
36 Loan Payment Due				
37 Broker's Fee				
SUBTOTALS				
Balance due to/from Seller				
Balance due to/from Buyer				
TOTALS				

WORKSHEET FOR REAL ESTATE SETTLEMENT

Page 2 of 2

FIGURE 8–14
(continued)

Ledger Summary

File #: 45781296351

Borrower(s):
  Borrower Name 1
  Borrower Name 2

Seller(s):
  Seller Name 1
  Seller Name 2

Settlement Date:

Property Address:
  Borrower Address 1
  Borrower City, NJ 12462-8888

Deposits

Date	Payee/Payor	Ref #	Amount
1/26/2009	Borrower Name 1		8,937.53
	Cash at settlement from buyer		
1/26/2009	Lender Name 1		483,728.79
	Loan proceeds		
	Total Deposits:		**492,666.32**

FIGURE 8–15
Courtesy of Easy Soft Inc., 212 North Center Drive, North Brunswick NJ 08902, www.easysoft-usa.com.
(continues)

Ledger Summary

Payments

Date	Payee/Payor	Ref #	Amount
1/26/2009	Washington Mutual Bank		98,553.85
	Payoff of first mortgage loan		
1/26/2009	Wachovia Bank		153,982.02
	Payoff of second mortgage loan		
1/26/2009	Borrower Name 1		207,968.45
	Cash at settlement to seller		
1/26/2009	Weichert Realty, Inc.		9,200.00
	Sales/Broker's Commission		
1/26/2009	Coldwell Banker		9,800.00
	Sales/Broker's Commission		
1/26/2009	Taxes to Towns		85.00
	Tax service fee		
1/26/2009	Floods R Us		25.00
	Flood certification		
1/26/2009	Borrower City		950.00
	2nd Qtr 09 Taxes		
1/26/2009	Moore Title Services, Inc.		4,852.00
	Title charges		
1/26/2009	S.Simon, Sr., Esq./Edward Montuck, Esq.		950.00
	Settlement or closing fee		
1/26/2009	S.Simon, Sr., Esq./Edward Montuck, Esq.		750.00
	Settlement or closing fee		
1/26/2009	County Clerk's Office		350.00
	Govt recording charges		
1/26/2009	County Clerk's Office		50.00
	Govt recording charges		
1/26/2009	County Clerk's Office		4,175.00
	State tax/stamps		
1/26/2009	Today's Survey Company, Inc.		800.00
	Survey w/stakes		
1/26/2009	Downtown Lawyers, PC		75.00
	Overnight charges-buyer/seller		
1/26/2009	Downtown Lawyers, PC		100.00
	Postage, copies, telephone/fax		

Total Payments: 492,666.32

Difference:

FIGURE 8–15
(continued)

- Sewage
- Water
- Pest infestation
- Survey
- Repairs

E. IRS Reporting

For nearly the last decade, the IRS has required the reporting of any real estate transaction, not statutorily excluded.[8] Reportable real estate is any present or future ownership interest in:

- Land (including air space)
- Inherently permanent structures (including residential, commercial, and industrial buildings)
- Condominium units and certain related property
- Stock in a cooperative housing corporation.[9]

The IRS policy is based on its desire to tax capital gains. The code specifies the person responsible for closing the transaction as being equally responsible for its reporting. Thus, closing agents, paralegals, and attorneys must complete a statement for submission to the IRS.

If the seller does not provide the attorney or paralegal with the necessary Taxpayer Identification Number for recording purposes, prepare an IRS Form W-9, have seller imprint signature, and pass it on to the IRS. See Figure 8–16.

If the parties are unclear to whom that reporting authority belongs, they can designate, by formal agreement, where the responsibility lies.

V. POST-CLOSING ACTIVITIES

A. Recordation

Upon the settlement's completion, the paralegal involved in the transactions should assure that the deed and mortgage are recorded. Recordation sets out a priority of rights over any other competing claim to the same real property. Recording puts the world, whether it be by adverse possessors, creditors, or long lost relatives, on notice of the time and the right of ownership. By failing to record the deed, one has an exposed flank in the event of challenge.

To record, fees are computed page by page or by transfer tax stamps. Over the years, recording costs have gone up dramatically, and the governmental expenses associated with maintaining such records have prompted a call for recording reform. Instead of being forced to record mortgages and notes, some argue they should be cross-referenced in the deed itself.

As a general rule, record *immediately* after closing.

B. Title Policy Issuance

As discussed previously, title insurance companies are usually willing to issue only an initial or preliminary binder covering the real estate transaction. Once all documents and other requirements are fulfilled, a title insurance policy of full legal effect will be issued. Make sure that a full premium is paid for both the bank and the purchaser.

C. Escrow or Repair Issues

Frequently, upon final inspection by the purchaser, corrective repairs are necessary. If the plumbing and electrical systems are inoperable, the attorney should escrow a designated amount, say

| Form **W-9**
(Rev. October 2007)
Department of the Treasury
Internal Revenue Service | **Request for Taxpayer**
Identification Number and Certification | **Give form to the**
requester. Do not
send to the IRS. |

Print or type
See Specific Instructions on page 2.

Name (as shown on your income tax return)

Business name, if different from above

Check appropriate box: ☐ Individual/Sole proprietor ☐ Corporation ☐ Partnership   ☐ Exempt payee
☐ Limited liability company. Enter the tax classification (D=disregarded entity, C=corporation, P=partnership) ▶ ....
☐ Other (see instructions) ▶

Address (number, street, and apt. or suite no.)

Requester's name and address (optional)

City, state, and ZIP code

List account number(s) here (optional)

Part I   **Taxpayer Identification Number (TIN)**

Enter your TIN in the appropriate box. The TIN provided must match the name given on Line 1 to avoid backup withholding. For individuals, this is your social security number (SSN). However, for a resident alien, sole proprietor, or disregarded entity, see the Part I instructions on page 3. For other entities, it is your employer identification number (EIN). If you do not have a number, see *How to get a TIN* on page 3.

Note. If the account is in more than one name, see the chart on page 4 for guidelines on whose number to enter.

| Social security number |
| **or** |
| Employer identification number |

Part II   **Certification**

Under penalties of perjury, I certify that:

1. The number shown on this form is my correct taxpayer identification number (or I am waiting for a number to be issued to me), and

2. I am not subject to backup withholding because: (a) I am exempt from backup withholding, or (b) I have not been notified by the Internal Revenue Service (IRS) that I am subject to backup withholding as a result of a failure to report all interest or dividends, or (c) the IRS has notified me that I am no longer subject to backup withholding, and

3. I am a U.S. citizen or other U.S. person (defined below).

Certification instructions. You must cross out item 2 above if you have been notified by the IRS that you are currently subject to backup withholding because you have failed to report all interest and dividends on your tax return. For real estate transactions, item 2 does not apply. For mortgage interest paid, acquisition or abandonment of secured property, cancellation of debt, contributions to an individual retirement arrangement (IRA), and generally, payments other than interest and dividends, you are not required to sign the Certification, but you must provide your correct TIN. See the instructions on page 4.

Sign
Here | Signature of
U.S. person ▶   Date ▶

General Instructions

Section references are to the Internal Revenue Code unless otherwise noted.

Purpose of Form

A person who is required to file an information return with the IRS must obtain your correct taxpayer identification number (TIN) to report, for example, income paid to you, real estate transactions, mortgage interest you paid, acquisition or abandonment of secured property, cancellation of debt, or contributions you made to an IRA.

Use Form W-9 only if you are a U.S. person (including a resident alien), to provide your correct TIN to the person requesting it (the requester) and, when applicable, to:

  1. Certify that the TIN you are giving is correct (or you are waiting for a number to be issued),

  2. Certify that you are not subject to backup withholding, or

  3. Claim exemption from backup withholding if you are a U.S. exempt payee. If applicable, you are also certifying that as a U.S. person, your allocable share of any partnership income from a U.S. trade or business is not subject to the withholding tax on foreign partners' share of effectively connected income.

Note. If a requester gives you a form other than Form W-9 to request your TIN, you must use the requester's form if it is substantially similar to this Form W-9.

Definition of a U.S. person. For federal tax purposes, you are considered a U.S. person if you are:

● An individual who is a U.S. citizen or U.S. resident alien,

● A partnership, corporation, company, or association created or organized in the United States or under the laws of the United States,

● An estate (other than a foreign estate), or

● A domestic trust (as defined in Regulations section 301.7701-7).

Special rules for partnerships. Partnerships that conduct a trade or business in the United States are generally required to pay a withholding tax on any foreign partners' share of income from such business. Further, in certain cases where a Form W-9 has not been received, a partnership is required to presume that a partner is a foreign person, and pay the withholding tax. Therefore, if you are a U.S. person that is a partner in a partnership conducting a trade or business in the United States, provide Form W-9 to the partnership to establish your U.S. status and avoid withholding on your share of partnership income.

The person who gives Form W-9 to the partnership for purposes of establishing its U.S. status and avoiding withholding on its allocable share of net income from the partnership conducting a trade or business in the United States is in the following cases:

● The U.S. owner of a disregarded entity and not the entity,

Cat. No. 10231X   Form **W-9** (Rev. 10-2007)

FIGURE 8–16
(continues)

● The U.S. grantor or other owner of a grantor trust and not the trust, and

● The U.S. trust (other than a grantor trust) and not the beneficiaries of the trust.

Foreign person. If you are a foreign person, do not use Form W-9. Instead, use the appropriate Form W-8 (see Publication 515, Withholding of Tax on Nonresident Aliens and Foreign Entities).

Nonresident alien who becomes a resident alien. Generally, only a nonresident alien individual may use the terms of a tax treaty to reduce or eliminate U.S. tax on certain types of income. However, most tax treaties contain a provision known as a "saving clause." Exceptions specified in the saving clause may permit an exemption from tax to continue for certain types of income even after the payee has otherwise become a U.S. resident alien for tax purposes.

If you are a U.S. resident alien who is relying on an exception contained in the saving clause of a tax treaty to claim an exemption from U.S. tax on certain types of income, you must attach a statement to Form W-9 that specifies the following five items:

1. The treaty country. Generally, this must be the same treaty under which you claimed exemption from tax as a nonresident alien.

2. The treaty article addressing the income.

3. The article number (or location) in the tax treaty that contains the saving clause and its exceptions.

4. The type and amount of income that qualifies for the exemption from tax.

5. Sufficient facts to justify the exemption from tax under the terms of the treaty article.

Example. Article 20 of the U.S.-China income tax treaty allows an exemption from tax for scholarship income received by a Chinese student temporarily present in the United States. Under U.S. law, this student will become a resident alien for tax purposes if his or her stay in the United States exceeds 5 calendar years. However, paragraph 2 of the first Protocol to the U.S.-China treaty (dated April 30, 1984) allows the provisions of Article 20 to continue to apply even after the Chinese student becomes a resident alien of the United States. A Chinese student who qualifies for this exception (under paragraph 2 of the first protocol) and is relying on this exception to claim an exemption from tax on his or her scholarship or fellowship income would attach to Form W-9 a statement that includes the information described above to support that exemption.

If you are a nonresident alien or a foreign entity not subject to backup withholding, give the requester the appropriate completed Form W-8.

What is backup withholding? Persons making certain payments to you must under certain conditions withhold and pay to the IRS 28% of such payments. This is called "backup withholding." Payments that may be subject to backup withholding include interest, tax-exempt interest, dividends, broker and barter exchange transactions, rents, royalties, nonemployee pay, and certain payments from fishing boat operators. Real estate transactions are not subject to backup withholding.

You will not be subject to backup withholding on payments you receive if you give the requester your correct TIN, make the proper certifications, and report all your taxable interest and dividends on your tax return.

Payments you receive will be subject to backup withholding if:

1. You do not furnish your TIN to the requester,

2. You do not certify your TIN when required (see the Part II instructions on page 3 for details),

3. The IRS tells the requester that you furnished an incorrect TIN,

4. The IRS tells you that you are subject to backup withholding because you did not report all your interest and dividends on your tax return (for reportable interest and dividends only), or

5. You do not certify to the requester that you are not subject to backup withholding under 4 above (for reportable interest and dividend accounts opened after 1983 only).

Certain payees and payments are exempt from backup withholding. See the instructions below and the separate Instructions for the Requester of Form W-9.

Also see *Special rules for partnerships* on page 1.

Penalties

Failure to furnish TIN. If you fail to furnish your correct TIN to a requester, you are subject to a penalty of $50 for each such failure unless your failure is due to reasonable cause and not to willful neglect.

Civil penalty for false information with respect to withholding. If you make a false statement with no reasonable basis that results in no backup withholding, you are subject to a $500 penalty.

Criminal penalty for falsifying information. Willfully falsifying certifications or affirmations may subject you to criminal penalties including fines and/or imprisonment.

Misuse of TINs. If the requester discloses or uses TINs in violation of federal law, the requester may be subject to civil and criminal penalties.

Specific Instructions

Name

If you are an individual, you must generally enter the name shown on your income tax return. However, if you have changed your last name, for instance, due to marriage without informing the Social Security Administration of the name change, enter your first name, the last name shown on your social security card, and your new last name.

If the account is in joint names, list first, and then circle, the name of the person or entity whose number you entered in Part I of the form.

Sole proprietor. Enter your individual name as shown on your income tax return on the "Name" line. You may enter your business, trade, or "doing business as (DBA)" name on the "Business name" line.

Limited liability company (LLC). Check the "Limited liability company" box only and enter the appropriate code for the tax classification ("D" for disregarded entity, "C" for corporation, "P" for partnership) in the space provided.

For a single-member LLC (including a foreign LLC with a domestic owner) that is disregarded as an entity separate from its owner under Regulations section 301.7701-3, enter the owner's name on the "Name" line. Enter the LLC's name on the "Business name" line.

For an LLC classified as a partnership or a corporation, enter the LLC's name on the "Name" line and any business, trade, or DBA name on the "Business name" line.

Other entities. Enter your business name as shown on required federal tax documents on the "Name" line. This name should match the name shown on the charter or other legal document creating the entity. You may enter any business, trade, or DBA name on the "Business name" line.

Note. You are requested to check the appropriate box for your status (individual/sole proprietor, corporation, etc.).

Exempt Payee

If you are exempt from backup withholding, enter your name as described above and check the appropriate box for your status, then check the "Exempt payee" box in the line following the business name, sign and date the form.

FIGURE 8–16
(continued)

Generally, individuals (including sole proprietors) are not exempt from backup withholding. Corporations are exempt from backup withholding for certain payments, such as interest and dividends.

Note. If you are exempt from backup withholding, you should still complete this form to avoid possible erroneous backup withholding.

The following payees are exempt from backup withholding:

1. An organization exempt from tax under section 501(a), any IRA, or a custodial account under section 403(b)(7) if the account satisfies the requirements of section 401(f)(2),

2. The United States or any of its agencies or instrumentalities,

3. A state, the District of Columbia, a possession of the United States, or any of their political subdivisions or instrumentalities,

4. A foreign government or any of its political subdivisions, agencies, or instrumentalities, or

5. An international organization or any of its agencies or instrumentalities.

Other payees that may be exempt from backup withholding include:

6. A corporation,

7. A foreign central bank of issue,

8. A dealer in securities or commodities required to register in the United States, the District of Columbia, or a possession of the United States,

9. A futures commission merchant registered with the Commodity Futures Trading Commission,

10. A real estate investment trust,

11. An entity registered at all times during the tax year under the Investment Company Act of 1940,

12. A common trust fund operated by a bank under section 584(a),

13. A financial institution,

14. A middleman known in the investment community as a nominee or custodian, or

15. A trust exempt from tax under section 664 or described in section 4947.

The chart below shows types of payments that may be exempt from backup withholding. The chart applies to the exempt payees listed above, 1 through 15.

IF the payment is for . . .	THEN the payment is exempt for . . .
Interest and dividend payments	All exempt payees except for 9
Broker transactions	Exempt payees 1 through 13. Also, a person registered under the Investment Advisers Act of 1940 who regularly acts as a broker
Barter exchange transactions and patronage dividends	Exempt payees 1 through 5
Payments over $600 required to be reported and direct sales over $5,000[1]	Generally, exempt payees 1 through 7[2]

[1] See Form 1099-MISC, Miscellaneous Income, and its instructions.

[2] However, the following payments made to a corporation (including gross proceeds paid to an attorney under section 6045(f), even if the attorney is a corporation) and reportable on Form 1099-MISC are not exempt from backup withholding: medical and health care payments, attorneys' fees, and payments for services paid by a federal executive agency.

Part I. Taxpayer Identification Number (TIN)

Enter your TIN in the appropriate box. If you are a resident alien and you do not have and are not eligible to get an SSN, your TIN is your IRS individual taxpayer identification number (ITIN). Enter it in the social security number box. If you do not have an ITIN, see *How to get a TIN* below.

If you are a sole proprietor and you have an EIN, you may enter either your SSN or EIN. However, the IRS prefers that you use your SSN.

If you are a single-member LLC that is disregarded as an entity separate from its owner (see *Limited liability company (LLC)* on page 2), enter the owner's SSN (or EIN, if the owner has one). Do not enter the disregarded entity's EIN. If the LLC is classified as a corporation or partnership, enter the entity's EIN.

Note. See the chart on page 4 for further clarification of name and TIN combinations.

How to get a TIN. If you do not have a TIN, apply for one immediately. To apply for an SSN, get Form SS-5, Application for a Social Security Card, from your local Social Security Administration office or get this form online at *www.ssa.gov*. You may also get this form by calling 1-800-772-1213. Use Form W-7, Application for IRS Individual Taxpayer Identification Number, to apply for an ITIN, or Form SS-4, Application for Employer Identification Number, to apply for an EIN. You can apply for an EIN online by accessing the IRS website at *www.irs.gov/businesses* and clicking on Employer Identification Number (EIN) under Starting a Business. You can get Forms W-7 and SS-4 from the IRS by visiting *www.irs.gov* or by calling 1-800-TAX-FORM (1-800-829-3676).

If you are asked to complete Form W-9 but do not have a TIN, write "Applied For" in the space for the TIN, sign and date the form, and give it to the requester. For interest and dividend payments, and certain payments made with respect to readily tradable instruments, generally you will have 60 days to get a TIN and give it to the requester before you are subject to backup withholding on payments. The 60-day rule does not apply to other types of payments. You will be subject to backup withholding on all such payments until you provide your TIN to the requester.

Note. Entering "Applied For" means that you have already applied for a TIN or that you intend to apply for one soon.

Caution: *A disregarded domestic entity that has a foreign owner must use the appropriate Form W-8.*

Part II. Certification

To establish to the withholding agent that you are a U.S. person, or resident alien, sign Form W-9. You may be requested to sign by the withholding agent even if items 1, 4, and 5 below indicate otherwise.

For a joint account, only the person whose TIN is shown in Part I should sign (when required). Exempt payees, see *Exempt Payee* on page 2.

Signature requirements. Complete the certification as indicated in 1 through 5 below.

1. Interest, dividend, and barter exchange accounts opened before 1984 and broker accounts considered active during 1983. You must give your correct TIN, but you do not have to sign the certification.

2. Interest, dividend, broker, and barter exchange accounts opened after 1983 and broker accounts considered inactive during 1983. You must sign the certification or backup withholding will apply. If you are subject to backup withholding and you are merely providing your correct TIN to the requester, you must cross out item 2 in the certification before signing the form.

FIGURE 8–16

(continued)

3. Real estate transactions. You must sign the certification. You may cross out item 2 of the certification.

4. Other payments. You must give your correct TIN, but you do not have to sign the certification unless you have been notified that you have previously given an incorrect TIN. "Other payments" include payments made in the course of the requester's trade or business for rents, royalties, goods (other than bills for merchandise), medical and health care services (including payments to corporations), payments to a nonemployee for services, payments to certain fishing boat crew members and fishermen, and gross proceeds paid to attorneys (including payments to corporations).

5. Mortgage interest paid by you, acquisition or abandonment of secured property, cancellation of debt, qualified tuition program payments (under section 529), IRA, Coverdell ESA, Archer MSA or HSA contributions or distributions, and pension distributions. You must give your correct TIN, but you do not have to sign the certification.

What Name and Number To Give the Requester

For this type of account:	Give name and SSN of:
1. Individual	The individual
2. Two or more individuals (joint account)	The actual owner of the account or, if combined funds, the first individual on the account [1]
3. Custodian account of a minor (Uniform Gift to Minors Act)	The minor [2]
4. a. The usual revocable savings trust (grantor is also trustee)	The grantor-trustee [1]
b. So-called trust account that is not a legal or valid trust under state law	The actual owner [1]
5. Sole proprietorship or disregarded entity owned by an individual	The owner [3]

For this type of account:	Give name and EIN of:
6. Disregarded entity not owned by an individual	The owner
7. A valid trust, estate, or pension trust	Legal entity [4]
8. Corporate or LLC electing corporate status on Form 8832	The corporation
9. Association, club, religious, charitable, educational, or other tax-exempt organization	The organization
10. Partnership or multi-member LLC	The partnership
11. A broker or registered nominee	The broker or nominee
12. Account with the Department of Agriculture in the name of a public entity (such as a state or local government, school district, or prison) that receives agricultural program payments	The public entity

[1] List first and circle the name of the person whose number you furnish. If only one person on a joint account has an SSN, that person's number must be furnished.

[2] Circle the minor's name and furnish the minor's SSN.

[3] You must show your individual name and you may also enter your business or "DBA" name on the second name line. You may use either your SSN or EIN (if you have one), but the IRS encourages you to use your SSN.

[4] List first and circle the name of the trust, estate, or pension trust. (Do not furnish the TIN of the personal representative or trustee unless the legal entity itself is not designated in the account title.) Also see *Special rules for partnerships* on page 1.

Note. If no name is circled when more than one name is listed, the number will be considered to be that of the first name listed.

Secure Your Tax Records from Identity Theft

Identity theft occurs when someone uses your personal information such as your name, social security number (SSN), or other identifying information, without your permission, to commit fraud or other crimes. An identity thief may use your SSN to get a job or may file a tax return using your SSN to receive a refund.

To reduce your risk:
● Protect your SSN,
● Ensure your employer is protecting your SSN, and
● Be careful when choosing a tax preparer.

Call the IRS at 1-800-829-1040 if you think your identity has been used inappropriately for tax purposes.

Victims of identity theft who are experiencing economic harm or a system problem, or are seeking help in resolving tax problems that have not been resolved through normal channels, may be eligible for Taxpayer Advocate Service (TAS) assistance. You can reach TAS by calling the TAS toll-free case intake line at 1-877-777-4778 or TTY/TDD 1-800-829-4059.

Protect yourself from suspicious emails or phishing schemes. Phishing is the creation and use of email and websites designed to mimic legitimate business emails and websites. The most common act is sending an email to a user falsely claiming to be an established legitimate enterprise in an attempt to scam the user into surrendering private information that will be used for identity theft.

The IRS does not initiate contacts with taxpayers via emails. Also, the IRS does not request personal detailed information through email or ask taxpayers for the PIN numbers, passwords, or similar secret access information for their credit card, bank, or other financial accounts.

If you receive an unsolicited email claiming to be from the IRS, forward this message to *phishing@irs.gov.* You may also report misuse of the IRS name, logo, or other IRS personal property to the Treasury Inspector General for Tax Administration at 1-800-366-4484. You can forward suspicious emails to the Federal Trade Commission at: *spam@uce.gov* or contact them at *www.consumer.gov/idtheft* or 1-877-IDTHEFT(438-4338).

Visit the IRS website at *www.irs.gov* to learn more about identity theft and how to reduce your risk.

Privacy Act Notice

Section 6109 of the Internal Revenue Code requires you to provide your correct TIN to persons who must file information returns with the IRS to report interest, dividends, and certain other income paid to you, mortgage interest you paid, the acquisition or abandonment of secured property, cancellation of debt, or contributions you made to an IRA, or Archer MSA or HSA. The IRS uses the numbers for identification purposes and to help verify the accuracy of your tax return. The IRS may also provide this information to the Department of Justice for civil and criminal litigation, and to cities, states, the District of Columbia, and U.S. possessions to carry out their tax laws. We may also disclose this information to other countries under a tax treaty, to federal and state agencies to enforce federal nontax criminal laws, or to federal law enforcement and intelligence agencies to combat terrorism.

You must provide your TIN whether or not you are required to file a tax return. Payers must generally withhold 28% of taxable interest, dividend, and certain other payments to a payee who does not give a TIN to a payer. Certain penalties may also apply.

FIGURE 8–16

(continued)

ESCROW AGREEMENT

The undersigned hereby agree that _____ as Escrow Agents, shall hold the sum of $ _____ from the Seller's net proceeds of the sale of _____ to secure the complaint of _____ for such property. Seller shall proceed with due diligence to complete such work on or before _____, 19 _____, weather permitting.

Upon completion of the work and a satisfactory inspection report by _____, the first mortgage lender, Escrow Agent shall disburse the escrowed funds to seller. In the event the required work is not completed as set forth in this agreement, purchaser and the first mortgage lender may use the escrowed funds to obtain such completion.

This the _____ day of _____, 19_____.

FIGURE 8–17

$500 or $1,000, to cover the cost of future repairs. The parties should execute an escrow agreement to protect their relative interests. See Figure 8–17.

The paralegal must monitor the situation to see that those repairs have taken place, and refund the balance if necessary.[10] Use the suggested flowchart at Figure 8–18[11] to track the history of escrow.

Finally, "review the closing statement and any closing memoranda to ensure that no matters are left unresolved. For example, certain documents or letters may need to be forwarded to different parties."[12]

► FLOW CHART ◄
FOR RESIDENTIAL USE ONLY

Subject Property: _____ Acceptance Date: _____ Close of Escrow Date: _____

Days from Acceptance	Due Date	Ordered	Received/ Completed	Responsible Party	CONTINGENCIES
3				BUYER:	Deposit of funds in escrow
3				SELLER:	Request from HOA required documents and disclosures
7				BUYER:	Lender letter stating Buyer is pre-qualified for the new loan ~ must include review of Buyer's written application and credit report.
7				BUYER:	Pre-Qualify or Pre-Approval letter, based on Buyers written application and credit report.
				SELLER:	
7					Pest Inspection, Water, Septic report, etc.
7					Delivery of all Inspections and Reports
7					Delivery of Statutory Disclosures (TDS, NHD, SSD, SDS, WHS, Lead, etc.)
7					Delivery of Booklets/Guides – Environmental Hazards, etc.
7					Delivery of Preliminary Title Report
17				BUYER:	Buyer to remove contingencies.
17				BUYER:	Complete all investigations; approve all disclosures and reports received from Seller (including lead-based paint and insurability). Within the time frame Buyer may request that Seller may make repairs or take other actions.
5 Days After Receipt				BUYER:	If Seller does NOT provide the following with the time specified above, Buyer has 5 days after receipt or until _____, or the time frame specified in 14 (B1) whichever is later, to remove the contingency; government-mandated reports Common Interest Disclosures (HOA Docs).
5 Days Before the COE				BUYER:	Final verification of condition (walk-through).

FIGURE 8–18

CHAPTER EIGHT **SUMMARY**

Chapter Eight discussed the following topics:

- Closing documentation necessary
- Compliance documentation
- Mortgage documents and escrow agreements
- Deed and title documentation
- Settlement sheet preparation and explanation in RESPA and non-RESPA settlements
- Preparation of a closing checklist
- Buyer and seller requirements at closing
- Disbursement of funds and proceeds
- When IRS reporting is necessary
- Recording of documents

REVIEW **QUESTIONS**

1. At settlement, the paralegal is responsible for a host of documents and mortgage and financing forms. List five examples.
2. What are some of the tasks that are the responsibility of the paralegal at closing?
3. What types of entries on a settlement sheet are prorated?
4. What circumstance may call for an escrow deposit at closing?
5. During the closing and settlement process, the paralegal must be certain that bills to governmental authorities are fully paid and properly prorated. What are some costs that are normally equally shared by the buyer and seller?
6. What are the types of charges a seller can expect to pay which are listed on the settlement sheet?
7. What types of government required documentation must be signed at closing?
8. What is the difference between a RESPA and non-RESPA settlement sheet?
9. What are the recordation procedure and costs in your area?
10. What types of funds are normally escrowed?

DISCUSSION **QUESTION**

What is the purpose of the Real Estate Settlement and Procedures Act? During a RESPA settlement, what additional information and documentation is required?

EXERCISE 1

Draft a Truth in Lending Disclosure Statement using the following facts:

Total of payments—$146,724.16

Finance charge—$78,490.08

Amount financed—$68,234.08

Annual percentage rate—10.904%

Life insurance—No

Security—Property being purchased

Recording fees—$50

Late charges—7% of principle and interest

Prepayment—2% penalty on outstanding principle and interest

Assumption—No

EXERCISE 2

Complete a HUD-1 Settlement Statement using the following facts:

Settlement Agent—Easy Settlement Inc., 3628 Easy Way, Mytown, US 00001

Type of Loan—Conventional

Name of Borrower—John Stokes, P.O. Box 000, Mytown, US 00000

Property Location—23 North Street, Mytown, US 00000

Name of Seller—Jake Smith

Name of Lender—National Bank, Plaza Two, Mytown, US, 00000

Place of Settlement—Settlement Agent's Office

Date of Settlement—November 3, 2009

Contract Sales Price—$68,500

Deposit—$6,000

Real Estate Commission—7% by seller

Loan Origination Fee—2 points

Credit Report—$15

Interest from 11/1–11/3—$14.62/days

Mortgage Insurance Premium—12 months—$540

Hazard Insurance—1 year—$326

County Property Taxes—3 months at $53.20

Title Insurance Binder—$20

Settlement Charge—$200 (buyer)

Title Insurance—$300

Recording Fees—$72.50

State Transfer Tax—$700 (buyer)

Survey—$200 (seller)

Pest Inspection—$70 (seller)

Seller's Mortgage Payoff—$25,874

Document Preparation Fee—$40

Notary Fees—$15

Federal Express Charges—$75

Appraisal Fee—$300

ASSIGNMENT FOR THE CASE OF JOHN AND MARTHA

Complete a HUD-1 Settlement sheet using the following additional information:

Settlement Agent—Settlements UR Way, 100 May Street, June USA

Type of Loan—Conventional

Name of Lender—USA Bank, July Plaza, June USA

Place of Settlement—Settlement Agent's Office

Date of Settlement—July 10, 2009

Real Estate Commission—7% by seller

Loan Origination Fee—1 point

Credit Report—$15

Interest Rate—6%

Interest from—1st—10th—at $12.03/day

Mortgage Insurance Premium—1 year—$350

Hazard Insurance—1 year—$425

County Transfer Taxes—1% of Sales Price—paid by buyer

City Transfer Taxes—0.5%—paid by buyer

School Taxes—$1574 paid until July 1, 2009

County Property Tax— $935—Paid until April 1, 2009

Title Insurance Binder—$40

Settlement Charge—$300—paid by buyer

Title Insurance—$350

Recording Fees—75.50

State Transfer Tax—1% of sale price

Survey—$200—previously paid by seller

Pest Inspection—$150—previously paid by seller

Seller's Mortgage Payoff—$35,600

Document Preparation Fee—$75

Notary Fees—$25

Federal Express Charges—$115

Appraisal Fee—$325

REFERENCES

1. John H. Kupillas Jr., *Attorney Etiquette at Residential Real Estate Closings*, 62 N.Y. State B. J. 44 (1990); Judy A. Long, Office Procedures for the Legal Professional (2004).
2. 12 U.S.C. §2601(a) (2008).
3. Robert E. Schreiner, Real Estate Closing 281 (1983).
4. 12 U.S.C. §2603 (2008).
5. Stevens A. Carey, *Prorations: Watch Out for Real Estate Taxes Paid in Arrears*, 8 Real Est. Fin. J. 11, 14 (1993).

6. Schreiner, *supra* note 3, at 218–19.

7. Easy Soft Inc., 212 North Center Drive, North Brunswick NJ 08902, www.easysoft-usa.com.

8. I.R.C. § 6045(e) (1994).

9. R. Clark Morrison & David F. Abele, *Reporting Real Estate Transactions to the IRS* (with Form), 8 PRAC. REAL EST. LAW. 63, 65 (1992).

10. Robert L. Flores, *A Comparison of the Rules and Rationales for Allocating Risks Arising in Realty Sales Using Executory Sale Contracts and Escrows* 59 MO. L. REV. 307 (1994).

11. *See* Tehama County Association of Realtors, *Flowchart*, 956 Walnut Street, Red Bluff, CA 96080(530) 529–0430 http://tcaor.com/PDF_Forms/Flow%20Chart.pdf.

12. INSTITUTE OF CONTINUING LEGAL EDUCATION, 1 MICHIGAN BASIC PRACTICE HANDBOOK 104 (1986).

Leases in the Real Estate Transaction

LEARNING OBJECTIVES

- To review the nature of a leasehold and when they are appropriate in a buy/sell transaction.
- To explain the various parties to a lease.
- To identify various elements of a lease and be able to draft a legally enforceable document.
- To recognize the various remedies available in the event that a lease is either breached or defaulted.

JOB COMPETENCIES

- In conjunction with an attorney, prepare a lease.
- To work cooperatively with landlords and tenants who may be clients of the firm.
- To prepare, in conjunction with an attorney, all eviction papers.
- To assist the attorney in enforcing the rights of landlord or tenant in a contractual dispute under the leasehold.
- To develop relationships with governmental agencies regarding statutory and code qualifications of leasehold housing.
- To draft specialized leases in conjunction with an attorney.

ETHICAL CONSIDERATIONS

The paralegal must be aware of the following ethical dilemmas during this phase of a real estate transaction:

- Unauthorized practice of law
- Lawyer supervision of nonlawyers

I. INTRODUCTION

KEY WORDS

ejectment	lessor
eviction	option
forcible entry and detainer	plain English
holdover	real estate management agreement
landlord	reentry
lease	tenancy
leasehold	tenant
lessee	trespass

Often the matter of leases seems contrary and irrelevant to the full transfer and alienation of a property. Upon closer inspection, leases play a frequent, but peripheral, role in the buy-sell transaction. This chapter summarizes those occasions and provides a series of working documents that:

1. Initiate leaseholds,
2. Protect both vendor/lessor and vendee/lessee during tenancy, and
3. Contractually set out the parties' rights and obligations, if the vendor seeks to transfer the real estate property permanently and without reservation.

Why, at times, would a lease be involved? What advantages does the lease arrangement have for traditional parties to the real estate transaction? Before considering these policy questions, a brief overview of lease elements is presented.

II. THE NATURE OF A LEASE

As noted in Chapter 1, freehold estates are generally limitless in regard to time. When a buyer buys fee simple, the buyer owns what was bought forever. By contrast, a lease, lacking a freehold, fee simple nature, contains a calculated, definite period of possession to specifically described real property. A **tenancy**, or lease, has limits of time and possessory interest. A lease is "defined as a conveyance or grant or demise of certain described land or tenement (usually in consideration of rent or other recompense) for a prescribed period or at will, but for less time than the lessor has in the premises. A lease embraces any agreement, whether express or implied, that gives rise to the relationship of landlord and tenant. When property is leased to a tenant, the law regards the lease as equivalent to a sale of the premises for the term."[1]

A lease is a contractual undertaking expressly entered into by one who leases out (the **landlord/lessor**) and one who desires to rent a certain property (the **tenant/lessee**). If the lease is for more than three years, the Statute of Frauds mandates writing. The Statute of Frauds acts primarily as an affirmative defense than a requirement. Only if, and when, a party asserts a claim or right under the provision of a lease, does the statute apply. Ohio's codification addresses its usage.

(A) A lease contract is not enforceable by way of action or defense unless one of the following applies:

(1) The total payments to be made under the lease contract, excluding payments for options to renew or buy, are less than $1,000.

(2) There is a writing, signed by the party against whom enforcement is sought or by that party's authorized agent, sufficient to indicate that a lease contract has been made between the parties and to describe the goods leased and the lease term.

(B) Any description of leased goods or of the lease term is sufficient and satisfies division (A)(2) of this section, whether or not it is specific, if it reasonably identifies what is described.

(C) A writing is not insufficient because it omits or incorrectly states a term agreed upon, but the lease contract is not enforceable under division (A)(2) of this section beyond the lease term and the quantity of goods shown in the writing.[2]

For all practical purposes, every lease regardless of its duration should be in writing.

To have legal effect, a lease needs:

- Lessor
- Lessee
- Premises
- Written document
- Specific term of possession
- Terms

The standard lease, usually seen in apartment complexes or residential rent circumstances, encompasses these criteria. See Figure 9–1[3] that includes:

- Parties to the lease
- Premises that will be the subject of the lease
- Right of usage and corresponding restrictions
- Rent amount
- Term and possession of the lease
- Rights to renewal
- Rights to possession
- Covenants to the lease

The language of leases is further buttressed by a wide array of statutory and legislative enactments that impact on tenant/landlord behavior. **Plain English** requirements represent this push and force landlords to redraft leases in understandable, nonlegalistic language. Pennsylvania has been in the forefront of this movement toward clarity in lease documents. Here is a part of the act that provides this protection.

Lease

This Lease is made on
BETWEEN the Tenant(s)

whose address is

referred to as the "Tenant,"
AND the Landlord

whose address is

referred to as the "Landlord."
The word "Tenant" means each Tenant named above.

1. Property. The Tenant agrees to rent from the Landlord and the Landlord agrees to lease to the Tenant the property known as

referred to as the "Property."

2. Term. The term of this Lease is for   starting on   and ending   . The Landlord is not responsible if the Landlord cannot give the Tenant possession of the Property at the start of this Lease. However, rent will only be charged from the date on which possession of the Property is made available to the Tenant. If the Landlord cannot give possession within 30 days after the starting date, the Tenant may cancel this Lease.

3. Rent. The Tenant agrees to pay $ as rent, to be paid as follows: $ per month, due on the   day of each month. The first payment of rent and any security deposit is due upon the signing of this Lease by the Tenant. The Tenant must pay a late charge of $ for each payment that is more than 10 days late. This late charge is due with the monthly rent payment. All rent and other payments due Landlord hereunder shall be made at the address given above or such other address as Landlord shall specify in writing.

4. Use of Property. The Tenant may use the Property only for the following purpose(s):

5. Eviction. If the Tenant does not pay the rent within   days after it is due, the Tenant may be evicted. The Landlord may also evict the Tenant if the Tenant does not comply with all of the terms of this Lease and for all other causes allowed by law. If evicted, the Tenant must continue to pay the rent for the rest of the term. The Tenant must also pay all costs, including reasonable attorney fees, related to the eviction and the collection of any moneys owed the Landlord, along with the cost of re-entering, re-renting, cleaning and repairing the Property. Rent received from any new tenant will reduce the amount owed the Landlord.

6. Payments by the Landlord. If the Tenant fails to comply with the terms of this Lease, the Landlord may take any required action and charge the cost, including reasonable attorney fees, to the Tenant as additional rent. Failure to pay such additional rent upon demand is a violation of this Lease.

7. Care of the Property. The Tenant has examined the Property, including all facilities, furniture and appliances, and is satisfied with its present condition. The Tenant agrees to maintain the property in as good condition as it is at the start of this Lease except for ordinary wear and tear. The Tenant must pay for all repairs, replacements and damages caused by the act or neglect of the Tenant or the Tenant's visitors. The Tenant will remove all of the Tenant's property at the end of this Lease. Any property that is left becomes the property of the Landlord and may be thrown out.

8. Quiet Enjoyment. The Tenant may remain in and use the Property without interference by Landlord or anyone claiming through Landlord, subject to the terms of this Lease.

9. Validity of Lease. If a clause or provision of this Lease is legally invalid, the rest of this Lease remains in effect.

251 - Lease - General
Ind. or Corp. Plain Language
Rev. 9/02   P11/07

©2002 by ALL-STATE LEGAL®
A Division of ALL-STATE International, Inc.
www.aslegal.com   800.222.0510   Page 1

FIGURE 9–1
(continues)

10. Lead Paint Lease Disclosure. The Landlord, Tenant and Agent (if any), have signed the "Disclosure to Tenants" form for lease of residential property (if the housing was built before 1978). For all such above leases the tenant has also been provided with a copy of the EPA pamphlet, "Protect Your Family from Lead in Your Home." 42 U.S.C. 4852d; 24 C.F.R. 35.88; 40 C.F.R. 745.107.

11. Private Well Testing Act (N.J.S.A. 58:12A-26 et seq.) In accordance with the Private Well Testing Act (the "Act"), if potable water for the Property is supplied by a private well, and testing of the water supply is not required pursuant to any other State law, Landlord is required to test the water (i) by March 14, 2004, and (ii) every five years thereafter, in the manner established under the Act and to provide a copy of the results thereof to each tenant. If such testing has been done prior to the date hereof, upon signing this Lease, Landlord shall provide Tenant with a written copy of the most recent test results.

12. Parties. The Landlord and each of the Tenants is bound by this Lease. All parties who lawfully succeed to their rights and responsibilities are also bound.

13. Entire Lease. All promises the Landlord has made are contained in this written lease. This Lease can only be changed by an agreement in writing by both the Tenant and the Landlord.

14. Signatures. The Landlord and the Tenant agree to the terms of this Lease. If this Lease is made by a corporation, its proper corporate officers sign and its corporate seal is affixed.

Witnessed or Attested by:

_____   _____ (Seal)
                                                     Landlord

_____   _____ (Seal)
                                                     Tenant

                                  _____ (Seal)
                                                     Tenant

LEASE	Dated:
	Expires on
Landlord	
TO	Rent $
Tenant	

251 - Lease - General
Ind. or Corp. Plain Language
Rev. 9/02   P11/07

©2002 by ALL-STATE LEGAL®
A Division of ALL-STATE International, Inc.
www.aslegal.com 800.222.0510   Page 2

FIGURE 9–1

(continued)

432 ▤ ▦ ▬ *Reality of Real Estate*

§ 2201. Short title

This act shall be known and may be cited as the Plain Language Consumer Contract Act.

§ 2202. Legislative findings and intent

(a) LEGISLATIVE FINDINGS.– The General Assembly finds that many consumer contracts are written, arranged, and designed in a way that makes them hard for consumers to understand. Competition would be aided if these contracts were easier to understand.

(b) LEGISLATIVE INTENT.– By passing this act, the General Assembly wants to promote the writing of consumer contracts in plain language. This act will protect consumers from making contracts that they do not understand. It will help consumers know better their rights and duties under those contracts.

§ 2203. Definitions

The following words and phrases when used in this act shall have the meanings given to them in this section unless the context clearly indicates otherwise:

"CONSUMER." Any individual who borrows, buys, leases, or obtains credit, money, services, or property under a consumer contract.

"CONSUMER CONTRACT" or "CONTRACT." A written agreement between a consumer and a party acting in the usual course of business, made primarily for personal, family, or household purposes in which a consumer does any of the following:

(1) Borrows money

(2) Buys, leases, or rents personal property, real property, or services for cash or on credit

(3) Obtains credit

§ 2204. Application of act and interpretation

(a) GENERAL RULE.– This act applies to all contracts that are made, solicited, or intended to be performed in this Commonwealth after the effective date of this act.

(b) EXCLUSIONS.– This act does not apply to the following:

(1) Real estate conveyance documents and contracts, deeds and mortgages, real estate certificates of title, and title insurance contracts.

(2) Consumer contracts involving amounts of more than $50,000.

(3) Marital agreements.

(4) Contracts to buy securities.

(5) Documents used by financial institutions, which financial institutions are subject to examination or other supervision by Federal or State regulatory authorities, or documents used by affiliates, subsidiaries, or service corporations of such financial institutions.

(6) Contracts for insurance or insurance policies.

(7) Contracts subject to examination or other supervision by the Pennsylvania Public Utility Commission or by the Federal Energy Regulatory Commission.

(8) Commercial leases.

(c) INTERPRETATION.– This act shall be liberally interpreted to protect consumers.[4]

Standard leases discuss both landlord obligation and **lessee** rights dealing with express and implied covenants, rights of quiet enjoyment, warranties, services, and repairs. In the same document, clauses covering maintenance and repair and indemnification for destruction are drafted. Both lessor and lessee have a series of rights and obligations, all of which are fully discernible in a well-drafted lease.

III. LEASES IN A BUY-SELL CONTRACT

There are times when a lessee may wish to test or try out a specific property before plunging into an outright purchase. Other times, a prospective buyer lacks the financial resources to purchase presently but wishes to lock up the property by promising to purchase in the future. In both of these cases, a lease purchase agreement may be appropriate. Before preparation of the lease by the paralegal, the prospective buyer should be screened, as any other tenant would be when entering into a lease. During the initial interview, a rental application, similar to Figure 9–2, should be completed.

RENTAL APPLICATION

NOTICE:　　Co-Applicant must complete a separate Rental Application Form.
The undersigned hereby makes application to rent _____ located at beginning on
_____, 20_____, at a monthly rent of $_____.

PLEASE TELL US ABOUT YOURSELF

FULL NAME _____ Phone (_____) _____
Date of Birth _____ Social Security No. _____
Name of Co-Applicant _____
Number of Dependents (excluding Co-Applicant) _____
Ages of Dependents _____
Other Occupants and their Relationship _____
Pets (Number and Kind) _____

PLEASE GIVE YOUR RESIDENCE HISTORY FOR THE PAST 3 YEARS
(Beginning with the most current)

CURRENT ADDRESS _____
Month & Year moved in _____
Reason for Leaving _____
Owner or Agent _____ Phone (_____) _____
PREVIOUS ADDRESS (if within 3 years) _____
Month & Year moved in _____ Moved out _____
Reason for Leaving _____
Owner or Agent _____ Phone (_____) _____

PLEASE GIVE YOUR EMPLOYMENT INFORMATION

YOUR STATUS　　　[ ] Employed Full-Time　[ ] Employed Part-Time
　　　　　　　　　[ ] Student　[ ] Retired　　[ ] Unemployed

EMPLOYER _____
Dates Employed _____ Employed as _____
Supervisor _____ Phone (_____) _____
Address _____
Salary $_____per _____

If employed by above less than six months, give name and address of previous employer or school.
_____

FIGURE 9–2
(continues)

```
LEASE LIST YOUR BANK AND CREDIT REFERENCE

Your Bank(s)      City-State       Branch  Type of Acct.     Acct. #
1. _____
2. _____
3. _____
Your Driver's License Number _____ State _____
Your Vehicle Make/Model _____ Year _____ Tag No. _____ State _____
Second Vehicle Make/Model _____ Year _____ Tag No. _____ State _____

I hereby deposit $_____ in earnest money to be refunded to me if this application is not
accepted within ____ business banking days, plus a $25.00 NONREFUNDABLE credit investigation
fee. Upon acceptance of this application, this deposit shall be retained as part of the security deposit.
When so approved and accepted I agree to execute a lease for _____ months and agree to pay the
balance of the security deposit within ____ business banking days after being notified of acceptance,
or the deposit will be forfeited as liquidated damages in payment for the agent's time and effort in
processing my inquiry and application, including making necessary investigation of my credit,
character, and reputation. If this application is not approved and accepted by the owner or agent, the
deposit will be refunded, the applicant thereby waiving any claim for damages by reason of
nonacceptance which the owner or his agent may reject without stating any reason for so doing.

The above information, to the best of my knowledge, is true and correct.
APPLICANT'S SIGNATURE _____ DATE _____
```

FIGURE 9–2
(continued)

If an application paints a positive portrait of a tenant, the landlord/seller may decide to enter into a temporary lease, but not necessarily an obligation to buy. In the instance cited previously, the prospective buyer wishes to "kick the tires" of the rental property without a binding commitment, and the lease contains an **option**. An option is mainly a right to purchase, exercisable solely by purchase, with no legal liability for failure to do so. Figure 9–3 contains a Lease Agreement and Option to Purchase contract.

IV. LEASES FOR SELLERS IN REAL ESTATE TRANSACTIONS

When the seller cannot vacate the premises subject to the conveyance until after the formal closing date, a lease for sellers' possession past the closing date may be desirable. It is customary that the agreement of sale reflect this status in an addendum with an extra clause, provision, or any other incorporated document. "If the agreement of sale provides that settlement is to be held prior to the date of possession, a lease should be prepared for execution by seller at the time of settlement."[5] If the sellers desire this accommodation, it is sound practice for the paralegal to memorialize it with a letter to the prospective buyers. See Figure 9–4.

In Figure 9–5, a short-term lease protects the buyer who allows the seller to remain in a **leasehold** capacity.

If for some legitimate reason, the short-term lease needs a temporary extension, an addendum to the sales contract or existing lease referencing this document is appropriate. See Figure 9–6.

V. LEASES BY BUYERS IN REAL ESTATE TRANSACTIONS

Witnessed with less regularity is the lease instrument granted on behalf of a buyer. In this case, the sellers have vacated the premises in advance of the official closing date and, at the same time, have no objection to the buyers having physical possession of the property.

LEASE AGREEMENT AND OPTION TO PURCHASE

THIS LEASE AGREEMENT ("Agreement" or "Lease"), made this ___ day of
_____.

BY AND BETWEEN:

1. PARTIES: _____ and _____, his wife, hereinafter referred to as "Lessor";

AND

_____ and _____, his wife, hereinafter referred to as "Lessee."

2. LEASE. In consideration of the covenants and promises hereby mutually undertaken to be kept and performed by the parties hereto, Lessor hereby leases to Lessee and Lessee hereby rents and takes the condominium unit located at _____, _____, State of _____, (hereinafter the "Demised Premises"). (For legal description see attached Exhibit "A").

3. TERMS. This lease shall be for a maximum of _____ (__) months commencing on the ____ day of _____, year__, and ending on the ____ day of _____,

4. TERMINATION OF LEASE. This Lease shall automatically terminate if the option set forth in paragraph 15 if not exercised by Lessee prior to _____,___ or, if there has been an unremedied default in accordance with paragraph 20 of this Lease.

5. RENT. Lessee hereby covenant and agree to pay Lessor, without notice, demand, or setoff at the address to be specified by Lessor, in equal monthly installments in advance, on or before the first day of each and every month during said term, and sum of _____ ($_____). Also due and payable shall be an option payment of _____ ($_____) as outlined in paragraph 15 hereof.

A. Further, Lessee agrees that if such rent and option payment are not paid on or by the tenth day of every month, Lessee shall be subject to a late charge of _____ ($____) per month.

B. Lessee is aware that the current condominium fee of _____ ($_____) is due and payable by Lessee to the Condominium Association on or before the first of each month. Furthermore, a late fee is imposed currently of $_____ for any fee paid after the ___ day of the month. All current and future condominium fees due during the term of special amounts and assessments which shall become due and payable or which are issued against or levied upon the Demised Premises during the term of this Lease.

7. UTILITIES. It shall be the Lessees' responsibility and expense to obtain the transfer of all utility accounts into the Lessee's name. Lessee shall pay all charges for gas, water, sewage, electricity, light, heat or power, telephone used or supplied in connection with the Demised Premises, and all other utility services used or supplied in connection with the Demised Premises during the term . f this Lease. Lessee shall supply proof of payment of the utilities upon request by the Lessor during the term of the Lease. Upon vacating the Demised Premises, Lessee shall submit proof of payment of all utilities used in connection with the Demised Premises.

FIGURE 9–3
(continues)

8. INSURANCE. Lessee agrees to hold harmless Lessor from any loss due to theft or other criminal act during the term of this Agreement. During the term of this Lease, the Lessor agrees to maintain and keep in force a residential dwelling policy with $_____ of liability coverage and $_____ in medical payment coverage.

Lessee, during the term of this Agreement, agrees to maintain and keep in force a renters' insurance policy with a minimum amount of $_____ in public liability insurance and $_____ in medical payment coverage. Lessee, at the time of the signing of this Agreement, will provide proof of such coverage to the Lessor and shall subsequently provide proof to the Lessor of such coverage upon every anniversary date of this Agreement thereafter.

The cost of all insurance coverage carried by Lessor during the term of this Agreement and required by this Agreement on the Demised Premises, shall be reimbursed to the Lessor within _____ (__) days after notice is given to Lessee of the premium then due and owing.

9. FURNITURE & APPLIANCES. Any appliance, furniture, draperies, or the like, left on the Demised Premises by the Lessor are left in an "as is" condition and as a convenience to the Lessee and they shall not be repaired or replaced by the Lessor during the term of the Lease. Regardless of the foregoing, Lessee shall be liable for any damages to any property on the Demised Premises which damage is the fault of the Lessee, their agents and invitees.

A. Lessee specifically acknowledges that the Demised Premises were equipped with the following items, in good working order, upon their occupancy: [list items]
[list any items removed by the Lessor prior to Lessees' occupancy]

10. REPAIRS. The Lessee acknowledges that the Demised Premises and all appliances are being accepted by the Lessee "as is" without any warranties or representations of any kind from the Lessor or their agents. The responsibility for repair of all appliances and the routine and normal repairs to the Demised Premises are the responsibility of the Lessee during the term of this Lease Agreement. If any repairs remain unfinished in whole or in part, the Lessor, after _____ (__) days written notice to the Lessee of the need of such repair, the Lessor may make such repair and charge the cost of the repair as rent due and owing to Lessor with the next month's rent.

11. DESTRUCTION OF PREMISES. Should the Demised Premises be destroyed or rendered unfit for use and occupancy by fire or other casualty, in whole or in part, Lessor shall, at his option replace or repair the same, or terminate the Lease. In the event this Lease is terminated for this reason, the option payments shall be retained by Lessor.

At the option of the Lessee, if the property or the building of which it is a part, shall be damaged by fire or other peril or casualty during the term of this Lease Agreement, the Lessee may repair such damage, at Lessee's cost and expense. Such repairs by Lessee, Lessor shall assign to Lessee the proceeds of the insurance policy maintained by Lessor. Damage to the property of the building by fire or other casualty shall not automatically cause a termination of this Agreement.

12. DEFECTS. Lessee agrees that the Demised Premises have been inspected prior to the execution of this Lease and Lessee has found the Demised Premises to be habitable and in good repair. Lessor shall not be liable to Lessee or any other person for any loss suffered during the term of this Lease on account of any defective condition of the Demised Premises. In this regard, Lessee shall indemnify Lessor against all suits, actions or claims made on account of the condition of the Demised Premises.

13. ALTERATIONS AND IMPROVEMENTS. Lessee shall not structurally alter nor substantially repair the Demised Premises or any item therein without the consent of the Lessor. Such consent shall not be unreasonably withheld by Lessor. Upon vacating the Demised Premises, Lessee shall make "broom clean" all carpeting, appliances and all other areas of the Demised Premises.

FIGURE 9–3
(continued)

14. USE OF PREMISES. The Demised Premises shall be used and occupied by Lessee exclusively as a private single family residence, and neither the premises nor any part thereof shall be used at any time during the term of this Lease by Lessee for the purpose of carrying on any business, profession, or trade of any kind, or for any purpose other than as a private single family residence. Lessee shall comply with all the sanitary laws, ordinances, rules and orders of appropriate governmental authorities and the Homeowners' Association affecting the cleanliness, occupancy and preservation of the Demised Premises, and the sidewalks connected thereto, during the term of this Lease. The only pet permitted on the Demised Premises shall be one dog.

15. OPTION TO PURCHASE. Lessor hereby grants to Lessee the option to purchase, at the time, for the consideration and upon the terms and conditions set forth hereafter:

A. Lessee may purchase the Demised Premises at any time after the effective date of the Lease Agreement and prior to the 15th month of the Lease Agreement by giving _____ (__) days written notice to the Lessor of their intent to purchase the Demised Premises. Such notice shall also be accompanied with a signed, standard multi-list sales agreement which shall incorporate all terms of the purchase set forth herein and provide a closing date within _____ (__) days of the mailing of the notice and sales agreement. The sales agreement will be reviewed by the Lessor and if it contains the terms and conditions of sale accurately set forth as herein, Lessor shall sign said agreement and return it to the Lessee.

The terms of purchase shall be as follows:

A. Sales price to be _____ DOLLARS ($_____) and shall include all appliances and drapes left on the Demised Premises. The closing costs shall be divided as outlined on a standard multi-list condominium sales agreement and as is the custom of buyers and sellers in the area of _____ at the time of this closing. Lessor acknowledges receipt of one note for _____ DOLLARS ($_____) to be redeemed for cash on or before _____,year____. Said note will be held by the Broker until the option is exercised by the Lessee. This note with interest will be forfeited if the option is not exercised by Lessee or his assigns. Any interest accumulating prior to closing will be the sole property of the Lessor.

B. The monthly option payment of _____ DOLLARS ($_____) shall be paid along with the rent due to the Lessor. If the option is not exercised by Lessee, all option payments shall be forfeited and become the exclusive sole property of the Lessor.

C. In addition to the monthly rent and option payment due Lessor from Lessee, there shall also be due and owing during the term of this Lease Agreement, quarterly option payments of _____ DOLLARS ($_____) which shall be due to Lessor on: [list dates]_____

D. In the event that Lessee properly exercises the option during the term of the Lease Agreement, full credit of all option payments shall be given to Lessee toward the purchase price of the Demised Premises.

E. The Demised Premises shall be conveyed by the Lessor to the Lessee free and clear of all liens or encumbrances and the transfer of the Demised Premises by the Lessor to Lessee shall be by a general warranty deed.

F. The right to exercise this option is conditioned upon the faithful performance by the Lessee of all the covenants, conditions and agreements required to be performed by it as Lessee under this Lease, and the payment by the Lessee of all rent and any other payments as provided in this Lease Agreement to the closing date.

G. Adjustments and proration of taxes, insurance premiums and similar items shall be made as of the closing date.

FIGURE 9–3
(continued)

16. ASSIGNMENT. Lessee shall not assign this Lease Agreement without the written consent of Lessor. Such consent shall be conditioned upon a credit check on the third party assignee acceptable to Lessor. Any assignee of this Agreement shall agree in writing to be bound by all the terms and conditions contained in this Agreement including the option provisions as contained herein.

17. INSPECTION. Lessor shall have the right upon _____ (__) hours oral notice to Lessee to enter the Demised Premises for the purpose of making inspections, or for other purposes of protection of such premises. Such notice shall be deemed waived in the event of an emergency.

18. SIDEWALKS AND DRIVEWAY. Except as provided in paragraph 12, Lessee shall be solely responsible for any damage caused by or for any accident due or allegedly due to the defective or dangerous condition of sidewalks and driveway, including any such condition due to ice or snow.

19. SURRENDER OF PREMISES. At the expiration or termination of this Lease, Lessee shall surrender the Demised Premises to Lessor in the same condition as when Lessee took possession, reasonable wear and tear excepted.

20. DEFAULT BY LESSEE. The Lessee further agrees to perform fully, obey, and comply with all the ordinances, rules, regulations and laws of all public authorities, boards, condominium association boards and officers relating to said premises, or the improvements thereon, or to the use thereof, and further, not to use or occupy, or suffer or permit any person or body to use or occupy the same premises, or any part thereof, for any purpose or use in violation of any law, statute or ordinance, whether federal, state or municipal, during the term of said Lease Agreement or any renewal thereof.

In the event of any default by the Lessee in the payment of any rent and any monies herein required to be paid, or any sum owed by the Lessee because of repairs made by the Lessor and payable by the Lessee pursuant to the terms of this Lease Agreement, and said default is not corrected by the Lessee within _____ (__) days of the date written notice of default is mailed to Lessee, or if the default be made at any time in any of the covenants or terms herein, and remains unremedied for a period of _____ (__) days after written notice is mailed to the Lessee, then this Agreement shall, at the sole discretion of Lessor, terminate, all option monies held by the Lessor shall become the sole property of Lessor and the Lessor shall be permitted to take whatever legal action is necessary in law or equity to enforce their rights to collect monies owed by Lessee and take possession of the Demised Premises.

Similarly, in the event of default by the Lessor in the payment of any monies herein required to be paid by Lessor, and said default is not corrected by the Lessor within fifteen (15) days of the date written notice of default is mailed to Lessor, or if the default be made at any time in any of the covenants or terms herein remain unremedied for a period of fifteen (15) days after written notice is mailed to the Lessor, then, at the election of the Lessee, this Lease Agreement shall (1) terminate and all option payments now being held by Lessor shall be returned to Lessee, or, (2) the Lessee shall be permitted to take whatever action in law or equity necessary to collect money owed by Lessor, and retain possession of the Demised Premises.

21. MERGER. This Lease Agreement constitutes the entire agreement between the parties hereto and there are no other understandings, representations or warranties, oral or written, relating to the subject matter hereof. This Lease Agreement may not be changed, modified or amended, in whole or in part, except as done in writing, signed by both parties.

FIGURE 9–3
(continued)

22. NOTICES. Any notice or other communication that shall be given hereunder, unless otherwise stated, shall be deemed to have been given when made in writing and mailed to the party to whom it is addressed, postage prepaid by registered or certified mail with the United States postal service at the address set forth below for such party or such address as may hereinafter be designated by notice in writing to the other party.

23. JOINT AND BINDING EFFECT. The understanding and obligations of the Lessor and Lessee shall be joint and several and this Lease shall be considered to be binding on the respective parties hereto, their heirs, executors, administrators, personal representatives, successors and assigns, except as provided in this Lease.

24. TIME OF THE ESSENCE. Time is of the essence for all payments, duties and obligations called for all payments, duties and obligations called for in this Agreement.

25. STRICT PERFORMANCE. The failure of either party to this Agreement, whether intentional or unintentional, to insist upon strict performance of any provision under this Agreement, shall neither be construed as a waiver, release, relinquishment nor forgiveness thereof.

26. CONDOMINIUM RULES AND REGULATIONS. Lessee acknowledges receipt of a copy of the _____Homeowners Association Handbook (approximately 39 pages), affecting the Demised Premises and agree for themselves and their guests to observe all applicable rules and regulations affecting the Demised Premises.

IN WITNESS WHEREOF, the said parties, intending to be legally bound, have hereunto set their hands and seals the day and year first above written.

WITNESS: LESSOR:

_____   _____(SEAL)
                            [Typed Name]

_____   _____(SEAL)
                            [Typed Name]

ADDRESS:_____

_____

WITNESS: LESSEE:

_____   _____(SEAL)
                            [Typed Name]

_____   _____(SEAL)
                            [Typed Name]

ADDRESS:_____

_____

FIGURE 9–3
(continued)

_____, year _____

Mr. and Mrs. Thomas Smith
c/o Mochnsky & Dublonsky
Attorneys at Law
58 Green Street
Anytown, PA 00000

RE: 237 Lock Street
       Anytown, Wherever County
       Your State

Dear Mr. and Mrs. Smith,

As the sellers of the above premises, pursuant to our contract dated _____, year _____, we are not entitled to remain in possession of the premises after closing. However, at our request, and your gracious acceptance, continued possession is being extended to us. We agree at the closing, all adjustments will be as of _____, year _____. During the time of extended possession, we will pay all maintenance and utilities of premises, including gas, oil, water, sewage, electricity, etc.
        [set out relationship of seller and buyer that will exist, e.g., tenant and landlord, or licensee and licensor.]

In the event that possession is not surrendered to you by _____, year _____, we agree that upon _____ days' notice, in writing from you, or your attorney/agent we will vacate the premises, being broom clean and in good condition. Full payment of the monthly rate of $_____ will then be made to you, as apportioned from _____, ____ to such date. Furthermore, in the event that we refuse to remove ourselves and possessions on the date set forth in any notice given, we hereby agree to reimburse you for all reasonable costs and expenses incurred by you in regard to recovering possession of the property, including reasonable attorney's fees and an additional $_____ per day for each day we continue in possession after the date of said revocation of [license/lease]. You are hereby authorized to deduct such sum from the amount of $_____ deposited at closing with your attorney/agent before returning the balance to us.

We acknowledge that you have the right to inspect said house after the premises are vacated. We agree that your closing of title, in reliance upon this letter agreement, shall not constitute an acceptance of the house in its present state and condition, and any representation, covenants, promises, or obligations made by us as set forth in said contract shall survive the closing of title and delivery and acceptance of the deed. Further, we agree that all of the personal property set forth in the contract as included in the sale shall be present in the house upon surrender of our [license/lease]. We further agree that while we are in possession of said house, after the closing of title, we shall take good care of the premises, make all necessary and reasonable repairs, and be responsible for any damage. We further agree to indemnify you and hold you harmless from all damages caused by our occupancy of said house. The money deposited at closing with your attorney/agent shall be held by him or her also as a fund out of which you shall be reimbursed for such damages, after the assessment of same. We agree to continue our insurance on the premises until such time as we turn over possession to you.

Agreed and Accepted: Very truly yours,

_____   _____
Thomas H. Smith   Roger A. Thomas

_____   _____
Nancy R. Smith   Susan C. Thomas

FIGURE 9–4

SHORT-TERM LEASE

Address: _____

Seller: _____

Buyer: _____

Date: _____

This short-term lease is to be read in conjunction with and be made part of the Agreement of Sale dated _____, year ___ by and between the same parties.

Whereas the sellers are desirous of remaining in possession of said property after delivery of the deed and in consideration whereof the sellers covenant to pay $____ without demand in advance for a term of _____ commencing on _____ and ending _____.
In addition, the parties agree as follows:

1.   That a settlement on the above-mentioned property shall take place on _____, _____, wherein buyer shall purchase from seller said property at the stipulated amount for consideration.

2.   Sellers' Fire & Liability Insurance will remain in effect to coincide with lease term. And a rider will be attached to their existing policy protecting the buyers (proof of said property to be given to buyers prior to settlement).

3.   Sellers shall be liable for all utilities (gas, electric, water and sewage) for the term of this lease.

4.   Sellers agree to hold harmless and release the buyers from any liability as a result of their possession.

5.   Sellers agree to escrow with buyer $_____ as security against any damage and/or maintenance and/or litigation that may result in their occupancy.

6.   Time is of the essence with respect to the dates and terms mentioned in this Lease. In the event the seller does not vacate the property as indicated above, sellers shall be liable for additional rent in the amount of $_____ per day, and buyer may take possession according to the terms stipulated in Paragraph #_____ of the Agreement of Sale and apply escrow monies towards any damages and/or legal expenses incurred.

_____   _____
Witness   Seller

_____   _____
Witness   Seller

_____   _____
Witness   Buyer

_____   _____
Witness   Buyer

FIGURE 9–5

ADDENDUM

I/we hereby agree to renew my/our present lease for the townhouse located at _____ the term of renewal will be from _____ to _____ at an annual rental of $___ to be paid in equal installments of $_____ and upon the same terms and conditions set forth in said lease.

This agreement to be attached and made part of said lease and, except as set forth herein, said lease and all its terms, provisions, conditions, covenants, confessions of judgement, waivers, remedies, and any and all of landlord's rights therein specially given and agreed to shall remain in full force and effect.

_____   _____
Agent   Tenant

_____   _____
Witness   Tenant

_____
Date

FIGURE 9–6

As in the event of a seller remaining after a closing date, the same **leasehold** principles apply, whether by independent lease or addendum, endorsement, or added provision to the agreement of sale. A buyer can take early possession even when a transfer of the possessed property has yet to take place.

A regular lease or a lease purchase clause (see Figure 9–7) can accomplish this end.

If buyers take early possession, a liability release clause protecting sellers should be drafted. See Figure 9–8. See another version of a buyers' Early Possession Agreement in Figure 9–9.

LEASE PURCHASE CLAUSE

Seller hereby agrees to deliver possession of the subject premises to buyer on, _____, 20_____, pursuant to the terms of the Lease, which is attached hereto and made a part hereof. (At the time of settlement on this transaction, buyer shall receive a credit of $_____ for each monthly rental payment made by tenant to lessor, said credit to be applied as hand money toward the purchase price of the subject premises.) Buyer agrees to pay for all utilities used on the premises during the term of said Lease. In the event the buyer fails to attend settlement on this transaction on the date provided for in this agreement, then buyer shall be considered to be in default and seller may retain all hand money and monthly payments made by buyer as a rent and liquidated damages or may apply said monies toward the purchase price or toward seller's loss as provided in Paragraph _____ hereof.

FIGURE 9–7

LIABILITY RELEASE

This addendum is attached to and made a part of the agreement of sale dated _____ by and between _____ (seller) and _____ (buyers) for the property located AT _____.

We grant permission for you to remain at _____ until _____.
We therefore request that in consideration of our granting permission for you to stay at the property, after closing date of _____ , you agree to the following:

1.   Release the record owner of the property from any and all liabilities for loss of property, or for personal injury which you may sustain in and about the property.
2.   Indemnify and hold harmless the record owner of the property from liability on account of loss or damage to the property of any person or persons, or on account of any injury sustained by, or the death of any person or persons resulting from the condition of the property, or caused in any manner by your acts or the acts of your agents.
3.   Maintain Homeowner Insurance policy up to and including the day of scheduled vacancy.
4.   I ay to the owner of record a rental charge of $_____ dollars per day up to and including the last day of your possession at said premises.

If the foregoing is acceptable to you, please indicate your agreement by signing.

_____	_____
WITNESS	BUYER
_____	_____
DATE	BUYER
_____	_____
WITNESS	SELLER
_____	_____
DATE	SELLER

FIGURE 9–8

These types of advance agreements are sometimes employed in construction loan agreements of sale. Buyers, anxious to have the job done right, prefer to take possession in advance of the completed construction. Review the Lease for Occupancy of New Construction Prior to Closing in Figure 9–10.

Closely aligned to the construction scenario would be when a buyer needs to make extensive repairs before the official transfer. See the Agreement to Enter Property Prior to Closing in Figure 9–11.

Some buyers or sellers may wish to avoid the daily responsibilities that are related to leasehold. **Real estate management agreements**, whereby the lessor/client wishes to delegate the daily responsibility of handling the lease to a professional company, may be the solution. "The key provisions of a management agreement vary with the property to be managed, the sophistication of the owner and manager, and the extent to which the owner does or does not want to be involved in or informed about the details of the operation of the property."[6] For an illustration of such an agreement, see Figure 9–12.

EARLY POSSESSION AGREEMENT

PROPERTY ADDRESS: _____

SELLERS: _____

BUYERS: _____

1. WHEREAS: The buyers are desirous of having possession of the above-captioned property prior to delivery of deed and full payment of purchase price, the sellers hereby in consideration of the sum of $_____ permit the buyers to enter into possession of said property for the sole purpose of:

2. Buyers hereby agree to make no material changes or to use said property except as stated above without prior written consent of the sellers.
    a.
    b.
    c.

3. Buyers have hereby obtained adequate fire, casualty and liability (but not limited to) insurance. Sellers assume no liability or responsibility for buyers' possessions or for anyone allowed to enter on and in said property by reason of the buyers having possession, and buyers assume said liability and responsibility.

4. Buyers have made final inspection of above-captioned property prior to the signing of this addendum and are purchasing the same solely upon that inspection and not by promises or guarantees of any person whomsoever. Buyers are purchasing the property in as is condition.

5. Sellers will pay all utilities until the time of settlement and buyers will have the utilities changed to their names prior to settlement.

6. If for any reason whatsoever the buyers are not able to close due to whatever reason on or before _____then either party may extend the terms of this agreement for an additional 30 days. Buyers will pay an additional $_____.

7. Should settlement not occur on or before _____ due to default by the buyers then the sellers may take all legal remedies as stated in the sales agreement. Buyers waive all rights against eviction in the State of _____ and will relinquish possession immediately. Time is of the essence in this agreement. In such case the Sellers shall receive the $ in hard money.

8. Buyers do hereby release and forever hold harmless the sellers and the listing broker, _____ and the selling broker, _____ and their agents, against all judgments, claims and/or actions arising from the above-captioned sale, purchase and early possession.

9. All other terms of the sale and purchase agreement remain in full force and effect.

10. Buyers intend to take possession on the following date for the above purpose: _____.

IN WITNESS WHEREOF the sellers and buyers have hereunto set their hands and seals, intending to be legally bound thereby this _____ day of, year.

Witness:_____   Seller:_____
                                        Seller:_____

Witness:_____   Buyer:_____
                                        Buyer:_____

FIGURE 9–9

LEASE FOR OCCUPANCY OF NEW CONSTRUCTION PRIOR TO CLOSING

This lease is made in conjunction with Sales Agreement dated_____by, _____Seller, and _____, Buyer,

THIS LEASE WITNESSETH, THAT _____, herein called LESSOR, hereby leases to _____, herein called TENANT for a per-diem term commencing on _____and ending on the settlement day, not later than _____ the following described premises and street to the center, subject to the public easement therein, in its present condition in _____,_____.

VIZ:

_____

TENANT hereby agrees to deposit the sum of _____ dollars, which represents the down payment on the purchase of aforesaid premises. Said deposit shall be presented at time of closing and credited to TENANT.

IN CONSIDERATION WHEREOF, the TENANT covenants to pay as rent in daily installments to be paid in full at final settlement from the beginning of the term: that is to say, the sum of _____ dollars per-diem until final settlement.

TENANT agrees to pay all gas and electricity used thereon, all garbage collection charges, all sanitary sewer charges or assessments, and all water rents assessed on the premises herein described.

IN WITNESS WHEREOF, the parties hereto set their hands and seals on this ___ day of _____, year.

_____   _____
Witness

_____   _____
Witness

FIGURE 9–10

VI. LANDLORD REMEDIES FOR HOLDING

One of the chief drawbacks to becoming a landlord is the possibility that the lessee may hold out and not allow repossession of the property in question. In a lease-purchase situation the landlord must, before any legal action can occur, follow step-by-step guidelines.

Some jurisdictions supply lessees with an increased right of protection under the doctrine of "implied warranty of habitability." Both rental and ownership markets must contend with the doctrine's influence. Applied to apartment complexes, this warranty may have some application, particularly for lessees. Here the lessor is expected to lease a property that is habitable, with all the fundamental services and utilities, and in the absence thereof, be held to have breached the

---

AGREEMENT TO ENTER PROPERTY PRIOR TO CLOSING

Agreement made this _____ between _____, Seller of property known as _____ and _____ being purchaser.

Purchaser agrees to accept property in "as is" condition.

Purchaser agrees to release seller of all liability against himself or workers on said property.

Purchaser also agrees that, _____ Realty and _____ will not be held responsible for payment of work completed on said property if sale is not consummated. Should purchaser place personal possessions on premises, it is agreed and understood that seller and Realty Cos. are released of all liability from damage or destruction to said possessions. This agreement is contingent upon buyers having already obtained a firm mortgage commitment for above property as per sales contract between seller and buyers dated. This Agreement is intended solely for purchasers to enter premises prior to closing and not intended to grant possession.

_____   _____
Purchaser   Witness

_____   _____
Purchaser   Witness

FIGURE 9–11

---

warranty. The warranty closely aligns with product warranty theories. "With the advent of mass production and consumption of goods, caveat emptor for sales of goods largely disappeared, consumers became accustomed to buying goods with implied warranties of merchantability and when applicable for fitness for a particular purpose. Following World War II, the demand for and construction of houses exploded. Instances of poor quality almost inevitably resulted due to hurried construction and skimping on materials. Unsophisticated purchasers streamed into court seeking relief. Accustomed to implied warranty for consumer goods, consumers logically expected the law to protect them when they purchased new homes."[7]

In the leasehold environment, "a tenant may vacate the premises if the breach is material.[8] In such instances, the tenant may surrender possession of the property and terminate his obligation to pay rent under the lease. Second, if the tenant remains in possession and issued by the landlord for possession and unpaid rent, the implied warranty of habitability may be presented as a total defense by the tenant. Where the landlord can be shown to not have delivered a premises that fails to meet the elementary standards, of the warranty of habitability, the tenant's obligation to pay rent would be abated in full—the action for possession would fail because there would be no unpaid rent."[9] Research local law to determine the doctrine's applicability.

Standard leases discuss both landlord obligation and lessee rights as to express and implied covenants, rights of quiet enjoyment, warranties, services, and repairs. In the same document, clauses covering maintenance and repair and indemnification for destruction are drafted. Both lessor and lessee have a series of rights and obligations, all of which are fully discernible in a well-drafted lease. (See Figure 9–13.)

Varied jurisdictional requirements govern the application of a security deposit. As a general principle, security deposits are refundable after a finding by the landlord that no destruction or

AGREEMENT FOR THE MANAGEMENT OF REAL ESTATE

This Agreement made and entered into this _____ day of, by and between
_____(hereinafter collectively called "Owner") and, (hereinafter called
"Agent").

WITNESSETH THAT:

In consideration of the mutual covenants herein contained and intending to be legally bound hereby,
the parties hereto do mutually covenant and agree as follows:

    1.   The Owner hereby employs the Agent exclusively to rent and manage the property
located at _____ (hereinafter called the "Property"), upon the terms
and conditions hereinafter set forth, for the period from _____ through
_____and including all subsequent lease and lease renewal periods. The
minimum monthly rental shall be $_____.

    2.   The Agent agrees:
        a.   To accept and does hereby accept the management of the property for the
period and upon the terms herein provided and agrees to furnish the services of its organization for
the renting, operation, and managing of the property.
        b.   To investigate carefully all references of prospective tenants.
        c.   To render monthly statements of receipts, expenses and charges and to remit
receipts less disbursements. In case the disbursements shall be in excess of the rents collected by the
agent, the owner agrees to pay such excess promptly upon demand.

    3.   The owner hereby gives the agent the following authority and powers:
        a.   To advertise the property or any part thereof for rent, at the owners expense,
to display signs thereon, and to rent the same; to sign review and/or cancel leases for the property or
any part thereof, with express authority to the agent to sign leases for terms not in excess of two (2)
years.
        b.   To collect rents due or to become due and give receipts therefore.
        c.   To make or cause to be made and supervise repairs and alterations and to do
decorating on the property: and to purchase supplies and pay all bills. The agent agrees to secure
services necessary to protect the property from damages or maintain services to the tenants as called
for by their tenancy. Such deductions for payments shall be paid from rental proceeds and so noted
on monthly statements.
        d.   The agent shall not be liable for any error of judgment or for any mistake or
fact of law, or for anything which it may do or refrain from doing hereunder, except in cases of
willful misconduct or gross negligence.
        e.   To make contracts for electricity, gas, fuel, water, telephone, window
cleaning, refuse removal, and other services or such of them as the agent shall deem advisable; the
owner to assume the obligation of any contract so entered into at the termination of this agreement.

    4.   The owner further agrees:
        a.   To indemnify and hold the agent harmless from all claims, damages, costs,
and expenses, including reasonable attorneys' fees, incurred in connection with the management of
the property.
        b.   To advise the agent in writing if payments of mortgages indebtedness,
property or employees taxes, special assessments or the placing of fire, liability, steam boiler or any
other insurance is desired.
        c.   To pay the agent each month for services rendered hereunder ____% of the
gross amount of money received from the operation of the property during the period herein
provided. And to pay a one-time "finder's fee" per new tenant secured in the amount of one-twelfth
(1/12th) of the expected rent from the lease.

    5.   This Agreement shall inure to the benefit of and be binding upon the parties hereto,
and their respective heirs, administrators, successors and assigns.

        IN WITNESS WHEREOF, the parties hereto have caused this Agreement to be
executed as of the day and year first above written.

_____   _____
Agent   Owner

FIGURE 9–12

RENTAL LEASE FORM

THIS RENTAL LEASE AGREEMENT (hereinafter referred to as the "Agreement") made and entered into this _____ day of _____, 20_____, by and between _____, whose address is _____ (hereinafter referred to as "Lessor") and

_____

(hereinafter referred to as "Lessee").

WITNESSETH:

WHEREAS, Lessor is the fee owner of certain real property being, lying and situate in _____ County, _____, such real property having a street address of _____.

WHEREAS, Lessor is desirous of leasing the Premises to Lessee upon the terms and conditions as contained herein; and

WHEREAS, Lessee is desirous of leasing the Premises from Lessor on the terms and conditions as contained herein;

NOW, THEREFORE, for and in consideration of the sum of TEN DOLLARS ($10.00), the covenants and obligations contained herein and other good and valuable consideration, the receipt and sufficiency of which is hereby acknowledged, the parties hereto hereby agree as follows:

TERM. Lessor leases to Lessee and Lessee leases from Lessor the above described premises together with any and all appurtenances thereto, for a term of _____ year(s), such term beginning on _____, and ending at 12 o'clock midnight on _____.

RENT. The total rent for the term hereof is the sum of _____ DOLLARS ($_____) payable on the _____ day of each month of the term, in equal installments of _____ DOLLARS ($_____) first and last installments to be paid upon the due execution of this Agreement, the second installment to be paid on _____. All such payments shall be made to Lessor at Lessor's address as set forth in the preamble to this Agreement on or before the due date and without demand.

DAMAGE DEPOSIT. Upon the due execution of this Agreement, Lessee shall deposit with Lessor the sum of _____ DOLLARS ($_____) receipt of which is hereby acknowledged by Lessor, as security for any damage caused to the Premises during the term hereof. Such deposit shall be returned to Lessee, without interest, and less any set off for damages to the Premises upon the termination of this Agreement.

USE OF PREMISES. The Premises shall be used and occupied by Lessee and Lessee's immediate family, consisting of _____ _____ _____, exclusively, as a private single family dwelling, and no part of the Premises shall be used at any time during the term of this Agreement by Lessee for the purpose of carrying on any business, profession, or trade of any kind, or for any purpose other than as a private single family dwelling. Lessee shall not allow any other person, other than Lessee's immediate family or transient relatives and friends who are guests of Lessee, to use or occupy the Premises without first obtaining Lessor's written consent to such use. Lessee shall comply with any and all laws, ordinances, rules and orders of any and all governmental or quasi-governmental authorities affecting the cleanliness, use, occupancy and preservation of the Premises.

CONDITION OF PREMISES. Lessee stipulates, represents and warrants that Lessee has examined the Premises, and that they are at the time of this Lease in good order, repair, and in a safe, clean and tenantable condition.

FIGURE 9–13
(continues)

ASSIGNMENT AND SUB-LETTING. Lessee shall not assign this Agreement, or sub-let or grant any license to use the Premises or any part thereof without the prior written consent of Lessor. A consent by Lessor to one such assignment, sub-letting or license shall not be deemed to be a consent to any subsequent assignment, sub-letting or license. An assignment, sub-letting or license without the prior written consent of Lessor or an assignment or sub-letting by operation of law shall be absolutely null and void and shall, at Lessor's option, terminate this Agreement.

ALTERATIONS AND IMPROVEMENTS. Lessee shall make no alterations to the buildings or improvements on the Premises or construct any building or make any other improvements on the Premises without the prior written consent of Lessor. Any and all alterations, changes, and/or improvements built, constructed or placed on the Premises by Lessee shall, unless otherwise provided by written agreement between Lessor and Lessee, be and become the property of Lessor and remain on the Premises at the expiration or earlier termination of this Agreement.

NON-DELIVERY OF POSSESSION. In the event Lessor cannot deliver possession of the Premises to Lessee upon the commencement of the Lease term, through no fault of Lessor or its agents, then Lessor or its agents shall have no liability, but the rental herein provided shall abate until possession is given.

Lessor or its agents shall have thirty (30) days in which to give possession, and if possession is tendered within such time, Lessee agrees to accept the demised Premises and pay the rental herein provided from that date. In the event possession cannot be delivered within such time, through no fault of Lessor or its agents, then this Agreement and all rights hereunder shall terminate.

HAZARDOUS MATERIALS. Lessee shall not keep on the Premises any item of a dangerous, flammable or explosive character that might unreasonably increase the danger of fire or explosion on the Premises or that might be considered hazardous or extra hazardous by any responsible insurance company.

UTILITIES. Lessee shall be responsible for arranging for and paying for all utility services required on the Premises.

MAINTENANCE AND REPAIR; RULES. Lessee will, at its sole expense, keep and maintain the Premises and appurtenances in good and sanitary condition and repair during the term of this Agreement and any renewal thereof. Without limiting the generality of the foregoing, Lessee shall:

(a) Not obstruct the driveways, sidewalks, courts, entry ways, stairs and/or halls, which shall be used for the purposes of ingress and egress only;

(b) Keep all windows, glass, window coverings, doors, locks and hardware in good, clean order and repair;

(c) Not obstruct or cover the windows or doors;

(d) Not leave windows or doors in an open position during any inclement weather;

(e) Not hang any laundry, clothing, sheets, etc. from any window, rail, porch or balcony nor air or dry any of same within any yard area or space;

(f) Not cause or permit any locks or hooks to be placed upon any door or window without the prior written consent of Lessor;

(g) Keep all air conditioning filters clean and free from dirt;

(h) Keep all lavatories, sinks, toilets, and all other water and plumbing apparatus in good order and repair and shall use same only for the purposes for which they were constructed. Lessee shall not allow any sweepings, rubbish, sand, rags, ashes or other substances to be thrown or deposited therein. Any damage to any such apparatus and the cost of clearing stopped plumbing resulting from misuse shall be borne by Lessee;

FIGURE 9–13
(continued)

(i) And Lessee's family and guests shall at all times maintain order in the Premises and at all places on the Premises, and shall not make or permit any loud or improper noises, or otherwise disturb other residents;

(j) Keep all radios, television sets, stereos, phonographs, etc., turned down to a level of sound that does not annoy or interfere with other residents;

(k) Deposit all trash, garbage, rubbish or refuse in the locations provided therefor and shall not allow any trash, garbage, rubbish or refuse to be deposited or permitted to stand on the exterior of any building or within the common elements;

(l) Abide by and be bound by any and all rules and regulations affecting the Premises or the common area appurtenant thereto which may be adopted or promulgated by the Condominium or Homeowners' Association having control over them.

DAMAGE TO PREMISES. In the event the Premises are destroyed or rendered wholly untenantable by fire, storm, earthquake, or other casualty not caused by the negligence of Lessee, this Agreement shall terminate from such time except for the purpose of enforcing rights that may have then accrued hereunder. The rental provided for herein shall then be accounted for by and between Lessor and Lessee up to the time of such injury or destruction of the Premises, Lessee paying rentals up to such date and Lessor refunding rentals collected beyond such date. Should a portion of the Premises thereby be rendered untenantable, the Lessor shall have the option of either repairing such injured or damaged portion or terminating this Lease. In the event that Lessor exercises its right to repair such untenantable portion, the rental shall abate in the proportion that the injured parts bears to the whole Premises, and such part so injured shall be restored by Lessor as speedily as practicable, after which the full rent shall recommence and the Agreement continue according to its terms.

INSPECTION OF PREMISES. Lessor and Lessor's agents shall have the right at all reasonable times during the term of this Agreement and any renewal thereof to enter the Premises for the purpose of inspecting the Premises and all buildings and improvements thereon. And for the purposes of making any repairs, additions or alterations as may be deemed appropriate by Lessor for the preservation of the Premises or the building.

Lessor and its agents shall further have the right to exhibit the Premises and to display the usual "for sale", "for rent" or "vacancy" signs on the Premises at any time within forty-five (45) days before the expiration of this Lease. The right of entry shall likewise exist for the purpose of removing placards, signs, fixtures, alterations or additions, but do not conform to this Agreement or to any restrictions, rules or regulations affecting the Premises.

SUBORDINATION OF LEASE. This Agreement and Lessee's interest hereunder are and shall be subordinate, junior and inferior to any and all mortgages, liens or encumbrances now or hereafter placed on the Premises by Lessor, all advances made under any such mortgages, liens or encumbrances (including, but not limited to, future advances), the interest payable on such mortgages, liens or encumbrances and any and all renewals, extensions or modifications of such mortgages, liens or encumbrances.

LESSEE'S HOLD OVER. If Lessee remains in possession of the Premises with the consent of Lessor after the natural expiration of this Agreement, a new tenancy from month-to-month shall be created between Lessor and Lessee which shall be subject to all of the terms and conditions hereof except that rent shall then be due and owing at _____ DOLLARS ($_____) per month and except that such tenancy shall be terminable upon fifteen (15) days written notice served by either party.

SURRENDER OF PREMISES. Upon the expiration of the term hereof, Lessee shall surrender the Premises in as good a state and condition as they were at the commencement of this Agreement, reasonable use and wear and tear thereof and damages by the elements excepted.

FIGURE 9–13
(continued)

ANIMALS. Lessee shall be entitled to keep no more than _____ (___) domestic dogs, cats or birds; however, at such time as Lessee shall actually keep any such animal on the Premises, Lessee shall pay to Lessor a pet deposit of _____ DOLLARS ($_____), _____ DOLLARS ($_____) of which shall be non-refundable and shall be used upon the termination or expiration of this Agreement for the purposes of cleaning the carpets of the building.

QUIET ENJOYMENT. Lessee, upon payment of all of the sums referred to herein as being payable by Lessee and Lessee's performance of all Lessee's agreements contained herein and Lessee's observance of all rules and regulations, shall and may peacefully and quietly have, hold and enjoy said Premises for the term hereof.

INDEMNIFICATION. Lessor shall not be liable for any damage or injury of or to the Lessee, Lessee's family, guests, invitees, agents or employees or to any person entering the Premises or the building of which the Premises are a part or to goods or equipment, or in the structure or equipment of the structure of which the Premises are a part, and Lessee hereby agrees to indemnify, defend and hold Lessor harmless from any and all claims or assertions of every kind and nature.

DEFAULT. If Lessee fails to comply with any of the material provisions of this Agreement, other than the covenant to pay rent, or of any present rules and regulations or any that may be hereafter prescribed by Lessor, or materially fails to comply with any duties imposed on Lessee by statute, within seven (7) days after delivery of written notice by Lessor specifying the non-compliance and indicating the intention of Lessor to terminate the Lease by reason thereof, Lessor may terminate this Agreement. If Lessee fails to pay rent when due and the default continues for seven (7) days thereafter, Lessor may, at Lessor's option, declare the entire balance of rent payable hereunder to be immediately due and payable and may exercise any and all rights and remedies available to Lessor at law or in equity or may immediately terminate this Agreement.

LATE CHARGE. In the event that any payment required to be paid by Lessee hereunder is not made within three (3) days of when due, Lessee shall pay to Lessor, in addition to such payment or other charges due hereunder, a "late fee" in the amount of _____ ($_____).

ABANDONMENT. If at any time during the term of this Agreement Lessee abandons the Premises or any part thereof, Lessor may, at Lessor's option, obtain possession of the Premises in the manner provided by law, and without becoming liable to Lessee for damages or for any payment of any kind whatever. Lessor may, at Lessor's discretion, as agent for Lessee, relet the Premises, or any part thereof, for the whole or any part thereof, for the whole or any part of the then unexpired term, and may receive and collect all rent payable by virtue of such reletting, and, at Lessor's option, hold Lessee liable for any difference between the rent that would have been payable under this Agreement during the balance of the unexpired term, if this Agreement had continued in force, and the net rent for such period realized by Lessor by means of such reletting. If Lessor's right of reentry is exercised following abandonment of the Premises by Lessee, then Lessor shall consider any personal property belonging to Lessee and left on the Premises to also have been abandoned, in which case Lessor may dispose of all such personal property in any manner Lessor shall deem proper and Lessor is hereby relieved of all liability for doing so.

ATTORNEYS' FEES. Should it become necessary for Lessor to employ an attorney to enforce any of the conditions or covenants hereof, including the collection of rentals or gaining possession of the Premises, Lessee agrees to pay all expenses so incurred, including a reasonable attorneys' fee.

RECORDING OF AGREEMENT. Lessee shall not record this Agreement on the Public Records of any public office. In the event that Lessee shall record this Agreement, this Agreement shall, at Lessor's option, terminate immediately and Lessor shall be entitled to all rights and remedies that it has at law or in equity.

FIGURE 9–13
(continued)

GOVERNING LAW. This Agreement shall be governed, construed and interpreted by, through and under the Laws of the State of _____.

SEVERABILITY. If any provision of this Agreement or the application thereof shall, for any reason and to any extent, be invalid or unenforceable, neither the remainder of this Agreement nor the application of the provision to other persons, entities or circumstances shall be affected thereby, but instead shall be enforced to the maximum extent permitted by law.

BINDING EFFECT. The covenants, obligations and conditions herein contained shall be binding on and inure to the benefit of the heirs, legal representatives, and assigns of the parties hereto.

DESCRIPTIVE HEADINGS. The descriptive headings used herein are for convenience of reference only and they are not intended to have any effect whatsoever in determining the rights or obligations of the Lessor or Lessee.

CONSTRUCTION. The pronouns used herein shall include, where appropriate, either gender or both, singular and plural.

NON-WAIVER. No indulgence, waiver, election or non-election by Lessor under this Agreement shall affect Lessee's duties and liabilities hereunder.

MODIFICATION. The parties hereby agree that this document contains the entire agreement between the parties and this Agreement shall not be modified, changed, altered or amended in any way except through a written amendment signed by all of the parties hereto. As to Lessor this _____ day of _____, 20_____.

Witnesses: "Lessor"

_____   _____

_____

_____

As to Lessee, this _____ day of _____, 20_____.

Witnesses: "Lessee"

_____   _____

FIGURE 9–13
(continued)

costs have been incurred on lessee's part because of destruction beyond "ordinary wear and tear." Tenants must contend with landlords who, without right or just cause, retain the security deposit. In landlord-tenant practice, paralegals are responsible for two fundamental aspects:

1. Preparing leases according to specific detail and
2. Preparing litigation documents for **eviction** or back-payment of rent

A. Notice

Written notice informing the tenant that they must quit, or leave, the premises is required. "The notice to quit must clearly and unequivocally notify the tenant to remove from the premises and must specify a time for the tenant to quit; a notice to vacate leased premises is to be strictly construed."[10] For a notice format, see Figure 9–14.[11]

Unless the lease states otherwise, tenants, if legally obligated, must vacate in thirty days. For attorneys, the initial step in the **eviction** process is to gather information and documents,

𝔑𝔬𝔱𝔦𝔠𝔢 𝔗𝔢𝔯𝔪𝔦𝔫𝔞𝔱𝔦𝔫𝔤 𝔏𝔢𝔞𝔰𝔢

TO: , Tenant(s)

1. PRESENT LEASE.   You now rent
located at

                                                                                      as Tenant(s).

2. TERMINATION OF LEASE.   Your lease is TERMINATED (ended) as of

3. DEMAND FOR POSSESSION.   You must leave and vacate this rented property on or before that date
(the date of termination). This means you must move out and deliver possession to me, your Landlord.

4. REASON.   Your lease is terminated because *

Dated: _____

_____
Landlord

By_____

*This Notice must specify in detail the cause of the termination of the lease.

52 - Notice Terminating Lease
Plain Language
Rev. 12/96   P1/05

Courtesy of:
©2005 by ALL-STATE LEGAL®
A Division of ALL-STATE International, Inc.
www.aslegal.com   800.222.0510

FIGURE 9–14

beginning with the demand and lease. If the landlord has already served the demand, it should be reviewed to ensure that it was properly prepared and served. If there is a written lease, double check the notice and remedy provisions. The landlord's attorney should request a copy of all communications between the parties. An exchange of hostile correspondence is often a sign that the issues will extend beyond the simple inability to pay. Knowledge gleaned from such correspondence will give the attorney some forewarning of issues that may be raised on the initial trial date.[12]

The landlord may select among a bevy of remedies to end **holdover**. He or she may collect the rent and opt to consider the tenant as a tenant by sufferance, or permit the lease to be continued. The landlord can also evict the tenant and sue for possession and damages if he or she decides to treat the tenant as a trespasser.

In addition, the landlord may bring an action for **trespass**, possession and **reentry**, liquidated damages, or breaches relating to lessee's failure to repair and maintain the property.

In general, an eviction complaint must:

- Comply with the general pleasing requirements
- Describe the premises
- Allege nonpayment of rent
- State the rental periods and rate
- State the amount due when the complaint was filed
- Indicate the dates on which additional payments will become due[13]

For a sample Complaint for Eviction see Figure 9–15.

COMPLAINT FOR EVICTION

1. By written lease, dated _____, year _____, the defendant leased from plaintiff, for [number] _____ [months or years] commencing _____, year _____, the premises at _____ Street, City of _____, State of _____, for $_____, payable as follows: _____ [specify amount and intervals of rental payments]. A copy of the lease is attached hereto as Exhibit "_____" and hereby made a part of this complaint.

2. Under Paragraph _____ of the lease, plaintiff was entitled to evict defendant for nonpayment of rent, to relet the premises, and to hold defendant liable for any deficiency in the rentals for the lease term.

3. Defendant failed to pay the rentals accruing on _____, _____, and on _____, _____. And in accordance with Paragraph _____ of the lease and plaintiff's right under _____ [cite statute], plaintiff duly evicted defendant on _____, _____ for nonpayment of rent for the leased premises.

4. Plaintiff reentered the leased premises on _____, ____, and exercised due diligence to relet the same on defendant's behalf, but was unable to obtain a tenant for the premises until _____, year _____.

5. On _____, year _____, plaintiff relet the leased premises to _____ [substitute tenant] on defendant's behalf, for a monthly rental of $_____, which was paid for the remainder of the lease term.

6. On _____, year _____, plaintiff served on defendant written notice that the reletting was on defendant's behalf.

7. Plaintiff received from defendant $_____ under the lease for the period _____, _____, to _____,_____, and from _____ [substitute tenant] $_____ for the rental of the premises during the lease term, leaving a remainder of $_____ due plaintiff from defendant under the terms of the lease.

8. Plaintiff has demanded payment from defendant of the $_____ for rentals due under the lease and unpaid; but defendant has refused and neglected to pay the same and still refuses to do so.

FIGURE 9–15

Statutes heavily guide eviction remedies. Force and aggressive recapture by landlords in **ejectment** is unacceptable. In New Jersey, for example, [l]andlords may not use "self-help" to gain entry to an apartment. The entry must be legal and peaceable. With regard to real property occupied solely as a residence by the party in possession, the entry must be with the consent of the party in possession or pursuant to legal process set out in N.J.S.A. 2A: 18-53 et seq. or N.J.S.A. 2A: 35-1 et seq.

A landlord is guilty of **"forcible entry and detainer** when entering real property and detaining or holding it by force, violence, threats to kill, maim or beat, or using words to excite fear or put out of doors or carry away the tenant's goods."[14] A complaint for reentry and rent may be the only route left. See Figure 9–16. Another remedy would be a complaint to recover possession. See Figure 9–17.

COMPLAINT FOR REENTRY AND RENT

1. On, year, plaintiff, as lessor, and defendant, as lessee, executed a certain lease agreement, for a term of ___ [months or years], beginning, year, for a total rental of $_____, payable in monthly installments of $_____, in advance, on the ___ day of each month, for the following described property: _____[description]. A copy of the lease is attached hereto, marked Exhibit "___," and hereby incorporated herein by reference.

2. Pursuant to Paragraph ___ of the lease, plaintiff, as lessor, has the right to reenter and resume possession of the leased premises on the breach by defendant, as lessee, of his covenant to pay rent; to hold defendant liable, as lessee, for rents then accrued; to relet the premises after notice to defendant, as lessee; to hold defendant liable for any deficiency in the rent resulting from a reletting; and to hold defendant liable for the rental for the full term of the lease if plaintiff, as lessor, is unable, with exercise of reasonable diligence, to relet the premises during the lease term.

3. On defendant's failure to pay the $_____ rental due _____, year___, plaintiff duly notified defendant in writing, as required by the lease, of the intent to reenter and resume possession of the leased premises on _____, year___, in the event of defendant's failure to pay the rental due then.

4. Thereafter, defendant failed to pay the rental due, and plaintiff, pursuant to the notice to defendant, reentered the leased premises and resumed possession on _____, year___.

5. On _____, ___, plaintiff duly notified defendant of plaintiff's intention to relet the premises and to hold defendant liable for any deficiency in rent resulting from the reletting or, in the event of plaintiff's inability, despite the exercise of reasonable diligence, to relet the premises, to hold defendant liable for the rent for the full term of the lease.

6. Thereafter, plaintiff exercised due diligence in the attempt to relet the leased premises, but was unable to rent the premises during the lease term.

7. Plaintiff has demanded payment from defendant of the rentals accruing under the lease on [specify due dates], but defendant has failed to pay the accrued rentals and still refuses to do so. There is now due and owing plaintiff from defendant and unpaid $____ in accrued rentals for the lease term.]

8. _____[Allege generally plaintiff's performance of any other conditions precedent to defendant's payment.]

FIGURE 9–16

COMPLAINT TO RECOVER POSSESSION

1. Plaintiff owns in fee the following described real property: _____
[description].

2. By written agreement dated _____, _____, plaintiff leased the above-described property to defendant for a term of _____ years, commencing _____, _____, subject to plaintiff's option to terminate the lease, as provided in Paragraph _____ thereof, by giving defendant days' written notice of termination, to permit the erection of a new building or buildings on the demised premises, or any part thereof. A copy of the lease is attached hereto as Exhibit "_____" and hereby made a part of this complaint.

3. On or about _____, _____, defendant took possession of the leased premises pursuant to the terms of the lease agreement and still occupies the same.

4. On _____, _____, plaintiff duly served on defendant written notice of plaintiff's election to terminate the lease, effective as of _____, _____, to permit the erection of a new building on the demised premises, and demanded that defendant quit the premises and surrender possession thereof to plaintiff not later than _____,_____. A copy of the notice and demand so served on defendant, in strict compliance with Paragraph _____ of the lease, is attached hereto as Exhibit "_____" and hereby made a part of this complaint.

5. Plaintiff intends, in good faith, to demolish the present building on the above-described property and to erect, in lieu thereof, a new building or structure.

6. By reason of the provisions of Paragraph _____ of the lease and the notice and demand served on defendant, as alleged above, the lease terminated as of _____, _____, and plaintiff was entitled to possession of the above-described property, as of that date, free of any further obligations thereunder.

7. Despite the service on defendant of such notice and demand and the elapse of _____ days after the service of such notice and demand, defendant refused and failed to quit the premises and surrender possession to plaintiff and still refuses to do so. Defendant continues in possession without plaintiff's permission or consent, express or implied.

8. _____ [Allege, in addition, service of statutory notice to quit if required.]

Wherefore, plaintiff prays:

1. For judgment awarding possession of the above-described premises to plaintiff together with costs herein; and

2. For the issuance of a warrant forthwith to remove defendant from the possession of the premises.

FIGURE 9–17

CHAPTER NINE **SUMMARY**

Chapter Nine discussed the following topics:

- Nature of a lease
- Standard lease provisions
- Leases in a buy-sell contract
- Option to purchase
- Leases for buyers and sellers in a real estate transaction
- Landlord remedies

REVIEW **QUESTION**

1. What is the definition of a lease?
2. What are the needed elements in a lease?
3. Why are plain English requirements applicable to leases?
4. Why would a person enter into a lease with an option to purchase?
5. If buyers in a real estate transaction enter into an early possession agreement, what additional documentation should be drafted to protect the seller's interests?
6. What is the purpose of a real estate management agreement?
7. Is a notice document required before a landlord begins any other remedial procedure?
8. What must a general eviction complaint include?
9. What are common remedies used by a landlord to recover his or her property?
10. What is forcible entry and detainer?

DISCUSSION **QUESTION**

One of the more predominant questions practitioners hear is "Do I have to pay the rent since the landlord won't fix the heat/water, etc.?" Could the answer be yes? If so, what types of things or conditions not fixed would qualify?

EXERCISE 1

Complete a Lease for Seller using the following information:

Sellers—Stephen and Donna Green
Buyers—Donald and Susan Brown
Property Address—87 Third Street, Mytown, US 00000
Agreement of Sale Date—July 10, 2009
Date of End of Extended Possession—October 10, 2009
Seller/Buyer Relationship after Closing—Landlord/Tenant
Monthly Rent—$650
Escrow Deposited with Attorney—$1,000

EXERCISE 2

Complete an Early Possession Agreement using the following information:

Sellers—Mark and Judy Meyers
Buyers—Darren and Morgan Heatherly
Property Address—3920 Hunters Run, Mytown, US 00000
Date of Agreement of Sale—May 5, 2009
Date of Early Possession Agreement—July 1, 2009
Projected Date of Settlement—August 1, 2009
Monthly Rent—$425
Purpose for Early Possession—Residency

EXERCISE 3

Complete a Complaint for Eviction and a Complaint for Reentry and Rent using the information provided in either Exercise 1 or 2. Use hypothetical information as needed.

Assignment for the Case of John and Martha

John would like to take possession of the house one month prior to closing to complete some repairs and upgrades. John and Martha have agreed that they would pay $600 per month to occupy the property early. Complete the necessary documents.

REFERENCES

1. SUMM. PA JUR. 2d, Leases, § 26:1; *see also* S. Owen Friffin, Kelli Hopkins, Scot L. Wiggins & Emily Woodward, *Student Project: Recent Developments: The Uniform Arbitration Act.* 2000 J. DISP. RESOL. 459 (2000); Professor Roger Alford, *Report to Law Revision Commission Regarding Recommendations for Changes to California Arbitration Law,* 4 PEPP. DISP. RESOL. L.J. 1 (2003); Carl W. Hernstein, *Annual Survey of Michigan Law June 1, 1998–May 31, 1999: Real Property,* 46 WAYNE L. REV. 1037 (2000); Nancy Hylden, Case Note: *Contracts—A Rose by Any Other Name: No Tolling of an Arbitration Agreement Limitation Period, Unreasonableness Achieves the Same End in Rose Revocable Trust v. Eppich,* 29 WM. MITCHELL L. REV. 635 (2002); Celeste H. Hammond, *A Real Estate Focus: The (Pre) (as)sumed "Consent" of Commercial Binding Arbitration Contracts: An Empirical Study of Attitudes and Expectations of Transactional Lawyers,* 36 J. MARSHALL L. REV. 589 (2003).
2. OHIO REV. CODE ANN. §1310.08 (2009).
3. All-State Legal, One Commerce Drive, Cranford, NJ, Form 251.
4. 73 PA. CONS. STAT. §§2201-2204 (2009).
5. William F. Hoffmeyer, THE PENNSYLVANIA REAL ESTATE SETTLEMENT PROCEDURES MANUAL 12 (1990).
6. John S. Hollyfield, *How to Draft a Real Estate Management Agreement* (with Form), 37 Prac. Law. 31, 32 (1991).
7. Note, *Implied Warranty of Habitability, Doctrine in Residential Property Conveyances: Policy Backed Change,* 62 WASH. L. REV. 742 43 (1947).
8. Christopher S. Brennan, *The Next Step in the Evolution of the Implied Warranty of Habitability: Applying the Warranty to Condominiums,* 67 FORDHAM L. REV. 3041 (1999).
9. PENNSYLVANIA BAR INSTITUTE, REAL ESTATE PRACTICE 98–99 (1982).
10. SUMM. Pa. JUR. 2d, Leases § 26.303.
11. All-State Legal, One Commerce Drive, Cranford, NJ, Form 52.
12. Lawrence Shoffner, *Real Property Law: Evictions: A Basic Roadmap for Handling Nonpayment Actions,* 82 MI BAR JN. 20 (2003).
13. Id.
14. 13A NEW JERSEY PRACTICE § 26.194 (1994).

Resolution of Real Estate Disputes

LEARNING OBJECTIVES

- To assess the value of informal adjudication and its advantages versus formal litigation.
- To recognize the importance of arbitration and mediation as a means of human conciliation, which will provide a quicker and more humane remedy in a dispute between parties.
- To compose pleadings and other legal documentation pertinent to the arbitration process.
- To define the legal actions that may be taken in the event Alternative Dispute Resolution (ADR) fails and to prepare the necessary pleadings.

JOB COMPETENCIES

- To describe to clients the various alternate remedies available.
- To prepare the necessary paperwork that accompanies the ADR process.
- To identify the various options available when ADR does not work and to assist in preparing the attorney's pleadings.

ETHICAL CONSIDERATIONS

The paralegal must be aware of the following ethical dilemmas during this phase of a real estate transaction:

- Unauthorized practice of law
- Lawyer supervision of nonlawyers
- Confidentiality issues
- Conflicts of interest
- Partnerships between lawyers and nonlawyers
- Communications with persons outside the law firm

I. ALTERNATIVE DISPUTE RESOLUTION

KEY WORDS

alternative dispute resolution	mediation
arbitration	nonbinding
binding	settlement
breach of contract	specific performance
demand for arbitration	submission to arbitration

Like all other human exchanges, the real estate transaction is fertile ground for disputes between the parties. All real estate transactions are extremely legalistic and fraught with forms and timetables. In a way, the whole project is nerve rattling, especially for the novice and uninitiated buyer.

For the average person, the buying and selling of real estate may occur only once or twice in a normal life span. Add to this already stressful situation the enormous dollar sum of the investment and the probability of a dispute increases. The dispute can range from a fuel oil breach to whether window blinds are part of the deal. It is up to the paralegals and other practitioners involved to keep all differences in perspective and to aid the parties as they seek amicable resolutions. Being adversarial and overly legal, for the most part, kills the deal. "If one thing is indisputable, it's that disputes are sure to result from home resales. Not all of them, of course, but some of them. Like a used car, a used house usually can be counted on to have its imperfections."[1]

For every player in the real estate transaction, the task is to aid the parties in reaching a settlement, but only on terms beneficial to the clients that the paralegal's supervising attorney represents. For the most part, the troubles seen between buyers and sellers can be resolved. Establishing a climate that is favorable to resolution is a crucial paralegal responsibility.

In place of formal, traditional litigation weigh the potential of **Alternative Dispute Resolution**, known as ADR. Alternative dispute resolution has become an integral part of the U.S. system of justice, and its role is expected to grow in the future.[2]

"The growth has been attributed to a number of circumstances—first, problematic and sometimes staggering court backlog has been the impetus for designing alternative dispute resolution mechanisms and for diverting cases to them; Secondly, the costs of prolonged litigation have prompted the consideration of alternatives to traditional judicial proceedings; and finally, there is a growing recognition that not all complaints require adversarial setting for their resolution and that, in some circumstances, such a setting may actually be detrimental to reaching a satisfactory resolution as receptivity to innovative mechanics increases."[3] Federal courts have instituted court-annexed arbitration, which provides for the involuntary assignment of an eligible case. Procedural rules are relaxed, and the Federal Rules of Evidence are generally used as "guides" rather than strict rules of admissibility. The power of subpoena is enforceable. A panel of three arbitrators hears the testimony of the parties and their witnesses. If a party is dissatisfied with the award, it may reject it by demanding a formal trial de novo within a set period (usually thirty days). If such a demand is not filed, the arbitration award will be entered as a judgment of the court after the expiration of the thirty days. The judgment has the same force effect as any civil judgment, except that it is not appealable. If a trial de novo is granted, the court may not admit evidence regarding the arbitration proceeding.[4] The United States Department of Justice has been promoting ADR through its Federal Mediation and Conciliation Service. *The Civil Justice Reform Act of 1990* [5] requires "each federal district court to develop a civil justice delay-and-expense-reduction, including consideration of the use of ADR."[6] Private sector involvement in dispute resolution has been substantial, including support from professional associations, like the American Bar Association Special Committee on Alternative Dispute Resolution and a host of for-profit providers. There are a variety of programs available. See Figure 10–1[7] for a flowchart from the National Arbitration Forum outlining the ADR process.

ADR is essentially a twentieth-century phenomenon. And while ADR is often touted as an intelligent replacement for formal litigation, there is a body of literature that weighs ADR effectiveness.[8]

■ The questions are worthy of assessment.

■ Why is there such a drive toward the privatization of dispute resolution?

■ Does arbitration really play a significant role in the reduction of court overload at both the federal and state level?

■ Is ADR merely a panacea or an anathema to our historical method of dispute resolution?

■ Is it more costly or more efficient?

■ Has there been an objective, quantifiable assessment of the arbitration process?[9]

According to the United States Department of Justice's, *Dispute Resolution: Techniques and Applications*, "Given the very nature of conflicts and conflicting parties, coupled with the need to resolve disputes more quickly and, in some cases, more personally than the traditional judicial system allows, the dispute resolution field promises to continue expanding into new areas."[10] Guided by relaxed rules of evidence, less rigorous standards of advocacy and generally operating in a common sense, common language approach, companies that provide dispute resolution services are experiencing a wave of popularity.[11]

The growth of ADR is fueled by a variety of forces, including the strain on the courts caused by the increasing number of cases filed each year and the inability of a large portion of the population to afford traditional litigation to resolve disputes. Also, there is a growing recognition that the adversarial nature of the U.S. legal system may not provide the best atmosphere for solving certain types of disputes. Litigation and trial tend to be destructive of any relationship the parties enjoyed prior to the lawsuit. Thus, where the parties hope to continue their relationship after the dispute is settled, ADR can offer resolution methods that are restorative and, in some situations, can promote better cooperation in the future. Alternative Dispute Resolution consists of two major options:

1. *Mediation* uses a neutral third party to act as a referee while the parties negotiate. Often the mediator will separate the parties into different offices or conference rooms and then will shuttle back and forth between them conveying messages, offering insights into how the opposite side is thinking and feeling, and other communications designed to bring the parties to a negotiated settlement. If the mediator is successful, the parties will reach an agreement they can both accept. If not, at least they will each have gained insight into how the other side views the dispute, which is information that may enable them to settle the matter at a later time.

2. *Arbitration* is the best-known form of third-party ADR and has been used for most of the twentieth century to resolve disputes between employers and unions. Arbitration is

**OVERVIEW OF THE FORUM
MEDIATION PROCESS**

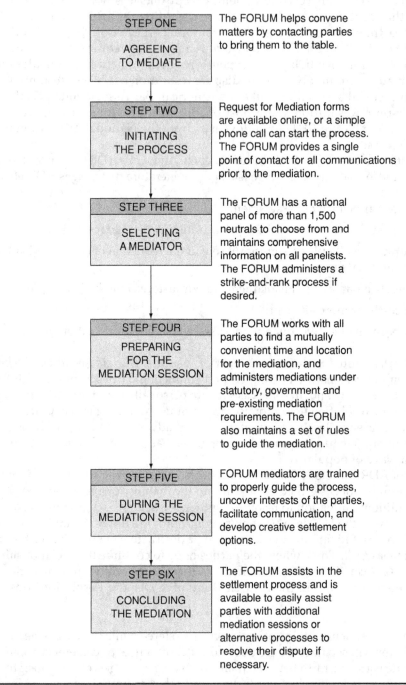

| STEP ONE
AGREEING
TO MEDIATE | The FORUM helps convene matters by contacting parties to bring them to the table. |

| STEP TWO
INITIATING
THE PROCESS | Request for Mediation forms are available online, or a simple phone call can start the process. The FORUM provides a single point of contact for all communications prior to the mediation. |

| STEP THREE
SELECTING
A MEDIATOR | The FORUM has a national panel of more than 1,500 neutrals to choose from and maintains comprehensive information on all panelists. The FORUM administers a strike-and-rank process if desired. |

| STEP FOUR
PREPARING
FOR THE
MEDIATION SESSION | The FORUM works with all parties to find a mutually convenient time and location for the mediation, and administers mediations under statutory, government and pre-existing mediation requirements. The FORUM also maintains a set of rules to guide the mediation. |

| STEP FIVE
DURING THE
MEDIATION SESSION | FORUM mediators are trained to properly guide the process, uncover interests of the parties, facilitate communication, and develop creative settlement options. |

| STEP SIX
CONCLUDING
THE MEDIATION | The FORUM assists in the settlement process and is available to easily assist parties with additional mediation sessions or alternative processes to resolve their dispute if necessary. |

FIGURE 10–1
Overview of the Forum Mediation Process.

similar to trial, but less formal. Like most ADR, the proceedings and outcome are confidential. An arbitrator, or panel of three arbitrators, who often are experts in the type of dispute involved, listen to evidence and arguments from each side and render a decision, called an award.

The decision of the arbitrator is either binding, meaning final, or nonbinding, meaning the parties can initiate formal legal action. A binding clause logically binds the parties to the result that arises from ADR. In the absence of some severe caprice or arbitrariness, courts give full effect to these provisions. A sample clause might be such as that shown in Figure 10–2.

Given this reality, the chapter commences with a conciliatory tone, urging paralegals and attorneys to first formally and cordially resolve disputes and, if not successful, consider ADR before

---

Pre-Dispute Binding Arbitration Clause

Agreement To Arbitrate

If any of the following disputes arise and are not resolved, it is agreed that the parties will not sue in court but will instead submit the dispute to binding arbitration by the Better Business Bureau located at

Any dispute arising under the agreement by and between:

_____ (Customer)

and

_____ (Business)

dated: _____

attached hereto. This does not include the following: disputes relating to alleged criminal violation, allegations of fraud or misrepresentation, mental anguish, or punitive damages.

In arbitration, an informal hearing will be held in accordance with the BBB's Rules for Binding Arbitration. A volunteer BBB arbitrator will render a decision that the arbitrator considers to be a fair resolution of the dispute, and in doing so the arbitrator will not be required to apply legal principles. The arbitrator's decision will be final and binding on both parties, and it is agreed that judgment on the decision may be entered in any court having jurisdiction. All administrative fees for the arbitration have been paid by the business.

The Better Business Bureau's address is _____. The BBB's telephone number is _____. Additional information about the BBB or BBB arbitration may be obtained by contacting the BBB at the above address or phone number.

This Agreement to Arbitrate affects important legal rights. By signing it, the parties are agreeing to waive their right to sue in court for disputes that must be submitted to arbitration. The customer does not have to sign this Agreement to Arbitrate, and should sip below only if the customer agrees to resolve disputes through arbitration as set out above.

Date: _____ _____
                 Customer

Date: _____ _____ _____
                 Business   Title

FIGURE 10–2

---

§ 7361. Compulsory arbitration

(a) GENERAL RULE.– Except as provided in subsection (b), when prescribed by general rule or rule of court such civil matters or issues therein as shall be specified by rule shall first be submitted to and heard by a board of three members of the bar of the court.

(b) LIMITATIONS.– No matter shall be referred under subsection (a):

(1) which involves title to real property; or

(2) where the amount in controversy, exclusive of interest and costs, exceeds $ 50,000.

(c) PROCEDURE.– The arbitrators appointed pursuant to this section shall have such powers and shall proceed in such manner as shall be prescribed by general rules.

(d) APPEAL FOR TRIAL DE NOVO.– Any party to a matter shall have the right to appeal for trial de novo in the court. The party who takes the appeal shall pay such amount or proportion of fees and costs and shall comply with such other procedures as shall be prescribed by general rules. In the absence of appeal the judgment entered on the award of the arbitrators shall be enforced as any other judgment of the court. For the purposes of this section and section 5571 (relating to appeals generally) an award of arbitrators constitutes an order of a tribunal.

FIGURE 10–3

running to the courthouse. In the event this tactic fails, the chapter ends its discussion with the traditional legal remedies: breach of contract and specific performance.

Examples of private ADR providers are:

- National Association of REALTORS®
- National Arbitration Forum
- American Arbitration Association
- Better Business Bureau
- National Arbitration and Mediation
- JAMS/Endispute
- State and Local Boards of REALTORS®

As to public arbitration, judicially sponsored compulsory arbitration programs for select claims or types of cases are increasing phenomena. See the Pennsylvania judicial arbitration statute in Figure 10–3.[12]

Web Exercise

You can review formal ADR programs, state by state, by visiting http://courtadr.org/.

Real estate industry groups sincerely promote the benefits of arbitration and mediation systems. The National Association of REALTORS® (NAR) has produced a Homebuyer/Homeseller Dispute Resolution System, which emphasizes the ADR philosophy. See the NAR promotion in Figure 10–4.[13]

State and local realty boards and associations ardently endorse local arbitration and mediation services. In some counties, the published Real Estate Agreement of Sale contains a clause on compulsory or voluntary arbitration. See Figure 10–5 for an example from the Minnesota Association of REALTORS®.

SAMPLE PRESS RELEASE

(Retype this release on Association stationery, filling in the appropriate information in the blanks as indicated. The contact at the top of the release should be the person who handles media calls. The retyped release should be mailed or hand delivered to area newspapers.)

FOR FURTHER INFORMATION CONTACT: **Media relations contact**
                                                                 Phone number _____

Local Association of REALTORS® Launches Mediation Service For Buyers, Sellers

   (Your Town) Date — "Area real estate buyers and sellers now have an alternative to expensive and time-consuming litigation when there is a problem with their transactions," according to (<u>Full Name of Association President</u>). President of the (<u>Association Name</u>).

   The mediation component of the Dispute Resolution System (DRS), was developed by the NATIONAL ASSOCIATION OF REALTORS® for implementation by its more than 1,800 local Associations of REALTORS® nationwide. Through the service, sellers and buyers have access to mediators who have agreed to conduct mediations under the DRS Rules and Procedures.

   "Although most real estate transactions are completed smoothly, occasionally there is a need to resolve a dispute," said (<u>Last Name of Association President</u>). "Many of the most common disputes, such as disagreements over earnest money deposits, are natural candidates for this type of service."

   (<u>Last Name of Association President</u>) added that DRS is a very economical and efficient method of settling conflicts that otherwise might take months to resolve through the courts or through outside arbitration services. (<u>Add sentence(s) briefly describing approximate fees involved for parties, indicating that fees may vary depending on the complexity of the case.</u>)

   In the mediation process, the parties meet with a trained, impartial mediator who helps them attempts to reach a mutually agreeable solution to the dispute. Unlike an arbitrator, the mediator cannot render a binding decision. If the parties cannot reach an agreement, they may pursue arbitration or litigation. Professional mediation groups around the country report a success rate of 80%-90%.

   "It's a "win-win" situation, with no risk involved for either party," said (<u>Last Name of Association President</u>). "If the parties reach a settlement, the dispute is over. If they don't they are free to take other courses of action without prejudice."

   For additional information on the DRS, contact the (<u>Association Name</u>).

FIGURE 10–4

**ARBITRATION DISCLOSURE AND
RESIDENTIAL REAL PROPERTY
ARBITRATION AGREEMENT**
This form approved by the Minnesota Association of REALTORS®,
which disclaims any liability arising out of use or misuse of this form.
© 2009 Minnesota Association of REALTORS®, Edina, MN

1. Page 1

2. **ARBITRATION DISCLOSURE**

3.   You have the right to choose whether to have any disputes about disclosure of material facts affecting the use
4. or enjoyment of the property that you are buying or selling decided by binding arbitration or by a court of law. By agreeing
5. to binding arbitration, **you give up your right to go to court**. By signing the RESIDENTIAL REAL PROPERTY
6. ARBITRATION AGREEMENT (ARBITRATION AGREEMENT) on page two, you agree to binding arbitration under the
7. Residential Real Property Arbitration System (Arbitration System) administered by National Center for Dispute Settlement
8. (NCDS) and endorsed by the Minnesota Association of REALTORS® (MNAR). The ARBITRATION AGREEMENT is
9. enforceable only if it is signed by all buyers, sellers and licensees representing or assisting the buyers and the sellers.
10. The ARBITRATION AGREEMENT is not part of the Purchase Agreement. **Your Purchase Agreement will still be**
11. **valid whether or not you sign the ARBITRATION AGREEMENT.**

12.   The Arbitration System is a private dispute resolution system offered as an alternative to the court system. It
13. is not government sponsored. NCDS and the MNAR jointly adopt the rules that govern the Arbitration System. NCDS
14. and the MNAR are not affiliated. Under the ARBITRATION AGREEMENT you must use the arbitration services of
15. NCDS.

16.   All disputes about or relating to disclosure of material facts affecting the use or enjoyment of the property, excluding
17. disputes related to title issues, are subject to arbitration under the ARBITRATION AGREEMENT. This includes claims
18. of fraud, misrepresentation, warranty and negligence. Nothing in this Agreement limits other rights you may have under
19. MN Statute 327A (statutory new home warranties) or under private contracts for warranty coverage. An agreement to
20. arbitrate does not prevent a party from contacting the Minnesota Department of Commerce, the state agency that
21. regulates the real estate profession, about licensee compliance with state law.

22.   The administrative fee for the Arbitration System varies depending on the amount of the claim, but it is more
23. than initial court filing fees. In some cases, conciliation court is cheaper than arbitration. The maximum claim allowed
24. in conciliation court is $7,500. This amount is subject to future change. In some cases, it is quicker and less expensive
25. to arbitrate disputes than to go to court, but the time to file your claim and pre-hearing discovery rights are limited. The
26. right to appeal an arbitrator's award is very limited compared to the right to appeal a court decision.

27.   **A request for arbitration must be filed within 24 months of the date of the closing on the property or**
28. **else the claim cannot be pursued. In some cases of fraud, a court or arbitrator may extend the 24-month**
29. **limitation period provided herein.**

30.   A party who wants to arbitrate a dispute files a Demand, along with the appropriate administrative fee, with
31. NCDS. NCDS notifies the other party, who may file a response. NCDS works with the parties to select and appoint an arbitrator
32. to hear and decide the dispute. A three-arbitrator panel will be appointed instead of a single arbitrator at the request
33. of any party. The party requesting a panel must pay an additional fee. Arbitrators have backgrounds in law, real estate,
34. architecture, engineering, construction or other related fields.

35.   Arbitration hearings are usually held at the home site. Parties are notified about the hearing at least 14 days in
36. advance. A party may be represented by a lawyer at the hearing if he or she gives five (5) days advance notice to the
37. other party and to NCDS. Each party may present evidence, including documents or testimony by witnesses. The arbitrator
38. must make any award within 30 days from the final hearing date. The award must be in writing and may provide any
39. remedy the arbitrator considers just and equitable that is within the scope of the parties' agreement. The arbitrator
40. does not have to make findings of fact that explain the reason for granting or denying an award. The arbitrator may
41. require the party who does not prevail to pay the administrative fee.

42.   **This Arbitration Disclosure provides only a general description of the Arbitration System and a general**
43. **overview of the Arbitration System rules**. For specific information regarding the administrative fee, please see the
44. Fee Schedule located in the NCDS Rules. Copies of the Arbitration System rules are available from NCDS by calling
45. (888) 832-4792 or on the Web at www.ncdsusa.org or from your REALTOR®. If you have any questions about arbitration,
46. call NCDS at (888) 832-4792 or consult a lawyer.

---

47.   **THE RESIDENTIAL REAL PROPERTY ARBITRATION AGREEMENT IS A LEGALLY BINDING CONTRACT**
48.   **BETWEEN BUYERS, SELLERS AND LICENSEES. IF YOU DESIRE LEGAL ADVICE, CONSULT A LAWYER.**
MN:ADRAA-1 (8/09)

FIGURE 10–5 Reproduced with permission from the Minnesota Association of REALTORS®.

Century 21
Luger Realty

ARBITRATION DISCLOSURE AND
RESIDENTIAL REAL PROPERTY
ARBITRATION AGREEMENT
49. Page 2

50. **THIS IS AN OPTIONAL, VOLUNTARY AGREEMENT.**
51. **READ THE ARBITRATION DISCLOSURE ON PAGE ONE IN FULL BEFORE SIGNING.**

52. **RESIDENTIAL REAL PROPERTY ARBITRATION AGREEMENT**

53. For the property located at _____ .

54. City of _____ , County of _____ , State of Minnesota.
55. Any dispute between the undersigned parties, or any of them, about or relating to material facts affecting the use or
56. enjoyment of the property, excluding disputes related to title issues of the property covered by the Purchase Agreement
57. dated _____ , 20 _____ , including claims of fraud, misrepresentation, warranty and
58. negligence, shall be settled by binding arbitration. National Center for Dispute Settlement shall be the arbitration service
59. provider. The rules adopted by National Center for Dispute Settlement and the Minnesota Association of REALTORS®
60. shall govern the proceeding(s). The rules that shall govern the proceeding(s) are those rules in effect at the time the
61. Demand for Arbitration is filed and include the rules specified in the Arbitration Disclosure on page one. This Agreement shall
62. survive the delivery of the deed or contract for deed in the Purchase Agreement. This Agreement is only enforceable if
63. all buyers, sellers and licensees representing or assisting the buyers and sellers have agreed to arbitrate as acknowledged
64. by signatures below.

65. _____   _____
     (Seller's Signature)   (Date)   (Buyer's Signature)   (Date)

66. _____   _____
     (Seller's Printed Name)   (Buyer's Printed Name)

67. _____   _____
     (Seller's Signature)   (Date)   (Buyer's Signature)   (Date)

68. _____   _____
     (Seller's Printed Name)   (Buyer's Printed Name)

69. _____   _____
     (Licensee Representing or Assisting Seller)   (Date)   (Licensee Representing or Assisting Buyer)   (Date)

70. _____   _____
     (Company Name)   (Company Name)

71. **THE RESIDENTIAL REAL PROPERTY ARBITRATION AGREEMENT IS A LEGALLY BINDING CONTRACT**
72. **BETWEEN BUYERS, SELLERS AND LICENSEES. IF YOU DESIRE LEGAL ADVICE, CONSULT A LAWYER.**

MN:ADRAA-2 (8/09)

FIGURE 10–5
(continued)

CASE DECISION

For a look into how powerful the Binding Arbitration language is in a contract, read Woodside.

Filed 8/21/06

IN THE COURT OF APPEAL OF THE STATE OF CALIFORNIA

THIRD APPELLATE DISTRICT

(San Joaquin)

WOODSIDE HOMES OF CALIFORNIA INC. et al.,
 	
        Petitioners,
 	
v.
 	
THE SUPERIOR COURT OF SAN JOAQUIN COUNTY,
 	
        Respondent;
 	
KIMBERLY WHEELER et al.,
 	
        Real Parties in Interest.
	C052432
	
	(Super. Ct. No. CV023718)

ORIGINAL PROCEEDINGS. Writ of mandate/prohibition. Granted.

Anwyl, Scoffield & Stepp, Lindy H. Scoffield and Richard A. Sullivan for Petitioners.

No appearance by Respondent.

Kahn Brown & Poore, Karen Kahn, Scott A. Brown and David M. Poore for Real Parties in Interest.

Woodside Homes of California Inc. (Woodside Homes) petitions for a writ of mandate to overturn orders vacating the appointment of a referee. The appointment was pursuant to a written contract providing that any controversy arising under it shall be submitted to a general judicial reference. The Superior Court vacated the appointment under the view that *Grafton Partners v. Superior Court* (2005) 36 Cal.4th 944 (*Grafton*), prohibiting predispute waiver of the right to jury trial in the judicial forum, precludes enforcement of such a predispute contract for reference. *Grafton* has no such effect and we shall grant the petition.

FACTS AND PROCEDURAL BACKGROUND

Real party in interest Kimberly Wheeler bought a new Stockton subdivision home from Woodside Homes in February of 2003. The written real estate purchase contract for the transaction contains a reference provision, in pertinent part as follows:

"JUDICIAL REFERENCE OF DISPUTES. If either BUYER or SELLER commences a lawsuit for a dispute arising under this Agreement or relating to the condition, design or construction of any portion of the Property, all of the issues in such action, whether of fact or law, shall be submitted to general judicial reference pursuant to California Code of Civil Procedure Sections 638[] and 641 through 645.1 or any successor statutes thereto."

In May of 2004 Wheeler filed a damages action in the San Joaquin County Superior Court against Woodside Homes alleging harm from construction defects. Woodside Homes answered the complaint and filed a motion for appointment of a referee for all purposes, pursuant to the contract. The motion was granted. Wheeler petitioned this court to overturn the appointment order and we denied the petition.

In August of 2005 the Supreme Court issued the *Grafton* opinion. Soon thereafter Wheeler made a motion to "invalidate" the reference provision in the contract on the ground it was a predispute jury trial waiver, which was unenforceable in light of *Grafton, supra,* 36 Cal.4th 944. The superior court granted the motion and vacated the reference order. Woodside Homes moved for reconsideration. The superior court denied the motion for reconsideration on the ground the holding in *Grafton, supra,* 36 Cal.4th 944, is applicable. Woodside Homes's writ petition followed. We sent a letter to the parties stating we were considering issuing a peremptory writ pursuant to *Palma v. U.S. Industrial Fasteners Inc.* (1984) 36 Cal.3d 171.

DISCUSSION

Woodside Homes contends that the trial court erred in reading *Grafton, supra,* 36 Cal.4th 944, as barring enforcement of "a written contract . . . that provides that any controversy arising therefrom shall be heard by a referee" under Code of Civil Procedure section 638. [1] Woodside Homes argues that such a contract provision results in a waiver of the right to jury trial "prescribed by statute" and thus permitted under *Grafton.* The contention of error is meritorious.

Grafton addresses the question of validity of a contract provision that the parties "agree not to demand a trial by jury in any action, proceeding or counterclaim arising out of or relating to [the subject of the contract]." (*Grafton, supra,* 36 Cal.4th 944, 950.) The proponent of the provision relied upon *Trizec Properties Inc. v. Superior Court* (1991) 229 Cal.App.3d 1616. *Trizec* had held that although the statute addressing jury trial waiver in the judicial forum, section 631, did not authorize a predispute waiver, such a waiver was permissible without statutory authorization.[2] (*Grafton, supra,* 36 Cal.4th at pp. 951–952.) The Supreme Court disapproved *Trizec* insofar as it permitted a waiver without statutory authorization. (*Grafton, supra,* 36 Cal.4th at pp. 956.)

The Supreme Court agreed with *Trizec, supra,* 229 Cal.App.3d 1616, that section 631 did not authorize such a waiver. The waiver proponent argued that section 631, subdivision (d)(2), provided for a predispute waiver as one: "By written consent filed with the clerk or judge." (*Grafton, supra,* 36 Cal.4th at p. 957; see fn. 2, *ante.*) The Supreme Court found this insufficient as it is ambiguous as to the time at which the written consent might be executed. It noted that the other subdivisions of section 631 clearly address circumstances after litigation had commenced:

"Similarly, the circumstance that five of the six subsections of section 631, subdivision (d) refer to an act or omission that, as a temporal matter, must occur entirely during the period following the commencement of litigation strongly suggests that the waiver described in subsection (2) also refers to an act that is undertaken entirely during the period after the lawsuit was filed. Specifically, a failure to appear, to demand jury trial, or to pay necessary fees—or an oral consent in open court—must occur in its entirety after the litigation has commenced. If the Legislature had intended a different temporal reach for section 631, subdivision (d)(2), we believe it would have explicitly stated so—as it did in connection with arbitration and reference agreements. (See §§ 638, 1281.)" (*Grafton supra,* 36 Cal.4th at p. 959.)

Thereafter the *Grafton* opinion observes:

"We also do not find any indication [in section 631] the Legislature intended the result proposed by real party. On the contrary, when the Legislature has authorized waiver of the right to trial in a court of law prior to the emergence of a dispute, it has done so explicitly. . . . [F]or example . . . Section 638, authorizing courts to transfer a dispute to a referee upon the agreement of the parties, initially provided that a referee may be appointed 'upon the agreement of the parties filed with the clerk, or judge, or entered in the minutes' (Stats. 1951, ch. 1737, § 93, p. 4117), but that statute was amended in 1982 to include predispute agreements, now authorizing a judicial reference 'upon the agreement of the parties filed with the clerk, or judge, or entered in the minutes, or upon the motion of a party to a written contract or lease that provides that any controversy arising therefrom shall be heard by a referee . . . .' (§ 638, as amended by Stats. 1982, ch. 440, § 1, p. 1810, italics added.)" (*Grafton, supra,* 36 Cal.4th at pp. 960.)

This passage cites a predispute agreement for reference under section 638 as one example of an explicit statutory authorization of waiver to the right to trial in the judicial forum and, a fortiori, the right to jury trial.

(continued)

The *Grafton* opinion explains the ostensible anomaly concerning predispute agreements as follows.

"In addition, arbitration (like reference hearings) conserves judicial resources far more than the selection of a court trial over a jury trial. It therefore is rational for the Legislature to promote the use of arbitration and reference hearings by permitting predispute agreements, while not according the same advantage to jury trial waivers." (*Grafton, supra,* 36 Cal.4th at p. 964.)

Notwithstanding these unmistakable statements that a predispute reference agreement is not governed by the rationale of *Grafton, supra,* 36 Cal.4th 944, Wheeler contends *Grafton* precludes enforcement of such agreement. She argues that because section 638 does not use the terms "jury" or "waiver" it does not unambiguously authorize a predispute jury trial waiver, as required for a statutory waiver by *Grafton.*

In a consensual general reference, as here, the dispute is resolved by the decision of the referee. (§ 644) A statute permitting agreement for a reference unambiguously results in a waiver of "jury trial" without the need to use those words. Such a reference (like arbitration) entails dispensing with trial in the judicial forum, including jury trial. (See, e.g., *Badie v. Bank of America* (1998) 67 Cal.App.4th 779, 806; *Woodside Homes of Cal. Inc. v. Superior Court* (2003) 107 Cal.App.4th 723, 729.)

The 1982 extension of the "temporal reach" of section 638 to permit predispute agreements for reference is an unambiguous statutory authorization for waiver of the right to jury trial before a dispute arises. "Indeed it has always been understood without question that parties could eschew jury trial . . . by agreeing to a method of resolving that controversy, *such as* arbitration, which does not invoke a judicial forum. [Citation.]" (*Grafton,* 36 Cal.4th at p. 957; italics added; original italics omitted.)

The trial court erred in vacating the judicial reference, and we shall issue a writ.

DISPOSITION

Having complied with the procedural requirements for issuance of a peremptory writ in the first instance, we are authorized to issue the peremptory writ forthwith. (See *Palma v. U.S. Industrial Fasteners Inc., supra,* 36 Cal.3d 171.) We issued a temporary stay to prevent an unnecessary trial. Upon finality of this decision the temporary stay order is vacated.

Let a peremptory writ of mandate issue directing respondent superior court to vacate its order granting the motion to "invalidate" the reference provision in the contract and vacating the reference. Petitioners shall recover their costs. (Cal. Rules of Court, rule 56.)

_____SIMS_____, Acting P.J.

We concur:

_____NICHOLSON_____, J.

_____RAYE_____, J.

1. Undesignated statutory references are to the Code of Civil Procedure. Section 638 provides as pertinent: "A referee may be appointed upon the agreement of the parties filed with the clerk, or judge, or entered in the minutes, or upon the motion of a party to a written contract or lease that provides that any controversy arising therefrom shall be heard by a referee if the court finds a reference agreement exists between the parties:

"(a) To hear and determine any or all of the issues in an action or proceeding, whether of fact or of law, and to report a statement of decision.

"(b) To ascertain a fact necessary to enable the court to determine an action or proceeding." (§ 638, subds. (a), (b).)

2. Section 631 provides as pertinent: "The right to a trial by jury as declared by Section 16 of Article I of the California Constitution shall be preserved to the parties inviolate. In civil cases, a jury may only be waived pursuant to subdivision (d).

"(d) A party waives trial by jury in any of the following ways:

"(1) By failing to appear at the trial.

"(2) By written consent filed with the clerk or judge.

"(3) By oral consent, in open court, entered in the minutes.

"(4) By failing to announce that a jury is required, at the time the cause is first set for trial, if it is set upon notice or stipulation, or within five days after notice of setting if it is set without notice or stipulation.

"(5) By failing to deposit with the clerk, or judge, advance jury fees as provided in subdivision (b).

"(6) By failing to deposit with the clerk or judge, at the beginning of the second and each succeeding day's session, the sum provided in subdivision (c)." (§ 631, subds. (a), (d).)

II. ARBITRATION

In arbitration, disputes are submitted to an arbitrator or a panel of arbitrators. Bradley Miller explains:

> Depending on the type of dispute, the parties may prefer to have a single arbitrator. For example, a single arbitrator may be preferable for straightforward valuation disputes, but not for disputes where there are unique aspects to the property, such as the presence of hazardous materials. This will minimize the cost of the arbitration. Alternatively, each of the parties may prefer to select its own arbitrator and let the party-appointed arbitrators select a neutral third arbitrator.[14]

The NAR gives a thumbnail summary of the arbitration process:

- If permitted under state law, parties to a real property transaction precommit to submitting their disputes to either binding or nonbinding arbitration. Parties must be notified that if they commit to binding arbitration, they give up their legal right to litigate the dispute in the future.

- A dispute arises and a request for arbitration is made to the endorsing association or arbitration company. This request may be accompanied by a written complaint.

- Notice is given to the other relevant parties with a request for response to the complaint.

- A list of qualified arbitrators is provided to the parties. Each party notes those arbitrators that are acceptable to them. The arbitrator lists are then matched and the arbitrator(s) are appointed. There will usually be the option to have one or three arbitrators on the panel.

- The arbitrators shall notify all parties to the dispute of the time and place for the hearing. Parties are also notified that legal counsel may represent them.

- Prior to the hearing, limited discovery is allowed.

- At the hearing, each party may open with a statement of their position on the dispute. Testimony from witnesses may be heard and the witnesses are cross-examined. Documents in support of a position are also received at this time.

- The hearing then ends and the arbitrators render an award within a specified time period following the hearing.[15]

The arbitrator(s) conduct hearings according to predetermined rules of process and evidence. Arbitrators have broad discretion in their decision-making and the award. In binding arbitration, the parties must generally accept the result, except in a few rare circumstances like:

- The award was procured by corruption, fraud, or undue means;
- There was corruption by any of the arbitrators;
- A party's rights were substantially prejudiced by misconduct of a neutral arbitrator;

- The arbitrators exceeded their powers and the award cannot be corrected without affecting the merits of the decision upon the controversy submitted; or
- A party's rights were substantially prejudiced by the arbitrators' refusal to postpone the hearing upon sufficient cause being shown therefor, by the arbitrators' refusal to hear evidence material to the controversy, or by other conduct of the arbitrators contrary to the arbitration law.[16]

In nonbinding cases, the parties are free to appeal or disregard the decision on any grounds and proceed to formal litigation.

III. MEDIATION

An even less formal means of resolving real estate disputes is mediation. To mediate means to entertain compromise facilitated by a third party.[17] According to J. A. Young, "The goal of mediation is to provide the participants with a mutually agreeable business resolution to their dispute. By not adhering strictly to the custom of obtaining a legal solution to their problems, the participants are able to bypass the rigidity of the rules of evidence and *stare decisis*, and fashion their own remedies. In the process, the parties to the dispute avoid legal expenses, such as billed hours and expert witness fees."[18]

The advantages of mediation are many, including:

- Relieving court congestion
- Reducing undue costs and delay in the litigation of cases
- Enhancing opportunities for personal and community involvement in the resolution of cases
- Facilitating access to justice
- Providing access to justice to all classes and groups
- Providing a more expeditious forum for decision-making.[19]

Mediation tends to foster an environment conducive to problem resolution, and this atmosphere, once experienced, is an easier sell the second time around. The culture of ADR, in the most general terms, is:

- **Informal.** The process is informal and flexible; attorneys are not necessary.
- **Confidential.** Mediation is a confidential process.
- **Quick And Inexpensive.** When parties want to get on with their business and their lives, mediation may be desirable as a means of producing rapid results. The majority of mediations are completed in one or two sessions.

In addition, the end result of mediation tends to be less brutal and without the real and stereotypical human costs so often suffered in the traditional courtroom. And just as compelling, the parties to the case exercise a greater deal of control over the case at hand. Parties who negotiate their own settlements have more control over the outcome of their dispute. Parties have an equal say in the process. Mediation leaves the parties intact or at least less emotionally spent.

At the heart of mediation is the desire to reach an amicable and mutually satisfactory solution. Finally, mediation fosters an environment that is conducive to problem solving, by replacing the contentious adversarial approach with the collegiality of parties seeking to fix a problem.

By any measure, the mediation process relies heavily on the interpersonal skills and acumen of the mediator, whose sole purpose is getting both parties comfortable in their positions. The mediator clarifies the problem, focuses on the pros and cons of the parties' relative arguments, and tries to develop a consensus and forge new options. During mediation sessions, the mediator moves back and forth among the parties hoping to find common ground. According to Professor

Robert J. Aalberts, "Since the parties may still be apart, the mediator must create doubts in their minds about maintaining their current, unbending positions. This is a job a disgruntled party often cannot do alone."[20]

The mediator should be a neutral, third party facilitator. The mediator should not:

- Become an advocate for either party;
- Violate the principles of confidentially about the disclosures made by either party;
- Let the discussion run rampant; and
- Let the parties think the mediator will determine the outcome of the mediation.[21]

Mediators and attorneys Yaroslav Sochynsky and Mariah Baird suggest the insertion of a mediation clause in the agreement of sale.

> While such a clause is no guarantee that the case will settle, it will require the parties to make an effort to mediate their dispute with a third-party neutral before they go to court. If one of the parties does not participate in the mediation in good faith, the mediation will be concluded. There is no requirement that a party provide information in a mediation where the other side is simply looking for free discovery. There are thus very few downside risks to including an embedded mediation clause in an agreement.[22]

Once the parties have weighed all the alternatives posed by the mediator, if one or more routes are acceptable, they will formalize their intentions by agreement or **settlement**. Here, the paralegal, in conjunction with a supervisor, will "formally draw up a settlement agreement to bring this conflict to a successful conclusion."[23]

For other insights into the mediation process, see the NAR question/response sequence in Figure 10–6.[24]

RESPONSES TO FREQUENTLY ASKED QUESTIONS ABOUT MEDIATION

Q: What is mediation?

A: Mediation is a non-adversarial process that brings disputing parties together with a neutral, unbiased third party (mediator) who assists the parties in reaching a mutually agreeable settlement of the dispute. The mediator does not render decisions or impose sanctions. Settlement terms reached and agreed to by the parties during the mediation become binding when parties sign a written settlement agreement.

Q: How does mediation differ from arbitration?

A: An arbitrator has the authority to render a binding decision, similar to a judge in a court of law. The parties, therefore, forfeit their right to have their dispute tried in a court of law. Mediators, on the other hand, have no authority to render a decision but merely assist the parties to arrive at a mutually agreeable solution. If the parties fail to reach a settlement, they are free to pursue other forms of dispute resolution including arbitration and litigation. In successful mediations all parties have a part in working out the terms of the eventual settlement and must agree to the final outcome for it to be enforceable.

Q: When the DRS mediation clause is presented to a buyer or seller, isn't the real estate salesperson raising a "red flag" by bringing up the issue of a potential dispute at the outset of the transaction?

A: Not if the salesperson presents mediation in a positive, non-threatening way. The salesperson should point out that the mediation clause is similar to other clauses in the contract that are

---

FIGURE 10–6

(continues)

designed to protect interests of the parties. The mediation clause in no way suggests that a dispute will arise, any more than the option to have a home inspection means that there will be defects in the property. The mediation clause provides parties with an efficient, less expensive alternative to litigation in the event a dispute should arise. The salesperson should emphasize that mediation does not involve high risks. Parties are not bound to agreements reached in mediation unless they sign a written settlement agreement, and if a settlement isn't reached, parties are free to submit their dispute to arbitration or go to court. Salespeople should stress that mediation is successful 80%-90% of the time.

Q: **If a party signs a contract or an addendum that contains a mediation clause, is the party required to mediate if a dispute arises?**

A: Yes. The signed agreement to mediate is binding and parties must submit the dispute to mediation. The agreement to mediate does not bind the parties to results that might be achieved during mediation, and parties retain the right to go to court in the event that mediation is unsuccessful. If a settlement is reached during mediation it becomes binding only when it is put into writing and signed by all the parties. Once the parties have signed a written settlement agreement, they are legally bound to abide by its terms and cannot subsequently litigate the dispute.

Q: **Who are the mediators?**

A: DRS mediators are trained professionals who have absolutely no personal interest in the outcome of the mediation. Under the NAR DRS program, Association's do not handle the mediations but refer the mediations to either one mediation provider or to a list of mediation providers who are acting in their own individual capacity.

Q: **Do the parties involved in a dispute have the option of choosing the mediator who will mediate their dispute?**

A: Yes, however, if the local association has entered into an exclusive DRS Service Agreement with a single mediation group, the parties mediating under the DRS Rules and Procedures must select a mediator affiliated with that group.

Q: **What types of disputes can be mediated?**

A: Almost any type of dispute between or among buyers, sellers, brokers and other parties to a real estate transaction can and should be mediated. These include: disputes over earnest money deposits, e.g., who gets the deposit if the sale falls through; cost of repairs to property when there is a question of possible negligence or failure to disclose a known defect, e.g., a defective roof or termite infestation; claims for damages when there is a charge of possible misrepresentation concerning the condition of the property, e.g., central air conditioning was never connected to the new addition on the house.

Q: **Are there any types of disputes that can't be mediated under DRS?**

A: Yes. Disputes that cannot or should not be mediated under the DRS Mediation Rules include: disputes that involve extremely complex legal issues or allegations of criminal misconduct, violations of a states real estate license laws, disputes and controversies including disputes between REALTORS® that are subject to arbitration or hearing before a Professional Standards panel, and disputes that are not directly connected to a real estate transaction.

Q: **Who pays for the mediation?**

A: Parties are free to negotiate their own arrangements. In most cases, parties split mediation fees equally.

Q: **How much does mediation cost?**

A: The cost of mediation varies depending on the size of the claim, the complexity of the issues, and the mediator. Fees are established by the mediator and can range anywhere from $50 to $1,500.

FIGURE 10–6
(continued)

It is important to note that because the fee is usually split among the parties, no party pays an excessive amount.

Q: **How long does the whole process take?**

A: Under the DRS Rules, the mediation conference must be held within 60 days from the date on which the mediator receives the "Request to Initiate Mediation Transmittal Form" from the party initiating mediation. Most mediation conferences, however, are scheduled and conducted within 30 days. The typical mediation conference lasts from between 1 to 4 hours, and a second conference is rarely needed.

Q: **Can parties be represented by counsel?**

A: Yes. DRS Rules and Procedures state that any party may be represented by counsel. If a dispute involves a small sum and does not raise complex issues, parties may choose not to be represented by counsel which means that a party does not have to pay the attorney to attend the mediation conference. The Rules also state that all parties must be notified, in advance of the mediation conference, of another party's intention to be represented by counsel.

Q: **Can commission disputes between REALTORS® be mediated under DRS?**

A: No. Disputes that are normally arbitrated under Article 14 of the REALTOR® Code of Ethics are specifically excluded from mediation under the DRS Rules.

Q: **Why should the Association adopt DRS when we already offer mediation services through our Professional Standards Committee.**

A: The DRS Mediation Program is not intended to replace or to be used in connection with arbitration or mediation activities conducted by an association's Professional Standards Committee. The program is designed to accommodate and provide for disputes that are not covered under Professional Standards Policies and Procedures.

Q: **Can DRS be used to resolve disputes for commercial real estate transactions?**

A: Yes. Provided all parties in the dispute agree to mediate the dispute under the DRS Rules and Procedures.

FIGURE 10–6
(continued)

IV. ADR RULES AND PROCEDURAL REQUIREMENTS

If the parties choose to arbitrate or mediate, the process will be guided by either formally mandated rules or negotiated terms and conditions as to how the process will take place. Most of the professional associations mentioned throughout this chapter promulgate rules of procedure for these processes. Some are pretty straightforward while others are fairly complicated. The American Land Title Association posts clear cut rules for how to initiate and participate in ADR. (See Figure 10–7.[25])

Web Exercise

Compare and contrast the rules of the National Arbitration Forum at www.adrforum.com/users/naf/resources/CodeofProcedure2008-print2.pdf.

In general, the rules of ADR tend to be slightly more flexible than traditional litigation. Even so, it is crucial for the participants to understand and abide by the ADR terrain. In a binding case of arbitration, the results are fixed and nonappeallable.

Web Exercise

Visit the State of Minnesota's ADR rules at www.courts.state.mn.us/documents/0/public/Alternative_Dispute_Resolution/Rule_114_-_Updated_January_1%2c_2005.doc.

TITLE INSURANCE ARBITRATION RULES OF THE AMERICAN LAND TITLE ASSOCIATION®

(Amended January 1, 2006, as a supplement to the Code of Procedure of the National Arbitration Forum. These Title Insurance Arbitration Rules are available at www.alta.org. The Code of Procedure of the National Arbitration Forum is available at www.arb-forum.com.)

1. Introduction

The Title Insurance Arbitration Rules, which are administered by the National Arbitration Forum effective January 1, 2006, are the rules of the American Land Title Association® ("ALTA®"). ALTA® has responsibility for their maintenance and publication. Parties to title insurance policies providing for arbitration shall consider these rules as governing such arbitrations subject to the terms of those policies.

2. Incorporation of the Code of Procedure of the National Arbitration Forum

The Title Insurance Arbitration Rules hereby incorporate by reference the Code of Procedure of the National Arbitration Forum ("NAF Code"). To the extent there is any variance between the Title Insurance Arbitration Rules and the NAF Code, the Title Insurance Arbitration Rules shall take precedence. The provisions of the NAF Code for Expedited Hearings shall not apply absent the agreement of all parties to the dispute.

3. Applicability

These Title Insurance Arbitration Rules (including these Rules as they may be amended) shall apply whenever the parties' arbitration agreement refers to the Title Insurance Arbitration Rules of the American Land Title Association®, the Title Insurance Arbitration Rules of the American Arbitration Association, the Title Insurance Arbitration Rules of the National Arbitration Forum, or where the parties otherwise mutually agree to use the Title Insurance Arbitration Rules.

4. Administration

Unless otherwise agreed to by the parties, disputes administered in accordance with the Title Insurance Arbitration Rules are administered by the National Arbitration Forum. The parties may, by mutual agreement, decide to administer the arbitration themselves, or by a third party selected by mutual consent.

5. Fixing of Locale

In cases where parties fail to mutually agree on the locale, the National Arbitration Forum shall have the power to determine the locale in the state in which the land is located.

6. Consolidation of Arbitrations

Rule 19 of the NAF Code addresses Joinder, Intervention, Consolidation and Separation. With respect to consolidation of two or more arbitrations, Rule 19.C is amended as follows:

"Consolidation of two or more arbitrations, to be heard in joint proceedings under the Title Insurance Arbitration Rules, shall be had where ordered by an arbitrator if a reasonable number of the following circumstances exist:

(a) Each of the parties to the arbitrations to be consolidated has agreed to arbitrate under the Title Insurance Arbitration Rules.

(b) Either (i) the title insurance policies on which the arbitrations are based are linked or (ii) the parties or subject matters of the arbitrations are related in some other way so that consolidation will promote a fair, economical or efficient disposal of the issues presented in all of the arbitrations.

(c) There exist common issues of fact that will be required to be determined in each of the arbitrations to be consolidated, the proof of which will or could be substantially the same. However, neither incomplete identify of factual issues nor varying policy terms or measures of damages shall be a reason for refusing consolidation, unless the differences are of a number and complexity that will make the determination of the liabilities by the arbitrator unwieldy or difficult."

FIGURE 10–7
(continues)

7. Evidence

The arbitrator shall not limit the rights and obligations under the policy concerning proof of loss or damage. The arbitrator must apply the attorney work product doctrine of the applicable state to prohibit the discovery of or introduction into evidence of attorney work product, irrespective of whether under the law of the particular state the attorney work product doctrine is considered to be a legal privilege or a procedural discovery rule.

8. Applicable Law

The law and rules of equity of the situs of the land shall apply to every arbitration under the Title Insurance Arbitration Rules, except the arbitrator shall have the power pursuant to the pertinent rules in the NAF Code to rule on his or her own jurisdiction.

9. Scope of Award

The arbitrator may grant any remedy or relief that the arbitrator determines to be just and equitable according to the applicable laws and the terms of the policy. The award may not exceed the amount of any claim or counterclaim as disclosed when filed or as later changed in accordance with the pertinent rule of the NAF Code. If the insured in an arbitration is the owner of the estate or interest covered by the title insurance policy and the estate or interest is subject to a mortgage insured by the insurer under that policy or any title insurance policy when arbitration is commenced, the arbitrator shall provide for payment of the award (or any part thereof) directly to the owner of the mortgage (and not to the insured), pursuant to written instructions signed by the insurer and received by the arbitrator prior to the closing of the hearing.

10. Fee Schedule for Arbitrations Under the Title Insurance Arbitration Rules

The provisions of the NAF Code regarding the payment of fees (including compensation for arbitrators) for the arbitration shall apply subject to the modification that parties who have agreed by mutual consent to administer an arbitration themselves or with the assistance of a third party, as set forth in paragraph 3, above, shall be responsible to decide their own arrangements concerning payment of the fees for the arbitration (including compensation of the arbitrator).

FIGURE 10–7
(continued)

V. ARBITRATION AND MEDIATION AGREEMENTS AND CLAUSES

There are numerous ways paralegals can memorialize the buyers' and sellers' intention to arbitrate or mediate. Whether the desire is formalized by a separate, independent agreement or as a clause or an addendum to a Real Estate Agreement of Sale, the terms and conditions should consider these factors:

1. Decision of the arbitration or mediation panel and whether it is binding or nonbinding
2. Possibility to appeal the decision
3. Constitution of the panel
4. Costs and how they are to be divided or assessed
5. Locus of decision-making
6. Rules of evidence
7. Discussion and labeling of appropriate exhibits including any contracts or documents as necessary
8. Court of jurisdiction with concurrent jurisdictions if applicable

Web Exercise

The National Arbitration Forum publishes at wide array of forms and documents at www.adrforum.com/main.aspx?itemID=330&hideBar=False&navID=357&news=3.

AGREEMENT TO MEDIATE

Note: This Agreement does not have to be executed if parties have previously committed to mediation via the contract for sale or other written agreement to mediate.

The undersigned parties agree that they are involved in a dispute concerning the purchase of real estate to the signed contract dated _____. A copy of the executed contract is attached and made part of this Agreement by addendum.

The following is a brief summary of the dispute:

_____

_____

The undersigned further agree to submit the above-described dispute to mediation in accordance with the mediation rules and procedures of the Dispute Resolution System. Any agreement signed by the parties, pursuant to the mediation conference, shall be binding.

The undersigned hereby acknowledge that they have received and read the Dispute Resolution System Information Brochure and understand its contents.

Seller(s)_____   Date_____

Buyer(s)_____   Date_____

Listing Broker_____   Date_____

Selling Broker_____   Date_____

Other(s) _____

Date_____

Date_____

FIGURE 10–8

A. Agreements or Contracts

The parties to a real estate transaction, including agents and brokers, can execute an independent, fully integrated contract to arbitrate or mediate in the event of dispute. The National Association of REALTORS® Agreement to Mediate, reproduced in Figure 10–8,[26] is a solid example of this approach.

B. Clauses and Addenda

Instead of an independent agreement, the paralegal may insert, attach, or reference by incorporation, a clause or provision in a basic real estate agreement that addresses arbitration or mediation. Figure 10–9[27] is an arbitration clause.

Two examples of mediation clauses covering NAR guidelines are reproduced in Figures 10–10[28] and 10–11.[29]

ARBITRATION OF DISPUTES (AGREEMENTS OF PURCHASE AND SALE)

By signing below you are agreeing to have any dispute settled by neutral arbitration as provided by law and you are giving up any rights you might posses to a court or jury trial. By signing below you are giving up your judicial rights to discovery and appeal, unless they are specifically included in the Arbitration of Disputes Provision. If you refuse to submit to arbitration after agreeing to this provision, you may be compelled to arbitrate under the authority of. Your agreement to this Arbitration Provision is voluntary.

We have read and understand the foregoing and agree to submit disputes arising out of matter included in the Arbitration of Disputes Provision to Neutral Arbitration.

Buyer: _____
      Signature

Seller: _____
      Signature

1. Binding Arbitration.

The submission to arbitration in accordance with the terms hereof shall be the exclusive method and procedure to resolve any and all disputes, claims, or controversies of any kind, (a "Dispute"), now existing or hereafter arising between the parties in any way arising out of, pertaining to, or in connection with

    a. the Purchase Agreement, or any related agreement, document, or instrument (collectively, the "Documents");

    b. any incidents, omissions, acts, practices, or occurrences causing injury to either party whereby the other party or its agents, employees, or representatives may be liable, in whole or in part, and which relate in any manner to the documents or the transaction contemplated therein; or

    c. any aspect of the past or present relationships of the parties with respect to the documents or the transactions contemplated therein. Any party to a dispute may, by summary proceedings, bring an action in court to compel arbitration of any dispute.

2. Governing Rules.

The arbitration shall be conducted in accordance with the Commercial Arbitration Rules (the AAA Rules) of the American Arbitration Association (the "AAA"), except to the extent modified herein.

3. Appointment of Arbitrators.

Qualifications of Arbitrators. All arbitrators shall be practicing attorneys licensed to practice law in the state of _____ with at least ten (10) years in practice and shall be knowledgeable in the legal issues which are the subject of the Dispute. No arbitrator shall have represented either party to the Dispute within the preceding ten (10) years.

Selection of Arbitrators. Within 30 days after receipt of a notice requesting arbitration and stating the basis of a party's claim, each party shall appoint an arbitrator. Notice of the appointment shall be given by each party to all other parties when made. Within fifteen (15) days after the date the last arbitrator is selected by a party,

FIGURE 10–9
(continues)

the arbitrators shall appoint a neutral arbitrator. If the two (2) arbitrators are unable to agree upon a third arbitrator within the fifteen- (15) day period, then either party, on behalf of both, may request the appointment of the third arbitrator by making an application to the presiding judge of the Superior Court of the State and County of _____, acting as an individual. The party making the application shall give the other party fifteen (15) days notice of the application.

4. Scope of Award; Modification or Vacation of Award.

The arbitrators may grant any remedy or relief that the arbitrator deems just and equitable. The arbitrators may also grant such ancillary relief as is necessary to make effective the award; provided, however, in no event may the arbitrators award punitive damages. To the extent permitted by applicable law, the arbitrators shall have the power to award recovery of all legal expenses (including, but not limited to, attorneys' fees, administrative fees, arbitrators' fees, and other professional fees and expenses) to the prevailing party. However, the award or potential award of legal expenses shall not be considered in determining the amount in controversy for purposes of determining the appropriate number of arbitrators for the dispute.

The arbitrators shall resolve all aspects of any dispute in accordance with the applicable substantive law. The arbitrator shall make specific, written findings of fact and conclusions of law. Judgment upon the award rendered by the arbitrators may be entered in any court having jurisdiction subject to
    a. the parties' statutory right to seek vacation or modification of an award pursuant to applicable law, and
    b. the parties' right to seek vacation or modification of any award that is based in whole, or in part, on an incorrect or erroneous ruling of law by appeal to an appropriate court having jurisdiction; however, any such application for vacation or modification of an award based on an incorrect ruling of law must be filed in a court otherwise having jurisdiction over the dispute within sixty (60) days after the date the award is rendered. The findings of fact by the arbitrators shall be binding upon all parties and shall not be subject to futher review, except as otherwise allowed by applicable law.

Other Matters and Miscellaneous. To the maximum extent practicable, an arbitration proceeding hereunder shall be concluded within 180 days after the request by the initiating party for arbitration. Arbitration proceedings hereunder shall be conducted in the city of _____ in _____ county, state of _____. Arbitrators shall be empowered to impose sanctions and to take such other actions as the arbitrators deem necessary to the same extent a judge could pursuant to the _____ Rules of Court, and applicable law.

FIGURE 10–9
(*continued*)

MEDIATION CLAUSE

In the event of a dispute between the parties arising out of the subject matter of this agreement, neither party shall pursue any legal action against the other until the party desiring to resolve the dispute shall have first requested and mediated the dispute. The requested mediation shall take place within ten (10) days after written notification is received by the other party, in the city of X at the Y Alternative Dispute Resolution Center. The mediator shall be selected in accordance with the rules then prevailing at the Y Alternative Dispute Resolution Center, or in the absence of any such rule, the director of the Y Alternative Dispute Resolution Center shall select one at random from the membership of the local board of realtors. Each participant shall pay a proportionate share of the fees associated with the mediation, including the cost of the mediator. Unless a settlement is mutually agreed to in writing, the participants shall not be bound by the discussions or outcome of the mediation.

FIGURE 10–10

MEDIATION CLAUSE

The undersigned hereby agree that any dispute or claim arising out of or relating to the attached contract dated _____, between _____ and _____, the breach of that contract or the services provided shall be submitted to mediation in accordance with the rules and procedures of the Dispute Resolution System. Disputes shall include representations made by the buyer(s), seller(s) or any real estate broker or other person or entity in connection with the sale, purchase, financing, condition or other aspect of the property to which this contract pertains, including without limitation allegations of concealment, misrepresentation, negligence and/or fraud. Any agreement signed by the parties pursuant to the mediation conference shall be binding.

The following matters are excluded from mediation hereunder:

- Judicial or nonjudicial foreclosure or other action or proceeding to enforce a deed of trust, mortgage, or land contract
- Unlawful detainer action
- The filing or enforcement of a mechanic's lien
- Any matter which is within the jurisdiction of a probate court or
- Violation of a state's real estate license laws.

The filing of a judicial action to enable the recording of a notice of pending action, for order of attachment, receivership, injunction, or other provisional remedies, shall not constitute a waiver of the right to mediate under this provision, nor shall it constitute a breach of the duty to mediate.

The parties hereby acknowledge that they have received, read and understand the standard announcement brochure for the Dispute Resolution System and agree to submit disputes as described above to mediation in accordance with the Dispute Resolution System.

Seller(s) _____   Buyer(s)_____

Date_____   Date_____

Date_____   Date_____

Listing Broker _____   Selling Broker _____

Date_____   Date_____

FIGURE 10–11

C. Demand/Submission

In both arbitration and mediation cases, the parties initiating the request for ADR submit either a **Demand for Arbitration** (see Figure 10–12[30]) or a mutual **Submission to Arbitration** (see Figure 10–13[31]).

In the demand, one party or the other asserts the right or obligation to mediate or arbitrate. In the submission, the parties mutually concur on the need for ADR.

D. Settlement

If the parties conclude their dispute successfully, they should reduce the terms and conditions of the resolution to a formal writing. The Mediation Settlement Agreement in Figure 10–14 is a representative document.

American Arbitration Association
Dispute Resolution Services Worldwide

_____**ARBITRATION RULES**
(ENTER THE NAME OF THE APPLICABLE RULES)
Demand for Arbitration

MEDIATION: *If you would like the AAA to contact the other parties and attempt to arrange mediation, please check this box.* ☐ *There is no additional administrative fee for this service.*	
Name of Respondent	Name of Representative (if known)
Address:	Name of Firm (if applicable):
	Representative's Address

City	State	Zip Code	City	State	Zip Code
Phone No.		Fax No.	Phone No.		Fax No.
Email Address:			Email Address:		

The named claimant, a party to an arbitration agreement dated _____, which provides for arbitration under the
_____Arbitration Rules of the American Arbitration Association, hereby demands arbitration.

THE NATURE OF THE DISPUTE

Dollar Amount of Claim $	Other Relief Sought: ☐ Attorneys Fees ☐ Interest ☐ Arbitration Costs ☐ Punitive/ Exemplary ☐ Other _____

Amount Enclosed $_____ In accordance with Fee Schedule: ☐Flexible Fee Schedule ☐Standard Fee Schedule

PLEASE DESCRIBE APPROPRIATE QUALIFICATIONS FOR ARBITRATOR(S) TO BE APPOINTED TO HEAR THIS DISPUTE:

Hearing locale_____ (check one) ☐ Requested by Claimant ☐ Locale provision included in the contract

Estimated time needed for hearings overall: _____ hours or _____ days	Type of Business: Claimant _____ Respondent_____

Is this a dispute between a business and a consumer? ☐Yes ☐No
Does this dispute arise out of an employment relationship? ☐Yes ☐No

If this dispute arises out of an employment relationship, what was/is the employee's annual wage range? Note: This question is required by California law. ☐Less than $100,000 ☐ $100,000 - $250,000 ☐ Over $250,000

You are hereby notified that copies of our arbitration agreement and this demand are being filed with the American Arbitration Association's Case Management Center, located in (check one) ☐ Atlanta, GA ☐ Dallas, TX ☐ East Providence, RI ☐ Fresno, CA ☐ International Centre, NY, with a request that it commence administration of the arbitration. Under the rules, you may file an answering statement within the timeframe specified in the rules, after notice from the AAA.

Signature (may be signed by a representative) Date:	Name of Representative
Name of Claimant	Name of Firm (if applicable)
Address (to be used in connection with this case):	Representative's Address:

City	State	Zip Code	City	State	Zip Code
Phone No.		Fax No.	Phone No.		Fax No.
Email Address:			Email Address:		

To begin proceedings, please send two copies of this Demand and the Arbitration Agreement, along with the filing fee as provided for in the Rules, to the AAA. Send the original Demand to the Respondent.

Please visit our website at www.adr.org if you would like to file this case online. AAA Customer Service can be reached at 800-778-7879

FIGURE 10–12

American Arbitration Association
Dispute Resolution Services Worldwide

SUBMISSION TO DISPUTE RESOLUTION

The named parties hereby submit the following dispute for resolution, under the rules of the American Arbitration Association.

To be completed and signed by all parties (attach additional sheets if necessary).

Rules Selected: ☐Commercial ☐Construction ☐Other (please specify) _____.

Procedure Selected: ☐Binding Arbitration ☐Mediation ☐Other (please specify)_____.

NATURE OF DISPUTE:

| Dollar Amount of Claim $ | Other Relief Sought: ☐Attorneys Fees   ☐Interest |
| | ☐Arbitration Costs ☐Punitive/ Exemplary ☐Other _____ |

PLEASE DESCRIBE APPROPRIATE QUALIFICATIONS FOR ARBITRATOR(S) TO BE APPOINTED TO HEAR THIS DISPUTE:

PLEASE FILE TWO SIGNED COPIES ALONG WITH THE FILING FEE AS PROVIDED FOR IN THE RULES, TO THE AAA.

Amount Enclosed $_____ In accordance with Fee Schedule: ☐Flexible Fee Schedule ☐Standard Fee Schedule

| HEARING LOCALE REQUESTED: _____ | Estimated time needed for hearings overall: _____ hours or _____days |

We agree that, if arbitration is selected, we will abide by and perform any award rendered hereunder and that a judgment may be entered on the award.

| Name of Party | Name of Party |
| Address: | Address: |

City:	State	Zip Code	City:	State	Zip Code
Phone No.		Fax No.	Phone No.		Fax No.
Email Address:			Email Address:		
Signature (required):		Date:	Signature (required):		Date:
Name of Representative:	Name of Representative:
Name of Firm (if applicable)	Name of Firm (if applicable)
Address (to be used in connection with this case)	Address (to be used in connection with this case)

City:	State	Zip Code	City:	State	Zip Code
Phone No.		Fax No.	Phone No.		Fax No.
Email Address:			Email Address:		

Please visit our website at www.adr.org if you would like to file this case online.
AAA Customer Service can be reached at 800-778-7879

FIGURE 10–13

MEDIATION SETTLEMENT AGREEMENT

In the matter of mediation between _____ and _____

Date:_____

Case Number:_____

Mediator:_____

Settlement

We, the undersigned, having mediated our dispute in accordance with the DRS rules and procedures agree as follows:

By:_____   By:_____

Title:_____   Title:_____

Date:_____   Date:_____

By:_____

Title:_____

Date:_____

FIGURE 10–14

VI. ACTIONS IN LAW

When mediation or arbitration proposals have been refused despite express provisions in the contract or the contract sets out no such terms, the aggrieved party has no choice but to employ actions in law.

A. Remedies for Refusal to Arbitrate or Mediate

Despite an agreement's explicit terms, one party may balk at the required arbitration or mediation. If the reluctant party refuses to cooperate in the appointment of an arbitrator, a petition and corresponding order should be directed to their attorney by the paralegal.

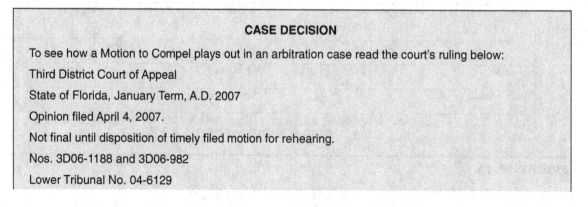

CASE DECISION

To see how a Motion to Compel plays out in an arbitration case read the court's ruling below:

Third District Court of Appeal

State of Florida, January Term, A.D. 2007

Opinion filed April 4, 2007.

Not final until disposition of timely filed motion for rehearing.

Nos. 3D06-1188 and 3D06-982

Lower Tribunal No. 04-6129

Coastal Systems Development Inc.,

Appellant,

v

Bunnell Foundation Inc.,

Appellee.

Appeals from nonfinal orders from the Circuit Court for Miami-Dade County, Scott M. Bernstein, Judge.

Holland & Knight and James D. Wing, for appellant.

Katz Barron Squitero Faust and Bernard Allen, for appellee.

Before RAMIREZ, WELLS, and LAGOA, JJ.

RAMIREZ, J.

The defendant, Coastal Systems Development Inc., appeals the trial court's nonfinal order denying its motion to compel arbitration. Coastal also appeals the trial court's nonfinal order denying its motion to compel mediation, for stay pending arbitration and to strike notice for trial. The cases were consolidated for appeal. We now affirm the order denying Coastal's motion to compel arbitration and dismiss the second appeal.

This action arose out of a contract between Coastal Systems Development Inc. and Bunnell Foundation Inc. The contract provided that upon completion of the Broward County Beach Restoration Project, the parties would share equally in all profits earned. Coastal refused to provide any financial information to Bunnell regarding profits, so Bunnell sued Coastal on March 15, 2004. Coastal moved to dismiss based on the mediation provision contained in the contract. The motion did not indicate that the action was subject to arbitration proceedings. Neither did Coastal's amended motion to dismiss seek arbitration.

On June 2, 2004, the trial court heard Coastal's motion to stay the proceedings pending mediation and denied it because Coastal would not provide Bunnell with a copy of Coastal's audit of the project, nor a breakdown of the expenses incurred by Coastal in connection with the project. The trial court reasoned that Bunnell could not determine the profits making mediation useless without Coastal's production of the requested documents.

Coastal then filed an Answer and Affirmative Defenses to the complaint, together with a counterclaim for breach of contract and breach of fiduciary duty.

Arbitration was not mentioned. Prior to filing this Answer, Coastal did not seek to compel arbitration, but it had begun to conduct discovery. Coastal later filed an Amended Answer, Affirmative Defenses and Counterclaim filed on July 6, 2004, which also failed to seek arbitration.

On August 17, 2004, pursuant to court order, Coastal's previous counsel was substituted by another law firm. New counsel filed a motion to compel mediation, even though the trial court previously had ruled on the issue when it entered its June 2, 2004 order. Coastal also sought to stay the action pending arbitration and to strike Bunnell's Notice of Trial, but did not specifically request the court to order arbitration.1 The trial court denied the motion by virtue of the order of June 2, 2004. Finally, on

April 19, 2006, approximately three years after Bunnell filed its action against Coastal, Coastal moved to compel arbitration pursuant to paragraph 13.9 of the contract. The trial court denied Coastal's motion.

First, the trial court properly denied Coastal's motion to compel mediation and for stay pending arbitration. This motion had been previously denied. The prior denial of mediation was not an appealable order. Thus, Coastal correctly argues that the prior order was a nonfinal, nonappealable order.

The second motion requesting mediation also applied for a stay pending arbitration. In essence, Coastal's renewed request to compel mediation filed on October 21, 2004, was the same as its previous request for mediation filed on August 19, 2004. The request in both motions was that the trial court compel mediation, not arbitration, of the underlying dispute. Both requests sought to abate the action pending mediation, according to paragraph 13.8 of the contract. As that issue was not appeal-

(continued)

able when previously denied, it is likewise not appealable now. In addition, the parties conceded at oral argument that mediation already has taken place. Accordingly, we dismiss the appeal of the Motion to Compel Mediation, for Stay Pending Arbitration and to Strike Notice of Trial.

As to arbitration, we conclude that the trial court properly denied Coastal's motion. When ruling on a motion to compel arbitration, under both the Federal Arbitration Act and Florida's Arbitration Code, the trial court must decide three things: (1) whether a valid written agreement to arbitrate exists; (2) whether an arbitrable issue exists; and (3) whether the right to arbitration was waived. *Raymond James Fin. Servs Inc. v. Saldukas*, 896 So. 2d 707, 711 (Fla. 2005). Contrary to Coastal's contention, an effective waiver of the right to arbitrate does not require proof of prejudice. *Id.* at 711. The trial court was eminently correct in denying Coastal's Motion to Compel arbitration because Coastal waived that right. Coastal did not seek to compel arbitration in either its Motion to Dismiss and Amended Motion to Dismiss and Motion to Stay Proceedings Pending Mediation filed on April 7, 2004 and May 19, 2004, respectively. It was not until April 19, 2006, two years into the litigation, that Coastal sought to compel arbitration. Coastal waived the right to seek arbitration. *Hardin Int'l. Inc. v. Firepak Inc.* 567 So. 2d 1019, 1020-21 (Fla. 3d DCA 1990).

In addition, Coastal has waived its right to arbitrate by actively participating in the lawsuit. A party who actively participates in a lawsuit waives the right to arbitration. *Doctors Assocs Inc. v. Thomas*, 898 So. 2d 159, 162 (Fla. 4th DCA 2005). Here, Coastal did not raise the right to arbitrate in its Answer in its Affirmative Defenses. Where a party defends on the merits by answering the complaint without demanding arbitration, a waiver is deemed to have occurred. *Marine Envtl. Partners Inc. v. Johnson*, 863 So. 2d 423, 427 (Fla. 4th DCA 2003). Coastal also waived its right to arbitrate when it filed its Counterclaim in the underlying action. *Owens & Minor Med. Inc. v. Innovative Marketing and Dist. Servcs Inc.* 711 So. 2d 176, 177 (Fla. 4th DCA 1998); *Coral 97 Assocs. Ltd. v. Chino Elec. Co.*, 501 So. 2d 69, 70-71 (Fla. 3d DCA 1987). Finally, Coastal proceeded with discovery in the underlying action, which also constitutes a waiver of its right to arbitrate. *Winter v. Arvida Corp*, 404 So. 2d 829, 830 (Fla. 3d DCA 1981) (the court held that a party waived its right to arbitrate by filing an answer and proceeding with discovery before moving to dismiss for failure to arbitrate) , 408 So. 2d 229, 238 (Fla. 3d DCA 1981). In sum, all of Coastal's actions demonstrate that it waived its right to compel arbitration two years into the proceedings. *See also Rolls v. Bliss & Nyitray Inc.*

We therefore affirm the trial court's denial of Coastal's motion to compel arbitration. With respect to the trial court's denial of Coastal's nonfinal order denying Coastal's motion to compel mediation, for stay pending arbitration and to strike notice for trial, we dismiss the appeal. Affirmed in part; dismissed in part.

---

[1]Although Coastal's motion stated that "the Court has previously entered discovery orders in aid of mediation . . .", referring to the trial court's ruling on June 2, 2004, it is not reflected in the record. Moreover, the trial court did not order mediation.

Web Exercise

Courts are not hesitant to uphold the language of mandatory Arbitration or Mediation clauses in real estate cases. See the Compendium of Cases compiled by the National Arbitration Forum at www.adrforum.com/users/naf/resources/FromTheBench-JudicialOpinions2.pdf.

Before commencing a formal action to compel arbitration or mediation, aside from informal requests, the parties should communicate by Demand method as an initial step. The National Arbitration and Mediation company publishes a form. See Figure 10–15.[32]

If the real estate dispute must be mandatorily resolved through arbitration, an action in law filed in disregard of arbitration can be stayed. See Figure 10–16 for a Motion for Stay format.

B. Action for Breach

Any party alleging a **breach of contract** may bring an action in law for the recovery of damages. An action on a contract is labeled a civil action. The only caveat to the maintenance of a breach suit is proof that the breach was material—that is, serious enough to undermine the underlying

National Arbitration and Mediation ("NAM
Comprehensive Dispute Resolution Rules and Procedui
990 Stewart Avenue, First Flo
Garden City, NY 115
Telephone: 1-800-358-25
Fax: 516-794-89
www.namadr.co

NAM COMPREHENSIVE DISPUTE RESOLUTION RULES AND PROCEDURES
DEMAND FOR ARBITRATION/ARBITRATION NOTICE

CLAIMANT INFORMATION

Name(s): _____

*Contact Person or Counsel: _____

Address: _____

_____

Phone: _____

Fax: _____

Email Address: _____

File/Claim Number: _____

RESPONDENT INFORMATION

Name(s): _____

*Contact Person or Counsel: _____

Address: _____

_____

Phone: _____

Email Address: _____

*Fax: _____

*File/Claim Number: _____

*if applicable

RESPONDENT(S): Please take notice that pursuant to NAM's Comprehensive Dispute Resolution Rules an
Procedures which provides for Arbitration of disputes arising thereunder the Claimant identified above **herel**
demands Arbitration of a claim against you. You have thirty (30) days to serve the Claimant and NA
with a Reply to this Demand for Arbitration/Arbitration Notice by messenger service, overnight delive
service by a nationally recognized courier company or by certified mail. **If you do not serve the Claimant ar**
NAM with a Reply within 30 days of service of this Notice, the Arbitrator may enter an award against you

Pursuant to the attached Arbitration Agreement, this matter is to be resolved by in-person oral Arbitration.

Revised as of 01/01/09

1

FIGURE 10–15
(continues)

CLAIMANT SECTION: EXPLANATION OF DEMAND

The Claimant is claiming the following relief, which may include the following:

Principal balance	_____
Interest accrued	_____
Legal expenses	_____
Cost of Arbitration*	_____
Other (specify)	_____
	_____
	_____
Total	_____

*The cost of the Arbitration is fully described in NAM's Fees and Costs for Homeowner/Realtor disputes involving agencies which are members of the Long Island Board of Realtors, Inc. (LIBOR). Binding Arbitration for Real Estate Transactions ("NAM's Fee Schedule"). In general, in a two-party Arbitration, the administrative fee is $540. There is also an hourly fee of $433 per hour for Arbitrator time. All fees are to be paid by the Claimant. The Claimant is to remit to NAM the payment for the administrative fee and 3 hours of Arbitrator time or $1,839 along with the Demand for Arbitration. To the extent that the Arbitrator time is less than 3 hours, the Claimant will receive a refund of up to 1 hour. Minimum billing is 2 hours. To the extent that additional time is needed beyond 3 hours, the Claimant will be billed at $433 per hour in excess thereof. **As part of the Demand for Arbitration, the Claimant who files the Demand for Arbitration may request that the Arbitrator order that all, or a portion of the cost of the Arbitration/Mediation, be reimbursed to the Claimant from the Respondent.** For a full description of the fees relating to various case types and circumstances, such as multi-party, Tri-panel, small claims cases, and/or adjournment, cancellation and/or settlement fees, please refer to NAM's Fee Schedule.

A description of the nature of the dispute and the injuries alleged follows (The Claimant should provide a detailed description herein and attach any evidence hereto):

_____

_____

_____

_____

_____

_____

_____

_____

_____

_____

Counsel or a party's representative accepts responsibility for payment of all NAM fees pertaining to this matter regardless of the outcome of this case.

_____

CLAIMANT by: (signature)

Name: _____

Title: _____   Date _____/_____/_____

National Arbitration and Mediation (NAM)
1-800-358-2550 / www.namadr.com

2

FIGURE 10–15
(continued)

RESPONDENT SECTION: REPLY TO DEMAND

The **Respondent** hereby responds to the demand made by the Claimant as follows (the Respondent should provide a response herein and attach any evidence hereto to support such position):

_____

_____

_____

_____

_____

_____

_____

_____

_____

_____

_____

_____

_____

_____

_____

_____

_____

_____

_____

_____

_____

_____

_____

_____

RESPONDENT by: (signature)

Name: _____

Title: _____   Date _____/_____/_____

FIGURE 10–15
(continued)

The parties are hereby notified that the Claimant has filed copies of the Arbitration Agreement (if applicable) and this Demand for Arbitration/Arbitration Notice at NAM's headquarters.

Either party may contact the NAM Administrator indicated below of the Comprehensive Dispute Resolution Rules and Procedures in writing at NAM, Comprehensive Dispute Resolution Rules and Procedures, 990 Stewart Avenue, First Floor, Garden City, New York 11530 or by telephone with questions regarding the Arbitration process or NAM's Comprehensive Dispute Resolution Rules and Procedures and Fee Schedule or to request a copy thereof.

Contact the NAM Administrator, _____at

1-800-358-2550 ext. _____.

FIGURE 10–15
(continued)

MOTION FOR STAY

Defendant, _____, moves the court for an order, staying the trial of the above-entitled action until arbitration has been had in accordance with the terms of the written contract between the parties hereto dated _____, _____.

This motion is made upon the following grounds:

1. On _____, _____, defendant and plaintiff duly entered into a contract in writing whereby defendant agreed to _____ and plaintiff agreed to _____. A copy of the contract is attached hereto, marked Exhibit _____ and made a part hereof.

2. The contract evidences a transaction involving commerce within the meaning of Sections 1 and 2 of Title 9 of the United States Code as is shown by the following facts: _____.

3. The contract contained the following arbitration clause: _____.

4. Differences have arisen between plaintiff and defendant over the contract, owing to the fact that _____.

5. On _____, _____, the above-entitled action was commenced by plaintiff, and is now pending, in which plaintiff seeks judgment against defendant in the sum of $_____ on the ground(s) that _____.

6. The issue(s) involved in the action (is or are) preferable to arbitration under the above-mentioned agreement.

7. (If a prior demand for arbitration has been made, add: On _____, _____, defendant submitted his demand to plaintiff to proceed to arbitration of the issues involved in the suit, which demand plaintiff has refused.)

This motion is based upon the complaint heretofore served herein, and upon the papers, records, and files in this action _____ (and the affidavit of _____ (name) filed herewith).

FIGURE 10–16

---

contract. When purchasers fail to show up at the settlement table, you can be assured a sufficient breach has taken place. Other examples of material breaches include:

- Failure to deliver deed
- Failure to make required deposits
- Failure to apply for mortgage
- Failure to make repairs
- Failure to make zoning application

In the event of a real, actual or anticipatory repudiation or breach of a contract, the aggrieved party to the contract has a right to file a complaint asserting either performance under the contract or payment of specific damages."[33] A sample breach complaint from Pennsylvania is outlined in Figure 10–17.

IN THE COURT OF COMMON PLEAS OF _____ COUNTY, PENNSYLVANIA
CIVIL DIVISION

_____, and _____, Plaintiffs,

　　　Vs.

_____, Defendant.

Type of pleading: Plaintiff's
complaint in assumpsit for
breach of a real estate
agreement

Code and classification:_____

Filed on behalf of: _____ and _____, Plaintiffs
Name, address and telephone of:
Counsel of record

_____

_____

_____

Attorney's State ID #

IN THE COURT OF COMMON PLEAS OF _____ COUNTY, PENNSYLVANIA
CIVIL DIVISION

_____)　　　Case No. _____
　　　　　　　　　　　)
_____,_____)
　　　　　　　　　　　)
　　　　　　　　　　　)
Plaintiff,　　　　　　)　　　Civil Action: LAW
　　　　　　　　　　　)
　　　Vs.　　　　　　)
　　　　　　　　　　　)
_____,_____)
　　　　　　　　　　　)
Defendant.　　　　　)

FIGURE 10–17
(continues)

NOTICE TO DEFEND

You have been sued in court. If you wish to defend against the claim set forth in the following pages, you must take action within twenty (20) days after this complaint and notice are served, by entering a written appearance personally or by attorney and filing in writing with the court your defenses or objections to the claims set forth against you. You are warned that if you fail to do so the case may proceed without you and a judgment may be entered against you by the court without further notice for any money claimed in the complaint or for any other claim or relief requested by the plaintiff. You may lose money or property or other rights important to you.

YOU SHOULD TAKE THIS PAPER TO YOUR LAWYER AT ONCE. IF YOU DO NOT HAVE A LAWYER OR CANNOT AFFORD ONE, GO TO OR TELEPHONE THE OFFICE SET FORTH BELOW TO FIND OUT WHERE YOU CAN GET LEGAL HELP.

IN THE COURT OF COMMON PLEAS OF _____ COUNTY, PENNSYLVANIA, CIVIL DIVISION

_____)
)
and _____)
)
)
)
Plaintiffs,   )
)
    Vs.   )
)   Case No. _____
)
_____)
)
)
Defendant.   )

COMPLAINT FOR BREACH OF A REAL ESTATE AGREEMENT

Come now, _____ and _____, who are residents of _____, _____, County of _____, Commonwealth of Pennsylvania, hereinafter known as Plaintiffs complaining:

1. Plaintiffs are owners, by tenants of the entireties, of a real property located at _____, _____, Pennsylvania.

2. Defendant _____, is a corporation, located and doing business in the County of _____, Commonwealth of Pennsylvania at _____, _____, _____.

3. PLAINTIFFS and DEFENDANT entered into an Agreement, dated _____, year_____, for the purchase and sale of the following-described real property at _____, _____, _____, _____, for a purchase price of $_____. A copy of the Agreement, marked Exhibit "A", is attached and made a part of this pleading by reference.

FIGURE 10–17
(continued)

4. Defendant made a $_____ earnest money deposit, one half of which was nonrefundable. At the same time, Plaintiffs and Defendant, within same Exhibit "A", negotiated additional provisions germane to this Agreement, and listed in Addendum form, effective _____, year_____. A copy of the Addendum, marked Exhibit "B" is attached and made a part of this pleading by reference.

5. The Addendum required Defendant to make an additional payment of "dollar;_____ upon either zoning approval of a particular site plan or within _____ (_) months of the signing of this Agreement whichever occurred first.

6. That same Addendum, at Exhibit "B", made $_____ of the additional payment described above, a non-refundable option payment.

COUNT I
BREACH OF CONTRACT

7. DEFENDANT has remitted only $_____ of the required $_____ deposit set out in the Agreement, and did not pay the balance owed effective _____, _____.

8. Upon DEFENDANT's failure to honor the terms of the Agreement, both PLAINTIFFS and Defendant attempted to renegotiate the Agreement, by a modified Addendum on _____, year_____. However, due to Defendant's bad faith, these negotiations failed to lead to a modified Agreement.

9. Plaintiffs are ready, willing, and able to convey said property, by a sufficient deed, on payment by defendant of the agreed sum. However, Defendant refused, and still so refuses, to accept the conveyance and honor the terms of said contract.

10. Defendant has not paid the agreed purchase price or any part thereof.

11. Defendant is also obliged, by the same Agreement of Sale, to seek zoning approvals and other municipal variances from the _____, as a condition to this Agreement. Defendant has not acted in good faith regarding these conditions. Defendant has neither submitted an acceptable plan for site variance nor made sufficient arguments in a zoning request to the _____.

12. By reason of the breach, Plaintiffs have been damaged in the sum of $_____

WHEREFORE, PLAINTIFFS requests:

1. Plaintiffs' damages in the sum of $_____;
2. Costs of this proceeding, including attorneys' fees and related expenses; and
3. Such other and further relief as the court deems justified.

Respectfully submitted,

_____
[Typed name]
Counsel for Plaintiffs
[Address]
[City] Pennsylvania [Zip]
Attorney ID No._____
[Phone number]

FIGURE 10–17
(continued)

VERIFICATION

The undersigned, _____ and _____, aver that the statements of fact contained in the attached complaint are true and correct to the best of our information, knowledge and belief, and are made subject to the penalties of 18 PA. R. CIV. PRO. §4904 relating to unsworn falsification to authorities.

Dated: _____

_____
[Typed name]
Plaintiff

Dated: _____

_____
[Typed name]
Plaintiff

COMMONWEALTH OF PENNSYLVANIA COURT OF COMMON PLEAS,
_____ COURT, PENNSYLVANIA

_____)
)
and)   Case No. _____
)
_____)
)
PLAINTIFFS,)
)
)
Vs.   )   CIVIL ACTION: LAW
)
_____)
)
DEFENDANT.)

AFFIDAVIT OF RETURN OF SERVICE OF COMPLAINT

I hereby certify and return that on the _____ day of _____, year _____ at _____ _____.m., I served this complaint, or other pleading as follows: _____.
Name of individual, company, corporation, etc., served:

Address where service was made: _____.

THIS AFFIDAVIT IS MADE SUBJECT TO THE PENALTIES OF 18 Pa.C.S.A. § 4904 RELATING TO UNSWORN FALSIFICATION TO AUTHORITIES.

BY: _____
(Signature of Process Server)

_____
(Typed or Printed Name—Process Server)

FIGURE 10–17
(continued)

C. Specific Performance

The equitable action of **specific performance** is usually a last ditch effort in one's effort to purchase a property or force a sale. Due to the unique nature of real estate, an aggressive buyer or seller can insist, by this action, on the buyer being able to buy or the seller being able to sell. A litigant elects this remedy over the damage action for breach. See Figure 10–18 for an example of a specific performance pleading.

Web Exercise

For an esoteric look at how to enforce an arbitration agreement, visit: http://floridaarbitrationlaw.com/materials/10_Steps_of_Arb.ppt#259,3,Slide3.

IN THE COURT OF COMMON PLEAS

OF _____ COUNTY, _____

CIVIL DIVISION

_____)
)

and   )

Plaintiffs,   )

Vs.   )   CASE NO. _____

Defendant.   )

COMPLAINT FOR SPECIFIC PERFORMANCE

1. On the ____ day of _____, _____, plaintiff and defendant entered into a written agreement, a copy of which is attached hereto and marked Exhibit "A," whereby defendant agreed to sell to plaintiff for the sum of $____ the following real property, of which defendant was then and is now owner in fee simple:

[Describe by metes and bounds, or record description]

2. Plaintiff paid defendant at said time the sum of $ ____ to apply to the purchase price of said property, and by the terms of said agreement the balance of the purchase price was to be paid upon delivery to plaintiff by defendant of a good and sufficient general warranty deed, free of encumbrances and dower rights, which the defendant agreed to do within not less than _____ from date of said agreement.

3. Within the stipulated period of time, and on the _____ day of _____, _____, plaintiff tendered to defendant the balance of such purchase price and demanded that defendant execute and deliver to plaintiff a deed in accordance with the terms of said agreement, with release of the inchoate dower rights of defendant's wife, but defendant neglected and refused to execute and deliver to plaintiff such deed, and has at all times since so neglected and refused, but plaintiff has been able, willing, and ready to perform the terms of said agreement on his part to be performed.

4. If defendant does not sell said real property the plaintiff, plaintiff will lose a profit of $_____ as his benefit of the bargain.

FIGURE 10–18

(continues)

WHEREFORE, plaintiff demands that defendant be ordered and directed to specifically perform said agreement on his part and to execute and deliver to plaintiff a good and sufficient general warranty deed for said premises, free from the inchoate dower right of his wife, that plaintiff be allowed an abatement of the purchase prior to the extent of the value thereof, and for the recovery of his costs herein. In the alternative, if specific performance is denied, plaintiff demands judgment against defendant for $_____ plus costs.

Respectfully submitted,

_____

[Typed name]
Counsel for Plaintiffs
[Address]
[City] [State] [Zip]

Attorney ID No.

FIGURE 10–18
(continued)

CHAPTER TEN **SUMMARY**

Chapter Ten discussed the following topics:

- Difference between mediation and arbitration
- ADR providers
- Arbitration process
- Mediation process
- Arbitration and mediation clauses and agreements
- Settlement process
- Remedies for refusal to submit to ADR

REVIEW **QUESTIONS**

1. What is the purpose of ADR?
2. What is the difference between mediation and arbitration?
3. Explain the difference between binding and nonbinding arbitration.
4. Are there any public arbitration programs? What kind are they, and who orders them? Find out if your state has a program such as this.
5. What is the process during an arbitration hearing?
6. Under what circumstances is "binding" arbitration not binding?
7. What are the advantages of mediation?
8. What is the difference between a demand for arbitration and a submission to dispute resolution?
9. What actions in law are available for real estate disputes?
10. Explain specific performance.

DISCUSSION **QUESTION**

Discuss the arbitration process from application to award.

EXERCISE 1

Draft an arbitration clause and a demand for arbitration using the Fact Pattern from Exercise 1 in Chapter 3. Use hypothetical information as needed.

EXERCISE 2

Draft a mediation clause and a mediation settlement agreement using the following information. Use hypothetical information as needed.

> Buyer—Ted Williams
>
> Seller—John Tuff
>
> Agreement of Sale—Date March 12, 2009
>
> Sale price—$78,000
>
> Mortgage Commitment to be Secured—Within 90 days
>
> Settlement to be held on or before June 18, 2009
>
> Pest inspection clause incorporated by addendum on March 29, 2009
>
> Title to be conveyed by general warranty deed

EXERCISE 3

Draft a complaint for breach of a real estate agreement using the information from Exercise 2 in this chapter. Create a scenario or use hypothetical facts as needed.

Assignment for the Case of John and Martha

A dispute has arisen from the sale of the property John and Martha have just purchased. The following items were missing after settlement:

- Six pairs of outside shutters
- Central air-conditioning unit
- One wooden garden shed, cement pad that the shed was on is still on the property
- 20 feet of porch railing from the front porch

Prepare the necessary documents to submit the dispute to either mediation or arbitration. Explain why you chose the specified method.

REFERENCES

1. Realtors Seek Arbitration for Sales Disputes, *Sacramento Daily Journal* at 2; *see also* Roger Alford, *Report to the Law Revision Committee Regarding Recommendations to California Arbitration Law*, 4 PEPP. DISP. RESOL. L. J. 1 (2003).

2. CHARLES P. NEMETH, PARALEGAL RESOURCE MANUAL at Chapter 14 (2008).

3. U.S. DEPARTMENT OF JUSTICE, DISPUTE RESOLUTION: TECHNIQUES AND APPLICATIONS, A SELECTED BIBLIOGRAPHY v (1985).

4. Irving R. Kaufman, *Reform for a System in Crisis: Alternative Dispute Resolution in the Federal Courts*, 59 FORDHAM L. REV., 17–18 (Oct. 1990).

5. Pub. L. No. 101-650, Tit. I § 103(A), 104 Stat 5091 (Codified at 28 U.S.C. § 473(A) (Supp. II 1990).

6. Eric D. Green, *Voluntary ADR: Part of the Solution*, 29 TRIAL 35 (April 1993).

7. Bradley S. Miller, *How to Draft Real Estate Arbitration Clauses* (with Forms), 10 PRAC. REAL EST. LAW. 27, 30–31 (1994).

8. National Arbitration Forum, P.O. Box 50191, Minneapolis, MN 55405-0191 available at www.adrforum.com/users/naf/resources/ConstructionADR2.pdf.

9. Greg Rinckey, *Using Alternative Dispute Resolution*, FEDERAL TIMES, July 15, 2009, visited July 23, 2009.

10. CHARLES P. NEMETH, LITIGATION, PLEADINGS AND ARBITRATION 591 (1990).

11. U.S. DEPARTMENT OF JUSTICE, DISPUTE RESOLUTION: TECHNIQUES AND APPLICATIONS, A SELECTED BIBLIOGRAPHY vi (1985).

12. For an assessment of a publicly annexed ADR program see generally Honorable Howard H. Dana Jr., *Court-Connected Alternative Dispute Resolution in Maine*, 57 ME. L. REV. 349 (2005); *See also* Joshua Isaacs, *Current Development 2004-2005: A New Way to Avoid the Courtroom: The Ethical Implications Surrounding Collaborative Law*, 18 GEO. J. LEGAL ETHICS 833 (2005).

13. 42 PA.C.S. § 7361 (2009) *See also* California is an aggressive promoter of ADR. The Dispute Resolution Programs Act of 1986 (Stats 1986, ch. 1313, SB 2064-Garamendi and Stats 1987, ch. 28, SB 123-Garamendi) provides for the local establishment and funding of informal dispute resolution programs. The goal of the act is the creation of a statewide system of locally funded programs which will provide dispute resolution services (primarily conciliation and mediation) to county residents. These services assist in resolving problems informally and function as alternatives to more formal court proceedings; Some states, like New Hampshire, are just now implementing a formal ADR system. See the announcement at www.courts.state.nh.us/ADR.pdf, visited July 23, 2009.

14. National Association of REALTORS®, Dispute Resolution System: Mediation/Arbitration (1994).

15. Miller, *supra* note 6.

16. National Association of REALTORS®, *supra* note 13.

17. Yaroslav Sochynsky & Mariah Baird, *Using Alternative Dispute Resolution in Real Estate Transactions*, 7 PRAC. REAL EST. LAW. 13, 18–19 (1991).

18. TANIA SOURDIN, ALTERNATIVE DISPUTE RESOLUTION AND THE COURTS (2004).

19. J.A. Young, *Mediate Your Real Estate Disputes* (with Forms), 6 PRAC. REAL EST. LAW. 25, 26 (1990); *see also* Christopher M. Fairman, *Growing Pains: Changes in Collaborative Law and the Challenge of Ethics*, 30 CAMPBELL L. REV 237 (2008).

20. CHARLES P. NEMETH, LITIGATION, PLEADINGS AND ARBITRATION, 456 (1991), 2nd ed., (1997).

21. Robert J. Aalberts, *The Use of Mediation in the Real Estate Industry*, 20 REAL EST. L.J. 347, 357 (1992).

22. Young, *supra* note 18, at 27.

23. Sochynsky & Baird, *supra* note 16, at 304.

24. Aalberts, *supra* note 20, at 358.

25. AMERICAN LAND TITLE ASSOCIATION, TITLE INSURANCE ARBITRATION RULES OF THE AMERICAN LAND TITLE ASSOCIATION (2006) at www.alta.org/standards/arbitration1.1.06.cfm.

26. National Association of REALTORS®, *supra* note 13.

27. National Association of REALTORS®.

28. National Association of REALTORS®. See Young, *supra* note 18, at 29–30.

29. National Association of REALTORS®.

30. National Association of REALTORS®.

31. American Arbitration Association, Form G2.

32. *Id.*, Form G1A.

33. National Arbitration and Mediation (NAM), 990 Stewart Ave., Garden City, NY 11530, *Demand for Arbitration*, at www.namadr.com/documents/LIBOR-Demand_for_Arb.pdf.

34. CHARLES P. NEMETH, THE PARALEGAL RESOURCE MANUAL, 2nd ed., 977 (1995).

Foreclosure

LEARNING OBJECTIVES

- To discuss the nature of foreclosure and when a foreclosure may occur.
- To identify the three methods of foreclosure, judicial foreclosure, power-of-sale foreclosure, and strict foreclosure, and the processes involved in each method.
- To summarize the concepts of sale surplus and the aligned concepts of deficiency judgments and redemption.

JOB COMPETENCIES

- To discuss the nature and process of foreclosure with a client.
- To assist the attorney in various foreclosure procedures.

ETHICAL CONSIDERATIONS

The paralegal must be aware of the following ethical dilemmas during this phase of a real estate transaction:

- Unauthorized practice of law
- Lawyer supervision of nonlawyers
- Confidentiality issues
- Communications with persons outside of law firm

I. THE ECONOMIC AND LEGAL LANDSCAPE OF FORECLOSURE

Recent economic conditions have made the process of foreclosure common parlance. What was once a rare event has not become a mainstream tragedy. Millions of American homes are descending into foreclosure annually. The data paints a dismal picture at Figure 11–1.[1]

Responses to this housing crisis have been many and largely ineffectual. The Federal Reserve, the Office of the President and Congress, both House and Senate, have infused government largesse, both in terms of money and policy, not witnessed since the Great Depression. Simple things like, temporary moratoria on foreclosure actions, in many states, have helped slow the march of foreclosures. Financial assistance to banks and homeowners so that these parties might renegotiate terms and conditions of a loan, and stave off the foreclosure has also been tried. The results are at best mixed. Legislative measures are well intentioned but still yet to be fully evaluated.

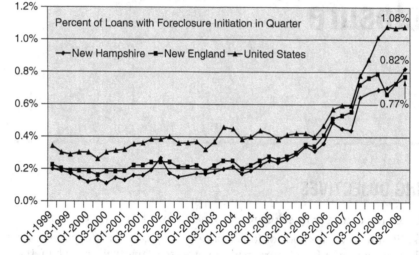

Foreclosure Rates For United States, New England and New Hampshire, through Q4-2008

FIGURE 11–1

The President has just signed the *Helping Families Save Their Homes Act of 2009*[2] into law; it also expands the Department of Justice's ability to prosecute at virtually every step of the process from predatory lending on Main Street to the manipulation on Wall Street. The new law creates a bipartisan Financial Crisis Inquiry Commission to investigate the financial practices. Other features of the legislation are:

■ Grants bankruptcy court judges the authority to reduce interest rates or extend the repayment period up to forty years for mortgages (Sec. 103).

■ Requires homeowners who receive assistance under this act and sell their home within the first year for a profit to pay their lender up to 90% of the difference between the sales price and the amount due under their original mortgage (Sec. 103).

■ Prohibits aid to homeowners who are able to meet their original or modified mortgage payments without assistance or who obtained credit through actual fraud (Sec. 105).

■ Amends standards for participation in the HOPE for Homeowners Program by excluding borrowers who intentionally defaulted on their mortgage, who have been convicted of fraud or those who earn more than $1 million (Sec. 202).

■ Raises FDIC depositor insurance to permanently cover $250,000 instead of $100,000 of each deposit at participating institutions (Sec. 204).

■ Establishes a Nationwide Mortgage Fraud Task Force to investigate mortgage fraud in and aid enforcement of mortgage fraud laws (Sec. 302).

 Web Exercise

Read about Congress' efforts to minimize the foreclosure crisis at http://thomas.loc.gov/cgi-bin/query/z?c111:S.895:

There are a host of other efforts as well. The public is well aware of TARP— *the Troubled Asset Relief Program*,[3] which was to assist banks in ridding themselves of "toxic assets."

Other solutions have been proposed including:

■ Allow qualified homeowners to restructure mortgages under court supervision (H.R. 1106/S. 61)

- Restore confidence in the housing market by strengthening mortgage lending practices and correcting perverse business incentives to make bad loans (H.R. 1728)
- Reduce tax burdens related to loan modifications that undermine foreclosure prevention
- Reduce or eliminate key obstacles to constructive loan modifications (S. 376)
- Increase modifications by providing legal protection for loan servicers and boosting participation in the Hope for Homeowners Program (H.R. 703)
- Strengthen oversight of the FHA and provide more resources
- Improve efforts to work with distressed homeowners
- Prevent predatory and reckless lending in the future[4]

Web Exercise

Find out about the role of the Federal Reserve in this mortgage, banking, and foreclosure crisis at www.federalreserveeducation.org/FRED/.

II. FORECLOSURE PROCESS

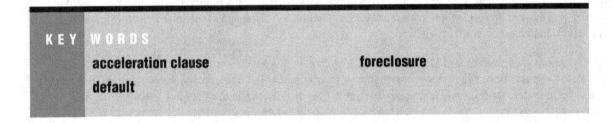

KEY WORDS	
acceleration clause	foreclosure
default	

Foreclosure is the process by which a mortgagee (seller or lender) terminates the mortgagor's (the purchaser's) interest in real property.[5] The mortgagee's right to do this typically arises when the mortgagor falls behind in making payments on the property. The varieties of ways a mortgagee can do this and the rights of the mortgagor to recover the property are the subjects of this chapter.

A. The Right to Foreclose

1. Default

The mortgagee's right to foreclose accrues on **default**. A mortgagee might default in a variety of ways—for example, by failing to pay property taxes, failing to maintain property insurance, or for damaging the property (sometimes called "committing waste"). But the most common cause of default is the mortgagor's failure to make regular payments on the debt that the mortgage secures. The fact that a mortgagor is in default does not, however, always mean that the mortgage will be foreclosed. The foreclosure process begins solely at the mortgagee's option. A mortgagee might, for example, wait awhile to begin foreclosure in the hope that the mortgagee will resume making payments. but if the mortgagee intends to begin foreclosure proceedings (or wants to spur payment from the borrower), the paralegal may need to draft a notice to the mortgagor as a warning of things to come. See Figure 11–2.

Sample of Notice Letter
(date)

(name of debtor)
(address of debtor)

Re: Demand for payment of past-due installments on promissory note dated (date) and notice of intent to accelerate unpaid principal balance and accrued interest owned on note.

Dear (name of debtor):

Our firm represents (name of noteholder), the noteholder, in connection with your indebtedness owed on the note executed by you, dated (date), payable to the order of (Mortgagee), in the original principal amount of $ (dollar amount).

You are delinquent in the payment of (number) installment of $ (dollar amount) each. These past-due installments shall accrue interest in accordance with the terms of the note until paid. You may contact me at the firm's address to obtain a complete statement and to arrange for payment of this debt.

Because you fail to pay the installments at the proper time they are accruing interest at the rate of (number) percent per annum, which is $ (dollar amount) per day.

Demand is hereby made for payment on or before (time) on (date), in full for the balance owed on these past-due installments plus interest and all reasonable attorney's fees incurred in collection of these amounts, which are permitted under the note and/or mortgage.

The loan documents executed by you provided that upon default in the punctual payment of the installments due on the note, the unpaid principal balance of the note may be matured at the option of the noteholder. You are notified that if the unpaid balance due on the past-due installments, interest on the past-due installments, and reasonable attorney's fees incurred by the noteholder are not paid before (time) on (date), the maturity of the unpaid balance of the principal of the note shall automatically be accelerated as of (time) on that date, and the entire unpaid principal balance plus all accrued and earned interest shall become immediately due and payable as of that time without further notice, demand, or other action. If you do not make up the delinquent payments with interest and pay any attorney's fees appropriate or reimbursable under the loan documents that have accrued as of (time) on (date), you shall owe and be immediately required to pay the noteholder the sum of (dollar amount) plus interest at the rate of (number) percent per annum from (date, which is $ (dollar amount) per day), and reasonable attorney's fees.

If the maturity of the indebtedness is acclerated, our client has instructed us to initiate foreclosure suite under the mortgage executed by you to secure the note. If a deficiency remains on your debt after the foreclosure sale, the noteholder may seek to hold you personally liable for any deficiency remaining after such foreclosure. The exercise of such rights shall not constitute a waiver of the other rights and remedies held by the noteholder.

Yours very truly,
(name of firm)

_____
(Name of attorney)

Certified Mail No. (number), Return Receipt Requested and by regular mail

FIGURE 11–2

2. Acceleration Clause

An **acceleration clause** gives the mortgagee the right to move up (that is, accelerate) the payment date for the entire loan amount if the mortgagor defaults on the loan. Most mortgages have this type of clause, and they are permitted in all states. Acceleration clauses usually come into play when a borrower fails to make regular payments. So how is the debt accelerated? Most jurisdictions require the mortgagee to send a notice to the mortgagor of the intent to accelerate. Some jurisdictions also require a separate notice that the loan has, in fact, been accelerated. This type of notice usually looks something like Figure 11–3.

a. Restrictions on Acceleration Borrowers do have some protection during the acceleration process. Legislation allowing the borrower to defeat acceleration by curing the default is becoming increasingly common. In Pennsylvania, for example, residential mortgagors may wait until one hour before the foreclosure sale to defeat the acceleration by paying all sums due at the time of the payment.[6] Some states give these kinds of protection to all—not just residential—mortgagors.

NOTICE OF ACCELERATION

(date)

(name of debtor or guarantor)
(address)

Re: Notice of acceleration of promissory note dated (date), in the original principal amount of $ (dollar amount), executed by (mortgagor), and payable in the order of (mortgagee)

Dear (name of debtor):

This letter is being sent to you as a (debtor/guarantor) on the indebtedness evidenced by the note described above. You were notified in our firm's letter of (date) that default had occurred in the payment of the note and that (name), the noteholder, would automatically accelerate the maturity of the note at (time) on (date), unless the default were cured before that time. Because of your failure to cure the default in payment of the note, the maturity date of the note was accelerated by the noteholder effective as of the time and date stated above. All unpaid principal and accrued interest on the note are due and payable at this time. The amount due on this indebtedness of the (date) is $ (dollar amount) in principal plus all unpaid accrued interest. The note will continue to accrue interest at the rate set forth in the note until paid. Additionally, the note and mortgage securing the note provide for reimbursement of reasonable attorney's fees incurred by the holder of these instruments in the collection of the indebtedness owed on the note.

You may contact me at the firm's address for further information concerning the exact amount due and owed on the note and for arranging the payment of your indebtedness.

Yours very truly,
(name of firm)

_____
(Name of attorney)

FIGURE 11–3

III. METHODS OF FORECLOSURE

There are three ways to foreclose on property: by judicial sale, by power of sale, and by strict foreclosure. Each of these will be discussed. Before beginning a foreclosure, always be sure to have a complete list of information. See Figure 11–4.

A. Judicial Foreclosure

Judicial foreclosure is the process by which mortgaged property is sold under the supervision of a court. This type of foreclosure is available in all states, and it is the exclusive or dominant method

Master Information List

1. Country where proceeding to be brought
2. Date of Substitution of Trustee, if any
3. Holder of indebtedness and address
4. Substitute Trustee
5. Original Trustee
6. Date of Note and Date of Trust or Mortgage
7. Name of original beneficiary
8. Assignment of instruments, if any
9. Special Proceeding or Civil Action Number
10. Defendants' Names
11. Recording information of Deed or Trust or Mortgage
12. Recording information of Substitution, if any
13. Original amount of indebtedness
14. Original debtor(s)
15. Acceleration option to be executed (check original instrument)
16. Description of Security
    a. Village/Parish/Township of
    b. County of (same as #1 above)
17. Name of default (nonpayment, etc.)
18. Amount needed to pay or cure
19. Per diem interest amount or rate of interest
20. Date of default
21. Date last payment made
22. Date of sale
23. Place of sale
24. Time of sale
25. Encumbrances (taxes, assessments, water, rents, prior indebtedness)
26. Date, time, and place of hearing to show cause
27. Date Notice of Hearing filed
28. Date of defendants served
29. Amount required for deposit
30. Period of publication required by instrument or statue
31. Period of posting of Notice request by instrument or statue
32. Dates of publication inclusive
33. Newspaper or publications
34. Date of Affidavit of publisher
35. Place of posting of Notice
36. Dates of posting inclusive
37. Name of purchases at sale
38. Date of resale
39. Name of purchaser at resale
40. Amount of sales for upset
41. Amount required for upset
42. Amount of resale price

FIGURE 11–4

of foreclosure in almost half of the states. Foreclosure by judicial sale has several advantages over power-of-sale foreclosure and strict foreclosure. The primary advantage is that it settles title disputes more definitely than either of the other two methods. If, for instance, a dispute arises among lienholders as to priority of the liens, a court's judgment on the issue—handed down after an evidentiary hearing on the matter—settles the matter authoritatively.

Further, some jurisdictions do not allow the mortgagee to receive a judgment for any deficiencies arising under power-of-sale foreclosure (discussed later in this chapter). So, where the value of the property exceeds the amount of the debt, the mortgagee has a strong incentive to foreclose judicially.

CASE DECISION

See how the laws of bankruptcy and foreclosure intersect in Neely.

UNITED STATES BANKRUPTCY COURT

MIDDLE DISTRICT OF FLORIDA

JACKSONVILLE DIVISION

In Re: CASE NO.: 00-01819-BKC-3F3

JERRY L. NEELY JR. and

VICTORIA E. NEELY,

Debtors.

JERRY L. NEELY JR. and

VICTORIA E. NEELY,

Plaintiffs,

v. ADV. NO.: 00-184

FIRSTPLUS FINANCIAL INC.,

Defendant.

FINDINGS OF FACT AND CONCLUSIONS OF LAW

This Proceeding came before the Court for a Final Pretrial Conference on August 8, 2000. The Court also considered Jerry L. Neely's and Victoria E. Neely's ("Plaintiffs") Objection to Firstplus Financial's ("Defendant") Claim #2 (Doc. 30) and Defendant's Motion for Relief from Stay as to Claim #2 (Doc. 20) filed in the underlying Bankruptcy Case. In a Joint Pretrial Statement the parties stipulated to consolidation of all pending issues between the parties in the form of a mutual ore tenus Motion for Summary Judgment. Upon review of the stipulated facts and applicable Florida law, the Court finds that Defendant is entitled to summary judgment. The Court will also grant Defendant adequate protection payments as stipulated to in the Joint Pretrial Statement.

FINDINGS OF FACT

On September 9, 1983, Plaintiffs granted American Home Funding Inc. a first mortgage on their homestead property located in Duval County, Florida. American Home Funding subsequently assigned this mortgage to Norwest Mortgage Inc. ("Norwest"). On June 11, 1997, Plaintiffs granted a junior mortgage on their homestead to Banc One Financial Services Inc. Banc One subsequently assigned this junior mortgage to Defendant. This junior mortgage constitutes the basis for the claim at issue. In

---

(continued)

1999, Norwest instituted foreclosure proceedings on the property. On February 28, 2000, the Circuit Court of Duval County issued a Final Summary Judgment of Mortgage Foreclosure on the property and scheduled a judicial sale for March 27, 2000. The Final Summary Judgment of Mortgage Foreclosure provides in pertinent part that:

On filing of the Certificate of Title with respect to the property described in paragraph 4 above, the Defendants named herein, and all persons claiming by, through, under or against them since the filing of the Notice of Lis Pendens in this action, are foreclosed of all estate, interest or claim in the property described in paragraph 4, and the purchaser or purchasers at the sale shall be let into possession of the property.

(Defendant's Exh. 4).

On March 9, 2000, Plaintiffs filed a voluntary Chapter 13 petition and their proposed Chapter 13 Plan. The Plan did not account for Defendant's junior mortgage, except to allege that "[t]he lien of this mortgage has been extinguished by the foreclosure of the first mortgage."

Having agreed to the above facts, the parties submit to the Court a single decisive question: Whether or not Defendant's junior mortgage was extinguished by the Final Summary Judgment of Mortgage Foreclosure. Plaintiffs contend that the mortgage was extinguished by the judgment. Defendants contend that the mortgage survives until the foreclosure sale is complete.

CONCLUSIONS OF LAW

Because the parties stipulated to the facts as outlined above, no genuine issues of material fact exist. Therefore, the Court will proceed to dispose of the sole legal question at hand: whether a junior mortgage is extinguished by the entry of a judgment of foreclosure.

The foreclosure action in Florida consists of three essential steps. First, the validity of claimed interests are determined. Second, the extent (amount) and priority of valid liens are determined. Finally, there is a window of opportunity during which junior lienholders may redeem the newly adjudged senior interests in order to protect themselves. Plaintiffs request that the Court eliminate the third step of the foreclosure process. Such a holding directly contradicts the plain language of Florida Statutes § 45.0315. To hold that junior interests are extinguished upon judgment of foreclosure would defy a long line of Florida case law to the contrary. Additionally, Plaintiffs are collaterally estopped from asserting that the judgment extinguished Defendant's mortgage when the judgment provides for exactly the opposite result.

Under Florida law, a junior mortgagee maintains a right to redeem its interest in mortgaged property being foreclosed by a senior mortgagee up until the issuance of a certificate of sale to a judicial sale purchaser by the clerk of the court. *See* § 45.0315 Fla. Stat. (West 2000). The existence of this right of redemption logically demands the concurring existence of the interest itself. Therefore, § 45.0315 stands for the proposition that a junior mortgage is not extinguished by the entry of a foreclosure judgment but survives until the completion of the judicial sale. Florida case law supports this interpretation of § 45.0315. *See e.g. Glendale Fed. Savings and Loan v. Guadagnino*, 434 So. 2d 54 (Fla. 4th DCA 1983) (holding untimely the attempt of junior mortgagee to exercise right of redemption after sale). Only the issuance of a certificate of sale extinguishes junior mortgages. *See Id.*

The Court will not allow Plaintiffs to assert that the Summary Judgment of Foreclosure extinguishes junior mortgages when the face of the Judgment says exactly the opposite. The terms of a judgment of foreclosure may modify or reinforce the provisions in § 45.0315 relating to the extinguishing of junior liens. *See Saidi v. Wasko*, 687 So. 2d 10 (Fla. 5th DCA 1997). In the instant case the Judgment provides that Defendant's lien is not extinguished until the filing of a certificate of title on Plaintiffs' homestead. (See Defendant's Exh. 4). The Defendant's junior mortgage cannot be extinguished at judgment if the Judgment itself provides for the mortgage to be extinguished upon the filing of a certificate of title subsequent to foreclosure sale. Plaintiffs are collaterally estopped from going behind the Judgment by the plain language of the Judgment. Plaintiffs rely on *Acosta v.*

Marion County (In re Acosta), 200 B.R. 57 (Bankr. M.D. Fla. 1996) to support their contention that junior mortgages are extinguished by a judgment of foreclosure. In *Acosta*, a homeowner facing foreclosure sale by the primary 1 The language of the Summary Judgment of Foreclosure differs from the language of § 45.0315 in that it provides that junior interests are extinguished at the filing of a new certificate of title rather than at the certificate's issuance. This discrepancy is due to the fact that the judgment form promulgated by the Florida Supreme Court has not been updated since § 45.0315 was amended in 1993. *See Saidi*, 697 So. 2d at 12. The difference is irrelevant in the instant case, as a new certificate of title has not been issued or filed. Mortgagee filed a voluntary Chapter 13 petition to prevent the judicial sale of his home. *See Id* at 58. The homeowner then objected to a secured claim filed against the estate by the holder of a junior mechanics' lien on the grounds that the lien had been extinguished by the judgment of foreclosure. *See Id.* at 58. Based on Florida Statutes § 713.21(5), the Court found that the lienholder's interest was extinguished by the foreclosure judgment.

See Id. at 59. Section 713.21 provides in relevant part:

A lien properly perfected under this chapter [a mechanics' lien] may be discharged by any one of the following methods. . . . . .(5) By recording in the clerk's office the original or a certified copy of a judgment or decree of a court of competent jurisdiction showing a final determination of the action.

§ 713.21, Fla. Stat. (West 2000).

The *Acosta* Court interpreted § 713.21(5) as standing for the proposition that all junior interests, including junior mortgages as well as mechanics' liens, are extinguished at the entry of a foreclosure judgment rather than at the time a judicial sale is complete. *See Acosta* at 58. Additionally, the *Acosta* Court mistakenly cited *Glendale Savings* as supporting the proposition that junior interests were extinguished by a judgment of foreclosure. *See Id.* at 58.

The Court declines to follow the holding and rationale of *Acosta*. The Court instead elects to follow an interpretation of the mechanics' lien statute that is more consistent with § 45.0315 and with the above-noted case law. The mechanics' lien statute, § 713.21, does not discharge mechanics' liens or other junior interests at the entry of a judgment of foreclosure. Rather, § 713.21(5) discharges mechanics' liens at the entry of a judgment related to the subject matter of the dispute which lead to the lien attachment, or, more specifically, at the entry of a judgment in favor of the plaintiff on the unusual statutory action of Complaint to Discharge a Mechanics' Lien, as provided

for in § 713.21(4). *See Matrix Const. Corp. v. Mecca Const. Inc.*, 578 So. 2d 388 (Fla.1991) (outlining special, informal procedure for lien discharge action).

This Court concludes that if the Florida legislature intended to establish entry of judgment as the moment of the eradication of junior interests in the event of foreclosure, then the legislature would not have passed the revised § 45.0315 in 1993, 26 years after § 713.21 was enacted. Additionally, no Florida court has applied § 713.21(5) to a junior mortgagee situation. The Court finds the Florida courts' findings as to the timing of the destruction of junior interests more persuasive than the finding of the *Acosta* Court.

The Court reiterates that Debtors' view of the law conflicts with the reality of foreclosure practice. As noted above, there are three stages to a foreclosure action. First, the state court determines the validity of liens claimed by plaintiffs. Second, the state court determines the extent (amount) and priority of those liens. Third, § 45.0315 freezes the action to allow plaintiffs to redeem their liens and to move up the priority ladder in order to protect their interests. Section 45.0315 provides that this redemption period is terminated by the issuance of a certificate of sale to the foreclosure sale purchaser or by some other event specified in the judgment. The Court will not eliminate the important third stage of the foreclosure process. Junior mortgagees would be deprived of the opportunity to make educated decisions on redemption. The amounts due for principle, interest, attorney's fees, and costs, if applicable, are not determined until judgment, at which time the debtor and junior lienors are given an opportunity to redeem. Plaintiffs would have the Court extinguish junior mortgages and attending redemption rights prematurely.

(continued)

CONCLUSION

The Court finds that valid junior mortgages survive the entry of a judgment of foreclosure by a senior interest, and are only extinguished upon the issuance of a certificate of sale subsequent to a foreclosure sale or as otherwise provided in a judgment of foreclosure. In the instant case, the Plaintiffs prevented the foreclosure sale of their homestead, scheduled for March 27, 2000, by filing a voluntary Chapter 13 petition on March 9. The event that would have extinguished Defendant's mortgage never occurred; therefore, Defendant's secured claim under its mortgage survives and Plaintiffs must provide for Defendant's secured claim in their Chapter 13 Plan.

The Court will enter a separate Judgment and Order Granting Adequate Protection in accordance with these Findings of Fact and Conclusions of Law.

Dated August 24, 2000 at Jacksonville, Florida.

JERRY A. FUNK

United States Bankruptcy Judge

The benefits of judicial foreclosure are offset to a considerable degree by its complexity. Notice of the proceeding must be sent out to persons who have an interest in the matter, and a hearing must be held. This means delay that, in turn, means greater expense.

 Web Exercise

Find out changes that states like Maryland are making in the foreclosure process at www.msba.org/departments/commpubl/publications/brochures/foreclosure.htm.

1. Parties

Judicial foreclosures typically begin with a title search to determine who might have an interest in the property and who should, therefore, be given notice of the lawsuit. The search will reveal who is a necessary party to the action and who is a proper party. A **necessary party** is a person who must be joined to accomplish the purpose of the foreclosure. The mortgagor, for instance, is a necessary party because without him the mortgagee will not be able to recover the property. Joining necessary parties is crucial to achieve the purpose of the foreclosure—to restore to the mortgagee the same title held when the mortgage was executed.

A **proper party**, on the other hand, is a person whose joinder is desirable—but not essential—to accomplish the purpose of foreclosure. A person who has no interest in the property but is personally liable for the debt, for example, is a proper (but not necessary) party to the action.

2. Confirmation and Adequacy of Sale Price

A judicial foreclosure is not final until the court confirms it. As a general rule, a low sale price is usually not a convincing reason for a court to refuse to confirm a sale. But some states have enacted legislation that requires the sales price to be a specified fraction of its appraised value (such as half or two-thirds). Despite this protection, in some of these jurisdictions, mortgagors commonly waive this right at the request of the mortgagee.

3. Purchaser

a. Purchaser's Title The purchaser of the property at a judicial sale receives the property title, as it existed at the time the mortgagor executed the mortgage. The mortgagor's interest in the property, along with the interests of **junior leinholders** who were included in the foreclosure action, is extinguished. If the proceeds from the sale are not enough to cover the outstanding debt, the purchaser acquires the right of the mortgagee.

b. Omitted Junior Lienholders   The interest of a junior lienholder survives the sale if he is not named a party to the foreclosure action. But what if the sale proceeds are not enough to cover the debt—how does the purchaser get clear title to the property? The purchaser has several options. First, the purchaser can pay off (that is, "redeem") the junior lienholder. Second, the purchaser—who has not acquired the mortgagee's right to foreclose—can foreclose on the property again by judicial sale, this time making sure to include the junior lienholder as a party to the lawsuit. Finally, in jurisdictions that allow strict foreclosure (discussed following), the purchaser can strictly foreclosure the rights of the junior lienholder.

c. Mortgagee Purchase   The mortgagee has the right to purchase the property at the sale. The mortgagee is entitled to receive as much of the sale proceeds necessary to pay the debt. So, the mortgagee can bid up to the amount of the sale without having to pay any cash. As a result, the mortgagee is often the highest bidder at the sale.

d. Mortgagor Purchase   The mortgagor can also buy the property at the sale. If the mortgagor buys the property back, unpaid junior liens survive the foreclosure because the purchase goes to pay off the **senior lienholder** (that is, the mortgagee's lien). Note that this is an exception to the rule that all junior interests properly joined in the foreclosure action are terminated by the foreclosure.

e. Disbursement of the Proceeds   Sale proceeds are disbursed in the following order:

1. Expenses of the foreclosure,
2. Payment of the mortgage debt, and
3. Satisfaction of junior liens in order of their priority.

Any sums left after payment of these expenses belong to the owner of the property (in most cases, the mortgagor).[7]

B. Power-of-Sale Foreclosure

With a **power-of-sale foreclosure**, the mortgage instrument grants the mortgagee permission to foreclose on the mortgagor's **equity of redemption** (discussed following) through nonjudicial means. Foreclosure by power-of-sale is allowed in approximately 60% of the states. Under this type of foreclosure, a public official (usually the sheriff) sells the property at a public sale by the mortgagee or by a third party.[8]

1. The Deed of Trust

The instrument used in most jurisdictions to accomplish a nonjudicial foreclosure is the **deed of trust**. The mortgagor, while keeping possession of the property, conveys title to a trustee who holds it in trust for the benefit of the mortgagee. At foreclosure, it is the trustee who holds a public sale of the mortgaged property. The simplified procedures of a power-of-sale foreclosure have made this method a popular alternative to judicially supervised foreclosure. A typical notice of this type of sale that a paralegal may have to draft looks like the sample shown in Figure 11–5.

2. Sale Procedures

The notice requirements for a power-of-sale foreclosure vary from state to state, but they are generally less stringent than those required for a judicially supervised foreclosure. Most states require

---

NOTICE OF SALE

STATE OF (name of state)   )

)   NOTICE OF SALE OF REAL ESTATE

COUNTY OF (name of county)   )

Under and by virtue of the power of sale contained in a certain Deed of Trust executed by (grantor) to (name of trustee), Trustee, dated (date), and recorded in Book (number at Page (number), in the office of the Register of Deeds of (name of county) County, (name of state); and under and by virtue of the authority vested in the undersigned, as Trustee, default having been made in the payment of the indebtedness thereby secured and the said Deed of Trust being by the terms thereof subject to foreclose, and the Holder of the indebtedness thereby secured having demanded a foreclosure thereof for the purpose of satisfying said indebtedness, the undersigned Trustee will offer for the sale of public auction to the highest bidder for cash at (location) of the (name of courthouse) at (time o'clock a.m. or p.m.) on the (number) day of (month), (year), all the property conveyed in said Deed or Trust, which property as of (date) was owned by (name of mortgagee) the same lying and being in (name of county) County, (name of state), and more particularly described as follows:

The property is to be sold subject to any City-County ad valorem taxes and any special assessments that are a lien against the premises.

The Trustee, after sale, shall require the highest bidder immediately make a cash deposit of (number) % of the amount of his bid up to and including $ (dollar amount) plus (number) % to any excess over $ (dollar amount).

The Notice of Sale hereby given is in satisfaction of the requirements of the aforementioned Deed of Trust and the requirements contained in (statute) with respect to posting or publishing notice of sale.

Time: (time) o'clock (a.m. or p.m.) on the (number) day of (month), (year)
Place: location, (courthouse), (county), (state)
Terms: (cash or other)

This is the (number) day of (month), (year).
(name of trustee), Trustee
Telephone: (area code and number)

FIGURE 11–5

---

that a notice be published in a local newspaper for a prescribed time, while some require only a public posting, usually at the county courthouse. A few jurisdictions, however, also require notice by mail or personal service. Almost no states require a judicial hearing before the sale.

3. Purchaser's Title

Though power-of-sale foreclosure is less costly and time-consuming than judicial foreclosure, the downside to this foreclosure method is that it can produce a less stable title. Court supervision tends to produce titles with fewer defects because having various parties before the court increases the likelihood that one of them would point out defects. Problems with the title could thus be dealt with before the court issues its judgment on the matter. In addition, simply having a court rule on a title enhances the title's stability.

Without court supervision, who is watching to make sure that the sale is held in a fair manner? By law, mortgagees are required to conduct the sale in an impartial manner. Because of this, mortgagees are not allowed to bid at the sale unless they are authorized to do so in the mortgage instrument. But note that this obstacle to a mortgagee purchase does not arise if the mortgage instrument is a deed of trust because the trustee, not the mortgagee, conducts the sale.

4. Overturning a Sale

As discussed previously, an inadequate sale price rarely invalidates a power-of-sale foreclosure. But a sale can be set aside if fraud or other impermissible actions by the mortgagee were committed. A variety of factors can lead a court to overturn the sale. If, for example, a completely inadequate price is obtained because the mortgagee told the mortgagor of the wrong sale date (or the sale was held at an unusual time) and if the sale price is grossly inadequate (such as, 5% of the property's fair market value), the mortgagor might have grounds to contest the sale's validity.

Another problem that can lead a court to overturn a foreclosure is **chilled bidding**. This occurs when the seller (either the mortgagee or a trustee named in a deed of trust) engages in collusive activity with a potential purchaser to artificially hold down the sale price. Under a deed of trust sale, for example, a mortgagee and trustee could pay off a potential purchaser in exchange for the latter's agreement not to bid. A sale can also be voided due to unintentional acts by the seller that lead to chilled bidding, as when a seller erroneously states that the property will be sold subject to a senior lien (that is, a lien that the foreclosure will not extinguish) when, in fact, there is no such lien.

C. Strict Foreclosure

Strict foreclosure, a rare procedure, gives the mortgagee title to the property without judicial oversight and without a sale. The mortgagee can do this if a defaulting mortgagor fails to pay the debt within a specified time, often one set by the court. Strict foreclosure is available in very few states, such as Connecticut, Vermont, and Illinois. But safeguards are usually available by legislation for the mortgagor. In Connecticut, for example, the defendant can by statute seek a court order requiring a judicially supervised sale.

Most courts now publish forms and formats for the litigants in a foreclosure case. See the New Jersey example at Figure 11–6.

IV. SALE SURPLUS

KEY WORDS

clog the equity of redemption	one action rule
deficiency judgment	redemption
equity of redemption	sale surplus
fair value legislation	statutory redemption
interpleader	

FORECLOSURE
CASE INFORMATION STATEMENT
(FCIS)

Use for initial Chancery Division — General Equity foreclosure pleadings (not motions) under Rule 4:5-1. Pleading will be rejected for filing, under Rule 1:5-6(c), if information is not furnished or if attorney's signature is not affixed.

FOR USE BY CLERK'S OFFICE ONLY

PAYMENT TYPE: ☐ CK ☐ CG ☐ CA

CHG/CK NO:

AMOUNT:

OVERPAYMENT:

BATCH NUMBER:

CAPTION

COUNTY OF VENUE

NAME OF FILING PARTY (*e.g.*, John Doe, Plaintiff)

DOCKET NUMBER (When available)

F-

DOCUMENT TYPE
☐ COMPLAINT ☐ ANSWER

ATTORNEY/SELF REPRESENTED NAME

TELEPHONE NUMBER ( )

FIRM NAME (If applicable)

ADDRESS

FORECLOSURE CASE TYPE NUMBER

☐ 088 IN PERSONAM TAX FORECLOSURE
☐ 089 IN REM TAX FORECLOSURE
☐ ORF RESIDENTIAL MORTGAGE FORECLOSURE
☐ OCF COMMERCIAL MORTGAGE FORECLOSURE
☐ OCD CONDOMINIUM OR HOMEOWNER'S ASSOCIATION LIEN FORECLOSURE
☐ 091 STRICT FORECLOSURE
☐ OPTIONAL FORECLOSURE PROCEDURE (NO SALE)

DEFENDANT (S) NAMES (i.e., debtors, mortgagors, subordinate mortgages, judgment creditors *et seq.*)

PROPERTY STREET ADDRESS:

MUNICIPALITY: COUNTY:

MUNICIPAL BLOCK: LOT (S):

ZIP CODE:

MORTGAGE FORECLOSURE TYPE

☐ RESIDENTIAL ☐ COMMERCIAL

PURCHASE MONEY MORTGAGE ☐ YES ☐ NO

RELATED PENDING CASE ☐ YES ☐ NO

IF YES, LIST DOCKET NUMBERS:

ATTORNEY SIGNATURE PRINT ATTORNEY NAME DATE

N: 10169-English, FCIS-(Appendix XII-B2)-9/1/2008

FIGURE 11–6

In general, the **sale surplus** represents the foreclosed real estate. Liens and interest that had previously attached to that property now attach to the surplus. They are entitled to be paid out of the surplus in the order of their priority before foreclosure. Further, any claim that the mortgagor has to the property is junior to the claims of valid liens extinguished by the foreclosure. If the proceeds exceed the amount of the debt, the mortgagee may deposit the surplus with the court for a judicial determination of who is entitled to the funds. This is known as an "**interpleader**" action, and it protects the mortgagee from liability that could arise from paying the surplus to the wrong party.

V. DEFICIENCY JUDGMENTS

If the sale proceeds are not enough to pay the mortgage debt, the mortgagee must bring an action for a **deficiency judgment** against a party who is liable for the debt, usually the mortgagor. Generally, this judgment can be obtained during (or shortly after) a judicial foreclosure action. The sale price usually determines the amount to be credited against the debt and so sets the size of the deficiency judgment for which the mortgagee can sue.[9]

Because a deficiency judgment can be enforced against other property of the mortgagor just like any other judgment, there are a number of procedural requirements that the mortgagee must surmount before receiving the judgment. Many states have rigorous notice requirements and strictly limit the time within which the mortgagee must bring suit to obtain a deficiency judgment. In fact, under a principle known as the **one action rule**, some states *require* the mortgagee to bring an action for a deficiency judgment at the same time as the foreclosure action, on pain of being forever barred from pursuing this type of judgment.

Much of the legislation that is in place to ensure that mortgagors are not taken advantage of during the deficiency judgment action stems from the Great Depression of the 1930s, when many borrowers suffered greatly when their land was sold for nominal amounts at foreclosure. Mortgagees would then resell the property at fair market value, but then continue to go after mortgagors through deficiency judgments.

Dissatisfaction with this state of affairs led many jurisdictions to enact some form of **fair-value legislation**. Under this legislation, courts can ascertain the fair value of the foreclosed property and take that value into consideration when determining the size of the deficiency judgment. The judge, a jury, or an appraiser, depending on the jurisdiction, determines this "fair value." This protection for the mortgagor is often available in judicial foreclosures and is sometimes available (depending on the jurisdiction) in power-of-sale foreclosures. Note that some states (such as Arizona and California) go a step further and flatly prohibit deficiency judgments that arise from a power-of-sale foreclosure.

VI. REDEMPTION

Redemption refers to the right of the mortgagor to recover the property after default by paying the outstanding debt. This right traditionally existed until foreclosure sale.

A. Equitable Redemption

At common law, a mortgagor could expect little chance of recovering property after default if the mortgagee was determined to cut off the mortgagor's interest in the land. If a mortgagor's payment was a day late, for instance, the mortgagee could foreclosure and recover the property. Over time, however, the courts of equity intervened to soften this harsh result. If the mortgagor could come up with a reasonable explanation for the failure to strictly abide the terms of the mortgage, the court would allow the mortgagor to recover the property by paying the entire debt. As this practice was gradually extended to all mortgagors, rather than only on a case-by-case basis, it came to be known as the **equity of redemption**.

Mortgagees, not surprisingly, disliked this right of late payment and so began to add causes in mortgages that impeded (or "clogged") this right. Courts responded by rejecting the validity of these clauses that **clogged the equity of redemption**. This equitable right to redeem property before foreclosure exists in all states. But, unlike statutory redemption, equitable redemption terminates at foreclosure.

B. Statutory Redemption

More than half the states allow the mortgagor a window of time (generally six to twelve months) to buy back the foreclosed property, usually by paying the sale price. This is known as **statutory redemption** because it is a legislative creation. This type of legislation has been criticized on the grounds that it removes an incentive for timely mortgage payments because the mortgagor knows that the property can be recovered after foreclosure. On the other hand, statutory redemption gives the mortgagor needed breathing space to arrange for new financing to recover the property. It also encourages potential purchasers to make fairer bids for the property because they know that if they bid too low that they may lose the property.

Note that unlike equitable redemption, which cannot be waived to the prohibition of clogs on the equity of redemption, statutory redemption can be waived in some jurisdictions.

VII. BANKRUPTCY LAW AND THE FORECLOSURE PROCESS

KEY WORDS

bankruptcy	Chapter 13	means test
bankruptcy estate	discharge	nonexempt property
Chapter 7	exemption	
Chapter 11	involuntary petition	trustee
Chapter 12	liquidate	voluntary petition

It is abundantly clear that foreclosure problems are inexorably entwined with the law of **bankruptcy**. Far too often, homeowners, struggling to stay afloat, have little choice but to declare bankruptcy. A cursory understanding of bankruptcy law is, therefore, crucial content for the paralegal.

Debt can unexpectedly overwhelm both individuals and institutions. Debt difficulties are caused by multiple factors, including careless management, crisis or trauma in the business market, or poor financial planning. Other times, bankruptcy results from catastrophic events, hard luck and a general turn of economic conditions and events that are unforeseeable. Today, the housing crisis or meltdown, directly correlates to the rise of bankruptcy petitions. See Figure 11–7.[10]

Housing, which was once considered a safe haven, a defensible long term investment that bore equity growth, has now become an albatross for many. Laden with housing debt in the form of first and second mortgages, home owners increasingly struggle to make ends meet. Bankruptcy is now considered a viable defense to foreclosure though that view is not universally held.

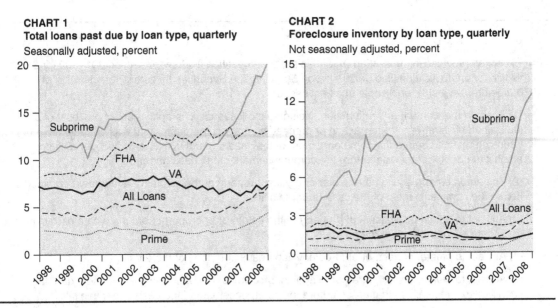

CHART 1
Total loans past due by loan type, quarterly
Seasonally adjusted, percent

CHART 2
Foreclosure inventory by loan type, quarterly
Not seasonally adjusted, percent

FIGURE 11–7

Critics of bankruptcy have long argued that the government should erect a legal process that allows bankrupt parties to avoid or eliminate debt. The numbers of legal actions borders on the hyperbolic as bankruptcy rates "have soared during the past twenty-five years. From 225,000 filings in 1979, consumer bankruptcies topped 1.5 million".[11] In a sense, the system encourages financial irresponsibility by providing "economic incentives" for going bankrupt.[12] Others argue that bankruptcy provides a free market means for business and individuals to restore their financial health. Some argue that the bankruptcy system is a form of rehabilitation for both individuals and businesses.[13] In the American experience, there has been a supportive and historical tradition for bankruptcy, both at common law and statutorily. The federal *Bankruptcy Act of 1898* has an obvious lineage. Bankruptcy laws have a constitutional basis as well.[14]

Bankruptcy legislation resides exclusively in the federal legislative process. Congress has the power to establish uniform laws on bankruptcy throughout the United States. In doing so, the federal government preempts state legislation on the practices and policies of bankruptcy.[15] Subsequent acts culminated in the *Bankruptcy Reform Act of 1978*, whose effective date of operation was October 1, 1979.[16] The 1978 Act is always referred to as the "code" since the *Bankruptcy Act of 1898* was repealed and subsequently codified in 1979. In 2004, the *Bankruptcy Act* was substantially revised and by most accounts makes the process a bit more difficult for individuals.

Ironically, creditors have in some ways benefited from the adoption of a bankruptcy code. Instead of a cataclysmic, nonproductive collapse of the debtor, whether an individual or an institution, debtors usually emerge from what could have been a total loss to a partial restoration of a debt. While this is not always true, in business bankruptcies, the bankruptcy process distributes by order of priority—and hopes that most interested parties receive some portion of what is owed.[17] Creditors also benefit from the orderly processes the bankruptcy procedure affords a distressed debtor. Creditors have fair opportunity to have their claims prioritized according to their interests and negotiating their interests with competing creditor in an open, deliberate forum. "It is the task of bankruptcy judges to balance competing interests and arrive at fair solutions."[18] Under recent reforms to the *Bankruptcy Act*, the debtor appears to have lost some of its footing when compared to the status of creditors.

In the housing sector, the Bankruptcy Act, as in all other debtor-creditor relationships, once a petition is filed, serves to stay the proceedings. Title 11 at 362 of the *Bankruptcy Act* makes this plain.

---

§ 362. Automatic stay

(a) Except as provided in subsection (b) of this section, a petition filed under section 301, 302, or 303 of this title, or an application filed under section 5(a)(3) of the Securities Investor Protection Act of 1970, operates as a stay, applicable to all entities, of:

(1) The commencement or continuation, including the issuance or employment of process, of a judicial, administrative, or other action or proceeding against the debtor that was or could have been commenced before the commencement of the case under this title, or to recover a claim against the debtor that arose before the commencement of the case under this title;

(2) The enforcement, against the debtor or against property of the estate, of a judgment obtained before the commencement of the case under this title;

(3) Any act to obtain possession of property of the estate or of property from the estate or to exercise control over property of the estate;

(4) Any act to create, perfect, or enforce any lien against property of the estate;

(5) Any act to create, perfect, or enforce against property of the debtor any lien to the extent that such lien secures a claim that arose before the commencement of the case under this title;

(6) Any act to collect, assess, or recover a claim against the debtor that arose before the commencement of the case under this title . . .[19]

Whatever the merits of these arguments, there is little dispute that bankruptcy has witnessed some serious abuse. Instead of the historic connection, that ties the filing rate to economic conditions, it is apparent that rates rise despite the health or distress of the economy. Todd Zywicki sees the sham of a system that rewards the irresponsible, that appears in a bankrupt class of repetitors—"the increased frequency of Americans choosing bankruptcy as the preferred response to those underlying problems."[20]

In the final analysis, bankruptcy is sometimes employed as a defense to foreclosure, and it is a worth a broad look.

The statutory framework of the bankruptcy code contains these titles and chapters:

Chapter 1:   Definitions and general provisions.

Chapter 3:   The Administration and Procedure to be followed in bankruptcy cases.

Chapter 7:   Liquidation processes and techniques in bankruptcy cases.

Chapter 9:   Adjustment of debts for municipalities.

Chapter 11:   Plans of reorganization for business entities and nonbusiness individuals.

Chapter 12:   Adjustment of Debts of a Family Farmer with regular Income.

Chapter 13:   Debt extension plans or other adjustments for individuals with regular income.

Chapter 15:   Discussion of the United States Trustee system.

Bankruptcy practice allows paralegals to perform many valuable tasks. Recent reforms to the Bankruptcy Act, appear to substantially benefit the paralegal profession.[21] Under the Debt Relief Agency component of the act, paralegals are essentially permitted to engage in representation of debtors and creditors. The act states in part:

"Debt Relief Agency", means any person who provides bankruptcy assistance to an assisted person in return for the payment of money or other valuable consideration, or who is a bankruptcy petition preparer under Section 110 . . .[22]

Bankruptcy paralegals will find a plethora of pleadings, forms, documents, and other necessary filings, as dictated by increasingly favorable legislation. Geoff Giles comments that "[p]aralegal firms are likely to flourish as they get to advertise that they are "debt relief agencies," just like lawyers."[23]

The bankruptcy process is also guided by specific bankruptcy rules adopted by a congressional advisory committee. Jurisdiction and venue is based on subject matter and the residence of the claimant or debtor. By a grant to the federal courts of original and exclusive jurisdiction, the task of handling bankruptcy has been delegated to a specialized court, namely, the Bankruptcy Court.[24] Bankruptcy judges are federal judges with limited tenure, unlike other federal colleagues on the bench. Much constitutional litigation has occurred about these courts, and more specifically as to whether such congressional right or authority can be delegated. An equally complicated and intellectual controversy has centered on the designation, title and duties of bankruptcy judges. Mired in a confused legal status, bankruptcy judges are continually searching for their place as either Article I or Article III judges under the United States Constitution. Bankruptcy judges are not granted life tenure and do not have the same protections and emoluments as other federal judges.[25] See Figure 11–8.[26]

USTP - Bankruptcy Fraud Scams

U.S. Department of Justice

U.S. Trustee Program

Contact Us   Search   Site Map

Home >> Press & Public Affairs >> Bankruptcy Fact Sheets & Consumer Notices >> Consumer Alert — Mortgage Foreclosure Scams

Consumer Alert — Mortgage Foreclosure Scams

**DON'T GET "LOCKED OUT" OF YOUR HOME
BY A BANKRUPTCY SCAM OPERATOR**

Are you having trouble making your home mortgage payments? Are you facing foreclosure on your home? Get all the facts before you pay someone to help you work out your mortgage problems.

"Bankruptcy foreclosure scams" target people whose home mortgages are in trouble. Scam operators advertise over the Internet and in local publications, distribute flyers, or contact people whose homes are listed in the foreclosure notices. Sometimes they direct their appeals to specific religious or ethnic groups.

These scam operators may promise to take care of your problems with your mortgage lender or to obtain refinancing for you. Sometimes they also ask you to pay your mortgage payments directly to the scam operator. They may even ask you to hand over your property deed to the operator, and then make payments to the operator in order to stay in your home.

But instead of contacting your lender or refinancing your loan, the scam operator pockets all the money you paid, and then files a bankruptcy case in your name -- sometimes without your knowledge.

A bankruptcy filing often stops a home foreclosure, but only temporarily. If a bankruptcy is filed in your name but you don't participate in the case, the judge will dismiss the case and the foreclosure proceedings will continue.

If this happens, you will lose the money you paid to the scam operator -- AND YOU COULD LOSE YOUR HOME. You will also have a bankruptcy listed on your credit record for years afterward.

Proceed with care if an individual or company:

- Calls itself a "mortgage consultant," "foreclosure service," or similar name.

- Contacts or advertises to people whose homes are listed for foreclosure.
- Collects a fee before it provides services to you.

- Tells you to make your home mortgage payments directly to the individual or company.

- Tells you to transfer your property deed or title to the individual or company.

http://www.usdoj.gov/ust/eo/public_affairs/factsheet/docs/fs06.htm (1 of 2)9/1/2009 6:22:59 PM

FIGURE 11–8
(continues)

If you can't pay your mortgage, call your mortgage lender or contact a lawyer for help. Your state or local bar association may be able to help you find low-cost legal help.

If you think an individual or company is running a mortgage foreclosure scam, contact the local office of the United States Trustee. The United States Trustee is a Justice Department official who monitors the bankruptcy system. Look for your local United States Trustee's telephone number in your telephone directory or on our web site at www.usdoj.gov/ust/eo/ust_org/office_locator.htm.

Press Contact:

Public Information Officer
Executive Office for U.S. Trustees
(202) 305-7411

Last Update: November 18, 2008 3:11 PM
U.S. Trustee Program/Department of Justice
usdoj/ust/smm

USTPHome| USTPRegions| BankruptcyReform| What'sNew| PrivacyPolicy| LegalPolicies&Disclaimers| DOJHome| USA.gov| Search| ContactUs| FOIA

UnitedStatesBankruptcyCourts| BankruptcyCode

FIGURE 11–8
(continued)

In reality, paralegals will be mostly concerned with the liquidation processes of a Chapter 7 Bankruptcy—and on occasion have some exposure to Chapter 12 which deals with family farmers. As for reorganization of business entity, or simply starting all over, paralegals will work extensively under Chapters 11 and 13.[27] Most forms and pleadings are now online for easy access—published in both html or pdf format.

Web Exercise

For the full set of forms, visit: www.uscourts.gov/bkforms/bankruptcy_forms.html.

Local jurisdictions may post additional requirements. Some excellent web locations for information on courts, codes and paralegals engaged in bankruptcy as well as updates on this ever changing are of law are charted at Figure 11–9.

U.S. Bankruptcy Trustee	www.usdoj.gov/ust/7_12n13.htm
	Names, addresses and contact information of all Trustees in all 50 states
Local Rules of Court for All Districts	www.uscourts.gov/rules/bk-localrules.html
	Local rules for all bankruptcy courts in all 50 states
Bankruptcy Code Online	www4.law.cornell.edu/uscode/11
	Easy look up for federal case law and codes
Chapter 7 Help Center	law.chapter7.com
	Chapter 7 information for consumers and attorneys
State Bankruptcy Exemptions	www.debtworkout.com/statex.html

FIGURE 11–9

VIII. LIQUIDATION PROCEEDINGS UNDER CHAPTER 7 BANKRUPTCY

Chapter 7 of the Bankruptcy Code permits individuals, partnerships, corporations and other entities with some exceptions, an opportunity to **liquidate** all existing assets and distribute the remainder to creditors. The debtor is then discharged from most debts except those that were fraudulently incurred or are priority claims under 11 U.S.C. §507. **Discharge** will only be granted to specific individuals rather than business entities. "A discharge covers all debts that arose before the date of the order for relief. . . . A discharge also operates as an injunction against all attempts to collect the debt—by judicial proceedings, telephone calls, letters, personal contacts or other efforts."[28] Once commenced, creditors are precluded from any attempt to collect a debt. Despite the liberality of discharge, the debtor can no longer be relieved of every type of obligation. Under the reforms of 2005, the debtor needs to compute and calculate income on a **means test**.[29] See Figure 11–10. The reform seeks to zero on those who take advantage of the system.[30] See the language of the statute below:

(10A) The term "current monthly income":

(A) Means the average monthly income from all sources that the debtor receives (or in a joint case the debtor and the debtor's spouse receive) without regard to whether such income is taxable income, derived during the six-month period ending on:

    (i) The last day of the calendar month immediately preceding the date of the commencement of the case if the debtor files the schedule of current income required by section 521(a)(1)(B)(ii) or

    (ii) The date on which current income is determined by the court for purposes of this title if the debtor does not file the schedule of current income required by section 521(a)(1)(B)(ii); and

(B) Includes any amount paid by any entity other than the debtor (or in a joint case the debtor and the debtor's spouse), on a regular basis for the household expenses of the debtor or the debtor's dependents (and in a joint case the debtor's spouse if not otherwise a dependent), but excludes benefits received under the Social Security Act, payments to victims of war crimes or crimes against humanity on account of their status as victims of such crimes, and payments to victims of international terrorism (as defined in section 2331 of title 18) or domestic terrorism (as defined in section 2331 of title 18) on account of their status as victims of such terrorism.[31]

See Figure 11–10 for a Statement of Monthly Income and Means Test Calculation.

In addition, debtor's are required to complete an instructional course that highlights financial management.

Web Exercise

Find out about approved Financial Management Classes in your jurisdiction at www.usdoj.gov/ust/eo/bapcpa/ccde/de_approved.htm.

Once the course is completed, the debtor must file an Affirmation. See Figure 11–11.

Once eligible for bankruptcy protection, the paralegal assists in the next task—the Petition.

A. Voluntary Petition

Bankruptcy cases commence in two ways. First, a **voluntary petition** is filed by a (See Figure 11–12) debtor entitled to relief under Chapter 7, Title 11 of the U.S. Code files the Petition.

Form B22A (Chapter 7) (10/05)

In re _____
Debtor(s)

Case Number: _____
(If known)

According to the calculations required by this statement:

☐ **The presumption arises.**

☐ **The presumption does not arise.**

(Check the box as directed in Parts I, III, and VI of this statement.)

STATEMENT OF CURRENT MONTHLY INCOME AND MEANS TEST CALCULATION
FOR USE IN CHAPTER 7 ONLY

In addition to Schedule I and J, this statement must be completed by every individual Chapter 7 debtor, whether or not filing jointly, whose debts are primarily consumer debts. Joint debtors may complete one statement only.

	Part I. EXCLUSION FOR DISABLED VETERANS
1	If you are a disabled veteran described in the Veteran's Declaration in this Part I, (1) check the box at the beginning of the Veteran's Declaration, (2) check the box for "The presumption does not arise" at the top of this statement, and (3) complete the verification in Part VIII. Do not complete any of the remaining parts of this statement. ☐ **Veteran's Declaration.** By checking this box, I declare under penalty of perjury that I am a disabled veteran (as defined in 38 U.S.C. § 3741(1)) whose indebtedness occurred primarily during a period in which I was on active duty (as defined in 10 U.S.C. § 101(d)(1)) or while I was performing a homeland defense activity (as defined in 32 U.S.C. §901(1)).

	Part II. CALCULATION OF MONTHLY INCOME FOR § 707(b)(7) EXCLUSION		
2	**Marital/filing status.** Check the box that applies and complete the balance of this part of this statement as directed. a. ☐ Unmarried. **Complete only Column A ("Debtor's Income") for Lines 3-11.** b. ☐ Married, not filing jointly, with declaration of separate households. By checking this box, debtor declares under penalty of perjury: "My spouse and I are legally separated under applicable non-bankruptcy law or my spouse and I are living apart other than for the purpose of evading the requirements of § 707(b)(2)(A) of the Bankruptcy Code." **Complete only Column A ("Debtor's Income") for Lines 3-11.** c. ☐ Married, not filing jointly, without the declaration of separate households set out in Line 2.b above. **Complete both Column A ("Debtor's Income") and Column B (Spouse's Income) for Lines 3-11.** d. ☐ Married, filing jointly. **Complete both Column A ("Debtor's Income") and Column B ("Spouse's Income") for Lines 3-11.**		

		Column A Debtor's Income	Column B Spouse's Income
	All figures must reflect average monthly income for the six calendar months prior to filing the bankruptcy case, ending on the last day of the month before the filing. If you received different amounts of income during these six months, you must total the amounts received during the six months, divide this total by six, and enter the result on the appropriate line.		
3	Gross wages, salary, tips, bonuses, overtime, commissions.	$	$

4	Income from the operation of a business, profession or farm. Subtract Line b from Line a and enter the difference on Line 4. Do not enter a number less than zero. **Do not include any part of the business expenses entered on Line b as a deduction in Part V.**		

	a.	Gross receipts	$		
	b.	Ordinary and necessary business expenses	$		
	c.	Business income	Subtract Line b from Line a	$	$

5	Rent and other real property income. Subtract Line b from Line a and enter the difference on Line 5. Do not enter a number less than zero. **Do not include any part of the operating expenses entered on Line b as a deduction in Part V.**		

	a.	Gross receipts	$		
	b.	Ordinary and necessary operating expenses	$		
	c.	Rental income	Subtract Line b from Line a	$	$

6	Interest, dividends and royalties.	$	$
7	Pension and retirement income.	$	$
8	Regular contributions to the household expenses of the debtor or the debtor's dependents, including child or spousal support. Do not include contributions from the debtor's spouse if Column B is completed.	$	$

FIGURE 11–10

(continues)

Form B 22A (Chapter 7) (10/05)   2

9	Unemployment compensation. Enter the amount in Column A and, if applicable, Column B. However, if you contend that unemployment compensation received by you or your spouse was a benefit under the Social Security Act, do not list the amount of such compensation in Column A or B, but instead state the amount in the space below: Unemployment compensation claimed to be a benefit under the Social Security Act Debtor $ _____ Spouse $ _____	$	$
10	Income from all other sources. If necessary, list additional sources on a separate page. **Do not include** any benefits received under the Social Security Act or payments received as a victim of a war crime, crime against humanity, or as a victim of international or domestic terrorism. Specify source and amount. a. _____ $ _____ b. _____ $ _____ Total and enter on Line 10	$	$
11	**Subtotal of Current Monthly Income for § 707(b)(7).** Add Lines 3 thru 10 in Column A, and, if Column B is completed, add Lines 3 through 10 in Column B. Enter the total(s).	$	$
12	**Total Current Monthly Income for § 707(b)(7).** If Column B has been completed, add Line 11, Column A to Line 11, Column B, and enter the total. If Column B has not been completed, enter the amount from Line 11, Column A.	$	

	Part III. APPLICATION OF § 707(b)(7) EXCLUSION	
13	**Annualized Current Monthly Income for § 707(b)(7).** Multiply the amount from Line 12 by the number 12 and enter the result.	$
14	**Applicable median family income.** Enter the median family income for the applicable state and household size. (This information is available by family size at www.usdoj.gov/ust/ or from the clerk of the bankruptcy court.) a. Enter debtor's state of residence: _____ b. Enter debtor's household size: _____	$
15	**Application of Section 707(b)(7).** Check the applicable box and proceed as directed. ☐ **The amount on Line 13 is less than or equal to the amount on Line 14.** Check the box for "The presumption does not arise" at the top of page 1 of this statement, and complete Part VIII; do not complete Parts IV, V, VI or VII. ☐ **The amount on Line 13 is more than the amount on Line 14.** Complete the remaining parts of this statement.	

Complete Parts IV, V, VI, and VII of this statement only if required. (See Line 15.)

	Part IV. CALCULATION OF CURRENT MONTHLY INCOME FOR § 707(b)(2)	
16	**Enter the amount from Line 12.**	$
17	**Marital adjustment.** If you checked the box at Line 2.c, enter the amount of the income listed in Line 11, Column B that was NOT regularly contributed to the household expenses of the debtor or the debtor's dependents. If you did not check box at Line 2.c, enter zero.	$
18	**Current monthly income for § 707(b)(2).** Subtract Line 17 from Line 16 and enter the result.	$

	Part V. CALCULATION OF DEDUCTIONS ALLOWED UNDER § 707(b)(2)	
	Subpart A: Deductions under Standards of the Internal Revenue Service (IRS)	
19	**National Standards: food, clothing, household supplies, personal care, and miscellaneous.** Enter "Total" amount from IRS National Standards for Allowable Living Expenses for the applicable family size and income level. (This information is available at www.usdoj.gov/ust/ or from the clerk of the bankruptcy court.)	$
20A	**Local Standards: housing and utilities; non-mortgage expenses.** Enter the amount of the IRS Housing and Utilities Standards; non-mortgage expenses for the applicable county and family size.	$

FIGURE 11–10
(continued)

Form B 22A (Chapter 7) (10/05)   3

	(This information is available at www.usdoj.gov/ust/ or from the clerk of the bankruptcy court).		
20B	**Local Standards: housing and utilities; mortgage/rent expense.** Enter, in Line a below, the amount of the IRS Housing and Utilities Standards; mortgage/rent expense for your county and family size (this information is available at www.usdoj.gov/ust/ or from the clerk of the bankruptcy court); enter on Line b the total of the Average Monthly Payments for any debts secured by your home, as stated in Line 42; subtract Line b from Line a and enter the result in Line 20B. **Do not enter an amount less than zero.**		
	a.	IRS Housing and Utilities Standards; mortgage/rental expense	$	
	b.	Average Monthly Payment for any debts secured by your home, if any, as stated in Line 42	$	
	c.	Net mortgage/rental expense	Subtract Line b from Line a.	$
21	**Local Standards: housing and utilities; adjustment.** if you contend that the process set out in Lines 20A and 20B does not accurately compute the allowance to which you are entitled under the IRS Housing and Utilities Standards, enter any additional amount to which you contend you are entitled, and state the basis for your contention in the space below: _____ _____ _____		$
22	**Local Standards: transportation; vehicle operation/public transportation expense.** You are entitled to an expense allowance in this category regardless of whether you pay the expenses of operating a vehicle and regardless of whether you use public transportation. Check the number of vehicles for which you pay the operating expenses or for which the operating expenses are included as a contribution to your household expenses in Line 8. ☐ 0 ☐ 1 ☐ 2 or more. Enter the amount from IRS Transportation Standards, Operating Costs & Public Transportation Costs for the applicable number of vehicles in the applicable Metropolitan Statistical Area or Census Region. (This information is available at www.usdoj.gov/ust/ or from the clerk of the bankruptcy court.)		$
23	**Local Standards: transportation ownership/lease expense; Vehicle 1.** Check the number of vehicles for which you claim an ownership/lease expense. (You may not claim an ownership/lease expense for more than two vehicles.) ☐ 1 ☐ 2 or more. Enter, in Line a below, the amount of the IRS Transportation Standards, Ownership Costs, First Car (available at www.usdoj.gov/ust/ or from the clerk of the bankruptcy court); enter in Line b the total of the Average Monthly Payments for any debts secured by Vehicle 1, as stated in Line 42; subtract Line b from Line a and enter the result in Line 23. **Do not enter an amount less than zero.**		
	a.	IRS Transportation Standards, Ownership Costs, First Car	$	
	b.	Average Monthly Payment for any debts secured by Vehicle 1, as stated in Line 42	$	
	c.	Net ownership/lease expense for Vehicle 1	Subtract Line b from Line a.	$
24	**Local Standards: transportation ownership/lease expense; Vehicle 2.** Complete this Line only if you checked the "2 or more" Box in Line 23. Enter, in Line a below, the amount of the IRS Transportation Standards, Ownership Costs, Second Car (available at www.usdoj.gov/ust/ or from the clerk of the bankruptcy court); enter in Line b the total of the Average Monthly Payments for any debts secured by Vehicle 2, as stated in Line 42; subtract Line b from Line a and enter the result in Line 24. **Do not enter an amount less than zero.**		
	a.	IRS Transportation Standards, Ownership Costs, Second Car	$	
	b.	Average Monthly Payment for any debts secured by Vehicle 2, as stated in Line 42	$	
	c.	Net ownership/lease expense for Vehicle 2	Subtract Line b from Line a.	$
25	**Other Necessary Expenses: taxes.** Enter the total average monthly expense that you actually incur for all federal, state and local taxes, other than real estate and sales taxes, such as income taxes, self employment taxes, social security taxes, and Medicare taxes. **Do not include real estate or sales taxes.**		
26	**Other Necessary Expenses: mandatory payroll deductions.** Enter the total average monthly payroll deductions that are required for your employment, such as mandatory retirement contributions, union dues, and uniform costs. **Do not include discretionary amounts, such as non-mandatory 401(k) contributions.**		$

FIGURE 11–10

(continued)

Form B 22A (Chapter 7) (10/05) 4

27	**Other Necessary Expenses: life insurance.** Enter average monthly premiums that you actually pay for term life insurance for yourself. **Do not include premiums for insurance on your dependents, for whole life or for any other form of insurance.**	$
28	**Other Necessary Expenses: court-ordered payments.** Enter the total monthly amount that you are required to pay pursuant to court order, such as spousal or child support payments. **Do not include payments on past due support obligations included in Line 44.**	$
29	**Other Necessary Expenses: education for employment or for a physically or mentally challenged child.** Enter the total monthly amount that you actually expend for education that is a condition of employment and for education that is required for a physically or mentally challenged dependent child for whom no public education providing similar services is available.	$
30	**Other Necessary Expenses: childcare.** Enter the average monthly amount that you actually expend on childcare. **Do not include payments made for children's education.**	$
31	**Other Necessary Expenses: health care.** Enter the average monthly amount that you actually expend on health care expenses that are not reimbursed by insurance or paid by a health savings account. **Do not include payments for health insurance listed in Line 34.**	$
32	**Other Necessary Expenses: telecommunication services.** Enter the average monthly expenses that you actually pay for cell phones, pagers, call waiting, caller identification, special long distance or internet services necessary for the health and welfare of you or your dependents. **Do not include any amount previously deducted.**	$
33	**Total Expenses Allowed under IRS Standards.** Enter the total of Lines 19 through 32.	$

	Subpart B: Additional Expense Deductions under § 707(b)		
	Note: Do not include any expenses that you have listed in Lines 19-32		
34	**Health Insurance, Disability Insurance and Health Savings Account Expenses.** List the average monthly amounts that you actually expend in each of the following categories and enter the total.		
	a.	Health Insurance	$
	b.	Disability Insurance	$
	c.	Health Savings Account	$
		Total: Add Lines a, b and c	$
35	**Continued contributions to the care of household or family members.** Enter the actual monthly expenses that you will continue to pay for the reasonable and necessary care and support of an elderly, chronically ill, or disabled member of your household or member of your immediate family who is unable to pay for such expenses.	$
36	**Protection against family violence.** Enter any average monthly expenses that you actually incurred to maintain the safety of your family under the Family Violence Prevention and Services Act or other applicable federal law.	$
37	**Home energy costs in excess of the allowance specified by the IRS Local Standards.** Enter the average monthly amount by which your home energy costs exceed the allowance in the IRS Local Standards for Housing and Utilities. **You must provide your case trustee with documentation demonstrating that the additional amount claimed is reasonable and necessary.**	$
38	**Education expenses for dependent children less than 18.** Enter the average monthly expenses that you actually incur, not to exceed $125 per child, in providing elementary and secondary education for your dependent children less than 18 years of age. **You must provide your case trustee with documentation demonstrating that the amount claimed is reasonable and necessary and not already accounted for in the IRS Standards.**	$
39	**Additional food and clothing expense.** Enter the average monthly amount by which your food and clothing expenses exceed the combined allowances for food and apparel in the IRS National Standards, not to exceed five percent of those combined allowances. (This information is available at www.usdoj.gov/ust/ or from the clerk of the bankruptcy court.) **You must provide your case trustee with documentation demonstrating that the additional amount claimed is reasonable and necessary.**	$
40	**Continued charitable contributions.** Enter the amount that you will continue to contribute in the form of cash or financial instruments to a charitable organization as defined in 26 U.S.C. § 170(c)(1)-(2).	$
41	**Total Additional Expense Deductions under § 707(b).** Enter the total of Lines 34 through 40	$

FIGURE 11–10
(continued)

	Subpart C: Deductions for Debt Payment			
42	**Future payments on secured claims.** For each of your debts that is secured by an interest in property that you own, list the name of the creditor, identify the property securing the debt, and state the Average Monthly Payment. The Average Monthly Payment is the total of all amounts contractually due to each Secured Creditor in the 60 months following the filing of the bankruptcy case, divided by 60. Mortgage debts should include payments of taxes and insurance required by the mortgage. If necessary, list additional entries on a separate page.			

42		Name of Creditor	Property Securing the Debt	60-month Average Payment	
	a.			$	
	b.			$	
	c.			$	
				Total: Add Lines a, b and c.	$

43	**Past due payments on secured claims.** If any of the debts listed in Line 42 are in default, and the property securing the debt is necessary for your support or the support of your dependents, you may include in your deductions 1/60th of the amount that you must pay the creditor as a result of the default (the "cure amount") in order to maintain possession of the property. List any such amounts in the following chart and enter the total. If necessary, list additional entries on a separate page.			

43		Name of Creditor	Property Securing the Debt in Default	1/60th of the Cure Amount	
	a.			$	
	b.			$	
	c.			$	
				Total: Add Lines a, b and c	$

44	**Payments on priority claims.** Enter the total amount of all priority claims (including priority child support and alimony claims), divided by 60.	$

45	**Chapter 13 administrative expenses.** If you are eligible to file a case under Chapter 13, complete the following chart, multiply the amount in line a by the amount in line b, and enter the resulting administrative expense.		

45	a.	Projected average monthly Chapter 13 plan payment.	$	
	b.	Current multiplier for your district as determined under schedules issued by the Executive Office for United States Trustees. (This information is available at www.usdoj.gov/ust/ or from the clerk of the bankruptcy court.)	x	
	c.	Average monthly administrative expense of Chapter 13 case	Total: Multiply Lines a and b	$

46	**Total Deductions for Debt Payment.** Enter the total of Lines 42 through 45.	$

	Subpart D: Total Deductions Allowed under § 707(b)(2)	
47	**Total of all deductions allowed under § 707(b)(2).** Enter the total of Lines 33, 41, and 46.	$

	Part VI. DETERMINATION OF § 707(b)(2) PRESUMPTION	
48	**Enter the amount from Line 18 (Current monthly income for § 707(b)(2))**	$
49	**Enter the amount from Line 47 (Total of all deductions allowed under § 707(b)(2))**	$
50	**Monthly disposable income under § 707(b)(2).** Subtract Line 49 from Line 48 and enter the result	$
51	**60-month disposable income under § 707(b)(2).** Multiply the amount in Line 50 by the number 60 and enter the result.	$

FIGURE 11–10
(continued)

Form B 22A (Chapter 7) (10/05) 6

52	**Initial presumption determination.** Check the applicable box and proceed as directed. ☐ **The amount on Line 51 is less than $6,000** Check the box for "The presumption does not arise" at the top of page 1 of this statement, and complete the verification in Part VIII. Do not complete the remainder of Part VI. ☐ **The amount set forth on Line 51 is more than $10,000.** Check the box for "The presumption arises" at the top of page 1 of this statement, and complete the verification in Part VIII. You may also complete Part VII. Do not complete the remainder of Part VI. ☐ **The amount on Line 51 is at least $6,000, but not more than $10,000.** Complete the remainder of Part VI (Lines 53 through 55).
53	**Enter the amount of your total non-priority unsecured debt** $
54	**Threshold debt payment amount.** Multiply the amount in Line 53 by the number 0.25 and enter the result. $
55	**Secondary presumption determination.** Check the applicable box and proceed as directed. ☐ **The amount on Line 51 is less than the amount on Line 54.** Check the box for "The presumption does not arise" at the top of page 1 of this statement, and complete the verification in Part VIII. ☐ **The amount on Line 51 is equal to or greater than the amount on Line 54.** Check the box for "The presumption arises" at the top of page 1 of this statement, and complete the verification in Part VIII. You may also complete Part VII.

Part VII: ADDITIONAL EXPENSE CLAIMS

56	**Other Expenses.** List and describe any monthly expenses, not otherwise stated in this form, that are required for the health and welfare of you and your family and that you contend should be an additional deduction from your current monthly income under § 707(b)(2)(A)(ii)(I). If necessary, list additional sources on a separate page. All figures should reflect your average monthly expense for each item. Total the expenses.

	Expense Description	Monthly Amount
a.		$
b.		$
c.		$
	Total: Add Lines a, b and c	$

Part VIII: VERIFICATION

57	I declare under penalty of perjury that the information provided in this statement is true and correct. *(If this a joint case, both debtors must sign.)*
	
	Date: _____ Signature: _____
	                                                   (Debtor)
	
	Date: _____ Signature: _____
	                                                (Joint Debtor, if any)

FIGURE 11–10
(continued)

The petition has a series of Schedules that compute both assets and liabilities which are:

Schedule A	Real Property
Schedule B	Personal Property
Schedule C	Property Claimed as Exempt
Schedule D	Creditors Holding Secured Claims
Schedule E	Creditors Holding Unsecured Priority Claims
Schedule F	Creditors Holding Unsecured Nonpriority Claims
Schedule G	Executory Contracts and Unexpired Leases
Schedule H	Codebtors
Schedule I	Current Income of Individual Debtor(s)
Schedule J	Current Expenditures of Individual Debtor(s)

Form 23
(10/05)

United States Bankruptcy Court

_____ District Of _____

In re _____,   Case No. _____
                    Debtor

                                              Chapter _____

DEBTOR'S CERTIFICATION OF COMPLETION OF INSTRUCTIONAL COURSE
CONCERNING PERSONAL FINANCIAL MANAGEMENT

[Complete one of the following statements.]

☐ I/We, _____. the debtor(s) in the above-
          (Printed Name(s) of Debtor and Joint Debtor, if any)
styled case hereby certify that on _____ I/we completed an instructional
                                    (Date)
course in personal financial management provided by _____,
                                                       (Name of Provider)
an approved personal financial management instruction provider. If the provider furnished a
document attesting to the completion of the personal financial management instructional
course, a copy of that document is attached.

☐ I/We, _____, the debtor(s) in the above-
styled
          (Printed Names of Debtor and Joint Debtor, if any)
case, hereby certify that no personal financial management course is required because:
[Check the appropriate box.]
☐ I am/We are incapacitated or disabled, as defined in 11 U.S.C. § 109(h);
☐ I am/We are on active military duty in a military combat zone; or
☐ I/We reside in a district in which the United States trustee (or bankruptcy administrator) has
determined that the approved instructional courses are not adequate at this time to serve the
additional individuals who would otherwise be required to complete such courses.

Signature of Debtor: _____

Date: _____

Signature of Joint Debtor: _____

Date: _____

FIGURE 11–11

(Official Form 1) (10/05)

United States Bankruptcy Court District of_____	Voluntary Petition

Name of Debtor (if individual, enter Last, First, Middle):	Name of Joint Debtor (Spouse) (Last, First, Middle):
All Other Names used by the Debtor in the last 8 years (include married, maiden, and trade names):	All Other Names used by the Joint Debtor in the last 8 years (include married, maiden, and trade names):
Last four digits of Soc. Sec./Complete EIN or other Tax I.D. No. (if more than one, state all):	Last four digits of Soc. Sec./Complete EIN or other Tax I.D. No. (if more than one, state all):
Street Address of Debtor (No. & Street, City, and State): ZIPCODE	Street Address of Joint Debtor (No. & Street, City, and State): ZIPCODE
County of Residence or of the Principal Place of Business:	County of Residence or of the Principal Place of Business:
Mailing Address of Debtor (if different from street address): ZIPCODE	Mailing Address of Joint Debtor (if different from street address): ZIPCODE

Location of Principal Assets of Business Debtor (if different from street address above):
ZIPCODE

Type of Debtor (Form of Organization) (Check **one** box.)
- [ ] Individual (includes Joint Debtors)
- [ ] Corporation (includes LLC and LLP)
- [ ] Partnership
- [ ] Other (If debtor is not one of the above entities, check this box and provide the information requested below.)

State type of entity: _____

Nature of Business (Check **all** applicable boxes.)
- [ ] Health Care Business
- [ ] Single Asset Real Estate as defined in 11 U.S.C. § 101 (51B)
- [ ] Railroad
- [ ] Stockbroker
- [ ] Commodity Broker
- [ ] Clearing Bank
- [ ] Nonprofit Organization qualified under 26 U.S.C. § 501(c)(3)

Chapter of Bankruptcy Code Under Which the Petition is Filed (Check one box)
- [ ] Chapter 7
- [ ] Chapter 9
- [ ] Chapter 11
- [ ] Chapter 12
- [ ] Chapter 13
- [ ] Chapter 15 Petition for Recognition of a Foreign Main Proceeding
- [ ] Chapter 15 Petition for Recognition of a Foreign Nonmain Proceeding

Nature of Debts (Check one box)
- [ ] Consumer/Non-Business
- [ ] Business

Filing Fee (Check one box)
- [ ] Full Filing Fee attached
- [ ] Filing Fee to be paid in installments (Applicable to individuals only) Must attach signed application for the court's consideration certifying that the debtor is unable to pay fee except in installments. Rule 1006(b). See Official Form 3A.
- [ ] Filing Fee waiver requested (Applicable to chapter 7 individuals only). Must attach signed application for the court's consideration. See Official Form 3B.

Chapter 11 Debtors
Check one box:
- [ ] Debtor is a small business debtor as defined in 11 U.S.C. § 101(51D).
- [ ] Debtor is not a small business debtor as defined in 11 U.S.C. § 101(51D).

Check if:
- [ ] Debtor's aggregate noncontingent liquidated debts owed to non-insiders or affliates are less than $2 million.

Statistical/Administrative Information   THIS SPACE IS FOR COURT USE ONLY
- [ ] Debtor estimates that funds will be available for distribution to unsecured creditors.
- [ ] Debtor estimates that, after any exempt property is excluded and administrative expenses paid, there will be no funds available for distribution to unsecured creditors.

Estimated Number of Creditors

1-49	50-99	100-199	200-999	1,000-5,000	5,001-10,000	10,001-25,000	25,001-50,000	50,001-100,000	OVER 100,000
[ ]	[ ]	[ ]	[ ]	[ ]	[ ]	[ ]	[ ]	[ ]	[ ]

Estimated Assets

$0 to $50,000	$50,001 to $100,000	$100,001 to $500,000	$500,001 to $1 million	$1,000,001 to $10 million	$10,000,001 to $50 million	$50,000,001 to $100 million	More than $100 million
[ ]	[ ]	[ ]	[ ]	[ ]	[ ]	[ ]	[ ]

Estimated Debts

$0 to $50,000	$50,001 to $100,000	$100,001 to $500,000	$500,001 to $1 million	$1,000,001 to $10 million	$10,000,001 to $50 million	$50,000,001 to $100 million	More than $100 million
[ ]	[ ]	[ ]	[ ]	[ ]	[ ]	[ ]	[ ]

FIGURE 11–12
(continues)

(Official Form 1) (10/05)

FORM B1, Page 2

Voluntary Petition *(This page must be completed and filed in every case)*	Name of Debtor(s):	

Prior Bankruptcy Case Filed Within Last 8 Years (If more than one, attach additional sheet)		
Location Where Filed:	Case Number:	Date Filed:

Pending Bankruptcy Case Filed by any Spouse, Partner or Affiliate of this Debtor (If more than one, attach additional sheet)		
Name of Debtor:	Case Number:	Date Filed:
District:	Relationship:	Judge:

Exhibit A	**Exhibit B**
(To be completed if debtor is required to file periodic reports (e.g., forms 10K and 10Q) with the Securities and Exchange Commission pursuant to Section 13 or 15(d) of the Securities Exchange Act of 1934 and is requesting relief under chapter 11.) ☐ Exhibit A is attached and made a part of this petition.	(To be completed if debtor is an individual whose debts are primarily consumer debts.) I, the attorney for the petitioner named in the foregoing petition, declare that I have informed the petitioner that [he or she] may proceed under chapter 7, 11, 12, or 13 of title 11, United States Code, and have explained the relief available under each such chapter. I further certify that I delivered to the debtor the notice required by § 342(b) of the Bankruptcy Code. X _____ Signature of Attorney for Debtor(s) Date

Exhibit C	**Certification Concerning Debt Counseling by Individual/Joint Debtor(s)**
Does the debtor own or have possession of any property that poses or is alleged to pose a threat of imminent and identifiable harm to public health or safety? ☐ Yes, and Exhibit C is attached and made a part of this petition. ☐ No	☐ I/we have received approved budget and credit counseling during the 180-day period preceding the filing of this petition. ☐ I/we request a waiver of the requirement to obtain budget and credit counseling prior to filing based on exigent circumstances. (Must attach certification describing.)

Information Regarding the Debtor (Check the Applicable Boxes)

Venue (Check any applicable box)

☐ Debtor has been domiciled or has had a residence, principal place of business, or principal assets in this District for 180 days immediately preceding the date of this petition or for a longer part of such 180 days than in any other District.

☐ There is a bankruptcy case concerning debtor's affiliate, general partner, or partnership pending in this District.

☐ Debtor is a debtor in a foreign proceeding and has its principal place of business or principal assets in the United States in this District, or has no principal place of business or assets in the United States but is a defendant in an action or proceeding [in a federal or state court] in this District, or the interests of the parties will be served in regard to the relief sought in this District.

Statement by a Debtor Who Resides as a Tenant of Residential Property
Check all applicable boxes.

☐ Landlord has a judgment against the debtor for possession of debtor's residence. (If box checked, complete the following.)

_____
(Name of landlord that obtained judgment)

_____
(Address of landlord)

☐ Debtor claims that under applicable nonbankruptcy law, there are circumstances under which the debtor would be permitted to cure the entire monetary default that gave rise to the judgment for possession, after the judgment for possession was entered, and

☐ Debtor has included in this petition the deposit with the court of any rent that would become due during the 30-day period after the filing of the petition.

FIGURE 11–12
(continued)

(Official Form 1) (10/05)	FORM B1, Page 3
Voluntary Petition *(This page must be completed and filed in every case)*	Name of Debtor(s):

Signatures

Signature(s) of Debtor(s) (Individual/Joint)	**Signature of a Foreign Representative**
I declare under penalty of perjury that the information provided in this petition is true and correct. [If petitioner is an individual whose debts are primarily consumer debts and has chosen to file under chapter 7] I am aware that I may proceed under chapter 7, 11, 12 or 13 of title 11, United States Code, understand the relief available under each such chapter, and choose to proceed under chapter 7. [If no attorney represents me and no bankruptcy petition preparer signs the petition] I have obtained and read the notice required by § 342(b) of the Bankruptcy Code. I request relief in accordance with the chapter of title 11, United States Code, specified in this petition. X_____ Signature of Debtor X_____ Signature of Joint Debtor _____ Telephone Number (If not represented by attorney) _____ Date	I declare under penalty of perjury that the information provided in this petition is true and correct, that I am the foreign representative of a debtor in a foreign proceeding, and that I am authorized to file this petition. (Check only one box.) ☐ I request relief in accordance with chapter 15 of title 11, United States Code. Certified copies of the documents required by § 1515 of title 11 are attached. ☐ Pursuant to § 1511 of title 11, United States Code, I request relief in accordance with the chapter of title 11 specified in this petition. A certified copy of the order granting recognition of the foreign main proceeding is attached. X_____ (Signature of Foreign Representative) _____ (Printed Name of Foreign Representative) _____ Date
Signature of Attorney X_____ Signature of Attorney for Debtor(s) _____ Printed Name of Attorney for Debtor(s) _____ Firm Name _____ Address _____ Telephone Number _____ Date	**Signature of Non-Attorney Bankruptcy Petition Preparer** I declare under penalty of perjury that: (1) I am a bankruptcy petition preparer as defined in 11 U.S.C. § 110; (2) I prepared this document for compensation and have provided the debtor with a copy of this document and the notices and information required under 11 U.S.C. §§ 110(b), 110(h), and 342(b); and, (3) if rules or guidelines have been promulgated pursuant to 11 U.S.C. § 110(h) setting a maximum fee for services chargeable by bankruptcy petition preparers, I have given the debtor notice of the maximum amount before preparing any document for filing for a debtor or accepting any fee from the debtor, as required in that section. Official Form 19B is attached. _____ Printed Name and title, if any, of Bankruptcy Petition Preparer _____ Social Security number (If the bankrutpcy petition preparer is not an individual, state the Social Security number of the officer, principal, responsible person or partner of the bankruptcy petition preparer.)(Required by 11 U.S.C. § 110.)
Signature of Debtor (Corporation/Partnership) I declare under penalty of perjury that the information provided in this petition is true and correct, and that I have been authorized to file this petition on behalf of the debtor. The debtor requests relief in accordance with the chapter of title 11, United States Code, specified in this petition. X_____ Signature of Authorized Individual _____ Printed Name of Authorized Individual _____ Title of Authorized Individual _____ Date	Address _____ X_____ _____ Date Signature of Bankruptcy Petition Preparer or officer, principal, responsible person, or partner whose social security number is provided above. Names and Social Security numbers of all other individuals who prepared or assisted in preparing this document unless the bankruptcy petition preparer is not an individual: If more than one person prepared this document, attach additional sheets conforming to the appropriate official form for each person. *A bankruptcy petition preparer's failure to comply with the provisions of title 11 and the Federal Rules of Bankruptcy Procedure may result in fines or imprisonment or both 11 U.S.C. §110; 18 U.S.C. §156.*

FIGURE 11–12
(continued)

Once all Schedules are calculated, the debtor prepares a Summary of said schedules and declares, under penalty of perjury that the calculation is correct. (See Figure 11–13.)

B. Involuntary Petition

A second option would be the **involuntary petition**. An involuntary case can be commenced by creditors or other interested parties by filing. An involuntary petition under a Chapter 7 scheme is at Figure 11–14.

Notice within its content that creditors whose unsecured claims total more than $5,000 must sign the involuntary petition.

Form 6-Summary
(10/05)

United States Bankruptcy Court
_____ District Of _____

In re _____,   Case No. _____
　　　　　　　Debtor

　　　　　　　　　　　　　　　　　　　　Chapter _____

SUMMARY OF SCHEDULES

Indicate as to each schedule whether that schedule is attached and state the number of pages in each. Report the totals from Schedules A, B, D, E, F, I, and J in the boxes provided. Add the amounts from Schedules A and B to determine the total amount of the debtor's assets. Add the amounts of all claims from Schedules D, E, and F to determine the total amount of the debtor's liabilities. Individual debtors must also complete the "Statistical Summary of Certain Liabilities."

AMOUNTS SCHEDULED

NAME OF SCHEDULE	ATTACHED (YES/NO)	NO. OF SHEETS	ASSETS	LIABILITIES	OTHER
A - Real Property			$		
B - Personal Property			$		
C - Property Claimed as Exempt					
D - Creditors Holding Secured Claims				$	
E - Creditors Holding Unsecured Priority Claims				$	
F - Creditors Holding Unsecured Nonpriority Claims				$	
G - Executory Contracts and Unexpired Leases					
H - Codebtors					
I - Current Income of Individual Debtor(s)					$
J - Current Expenditures of Individual Debtors(s)					$
TOTAL			$	$	

FIGURE 11–13
(continues)

Form 6-Summ2
(10/05)

United States Bankruptcy Court

_____ District Of _____

In re _____,   Case No. _____
                    Debtor

                                                    Chapter _____

STATISTICAL SUMMARY OF CERTAIN LIABILITIES (28 U.S.C. § 159)
[Individual Debtors Only]

Summarize the following types of liabilities, as reported in the Schedules, and total them.

Type of Liability	Amount
Domestic Support Obligations (from Schedule E)	$
Taxes and Certain Other Debts Owed to Governmental Units (from Schedule E)	$
Claims for Death or Personal Injury While Debtor Was Intoxicated (from Schedule E)	$
Student Loan Obligations (from Schedule F)	$
Domestic Support, Separation Agreement, and Divorce Decree Obligations Not Reported on Schedule E	$
Obligations to Pension or Profit-Sharing, and Other Similar Obligations (from Schedule F)	$
TOTAL	$

The foregoing information is for statistical purposes only under 28 U.S.C. § 159.

FIGURE 11–13
(continued)

Title 11 at § 501 publishes guidelines for a Proof of Claim.

(a) A creditor or an indenture trustee may file a proof of claim. An equity security holder may file a proof of interest.

(b) If a creditor does not timely file a proof of such creditor's claim, an entity that is liable to such creditor with the debtor, or that has secured such creditor, may file a proof of such claim.

(c) If a creditor does not timely file a proof of such creditor's claim, the debtor or the trustee may file a proof of such claim.

(d) A claim of a kind specified in section 502(e)(2), 502(f), 502(g), 502(h) or 502(i) of this title may be filed under subsection (a), (b), or (c) of this section the same as if such claim were a claim against the debtor and had arisen before the date of the filing of the petition.[32]

Of course, a debtor in a Chapter 7 case has every right to challenge the actions within the petition. The court is not permitted or entitled to grant relief if there exists any of the following:

  a genuine issue of material fact that bears upon the debtor's liability, or a meritorious contention as to the application of law to undisputed facts, then the involuntary petition must be dismissed.[33]

FORM B5
(10-05)

United States Bankruptcy Court	INVOLUNTARY
_____District of_____	PETITION

IN RE (Name of Debtor - If Individual: Last, First, Middle)	ALL OTHER NAMES used by debtor in the last 8 years (Include married, maiden, and trade names.)

LAST FOUR DIGITS OF SOC. SEC. NO./Complete EIN or other TAX I.D. NO. (If more than one, state all.)

STREET ADDRESS OF DEBTOR (No. and street, city, state, and zip code)	MAILING ADDRESS OF DEBTOR (If different from street address)

COUNTY OF RESIDENCE OR PRINCIPAL PLACE OF BUSINESS	ZIP CODE		ZIP CODE

LOCATION OF PRINCIPAL ASSETS OF BUSINESS DEBTOR (If different from previously listed addresses)

CHAPTER OF BANKRUPTCY CODE UNDER WHICH PETITION IS FILED

☐ Chapter 7   ☐ Chapter 11

INFORMATION REGARDING DEBTOR (Check applicable boxes)

TYPE OF DEBTOR

Petitioners believe:
☐ Debts are primarily consumer debts
☐ Debts are primarily business debts

☐ Individual   ☐ Stockbroker
☐ Partnership   ☐ Railroad
☐ Corporation   ☐ Health Care Business
☐ Clearing Bank   ☐ Commodity Broker
☐ Other: _____

BRIEFLY DESCRIBE NATURE OF BUSINESS

VENUE	FILING FEE (Check one box)
☐ Debtor has been domiciled or has had a residence, principal place of business, or principal assets in the District for 180 days immediately preceding the date of this petition or for a longer part of such 180 days than in any other District.	☐ Full Filing Fee attached
☐ A bankruptcy case concerning debtor's affiliate, general partner or partnership is pending in this District.	☐ Petitioner is a child suport creditor or its representative, and the form specified in § 304(g) of the Bankruptcy Reform Act of 1994 is attached.

PENDING BANKRUPTCY CASE FILED BY OR AGAINST ANY PARTNER OR AFFILIATE OF THIS DEBTOR (Report information for any additional cases on attached sheets.)

Name of Debtor	Case Number	Date
Relationship	District	Judge

ALLEGATIONS
(Check applicable boxes)

COURT USE ONLY

1. ☐ Petitioner(s) are eligible to file this petition pursuant to 11 U.S.C. § 303(b).
2. ☐ The debtor is a person against whom an order for relief may be entered under title 11 of the United States Code.
3.a. ☐ The debtor is generally not paying such debtor's debts as they become due, unless such debts are the subject of a bona fide dispute as to liability or amount;
        or
  b. ☐ Within 120 days preceding the filing of this petition, a custodian, other than a trustee, receiver, or agent appointed or authorized to take charge of less than substantially all of the property of the debtor for the purpose of enforcing a lien against such property, was appointed or took possession.

If a child support creditor or its representative is a petitioner, and if the petitioner files the form specified in § 304(g) of the Bankruptcy Reform Act of 1994, no fee is required.

FIGURE 11–14

Name of Debtor_____

OFFICIAL FORM 5 - Page 2
Involuntary Petition
(10/05)

Case No._____

TRANSFER OF CLAIM

☐ Check this box if there has been a transfer of any claim against the debtor by or to any petitioner. Attach all documents evidencing the transfer and any statements that are required under Bankruptcy Rule 1003(a).

REQUEST FOR RELIEF

Petitioner(s) request that an order for relief be entered against the debtor under the chapter of title 11, United States Code, specified in this petition. If any petitioner is a foreign representative appointed in a foreign proceeding, a certified copy of the order of the court granting recognition is attached.

Petitioner(s) declare under penalty of perjury that the foregoing is true and correct according to the best of their knowledge, information, and belief.

X_____
Signature of Petitioner or Representative (State title)

X_____
Signature of Attorney   Date

Name of Petitioner   Date Signed

Name of Attorney Firm (If any)

Name & Mailing
Address of Individual
Signing in Representative
Capacity

Address

Telephone No.

X_____
Signature of Petitioner or Representative (State title)

X_____
Signature of Attorney   Date

Name of Petitioner   Date Signed

Name of Attorney Firm (If any)

Name & Mailing
Address of Individual
Signing in Representative
Capacity

Address

Telephone No.

X_____
Signature of Petitioner or Representative (State title)

X_____
Signature of Attorney   Date

Name of Petitioner   Date Signed

Name of Attorney Firm (If any)

Name & Mailing
Address of Individual
Signing in Representative
Capacity

Address

Telephone No.

PETITIONING CREDITORS

Name and Address of Petitioner	Nature of Claim	Amount of Claim
Name and Address of Petitioner	Nature of Claim	Amount of Claim
Name and Address of Petitioner	Nature of Claim	Amount of Claim
Note: If there are more than three petitioners, attach additional sheets with the statement under penalty of perjury, each petitioner's signature under the statement and the name of attorney and petitioning creditor information in the format above.		Total Amount of Petitioners' Claims

_____continuation sheets attached

FIGURE 11–14
(continued)

C. Appointment of a Trustee

In both Chapter 7 and thirteen cases, a judicial appointment of a **trustee** takes place. The representative of the bankruptcy estate, who exercises statutory powers, principally for the benefit of the unsecured creditors, under the general supervision of the court and the direct supervision of the U.S. trustee or bankruptcy administrator, is the trustee. The trustee is a private individual, business entity or other legal authority. The trustee's responsibilities include reviewing the debtor's petition and schedules and bringing actions against creditors or the debtor to recover property of the bankruptcy estate. In Chapter 7, the trustee liquidates property of the estate and makes distributions to creditors. Trustees exercise statutory powers, principally for the benefit of the unsecured creditors, under the general supervision of the court and the direct supervision of the U.S. trustee or bankruptcy administrator. Bankruptcy trustees are granted wide discretion and authority and have been criticized for their liberal exercise of their power. Title 11 § 704 states:

The trustee shall:

(1) Collect and reduce to money the property of the estate for which such trustee serves, and close such estate as expeditiously as is compatible with the best interests of parties in interest;

(2) Be accountable for all property received;

(3) Ensure that the debtor shall perform his intention as specified in Section 521 (2)(B) of this title [U.S.C.S. § 521 (2)(B)];

(4) Investigate the financial affairs of the debtor;

(5) If a purpose would be served, examine proofs of claims and object to the allowance of any claim that is improper;

(6) If advisable, oppose the discharge of the debtor;

(7) Unless the court orders otherwise, furnish such information concerning the estate and the estate's administration as is required by a party in interest;

(8) If the business of the debtor is authorized to be operated, file with the court and with the governmental unit charged with responsibility for collection or determination of any tax arising out of such operation, periodic reports, and summaries of the operation of such business, including a statement of receipts and disbursements, and such other information as the court requires; and

(9) Make a final report and file a final account of the administration of the estate with the court.[34]

In a Chapter 7 case, trustees are required to calculate and reduce all nonexempt property or property that is subject to a valid security interest to cash and then distribute the money to creditors expeditiously. The trustee must also ensure that the debtor performs his obligations and that the debtor makes no unauthorized transfers. Trustees have the authority and power to set aside what are deemed preferential transfers. The preferential transfers are:

1. The trustee transfer was to pay a debt incurred at some earlier time;

2. The transfer was made when the debtor was insolvent and within 90 days before filing the bankruptcy petition;[35] and

3. By the transfer, the creditor received more than such creditor would have received in a liquidation of a debtor's estate.

A trustee can, depending on the nature of the transaction, avoid the improper transfer of an interest of the debtor. Fraudulent transfers may also be avoided.

(a)(1) The trustee may avoid any transfer of an interest of the debtor in property, or any obligation incurred by the debtor, that was made or incurred on or within one year before the date of the filing of the petition, if the debtor voluntarily or involuntarily:

(A) Made such transfer or incurred such obligation with actual intent to hinder, delay, or defraud any entity to which the debtor was or became, on or after the date that such transfer was made or such obligation was incurred, indebted; or

(B)(i) Received less than a reasonably equivalent value in exchange for such transfer or obligation; and

(ii)(I) Was insolvent on the date that such transfer was made or such obligation was incurred, or became insolvent as a result of such transfer or obligation;

(II) Was engaged in business or a transaction, or was about to engage in business or a transaction, for which any property remaining with the debtor was an unreasonably small capital; or

(III) Intended to incur, or believed that the debtor would incur, debts that would be beyond the debtor's ability to pay as such debts matured.[36]

Paralegals often are major players in this world—a trend likely to continue.[37]

CASE DECISION

For the complexities of integral involvement versus unauthorized practice, see the Ethical Opinion from the State Bar of Montana

ETHICS OPINION

871008

QUESTION PRESENTED: Can paralegals employed by law firms appear on behalf of creditors at Section 341 hearings in bankruptcy proceedings to question and examine debtors?

ANSWER: No. The appearance of a paralegal without a supervising attorney would constitute an unauthorized practice of law.

ANALYSIS: It is true that a bankruptcy trustee is not required to be a lawyer pursuant to 11 U.S.C. Section 321. However, a trustee is an individual who is "competent" to serve as trustee, who is required to furnish a bond, and who is fully subject to review by the Court. It is often the case as well, that the bankruptcy judge's law clerk is not a licensed attorney, but assists the judge in writing opinions and performing legal research. The heart of the concept in these matters, is that these individuals are, in essence, arms of the Court, and assist the Court in its proper functioning. In Montana, Section 37-61-101, M.C.A. 1987, states unequivocally that the Supreme Court has the authority to determine whether any agents or employees of any law firm are possessed of the requisite skill, competence and ethics necessary to practice law in the State of Montana. The Supreme Court has that power to make that determination through a bar examination, yearly continuing legal education requirements and the Code of Professional Responsibility. In the case of *Bennion, Van Camp, Hagen and Ruhl, v. Kassler Escrow Inc.*, 635 P.2d 730 (1981), the Supreme Court of the State of Washington stated, "The 'practice of law' does not lend itself easily to precise definition . . . selection and completion of pre-printed form legal documents has been found to be 'practice of law'." *Id.* at page 732. The Washington Supreme Court in the Bennion decision, referred to another case, *Washington State Bar Association v. Great Western Union Federal Savings and Loan Assoc.*, 586 P.2d 870 (1978), which stated that it was the duty of the Court to "protect the public from the activity of those who because of lack of professional skills, may cause injury whether they are members of the bar of persons never qualified for or admitted to the bar." In another case, *Washington State Bar Assoc. v. Washington Assoc. of Realtors*, 251 P.2d 619 (1952), the Court stated that "there is no such thing as a simple legal instrument in the hands of a layman."

(continued)

In Montana, Section 37-61-201, M.C.A. 1987, states that "any person who shall hold himself out . . . or who shall appear in any court of record or before a judicial body, referee, commissioner, or other officer appointed to determine any question of law or fact by a court or who shall engage in the business and duties and perform such acts, matters, and things as are usually performed by an attorney at law in the practice of his profession for the purposes of Parts 1 through 3 of this chapter, shall be deemed practicing law." It seems pretty clear from this statutory definition, which dates back to the laws of 1917, that a paralegal appearing in a Section 341 meeting would be deemed to be practicing law in Montana.

In *Florida Bar vs. Pascual*, 424 So.2d 757 (1982), the Supreme Court of Florida ruled that a "paralegal who represented a party in purchase and closing of restaurant purchase without supervision of attorney . . . engaged in the unauthorized practice of law . . ." In this particular case, the paralegal was also the president of the Atlantic Title Corp., and had a great deal of expertise, but held the closing of the restaurant without the active supervision of the attorney involved.

In the Matter of Bradford Arthur, U.S. Bankruptcy Court (E.D. Penn. 1981), involved the activities of a paralegal advising and counseling "clients" as to the various provisions of the bankruptcy code, including exemptions, dischargability and automatic stay, advising and counseling members of the general public on the relative advantages of filing a petition for liquidation under Chapter 7 petitions, and preparing and filing applications to pay filing fees in installments. The Bankruptcy Court held that such activities constituted the unauthorized practice of law in a bankruptcy proceeding whenever such an individual was not a member of any bar, not authorized to practice law in any jurisdiction, and cited 11 U.S.C. Sections 701 *et seq.*, 1101 *et seq.* and 1301 *et seq.* Further, the Bankruptcy Court held that "courts have the inherent authority, independent of the statute, to decide what acts constitute the practice of law." The Court also went on to say that "as generally understood the practice of law involved the performance of services in a court of law in conformity with adopted rules of procedures." Perhaps the strongest statement that the Bankruptcy Court made in this case was the holding that "when a judgment requires the abstract understanding of legal principles, and a refined skill for their concrete application, the exercise of legal judgments is necessary, and the 'practice of law' is involved."

In the case of *In re Bryan W. Pearson*, U.S. Bankruptcy Court (S.D. Fla. 1986), the Bankruptcy Court discharged an attorney as debtor's attorney, and enjoined the attorney from further practice in the Bankruptcy Court until such time as he completed a minimum of nine hours in continuing legal education in the area of bankruptcy and filed an affirmative statement that he was now conversant with bankruptcy matters and qualified to represent a client in bankruptcy matters in accordance with D.R. 6-101 and E.C. 6-1, 6-2, 6-3 and 6-4 of the Rules of Professional Responsibility. In this case, before the Bankruptcy Court, the attorney admitted in a motion to vacate the Court's dismissal of a Chapter 13 case, that he had not undertaken a bankruptcy petition in a number of years and was not aware of a Chapter 13 statement and plan requirement. The attorney stated that he had relied upon the advice given by the assistant clerks in the bankruptcy clerk's office, who told him that he had submitted all required forms and schedules and that the forms and schedules were purchased at an office supply store pursuant to the clerks instructions. The Bankruptcy Court stated, "It is outrageous that an attorney, who has achieved a law degree and obtained admission to the Florida Bar, publicly admits that he practices based on advice of assistant court clerks and products available in a stationary store." Inherent in this statement is the obvious injunction that a paralegal, no matter how knowledgeable, must be subject to a qualified attorney's active supervision.

THIS OPINION IS ADVISORY ONLY

State Bar of Montana

7 West 6th Avenue, Suite 2B

P.O. Box 577

Helena, MT 59624

406.442.7660

D. Duty of a Debtor

In Chapter 7, a debtor must comply with a various obligations regarding documentation, cooperation with the trustee and attendance at legal hearings and meetings with creditors. A Statement of Financial Affairs needs preparation and filing under the original Petition. (See Figure 11–15.)

Official Form 7
(10/05)

UNITED STATES BANKRUPTCY COURT

_____ DISTRICT OF _____

In re: _____ ,   Case No. _____
                    Debtor   (if known)

STATEMENT OF FINANCIAL AFFAIRS

This statement is to be completed by every debtor. Spouses filing a joint petition may file a single statement on which the information for both spouses is combined. If the case is filed under chapter 12 or chapter 13, a married debtor must furnish information for both spouses whether or not a joint petition is filed, unless the spouses are separated and a joint petition is not filed. An individual debtor engaged in business as a sole proprietor, partner, family farmer, or self-employed professional, should provide the information requested on this statement concerning all such activities as well as the individual's personal affairs. Do not include the name or address of a minor child in this statement. Indicate payments, transfers and the like to minor children by stating "a minor child." See 11 U.S.C. § 112; Fed. R. Bankr. P. 1007(m).

Questions 1 - 18 are to be completed by all debtors. Debtors that are or have been in business, as defined below, also must complete Questions 19 - 25. **If the answer to an applicable question is "None," mark the box labeled "None."** If additional space is needed for the answer to any question, use and attach a separate sheet properly identified with the case name, case number (if known), and the number of the question.

DEFINITIONS

"In business." A debtor is "in business" for the purpose of this form if the debtor is a corporation or partnership. An individual debtor is "in business" for the purpose of this form if the debtor is or has been, within six years immediately preceding the filing of this bankruptcy case, any of the following: an officer, director, managing executive, or owner of 5 percent or more of the voting or equity securities of a corporation; a partner, other than a limited partner, of a partnership; a sole proprietor or self-employed full-time or part-time. An individual debtor also may be "in business" for the purpose of this form if the debtor engages in a trade, business, or other activity, other than as an employee, to supplement income from the debtor's primary employment.

"Insider." The term "insider" includes but is not limited to: relatives of the debtor; general partners of the debtor and their relatives; corporations of which the debtor is an officer, director, or person in control; officers, directors, and any owner of 5 percent or more of the voting or equity securities of a corporate debtor and their relatives; affiliates of the debtor and insiders of such affiliates; any managing agent of the debtor. 11 U.S.C. § 101.

_____

1. **Income from employment or operation of business**

None
☐

State the gross amount of income the debtor has received from employment, trade, or profession, or from operation of the debtor's business, including part-time activities either as an employee or in independent trade or business, from the beginning of this calendar year to the date this case was commenced. State also the gross amounts received during the **two years** immediately preceding this calendar year. (A debtor that maintains, or has maintained, financial records on the basis of a fiscal rather than a calendar year may report fiscal year income. Identify the beginning and ending dates of the debtor's fiscal year.) If a joint petition is filed, state income for each spouse separately. (Married debtors filing under chapter 12 or chapter 13 must state income of both spouses whether or not a joint petition is filed, unless the spouses are separated and a joint petition is not filed.)

AMOUNT   SOURCE

FIGURE 11–15
(continues)

2

2. Income other than from employment or operation of business

None ☐

State the amount of income received by the debtor other than from employment, trade, profession, operation of the debtor's business during the **two years** immediately preceding the commencement of this case. Give particulars. If a joint petition is filed, state income for each spouse separately. (Married debtors filing under chapter 12 or chapter 13 must state income for each spouse whether or not a joint petition is filed, unless the spouses are separated and a joint petition is not filed.)

AMOUNT   SOURCE

3. Payments to creditors

Complete a. or b., as appropriate, and c.

None ☐

a. *Individual or joint debtor(s) with primarily consumer debts:* List all payments on loans, installment purchases of goods or services, and other debts to any creditor made within **90 days** immediately preceding the commencement of this case if the aggregate value of all property that constitutes or is affected by such transfer is not less than $600. Indicate with an asterisk (*) any payments that were made to a creditor on account of a domestic support obligation or as part of an alternative repayment schedule under a plan by an approved nonprofit budgeting and creditor counseling agency. (Married debtors filing under chapter 12 or chapter 13 must include payments by either or both spouses whether or not a joint petition is filed, unless the spouses are separated and a joint petition is not filed.)

NAME AND ADDRESS OF CREDITOR	DATES OF PAYMENTS	AMOUNT PAID	AMOUNT STILL OWING

None ☐

b. *Debtor whose debts are not primarily consumer debts:* List each payment or other transfer to any creditor made within **90** days immediately preceding the commencement of the case if the aggregate value of all property that constitutes or is affected by such transfer is not less than $5,000. (Married debtors filing under chapter 12 or chapter 13 must include payments and other transfers by either or both spouses whether or not a joint petition is filed, unless the spouses are separated and a joint petition is not filed.)

NAME AND ADDRESS OF CREDITOR	DATES OF PAYMENTS/ TRANSFERS	AMOUNT PAID OR VALUE OF TRANSFERS	AMOUNT STILL OWING

None ☐

c. *All debtors:* List all payments made within **one year** immediately preceding the commencement of this case to or for the benefit of creditors who are or were insiders. (Married debtors filing under chapter 12 or chapter 13 must include payments by either or both spouses whether or not a joint petition is filed, unless the spouses are separated and a joint petition is not filed.)

NAME AND ADDRESS OF CREDITOR AND RELATIONSHIP TO DEBTOR	DATE OF PAYMENT	AMOUNT PAID	AMOUNT STILL OWING

FIGURE 11–15
(continued)

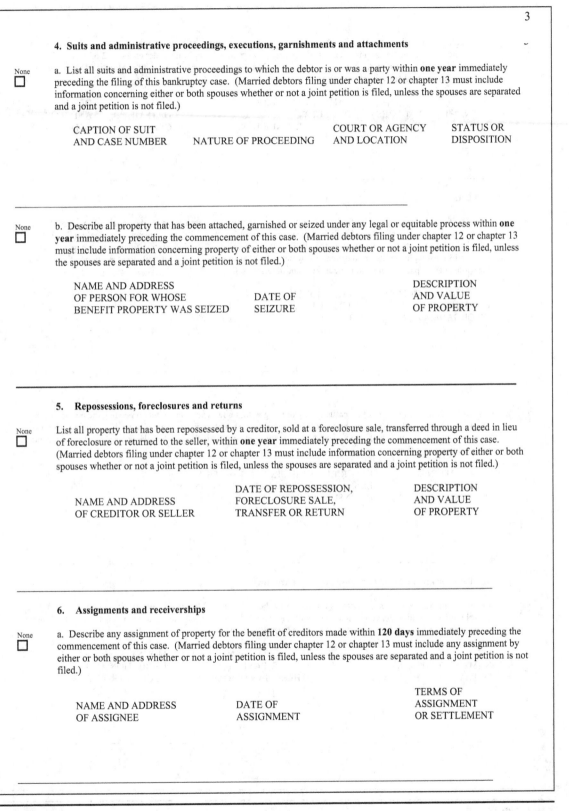

3

4. **Suits and administrative proceedings, executions, garnishments and attachments**

None ☐   a. List all suits and administrative proceedings to which the debtor is or was a party within **one year** immediately preceding the filing of this bankruptcy case. (Married debtors filing under chapter 12 or chapter 13 must include information concerning either or both spouses whether or not a joint petition is filed, unless the spouses are separated and a joint petition is not filed.)

CAPTION OF SUIT AND CASE NUMBER	NATURE OF PROCEEDING	COURT OR AGENCY AND LOCATION	STATUS OR DISPOSITION

None ☐   b. Describe all property that has been attached, garnished or seized under any legal or equitable process within **one year** immediately preceding the commencement of this case. (Married debtors filing under chapter 12 or chapter 13 must include information concerning property of either or both spouses whether or not a joint petition is filed, unless the spouses are separated and a joint petition is not filed.)

NAME AND ADDRESS OF PERSON FOR WHOSE BENEFIT PROPERTY WAS SEIZED	DATE OF SEIZURE	DESCRIPTION AND VALUE OF PROPERTY

5. **Repossessions, foreclosures and returns**

None ☐   List all property that has been repossessed by a creditor, sold at a foreclosure sale, transferred through a deed in lieu of foreclosure or returned to the seller, within **one year** immediately preceding the commencement of this case. (Married debtors filing under chapter 12 or chapter 13 must include information concerning property of either or both spouses whether or not a joint petition is filed, unless the spouses are separated and a joint petition is not filed.)

NAME AND ADDRESS OF CREDITOR OR SELLER	DATE OF REPOSSESSION, FORECLOSURE SALE, TRANSFER OR RETURN	DESCRIPTION AND VALUE OF PROPERTY

6. **Assignments and receiverships**

None ☐   a. Describe any assignment of property for the benefit of creditors made within **120 days** immediately preceding the commencement of this case. (Married debtors filing under chapter 12 or chapter 13 must include any assignment by either or both spouses whether or not a joint petition is filed, unless the spouses are separated and a joint petition is not filed.)

NAME AND ADDRESS OF ASSIGNEE	DATE OF ASSIGNMENT	TERMS OF ASSIGNMENT OR SETTLEMENT

FIGURE 11–15
(continued)

4

None ☐ b. List all property which has been in the hands of a custodian, receiver, or court-appointed official within **one year** immediately preceding the commencement of this case. (Married debtors filing under chapter 12 or chapter 13 must include information concerning property of either or both spouses whether or not a joint petition is filed, unless the spouses are separated and a joint petition is not filed.)

NAME AND ADDRESS OF CUSTODIAN	NAME AND LOCATION OF COURT CASE TITLE & NUMBER	DATE OF ORDER	DESCRIPTION AND VALUE Of PROPERTY

7. Gifts

None ☐ List all gifts or charitable contributions made within **one year** immediately preceding the commencement of this case except ordinary and usual gifts to family members aggregating less than $200 in value per individual family member and charitable contributions aggregating less than $100 per recipient. (Married debtors filing under chapter 12 or chapter 13 must include gifts or contributions by either or both spouses whether or not a joint petition is filed, unless the spouses are separated and a joint petition is not filed.)

NAME AND ADDRESS OF PERSON OR ORGANIZATION	RELATIONSHIP TO DEBTOR, IF ANY	DATE OF GIFT	DESCRIPTION AND VALUE OF GIFT

8. Losses

None ☐ List all losses from fire, theft, other casualty or gambling within **one year** immediately preceding the commencement of this case **or since the commencement of this case**. (Married debtors filing under chapter 12 or chapter 13 must include losses by either or both spouses whether or not a joint petition is filed, unless the spouses are separated and a joint petition is not filed.)

DESCRIPTION AND VALUE OF PROPERTY	DESCRIPTION OF CIRCUMSTANCES AND, IF LOSS WAS COVERED IN WHOLE OR IN PART BY INSURANCE, GIVE PARTICULARS	DATE OF LOSS

9. Payments related to debt counseling or bankruptcy

None ☐ List all payments made or property transferred by or on behalf of the debtor to any persons, including attorneys, for consultation concerning debt consolidation, relief under the bankruptcy law or preparation of a petition in bankruptcy within **one year** immediately preceding the commencement of this case.

NAME AND ADDRESS OF PAYEE	DATE OF PAYMENT, NAME OF PAYER IF OTHER THAN DEBTOR	AMOUNT OF MONEY OR DESCRIPTION AND VALUE OF PROPERTY

FIGURE 11–15
(continued)

5

10. Other transfers

None ☐ a. List all other property, other than property transferred in the ordinary course of the business or financial affairs of the debtor, transferred either absolutely or as security within **two years** immediately preceding the commencement of this case. (Married debtors filing under chapter 12 or chapter 13 must include transfers by either or both spouses whether or not a joint petition is filed, unless the spouses are separated and a joint petition is not filed.)

NAME AND ADDRESS OF TRANSFEREE, RELATIONSHIP TO DEBTOR	DATE	DESCRIBE PROPERTY TRANSFERRED AND VALUE RECEIVED

None ☐ b. List all property transferred by the debtor within **ten years** immediately preceding the commencement of this case to a self-settled trust or similar device of which the debtor is a beneficiary.

NAME OF TRUST OR OTHER DEVICE	DATE(S) OF TRANSFER(S)	AMOUNT OF MONEY OR DESCRIPTION AND VALUE OF PROPERTY OR DEBTOR'S INTEREST IN PROPERTY

11. Closed financial accounts

None ☐ List all financial accounts and instruments held in the name of the debtor or for the benefit of the debtor which were closed, sold, or otherwise transferred within **one year** immediately preceding the commencement of this case. Include checking, savings, or other financial accounts, certificates of deposit, or other instruments; shares and share accounts held in banks, credit unions, pension funds, cooperatives, associations, brokerage houses and other financial institutions. (Married debtors filing under chapter 12 or chapter 13 must include information concerning accounts or instruments held by or for either or both spouses whether or not a joint petition is filed, unless the spouses are separated and a joint petition is not filed.)

NAME AND ADDRESS OF INSTITUTION	TYPE OF ACCOUNT, LAST FOUR DIGITS OF ACCOUNT NUMBER, AND AMOUNT OF FINAL BALANCE	AMOUNT AND DATE OF SALE OR CLOSING

12. Safe deposit boxes

None ☐ List each safe deposit or other box or depository in which the debtor has or had securities, cash, or other valuables within **one year** immediately preceding the commencement of this case. (Married debtors filing under chapter 12 or chapter 13 must include boxes or depositories of either or both spouses whether or not a joint petition is filed, unless the spouses are separated and a joint petition is not filed.)

NAME AND ADDRESS OF BANK OR OTHER DEPOSITORY	NAMES AND ADDRESSES OF THOSE WITH ACCESS TO BOX OR DEPOSITORY	DESCRIPTION OF CONTENTS	DATE OF TRANSFER OR SURRENDER, IF ANY

FIGURE 11–15
(continued)

6

13. Setoffs

None ☐ List all setoffs made by any creditor, including a bank, against a debt or deposit of the debtor within **90 days** preceding the commencement of this case. (Married debtors filing under chapter 12 or chapter 13 must include information concerning either or both spouses whether or not a joint petition is filed, unless the spouses are separated and a joint petition is not filed.)

| | DATE OF | AMOUNT |
| NAME AND ADDRESS OF CREDITOR | SETOFF | OF SETOFF |

14. Property held for another person

None ☐ List all property owned by another person that the debtor holds or controls.

| NAME AND ADDRESS OF OWNER | DESCRIPTION AND VALUE OF PROPERTY | LOCATION OF PROPERTY |

15. Prior address of debtor

None ☐ If debtor has moved within **three years** immediately preceding the commencement of this case, list all premises which the debtor occupied during that period and vacated prior to the commencement of this case. If a joint petition is filed, report also any separate address of either spouse.

| ADDRESS | NAME USED | DATES OF OCCUPANCY |

16. Spouses and Former Spouses

None ☐ If the debtor resides or resided in a community property state, commonwealth, or territory (including Alaska, Arizona, California, Idaho, Louisiana, Nevada, New Mexico, Puerto Rico, Texas, Washington, or Wisconsin) within **eight years** immediately preceding the commencement of the case, identify the name of the debtor's spouse and of any former spouse who resides or resided with the debtor in the community property state.

NAME

FIGURE 11–15
(continued)

7

17. Environmental Information.

For the purpose of this question, the following definitions apply:

"Environmental Law" means any federal, state, or local statute or regulation regulating pollution, contamination, releases of hazardous or toxic substances, wastes or material into the air, land, soil, surface water, groundwater, or other medium, including, but not limited to, statutes or regulations regulating the cleanup of these substances, wastes, or material.

"Site" means any location, facility, or property as defined under any Environmental Law, whether or not presently or formerly owned or operated by the debtor, including, but not limited to, disposal sites.

"Hazardous Material" means anything defined as a hazardous waste, hazardous substance, toxic substance, hazardous material, pollutant, or contaminant or similar term under an Environmental Law.

None ☐
a. List the name and address of every site for which the debtor has received notice in writing by a governmental unit that it may be liable or potentially liable under or in violation of an Environmental Law. Indicate the governmental unit, the date of the notice, and, if known, the Environmental Law:

SITE NAME AND ADDRESS	NAME AND ADDRESS OF GOVERNMENTAL UNIT	DATE OF NOTICE	ENVIRONMENTAL LAW

None ☐
b. List the name and address of every site for which the debtor provided notice to a governmental unit of a release of Hazardous Material. Indicate the governmental unit to which the notice was sent and the date of the notice.

SITE NAME AND ADDRESS	NAME AND ADDRESS OF GOVERNMENTAL UNIT	DATE OF NOTICE	ENVIRONMENTAL LAW

None ☐
c. List all judicial or administrative proceedings, including settlements or orders, under any Environmental Law with respect to which the debtor is or was a party. Indicate the name and address of the governmental unit that is or was a party to the proceeding, and the docket number.

NAME AND ADDRESS OF GOVERNMENTAL UNIT	DOCKET NUMBER	STATUS OR DISPOSITION

18 . Nature, location and name of business

None ☐
a. *If the debtor is an individual*, list the names, addresses, taxpayer identification numbers, nature of the businesses, and beginning and ending dates of all businesses in which the debtor was an officer, director, partner, or managing executive of a corporation, partner in a partnership, sole proprietor, or was self-employed in a trade, profession, or other activity either full- or part-time within **six years** immediately preceding the commencement of this case, or in which the debtor owned 5 percent or more of the voting or equity securities within **six years** immediately preceding the commencement of this case.

If the debtor is a partnership, list the names, addresses, taxpayer identification numbers, nature of the businesses, and beginning and ending dates of all businesses in which the debtor was a partner or owned 5 percent or more of the voting or equity securities, within **six years** immediately preceding the commencement of this case.

If the debtor is a corporation, list the names, addresses, taxpayer identification numbers, nature of the businesses, and beginning and ending dates of all businesses in which the debtor was a partner or owned 5 percent or more of the voting or equity securities within **six years** immediately preceding the commencement of this case.

FIGURE 11–15
(continued)

8

NAME	LAST FOUR DIGITS OF SOC. SEC. NO./ COMPLETE EIN OR OTHER TAXPAYER I.D. NO.	ADDRESS	NATURE OF BUSINESS	BEGINNING AND ENDING DATES

None ☐   b. Identify any business listed in response to subdivision a., above, that is "single asset real estate" as defined in 11 U.S.C. § 101.

NAME	ADDRESS

The following questions are to be completed by every debtor that is a corporation or partnership and by any individual debtor who is or has been, within **six years** immediately preceding the commencement of this case, any of the following: an officer, director, managing executive, or owner of more than 5 percent of the voting or equity securities of a corporation; a partner, other than a limited partner, of a partnership, a sole proprietor, or self-employed in a trade, profession, or other activity, either full- or part-time.

*(An individual or joint debtor should complete this portion of the statement **only** if the debtor is or has been in business, as defined above, within six years immediately preceding the commencement of this case. A debtor who has not been in business within those six years should go directly to the signature page.)*

19. Books, records and financial statements

None ☐   a. List all bookkeepers and accountants who within **two years** immediately preceding the filing of this bankruptcy case kept or supervised the keeping of books of account and records of the debtor.

NAME AND ADDRESS	DATES SERVICES RENDERED

None ☐   b. List all firms or individuals who within **two years** immediately preceding the filing of this bankruptcy case have audited the books of account and records, or prepared a financial statement of the debtor.

NAME	ADDRESS	DATES SERVICES RENDERED

None ☐   c. List all firms or individuals who at the time of the commencement of this case were in possession of the books of account and records of the debtor. If any of the books of account and records are not available, explain.

NAME	ADDRESS

FIGURE 11–15
(continued)

9

None ☐   d. List all financial institutions, creditors and other parties, including mercantile and trade agencies, to whom a financial statement was issued by the debtor within **two years** immediately preceding the commencement of this case.

NAME AND ADDRESS   DATE ISSUED

20. Inventories

None ☐   a. List the dates of the last two inventories taken of your property, the name of the person who supervised the taking of each inventory, and the dollar amount and basis of each inventory.

DOLLAR AMOUNT
OF INVENTORY
DATE OF INVENTORY   INVENTORY SUPERVISOR   (Specify cost, market or other basis)

None ☐   b. List the name and address of the person having possession of the records of each of the inventories reported in a., above.

NAME AND ADDRESSES
OF CUSTODIAN
DATE OF INVENTORY   OF INVENTORY RECORDS

21 . Current Partners, Officers, Directors and Shareholders

None ☐   a. If the debtor is a partnership, list the nature and percentage of partnership interest of each member of the partnership.

NAME AND ADDRESS   NATURE OF INTEREST   PERCENTAGE OF INTEREST

None ☐   b. If the debtor is a corporation, list all officers and directors of the corporation, and each stockholder who directly or indirectly owns, controls, or holds 5 percent or more of the voting or equity securities of the corporation.

NATURE AND PERCENTAGE
NAME AND ADDRESS   TITLE   OF STOCK OWNERSHIP

22 . Former partners, officers, directors and shareholders

None ☐   a. If the debtor is a partnership, list each member who withdrew from the partnership within **one year** immediately preceding the commencement of this case.

NAME   ADDRESS   DATE OF WITHDRAWAL

FIGURE 11–15
(continued)

10

None ☐   b.   If the debtor is a corporation, list all officers, or directors whose relationship with the corporation terminated within **one year** immediately preceding the commencement of this case.

         NAME AND ADDRESS   TITLE   DATE OF TERMINATION

23 . Withdrawals from a partnership or distributions by a corporation

None ☐   If the debtor is a partnership or corporation, list all withdrawals or distributions credited or given to an insider, including compensation in any form, bonuses, loans, stock redemptions, options exercised and any other perquisite during **one year** immediately preceding the commencement of this case.

NAME & ADDRESS OF RECIPIENT, RELATIONSHIP TO DEBTOR	DATE AND PURPOSE OF WITHDRAWAL	AMOUNT OF MONEY OR DESCRIPTION AND VALUE OF PROPERTY

24. Tax Consolidation Group.

None ☐   If the debtor is a corporation, list the name and federal taxpayer identification number of the parent corporation of any consolidated group for tax purposes of which the debtor has been a member at any time within **six years** immediately preceding the commencement of the case.

NAME OF PARENT CORPORATION   TAXPAYER IDENTIFICATION NUMBER (EIN)

25. Pension Funds.

None ☐   If the debtor is not an individual, list the name and federal taxpayer identification number of any pension fund to which the debtor, as an employer, has been responsible for contributing at any time within **six years** immediately preceding the commencement of the case.

NAME OF PENSION FUND   TAXPAYER IDENTIFICATION NUMBER (EIN)

* * * * * *

FIGURE 11–15
(continued)

11

[If completed by an individual or individual and spouse]

I declare under penalty of perjury that I have read the answers contained in the foregoing statement of financial affairs and any attachments thereto and that they are true and correct.

Date _____   Signature _____
                                                              of Debtor

Date _____   Signature _____
                                                              of Joint Debtor
                                                              (if any)

_____

[If completed on behalf of a partnership or corporation]

I, declare under penalty of perjury that I have read the answers contained in the foregoing statement of financial affairs and any attachments thereto and that they are true and correct to the best of my knowledge, information and belief.

Date _____   Signature _____

                                                              Print Name and Title

[An individual signing on behalf of a partnership or corporation must indicate position or relationship to debtor.]

_____ continuation sheets attached

Penalty for making a false statement: Fine of up to $500,000 or imprisonment for up to 5 years, or both. 18 U.S.C. §§ 152 and 3571

DECLARATION AND SIGNATURE OF NON-ATTORNEY BANKRUPTCY PETITION PREPARER (See 11 U.S.C. § 110)

I declare under penalty of perjury that: (1) I am a bankruptcy petition preparer as defined in 11 U.S.C. § 110; (2) I prepared this document for compensation and have provided the debtor with a copy of this document and the notices and information required under 11 U.S.C. §§ 110(b), 110(h), and 342(b); and, (3) if rules or guidelines have been promulgated pursuant to 11 U.S.C. § 110(h) setting a maximum fee for services chargeable by bankruptcy petition preparers, I have given the debtor notice of the maximum amount before preparing any document for filing for a debtor or accepting any fee from the debtor, as required by that section.

_____   _____
Printed or Typed Name and Title, if any, of Bankruptcy Petition Preparer   Social Security No.(Required by 11 U.S.C. § 110.)

If the bankruptcy petition preparer is not an individual, state the name, title (if any), address, and social security number of the officer, principal, responsible person, or partner who signs this document.

_____

_____
Address

X _____   _____
Signature of Bankruptcy Petition Preparer   Date

Names and Social Security numbers of all other individuals who prepared or assisted in preparing this document unless the bankruptcy petition preparer is not an individual:

If more than one person prepared this document, attach additional signed sheets conforming to the appropriate Official Form for each person.

A bankruptcy petition preparer's failure to comply with the provisions of title 11 and the Federal Rules of Bankruptcy Procedure may result in fines or imprisonment or both. 18 U.S.C. § 156.

FIGURE 11–15
(continued)

The provisions of the bankruptcy code permit payment of legal fees and compensation that is reasonable in light of services rendered. Following is a statement for attorneys' fees, a standardized form that is regularly used in the bankruptcy division. An official form, *Disclosure of Compensation of Attorney for Debtor* is either filed with Voluntary Petition or no more than 15 days after the Order of Relief is issued.[38] See Figure 11–16 for a Compensation Statement.

B 203
(12/94)

United States Bankruptcy Court

_____ District Of _____

In re

Case No. _____

Debtor

Chapter _____

DISCLOSURE OF COMPENSATION OF ATTORNEY FOR DEBTOR

1. Pursuant to 11 U.S.C. § 329(a) and Fed. Bankr. P. 2016(b), I certify that I am the attorney for the above-named debtor(s) and that compensation paid to me within one year before the filing of the petition in bankruptcy, or agreed to be paid to me, for services rendered or to be rendered on behalf of the debtor(s) in contemplation of or in connection with the bankruptcy case is as follows:

   For legal services, I have agreed to accept ....$_____

   Prior to the filing of this statement I have received .... $_____

   Balance Due .... $_____

2. The source of the compensation paid to me was:

   ☐ Debtor   ☐ Other (specify)

3. The source of compensation to be paid to me is:

   ☐ Debtor   ☐ Other (specify)

4. ☐ I have not agreed to share the above-disclosed compensation with any other person unless they are members and associates of my law firm.

   ☐ I have agreed to share the above-disclosed compensation with a other person or persons who are not members or associates of my law firm. A copy of the agreement, together with a list of the names of the people sharing in the compensation, is attached.

5. In return for the above-disclosed fee, I have agreed to render legal service for all aspects of the bankruptcy case, including:

   a. Analysis of the debtor's financial situation, and rendering advice to the debtor in determining whether to file a petition in bankruptcy;

   b. Preparation and filing of any petition, schedules, statements of affairs and plan which may be required;

   c. Representation of the debtor at the meeting of creditors and confirmation hearing, and any adjourned hearings thereof;

FIGURE 11–16

(continues)

DISCLOSURE OF COMPENSATION OF ATTORNEY FOR DEBTOR (Continued)

d. Representation of the debtor in adversary proceedings and other contested bankruptcy matters;

e. [Other provisions as needed]

6. By agreement with the debtor(s), the above-disclosed fee does not include the following services:

CERTIFICATION

I certify that the foregoing is a complete statement of any agreement or arrangement for payment to me for representation of the debtor(s) in this bankruptcy proceedings.

_____   _____
Date   *Signature of Attorney*

                                              _____
                                              Name of law firm

---

FIGURE 11–16
(continued)

E. Distribution of the Bankruptcy Estate

Upon the filing of the bankruptcy petition and the commencement of the case, a new entity entitled the **bankruptcy estate** comes into being. "The estate consists of all the debtors' interests in real and personal property as of the date the petition is filed."[39] It is this sum that need be distributed to the interested parties. This total sum of property also must be finally calculated when specific federal and state **exemptions** as to forms of property are subtracted. Various federal exemptions exist which are excluded from the distribution. In this case, our chief interest lies with the exemption for a personal residence. While it is not a dramatic amount, $17,425, it is the sum permitted under the statute. Other exemptions are charted below at Figure 11–17.[40]

Type of Property	Amount of Exemption	Statute Creating Exemption
Debtor's interest in real or personal property that debtor uses as residence	$17,425	11 USC 522(d)(1)
1 Motor vehicle	$2,775	11 USC 522(d)(2)
Household furnishings	$9,300 aggregate value limitations with $450 limitation on value of each item	11 USC 522(d)(3)
Jewelry	$1,150	11 USC 522(d)(4)
Any property selected by debtor	$925 plus up to $8,725 of unused portion of 11 USC 522(d)(1) exemption	11 USC 522(d)(5)
Implements, professional books, or tools, of the trade of debtor or a dependent of the debtor	$1,750	11 USC 522(d)(6)
Unmatured life insurance contracts owned by debtor except credit life insurance contracts	100%	11 USC 522(d)(7)
Accrued dividends or interest under, or loan value of, any unmatured life insurance contract owned by debtor in which the insured is the debtor or a person of whom the debtor is a dependent	$9,300 less any amounts transferred by insurer for payment of premiums	11 USC 522(d)(8)
Professionally prescribed health aids	100%	11 USC 522(d)(9)
Social security, unemployment compensation, or public assistance benefits	100%	11 USC 522(d)(10)(A)
Veterans benefits	100%	11 USC 522(d)(10)(B)
Disability, illness or unemployment benefits	100%	11 USC 522(d)(10)(C)
Alimony, support, or separate maintenance	100% of amount reasonably necessary for support of debtor and dependents	11 USC 522(d)(10)(D)
Payments under stock bonus, pension, profitsharing, annuity, or similar plan or contract on account of illness, disability, death, age, or length of service	100% of amount reasonably necessary for support of debtor and dependents	11 USC 522(d)(10)(E)
Crime victims reparation law benefits or awards	100%	11 USC 522(d)(11)(A)

FIGURE 11–17

(continues)

Payments on account of the wrongful death of individual of whom debtor was a dependent	100% of amount reasonably necessary for support of debtor and dependents	11 USC 622(d)(11)(B)
Payment under life insurance contract insuring life of an individual of whom debtor was a dependent	100% of amount reasonably necessary for support of debtor and dependents	11 USC 522(d)(11)(C)
Payments on account of personal bodily injury (does not include compensation for pain and suffering or actual pecuniary loss)	$17,425	11 USC 522(d)(11)(D)
Payments in compensation for loss of future earnings	100% of amount reasonably necessary for support of debtor and dependents	11 USC 522(d)(11)(E)

FIGURE 11–17
(continued)

CHAPTER ELEVEN **SUMMARY**

Chapter Eleven discussed the following topics:

- The purpose of foreclosure
- The right to foreclose
- Acceleration and restrictions on acceleration
- Judicial foreclosure
- Power-of-sale foreclosure
- Strict foreclosure
- Sale surplus and deficiency judgments
- Equitable and statutory redemption
- Bankruptcy laws and rules
- Chapter 7 Bankruptcy
- Debt agent
- Bankruptcy relation to foreclosure
- The role of the paralegal in bankruptcy
- The role of a bankruptcy trustee
- Calculation of the bankruptcy estate
- Petitions, discharge and distribution formats
- Federal exemptions

REVIEW **QUESTION**

1. What is a foreclosure?
2. What is the purpose of an acceleration clause?
3. How does a party satisfy their obligations to omitted junior lienholders?
4. What is the order in which judicial foreclosure proceeds are distributed?

5. What is a strict foreclosure?
6. How does a power-of-sale foreclosure differ from a judicial foreclosure?
7. What are the two forms of redemption?
8. When is an action for deficiency judgment initiated?
9. What are the differences between a voluntary and involuntary petition for bankruptcy?
10. Outline the process, and list the forms used for filing bankruptcy.

DISCUSSION **QUESTION**

Discuss the process and advantages of judicial foreclosure.

EXERCISE 1

Draft a sample notice letter and separate notice of acceleration using the following facts and hypothetical information as necessary.

Name of Debtors—Robert and Samantha Morgan

Address of Debtors—405 Thirteen Street, Mytown, US, 00000

Date of Mortgage Note—April 8, 2001

Name of Bank issuing Note—National Bank, Plaza Two, Mytown, US, 00000

Original Loan Amount—$85,000

Number of payments delinquent—7

Amount of monthly payment—$874.32

Default interest rate—23.7%

Date default rate is effective—April 8, 2009

Last day for payment before total amount is due—August 8, 2009

EXERCISE 2

Using hypothetical information, complete a master information list and a notice of sale.

EXERCISE 3

Using the information from Exercise 1 and hypothetical information as needed, complete a Voluntary Petition for Bankruptcy, as well as Schedule A (Form B 6A)—Real Property. Schedule A, as well as the Voluntary Petition can be found at www.uscourts.gov/bkforms/bankruptcy_forms.html.

REFERENCES

1. New Hampshire Housing, www.nhhfa.org/rl_docs/housingdata/Foreclosure Update_03-25-09.htm.
2. Public Law No. 111-22, signed May 20, 2009.
3. Public Law 110-343, 122 Stat. 3765, enacted October 3, 2008.
4. See the findings of the Michigan Foundation on the price and turmoil caused by the foreclosure crisis at www.michiganfoundations.org/s_cmf/bin.asp?CID=7710&DID=26266&DOC=FILE.PDF.

5. RALPH E. BOYER et al., THE LAW OF PROPERTY: AN INTRODUCTORY SURVEY, 5th ed., 640 (2001).

6. 41 PA. STAT. ANN. § 404(b)(1).

7. EDWARD H. RABIN, FUNDAMENTS OF MODERN REAL PROPERTY LAW, 1087 (1974), 3rd ed. (1992).

8. JOSEPH WILLIAM SINGER, PROPERTY LAW: RULES AND PRACTICES, 914 (1993), 3rd ed. (2002).

9. A. JAMES CASNER et al., CASES AND TEST ON PROPERTY, 746, 3rd ed. (1984), 4th ed. (2000).

10. MORTGAGE BANKERS ASSOCIATION, NATIONAL DELINQUENCY SURVEY, 1 (Sept. 30, 2008), at www.mortgagemaine.com/pdfs/Natl_Delinquency_State_Results.pdf.

11. *See* Todd, J. Zywicki, *Institutions, Incentives, and Consumer Bankruptcy Reform,* 62 WASH. & LEE L. REV. 1071 (2005); *see also* Robert M. Zimman and Novica Petrosvski, *The Home Mortgage and Chapter 13: An Essay in Unintended Consequences,* 17 AM. BANKR. INST. L. REV. 133 (2009).

12. *Id.* at 1072.

13. *See* Harvey R. Miller & Shai Y. Waisman, *The Future of Chapter 11: A Symposium Cosponsored by the American College of Bankrupt: Is Chapter 11 Bankrupt?* 47 B.C. L. REV. 129 (2005).

14. U.S. CONST., art. I, § 8, Cl. 4.

15. International Shoe v. Pinkus, 278 U.S. 261 (1929).

16. 11 U.S.C. § 101 et seq. (2009).

17. "Two events have helped to raise the prestige and profitability of the field. One is the Bankruptcy Reform Act of 1978, which created a Bankruptcy Code that made it easier for people to file, and that also raised attorneys' fees, making the field more lucrative. The other factor behind the boom is the recession. With so many people declaring bankruptcy, it's become an acceptable way of cleaning up one's debts. And when well-known corporations like R.H. Macy's and TWA file for reorganization, it even becomes respectable." Verna Safran, *The Boom in Going Bust, Opportunities for Paralegals in Bankruptcy Law,* 9 LEGAL ASS'T TODAY, May/June 1992, at 99.

18. INSTITUTE FOR CONTINUING LEGAL EDUCATION, 2 MICHIGAN BASIC PRACTICE HANDBOOK 990 (1988).

19. 11 U.S.C. § 362 (2009).

20. Zywicki, *supra* note 11, at 1076.

21. *See* The Bankruptcy Abuse Prevention and Consumer Protection Act of 2005, Public Law No: 109-8, 119 STAT. 23 (2005).

22. 11 U.S.C. § 101(12A) (2005).

23. Geoff Giles, *Bankruptcy: The New Bankruptcy Law: Bad News for Debtors, Worse News for Lawyers,* 13 NEV. LAW., Sept. 2005 at 8, 17.

24. 28 U.S.C. § 1334(a) (2005).

25. *See* Charles P. Nemeth, *The District of Columbia Retired Judges' Services Act: Can It Pass Constitutional Muster?* JUDICATURE, Feb./Mar. 1990, at 253.

26. US Dept. of Justice, US Trustee Program, *Consumer Alert—Mortgage Foreclosure Scams* www.usdoj.gov/ust/eo/public_affairs/factsheet/docs/fs06.htm.

27. For some excellent resources on bankruptcy law, *see* DOUGLAS G. BAIRD, ELEMENTS OF BANKRUPTCY (2005); RICHARD E. BOYEER, PRACTICAL BANKRUPTCY LAW FOR PARALEGALS, 3rd ed. (2005); BRIAN BLUM, BANKRUPTCY AND DEBTOR/CREDITOR (Examples and Explanations) (2004); DAVID G. G. EPSTEIN, BANKRUPTCY AND RELATED LAW IN A NUTSHELL (2005); THE NEW BANKRUPTCY CODE: U.S. BANKRUPTCY CODE & RULES BOOKLET, Dahlstrom Legal Pub. Ed. (2005)

28. Robert N. Corley, Eric M. Holmes, & William J. Robert, Principles of Business Law 537 (1987); *See also* 11 U.S.C. § 362.

29. *See* 11 U.S.C. 101(10A) (2005).

30. *See* Henry J. Sommer, *Trying to Make Sense Out of Nonsense: Representing Consumers Under the "Bankruptcy Abuse Prevention And Consumer Protection Act Of 2005,"* 191, 79 Am. Bankr. L. J. 191, 195 (2005); *See also* Official Form B22a, Statement of Current Monthly Income and Means Test Calculation.

31. 11 U.S.C.S. § 101(10A) (2005).

32. 11 U.S.C.S. § 501 (2005).

33. *In re* Lough, 57 BANKR. 993 (Bankr. E.D. Mich. 1986).

34. 11 U.S.C.S. § 704(9) (2005).

35. 11 U.S.C. § 547(B)(4)(a) (2005).

36. 11 U.S.C. § 548 (2005).

37. David L. Buchbinder, Basic Bankruptcy Law for Paralegals (with CD) (2005); *see* the ethical implications in Ellen Lockwood et al., The Paralegal Ethics Handbook (2008).

38. 11 U.S.C.S. § 329 (2005).

39. Institute for Continuing Legal Education, 2 Michigan Basic Practice Handbook 1009 (1988); 11 U.S.C. § 541 (2005).

40. 11 U.S.C. § 522 (2005).

Index